Chechnya

In memory of Rory Peck,
cameraman and good friend, killed at Ostankino, Moscow
3 October 1993

Apellé 'le brave' par les braves eux-mêmes
– Epitaph of Marshall Crillon

Chechnya

Tombstone of Russian Power

Anatol Lieven
With photographs by Heidi Bradner

Yale University Press
New Haven and London

Set in Simoncini Garamond by Northern Phototypesetting Co. Ltd., Bolton, Lancs
Printed and bound in the United States of America

Library of Congress Catalog Card Number 98–84479
ISBN 0–300–07398–4

A catalogue record for this book is available from the British Library.

10 9 8 7 6 5 4 3 2 1

Contents

Preface

This book seeks to explain the Russian defeat in Chechnya in terms of the condition of the Russian state, Russian society and the Russian psyche in the 1990s. It does so against the background not just of Russian history but also that of the process of capitalist modernisation in countries with weak states and weak civil societies, as this has taken place over the past two hundred years. It also examines the reasons for the Chechen victory, which I explain in terms of Chechen history, society and culture. The introduction dissects some common fallacies in the Western interpretation of Russia, and the conclusion examines the nature and possible future courses of Russian nationalism.

In the course of the book I also try to use evidence from Russia, Chechnya and the war between them to make contributions to wider debates, whether academic or policy-oriented. Thus in part I, I look at the lessons of the Chechen War for modern armies, emphasising the importance of morale for victory. The outcome of the Gulf War has encouraged a belief among military experts in the supreme importance of technology and professionalism. Chechnya shows that in certain circumstances, victory can still go to 'the Nation in Arms'. In parts II and III, I touch in various places on the academic debate (which, thanks to the Yugoslav wars, has spilled over into the policy domain) on the origins of nationalism and national conflicts, the 'invention of tradition' and the 'construction of culture'.

Russian and Chechen nationalism are very different from each other, and both also diverge greatly from many of the standard models of nationalism drawn up by Western scholars in recent decades. The Chechens, as I will argue in part III, have many of the characteristics of a 'primordial ethnic nation', and their nationalism was not created or even significantly shaped by processes of state formation and economic development, or by mass literacy. They have indeed been able to fight and win without possessing either a real state or an organised national movement. The Russians by contrast are a people who have never been able fully to develop a modern national identity of their own because from the seventeenth century on, their states were so strong as to subsume Russian identity; and because those states defined themselves more in imperial and ideological than in Russian ethnic terms. The collapse of the last imperial state, the Soviet Union, has therefore left Russian nationalism in an extremely weak and confused state – as Chechnya demonstrated.

Different chapters also contain what are in effect individual short essays on various related themes: thus chapter 5 contains a discussion of the importance of changing demographic patterns for Russia today and in the past; and another of the relationship between democracy and modern wars, in the context of Chechnya and various other imperial campaigns. I also emphasise that modern culture in general, and especially the spread of television, seems to have a demilitarising effect, in Russia as elsewhere.

This book is not intended to be a complete or continuous history of Russia in the period of the Chechen War, and part I is only intended to set the scene with a personal description and a general chronological picture of events and an analysis of the causes of the war, the level of casualties and atrocities, the personal role of General Dudayev, and other specific aspects of the war and its genesis. This self-imposed limitation is for two reasons. First, such a history would be a monumental work, and as a journalist on a one year's sabbatical I have simply not had the time to attempt it. Second, we are still close to the events themselves, and there has not been time for the full picture of the causes of events in 1994–6 to emerge. Concerning the Chechen side, it may never do so. For a non-Chechen outsider, the underlying reasons for developments within Chechnya are habitually shrouded in several layers of opacity: anthropological, religious, linguistic and indeed criminal. On the Russian side, however, we can hope that a fuller picture will emerge as some of those responsible for the war eventually write their memoirs or flee abroad.

While the various bits of this book are strung together along a single thread – the Russian defeat in Chechnya – they can also be read separately. The first part tells the story of the war, beginning with what I saw and experienced myself. It is interspersed with passages discussing particular features of the conflict, such as the chaotic nature of the Russian government's decision-making process in 1994, the nature of Russian strategy, and the extent of Russian excesses against the civilian population. The second part, which may be the most relevant for analysts and journalists, looks at Russia today through a variety of prisms in an effort to explain the defeat and the weakness of Russian militant nationalism in the 1990s. The third part is an anthropological portrait – to the best of my knowledge, the first in English – of the Chechens, geared to understanding both their remarkable fighting qualities and their difficulties in creating a modern state.

The memoir of my own experiences in Chechnya, with which the book begins, may seem immodest, superfluous or both. On the other hand, being bombed does yield certain special insights. I also make no apology for having included so many direct quotations and personal portraits in the rest of the text. One advantage journalists have over academics is precisely their greater freedom to travel and talk to people, and it seemed a pity not to exploit this to the full.

Soon after the war began, I visited one of the great oil refineries on the southern outskirts of Grozny. This city was formerly the greatest oil-refining centre of the largest oil-producing state in the world, and its industries were on a scale to match; the rows of gargantuan machines, entwined with huge pipes like the arms of monsters and demons, stretched away into the distance until they vanished into the December mist. I thought of the great temple of a vanished religion, full of great idols whose awesome names had long been forgotten – and these Soviet industrial Molochs had claimed their share of human sacrifice in their time. All was dead, cold and silent, until a small group of Chechen fighters came past, grinning and raising their fists in a victory sign, crying 'God is Great' before they too passed into the mist to take up their positions, like small parasites moving through the bony carcass of a dead dinosaur.

This scene was like the epitaph to a whole world: for to most of its inhabitants, the Soviet Union was more than just a civilisation, or a warped version of modernity. It was indeed a world, the only one they knew, and – according to its founders and mentors – the greatest of all worlds, the summit of human history, knowledge and achievement. The huge Soviet factories were that world's greatest monuments. The idea that Soviet industry as a whole would one day largely collapse and fall silent would have seemed as utterly inconceivable only a few years ago as the idea that the whole Russian army could be humiliated by tiny groups of badly armed guerrillas. But it has happened, and it must be recognised, analysed and, if possible, understood.

Acknowledgements

First of all I must pay an affectionate and admiring tribute to the colleagues with whom I travelled in Chechnya, especially Heidi Bradner, Sebastian Smith, Andrew Harding, Robert Parsons, Victoria Clarke, David Filipov, Thomas de Waal, Carlotta Gall, Bill Gasperini, David Brauchli, Paul Lowe, Stanley Greene, Peter Jouvenal, Sonia Mikich, Colin Peck, Thomas Dvorzak, Petra Prokhazkova, David Remnick, Lee Hockstader, Stephen Erlanger and others. Joan Beecher Eichrodt set an example to us all for stamina and dedication, and in Washington was generous both with her food and wine and with her knowledge of Chechnya.

From previous wars mentioned in the text, Thomas and Hicran Goltz, Alexis Rowell, and Natalie Nougayrede have all been good friends and companions. Richard and Natasha Beeston were extremely thoughtful and helpful during our time working together in Moscow. I am also grateful to Francis and Susan Richards, for their hospitality and the pleasure of their conversation. Among the many people of Chechnya who helped my colleagues and me, sometimes at difficult moments, I should like to mention my driver Abubakr, who drove unhesitatingly into some fairly rough situations; Maqsharip Chadayev, whose help after the tragic death of our colleague Cynthia Elbaum showed nobility as well as kindness; Hasman Umarova, who kindly arranged our meeting with General Dudayev in December 1995; Professor Aslan Dukayev, who told me a great deal about Chechen society; Musa Damayev and his family in Shali; Aissa Abbasova, my interpreter in 1992, Islam Gunayev and his wife in Haji Yurt, and Azamat Nalgiyev at the Ingush press centre in Nazran.

I am grateful to Tyotya Natasha, who housed and fed so many of us; the owners and staff of the Frantsusky Dom, who also housed what must have been one of the largest and most nervous heap of journalists ever to cram themselves into a small hotel; and the people of the Lazania restaurant, who in December 1994 kept the beer flowing to the very last possible moment. Shamil Basayev and his followers and relatives extended hospitality on a number of occasions, and he himself showed courtesy to my colleagues and myself even in the most trying of circumstances.

I also extend thanks to the men of the Russian Special Rapid Reaction Force (SOBR) who served in Grozny in February 1995, and especially to Senior Lieutenant Oleg Svartsov, later killed in action. Although our introduction was not all it might have been, they later showed us true hospitality.

In general, I should say that while I had a number of unpleasant experiences with Russian soldiers during the war, there were other occasions when they showed surprising toleration and friendliness to the western journalists buzzing so irritatingly around their ears.

In Moscow, I am grateful for the help of Lieutenant Colonel Dmitri Trenin and Sergei Markov at the Carnegie Institute, as well as Sergei Karaganov, Andrei Piontkovsky, Emil Payin, and Alexander Goltz. Professor Sergei Arutiunov, of the Ethnography department of the Russian Academy of Sciences, was most helpful, as was Professor Valery Tishkov. Although I have never met him, I feel I should also mention Dr Jan Chesnov, whose work on teips first got me interested in this fascinating though frustrating subject.

The writing of this book was made possible by the award of a year's Senior Fellowship at the United States Institute of Peace in Washington D.C., for which I am extremely grateful. In particular, I must thank Joe Klaits and Sally Blair for their consideration and help during my stay, and Ivan Kachanovski for all his assistance with my research while in the States. Research in parts of the former Soviet Union in 1995 was made possible by research grants from the Nuffield Foundation and the Leverhulme Trust in the UK.

My thanks are due to Owen Harries, of the *National Interest*, and Michael Mazarr, of the *Washington Quarterly*, for permission to use for this book material which originally appeared in articles for their journals, and for their interest in my work.

Among my colleagues in Washington, I owe a great debt of gratitude to Dr Georgy Derluguian. His deep knowledge of the Soviet Union and the Caucasus, and insights into their societies, were most generously shared. I am also very grateful to Georgy and Lyuba for the number of times they fed my wife and me in D. C. Talking with Steven Sestanovich, Sherman Garnett, Michael McFaul and Anders Aslund at the Carnegie Institute in Washington was also of immense value in understanding contemporary developments in Russia, as were the seminars and conferences at the Carnegie, organised by Ann Stecker. I benefited from several fascinating conversations with Peter Reddaway, Charles Fairbanks, Abraham Brumberg, Josephine Woll and Vladimir Petrov. The 'Russia List' on the internet, organised by David Johnson of the Centre for Defence Information, was an invaluable source of the latest material from and about Russia.

Colonel James Warner and Professor Ephraim Kleiman in the USA, and Colonel Charles Blandy in the UK kindly provided the perspectives of trained military men on some of what I had written, as did some of the officers to whom I lectured at the National War College at the invitation of Professor Melvin Goodman. Roman Wassiliewski and Philip Remler of the US Foreign Service kindly shared some of what they had experienced during their courageous and valuable work with the OSCE mission in Grozny.

Finally, this book is for my wife Sasha, with my dearest love, and regret at having caused her so much worry while covering the war.

Introduction

Russia: Still a Bear
> Headline in the *Washington Post*, 9 July 1996

Wooing a Bear
> Headline in *The Economist*, 14 December 1996

Still within Reach of Russian Bear
> Headline in the *Washington Post*, 5 January 1997

There's more nonsense talked about the grizzly bear than any other animal, barring the wolf. Grown men will look you straight in the eye and tell of the hair-raising experiences they've had with bears; how a grizzly will charge a man on sight, how they can outrun a horse, tear down a tree and create hell generally with no provocation. The truth is that a bear is just like any other animal and has more sense than to tangle with a man without good reason. True, they're apt to be bad-tempered in the spring when they've just come out of hibernation, but a lot of people are like that when they've just got out of bed.

And they're hungry in the spring, too. The fat has gone from them and their hide hangs loose and they want to be left alone to eat in peace, just like most of us, I guess...Most of the tall tales about bears have been spun around camp fires to impress a tenderfoot or tourist, and even more have been poured out of a bottle of rye whisky.

> Desmond Bagley, *Landslide*

The war between Russia and the Chechen separatist forces, which lasted from December 1994 to August 1996, may be seen by future historians as a key moment in Russian and perhaps world history – not so much because of its consequences, as because of the stark light which this war has thrown on one of the most important developments of our time: the end of Russia as a great military and imperial power. The impossibility of Russia maintaining the Soviet Union's global role was obvious even before the USSR collapsed; what Chechnya has shown is that even the Russian effort to maintain itself as the hegemonic power within the former Soviet space will, for the forseeable future, labour under very severe constraints of strength and, even more importantly, of will. Since the Russian defeat in Chechnya, the growth of self-confidence in some of Russia's neighbours has been very marked.

A much greater threat to Western interests is posed precisely by Russian state and military weakness – if this were to lead to the illicit sale of nuclear materials or even weapons to rogue regimes. For this reason, the suicide on 30 October 1996 of Professor Vladimir Nechay, director of a formerly secret state nuclear research station at Chelyabinsk-70 (Snezhinsk), should have attracted more Western press attention and concern than all the endless column inches about a 'Russian threat to the Baltic States' and so on. Dr Nechay killed himself out of despair because the pay for his staff and the money for the upkeep of his centre was months in arrears. Even more sinister are the indications that to cover expenses he may have borrowed money from 'commercial structures' (most likely mafia linked) which he was then unable to repay. In July 1997, *Izvestia* reported that 141 officers of Russia's Northern Fleet (controlling most of the nuclear missile submarines) attempted suicide in 1996. The navy itself admitted thirty-two suicides and attempted suicides, above all because of lack of pay.[1]

The reasons for the Russian defeat in Chechnya therefore go far deeper than the specific problems of the Russian armed forces in the 1990s. They reflect both longstanding processes in Russian demography, society and culture, and fundamental weaknesses in the contemporary Russian state. The latter are the result not merely of the collapse of the Soviet Union and the attendant convulsions and changes, but of a process of the privatisation of the state and state power which in its origins goes back more than thirty years.

The depth of the weakness of the Russian state has been partly masked, however, because of the equal or greater weakness – due to seventy years of Communist rule – of Russian society, which can generate neither the forces of protest which elsewhere in the world might have brought the whole structure crashing down, nor the forces of national mobilisation (especially among the Russian populations outside Russia's borders) which would have compensated for the state's inability to project its power.

It follows that those who believe strongly in what they call the process of 'economic reform' in Russia and its neighbours ought to be very grateful for the absence of a civil society in these countries: because it is very unlikely that a population possessed of spontaneous means of socio-political organisation and mobilisation would have tolerated either the sufferings they have endured or the deeply rotten nature of the new order.

A central thesis of this book is that rather than making comparisons between the Russia of today and either the Soviet Union or the Russia of the Tsars, which are endlessly invoked by so many expert and non-expert observers, it would make more sense to look for parallels and models in the 'liberal' states of southern Europe and Latin America in the later nineteenth and early twentieth century, and among developing countries in other parts of the world today – with the key difference that while their populations are growing, that of Russia is falling steeply. I shall suggest therefore that

Gramscian concepts such as 'passive revolution' and 'hegemony' can provide an unexpectedly useful prism for understanding Russia today.

In particular, the rise to Russian state power during the period under study of a group of business and media magnates marks a completely new epoch in Russian history. Not only are several of them Jewish, but the nature of their power and influence is totally unlike anything which has previously existed in Russia. While in Washington I repeatedly heard parallels drawn between the Russian state today and that of one or other of the Tsars, with the implication that Russia is 'only returning to its ancient patterns of autocracy' (or anarchy, or corruption, or feudalism). Yet the sketchiest knowledge of Russian history is enough to tell us that Boris Berezovsky would not have become a senior security official in any government of Nicholas II.

A figure of this type is however extremely typical for the political elites of many 'developing' countries; and in so far as this is to a considerable extent an elite of a traditional Latin American 'comprador' type (with of course specific post-Soviet features), dependent for most of its wealth on controlling the state so as to extract soft loans, evade taxes and allow the unrestricted export of raw materials, it may very well play a key and malignant role in frustrating constructive economic growth.

But as political developments in Russia contemporaneous with the Chechen War – especially the presidential elections of June 1996 – have demonstrated, while the Russian state today is weak, like many such states it is probably also relatively stable. The coming years may see considerable political instability among the ruling elites, local mass protests, and possibly even coups d'état. They are very unlikely to see either a complete failure of the state, or its transformation by some revolutionary force and the recreation of Russia as a great military, expansionist and ideological power.

In examining the reasons for the political passivity of most ordinary Russians, I shall suggest that Francis Fukuyama's vision of the triumph of liberal democracy in contemporary societies is a good way of looking at Russia and the world today – but only if heavily diluted with a mixture of Antonio Gramsci, historical experience and plain historical horse-sense.

Of secondary importance for world politics but of very great interest both to military men and anthropologists is, or should be, the nature of the war on the ground and the character of the Chechen resistance. Russian weakness aside, the victory of the Chechens against such tremendous odds is a striking moment in military history, with lessons to teach on matters as diverse as military anthropology, national mobilisation, the limited effectiveness of air-power, the nature of urban combat and indeed the nature of warfare itself.

The victory of the Chechen separatist forces over Russia has been one of the greatest epics of colonial resistance in the past century. Whether it will be comparable in its historical effects to Dien Bien Phu or the FLN's victory in Algeria will depend on what now happens within Russia. In terms of sheer military achievement, however, the Chechens have already equalled the Vietcong, and Colonel Aslan Maskhadov has earned the right to be mentioned in the same breath with their General Giap, as a commander of rare and original genius.

I have dwelt on these questions in part because during a year spent in Washington DC it has struck me with increasing force how few American military analysts and advisers today have personal experience of combat or even of being and commanding soldiers; and of course even fewer have themselves been exposed to prolonged and heavy aerial bombardment. In particular, many have no way of understanding from the inside the factors which make individual soldiers fight or run away, and the whole nature of morale. This leads to distortions in their analysis, with potentially serious consequences for Western policy.

The Chechen War is also of significance and interest for historians, and not just Soviet or Russian specialists, for it involved a clash, epochal in its implications, between two utterly different nations, which can be seen as representing forces which have confronted each other since the very beginnings of recorded human history. The Russians, whose national identity has long been subsumed in a series of bureaucratic states, faced the Chechens, who have barely had any state at all in their history, and whose formidable martial attributes stem not from state organisation but from specific ethnic traditions. In the streets of Grozny, the demoralised conscript armies of Babylon, commanded not by warriors but by eunuch courtiers and corrupt officials, under the images of gods who had manifestly failed them, went down once more before the tribesmen from the hills.

To find a parallel for the triumph of such seemingly 'disorganised' , 'primitive' forces over a modern European army one would have to go back to the defeat of the Italians by the Ethiopians at Adowa, or of the Spanish by the Moroccans at Anual, or even to Red Indian victories over the British and Americans.

On the one hand, of course, this says a great deal about the Russians – for if the Russian army of today is no better than the Italians or the Spanish a century ago, then the world military order really has been turned upside down; but on the other, the Chechen victory is a testimonial to the extraordinary military qualities and fighting spirit of the Chechen tradition, as worked upon by twentieth-century influences and events.

In emphasising the striking nature of the Chechen victory, one must also remark the small size of the Chechen population and of the separatist armed forces. Consider: apart perhaps from during the Russian assault on Grozny at the beginning of the war, and the Chechen counter-attack of August 1996, when the Chechen forces in Grozny and elsewhere may have numbered up to 6,000 men, the most common estimate is that the Chechen independence forces never had more than 3,000 fighters actually in the field at any one time, as against up to fifteen times that number on the Russian side. Of course, the total number of Chechens who have fought at one time or another is very much larger. None the less, in most battles the Russians enjoyed a vastly greater superiority in numbers than was possessed by the French and Americans in Indo-China, the French in Algeria, or for that matter the Soviet forces in Afghanistan. Moreover, at around 6,000 square miles (excluding Ingushetia), Chechnya is only a fraction of the size of these countries. It is rather as if the entire Vietnam war had been restricted to the province of Hue – and the Americans had *still* been beaten.

Moreover, the usual problem for armies fighting against 'primitive' or guerrilla enemies – from the Romans to the US Rangers – is to get the enemy to stand and fight. According to Colonel Sir Charles Callwell's maxim, 'Tactics favour the regular army while strategy favours the enemy – therefore the object is to fight, not to manoeuvre.'[2] The Chechens accepted this challenge – and beat the Russian regulars, fair and square. Their triumph therefore is a reminder that because war for the individual fighting soldier so often comes down to a test of spirit and morale, the victory of the 'civilised' and 'modern' side can never be taken for granted. There will be room in the future of warfare for more Adowas and Little Big Horns.

This book aims therefore both to mark this 'clash of civilisations' and to make a small but I hope useful contribution to the continuing academic debate on the origins of nations and nationalisms. To be quite honest, while maintaining I hope a due scholarly and journalistic objectivity, I also wanted to honour the courage and tenacity of the Chechen people, for whom I have developed a deep admiration.

Much of the thrust of this book – and, I would say, of the facts themselves – is directed against three closely intertwined and extremely influential Western schools of thought concerning Russia. The first – associated above all with the name of Professor Richard Pipes, but very widespread in the worlds of academia, journalism and government – sees deep continuities running through and even largely determining the course of Russian history from the Middle Ages through the Tsarist empire and the Soviet Union to the post-Soviet present. The second school, which derives to a great extent from the first, sees the Russians and Russian culture as deeply, perennially and primordially imperialist, aggressive and expansionist.

The third school appears to be absolutely opposed to the first two, but in fact frequently plays into their hands. This is the approach characteristic of the more optimistic Western economic commentators on Russia, such as Anders Aslund and Richard Layard, who deny that Russian history and special characteristics of contemporary Russia are of major importance when it comes to the nature and progress of Russian reform. They assert, by contrast, that Russia is well on the way to becoming a 'normal' country.

To dissect these approaches in order. In a 1996 article, Professor Pipes wrote of an apparently fixed and unchanging 'Russian political culture' leading both to the adoption of the Leninist form of Marxism in 1917 and to the problems of Russian democracy in 1996 – as if this culture had not changed in the past eighty years, and as if the vote of ordinary Russians for the Communists in 1996 were motivated by the same sentiments which drove Lenin's

Red Guards.[3] This approach leads to extreme scepticism about whether Russia can ever be a 'normal' country – 'normal' of course meaning a country situated in the north-western part of the Northern hemisphere in the last quarter of the twentieth century.

Pipes also makes no distinction between the Communists and the 'nationalists' (by which he presumably meant Lebed), 'since both wish to reconquer the lost empire' – differences over economic policy and attitudes to private property, it seems, are simply not issues to be considered when such primordial ethnic forces are at work.

Representative of the second school, which believes in a unique and uniquely malign Russia, are the words of Dr Ariel Cohen: 'It is not prudent to deny or forget a thousand years of Russian history. It is replete with wars of imperial aggrandizement, the Russification of ethnic minorities, and absolutist, authoritarian, and totalitarian rule.'[4] (Neither the USA nor any other Western country having of course ever expanded, conquered indigenous peoples, or imposed on them its language and culture, or been themselves under an authoritarian regime.)

The historicist fallacy and that of Russia's uniqueness have often been accompanied by a tendency to exaggerate first Soviet and now Russian military strength. In the USA, this is associated with numerous 'analysts' and indeed with the now highly discredited portrait of the Soviet Union drawn by the Central Intelligence Agency in the 1980s, under William Casey and Robert Gates.[5]

At its crudest, this attitude can take forms which are virtually racialist; as for example in the words of the American conservative columnist George Will, 'Expansionism is in the Russians' DNA.'[6] Or Peter Rodman: 'The only potential great-power security problem in Central Europe is the lengthening shadow of Russian strength, and NATO has the job of counter-balancing it. Russia is a force of nature; all this is inevitable.'[7] The tone of such statements is partly due to the influence in America of ethnic minorities from the former Russian empire, who have retained bitter memories of past oppression, and in consequence a deep, abiding and seemingly unchangeable hatred for Russia and Russians.

These are extreme versions; but something very like this attitude underlies the whole approach to Russia of Western journals like the *Wall Street Journal*. Even a milder and more balanced version of Russian preoccupations can be seriously misleading. Thus in the words of Professor Pipes 'Nothing so much troubles many Russians today, not even the decline of their living standards or the prevalence of crime, and nothing so lowers in their eyes the prestige of their government, as the precipitous loss of great power status.'[8] On some occasions in recent years, this appeared to be borne out by the statements of Russian politicians, the behaviour of the Russian government, and the heavy vote (albeit in only one election) for Vladimir Zhirinovsky. One of the points of my book, however, is that the statements of politicians, and even of ordinary Russians, on this score need to be taken with a massive pinch of salt. The question is: they talk the talk, but do they walk the walk? For the world is full of nations which regularly indulge in outbursts of nationalist rhetoric, and still more of elites who use such rhetoric to mask their real and ugly motives for holding on to state power. How many, though, actually have the ability or the will to act out their rhetoric in reality?

Every single reputable opinion poll in Russia in the years 1994–6 showed exactly the opposite of what Pipes is alleging about the priorities of ordinary Russians. They all put living standards, job security and crime at the top of ordinary Russians' concerns, far above questions of foreign policy or great power status.[9] Thus in answering the open-ended question as to 'the single most serious problem facing the country' in an opinion poll of April 1996, 56 per cent of respondents pointed to various economic problems, 17 per cent to ethnic conflicts, 8 per cent to crime and corruption, and less than 1 per cent to the issues related to national security and similar issues.

It is true that polls have always shown a very strong desire for the restoration of the Soviet Union, but this has also been true among many Ukrainians, Caucasians and Central Asians; the key reason, especially among the elderly, is a desire not for empire and glory but for a return to security. Furthermore, most Russian politicians together with the vast majority of ordinary Russians stress that reunification must be voluntary or at least peaceable. Less than 10 per cent of Russians, according to polls conducted in 1996, were willing to contemplate the use of force either to recreate the USSR or to 'reunite' Russia with Russian-populated areas beyond its borders.

This book is also intended as a form of accounting with my own previous mistakes in analysing contemporary Russia. In the light of subsequent events, many readers of my previous book, *The Baltic Revolution*, written in 1992, have felt that I exaggerated the degree of threat to the Baltic States both from Russia and more importantly from their own Russian minorities. In the run-up to the Chechen War, like every other observer I also greatly overestimated the strength of the Russian army – or rather underestimated its extreme decline.

If I write with a certain anger about the more Russophobe or paranoid Western school of thought concerning Russia, this is partly because I was too much influenced by the picture of Russia and Russians drawn by analysts such as Richard Pipes, Zbigniew Brzezinski, Paul Goble and Ariel Cohen.[10] For it is crucial to remember that if the kind of Russian nation they portray had really existed – if indeed the contemporary Russians had resembled other European imperial nations in the past – then the history of the former Soviet Union in the mid-1990s would have been very different and very much nastier. Would Russians in the Baltic States who were obsessed with national power and status have sat so quietly by while their civic rights were severely restricted and their language driven from public life? If national pride and identity had been the top concern of Russians in Crimea, would they not have struggled very much harder for their independence? Would Russian elites for whom the restoration of imperial power was of paramount importance have starved the Russian army until it could be defeated by the Chechens? And even if starving, wouldn't ordinary Russian soldiers fired up with real national feeling have fought hard and well at least to preserve Russian territorial integrity against Chechen secession?

Even after Chechnya, Western belief in and fear of Russian military power remains extraordinarily tenacious. Thus on 5 January 1997, the *Washington Post* published an article on the former Western Soviet republics entitled 'Still within Reach of Russian Bear', datelined Kiev. It spoke of Russia 'projecting its military power' throughout the region and menacing its neighbours, of the Baltic States' 'utter military vulnerability' to Russia, of the 'heavily militarised' enclave of Kaliningrad 'effectively encircling' Latvia, Lithuania and Estonia. All this is tied to a historical process by which 'Russian rulers from Catherine the Great to Stalin [*sic*]' 'seized these lands' for 'Russia'.

The really extraordinary thing about this article was the date. January 5th 1997 was one day after the last Russian troops were withdrawn from Chechnya, after having been humiliatingly defeated by an apparently hopelessly outnumbered and outgunned adversary; and indeed, after years in which Russia had not in fact attempted military coercion of any of its Western neighbours.

The third approach, which believes that there is little to stop Russia becoming a 'normal' country, has recently been summed up by Richard Layard and John Parker. In a chapter entitled 'Is Russia Different?' they briefly discuss the way in which previous attempts to 'liberalise' Russia have failed, and ask whether this means that contemporary Russian reform and democracy are doomed. They reply:

> The short answer is that 'history is bunk', that the historical record provides no real guide to present behaviour and that historically formed cultural characteristics do not necessarily stand in the way of a country's ability to change. If culture is so important, how can they explain a culture's success in one era and failure in another?[11]

On the one hand, this approach is obviously more rational than the historicist one; but it also risks leading straight back to it. This is because of its very culturally constrained and indeed time-bound version of the 'normality' towards which Russia should be working, with 'normal' defined as a sanitised and homogenised version of the late twentieth-century West. For while there is no unique or mysterious historical, cultural or spiritual reason why contemporary Russia should not be able to achieve stable democracy and an effective free market system that will lead to prosperity for the mass of its population, a lot of good reasons do exist, and far from being uniquely Russian they are present in many countries of the world: a weak state and legal order, a weak civil society, extreme and cynical individualism, corruption, ignorant, shallow and greedy leaders, the entrenched rule of economically counterproductive elites. Unfortunately, over the past hundred and fifty years there has been nothing at all 'abnormal' about such states, with politically apathetic or disorganised populations, ruled by small elites who derive their wealth from the export of commodities, and from their ability, through control of the state, to evade taxation; and who spend that wealth on property abroad or the consumption of foreign luxuries; and who sometimes whip up chauvinist nationalism to consolidate their own rule and mask its vices.

A huge proportion of the Western and especially the American press tends to take the 'monolinear' approach to the 'transition' of Russia and the other former Communist states, according to which they are all on one 'path' to 'democracy and the free market'. They may proceed at different speeds, stop, or even go backwards, but the assumption is that the ultimate goal is one and indivisible, and you can take only one monorail route to go there. The most sophisticated contemporary version of this is, of course, Francis Fukuyama's 'end of history' thesis – much scorned by academic critics, and in part deservedly. However, his analysis is useful as a basis for argument, and he is careful to give a sophisticated and fair analysis of various challenges to his position.[12]

In the American media, by contrast, a shallow, bland version of Fukuyama's thought is so omnipresent that it is rarely noticed, let alone analysed or criticised. A classical, and typical, example was in a *Washington Post* article of 1996. The subject was the Armenians, but exactly the same formula has been used about all of the former Communist countries which have undergone 'reform'. The correspondent wrote that 'after Soviet rule and war with Azerbaijan, They are getting back on the path of free markets and democracy, albeit with growing pains.'[13]

Leaving aside the truly horrible mixed metaphor – for after all, what do you do if you suffer growing pains while on a path? Retire behind a tree? – this sentence in its short life succeeds in promiscuously coupling with no fewer than four ideological assumptions, all of them of doubtful character. The first is the religious and mystical imagery bound up with the metaphor of a 'path', evocative of spiritual quests, pilgrimages, adventures and the pursuit of various species of Grail. It must be pointed out that except for rare revolutionary moments, the use of religious metaphors for political processes is usually a mistake. Everywhere and most of the time, the principal business of politics is politics: it is the process by which people try to acquire and keep some form of power, the wealth that comes from power, or the power to protect wealth. We all know this instinctively when we look at our own politicians; but too often, when reporting on other countries, the assumption is made that their political processes are somehow much more driven by ideological 'quests'.

Secondly, reinforcing the religious metaphor in this passage, with its implications of the nobility and grandeur of the aim, is the organic metaphor of 'growing pains', which implies an inevitable and scientifically determined process, by which a life, unless artificially 'cut short', develops according to certain fixed rules towards an inevitable end. (The rather comical thing of course is that this end is death, which was presumably not what the writer meant to imply.) Actually, states and nations, while they may well develop in some sense organically, do not do so after the fashion of individual human organisms. Rather they are like complex ecosystems, in which one element changes, unpredictably influencing the rest, and so on, until in the end the whole system has been transformed.

Thirdly, there is the assumption that before this organic process was temporarily interrupted by Soviet rule, Armenia and other nations in the region were in fact proceeding along this path to 'democracy and the free market'. This was true of Estonia and Latvia, and possibly of Georgia; but in the case of Armenia and other areas, their actual history before the Soviet annexation, and the ideology of their leading nationalist parties, allows no such confidence.

Finally, there is the monolithic attitude that colours the entire passage and approach. It speaks of *the* path to democracy (evidently viewed as a single form, already fixed and fully understood) and *the* free market. Now it is obviously true that modernising and globalising tendencies both in economics and American culture are leading to a certain homogenisation of human society. It is also true that ostensibly free elections are now very widespread. But that said, it is equally obvious that the way that capitalist economies work and are influenced by states differs immensely from country to country;[14] that the paths by which countries have developed capitalism are highly varied; and that for every truly 'free' electoral system (whatever free really means in this context), there is another which in one way or another is rigged, bought, managed, guided or shaped according to local patterns and traditions. It is also true of course that for every fully successful capitalist state there are two or three where for many decades progress has proved halting and ambiguous, especially as far as the mass of the population is concerned. There is nothing 'abnormal' in the world today about the states of Egypt, Mexico or Pakistan.

In the words of Professor Jim Millar, 'the default mode in today's world is not a market economy. It is stagnation, corruption and great inequalities of income.' And ironically, as the *Washington Post* article on Armenia with the above passage appeared, the Armenian government was itself following a 'normal' pattern by preparing to rig the Armenian elections and crack down on the opposition.

Analysis based on the monolinear view of developments is mistaken with regard to most countries in the world. In the case of Russia, it can become actively dangerous, because it can so easily tie in with prejudices about the 'perennial' Russian character, criticised above. This is because if there is only one path forward, then this logically means that there is only one path back: – *either* the development of a pro-Western, free market democracy, *or* reversion to 'dictatorship and aggressive external policies' – is a complete misunderstanding. The fact is that both a Russian 'democracy' and a 'dictatorship' would desire to restore Russian hegemony over the other states of the former Soviet Union, but both would be headed by pragmatists (this is clear from the present line-up of potential future leaders – Lebed, Chernomyrdin and Luzhkov may be personally disagreeable, but they are all in their different ways rational and sensible men, and certainly not fanatics) and these prag-matists will realise that Russia has to operate under the most severe economic, military, social and international constraints on its behaviour. And because of all the changes that have taken place, any dictatorship in Russia today would not be a 'reversion' to the past but something qualitatively different from any previous Russian authoritarian regime, with a new nature and a new power base.

When this Western belief in a single road to democracy becomes mixed up with the ideological belief that 'democracies do not go to war with each other', whereas dictatorships are naturally prone to aggression, then the layers of mystification become almost impenetrable. This book is, among other things, an attempt to pierce through some of these mists.

Part I: The War

And drowning in their hearts their despair by means of songs, debauches and vodka, hundreds of thousands of simple, good people torn away from their wives, mothers and children, will march, with weapons of murder in their hands, whither they will be driven. They will go to freeze, to starve, to sicken, to die of disease, and finally they will arrive at the place where they will be killed by the thousand and will kill by the thousand – themselves not knowing why – men whom they have never seen and who have done them and can do them no harm.

Leo Tolstoy, 'Christianity and Patriotism'

A striking thing about the Chechen War, as seen from the perspective of the year after its close, is how little difference it seems to have made to the governments or the underlying political and economic orders in either Russia or Chechnya. In Russia, despite the utter humiliation he had brought on his administration and the Russian army, Boris Yeltsin remained President, and Victor Chernomyrdin remained his Prime Minister, as he had been in December 1994. Anatoly Kulikov, the Interior Minister in charge during several of the disasters in Chechnya, remained at his post. Sergei Stepashin, the secret service chief whose personal intrigues and total misreading of Chechen military potential was directly responsible for the intervention, was removed in 1995, but reappointed in 1997 as Justice Minister. The Yeltsin regime proved too strong to be shifted even by such a national humiliation as Chechnya, and in defiance of the great majority of predictions, survived both the presidential elections of 1996 and the subsequent attempt by General Lebed to take over from within.

It is worth pointing out how very unusual Yeltsin's victory was in terms of history, global patterns, and stereotypes of Russia. According to all these models, it should have been Lebed who won in 1996, impelled to power by a wave of popular fury at the way the Yeltsin regime had betrayed the army and humiliated the nation in Chechnya, on top of all the other sacrifices of Russian power and international position that he had made from 1991 on.

The reasons for the regime's survival, however, have little to do with its own inner strengths. Rather it was saved by two external factors, which will be analysed in part II, and which run beneath the events described in part I: in the first place, the political apathy and fear of chaos of the Russian population meant that no mass political opposition to Yeltsin developed; and secondly, in 1995–6 the most powerful section of the new Russian elites – the comprador-bankers – came to the rescue of the regime in return for being given an even larger share of control over Russia's raw materials. This deal was apparently brokered by Anatoly Chubais, then Privatisation Minister.

They came to Yeltsin's aid of course to secure their own position and weath, and not for any other reason; for, as this book will emphasise, it would be utterly wrong to see Russia's new dominant elites as concerned by Russian national power or even Russian national interest. In the words of Yegor Gaidar, who after all got to know them very well during his time as acting Prime Minister in 1992, the goals of the new Russian policy-makers 'are of a purely private character: strengthening the state for the purpose of quick enrichment'.[1]

Through the 'loans for shares' deal in the autumn of 1995, the 'group of seven' great bankers ('semibankirshchina') received control of leading Russian oil and metal industries at risibly small prices in return for agreeing to fund and support Yeltsin the following year, whether he decided to run in the elections or cancel them. They and other businessmen provided 500 million dollars or more in campaign funds (the legal spending limit was $3 million), and media magnates Boris Berezovsky and Vladimir Gusinsky used their television channels relentlessly to attack the Communists. The Yeltsin team was advised on the use of the media by a group of American PR men, including former Republican campaign staffers.[2] In the weeks immediately before the elections, the media were also used to build up General Alexander Lebed, presumably after he made a secret deal to support Yeltsin and not the Communist candidate, Gennady Zyuganov, in the second round.

There is no space in this book to tell the history of Russian politics in these years – and in any case, the full story will doubtless remain hidden for a long time, if not forever. Voting patterns in the elections will be analysed in chapter 5. The culminations of both the political process and the Chechen War came on the same day, 6 August 1996. On that day, Yeltsin was inaugurated in Moscow for his second term as President, and the Chechens launched a victorious offensive that swept the Russians out of Grozny and convinced key elements in the Yeltsin regime that the war could not be won. The result was the peace settlement between the new security chief General Lebed and the Chechen military commander General Aslan Maskhadov, by which the Russians agreed to withdraw from most of Chechnya.

The peace settlement was immensely popular with the Russian people; but this did not save Lebed, who was removed by Yeltsin in October 1996 after making too obvious a push to take over much of his power. As usual in Russia, despite Lebed's popularity, no public demonstrations of protest occurred. The deal with Maskhadov had been used by Anatoly Chubais,

General Kulikov and other enemies of Lebed to discredit the general and prepare for his removal, on the grounds that he had 'betrayed Russian interests'; but in fact, the bulk of the regime was only too grateful to have been extricated from Chechnya, and as will be seen, later themselves pulled out more totally than Lebed seems to have envisaged.

Was the Chechen War, however symbolic of the condition of Russia and the Russian state, therefore essentially irrelevant to the main political processes at work in Russia during these years? Hardly. Without the defeat in Chechnya, it is possible that the presidential elections of 1996 would not have taken place at all. There were powerful elements in the Yeltsin administration who believed, especially after the Communist success in the Duma elections of December 1995, that the elections should not be risked, and that instead they should be postponed under a state of emergency, either by agreement with the Communists or by authoritarian means. The leader of this school of thought was Yeltsin's personal security chief and old crony, General Alexander Korzhakov. He reportedly warned among other things that the President was simply not well enough to face elections – and in this, of course, Korzhakov came within a few days of being proved right, when Yeltsin had a heart attack just after the first round. On 15 February, when the President announced definitively that he would run in the elections, several of his staff are reported to have stood in the background crying, convinced that he would lose.[3] Korzhakov also claimed, quite wrongly, that the 'radical opposition' would refuse to accept a Yeltsin victory, and would start mass protests.

In fact, the Communists had no such plans. But in late April, the 'group of seven' were sufficiently worried that they joined other leading businessmen in writing an open letter calling for a deal with the Communists and the postponement of the elections.[4] However, by then Chubais, now serving as Yeltsin's campaign manager, had persuaded the President to risk the elections. A key moment in the defeat of Korzhakov's plans was at a meeting of Yeltsin's senior aides on 20 March. Two days earlier, the Communist-dominated Duma had passed a motion denouncing the Byelovezhskaya Pushcha agreement of December 1991 between the presidents of Russia, Ukraine and Belarus by which the Soviet Union was dissolved. The vote was widely (though not entirely fairly) interpreted as one for the overthrow of the existing post-Soviet states and the restoration of the Soviet Union, and Korzhakov argued that this threat could be used as a pretext for declaring a state of emergency and postponing the elections. After a stormy discussion, Chubais and his supporters persuaded Yeltsin to overrule him – a decision which seems to have been due above all to the influence of Yeltsin's daughter, Tatyana Dyachenko, closely linked to Chubais and reputed to be his lover. Korzhakov was finally removed after the first round of the elections, and went into opposition.

It seems possible that if the Russian armed forces had not suffered their humiliating reversals in Chechnya, the prestige and strength of the security clique around Yeltsin would have been greater, and they might in fact have persuaded the President to cancel the elections. If so, the political history of Russia would have changed in a number of incalculable ways. The Chechen resistance fighters might be said therefore to have saved not just themselves but also Russian democracy – for what that is worth.

The ability of the Chechens to generate a democratic or even an effective state of their own is much more questionable. Even more surprising than Russia's failure to change in response to the Chechen War was Chechnya's failure to do so – something which indicates the tremendous underlying strengths of Chechen 'ordered anarchy'. Formidable mobilising mechanisms in the face of outside invasion, these aspects of Chechen society, which will be analysed in part III, are almost equally formidable obstacles to the creation of a modern Chechen state by the Chechens themselves. Up to the war, the regime of Dzhokhar Dudayev had had very little success, and indeed made very little real effort, to replace the collapsed institutions of the Soviet state in Chechnya with indigenously generated ones.

One might have expected that the tremendous pressures of war would have forced the Chechens to create modern centralised institutions; but as of mid-1997, the government of Aslan Maskhadov was having the greatest difficulty in establishing modern state authority in Chechnya, as the spate of kidnappings and raids into Russia demonstrated. Above all, of course, it was far from establishing a monopoly of major armed force, usually taken as *the* defining characteristic of the modern state. The old Chechen order, like the new Russian one, emerged from the Chechen War bloodied, but unbowed and to a remarkable degree unchanged.

1 A Personal Memoir of Grozny and the Chechen War

The fight was over. All was still.
The bodies made a grisly hill.
Blood trickled from them, steaming, smoking...
'Just tell me, my kunak,
What do they call this little river?'
'They call it Valerik', he said,
'Which means The River of the Dead.
Those who named it are in Heaven...'
Then someone else's voice I heard,
'This day is for the war decisive'.
I caught the Chechen's glance derisive.
He grinned but did not say a word.

Mikhail Lermontov, 'Valerik'

Journey to Grozny

'Good luck!' said the Azeri colonel, with a leer. 'And when you see Dudayev, tell him that I drink to him as a hero not just of Chechnya, but for every true Muslim of the Caucasus!' Upon which he downed a large glass of Russian vodka.

The date was January 1992, the place a shabby but well-stocked black-market restaurant in the grim Azerbaijani industrial town of Sumgait, north of Baku on the Caspian Sea. From the distance – a pretty long distance – Sumgait, like Baku, can look rather grand, in an archaic kind of way. Especially at sunset, the gold-grey stone of its buildings seems to glow from within, and flows upwards from the golden dust of the surrounding semi-desert, until it meets the azure sea. Close to, the big picture disappears, and what is left is the grimly repetitive boredom of run-down Soviet provincial architecture.

Sumgait is poor, but even in 1992 some of its people were already rich. The restaurant was a curious pseudo-Moorish affair – 'built in the traditional Azeri style' – raw with newness, in the middle of a courtyard walled in grey concrete. It was richly stocked with the simple but pleasant food of Azerbaijan: sturgeon kebabs, lamb kebabs, herb salads and so on.

My host, a leading Soviet Azeri intellectual and Communist Party official,

17

was a man of three worlds, all of which he disliked. The Soviet Union he had served not just from opportunism but also from the same motives as many Asian former colonial servants, because it represented 'modernity' and 'progress'; yet he also hated it, because it meant the rule of crude and alien Russians. But Turkey he feared because pan-Turkic nationalism was a threat to the dominance of his own Soviet elite class, and indeed to his Azeri identity. As he put it, 'The love of Turkey you hear so many people expressing is the new religion of the village schoolteacher. He was brought up to be absolutely Communist, and now he is looking for a new identity, something simple and above all given from outside.'

In his disdain for the Turks was something of the attitude of his third world, his ancestors from the old Azeri elites of Baku and Shirvanshir, older by far than the powerful vulgarities of Soviet Moscow or Kemalist Ankara. Though of Turkic blood, they spoke Persian and looked for cultural inspiration to Iran, 'the greatest kingdom of this world'. But Iran's new rulers, the Ayatollahs, would have put him in gaol at once – and well he knew it. For he was a committed secularist – albeit one who would also never allow a stranger to meet his womenfolk. Whether because of his tradition or his confusion, he was the most interesting and detached person I met in Azerbaijan. He was even detached and objective about the growing war with the Armenians – detached enough at least to have no desire to see his relatives fight in it.

As for the colonel who offered the toast, he was made of simpler stuff. He was the police chief of the town, and reportedly deeply implicated in the infamous anti-Armenian pogrom there four years before – a pogrom which according to him had never occurred, or if it had, was the work of the Armenians themselves, instigated by the KGB.

His law enforcement record aside, the colonel's speech contained a variety of ironies. A 'true Muslim' drinking Russian vodka has become a cliché of the newly independent Muslim republics of the former Soviet Union, and hardly needs elaboration. The colonel's admiration for the Chechens was also ambiguous. Moments earlier, he had been warning me that 'they are all bandits, dangerous people,' and advising me strongly not to go to Grozny. Hence the 'Good luck!' – and the leer.

A further irony was that far from preparing himself to go and help the Chechen cause, the colonel had so far shown no apparent desire to go and fight for his own Muslim country of Azerbaijan, in its own backyard of Karabakh. This behaviour was highly characteristic of most Azeri colonels of my acquaintance; it helps explain the equal unwillingness of most Azeri privates to risk their lives. A single month in Azerbaijan had already been enough to give an impression of a deeply demoralised society, for reasons that appeared to go deeper than Soviet rule alone; or rather, as I noted at the time, 'unlike the Balts or the Georgians, Sovietism is a disease to which the Azeris have proved especially susceptible.'

Although the Chechen victory, and the humiliation of the Russian army, has greatly strengthened the hands of Azeris and Georgians in dealing with

Moscow, curiously enough it has been a humiliation for them as well. This is because for years these peoples comforted themselves for their defeats at the hands of the Armenians and the Abkhaz by saying that behind these peoples stood Russia, 'and who can win against Russia?'

Repeated Chechen victories have proved the hollowness of this excuse. The Azeris and Georgians were defeated fair and square – and still more, they defeated themselves. The Chechens played a leading part in the defeat of the Georgians (see below), and as for the military failure of the Azeris, the Chechens would never have predicted anything else. Their contempt for their Caucasian neighbours, Muslim as well as Christian, is deep and generally unconcealed. In Moscow, a Chechen mafia leader once told me that 'the Azeri groups here are just about up to bullying fruit-sellers in the market; but for real protection, they themselves have to come to us, the Chechens. On their own they're nothing.' This kind of attitude, however justified, has not made the Chechens much loved among their neighbours, and it has been partly responsible for the overwhelming absence of real support for them in the region since their struggle against Russia began.

The Azeris in my train compartment during the eighteen-hour journey to Grozny, through northern Azerbaijan and Daghestan, made no attempt to hide their hostility to the Chechens, an attitude of fear mixed with unwilling respect. They had some reason: the next three years saw repeated attacks by armed Chechen criminals on that particular train as it made its laborious way from Baku through Chechnya and north into Russia.

The passengers were by turns tragic, pitiable and disgusting, human flotsam from the wreck of the Soviet Union, which had finally sunk barely a month earlier. There were 'Russians' (some of whom looked Armenian to me, which would explain their flight) leaving their homes in Baku for an uncertain future in Russia, with relatives who, as one old woman, Lyudmilla Alexandrovna, told me, 'probably don't want us at all. I've lived in Baku for thirty years, my husband is buried there, I'll be a foreigner in Russia. But my son and his family are in Rostov, and he said to join them while I still can.' There were engineers fleeing Azerbaijan's collapsing economy for the slightly brighter prospects of Russia; many ordinary Azeris who had taken jobs elsewhere in the Union when it still was a Union, and were trying to rejoin their jobs or their families; some Soviet servicemen unsure of whether they still had a state, an army or even a country – as one teenage conscript said, 'I am half Russian and half Ukrainian, and one grandfather was a Tatar. I was a Soviet citizen. Now what am I, you tell me?' He had a look I was to find characteristic of many Russian conscripts, a strange mixture of extreme youth and vulnerability overlain with cynicism and coarseness, which in turn barely concealed a deep misery; like so many Soviet-made things, shiny with newness yet already scarred and battered – perhaps even broken for good.

And everywhere were the petty traders, former black marketeers now enjoying a still precarious legality, and swelling and oozing almost visibly before our eyes. There were fat ones, bulging in odd places like their own sacks of fruit and vegetables; there were leaner, younger ones, all with hard faces, some with heavily scarred ones. When travelling, they were not, I noticed, wearing the heavy gold jewellery which that class already liked to sport on its home turf; but one of them was wearing a suit apparently made entirely from imitation silver thread, which shone faintly in the dim light as he made undulating lunges in my direction, hinting at various things he could sell me, including the mercenary favours of the conductress, a plump, heavily made-up, resilient-looking Russian woman in her mid-thirties.

The train itself was close to being a wreck, icily cold, filthy, enveloped in a fug of cigarette smoke, urine, sweat, alcohol and cheap scent. As evening drew on, it crawled clanking through a hellish landscape – the oilfields of northern Azerbaijan, perhaps the ugliest post-industrial environment in the world. Hundreds, no thousands of abandoned, stunted, archaic-looking derricks sit amidst pools of oil and fragments of rusted machinery. In summer, the stench can make you physically ill; in winter, grey sky, black oil and brown desert merge into a symphony of gloom.

The whole tragedy of Soviet 'development' was in that scene. There in those countless lakes of oil was the potential wealth of Azerbaijan, pumped out to power the Soviet Union's megalomaniac visions, much of it lost on the spot through leaks and wastage, and as far as the people of Azerbaijan were concerned, almost all of it ultimately thrown away. Scattered among the oilfields are shanty-towns of mud-brick, the roofs covered with corrugated iron and plastic sheeting. Since 1992, these have been swelled by tens of thousands of refugees from the areas of Azerbaijan lost in the war with Armenia, then already gathering pace.

To complete the picture and my mood, all that was lacking was an albatross. Instead I had a whole trainload of ancient mariners. On the subject of their own countries they were bad enough. All expected civil war; the Azeris thought, quite rightly as it turned out, that they would soon be fighting each other as well as the Armenians, and several said with conviction that independence would not last, that Moscow would soon restore its rule. There was only one Azeri optimist, and he was very optimistic indeed. Breathing beer into my face, he began cursing the West for its backing of the Armenians – 'You always hated us Muslims, and wanted to destroy us! But you wait! You wait! The next century will be Turkish! First we will destroy the Armenians and then we will conquer you, and rule the world!' – until others in his group pulled him away.

As for the Russians, they seemed numbed and bewildered. Most of all they were afraid of famine – which in that bleak and chaotic winter of 1992 seemed a real possibility. Food was desperately short in many places, and queues were appalling even by past Soviet standards. 'I lived through the war and the hungry years afterwards,' Lyudmilla Alexandrovna told me. 'Now it looks as if we shall have to bear hunger again. But still, if you are to starve, it is better to starve among your own people.'

If the picture of Russia in the 1990s that I draw in this book is a grim one, it is worth remembering that things could have been a great deal worse. Yegor Gaidar's freeing of prices, which took place a few weeks after this journey, was as much an emergency response to the collapse in the supply of essential goods to the cities as it was the planned basis for free-market reform.

The sheer spiritual confusion and physical misery of that winter of the Soviet Union's death may hold part of the explanation for the central theme of this book: the subsequent apathy of ordinary Russians in the face of loss of empire, military defeat, international humiliation and unparalleled thieving by their own rulers. Psychologically, they had already touched bottom. During the presidential election campaign of 1996, the pro-Yeltsin media's harping on the famines and sufferings under Communist rule was so effective partly because in 1991–2 many Russians had felt they were once more facing famine and mass violence between Russians themselves. They recognised that however awful Yeltsin's rule had been, it had at least spared them that.

But the Baku–Grozny train, although it felt like the bottom of the pit, also symbolised something else: the way in which the Soviet infrastructure has continued to function, and so to support the population, partly because of the resilience and residual sense of duty of some of the people serving that infrastructure. This also was part of the explanation why the former Soviet Union did not in fact become like parts of Africa. The train groaned, it stank, it probably left pieces of itself behind on the rails – but it moved, and carried its passengers with it, even if few of them had any real idea where they were going. *E pur si muove.*

As this miniature Soviet world approached the borders of Chechnya, the Soviet nations aboard seemed to draw together in the face of a common threat. I can't remember which worried me more – the drunken Azeri 'businessman' who drew his hand over various parts of his anatomy, laughing uproariously, to indicate which bits of me the Chechens would cut off first; or the motherly Azeri woman, pushing a piece of bread into my hand and imploring me not to get off in Grozny. 'You are so young! You must think of your family!' Their news on Chechnya came exclusively from the former Soviet, now Russian television in Moscow, which painted a picture of Grozny in the grip of chaos, with looting and murder running rife.

The train halted in Grozny, five hours late, shortly before 4 a.m. Everything was dark. From the distance came an occasional shot. It may have been my own feelings which made me think that the train stopped for an unusually short time, and lumbered off again with more than its habitual speed. The handful of other people who had got out disappeared into the night. And I – as a good member of the British middle classes on unfamiliar ground – I went to find a policeman; or rather a group of heavily armed Chechen policemen and their friends, who refused as a matter of hospitality even to look at the passport I offered them, shared their meagre breakfast with me, and delivered me, through the curfew, to a sort of hotel, the Kavkaz.

This stood opposite a large white Soviet official building then at the beginning of its confused series of transmogrifications from Central Committee of the Communist Party of the Soviet Socialist Autonomous Republic of Checheno-Ingushetia, to the Parliament of the Sovereign Republic of Chechnya-Ichkeria, to the Presidential headquarters, to a shattered wreck and world-famous symbol of Chechen resistance, to an empty space, a clearing in a forest of ruins.

But looking at it from my window that morning I noted the following in my diary 'more like a babbling travel writer at a new resort than a supposedly serious correspondent in the middle of a revolution':[1] 'A delightful first impression. Open, cheerful, friendly without the odious oily familiarity of the Azeris. Also not subservient, either to me or their own officers. Self-respect and personal dignity. And none of the Soviet surliness. What a change from Baku! Chechen contempt for the Azeris – "all bandits", of course. But also cowards, weaklings, corrupt, Soviet slaves etc. Interesting: the Azeris and Russians dislike the Chechens, but also obviously fear and respect them; the Chechens don't respect anyone else at all. The police captain stresses the unity, pride and egalitarianism of the Chechens: "From millionaire to tractor driver, the important thing is to be a Chechen. We have very strict rules about how we behave to each other. Everyone has a gun here now, but you will see for yourself that we never shoot each other. But against our enemies, we will fight to the end"'.

Parts of the captain's speech were of course an exaggeration – but an exaggeration of the truth. Visually, the journey from Baku to Grozny had been simply a trip from an interesting Soviet oil town, intermittently hideous and strangely beautiful, on a lovely bay, to a banal and ugly one amidst nondescript rolling hills. Culturally and spiritually, it turned out to be a journey between worlds. And irritating, and sometimes terrifying, as I often subsequently found the Chechens, and terrible as has been the Chechen War, I never wholly lost the sense that to go among the Chechens is to go into a certain kind of morning, cold and stormy, but bright and somehow transcending the normal run of existence.

The longer I knew them, the more the Chechens seemed to me a people who had rejected not just much of the Soviet version of modernisation and the modern state – with all its works and all its empty promises – but modernisation in general. In this they reminded me somewhat of the Afghan Mujahidin, but with many times the latter's capacity for self-discipline, organisation and solidarity. This may make them remarkably suited for the postmodern age; but whether for the good or the bane of mankind remains to be seen. Perhaps it doesn't matter. Since December 1994, I have come to look on the Chechen people almost as on the face of Courage herself – with no necessary relation to justice or morality, but beautiful to see.

From Russian Fortress to Soviet Oil Town

Before its destruction, there was nothing about the city of Grozny to suggest that it was the capital of an extraordinary people – the reason, of course, being that it was not in fact a Chechen city. It was founded on 10 June 1818 by General Alexei Yermolov as one of the fortresses of the Cossack line, and served as the Russian headquarters in the campaigns first to contain, and then to conquer and suppress the Chechens. It was named Grozny, meaning 'Terrible', or more accurately 'Formidable', though a longstanding pun, which needs no explanation, renders it as 'Gryazny', or 'Dirty'.[2]

Originally Grozny was simply an earthen fort, a knot of earthen roads and a cluster of wooden or plaster houses, of a kind familiar in the writings of nineteenth-century Russian officers who served in the Caucasus. It is set between low hills in the rolling plain between the main Caucasus range and the much lower hills which run a few miles south of the Terek River. Until the mid-nineteenth century, the whole region was covered with thick forests of beech, oak and nut – until the Russians cut them down as part of their campaign against Shamil and his Chechen followers, who used them as their chief ally.

Today, the forests have been pushed back into the foothills of the Caucasus, where they cling to the mountainsides, deeply shaded, spiny, secretive and tenacious. Most of lowland Chechnya has come to be covered with wide, bare fields, glaringly hot in summer, grey and desolate in winter – and since the population explosion of the past forty years, thickly sprinkled with villages and small towns, endless sprawls of one-storey houses and compounds, with the odd drab Soviet official building; and now, towering over them, the minarets of the new great mosques.

It is no longer a particularly interesting landscape; but to the south, across the plain, are the fantastically shaped peaks of the Caucasus, white and blue, hung like a curtain across the sky; and to the north, the bare hills of the Terek range bloom in spring and autumn with a range of wild flowers, gorse and grasses, and as the sky changes above them, the colours shift like a kaleidoscope, the rolling hills seeming to stretch themselves and lift their breasts to the sun. It is hardly surprising that this country had such a romantic and inspiring effect on all those nineteenth-century Russian writers who saw it, and took time off from fighting the Chechens to describe its charms.

Grozny's day really dawned, however, not in the military and romantic, but in the new industrial age of the 1890s with the beginnings of oil extraction. The British historian and traveller John Baddeley, visiting it during that decade, wrote that it was clearly destined to become a major industrial centre, but:

> At this time, however, it was chiefly remarkable for streets which without exaggeration might be set down as among the worst in the world. In dry weather they were ankle deep in dust, in wet they were quagmires of mud, with ponds of green filth here and there, in which ducks and geese paddled, pigs wallowed, and frogs swam.[3]

Thanks to the decay of services and repair under Dudayev's rule, coming on top of decades of slow Soviet decrepitude, Grozny by 1994 had once again become rather like this, even before the war smashed it to pieces. There are, however, no longer any pigs – for Grozny when Baddeley was there was still overwhelmingly Russian, not Muslim.

But in the intervening decades Grozny was a major industrial metropolis first of the Russian and then of the Soviet empire, and already by 1917 was second only to Baku as an oil producing centre of Russia and indeed the world. Oil brought in both a flood of mainly Russian migrant workers, and a smaller flow of Western entrepreneurs and engineers. An undistinguished, vaguely neo-Gothic brick house on Victory Prospect in Grozny (now in ruins) is often pointed out as having been built for the 'English engineers' who came to work in the oilfields.

The Chechens, however, remained largely peripheral to this development at least until the 1920s, when the rapid development of the oilfields under Soviet rule, together with the Soviet onslaught on the economic and social life of the Chechen villages, began to draw or drive many Chechens into the city. Even so, it was not until the 1970s that Grozny really became a Chechen city; and since this development took place under Soviet rule, there were no architectural signs of it. Not a single mosque was allowed to be built or rebuilt anywhere in Checheno-Ingushetia until 1978. No mosques were allowed in Grozny until 1988, and at first services had to be held in sanctified railway wagons.

When the Chechen national revolution began at the end of the 1980s, the sole formal place of worship in the city, and the only symbol of the old Russian empire, was one ochre-painted Orthodox church – later wrecked by Russian bombardment. As usual on the ethnic frontiers of Russia, an Orthodox church was left in place by the atheist Soviet regime, when in much of the Russian heartland it would have been demolished or turned into something else.

By the eve of the war, in 1994, the church had been joined by a number of mosques, notably a soaring but unfinished one dedicated to the eighteenth-century religious and military leader Sheikh Mansur (strangely enough, begun with ten tons of bricks donated in 1991 by the Mayor of Petersburg, Anatoly Sobchak, as a gesture of national reconciliation). After 1991, the Chechens threw themselves into mosque-building, and it became one of the chief ways in which Chechen 'businessmen', whether from Grozny or Moscow, displayed their wealth and their attachment to their communities, and boosted their prestige.

Architecturally, these new mosques are to my eyes often very beautiful, but also rather curious, in a style I have seen nowhere else in the Muslim world. To judge by old pictures, they bear little resemblance to the old, simple whitewashed Chechen mosques which existed before they were all demolished after Stalin's deportation of the Chechen people in 1944. The difference is a sign of a deepening transformation in Chechnya's traditionally extremely egalitarian, clan-based society. The new ones are often enormous, and almost all made of red brick. Rather than traditional minarets, many of these mosques have soaring towers, sometimes equipped with battlements, and sometimes with a clock. The exterior decoration, and the shape of the windows is usually more or less 'Islamic', but the overall effect is more neo-Gothic – appropriately, perhaps, for mosques built by 'businessmen' whose character and role can to an extent be described as 'bastard feudal'.

It may be in fact that this was also, unconsciously at least, the effect the architects were thinking of. The architecture of the mosques is closely related to that of the castle-like, battlemented and terraced houses, with their great arched loggias, which before the war the 'businessmen' were building in every Chechen town and village. I asked a Chechen friend whether their style was neo-Chechen. 'No, more neo-English,' he replied, quite seriously. 'Isn't that the kind of house English lords live in? At least, that's the impression of England we were always given in Soviet days.'

If so, this would surely be one of the odder footnotes to architectural history: that a style pioneered for nineteenth-century English Christian churches and public monuments, picked up as a cliché of England by Russians before the Bolshevik Revolution, fossilised by Russian Communists cut off from the outside world and intent on showing England as a class-ridden neo-feudalism, should have ended after many transmogrifications as a symbol of the national pride and Islamic loyalty of a small people of the North Caucasus.

A curious feature of the new Chechen mosques is that relatively few were built in Grozny under Dudayev, despite the fact that by the 1991 it was by far the biggest Chechen population centre. The mosque of Sheikh Mansur, like another one planned for the central square but never begun, were initiatives of the Chechen government. The wealthy Chechens who have paid for the great majority of mosques have built them not in the capital, but in the villages and small towns from which their families and clans originated. For that matter, this has also been true of many of the palatial residences. A familiar sight in Chechnya is to enter some small village of straggling one-storey houses, and suddenly to come up against a towering, half-finished three-storey mansion behind high walls, and to be told that it was being built by a businessman in Moscow, whose mother and other relatives had remained in the village.

But above all, this is true of the graves. The overwhelming majority of Chechens who die in Grozny, in peace and war alike, have been buried by their relatives not in the city cemeteries, but in those of their ancestral villages, often near the shrine of an ancestral saint. The bodies in Grozny's cemeteries are usually local Russians, while the mass graves contain unidentified and unrecoverable Chechens who were buried in the ruins and dug out later by the Russian army. This was one of the things which made accurate assessment of the numbers killed in the battle for Grozny so extremely difficult.

In appearance, until it became a surrealist nightmare, central Grozny was entirely Soviet Russian. It had a certain southern cast, but of the kind you see from the Ukraine to Central Asia. The centre was dominated by the usual pompous, ugly official buildings, the same from Minsk to Magadan. These are occasionally relieved by a neo-classical official building from imperial times, equally standardised but far more attractive. Beyond that, and clustered in half a dozen *mikro-rayony* (micro-districts, or housing estates) in the suburbs, are the dreary 'Khrushchevka', the shoddy high-rises of the 1950s and 1960s, which at first represented liberation and luxury for so many wretched inhabitants of overcrowded communal flats.

But beyond and around them the true North Caucasian town begins: hundreds of streets, roughly asphalted or sometimes still of earth, with one-storey, whitewashed houses. The Russian ones open directly on to the street, and often have carved wooden window-frames with designs from the villages of Great Russia, the former Cossack provinces and the Ukraine. The Chechen houses, as commonly throughout the Muslim world, are generally hidden behind high walls and painted steel gates. These give on to enclosed yards, often inhabited by a mixed population highly characteristic of prewar Chechnya – children, chickens, ferocious dogs, a tractor, and a luxury Volvo or BMW, sometimes with German number plates still attached. Since it was mainly the centre of Grozny which was shattered in the bombing of December 1994 and the fighting of January and February 1995 and August 1996, while the suburbs were largely spared, it is this Caucasian Grozny which has endured.

Still, except in its inhabitants, the modern capital of Chechnya was never very Chechen; and I have sometimes wondered if the willingness of the Chechen independence forces to stand and fight in central Grozny, even at the cost of its destruction, was not unconsciously at least partly due to the fact that it had been built and developed not by Chechens, but as the local military outpost of their oppressors, from whom its very name derives – or did, before it was renamed Djoltkar Ghala in honour of Dudayev. But whatever its name, the Chechen blood shed there in its defence has now made it a Chechen city forever.[4]

Elders, Bandits and Heroes

Shortly before the Russian invasion, I met an elderly Chechen who represented the most positive and powerful face of his national tradition, which explained why it has endured so long and resisted so strongly – and who was by birth an ethnic German: Wilhelm Weisserth, who was deported from Ukraine to Kazakhstan by Stalin in 1941, met there a deported Chechen girl, fell in love first with her and then with her whole people, converted to Islam, and became first Mahomet and then – after visiting Mecca when this became possible under Gorbachev – Haji Mahomet.

He returned to Chechnya with his wife's family in 1957, and eventually became an elder of his village and his teip (clan). At the same time, he did not wholly lose his German characteristics – as a Chechen friend said of him, 'He's studied Islam so thoroughly he knows much more about it than we do ourselves!' This adoption is not quite so odd or unusual as it may seem. As I shall point out in chapter 10, the Chechens have a tradition of assimilating individuals or groups from outside their own ethnic group, which is one reason why they have remained the largest North Caucasian people.

I talked with Haji Mahomet at his home in the eastern village of Mekekhi. Round him were his wife (a round, smiling, deeply lined old lady in Soviet peasant clothes and a bright headscarf, like a bagful of wrinkled apples wrapped up in a particoloured bag), four sons, four daughters, seventeen grandchildren, eighty sheep, eight cows and a number of turkeys. One of his grandsons was studying at the Muslim university of al-Azhar in Cairo. In Haji Mahomet's words,

> When I married my wife in Karaganda, she was like me an orphan. Her father had died in a camp, her mother in a fire. She was already married, but her husband had abandoned her... The rest of her family were in Frunze. They were horrified. Her brother threatened to kill her and me. But when we met, I was already studying Islam, and I was able to convince him that I was a good man. Also by then we had a child... So I accepted Islam, her family became my friends, and we all live together to this day...
>
> They were also impressed because for a non-Muslim to accept Islam in those days in the Soviet Union was very dangerous. I was continually being questioned by the NKVD. One time when I was twenty-five years old, I was questioned by a Tatar NKVD officer. He began to interrogate me about why I had taken Islam. I replied, 'You are a Muslim, why aren't you glad?' He walked twice up and down the room, then he tore up the enquiry form, gave me a pass, told me to get out of there and not come back...
>
> Why did I accept Islam, apart from because of my wife? Islam seemed to me the most rational of religions, the Chechens I knew in exile were very impressive people, and the old ones had a very special tradition. In such a difficult time, when so many people behaved like beasts, they taught the Shariat and their national customs to their children and grandchildren, they stuck together as a community, and they shared everything with each other.

I asked him if he had ever been tempted to move to Germany with the rest of his surviving Ukrainian-German relatives. He replied, 'Why should I go to Germany? Here I am respected, and I play a useful role as an elder, reconciling conflicts and bringing people together. What could I do in Germany that would be useful?' It was difficult not to agree. With his healthy, sunburnt face, white beard, rough working jacket and patched trousers, in his plain, rather bare whitewashed house (bitterly cold in a Caucasian December) he could have been one of his own seventeenth-century ancestors, a Schwabian peasant farmer, tough, hardworking, religious, honoured by his peers. In modern Germany, he would look like a tramp, and as a 'Russian-German returnee', presumably be charitably assigned a pension and a one-room flat , where a social worker would visit him and his wife once a week, until it was time to go into a home.

He described for me the role of an elder in Chechen society, bringing out in the process the tension between Islamic law (the Shariat) and Chechen traditional custom (Adat):

> In our village, for example, the elders are responsible for arranging funerals, depending on which vird [Sufi brotherhood] the dead person belonged to. The rules on this are very strict, and the elder has to know them...
>
> Ideally, an elder should be just and impartial, for in the past at least, he regulated the whole structure of society, and looked after justice and order. If a man in the village drinks too much or mistreats his wife, the elder will rebuke him. In the past, you see, the Chechens had no police, and even under Soviet rule, they tried to sort out problems and disputes quietly in their own way whenever possible.

This was confirmed for me by a former KGB major, who said that from the 1970s, the KGB in Chechnya, except when Moscow was breathing down their necks, generally tried to cooperate with Chechen society over crimes, rather than enforcing the Soviet law – 'otherwise, on the occasions when for some reason we really *had* to get a result, no one would have even talked to us.' Of course, in the process, the police were also progressively taken over by the world of 'business'.

Haji Mahomet continued that:

> One problem for the elders is of course the question of revenge. In the Chechen tradition (Adat), if a member of your family is killed or wounded, you have the right of revenge. There was a case in the mountains, resolved this year, where members of a family got drunk and beat another man while stealing his car, and he died. The blood-feud went on for twenty-three years. The Soviet law gave the men ten years in gaol, but when they were released, it began again.
>
> But the Shariat lays down quite different rules, it absolutely forbids revenge against innocent relations – though many Chechens don't know that, or don't want to... We religious elders appeal to the Koran, tell people that Allah does not allow murder, whatever the reason.
>
> But when trouble has occurred, then our task is to reconcile the parties so that it doesn't spread, and to bring forgiveness. This is our religious duty. Elders may arrange compensation (*mekha*) – though strictly speaking this is wrong. If a breadwinner has been killed, then the other side will sometimes buy a car, provide food, support the children until they are aged fifteen...
>
> One reason for the killings and the feuds is that the Chechen people always loved arms. Every man who was a man had to carry arms, and

know how to use them. A man without arms would be continually humiliated, challenged to fight... Though as a result men did not hit each other, because the other man would immediately go for his weapon, and in general, quarrelsome men were not respected; the man with respect was the man who did not look for fights but would defend himself bravely if attacked.

Today, there is not such respect for tradition. Youths hit each other more easily, use their weapons more easily, partly because of the spread of alcohol, a great disgrace, and of crime – thanks to Soviet rule. We are trying to bring them back to a love of tradition, of solidarity and coop-erating with their neighbours, not being so ready to use guns, but this will be a long process.[5]

The previous day, I had interviewed an extreme representative of the neg-ative aspect of Chechen society, and of the corrupting influences disapproved of by Haji Mahomet: Ruslan Labazanov, originally a martial arts trainer and criminal boss from Krasnodar. The tension between these old and new worlds in Chechnya will determine the country's future. Convicted of armed robbery and murder – allegedly of a Russian KGB officer, which made him a Chechen hero, though this may have been invention on his part – Labazanov was released by the Chechen government in 1991 and became one of Dudayev's chief bodyguards, before breaking with him in 1994. He then became the chief military supporter of Ruslan Khasbulatov's 'peacemaking' effort, joined the Russian side, and was finally killed in obscure circumstances in May 1996, shortly after Yeltsin's fake 'peace deal' with Yandarbiyev.

One version of his death that I heard from several sources was that by way of a cost-free concession to the separatist side, the Russians had either killed him themselves or allowed the separatists to kill him, because he had been in the habit of taking money from Chechen families to kill individual Russian officers whom they held responsible for the death of relatives. This seems quite possible – but given how much he was hated, he may well have been assassinated either by the separatists without Russian assistance, or as part of a private feud.

This happened to another notorious criminal, Alauddi 'Abrek', with some of whose followers I travelled briefly in the Chechen mountains in May 1995.[6] Many years before, Alauddi had killed two people in Chechnya (allegedly, a Mullah and a woman he thought had put a spell on him – for as Haji Mahomet suggested, not all traditional beliefs in Chechnya are Islamic) and fled to Kazan, then the biggest criminal centre of the Soviet world, where he became a criminal boss. He returned to Chechnya with some of his followers under Dudayev, balancing himself between regime and opposition, supporting Dudayev but also giving protection to Labazanov when he was wounded by Dudayev's men in June 1994. Alauddi then fought in January and February against the Russians. After we returned from the mountains in May 1995, our host, Musa Damayev, said that we had had a lucky escape. I asked him whether men like Alauddi and Labazanov represented a danger to Chechnya. He replied,

> He is dangerous to anyone who has money and no family at his back. With me, it would be different. If I go up there, in principle I'm at his mercy, but he knows that my family knows where I've gone, and if he does something to me, they'll find out and have their revenge. To someone whose death wouldn't mean the possibility of a blood feud, yes, he could be very dangerous. To you, Alauddi himself wouldn't have done anything. He's a big man after all, and more or less rational. He invests in large-scale crimes, bank fraud and so on. But Asab [Alauddi's sidekick] – he's different: a little man, greedy. If you had gone up there without my letter, he would have smiled at you in that way he has, but then he might well have attacked you, to see what he could get.

Later that year, Alauddi was indeed killed in a blood-feud – though it is said that this was also by order of the Chechen leadership, for continuing to rob and kill other Chechens despite the war. After the war, it looks very much as if the little men have come into their own – encouraged by the promise of high ransoms for kidnapped Westerners.

Labazanov and Alauddi represent exactly the image Russian chauvinists have of the Chechens in general; his type also represented a major threat to the Chechen's own society, to attempts to create an effective Chechen state, and indeed to the Chechen traditions which have brought victory in the latest war (see chapter 10). Following the end of the war, the wave of kidnappings carried out by such men is gravely endangering Chechen hopes of reconstruction and prosperity.

The first time I had met Labazanov was in February 1992, when he was serving as one of Dudayev's bodyguards, and we had a sharp argument over the use of a phone at the presidential headquarters. I didn't at that time know about his previous career, or I'd have offered him the whole telephone exchange – it wasn't much good anyway. Though for that matter, his general aspect suggested that he wasn't a good man to argue with. 'He is the only chief bodyguard who's not a member of Dudayev's own teip,' one of the presidential staff told me. 'He feels insecure, that's why he throws his weight around so much.'

He was not an especially tall man, but so solidly built that he seemed much larger, with thick forearms and enormous fists. On the rare occasions when his small eyes weren't covered by dark glasses, they had a sort of amusement in them, and a reddish look – as if he were a large and ferocious animal congratulating itself on the fact that it could eat you whenever it wished, but couldn't be bothered to do so. He wore two enormous *stechlin* pistols in his gold-studded belt, and a black headband, and by the time we met again, in August 1994, he had added to this a big gold watch set with rubies, a gold and ruby ring (rubies were obviously the thing to wear in Grozny that year), a heavy gold bracelet, and a golden chain around his bull neck.

By this time, he had fortunately forgotten our argument. It was three months after he had broken with Dudayev, and the subsequent fighting ended with Labazanov's men being driven from Grozny and three of them being publicly beheaded, as revenge for killing members of the families of other Dudayev bodyguards. Labazanov himself was badly wounded and reportedly saved by Alauddi. I was told that the basic cause of the split was that Dudayev considered that Labazanov was becoming too powerful and arrogant, but that the precipitant was a dispute between Labazanov and some members of Dudayev's family over the proceeds of a bank fraud in Moscow.

Labazanov then cast around for new allies, and by August had aligned himself with Ruslan Khasbulatov and his 'peace mission', for which he provided the armed protection. I saw him riding with his men in Khasbulatov's motorcade, which swept along the bumpy roads with pennants fluttering from the aerials, rifles and machine guns pointing from the windows, horns blaring, men yelling, rows of lights glaring from the roofs of the big Nissan jeeps, the Cherokees and the Pajeros. Lesser vehicles swerved from the road to avoid them. Journalists and camp followers panted along behind them.

As Khasbulatov spoke from the back of a truck about a 'peaceful, civilised solution to Chechnya's problems', Labazanov stood beside him with an AK-74, arms akimbo, the barrel outlined against the pitiless August sky. Khasbulatov for his part, with his pasty, rubbery face and blank eyes, looked, as I wrote in my notebook, 'more than ever like something found underneath a stone'. Not everyone was happy with Labazanov's presence. When he spoke of how he had come to protect Khasbulatov's peace mission, because 'Dudayev is a murderer and Chechnya must be cleansed of him', a man yelled from the back, 'Where were you before?' – and was hustled away.

Khasbulatov himself, and his more respectable supporters, were embarrassed by questions about Labazanov from Russian and Western journalists, as indeed was Dudayev when reminded of his previous role. I was surprised however by how many Chechens – and not just from the opposition – were prepared to praise him, at least until he threw in his lot openly with the Russians in 1995. Ordinary Chechens called him an *abrek*, a 'bandit of honour'; the more educated, speaking to a British journalist, of course called him a 'Robin Khud'. He did indeed seem to have made some effort to buy popularity – in accordance of course with the whole tradition of figures of his kind. The director of a biscuit and sweets factory in Grozny, who gave me a lift just before the war, said of him that

> You should not be too hard on Labazanov. This is a harsh society, you know – a man who wants to play a part in politics, or even to make money, needs to be able to protect himself, his family and his friends. You shouldn't believe all the stories about him killing babies and so on – that is just his enemies talking. He may have made some money ille-

gally – who hasn't? – but he has also been very generous. He has given money to hospitals, to schools, to widows and orphans, and he has protected them against oppression. You know that under Dudayev state support for all services of this kind has just collapsed. It is only thanks to Labazanov and others like him that there hasn't been real hunger here, and he has been more generous than anyone.

To be fair, it should also be admitted that Khasbulatov did need protection – the previous day, 13 August 1994, a rally of his in the town of Stary Atagi had been blocked by Dudayev's guards with armoured vehicles, led by 'Colonel' Ilyes Arsanukayev, the commander of Dudayev's presidential guard – a man who closely resembled his former colleague Labazanov, even down to the dark glasses (his relative, Abu, a former Soviet sergeant, was at that time commander of the secret service, or DGB). When I tried to go through to find Khasbulatov, he threatened my driver with arrest, pointed a gun at us and made a move to confiscate my car. This was the reality behind the words to me the previous day of Mavlen Salamov, Dudayev's chief aide, that 'the people of Stary Atagi have vowed not to let Khasbulatov speak there.'

The next month, Dudayev's guards drove Labazanov from his base in Argun, and he set up in Khasbulatov's home-town of Tolstoy Yurt, where I saw him for the last time in November 1994, in a large but otherwise ordinary house in an ordinary muddy street – except for the four T-72 tanks, evidently supplied by Russia. His band seemed to come from all over the place – there were Chechens, but also Russians and Daghestanis. With them were their camp-followers, women who teetered on high heels or plodded in slippers through the mud of the village street. Some seemed to have fairly long-established relationships – one enormous, savage-looking character emerged from a jeep carrying a gun in one hand and a tiny child in another, illustrating the domestic character of Chechnya's low-intensity civil war before the Russian intervention.

The whole set-up looked like something out of *Mad Max*. Or rather, this wasn't like *Mad Max* – this *was Mad Max*, or at any rate these men's recreation of themselves in line with all the Hollywood action films they had seen. When we were ushered into the kitchen, where Labazanov was sitting – he had clearly come down in the world – he was ostentatiously playing with a new pistol with a laser sight, the red dot of which danced over the walls and our bodies as we talked – just like The Terminator.

He was sitting underneath a shelf with a big brass or bronze figure of an eagle, like a would-be bandit Napoleon, or maybe the Emperor Bokassa. Intermittently sharing the shelf with the eagle was a small grey cat, which had evidently come to the kitchen to bask in the glow of Labazanov's presence. The great man himself introduced a third animal, referring to Dudayev repeatedly as a 'goat' (*kozyol*, a Russian insult the exact meaning of which I will not translate) 'who ought to be beheaded', and boasted that he could have defeated him in the previous week (on 26 November) if he hadn't been 'let down' by the rest of the opposition.

Labazanov certainly could not have seen to aim with his new toy, because as we came in, he deliberately put on his dark glasses, so in the November gloom, and in the dimly lit kitchen, he can hardly have seen anything at all. This was just as well, because I spent most of the interview staring at a most extraordinary vision, a strange steel orchid, which had come in from the bedroom and was standing beside me. His 'wife' looked to be aged about seventeen, and was of a remarkable beauty, with a triangular face, huge eyes and a perfect mouth, but with vampirical white make-up and what looked in the dark like purple eye-shadow and lipstick – like something out of the Addams family, as I noted at the time. Her legs were also long and beautifully shaped – I could see a good deal of them, because she was wearing a black leather mini-skirt and boots. She was also wearing both an AK-47 and a machine-pistol, and a bandolier, together with a belt of bullets and bracelets, buttons, necklaces and rings of steel (if all this seems too good – or bad – to be true, let me say that Victoria Clarke, of the *Observer*, also witnessed it). We had come a long way from Haji Mahomet's vision, and it was difficult to see how either the Shariat or the Adat tradition of Chechnya could accommodate Ruslan Labazanov and his wife.

On the other hand, entirely in line with Chechen tradition was Shamil Basayev, the greatest Chechen commander after Maskhadov. His raid on the Russian town of Budennovsk in June 1995 played a major part in bringing the Russians to the negotiating table, and winning a critical few months' breathing space for the Chechens until the war resumed with full force in the winter. The hostage-taking, and the occupation of a hospital in Budennovsk by Basayev and his force, caused understandable outrage in Russia, and even in the West led to him being labelled a 'terrorist'. That his actions in Budennovsk were against the laws of war is certain – but then again, the Russian side (like the British in Ireland in 1919–21, and the French in Algeria) had repeatedly refused to recognise the Chechen fighters as legitimate combatants, or to treat them accordingly. Six weeks before the Budennovsk raid, a large part of Basayev's family had been wiped out in a Russian air-raid on Vedeno. In Basayev's own words to me in December 1995: 'You talk about terrorism forfeiting our moral superiority before world public opinion. Who cares about our moral position? Who from abroad has helped us, while Russia has brutally ignored every moral rule? If they can use such weapons and threats, then so can we.'[7] (In this context, it should be noted that while Basayev repeatedly threatened to plant bombs to kill civilians, there is no proof that he ever actually did so. Nor did the Russians ever use napalm or its equivalent in Chechnya – they were accused of doing so, but neither I nor any other Western journalist I knew ever saw any evidence of it.)

I first met Basayev in Abkhazia in October 1993, sitting on the pavement in the temporary Abkhaz capital of Gudauta with other leaders of the volunteers from the 'Confederation of Mountain Peoples' who had played a major part in the Abkhaz victory against the Georgians. Although only 28 years old, he himself had commanded the Chechen battalion. He grinned cheerfully –

not bothering to deny it – when we asked him about Russian help for the Abkhaz, and congratulated us on not having run into his men when we had been on the Georgian side.

In this he was dead right. Three months earlier, in July 1993, I might have met Basayev and his men while I was reporting from the Georgian side in Sukhumi. Most foolishly, I had joined a Georgian column headed up into the wooded hills around Mount Zegan, above the Georgian-held front-line village of Shroma. Supposedly the column was to look for the enemy, and drive back their advanced posts. In this sector, the 'enemy', as I later discovered, were indeed the Chechens.

I'm thankful we didn't meet them; for in terms of military preparedness, the Georgians and I just about deserved each other. My water flask was already half empty, the rest of the column had none either, and after several hours climbing in the blazing heat we ended by frantically drinking water from the radiator of a lorry.

The Georgian column consisted of about two hundred men, of whom no fewer than a dozen were 'senior officers', including two generals. Most were in civilian dress with bits and bobs of military uniform. Only a few had proper boots. They came from three different groups: the embryonic Georgian national army; the Mkhedrioni, a paramilitary force loyal to Djaba Yosseliani, a former bank robber and criminal boss who had played a leading part in the December 1991 coup against Gamsakhurdia; and local volunteers from the Georgian population of Sukhumi, who made up the majority.

The Mkhedrioni looked like what they were – unemployed youths from the grim industrial slums of Tbilisi and Rustavi, hard-faced but soft-bodied, and in many cases clearly addicted to alcohol or something stronger. They had already gained an odious reputation for looting, rape, vandalism and general mayhem, not just against the Abkhaz, but also in Georgian areas which supported Zviad Gamsakhurdia. By contrast, the local Georgian troops from Sukhumi were much more attractive, and their morale seemed higher, but they were very far from being natural fighters. I offered my flask to a plump middle-aged dentist called Gia, an intelligent, humorous-looking man with a balding head who was suffering badly from the steep climb in the stifling heat of the forest. 'Please don't think we want to fight and kill people,' he gasped, leaning against a tree. 'I wouldn't be here if it wasn't to defend my family.' He admitted he was himself pro-Gamsakhurdia, and in private made no secret of his loathing for his Mkhedrioni comrades.

Particularly striking was the absence of many volunteers from elsewhere in Georgia. It was just the same on the Azeri side in the Karabakh War – most of the fighters, at least up to 1994, were Azeris from Karabakh and the surrounding regions, whose homes were directly threatened. Throughout, Baku and its people felt very distant from the war raging less than 150 miles away. In this sense, Chechnya's small size may have worked to its advantage: there was no area that did not feel threatened by the invader, and few areas that were not occupied at one point or another; and so volunteers for the resistance came in from all over the country.

This was also a factor which was very visible in the high morale, discipline and endurance of the Abkhaz forces I met, compared to their Georgian enemies, and of the Karabakh Armenians compared to the Georgians. All were fighting with their backs to the wall. Several former Soviet soldiers among the Armenians in Stepanakert quoted to me the words of the Soviet battle order to the troops defending Moscow in December 1941: 'We have nowhere to retreat. Behind us lies Moscow.' Or in the words of my colleague Alexis Rowell about Armenian Karabakh, which could have been repeated for Abkhazia and Chechnya but emphatically not for Georgia, Azerbaijan or Russia: 'This is a completely military society. The men are all fighting and the women are all cooking for them, nursing their wounds and bringing up their children.'

I encountered Basayev again in August 1994, at a tea-party. A friend of his – whom I had met with him in Abkhazia – was serving as the chief guard at my hotel, incongruously named the Frantsuski Dom, or 'French House', and invited both Basayev and myself to drink tea with the manager and his wife in their flat on the first floor of the hotel. The 'hotel' was simply a converted block of flats, and the 'rooms' were the flats themselves, with their ordinary Soviet furniture and wallpaper. In principle, therefore, they were very roomy – except that by the autumn of 1994 there were half-a-dozen journalists to every room. But after the restaurant ceased to function and we were reduced to buying and cooking our own breakfasts, it still had a curiously domestic feel about it.

The tea-party was an unusual experience. Basayev's comrade, Vaqa, was one of the largest and most formidable-looking men I've ever met (he was killed during the war, fighting on the separatist side); some six foot seven in height, and with an enormous craggy face and huge nose, with the obligatory pistol in his belt. For the tea-party, he had produced a chocolate cake, with little flowers of pink and white icing on top. This he cut with a tremendous flourish, like a salute, using for the purpose an enormous locally produced saw-edged bayonet, with runnels down the side for blood – a scene beyond the imagination of a Fellini.[8]

During my conversation with Basayev, he reminisced about the fighting in the hills above Shroma, and described one incident in a way that struck a chord with my memories: 'It took us more than an hour to climb the hill. Every few minutes we'd stop and howl in chorus like wolves, and shout, "The Chechens are coming! The Chechens are coming!" And when we got to the top, the Georgians had all gone.'

When asked about Dudayev, he seemed to feel little personal enthusiasm for him. He only said, as so many fighters were to do, that he was for an independent Chechnya, and that Dudayev was the President. Speaking about Islam in Chechnya – at least to a Western journalist – he said nothing about the need for an Islamic state. His later support for this project seems therefore to have come out of the war. He recalled his time in the Soviet army, stressing that he'd only been a fireman, and his real military experience was all in Abkhazia, 'But we don't really need the Soviet army to teach a Chechen how to fight'. In those days, Basayev was a pleasant man to meet and talk with – obviously a leader of men, but with a humorous and open face. He told me – in part mistakenly as it turned out – that 'if the Russians invade, of course we won't be able to carry out frontal war, but we will be able to rely on the crudity of Russian tactics. We will inflict huge casualties on them. We will also carry the war to Russia, not with terrorism but with diversionary actions.'

He also talked about his time as a building worker and computer salesman in Russia:

> Officially, there used to be 200,000 unemployed Chechens before 1990. In fact, all of us were working, but none of us was registered with the authorities. We never lived from the state. We always lived on the side, unofficially. We made money, and we also always helped each other in time of need. That is why other peoples hate us so much, but that is why we are a strong people, and why so far we have been able to beat this Russian blockade, for example.

Not surprisingly, his face changed as the war continued. I met him again on 18 January 1995, at a former Soviet military base in southern Grozny, which was being used by the Chechens as a headquarters. He had been wounded in the hand, nose and scalp by shrapnel, and to this day bears a deep scar above his forehead. His eyes had sunk deeper into his head, and over the next years were to sink further and further; meanwhile his beard, which had been short and piratical, grew longer and bushier, until by the end of the year he really did resemble a Mujahid of old.

He was sitting on the edge of a filthy camp bed, on which sprawled an exhausted Chechen fighter. The latter was so exhausted that he barely stirred during the repeated hammerings of a heavy machine gun, just outside the window, firing at the Russian SU-25 fighter bombers ('Frogfeet' in NATO parlance) circling and swooping around the hill on which the base was situated. Again and again came the roar of the planes and the beating of the gun, while Basayev and Information Minister Mauvladi Udugov sat there unmoving, and my colleague and I sat there with idiotic expressions on our faces, pretending to be as unmoved as they were.

But Basayev and Udugov already had the measure of the Russian air force. In his words, 'They're frightened of our gun. Admittedly, it's not easy for them – because of the low cloud and the hill, they have to come in low, and that gives us a chance. But all the same – so many planes, and only one gun, and they still won't manage to hit us, I promise you.'

My next meeting with Basayev was in the mountain town of Vedeno – a headquarters of his namesake Shamil during the wars of the nineteenth century – in May 1995, after the Russians had temporarily cleared the Chechen fighters from the plains. This was the lowest ebb of Chechen fortunes during the entire war: ammunition was running very low, the men were exhausted, and it was the only time that I saw Chechen fighters show signs of panic – we had met a carload of them fleeing from the front, declaring wrongly that the Russians had broken through (they were actually to do so barely a week later).

Basayev came into the office being used by General Maskhadov in a former school situated within the old fort, once a stronghold of Shamil. The two great commanders of the Chechen War were interesting both in their differences and their similarities. Physically, they were very unalike. While Basayev was looking more and more like a Mujahid, Maskhadov was still very much the Soviet officer, clean-shaven and in faded and dirty battledress – and not even a very imposing one, with his long, sallow, yellowish face, his big nose, receding chin and jug ears, like a Chechen Mickey Mouse. He was sitting in the room of the school janitor, and looked indeed as if he might have been an elderly lieutenant minding the door of some distant, isolated, boring military outpost at a time of peace.

The difference in appearance between them reflected political differences that appeared later when they ran for President against each other in January 1997, with Basayev coming out more strongly for Islam and Chechen tradition, and Maskhadov standing for independence, but also for compromise with Russia. Maskhadov's Soviet military background was also, of course, a great help in his negotiations with those Russian commanders who were sincere about talks: first General Anatoly Romanov, then General Alexander Lebed.

What they had in common was an essential modesty of style; neither of them dressed, or even behaved, except in the line of command, in any way that would have distinguished them from their followers. They didn't 'give themselves airs'. There could hardly have been a greater contrast with Dudayev, or his nephew and acolyte Salman Raduyev – let alone with Labazanov. It is worth noting that in this clash of styles, by far the most brilliant and dedicated leaders were the ones who did not try visibly to elevate themselves above their followers.

The next day, we met Basayev again while we were visiting a Chechen armoured unit behind the front at Serzhen Yurt, a village at the mouth of the valley which winds up towards Vedeno. We had trekked over the hills for fear of air attack on the roads. He drove up in a bright red Niva, an excellent target; and he was not at all pleased to see us. This was because the state of the unit made the general Chechen position all too clear. Most of the handful of vehicles were immobilised, and there seemed very little ammunition. He tore a strip off the Chechen commander – without raising his voice, but with a severe effect on the poor man. To us however he was as always perfectly polite, and despite his obvious irritation at our presence, he gave no orders to stop us proceeding towards the front. This intelligent and generous recognition that we did not represent a threat to his cause marked Basayev out both from the bureaucratic and paranoid Azeris and from many other Chechen fighters, who became more and more hostile to Western journalists as the war went on.

I benefited once again from Basayev's hospitality in December 1995, when together with other Western correspondents I stayed in his aunt's house in Vedeno while waiting to interview him. (His uncle, or cousin – exact Chechen relationships are hard to fathom – turned out also to be related to both

Labazanov and Alauddi: 'We don't agree with each other, but because we are relatives, we don't trouble each other.') The house was a large one by Soviet standards, as Chechen houses often are, because they frequently contain several elements of an extended family.

Despite the war, we were fed well on shashlik and dumplings with fiery sauce, and courteously entertained, with the host producing a chess set. There was of course no alcohol, but otherwise – though there was no doubting the commitment to Islam – the atmosphere was far from being rigidly 'Islamic' in the sense that it is usually understood in the West. At the start of the evening the women of the family entertained Andrew Harding (BBC) and myself to tea, chatted with us, practised their English, talked about the elections, and even flirted a little, in a decorous sort of way. Thanks to Soviet rule, and in part their own pre-Islamic traditions, even religious Chechens are often a great deal less strictly Islamic than they think they are. The next day, when we interviewed him, Basayev sat there on the sofa, heavily armed, a natural leader of men, and one of the great guerrilla commanders of his age – but also a man drinking tea at the home of his relatives; a figure greatly respected by his community and completely rooted in it and its traditions.

The following day, we watched Basayev address a meeting of local notables in the town of Vedeno, persuading them not to allow the Russian-backed Zavgayev government to hold elections in the area. This incident showed Basayev's own astuteness and self-restraint, but also the effects of the various cultural barriers against Chechen killing Chechen. For several of the men on the platform were former Soviet figures who were secretly trying to sit on the fence between the separatists and the Russian-backed authorities. They sat there in their shabby, baggy suits and astrakhan hats, shifting uneasily, like elderly schoolboys waiting to be punished. But rather than criticise or threaten them directly, Basayev only singled out one of them, the newly appointed police chief, a stranger to the area. With him, too, Basayev did not use threats but rather the weapon of public shame:

> Aren't you ashamed to sit here before us when the Russians whom you serve are committing such crimes? Are you a Chechen? Are you a man? You were born a Muslim, but tell me, can you now say 'La illaha il'Allah', when you serve the Russian murderers? What would it cost you just to leave here and go back to your family? Would they shoot you for it? We could get the Russian army out of here peacefully if it were not for people like you helping them. We are not asking you to fight, just to stand aside and not harm your own nation.

After reducing the policeman to a quivering, almost tearful wreck, Basayev addressed the other notables present. But as his – completely empty – words about getting the army out peacefully indicated, rather than uttering fiery nationalist rhetoric he stressed that his men in Vedeno were not looking for trouble with the Russians. He said that they had not taken part in a recent capture of three Russian soldiers on the contrary, that had provoked the Russians to fire some shells into the town. He claimed, in fact that he had been on his way to the Russian commander to explain what had happened when the Russians opened fire.

I have no idea whether any of this was true; but the real point was not the truth or otherwise of what Basayev said to these men, but the fact that he bothered to say it at all. In other wars, his equivalents would simply have killed all the ex-Soviet officials in their beds, and then murdered their families. Not, of course, that the implicit threat of force was absent, and it would certainly have been used – in moderation – if anyone had in fact been mad enough to hold the elections in Vedeno.

Grozny under Dudayev: Ordered Anarchy

Robert Graves once wrote that revisiting the former No Man's Land of the Somme after the First World War, and comparing what he saw with his memories of fighting there, was like seeing the actual size of a hole in a tooth, compared with the way it feels to your tongue.[9] It was just the same for me in Grozny, but with the time reversed; for I visited Grozny several times in peacetime before I saw it destroyed by war.

I felt like this for example at Minutka, a small roundabout surrounded by undistinguished eight-storey buildings, with a café and a food shop (*gastronom*), at the top of a gentle hill down which the main street in Grozny, Avturkhanov Prospekt (formerly of course Lenin Prospekt) slopes down to the Sunja River, the main square and the centre of town, a bare mile away.

Minutka is at the start of the main roads leading out of Grozny to the east and south. On previous visits, I must have driven through it literally dozens of times without even noticing it or asking its name. In January 1995, however, it became a place of the most intense significance; with Russian forces in the centre of town and attacking the area around the presidential palace, Minutka became the marching-off point for Chechen forces heading for the front, a meeting place for civilians seeking relatives or trying to get a ride out of town, a distribution point for food and medicine, and a gathering place for journalists. Looking back, of course, we must have been crazy to gather at such an obvious spot during bombardment, and the fact that we were not all blown to pieces six times over is a testimony to the incompetence of the Russian air force and artillery (though they did in the end hit it again and again, killing a great many people there).

The undistinguished, mass-produced modern architecture of Minutka and the rest of the city initially made it seem an odd backdrop for the Chechen national epic being waged there. But in January 1995 its appearance became dramatic enough, especially at night, with gas flaring from fractured pipes casting a lurid light over the scene, and fighters, civilians, stray dogs and cats, journalists and the odd homeless tramp or drug addict all huddling as close as they dared to the flames to keep out the damp and icy chill. Before the war, I had sometimes wondered – mistakenly, of course – whether Grozny could get any more decrepit; between January 1992, when I first visited it, and November 1994, the increase in dilapidation was extremely marked, as was the gradual collapse of most municipal services, as Dudayev's government ceased to pay for them. Roads disintegrated, enormous heaps of rubbish accumulated, the telephone system broke down, a foretaste of the end of modernity as we have known it.

For after all, Grozny was not some small, half-baked provincial town of the Third World; it was a large industrial city, the second biggest oil-refining centre of the world's biggest oil-producing country, and formerly the world's second biggest industrial power. The oil refineries around Grozny are themselves whole cities, stretching for dozens of square miles. During the first days of the bombing, in December 1994, some colleagues and I went looking for the site where a bomb had fallen on one of the refineries – and ended up completely lost, as completely as if we had wandered into a steel jungle.

But this was by no means simply a collapse into barbarism; for if on the one hand the works of the Soviet state were decaying, on the other Grozny under Dudayev was characterised by a commercial vitality unmatched in any other area of provincial Russia; and if much of this activity was criminal, it was an organised criminality, shaped and regulated by tradition, and no mere banditism, though in the context of a population privately armed to a degree that would render insignificant the wildest dreams of the American National Rifle Association. The potholed streets were home to a splendid assortment of Western luxury cars, and since they suffered badly from the potholes, and were driven with scant regard for their sensitive Western feelings, the business of repairing them was one of the biggest in town.

All of these aspects of Grozny came together in its bazaar. Compared to the great bazaars of the past, this was perhaps nothing very remarkable: no architectural grandeur, no exotic spices or rugs, just an average Soviet street of offices and apartment blocks lined with roughly built stalls, in a sea of mud and festering rubbish. The amount of wares on sale was tremendous, but the range was not very large. Most were the standard wares of the Caucasus and southern Russia: great heaps of local fruit and vegetables, sausages and smoked chickens, fruit sauces and pickled carrots; and a mass of cheap imported goods, mainly from the Middle East – Turkish beer and jeans, scent from the Gulf, children's furry toys from Pakistan, and a seemingly endless supply of cheap male aftershave and dubious-looking alcohols and liqueurs, including a 'Scotch' whisky with the frightening name of 'Black Willie'.

At night, the street lamps long since having failed, the bazaar was lit by heaps of burning garbage. Their wavering glare gave exoticism and romance to the scene, making me think of nomads camping amidst the crumbling architecture of a Roman provincial town sometime in the Dark Ages. The smell of course was less romantic – but then, on the basis of my former Afghan experience, I should say that the romance of barbarian existence was always much exaggerated in Western literature.

All the same, this was a very remarkable market for Russia, if only because Russia in principle had been trying to shut it for years, with total lack of success. It was so large and vibrant because under Dudayev, Grozny airport functioned in effect as a free port of entry into Russia, without Russian customs or border guards (for what they are worth). For whatever reason, until November 1994 Russia took no steps to close the airport, while the corruption of the Russian army and police meant that on payment of unofficial fees, goods from there flowed into Russia, and in return goods from Russia flowed to the bazaar in Grozny.

It was in fact a market which encapsulated the weakness of the Russian state today, and the rather frightening strengths of Chechen society. This was to be seen especially at the end furthest from the government headquarters. On this street, incongruously still named 'Rosa Luxemburg' after the murdered German Communist leader, stood the only entirely public arms market on the territory of the former Soviet Union. On this pavement, beside the main post office, all the collapse of the Soviet army, and the dangers this presents for the world, were made manifest – everything from simple grenades to highly sophisticated snipers' rifles, all originally Soviet, most of them from the Russian army, most of them eventually to be used to kill Russian soldiers. There they were, simply lying on tables in the street; or, if it was raining, covered by plastic bags or sheeting. Next to the arms market was the patch of pavement where the money-changers did tens of thousands of dollars worth of daily business. A recipe for disaster? Not at all; this was probably the safest place in the whole of Grozny.

For while the bazaar appeared chaotic and disorderly to Western eyes, it was not a chaos but an anarchy, an absence of government, not of order. The stallholders, arms sellers and money-changers themselves cooperated freely to prevent theft, just as they did to standardise (or, if you prefer, rig) the prices of their goods. In December 1994, shortly before the end of that period of Grozny's existence, I spoke to a Russian man named Sasha, selling a strange assortment of goods, some of them brought in from Russia, others bought during a commercial shopping trip to Istanbul:

> I am a Russian, but no one here gives me any trouble. In fact I like working here, I prefer it to Russia – people are more decent. Here in the market for example, the Chechens have rules, and as long as you respect those rules and pay your dues, you can rely on your neighbours to protect you whatever your nationality. The Chechens are very strict about these things, when they want to be. Yesterday, for example, a Chechen man tried to grab a jar of honey from a Russian trader, and you should have seen the beating the crowd gave him!

A tough and humorous-looking Chechen woman called Meriam, selling Polish-made powdered soup with American labels, said that

We are going on working here because we are not afraid of the bombing, and anyway we have to live. When Russia cut off payments three years ago, the bazaar grew enormously, just because people had to buy and sell things to stay alive. The Russians thought they would starve us out, but we are intelligent and hard-working. We have survived. It's not just Chechen men who are strong, you know... There used to be an administration which ran the bazaar, but now we run it ourselves, and keep good order, as you see.

Her neighbour, a Russian named Ruslan, nodded, and said: 'We Russian traders have had no trouble from the Chechens, none. But if the Russian army comes here, they'll loot this place down to the last cigarette. They won't care who's a Russian and who's a Chechen. We'll all have to get out of here damned quick.'

On 22 December 1994, with the Russian bombardment intensifying and dozens of civilians already killed, I once again visited the much depleted bazaar. One of the few old women remaining sold me a dozen eggs, which I carried away in my helmet, and gave me a loaf of bread for free, possibly because my expression by then was probably as haggard as hers – 'You are our guest, and it's a bad time.' A few yards away, Chechen men were desperately trying to buy or barter for the last remaining weapons in the arms market. One man, who gave his name as Ahmed, was carrying a rocket-propelled grenade launcher, which he was trying to barter for four kalashnikovs. He said rather sadly that he had got hold of the RPG – to which he was obviously passionately attached – when the Russian army pulled out in 1992: 'I was keeping it for just this moment. But now, you see, all my brothers want to fight. They all have pistols, but only two have rifles. So I've been told I must give up this thing, so we can all go to fight together. But as you see, the rifles are all gone. Today, every Chechen man wants to fight.'

The central bazaar ceased to operate towards the end of December, and in January was the scene of some of the fiercest fighting in the war, as the Russians tried to move through it to attack the 'presidential headquarters'. In February 1995, when I returned, it was like a pond of viscous mud, half-filled with rubble and surrounded by jagged and blackened ruins. In the southern suburbs, however, small bazaars continued to work almost throughout the fighting – a testimony to the fact that Chechen women are indeed as tough as the men. Towards the end of the previous month, I visited a street market in Chernorechie, the southern suburb of Grozny still occupied by the separatist forces. Working there was Asya, a forty-nine-year-old Chechen woman who had formerly had a stall in the central market, and had fled from the centre with a carload of frozen chickens and Russian-made women's boots, which she was now busy selling. She said that several people had already been killed while coming to buy or sell. In her words,

I have been a refugee for a month now. Since my flat in Grozny was bombed, I have been living with relatives in Goiti, south of here – but I can't just live off them, I want to work myself, to feed my children myself. All the rest of us feel the same. There are twenty-five of us in one room in Goiti, but we are not talking about surrender. The Russians will never beat us. I have lost everything, and I tell you that.'[10]

Though of course the point was that she had not lost everything; she had kept her extended family, her business acumen, her capacity for hard work – and her chickens. When I returned in May 1995, street markets had sprung up again in many parts of the battered and Russian-occupied town. They reminded me of the high spring grass which was already growing all over the wasteland around the central square, the thrusting, twining creepers of vivid green growing over the stumps of the shattered trees, and eclipsing the grey and brown of the rubble which stood where thousands of people had suffered and died – an imposing and almost frightening sign of the vigour of nature amidst the fragility of the works of civilisation, or indeed of man.[11]

The Bombardment of Grozny

The worst experience of the Chechen War for me was the bombing in December, despite the fact that it was a great deal more sporadic and less intense than the mixture of bombing and artillery bombardment which accompanied the ground assault. This was indeed one of the most intense bombardments of recent decades – a large part of the artillery of the former Soviet colossus pouring its fire into an area of a few square miles. Colleagues who had been in Beirut and Sarajevo said that it dwarfed those battles.

Perhaps the bombing felt worse just because it was so sporadic and random; another reason was that the bombs were falling on a town which was still not under ground assault, and so had a semblance of normality; and then, of course, it was obviously intended to kill and terrorise civilians. Perhaps, too, because among the first victims was a personal acquaintance, Cynthia Elbaum, a young American photographer covering her first war, killed when bombs fell on a crossroads that had been hit the previous night, and where we had gone to inspect the damage.

But above all it was the sense of a great iron hand swooping down from the sky and crushing and tearing to pieces innocent people at random, while they lay in their beds or struggled to find food, with their husbands and children beside them, that gave the bombing its particular horror for me – compounded of moral shock and personal terror. Every morning when we got up, we would find that a malign giant had taken another bite out of the familiar streets, leaving a blackened hole in an otherwise untouched row of houses, and in it limbless, obscenely mangled corpses dressed in the remnants of nightclothes and slippers. In the long intervals between the air strikes, there was a deep silence, with the snow muffling every sound in the deserted streets. In those days, Grozny often felt like a city stricken not by war, but by plague.

In January, the difference was that the planes had switched to a ground attack role. The sheer number of planes was extraordinary, and terrifying. In the drizzling murk of a Grozny January, made worse by the thick clouds of smoke from the burning city and its oil refineries, it was like being at the bottom of a grey, turbid sea, watching great grey sharks wheeling and diving above your head, disappearing in and out of the grey clouds. Sometimes they seemed even to be moving slowly and silently. On one occasion, when I was observing a battle in the centre from the seventh floor of a wrecked block of flats, I could swear one of them actually flew past below the level of my window, with the pilot clearly visible.

The stamina of the Chechen fighters under this pressure (as much of a pressure on the nerves as a physical danger), for weeks on end, was deeply impressive; and as for the defenders of Bamut, in the Caucasus foothills, who defended their village for *fifteen months* in the face of a bombardment to which they could make no reply, their performance places them in the ranks of the great epic defenders of history, alongside the men of Verdun and Masada.

Many male civilians, with nothing to do but sit still and be bombed, took to drink during these terrible weeks. The contrast between the men and the women in this context was rather striking. It came out especially in visits I made in January to a particular cellar at Pionerskaya 87, half a mile from the central square, where the remaining inhabitants of the surrounding blocks of flats had taken refuge. Most of these buildings were already in ruins, and over the next few weeks were to be reduced in some cases virtually to the staircases alone, with odd bits of masonry clinging to them like tattered washing on a sagging line.

Our first meeting was when I helped them remove the surviving beds from the wreckage of a nearby polyclinic on the main avenue. The men, both Russians and Chechens, were every one of them drunk at 11 a.m., and showed it. The women, by contrast, were quiet and dignified – probably because they had something to do; they had brought to the cellar some semblance of order, with beds arranged in rows and blankets folded, and they were also busy looking after the children, and concealing their own fear so as not to make them afraid.

Some of them complained of marauders, whether from the separatist forces or simply bandits, who were looting abandoned flats, especially those belonging to Russians. But as Neila Bogdanova, an accountant (*bukhgalter*), told me, 'we don't have that problem here, because the Chechen boys from our neighbours' families guard these blocks, and the marauders don't want to fight other Chechens. Our problem is our own people, the Russian army,' she added with a grim laugh. 'Another few days of this bombardment and there won't be anything left to loot.' In an extraordinary triumph of hope over experience, not far away a man called Mikhail Grechko, a cousin of the famous Marshal, was hammering planks of wood over the wreckage of his door, blown in by a bomb blast. 'Yes, I know it won't do any good, but I can't just leave it open for anyone to walk in.'

They were all of them, Russians and Chechens, full of hate for the Russian government, but many were also extremely hostile to Dudayev. Vaqa Saidov (a former factory director, in other words from the Soviet elite), said, with the others murmuring agreement,

> If you'd like Dudayev in England, you're welcome to him. We've suffered from him enough these past three years, with his ambition and his dictatorship. He's as much to blame for this war as Yeltsin and Grachev. He should have looked for a compromise with Moscow, for the sake of the people. Whatever those 'Mujahidin' of his say, I don't know any ordinary Chechen who would have opposed a reasonable compromise, so we could live in peace. I know none of us here would have.

These people were not fighters, but I found many fighters as well expressing such sentiments about Dudayev, though usually without the point about compromise with Russia, which after the outbreak of war (though in many cases, not before it) most had come to oppose.

The Russian Population

But at least Chechen civilians who opposed Dudayev could still suffer and die in the war with some sense of meaning and purpose, feeling themselves part of a national tradition of suffering and resistance, and of a national movement for freedom – although those who had always warned against Dudayev's policies did so with a very bitter smile on their lips, as some of their conversations with me indicated.

Utterly pitiable from this point of view was the Russian population of Grozny, and especially the pensioners. At the time of the national revolution of 1991, almost half the population of Grozny were still Russian, but over the next three years, around two-thirds of these are estimated to have left. Of those who remained behind, some had established personal links of some kind to Chechen society – there were a disproportionate number of pretty young Russian girls in Grozny, presumably acting as mistresses to wealthy Chechens, because sexual relations among Muslim Chechens are very restricted. But very many more were lonely pensioners, people who had no money, no relatives in Russia who could or would receive them, and were therefore simply trapped in Chechnya. When war broke out, they were doubly trapped. When the bombardment began, a majority of the Chechens in Grozny were able to find relatives to stay with in the countryside or one of the smaller towns. Lacking this, the Russians left in Grozny had no choice but to remain, crouching in their cellars as their homes were blasted to pieces over their heads. No reliable statistics are available or could be under the circumstances, but to judge from the evidence of my own notebooks from Grozny during the bombing in December 1994, and the anecdotal evidence of my colleagues, it seems clear that a majority of civilians killed by the bombing in Grozny were ethnic Russians, and of these a very large proportion were pensioners.

Again and again, my colleagues and I heard words like the following, spoken on the bitter morning of 21 December by Lydia Mukashenko, an elderly Russian widow whose flat had just been destroyed by a bomb while she was sheltering in the cellar. Standing by the ruins in a nightdress with an overcoat flung over it, her thickly veined legs and bare, swollen feet in their slippers turning blue in the snow, she moaned,

> The Russian Federation is killing us Russians. Two of my neighbours are dead. Why? For what? Russian television said that Grozny is empty of people, that it's a military target. Are they lying, or do they really not know that there are still women and children here? Tell them, you must tell them that we are still here, that they are killing us, that the Russian army is killing its own people.

The evidence of what their own forces had done to Russian grandmothers was one factor in undermining the will of Russian soldiers to fight in Chechnya. I wrote at the time that, 'when the knowledge of what has happened to Russians in Grozny reaches ordinary Russians in Russia, Yeltsin will have to account for his crimes to the Russian people.' Under the impact of scenes like these and of the sheer humiliation suffered by the Russian army, when I returned to Moscow I wrote an editorial article entitled 'Be Ready for Yeltsin's Demise',[12] suggesting that, for all these reasons, Yeltsin was doomed and could not possibly either win a future election or rely on security forces whom he had so betrayed.

It didn't happen like that. But the fact that Russians did forgive Yeltsin for what happened says a lot about the apathy and cynicism of the bulk of the Russian electorate today, as well as showing their fear of the Communists and of disorder.

The Russian Army in Grozny

When I returned to Grozny in mid-February 1995, most of the city was under Russian occupation, but fighting continued in the southern suburb of Chernorechiye. As I wrote in my notebook at the time, the wrecked city in the freezing rain resembled 'a smashed and sodden ants' nest, with bewildered, leaderless ants scurrying in all directions, dragging burdens'. Everywhere were people carrying or pulling bundles of possessions, either refugees trying to get out, or ones coming back in a desperate attempt to find their relatives or protect their homes. Down the torn-up, muddy roads roared Russian armoured personnel carriers (BTRs), like giant grey female woodlice covered with babies – their infantry crews. The Chechens looked down as they passed. As one of them told me, 'during the battle in the city, if the men on the BTRs saw someone on the street, they'd shoot at them like game. They don't do that now, unless they're very drunk, but if they don't like the look of you, they will stop and arrest you, or maybe just beat and rob you.' As my colleagues and I found to our cost, it was indeed a very bad idea to attract their attention.

However, one thing struck me: in the whole week I spent in the city at that time, only once did I see Russian soldiers on foot patrol, away from their checkpoints and fortified headquarters. The rest clung to their armoured vehicles with limpet-like strength. At night, they huddled behind their barricades. Even in the immediate aftermath of the Russian victory in Grozny, it was already hard to tell who was besieging whom.

The really gross destruction of buildings was limited to an area of some five square miles of the city centre, where the main battles of January-February 1995 were concentrated (it has since spread, of course, due to the fighting of March and August 1996). One broad finger of ruins extended from the north down and around Pervomaiskoye Chaissee to the centre, where the Russians fought their way in from one side; another ran from the west to the railway station; a third extended south-eastwards down Prospect Lenina, where the Russians advanced outwards in February 1995. Along this street, every building was destroyed.

The whole centre around the presidential headquarters was also one field of jagged ruins (today, much of it is a field pure and simple, for most of the ruins were demolished by the Russians in 1995–6). In this area, the destruction was fully comparable to pictures of Stalingrad in 1943, Berlin in 1945, or Hue in 1968. Elsewhere, in the sprawling suburbs that extend on all sides of the city, the destruction was more sporadic. But all over the city centre I found here and there in the courtyards of apartment blocks, in ones and twos and fours, fresh graves of people who had been killed or – if old and sick – had simply died of cold, hunger and exhaustion in the cellars where they were hiding.

What was almost universal was the evidence of looting and vandalism, in some cases by Chechen fighters – or armed robbers posing as them – but in the overwhelming majority by Russian soldiers. I was shown literally dozens of houses and flats with the doors shot off by automatic rifle fire, and all the furniture either gone, or smashed in an ecstasy of destruction, along with anything else that could be broken. In two cases I saw, flats had also been used as latrines. During the fighting, the destruction had been purely wanton; by the time I came back, it was mostly taking place as part of raids for arms.

There was also a great deal of harassment of Chechen civilians. This and the looting affected all Chechens, irrespective of political allegiance, and a good many local Russians besides. Our host in Grozny, a builder called Musa (a relative of the former anti-Dudayev mayor, Bislan Gantemirov, and a supporter of the Russian-backed Provisional Council), declared:

Not a night goes by in this area without a house being looted or burnt. Those shots you hear, they're not fighting, they're the Russians shooting down doors… They don't give a damn who is for Dudayev or not, as long as you are a Chechen. You show them your Provisional Council pass, and they say 'we'll make you eat it,' and sometimes they even do, after mixing it with vodka. For that matter, they don't always even respect their own passes… My own house was wrecked by them, and there's no point trying to repair it, because they'd only smash it again… Now ordinary Chechens like me, who only want peace, have to fear everyone – Dudayev's Mujahidin and the Russian troops as well.

He and others described numerous cases of wanton shootings; from several people I heard of a soldiers' habit of dropping a cartridge into the pocket of a man they were searching, then 'finding' it, declaring him a 'terrorist', and killing him on the spot. Women, however, were apparently usually spared, somewhat unusually for this kind of war. (For a general assessment of Russian military atrocities, see chapter 3.)

The mood among the ordinary Russian civilians was mixed. Many had themselves suffered, either from the bombardment or the looting, but there was also a measure of grim satisfaction at the Chechens' plight, after what they had meted out to some of the Russians over the previous three years. I spoke to a small Russian girl called Anya, aged eight, who with her father and two even smaller brothers had gone to loot the remains of a jam and conserves factory. (I thought ordinary mud in Grozny was viscous until I discovered what it was like after it had been mixed with large quantities of apple puree and bottled plums. Through the mire waded Chechen and Russian civilians, desperately clutching their bottles and jars.) Looking out of tiny ancient eyes, like a haggard female leprechaun, she told me that

We saw the whole war, but they say the worst is now over. What was the worst? That was when we saw the Chechens put a Russian tankist against a wall and shoot him … and how the Russian soldiers beat up the Chechens. We were always afraid of the Chechens, ever since I can remember, but now it is the Chechens who are afraid… Am I glad? Well, there are good and bad Chechens. The bad ones used to curse us in the streets, and frighten us. Now it is good because the Russian army will come, and they will create order.

This was what you might call the naive Russian view; but their father, Niko-lai Fyodorovich, who had come up and was standing beside me, declared that

I'm glad to be free of Dudayev of course but that doesn't mean there's anything good about the situation. Look around you. The town is destroyed, there is no work, there's nothing to eat. The army keeps promising help for civilians, but they make you wait and wait and then give you nothing. What can you expect of a government like Yeltsin's – thieves, the lot of them.

As to the Russian army itself, the evidence of demoralisation in the Russian conscript units – whether army or Interior Ministry – was universal and overwhelming. Far from trying to deny it, the officers I met were perfectly open on the subject, lacing their remarks with black humour. At a base in northern Grozny, a drunken Interior Ministry major, surrounded by even drunker Cossack volunteers (for a portrait of the neo-Cossacks, see chapter 6), put his arms round two of his embarrassed soldiers, pale, scrawny creatures who looked about sixteen, and hiccuped, 'Look at these kids. They didn't ask to come here. You know what they're paid a month? Twenty thousand roubles, that's what, five dollars? Would you risk getting yourself killed for five dollars a month? Would you do *anything* for five dollars a month?'

At a Russian post outside Samashki, an OMON (paramilitary police) major pointed to a heap of army-ration cans of beef and declared, 'We don't eat that – it's only fit for dogs'; at which point one of his soldiers got down on his hands and knees and went 'woof woof'. As a matter of fact, these soldiers – all regulars, not conscripts, and supposedly an 'elite' unit – looked better cared for than most; but they also made no secret whatsoever of their hatred for the war. Standing in front of his men, the Major said that

> The only good that we can do here is if we go home, and it would be better if that so-called Provisional Government got out as well. We should have let the Chechens go three years ago, to sort things out on their own. If we left, 90 per cent of the people here would put down their guns and go home, and if the others wanted to go on killing each other, well that's their business.

However, the Major continued with words which pointed forwards to the massacre by Russian troops when they stormed Samashki two months later (and which of course has echoes of innumerable other such statements in the history of partisan war):

> We have constant negotiations with the local people to try to get the fighters to leave. We don't want to bombard the town. But the fighters don't want to leave, and they keep sniping at us, and we don't know who they are. One minute you'll see a couple of peaceful civilians in a car or working in a field – the next minute, bang, you're dead with a bullet in the back… The worst day here was when an ambulance brought back three army soldiers who had been ambushed and killed in Samashki. One of them was literally shot to pieces, as if it had been done deliberately.[13]

I was told by Chechen civilians that the Interior Ministry troops, or at least the regulars among them, were more disciplined and less uncontrolledly brutal than the army conscripts – though that may be in part because they had not participated in the worst of the fighting in January, and so had not suffered so many casualties. In the words of Aslanbek Elmakhanov, another relation of Gantemirov and an anti-Dudayevist:

> Thank God there has been a change in the troops. It was worse when the town was occupied by the military, after the Russians came in. The army troops who fought were extremely savage – hysterical, terrified, drunken – they would kill for no reason at all. These Interior Ministry soldiers are older, more responsible.

My own introduction to an Interior Ministry elite, or Spetsnaz, unit called SOBR (Spetsialniy Otryad Bystrogo Reagirovaniya, or Special Rapid Reaction Force) was one of the most terrifying experiences of my life. However, it is probably true that their relative restraint and discipline also saved the lives of my colleagues and myself, and our later acquaintance proved very interesting, so I am not complaining. If the Russian Interior Ministry forces have an elite – if indeed Russia today has any elite units at all – then SOBR units are it; and my experience of them suggests that while their men would probably become crack troops in the right circumstances – such as facing an invasion of Russia proper – they are nothing like that at present.

The encounter of my colleagues Victoria Clarke, Heidi Bradner, Ellen Binder and myself with SOBR was due to a mixture of our foolishness and their over-reaction, compounded by their belief in a particularly fatuous Russian legend.[14] We had been invited to stay by a Mr Elmakhanov, mentioned above, and foolishly imagined that the local Russian forces would either know or care that he was the cousin and aide of Gantemirov, whom they were even then restoring as Mayor of Grozny; and so, since it was already evening and the curfew was being savagely enforced, we had decided to leave it until the next day to make ourselves known to the local Russian command post.

They for their part had heard that there were people speaking Russian with foreign accents staying in the locality, and to their natural suspiciousness was added the fact that some of these people were women. This started a train of thought which led to the 'White Tights', a legendary unit of Latvian (or Estonian, or both) women sharpshooters who turn up in every post-Soviet war fighting on the anti-Russian side. Not a scrap of evidence for their existence has ever been produced – but every Russian soldier I have met (and the Abkhaz and Armenians to boot) has believed in them implicitly.[15] In Chechnya, they formed part of the general legend of the 'six thousand mercenaries' (or 'Afghan Mujahidin volunteers', depending on who you were talking with). This was a myth assiduously peddled by the Yeltsin administration and the Russian High Command, but unlike the rest of official misinformation on Chechnya, which the soldiers treated with utter contempt, this one they believed – mainly, no doubt, because it allowed them to hide from themselves the extent of their military humiliation by the Chechens.

Be that as it may, on the evening of 20 February the SOBR unit in Grozny came looking for the White Tights. They showed their professionalism by coming over the garden wall in dead silence – and in the garden, they found our host, washing the dishes. Thankfully, because they put a gun to his head and asked him who was in the house, and he replied 'Western journalists'. Without that, as one of them told us later, 'we'd have chucked a grenade into the room first and checked your documents afterwards. That's what we'd normally do in a case like that.'

The first we knew of their presence was a moment of the purest terror. We had just finished our dinner when I looked up to see a figure in a black mask framed in the doorway, rifle levelled at us. There was perhaps a second of dead silence, then a yell of 'Stoi!' ('stay still!'), and the room was suddenly full of uniformed figures, all in black masks, roaring orders and curses, pushing us against the walls, seemingly on the verge of hysteria (in part, this was no doubt standard technique for bewildering and terrifying any opposition – it certainly had that effect on me – but it also reflected genuine fear on their part).

Despite the fact that our identity must have been obvious from the start, the next hour or so, until we were finally brought to the local commandant's office was extremely unpleasant. Walking in darkness with your hands clasped over your head, and getting in and out of an armoured personnel carrier in that position, are not easy, but a rap over the head with a rifle butt will teach you to keep your balance. I collected several, together with a number of kicks, both at the scene of arrest and more systematically on arrival at the Kommendatura. The brutality there seemed to be a more or less standard roughing up for every male prisoner brought in – against the wall opposite, my colleagues saw three Chechens being beaten, one of them an elderly man. They themselves were not maltreated, which shows a measure of restraint and discipline on the part of SOBR – and also, that the soldiers weren't drunk.

After the Commandant, Colonel Nikolai Yefimenko, had checked our documents, our captors became extremely apologetic, mainly no doubt at having shown so much aggression in arresting three unarmed women. Incongruously enough, they even took us back home in the same BTR in which they had carried us to the Kommendatura. We ended up spending most of the next week with them, and became sufficiently good friends that on returning to Russia, we rang up several of their families to tell them that they were all right; and one of them, Andrei, later brought his wife and children to see me in Moscow, and invited me to visit them at their dacha in Kerch.[16]

Edik Ponomarev, one of the SOBR men, told me the next day, 'We're very sorry for what happened. You must understand, we've taken several casualties, and we're all on edge.' They had some reason: a few days after we left, one of them, Oleg Svartsov, was killed and two others wounded when their BTR drove over a Chechen mine in Grozny.

There was a sharp difference between the SOBR troops and the conscript units, whether Interior Ministry or army – something they themselves repeatedly emphasised. When we first talked with them, they tried to stress their higher motivation, though this attempt soon slipped. Sergei from Khabarovsk (most would not give their surnames, for fear of Chechen revenge against their families) said that

> You know, back home our job is to fight the mafia, and you could say we're doing the same here, fighting the Chechen mafia... So we know why we're here, even if we don't like being here any more than anyone else. We're not really soldiers, we're policemen. But on the other hand we're all ex-soldiers, most of us *Afghantsi*, and we are certainly better trained and equipped than most of the soldiers. As for the conscripts, it was simply a crime to send those kids here to be slaughtered. Lebed was right: they should have sent the sons of generals and ministers, maybe then they'd have been more careful.

In one way, this SOBR unit displayed a feature that the Russian and Soviet armies used to be distinguished for, but the bulk of the present army has completely forgotten – a certain talent for improvised construction. They had made the Kommendatura – incongruously a former honey-bottling plant – as comfortable as possible for themselves, and in one corner had erected that staple of Russian military life, a *banya* or steam bath, which they kindly invited us to use. In consequence they both looked and smelled better than much of the rest of the army.

In common with most soldiers far from home, they had adopted a temporary pet or mascot – a cat rescued from a burnt-out flat, and christened by immemorial Russian military tradition 'Mashka'. It was a strange sight – but one I have seen in every war – to see these hard-faced men with the cat on their knees, gently stroking its fur. I strongly suspected them of regarding the four of us in the light of additional mascots (or at least the women – I was probably decidedly *de trop* as far as they were concerned). They certainly took great delight in showing us off to other units we met when they drove us around town.

All the same, I was never in danger of sentimentalising this unit. A large lump on the head and several aching ribs reminded me of the mildest aspect of their behaviour to prisoners; and if they did regard us as mascots, then I have no doubt that in a crisis they would have killed and eaten Mashka. While with them, I repeatedly thought of a description in Czeslaw Milosz's memoir, *Native Realm*, of a scene that he witnessed during the Soviet invasion of East Prussia in January 1945. A group of Russian soldiers comfort a German prisoner with genuine humanity and kindness, and then with apparently equally genuine regret take him outside and shoot him, out of 'necessity' – the necessity in this case, as Milosz remarked, consisting of either the prisoner's warm sheepskin coat, or the difficulty of transferring him to the rear.

The high point of our acquaintance with the SOBR troops was when they invited us to dinner on Army Day, 23 February, producing a grilled goat and several bottles of captured Chechen brandy. Much of this of course they insisted on pouring down my throat; but I noticed that none of them drank more than three glasses – which to anyone who knows how the Russian armed forces usually behave on such days is a really striking example of their discipline. When they escorted us home on foot after the dinner (they had found us a place to stay nearby, with the family of a Russian woman working for the Kommendatura), they moved like men trained for urban warfare, in open order, covering the different angles of possible attack.

On this and other occasions, they gossiped a bit about themselves and their unit. Part of what they said could be discounted as boasting, both to us and to a couple of nervous-looking staff officers from headquarters, whom they obviously delighted in frightening. However, a number of interesting things emerged. One was the crazy way their unit had been put together – from volunteers taken in January in ones and twos from different regional units all the way from Murmansk to Vladivostok. After sitting around for a few days at a base near Moscow, waiting for a plane, they had finally been sent down to Grozny without the chance to train together for so much as an hour, hardly the way to create an 'elite' unit. (SOBR as a whole was put together about a year earlier, after the October 1993 events, and made up of volunteers from the Interior Ministry troops, the police, and armed units of Counter-Intelligence (the FSK).)

Another thing was that despite Dima's words about fighting the mafia, these elite troops were all fed up both with the war in Chechnya and with their service in general. Their commander, a major called Andrei – a rather impressive figure with an air of natural command, not altogether unlike Shamil Basayev – confessed to me that he was thinking of leaving the service to become a private security guard. Having served for the time as a government bodyguard in Moscow, he was sure he could get a good position:

> I don't much want to, because I've been a soldier all my life. But a man has to think of his family, after all, and the pay would be five times or more what I'm getting now, even with the bonus for serving here. Anyway, the government has shown that it doesn't give a damn for its soldiers or policemen. That's just the way it is these days. Who would be a soldier if you can work in a bank?

The feeling of disillusionment and pessimism was universal, even though it had not had as bad an effect on morale as elsewhere in the army. I asked Dima whether the struggle against the mafia wasn't hopeless, in view of the growing criminalisation and corruption of the Russian state itself. He shrugged his shoulders sadly: 'Maybe, but we have to go on trying. Otherwise everything will go to hell, and any kind of decent, normal life in Russia will be impossible.'

Another thing which came out over the brandy – not that it had been particularly hidden before – was the extent to which they hated and despised the Russian government and their own commanders. Oleg, who died three days after I last saw him, was a round-faced cheerful officer from Tsiktsikvar, with a short beard and a blue and white woolly hat, like a traditional seaman, and was often ribbed by the others for absent-mindedness. He said that

Russia's a country of fools, and more important, it's governed by scumbags. I suppose they hoped for the best, but it turned out as usual [a Russian saying]. In your country, I imagine, the army trusts the government. Here, the soldiers don't trust the government or even their own generals. They're quite convinced firstly that they're all thieves and secondly that they're so incompetent they'll make a stupid mistake and get them all killed. Can you blame them? Just look at what's happened here.

Andrei was even blunter: 'Yeltsin, Grachev – they're all pieces of shit. All they think about is staying in office and making money. The government and the mafia are virtually the same. Not one of them thinks about the country or the army.'

These men were from the Interior Ministry, the troops who would be in the front line to defend the Yeltsin regime or its successors if there were any mass unrest. My impression from them was that they might conceivably fight against an attempt by other services, or individual politicians, at a coup d'état, but that under no circumstances would they fire on ordinary demonstrators. This makes the Yeltsin and perhaps any other Russian administration seem rather brittle. If the masses ever did come out on to the streets in really large numbers, any specific government might fall with surprising speed – even though the next government to take power would probably be little different in its essence. Again and again, from army and Interior Ministry troops alike, I heard variants of the phrase from one of the SOBR men, 'If Yeltsin thinks the army and OMON will save him again the way they did in October 1993, he can think again.'

From the point of view of their military effectiveness, the SOBR men, it seemed to me, were and were not suitable as 'elite' troops. On the one hand, they had all spent years in the military. All but two had been in Afghanistan, and several in other operations as well – Andrei, an ex-paratrooper (and great admirer of Lebed as a commander) had six under his belt, including Baku in 1990. On the other hand, they mostly were in their late twenties and early thirties, with families – too old, and with too many personal responsibilities, for the kind of instinctive recklessness that makes for really good fighting troops, except in circumstances where the threat to the whole country, and their own families, is obvious and overwhelming.

As Dima – one of the youngest at twenty-three – said to me,

You know, at eighteen everyone thinks they're Rambo. But I'm married, with a ten-month-old child [he said with a chuckle that he had been married for six months – 'in a bit of a hurry, you see']. The rest of us are the same, all family men. All we want is to do our jobs here properly, and then go home to our families. We're not looking to do stupid heroics...Above all, we are just determined not to let each other down, not to let down our friends.

Moreover, they did not swagger and boast. Dima said that he had joined SOBR from being a lieutenant in the army, 'because I liked the army life, but not the army pay! Also, the way things are going, the army today is just not a career for life.'

Finally, in certain ways the SOBR men were quite unlike other Russian troops, but bore a certain, incongruous resemblance to their Chechen enemies. The most visibly striking aspect of this was their beards. Andrei, with his tufty, reddish beard, broad, high cheekbones, small, slightly slanting eyes and rather sly grin, looked like one of those coarse, competent, humorous and intermittently ruthless Russian peasants who populate the pages of nineteenth-century Russian literature. What he did not look like was a Soviet officer, or a contemporary Russian officer from any of the standard line units. All but two out of the twelve-man SOBR group had them (Dima, to fit in, had obviously just begun to grow one that was still thinnish). Until the very end of the 1980s, a beard in the Soviet armed forces would simply never have occurred; it would have been not just against every rule, but a sign of dissidence. They looked to me like an attempt to mark the men off from the boys, the hardened SOBR professionals from the weedy conscripts – but also perhaps the faint beginnings of a new post-Soviet spirit, for 'beards are an old Russian tradition', as Oleg told me. So too were their numerous touches of personal display – like Oleg's red and white spotted scarf, or Andrei's small gold cross, or the bandannas several of them wore: all strictly non-regulation.

Much more important was the discipline of the SOBR group. So unlike was it to that of the rest of the army that for the first two days I did not realise that Andrei was the commander. Not merely did he wear no badges of rank, but he gave orders through polite requests rather than barked commands. Much of the time indeed they seemed to know what to do without him giving an order at all. This was not surprising. The group was almost entirely made up of officers, with an easy camaraderie and a spontaneous discipline – by far the best kind of discipline there is.

It struck me that here was a spirit out of which something could be made for the future – if they were given a state and a cause worth fighting for. Or in the words of Andrei, 'Russian soldiers will fight hard to defend their country if it is attacked, make no mistake about it. They just need to be told why they are fighting, and to be sure they are being told the truth.'

2 Russia and Chechnya, 1991–1994: The Origins of War

You and I together form the tempest. You are the furious wind; I am the calm sea. You arrive and you blow irritatingly, and I burst into a fury of foam. Now we have a great storm. But between you and me there is a difference. I, like the sea, never leave my place, while you, like the wind, never remain in yours.

Mulay Ahmed er-Raisuli to a Spanish colonial officer, 1913

The Chechen Revolt of the 1990s

In the early 1990s, both the Russian central state and the Chechen state got much weaker; but both in fact were stronger than they appeared. The Chechen state was stronger because, as the event proved, it could in the last resort rely on the support of the great majority of its members in the face of outside attack. The Russian state was stronger than many thought because, with the sole exception of the Chechens, it did not face really determined ethnic secessionist movements from its federal elements. This was a key difference between the new Russian Federation and the old Soviet Union, and a key reason why the new Russia has endured even in the face of military defeat.

Apart from the Abkhaz, who could rely on a measure of central Soviet encouragement and support against the Georgians, the Chechens and Ingush were the first North Caucasian peoples to start making open national claims under Soviet rule. In 1973, Ingush protests against the loss of the Prigorodny District to Ossetia were joined by the Chechens, who as a result succeeded in forcing Moscow to appoint more Chechens to official posts in the republic (see chapter 9). These protests were almost certainly covertly encouraged by leading Chechen Communist Party officials.[1]

Protests resumed in the late 1980s under Gorbachev, and focused initially – as in the Baltic States – on environmental protest (against a plan, revealed in 1988, to build a biochemical plant in the city of Gudermes), on the protection of the Chechen language and national culture, and on demands for religious freedom. These protests were orchestrated by the Popular Front of Checheno-Ingushetia, a body ostensibly loyal to the Soviet Union, and closely linked to Chechen party officials, KGB officers and policemen who wanted to displace the conservative Russian First Secretary, Vladimir Foteyev, and replace him with a Chechen.[2] This helped lead in 1989 to the appointment of Doku Zavgayev, a former collective farm manager and senior Communist Party official, as the first Chechen First Secretary of the autonomous republic since the Chechens' return in 1957. The Popular Front (as initially in the Baltic States and elsewhere) was dominated by the intelligentsia, and had moderate aims. It used mainly Russian in its propaganda, and a considerable number of local Russians were in its ranks.

Part of the motive for these protests was socio-economic. Soviet official statistics showed Chechnya close to the bottom of the list of Russian autonomous republics and regions in most socio-economic and educational indicators – though as in Georgia and elsewhere, this of course ignored the huge unofficial, black market sources of income. What undoubtedly has been of great importance however – and could be a great danger in future, not just to Russia, but to Chechen governments themselves – is that the high birthrate produced large numbers of unemployed young men (for the contrast with Russia, see chapter 5). In the 1970s, an estimated 25,000 young men left Chechnya for other regions each spring to work as part-time labour, mostly in building.[3] By this stage, the Chechen oil-wells, in the 1940s second only to those of Baku and among the most productive in the world, were almost worked out, and by the early 1980s accounted for only 3 per cent of Russia's oil production.

Initially, and unusually, the Ingush took the lead over the Chechens in national protest. This was because, like the Karabakh Armenians, they had a particular grievance that could be voiced while remaining publicly loyal to the Soviet Union and without alienating Russians: their demand for the return of the Prigorodny District, transferred to North Ossetia when the Ingush were deported in 1944, was directed against another minority people. However, by calling for a separate Ingush ASSR the Ingush also pointed towards a split with the Chechens, and to some extent caused delays in the development of Chechen nationalism.

In the Soviet parliamentary elections of 1989, Zavgayev was able to pack most of the seats with his own candidates, except for the victory of an economics professor from the Chechen diaspora in Moscow, a 'democrat' and supporter of Boris Yeltsin – Ruslan Khasbulatov. He owed his prestige in Chechnya partly to the fact that his ancestors had been respected Muslim clerics. The split between Khasbulatov and the Communist faction of Zavgayev was to have fateful consequences for Chechnya, contributing to Chechen independence in 1991, the ascendancy of Dudayev, and the failure of the anti-Dudayev Chechen opposition.

In the spring of 1990, protests among the Chechens themselves spread even to the villages, and all over Chechnya unpopular officials, and ethnic Russians, were forced to resign. Zavgayev used his new position to replace them as far as possible with members of his own clan, kinship group and bureaucratic following. He was also able to gain considerable control over the Popular Front, thereby contributing to its collapse.

By 1991, the national protests had developed into a movement for Chechnya to become a full republic of the Soviet Union, outside the Russian Federation. This, it is interesting to note, remained the formal position of General Dudayev until his death. He always portrayed himself as a Soviet loyalist, who would like to see the Soviet Union reconstituted 'on new principles', with Chechnya as an equal member alongside Russia.[4] He also repeatedly offered to join the Commonwealth of Independent States, for what that is worth.

More extreme Chechen national demands were articulated by the Chechen National Congress, founded in November 1990 with the approval of Zavgayev, who presumably thought it might act as a safety-valve. However, it was also entered on a large scale by more radical members of the Popular Front and new nationalist elements like Zelimkhan Yandarbiyev. Dudayev, then (since 1987) a major-general commanding a wing of Soviet nuclear bombers stationed in Tartu, Estonia, attended the Congress, and was elected the chairman of its Executive Committee and commander of the National Guard. These were supposed to be honorary posts, for at that time Dudayev had not indicated that he was about to quit the air force. He did so after refusing to participate in the Soviet military intervention in the Baltic States in January 1991, and covertly helping Boris Yeltsin.

Dudayev was born in 1944 in the (partly Cossack) village of Pervomaiskoye in Chechnya. Almost immediately afterwards, his family was deported with the rest of the Chechen people to Kazakhstan, where he spent his childhood (for an account of the deportation, see chapter 9). He returned to Chechnya with his family in 1957, but soon left to join the military flying school in Tambov, and served in the Soviet air force from 1966 to 1990, winning the orders of the Red Star and the Red Banner. He married a Russian from Estonia.

The reasons for the political rise of Dudayev within Chechnya are now inevitably clouded by controversy and rumour. Delegates were undoubtedly impressed by his fiery speech at the Congress. The fact that he was a general, the only Chechen to hold this rank in the Soviet armed forces, also impressed them – throughout the North Caucasus, former Soviet officers have played leading political roles, presumably because of the instinctive respect that Caucasians feel for the profession of arms.

General Dudayev had reportedly signalled his sympathy for national liberation movements in the Soviet Union as early as 1989, when he allowed an Estonian flag to be hoisted above his base in Tartu. Until then, as a Soviet officer he had presumably had to cover up his national feelings totally, the more so as he came from a nationality which was always distrusted and disliked by many Russians – though there seems also to have been a deliberate Soviet policy of nominating certain picked Chechens to senior positions.

A subsidiary reason for the choice of Dudayev by the Congress may have been that as a member of a relatively small and insignificant teip, and as a man who had always lived outside Chechnya, he was a good compromise candidate for the representatives of larger, rival clans, followings and interest groups.

One aspect of the formation of the Congress and of the Chechen national movement was resentment of other clans at the domination of the Soviet bureaucracy and especially the oil industry in Chechnya by members of Zavgayev's clan. (As chapter 10 will point out, the importance of the teip as such in contemporary Chechen politics has been exaggerated. I am using 'clan' here in a much looser sense.)

Dudayev had also forged links with an important Chechen state manager turned businessman, with alleged mafia links, Yaragi Mamadayev, who until 1990 was head of the biggest state construction company in Chechnya, Chechenstroi. He is believed to have mobilised financial support for Dudayev, as well as the help of sections of the local bureaucracy and management who were opposed to Zavgayev. He was to become acting Prime Minister from 1991 to 1993.

Among the Chechen intelligentsia, Dudayev's closest ally was his later Vice-President and successor, Zelimkhan Yandarbiyev, a nationalist poet who worked as a very junior official in the state publishing house (in contrast to the better known and moderate intellectual figures who had founded the Popular Front). Yandarbiyev reportedly introduced Dudayev to the potential of Islamic politics, or at least imagery. He was leader of the Bart (Harmony) Party, which in 1990 became the Vainakh Democratic Party (*vainakh* being the common name for Chechens and Ingush).

A third, extremely sinister figure of great importance in this period was Yusup Soslambekov, a 'businessman' who had served time in prison for rape. He is reportedly something of an organisational genius, and played an important part in the revolution of 1991. From 1991 to 1993 he was chairman of the 'parliament' of the Confederation of Mountain Peoples, which linked the various Muslim North Caucasian Autonomous Republics, and helped mobilise some support for Chechnya – although very much less than the Chechens hoped for. He is also believed to have played a key role in sending Chechen and other North Caucasian volunteers to fight in Abkhazia against the Georgians – which served Russia's interests at the time, but also gave Shamil Basayev and his Chechen battalion fighting experience which they were to use with devastating effect against Russia later.

A similar figure was a former police sergeant, used car dealer and gangster from Moscow, Bislan Gantemirov, whose armed followers played a considerable part in the 1991 events and who became Mayor of Grozny.[5] (For Gantemirov's foundation of the 'Islamic Path Party', and what this says about Islamic politics – or rather the lack of them – in Chechnya, see chapter 11.)

Most of the tiny Chechen intelligentsia, by contrast, has remained distrustful of Islam in politics, and nostalgic for the security and funding of Soviet rule – which had, after all, created their class, and which emplyed them. In this they resembled the intellectual establishment in Azerbaijan and elsewhere. During the war, out of anger with the Russian invasion and atrocities by Russian troops, many of them rallied to the separatists. However, their sympathies went above all to Colonel Aslan Maskhadov, whom they regarded as more moderate and sensible than Dudayev, and less religious than Yandarbiyev or Basayev. The difference between Maskhadov's staff, made up of professional people (doctors, engineers and so on), and that of Basayev, containing much less educated and more religious people, was very striking.[6]

The Chechen National Congress called for the dissolution of the Chechen-Ingush Supreme Soviet, elected in 1990 and dominated by Communists. The Communist leadership reacted by suppressing opposition propaganda and meetings. But when the attempted counter-revolution of 19 August was carried out by conservative Soviet elements in Moscow, the Chechen-Ingush Communist leaders were apparently taken by surprise, and had obviously not been let in on the plot. Zavgayev and his chief aides were in Moscow for the signing of the planned Union Treaty (Gorbachev's constitution for a looser, more confederal Soviet Union) two days later, and those left in charge were split in different directions, with some supporting the coup, some denouncing it and others developing a wide variety of diplomatic illnesses so as to avoid having to commit themselves. Crucially, the republic's Interior Minister, General Umar Alsultanov, swung over to the opposition. When the coup failed, Zavgayev returned to Grozny, and like so many local Communist bosses, denounced the coup plotters.

But in the meantime, the coup and its failure had given Dudayev and the National Congress their chance. On the first day of the coup, Dudayev denounced it as criminal and called for a mass movement of resistance. He went on to demand the resignation of the government and the dissolution of the parliament for having supported the coup, and the transfer of power to the Executive Committee of the Congress.

Of great importance in this period was the attitude of Boris Yeltsin and his leading supporter Ruslan Khasbulatov, responsible for formulating Yeltsin's Chechen policy. At this stage, both men were evidently obsessed with consolidating their power and getting rid of the remaining pro-Gorbachev elements in the administration. They evidently saw Dudayev and the Chechen Congress as allies in this struggle, and it was presumably on their orders that when the highest Chechen within the Russian administration, Police Major-General (and RSFSR parliamentary Deputy) Aslanbek Aslakhanov visited Grozny at the end of August, he gave a strong warning to Zavgayev not to use force to crush the protests.

Meanwhile, the protests themselves were becoming more and more forceful. The Congress supporters launched a general strike and a series of mass demonstrations. Armed men began to occupy official buildings, including the TV and radio station in Grozny, beating and occasionally shooting those who resisted. Finally, on 6 September, they seized and occupied the Supreme Soviet, having previously declared it dissolved. This then was a real, violent revolution and not the largely 'passive' one occuring elsewhere in Russia, Ukraine and most Soviet republics.

When the Supreme Soviet was stormed, the Russian Communist Party Second Secretary was either thrown out of a window, or fell to his death while trying to escape. On 15 September, Zavgayev resigned and fled from the republic to Moscow, where he became a senior adviser to Yeltsin. Subsequently, the violent nationalist seizure of power in Chechnya allowed the Yeltsin administration to charge Dudayev himself with having staged an illegal coup d'état. Also on 15 September, a congress of Ingush radicals declared Ingushetia separated from Chechnya and a republic within the Russian Federation, a decision formalised by the Ingush parliament several months later.

In early September, however, Yeltsin and Khasbulatov had still been trying to work with Dudayev – this was after all only a few months after Yeltsin, in the campaign for the Russian presidency in June 1991, had told the Russian autonomous republics to take 'all the sovereignty you can swallow'. The Yeltsin administration had therefore put pressure on the Chechen-Ingush Supreme Soviet to declare itself dissolved, and on Zavgayev formally to quit. Power was ostensibly transferred to a provisional supreme council, under a neutral establishment academic, Professor Hussein Akhmadov.

In fact, Dudayev and the radicals never allowed Akhmadov to assume even the appearance of power. On 5 October the national guards dissolved the provisional council and occupied its building. As a response, the Russian parliament the next day despatched a delegation to Grozny headed by Vice-President Alexander Rutskoy, whose military nationalism quickly detected the threat posed by Chechen and other independence movements to the unity and borders of the Russian Federation. He argued sharply with Dudayev and returned to Moscow calling for military intervention.[7] Rutskoy described Dudayev's Executive Committee as 'a gang terrorising the population', and in the first of many Russian miscalculations, described their supporters as numbering only 250 men.[8] The Chechen crisis marked the beginning of the split between Rutskoy and Yeltsin, which two years later was to lead the Vice-President to take up arms in defence of the parliament and against Yeltsin's presidency.[9]

As demands for full Chechen independence from Russia gathered pace, the Russian government began to react, but the interval had allowed Dudayev several vital weeks in which to consolidate his power, take control of the police and their weapons, and buy, steal or extort weapons from Soviet troops in the republic. The Soviet armed forces at that time were effectively leaderless and in a state of complete confusion, with Yeltsin, Gorbachev and the different republican leaders (especially of course of Ukraine) all vying for their support. Under the circumstances, it is not surprising that so many of those in Chechnya chose to surrender their weapons, or sell them, rather than fight to keep them.

Dudayev was also able to procure the transfer to gaols in Grozny of Chechen criminals being held in gaols elsewhere in the North Caucasus. Others, like Labazanov, had already been transferred back to Chechnya from other parts of the Russian Federation at the request of the Chechen-Ingush Communist authorities, themselves under pressure from the men's families. As Russian pressure mounted in October, these were then released to swell the ranks of Dudayev's national guard.

Labazanov later described what happened as follows (allowance for boasting needs to be made):

> I began to take an interest in politics in 1990 when I was imprisoned in Rostov for murder. Then I was transferred to the investigation section in Grozny. During the coup of 1991 I set the whole prison free ahead of time – nearly 600 people. They listened to me. Then I formed my group out of those I had set free. We 'teamed up' with the new government, with Dudayev, and guarded him.[10]

None of these men of course allowed their new commitment to the national cause to prevent them from exploiting the new opportunities for criminality. In February 1992, outside Dudayev's headquarters in Grozny, I saw an incident which has probably been characteristic of many revolutions. A little man with hot eyes and the face of a gangster came out of the building – one Issa Akhyadov, a member of the national guard (and, I was told, a former KGB officer). He declared to the crowd that some of his men had been unjustly arrested by the police – for robbing shops, as I was told later. He then launched into a fiery speech about how the state managers of the shops had been stealing the food for themselves and fixing high prices. Waving a sheaf of papers, he yelled that

> I am the head of Special Commission 0001 on food, and I have here proof of the corruption of the Communist nomenklatura managers. We wanted to show this to the President, to tell him that they should be removed and punished so the people can eat, and that is why they are persecuting and imprisoning us… During the revolution, we risked our lives for the people. We should not be persecuted by traitors…The old Communists have infiltrated themselves into our revolution, and now they control parliament and are trying to reimpose their rule.

Part of the crowd howled its approval; others yelled back, 'This is just a drunken show, you are splitting the people.' Another: 'Tell us where they are hiding the food!'

At Rutskoy's instigation, the Russian parliament called for the disbanding of armed groups in Chechnya. On 23 October, the Russian General Procuracy issued an order banning groups whose demands 'violated the integrity of the Russian Federation'. This Russian pressure seems – as might have been predicted, and as happened again and again later – only to have increased support for Dudayev and the radicals. Thus a few months later, in February 1992, I interviewed Musa Temishev, editor of the newspaper *Kavkaz* and a strong critic of Dudayev from the side of the moderate Chechen intelligentsia. He was already warning of the threat of 'Islamic fundamentalism' and 'unrestrained banditry' in Chechnya, and described the Committee of Public Safety that Dudayev had set up as the 'Committee for Theft from the Public'.

He said that there should be a 'Russian Commonwealth of Nations', including Chechnya, and that there should be no borders between the two countries.

But when I asked about the possibility of Russian intervention, he said that in that case, Chechens should blow up Russian nuclear power stations, and burst out,

> I am against Dudayev, but if the Russians came here, I, Musa Temishev, would be the first to carry out such acts, and so would every Chechen. A Russian intervention would be the third Russian genocide against the Chechen nation... Why should we be the only ones to fear? The only reason the Russian parliament vetoed Yeltsin's state of emergency last autumn was that we had blockaded the airport and shown that we were ready to die. That is the only language the Russians understand.

On 27 October, Dudayev held presidential and parliamentary elections in which he won 85 per cent of the presidential vote and nationalist groups captured all the parliamentary seats. Observers at the time alleged numerous irregularities, including intimidation of the local Russian population, but on the whole the results seem to have reflected fairly enough the Chechen national mood at that time. Immediately on taking office, General Dudayev gave himself emergency powers for a month – powers which he was never in fact to surrender. Yeltsin responded by demanding the dissolution of the armed groups, the return of the seized buildings, elections for the Supreme Soviet, and a referendum on the Chechen state system.[11]

On 2 November, the Chechen parliament proclaimed full independence from Russia, and this was confirmed by a new constitution passed the following March. Meanwhile, supporters of Zavgayev and the ousted Communist leadership, who had retained control of his home district, Nadterechny, in north-western Chechnya, began to organise an armed opposition there.

President Yeltsin reacted to the declaration of independence by declaring a state of emergency in Chechnya on 8 November and threatening to restore order by force. This was, however, criticised by sections of the media and liberal politicians in Moscow – including, oddly enough, the liberal deputy Sergei Stepashin, who three years later, as head of the domestic intelligence service (the FSK, successor to the KGB), was to play a critical role in bringing on the Chechen war. Yeltsin's moves were also denounced by Mikhail Gorbachev and his remaining followers in the Soviet government and Interior Ministry.

On 10 November, the Supreme Soviet in Moscow met to discuss the President's decree. None the less, on the same day Yeltsin despatched 600 Interior Ministry troops to Chechnya – as was to be the case in 1994, far too few to do the job, but perhaps all the Russian government had available, given the chaos in the armed forces at that time. In the first of a series of military humiliations, Chechen gunmen met the Russian troops at the airport, surrounded them and confined them within the airport buildings. The Soviet army was not used, since it still came under the theoretical authority of Gorbachev, and in any case its commanders had no enthusiasm for this task. Referring to the declaration of the state of emergency in Chechnya and the sending of troops, Khasbulatov claimed later to a committee of the Russian Duma investigating the origins of the Chechen War that 'We cancelled the decree after it had already failed. The Soviet ministers simply did not want to obey the orders of the Russian President. So they punched Yeltsin's nose from the side of Gorbachev, and as a result a month later they got Byelovezhskaya Pushcha' (the agreement between Yeltsin, Kravchuk and Shushkevich to dissolve the Soviet Union).[12]

After the Russian Supreme Soviet on 11 November denounced the state of emergency and the introduction of the troops, an agreement was reached – portrayed by the Chechens as a surrender on terms – by which the soldiers got on to buses and were escorted out of Chechnya by the Chechen national guard.[13] Yeltsin subsequently withdrew his own decree, and in what was to become a melancholy pattern of inconsistency, evasion of responsibility and moral cowardice over Chechnya, tried to claim that he had never been in favour of it anyway. In the words of his spokesman: '[The President] agrees with the decision of the Supreme Soviet and will take the steps necessary to implement it. He was never in favour of solving the conflict at any price – only by political means, only by negotiations, no matter how hard these may be.'[14]

As later, in December 1994, the Chechen separatists' success was not simply a matter of Chechen courage and toughness. The Russian troops and their commanders were thoroughly bewildered about their orders and the purpose of their operation. The move by Yeltsin also came at the worst possible moment from the point of view of military morale, with the Soviet Union collapsing and the soldiers utterly unsure about who was in charge and where their loyalties lay.

An obscure role in these developments was played by Ruslan Khasbulatov. His Russian enemies allege that all the time he was secretly aiding the Chechen nationalists, while many Chechens claim on the contrary that he was supporting a tough line so as to establish his credentials with the Russian nationalists. In the atmosphere of near-universal mendacity now prevailing in Russian politics, the real truth may never be known. Khasbulatov himself says that he realised the threat from Dudayev in September, and asked Yeltsin to 'add one more star to Dudayev's epaulettes and send him back to the army' – but it was already much too late for that.

In the months between the collapse of the attempted intervention and June 1992, when the last forces left after an ultimatum from Dudayev, the Chechen government and national guard and various individual Chechen political and criminal groups succeeded in effect in driving the Soviet and Russian armed forces out of Chechnya. Some bases were overrun, including that of the 566th Regiment of Interior Ministry troops in Grozny, between 6 and 9 February 1992; others handed over their arms in return for being allowed to leave in peace; and finally the Russian Defence Ministry under Pavel Grachev itself made a deal handing over many arms to the Chechens in return for a promise of safe passage. It was these arms which two and a half years later formed the backbone of the Chechen defence.

The report of the Duma commisssion of investigation into the Chechen War, chaired by Stanislav Govorukhin, alleged that in these months the Chechens seized or were given 42 tanks, 56 armoured personnel carriers, 139 artillery systems and 24,737 automatic weapons.[15] Neither I nor any other correspondent ever saw anything like this number of tanks on the Chechen side, but the number of automatic rifles seems pretty accurate. (However, it must be said that while useful and full of fascinating if dubious information, this report is also deeply tendentious and marred by hysterical rhetoric and completely unsubstantiated claims, especially as regards the fate of ethnic Russians in Chechnya under Dudayev.)

Extraordinarily, the Chechens had managed to acquire a considerable number of handguns, and a few automatic rifles, even during the depths of Soviet state control in the 1960s. Between 1968 and 1970, the Soviet police confiscated a total of 20,530 guns from people in the North Caucasus, Kazakhstan and Kirghizia, and a disproportionate number of these were in the hands of Chechens.[16]

General Dzhokhar Dudayev

I first met Dudayev in February 1992, and I must say that except for his physical courage, which was undoubted, my impression of him did not improve with time. In that month, he was still camping in the former Grozny city council building next to my hotel. Understandably enough, everything was very chaotic. I waited in the antechamber for about three hours, surrounded by several Labazanov-looking characters, all heavily armed, unshaven and genially menacing. One of them kept playing with a flick-knife.

Walking from their room into that of Dudayev was like exchanging the company of a group of large, shaggy and potentially savage dogs for that of a well-groomed but irritable Siamese cat. Dudayev was a smallish man with a well-organised, aquiline face, a neat pencil moustache, and dark, hooded eyes. He was trim, almost finicky in his dress as well as his manner and his speech. When he wore military uniform, it was always clean, pressed and ironed; if a suit and tie, the shirt was white and the tie was dark and always neatly tied at the collar – a most unusual thing for the post-Soviet Caucasus. This was still true the last time I saw him, not long before his death, at a farmhouse somewhere in the Caucasus foothills. He sat in the small, shabby parlour, still in the same clothes, with the Chechen flag on the wall and two tables placed one on top of the other to make a presidential desk, and on top of them a small heap of presidential files. There was something genuinely heroic about this defiance of circumstance – but once again, it was a self-consciously posed heroism, not the instinctive heroism and leadership of a Basayev.

Dudayev had the cat's neatness and physical poise, the self-possession and self-satisfaction – so much so that I remember him as having had pointed ears, though this was not in fact the case. You could almost imagine him licking his suit to keep it clean, and grooming his moustache with his paws. Instead of gestures, he had a mirthless, artificial smile, which he flicked on and off by way of emphasis, sometimes accompanied by a theatrical, metallic laugh. But he did not have the cat's repose. Inwardly, he twitched and bristled.

Three things struck me at the first interview. The first was the obvious fear felt by my Chechen interpreter. My Russian at that time was not good, but it was good enough to realise that she toned down several of my questions, and prefaced others with obsequious apologies. This was hardly surprising, but it was also not at all characteristic of the Chechens, who are on the whole – as the third part of this book will seek to bring out – a notably democratic people in their traditions and manners.

Another thing that struck me from the first was that this was a play-actor. His speech was exaggeratedly clipped, emphatic, martial and authoritarian. When speaking in public, he combined this with a heavy stress on the last syllables of words. That these were consciously adopted mannerisms seemed to me to be indicated by his press conference in the cellars of the presidential headquarters in Grozny on 15 December 1994, after the Russian invasion. He looked exhausted, and presumably as a result of this and the general strain of the situation, he spoke normally, and most of his habitual emphases and repetitions had disappeared.

What part exactly he thought he was playing I've never quite been able to work out, but it was probably a fairly hackneyed one of national hero/wise ruler/visionary prophet. That aside, an element of play-acting was perhaps also intrinsic to his position. He was after all a Soviet general, a man who had spent by far the greater part of his life in the Soviet armed forces; and there may well have been moments when he wondered what the hell he had got himself into by joining the Chechen revolution.[17]

Culturally, Dudayev did indeed seem to me and many of my colleagues who met him to be a man who was curiously un-Chechen in some ways, and who gave the impression of being uncomfortable in his new Chechen skin. This was my third impression at that interview and it may also have been partly responsible for his frequently wild rhetoric: because of a personal feeling of insecurity, a feeling that because of his long service in the Soviet military, away from Chechnya and Chechen society, and because of his Russian wife (who never even pretended to convert to Islam)[18] and half-Russian children, and his initially poor grasp of the Chechen language, he was not really a Chechen in the full sense and therefore had to present himself as a 200 per cent Chechen nationalist by way of compensation.

This un-Chechen aspect of Dudayev was also remarked by many Chechens, and not just among his enemies. A Chechen fighter told me that 'I am fighting to defend Chechnya, not for Dudayev. I don't like him and never have, in his Soviet uniform, giving us orders and setting himself up over us as a dictator, when he is nothing but a Soviet general and always will be. Everything about him speaks of it. But we Chechens recognise no ruler but God.' (Though, on the other hand, Maskhadov is also of course a professional Soviet officer, but has never indulged in this ultra-Chechen business.)

For me, the most striking way in which Dudayev revealed his lack of a natural feeling for the Chechen tradition was in his lack of hospitality, something which is an iron law among Chechens. Just like the Afghan Mujahidin, every group of Chechen fighters with whom I have spent more than a few minutes has offered me a cup of tea, or apologised for not being able to do so. At my last meeting with Dudayev in December 1995 we were not offered so much as a glass of water. This of course is typical enough for high officials and officers of the former Communist world; it is absolutely *untypical* for a Chechen, however important.

Many aspects of Dudayev's behaviour almost corresponded to a Western parody of a Third World tinpot dictator, a sub-Ghadaffi. Typical in this regard were his long monologues, in which he would philosophise about history, religion and the world. In one of these, he spoke for eleven minutes without a pause in answer to a journalist's question. When someone yawned, or their head drooped, Dudayev would snap 'You're tired?' and we would all murmur dutifully, 'No, no'.

There were indeed moments when I thought Dudayev was mad – or, shall we say, psychologically unstable, with strong features of both paranoia and megalomania, in the clinical sense (this is also the private view of two Western diplomats from the Organisation for Security and Cooperation in Europe (OSCE) who met with Dudayev in 1995, and with whom I have spoken – and this man once commanded a wing of nuclear bombers!). Nothing else, it seemed, could explain his reckless and totally unnecessary verbal provocation of Yeltsin and Russia on several occasions. In one of his first speeches as President on Chechen TV, he accused the Russian secret services of preparing to attack Chechnya with an artificial earthquake – when I visited Chechnya in February 1992 people were still talking about this supposed threat.

On at least two occasions, Dudayev's language had disastrous results for Chechnya. The first was in March 1994, in the context of the Yeltsin administration's signature of the federal treaty with Tatarstan. It has often been suggested, and perhaps rightly, that if Yeltsin had invited Dudayev to a face-to-face meeting, as quasi-equals, then for reasons both of personal vanity and personal prestige within Chechnya, Dudayev might have felt that his face had been saved sufficiently for him to be able to follow Tatarstan in signing some kind of federal or confederal treaty with Russia. In this case, from the Yeltsin government's point of view the all-important question of 'secession' would have been solved, and the later war would almost certainly have been avoided.

Most Chechens would probably have been ready to accept this – again and again I was told that 'we are always ready to sign a treaty with Russia, but only as between equals,' so something that could have been presented as an equal confederation might well have passed. Most ordinary Chechens I met before the war, and especially of course older ones with wives and families, were on the whole not fanatical nationalists, and were afraid of war. It is true however that such a treaty would have been very unpopular among some of the young firebrands in Dudayev's guards, and this might well have spelled his personal doom.

In any case, it was not to be. According to the President of Tatarstan, Mintimer Shaimiyev, speaking to Professor Valery Tishkov in August 1996,

> At the moment of visiting our republic in March 1994, Yeltsin was almost ready for talks with Dudayev on the Tatarstan model, but then he was told that Dudayev was speaking negatively of him. 'How can I meet him when he insulted me?' Yeltsin asked me. I would guess that those reports on Dudayev's comments were deliberately placed in newspapers so as to influence Yeltsin against a meeting with Dudayev, because unfortunately, not all the members of the Security Council were in favour of such a meeting.[19]

The point is that while it is very likely that there was in fact a hardline plot along these lines within the Yeltsin administration, (probably led at that stage by Sergei Shakhrai and Sergei Filatov), it is also true that the public and very personal insults by Dudayev against Yeltsin in the period up to March 1994 were real, and very undiplomatic. Another disastrous example was Dudayev's threat to execute Russian prisoners captured in the opposition assault on Grozny of 26 November 1994, something which destroyed any possibility that the Russian government, having received a bloody nose, might quietly have backed away from further direct intervention and gone back to covert subversion.

The threat was soon afterwards retracted (an additional proof that he had quite simply been talking without thinking)[20] but the damage was done. In the words of Musa Damayev, a businessman and notable of the town of Shali, in May 1995,

> We don't need a brave president, because the people itself is brave, even the women and children. What we need is a wise president, who keeps his head, gets things done and doesn't talk too much. There was no need to insult the Yeltsin government so much before the war; and above all, there was no need to show off how many weapons we had. That was stupid. He should have simply kept them hidden, ready for use if needed.

Even odder in some ways were his various public statements trying to hold out an olive branch to Moscow in the fortnight immediately before the Russian invasion, and made for example at a press conference on 1 December which I attended with other colleagues. I believe that these efforts on his part were quite genuine, and indeed the first few minutes sounded rational enough. Then, however, he would rapidly degenerate into hysterical insults and rambling, philosophical, racial and historical speculations, almost as if possessed by some evil demon. In the course of that press conference, after declaring that a Chechen delegation had left for Moscow for talks, he three times quoted Harry Truman's alleged words that 'there is no language in which you can talk with Russians,' and four times called Russia a 'satanic power'.

Partly, of course, this ultra-nationalist position was forced on Dudayev because of the weakness of other bases of support in Chechnya. The absence of structures and traditions of state power left Dudayev no choice but to play the constant role of an actual or potential war leader. None the less, the fact that personality, as well as calculation, played a major part in this is demonstrated by the very different, and very much more diplomatic approach of his Vice-President and successor, Zelimkhan Yandarbiyev. The latter is certainly no less nationalist than General Dudayev, and as his meeting with Boris Yeltsin in the Kremlin in May 1996 showed, he can be both tough and morally brave in negotiation.

For reasons I cannot fathom, a film of this meeting was shown on NTV, the private Russian television channel. When the Chechens came in, Yeltsin, coarse and bloated, ordered Yandarbiyev roughly to sit on one side of him, and Yandarbiyev courteously but firmly stated that as the head of the delegation of an independent state, he insisted on sitting opposite Yeltsin, or the talks were off. After several minutes of bluster, it was Yeltsin who backed down – on his own ground, in his own palace. This was a small but highly typical example of Chechen determination, moral courage and iron will, from a man who had not generally been thought to possess these qualities.

But in his public rhetoric about Russia, Yandarbiyev was always far more moderate than his leader; and when I interviewed him on 16 December 1994, a few days after the start of the war, he showed the true diplomat's skill of sounding ready for compromise on confederation with Russia, while in fact (as I discovered on reading my notes) making no concrete surrender of substance. Meanwhile Dudayev was raving that 'Russism is worse even than Nazism,' and that 'Boris Yeltsin is the leader of a gang of murderers' and his regime the 'diabolical heir of the totalitarian monster'.[21]

An interesting example of both men's characters came in a meeting that a colleague, Andrew Harding of the BBC, and I had with them in December 1995, at a secret location in the foothills. As was his habit, Dudayev went out of his way to insult his interlocutors, going on about how Western journalists were 'cowards' and 'Russian slaves'. When we reacted and the atmosphere threatened to become really unpleasant, Yandarbiyev stepped in and smoothed things over. This was of course a wholly unimportant incident, but one of the Russian Deputies who tried to negotiate a compromise with Dudayev in December 1994, and prevent war, also told me that Dudayev spent the first half hour of the meeting insulting them.

After the end of the war, Dudayev's nephew, the guerrilla commander Salman Raduyev, continued to have a malign effect with his rhetoric, continuing the General's tradition.[22]

Chechens, Ingush and Ossetes

From early 1990 the small Ingush people, joined with the Chechens in the Chechen-Ingush Autonomous Republic, had been moving towards a break with the Chechens – despite the fact that the Chechens and Ingush are very close ethnically and linguistically; in fact most of the time their languages are mutually intelligible, and there are suggestions that Dudayev's own clan may be of Ingush origin. They also share the Muslim religion, though the Ingush are much less committed as Muslims than the Chechens, for reasons that will be explored in part III.

Although the political movement founded by General Dudayev in 1991 called itself the Vainakh Party, a name which covers both Chechen and Ingush, in fact from the very beginning of the Chechen national movement there was little attempt to appeal to the Ingush in terms of either interest or sentiment. No Ingush were present at the founding meeting of the Chechen National Congress in November 1990, and no Ingush leaders took part in the national revolution in Grozny in August–November 1991. The Ingush did not participate in the Chechen elections or the referendum on independence. In November 1991 they declared a republic of their own separate from the Chechens, and the next year a Soviet general (but a very different one from Dudayev), Ruslan Aushev, was elected President. The details of the border between the two republics remain undefined.

Most of the central reasons for the Ingush–Chechen split were summed up in an interview I had in February 1992 with Magomed Mamilov, a former collective farm chief, and now Deputy Chaiman of the Ingush People's Council. He stressed in particular the critical issue of the lands to Ossetia when the Ingush were deported in 1944, and never returned (the Prigorodny District).

> It is difficult at this moment to say whether a Chechen-Ingush Republic still exists, or what our status is. There is certainly no question of our joining an independent Chechen-Ingushetia. We have had discussions with Dudayev, and he has said that he wants a united Vainakh state, independent of Russia, but that he will not try to force us into this against our will. But we told him that for us, until our territory is returned, no other question has any importance, and we won't take part in any other long-term plans. Besides, we regard the Yeltsin government as our ally in this. We have had several discussions with Yeltsin, and he has promised us that Ingushetia will be returned to its borders of 1944...
>
> This is all-important to us. You probably don't know this, but the Russian name 'Ingush', by which we are now known in the world, comes

from a village called Angusht. Our own name for ourselves is Ghalghi. And this village Angusht is now not in our territory, but thanks to 1944, is in Ossetia! My own family's home was in Ordzhonikidze [Vladikavkaz]. After we were deported, they destroyed it, and built a block of flats there. And now, they not only refuse to return us our land, they won't even give us one flat in that block! In any case, in my personal opinion, an independent Vainakh Republic outside Russia is simply not possible. And in the referendum we organised on November 30, 92 per cent of Ingush also voted against this, and for autonomy within Russia. Historical experience shows that completely independent tiny states cannot exist, especially if they are surrounded by someone else's territory. So we should remain in the Russian Federation, but with full autonomy and respect for our national rights and democracy...

Unlike the Chechens, we Ingush have always got on well with the Russians, though not always with the Cossacks, it's true. Also we have a calmer attitude to religion. We are good Muslims of course, but not fanatics... Some of us fought with Shamil, but ever since the 1770s, most have fought on the side of Russia. One of my own ancestors signed a treaty with Russia in 1776. Many of them became officers in the Russian army, and even despite the Soviet repressions and deportation, we are now the core of the Ingush national intelligentsia. We are also present in Moscow. There are only about 6–7,000 Ingush there, but we are playing an important role, and you will see that we will be more and more prominent in future. My cousin is already a powerful businessman there, and a multimillionaire. He is a great supporter of Ingush culture. We are planning our own television channel and other developments of our state. Perhaps we could make it a free trade zone and the economic centre of the whole region... The problem about the Chechens is that they are in too much of a hurry. They want to rush us into dangers without thinking properly, and we don't like that.

In part, Chechen–Ingush alienation therefore was due to history: although both peoples were deported together to Central Asia in 1944, an enduring feeling remained among the Chechens that the Ingush had betrayed them by siding with the Russians in the nineteenth century, while the Ingush have always resented what they see as Chechen arrogance towards them, an arrogance abundantly demonstrated in recent years.[23]

This Ossete–Ingush territorial dispute is one of those Caucasian conflicts which gives some support to Russians who argue that given the way ethnic populations are mixed up together, only a quasi-imperial state is capable of maintaining any kind of peace and order in the region. Traditionally, the Ingush and Ossete populations across much of what is today North Ossetia lived in separate villages but not in distinct areas, as was also true of the Ossetes and Georgians in the mountains to the south.

Following the introduction of Soviet rule, the area went through a whole series of different administrative configurations, reflecting the impossibility of reaching any generally satisfactory arrangement. First both Ingush and Ossetes formed part of the Mountain Autonomous Republic; then between 1924 and 1934 they had separate units, but shared Vladikavkaz (renamed Ordzhonikidze in the 1930s, and today the capital of North Ossetia), with the Ingush on the right bank of the Terek River, in the ethnically mixed Prigorodny District, and the Ossetes on the left bank. In 1934, the Ingush were joined with the Chechens in one autonomous republic, and they were deported together to Central Asia in 1944.

When the Ingush returned from exile after 1957 they were once again put together with the Chechens. The Prigorodny District, making up almost half of what had been Ingush territory, remained in North Ossetia, however, though some 35,000 Ingush were eventually able to return to their homes there. As with Armenia and Karabakh, as soon as Gorbachev's perestroika allowed a measure of democratic politics, the 'return' of the district to Ingushetia became the central and defining question in Ingush politics, and one which made Russian goodwill a necessity.

The more the Ingush agitated over the issue, the more embittered was the reaction from the Ossetes and the local Russian Cossacks, who had also profited from the transfer of Ingush land, but who claimed that this was in fact the land of White Cossacks confiscated by the Soviet state as a punishment after the Civil War. The Ingush reply that this was originally Ingush land given to the Cossacks by the Russian empire in the eighteenth and nineteenth centuries – and so on. Clashes between Ingush and Cossacks escalated after an incident at the end of 1991 when a local Cossack Ataman and several of his men were killed in a fight with Ingush youths – according to the Ingush, because he had staggered drunk out of a wedding party and relieved himself in front of some of their womenfolk.

Meanwhile North Ossetia had its own problems, since it had had to absorb up to 100,000 southern Ossete refugees from the war in the Georgian region of South Ossetia, and argued with some reason that it could not afford to surrender any land.

The Ingush movement faced Moscow with a dilemma. On the one hand, the Ossetes have always been Russia's most loyal ally in the Caucasus; they are closely allied with the local Russian Cossacks; they provided a disproportionate number of officers, and especially senior officers to the Soviet army (and claim to have won more decorations as Hero of the Soviet Union, the highest Soviet award for valour, proportionate to their numbers than any other Soviet people); the southern Ossete revolt had played a major part in defeating Georgian national ambitions; and there was great sympathy in Moscow for North Ossetia's problems with its huge numbers of refugees. On the other hand, Moscow was very anxious to split the Ingush from the Chechens, and thereby weaken the separatist forces of General Dudayev. In addition, President Boris Yeltsin's authority in 1992 was still rather weak. As a result, the Russian government sat on the fence until events on the ground forced its hand; for more than a year in 1991–2, the Yeltsin administration tried to balance between the Ossetes and Ingush.

After an escalating series of clashes, the apparently accidental killing of an Ingush girl by an Ossete police armoured personnel carrier on 20 October 1992 sparked off an Ingush revolt in the Prigorodny District and large-scale fighting. The Ingush villages of the District declared themselves part of Ingushetia and barricaded themselves against the Ossete police, paramilitaries and Cossacks. Both sides were revealed to have accumulated large quantities of arms. Ingush forces crossed the border from Ingushetia, dozens of people were killed on both sides and several villages were 'ethnically cleansed'. By the time the heavy fighting was ended by Russia several weeks later, 261 people had been killed, with the reported numbers almost equally divided between Ossetes and Ingush. However, some 800 people had also disappeared, and though in some cases these were prisoners who were later exchanged, others disappeared for good and a majority of these were Ingush. Twelve Russian soldiers also died.

On 31 October, Moscow despatched some 3,000 Interior Ministry troops and paratroopers to the area. What happened next is a matter of bitter dispute. The Russian authorities say that they merely separated the two sides, and point out that to this day, Russian troops are protecting some 3,000 remaining Ingush in the Prigorodny District. The Ingush say that the Russian troops simply drew a line against the Ingush forces along the existing border between Ossetia and Ingushetia, and thereby either passively or in some cases actively helped the Ossetes. As a result, some 31,000 Ingush were driven from the Prigorodny District, nine-tenths of its Ingush population and a vast burden on the small population of Ingushetia, only 160,000 before the refugee influx.

A few Russian soldiers have admitted that in some cases they were ordered to stand by without acting while Ossetes attacked Ingush settlements. In other cases, however, they did help the Ingush, and in April 1993 the second Russian emergency administrator, Vladimir Lozovoi, was wounded while trying to release Ingush hostages captured by the Ossetes. The first, Vladimir Polyanichko, had been killed by unknown assailants in November 1992. On 2 November 1992, after eighty Russian soldiers were taken hostage by the Ingush, Moscow declared a state of emergency in the area. As of 1997, the situation on the Ingush-Ossetes border had now been relatively calm for some two years, though with occasional clashes, and although a few miles away in 1995 and 1996, Ingush villages were intermittently bombarded or harassed by Russian troops as part of the overspill from their war in Chechnya.

In the end, therefore, Ingushetia has been an example of how even in the most violent situations, Moscow will usually maintain its control over much of the North Caucasus through the Caucasians' own feuds and conflicting ambitions. The Ingush–Ossete conflict is also, however, an example of how in certain circumstances, the region's own bitter disputes can escape from Moscow's control and force a crisis against Moscow's will.[24]

Chechnya under Dudayev, 1991–1994

The movement of Russian troops to the Chechen border during the Ingush–Ossete clashes was the only armed attempt by Moscow to put pressure on Dudayev between November 1991 and July 1994. Apart from occasional verbal salvoes, the Russian government contented itself with imposing an extremely ineffective trade blockade and cutting off central subsidies to Chechnya. The 'blockade' also received no help from the police of neighbouring Ingushetia and Daghestan.[25]

The financial cut-off was eventually much more effective. Up to June 1993, in an effort to woo Dudayev's regime back into the fold, and to help local Russians (or rather to keep them from leaving Chechnya and consolidating still further the separatist position), the Russian state was still transferring some money for the payment of pensions – 2.5 billion roubles in all, though how much of this was ever seen by the pensioners in question is of course another matter. Professor Valery Tishkov, a leading Russian anthropologist and former advisor to the Yeltsin administration on nationality affairs, claims that 4 billion roubles in different state payments was transferred in 1992 alone. However, this still represented a great reduction on more normal times, and added to the chaos and corruption of Chechen officialdom, it meant that the Dudayev administration was soon unable to pay many salaries – to an even greater degree than was true in Russia in the same period.

By mid-1993, this had led to widespread disillusionment with Dudayev and growing support for the Chechen opposition. Chechen entrepreneurship, trade in untaxed goods, the financial power of Chechen businessmen (often organised criminal bosses) across much of Russia, coupled with Chechen family and clan solidarity, meant however that the Chechen population did not suffer as much as might have been expected. One bank fraud by Chechen criminals in Moscow in 1992 reportedly netted a staggering 700 million dollars, much of which was sent back to Chechnya. In general, Grozny's emergence as a centre of smuggling, money-laundering and fraud gained the Chechens many allies, as well as enemies, throughout the world of Russian business.[26]

Whether for corrupt reasons or as part of a quid pro quo in return for the maintenance of the oil pipeline from Baku, throughout this period the Russian authorities allowed Chechnya to go on importing Russian oil for processing at Chechen plants and re-exporting the refined product. Yegor Gaidar, Russian Prime Minister in 1992, gave the following excuse to a Duma investigative committee four years later:

> The Grozny oil refinery is the largest oil-refining enterprise in Russia, and used to supply a considerable part of the North Caucasus, Stavropol Kray, Krasnodar Kray, etc. In this regard, turning off the petroleum faucet all at once meant, at least, leaving them without fuel

for sowing operations, and that would have punished not only Chechnya, but also Russia.

In all, between 1991 and 1994 Chechnya exported some 20 million tonnes of oil to international markets. Given the corruption of the Russian bureaucracy and border guards, there can be little doubt that Chechens in fact exported very much more than this total (just as on the borders of the Baltic States in this period, Russian attempts to control the flow of oil and metals failed almost completely, allowing Estonia – which does not itself produce an ounce of metal – to become for a couple of years one of the biggest exporters of non-ferrous metals in the world).[27]

At least 300 million dollars in profits from oil went to the Chechen government in this period, but never showed up in the state budget (some Russian estimates put the figure as high as 1 billion dollars).[28] The question of whether General Dudayev himself was personally corrupt and criminal is in a sense irrelevant. Those with a knowledge of his character suggest that this was not the case, and that many of these dollars were in fact going to buy arms for national defence. However, Dudayev certainly recruited large numbers of criminals into his national guard and tolerated their activities. He did little or nothing to prevent the siphoning off of Azeri oil from the pipeline running across Chechen territory into Russia, and repeated looting of Russian trains passing through Chechnya – though on the other hand, given the nature of Chechen society and the collapse of the old Soviet state institutions in Chechnya, it is very doubtful that he could have done anything about this even if he had wanted to.[29]

Meanwhile, state services of all kinds in Chechnya continued to collapse, far faster even than in Russia. The effects of this on individuals were modified by Chechen traditions of solidarity in the extended family, so that rich Chechen 'businessmen' often supported large numbers of relatives who would otherwise have been indigent. The Russian population, however, suffered especially badly. Because of this and growing physical insecurity, many left, and since they occupied jobs in many essential services, the decline of these accelerated still further.

By April 1993, discontent with Dudayev among Chechens had reached a point where a majority of parliamentary deputies appeared ready to support an impeachment motion against him, and the opposition launched a series of mass protests. By this stage, Dudayev had fallen out with most of the allies who had helped him to power, with the exception of Yandarbiyev. Of the others, Khasbulatov was fighting his own battle in Moscow with Yeltsin, and had allied himself, bizarrely, with the Russian nationalist and Communist forces (I saw him declare on Russian television that 'what is good for the Russian nation is good for all the peoples of Russia'); Gantemirov, Mamadayev, and Soslambekov had all joined the opposition to Dudayev.

One motive for this may have been Dudayev's rejection of a draft treaty on confederation with Russia which Mamadayev and Soslambekov had worked out with a Russian delegation led by Sergei Shakhrai and Ramazan

Abdullatipov in December 1993. The previous year they had also established working relations with Rutskoy, still part of the Yeltsin administration. Although he was generally regarded as bitterly anti-Chechen, agreement was reached for Russian economic sanctions to be lifted and for respective missions to be established in Grozny and Moscow.[30]

Dudayev also persuaded the Chechen Congress to reject the treaty, and when Shakhrai and Abdullatipov arrived in Grozny to initial the treaty, Dudayev refused to meet them and had them turned away by his guards. Fury at this treatment may have been partly responsible for the hatred of Dudayev shown later by both Shakhrai (a Cossack) and Abdullatipov (a Daghestani Avar), and is an example of Dudayev's remarkable ability to insult people and unite them in hostility to him – something which was not the least among the causes of the Chechen War.

However, Dudayev's wild nationalist rhetoric was not, of course, simply a reflection of his own character. In a not unfamiliar historical pattern from around the world, Dudayev may have reckoned that the only way he could unite the country around his government, or at least attract the genuine loyalty of parts of Chechen youth, was by keeping nationalist feeling and fears of the 'country in danger' at white-hot levels. His rhetoric may therefore not have been quite as 'irrational' as it seemed.

This fits in with my analysis of Chechen society in chapter 10 as an 'ordered anarchy' which could only take effective common action when presented with a very specific stimulus, and which could only accept one kind of leader, a war leader in the context of mobilisation against the ancient enemy. In this context, Maskhadov is luckier – he has already proved himself as a war leader, and presumably doesn't need to go on doing so.

In this connection, it is interesting to compare Chechnya under Dudayev with the other Russian autonomous republic which went furthest in its push for independence, and in the end achieved the greatest autonomy: Tataria, now Tatarstan. Tatarstan has been what Chechnya would have been if Zavgayev had stayed in power, and if the Chechen nationalists had not been so numerous and well armed, and the Chechen people so anarchistic and rejecting of authority. The difference between the behaviour of the two nations in the 1990s is partly due to the much greater changes that had occurred in Tatar society, both under Russian rule (since the sixteenth century, three hundred years longer than in Chechnya) and in Soviet times, which led to Tatars closely resembling Russians sociologically and culturally.[31]

The Tatars have, however, been tougher and more consistent in their push for sovereignty than many observers think. The Communist leadership of the Tatar ASSR twice asked for upgrading to the status of a union republic, constitutionally separate from Russia: during the discussions on the introduction of new Soviet constitutions under Stalin in 1936 – when several were executed as a result; and under Brezhnev in 1977, when in keeping with the late Soviet and Brezhnevite approach, they were bought off with more central investment for Tataria's industry.

The key difference between Tatarstan and Chechnya since 1990 has obviously been that in 1991 Chechnya experienced a national revolution which overthrew the local institutions of the Soviet state, and Tatarstan did not. The Tatar Communist Party First Secretary, Mintimer Shaimiyev, stayed in power, defeated the radical nationalist opposition by a mixture of coercion and cooptation, and transformed the regional Communist Party into a moderate, statist national party under his absolute control. This was not easy, and at certain moments it seemed that a wave of radical Tatar nationalism, leading to a declaration of independence, was a real possibility. If this had recurred, there is no reason to doubt that the Yeltsin administration would have taken ruthless measures against the Tatars.[32]

It is easy to dismiss Shaimiyev's strategy as a cynical and corrupt nomenklatura manoeuvre; but it must also be admitted that as a result Tatarstan did achieve an impressive degree of real autonomy, and took control of important and effective state powers, including police control, revenue-raising capacity and control of the economy and especially oil production and exports – despite the lack of international status or an army. A visitor to Tatarstan in 1995 could not help but be struck by just how many signs of Tatar statehood really were present. The Chechens under Dudayev by contrast struck out for full independence, but in the process lost the state structures which could have underpinned that independence without war.

This picture of state collapse in Chechnya is by no means contradicted either by the mushrooming of Chechen ministries and bureaucrats or by the increase in the secret police. The first was simply a reflection of the privatisation of the state, as in Russia, and the buying off of individuals and groups by giving them non-working state jobs; the second was to defend Dudayev. This it may have done efficiently enough – assuming that the Russian intelligence service was trying to kill him – but it certainly did not increase his popularity with his people.

The resulting anarchy – unrule – contributed in three ways to the road to war: by encouraging Dudayev to fall back on radical nationalist rhetoric in an effort to compensate for his lack of real state authority; by allowing a growth of banditry which spilled over into Russia and infuriated the Russian government; and by encouraging the growth of a domestic violent opposition (that it was extraconstitutional goes without saying, given that there was no real constitution) which gave ample opportunity for Russia to interfere and play at divide and rule.

As for the desire of Soslambekov, Mamadayev and Gantemirov for compromise with Russia, this in my view reflected above all the groups they represented: Mamadayev the Chechen businessmen drawn from the Soviet managerial elite, Soslambekov and Gantemirov new businessmen and the mafia. Khasbulatov drew his support from the Soviet educated classes and from his own extensive lineage network. He came from one of those Muslim clerical families who under Soviet rule had switched to secular academia. He himself is an economist by training, and his elder brother, Aslanbek , a leading historian.

However, Khasbulatov also had his own criminal contacts, and was reportedly encouraged to return to Chechnya in August 1994 by Suleiman Khosa, a leading Moscow gangster. These groups of course merged into each other, and all were well aware that their own commercial interests, and indeed commercial survival, depended on Chechnya remaining in some sense within Russia, so that Chechens could go on living and working throughout the Russian Federation, and using the rouble freely as a currency. They may also genuinely have feared the terrible consequences of a war in Chechnya for the Chechen population.

They were also becoming alarmed, or so Chechen acquaintances in Moscow have told me, by the growing anti-Chechen chauvinism in Russia and in the Yeltsin administration, inspired partly by old hatreds, but also by resentment both at Dudayev and more importantly at Ruslan Khasbulatov and his orchestration of opposition to Yeltsin ('If only we could shoot that Chechen' was a sentiment often heard among Yeltsin supporters at that time). They feared the kind of expulsions of Chechens from Moscow which took place, albeit on a limited scale, after Yeltsin's overthrow of the Russian parliament in October. The Moscow-based business and mafia leaders had reason to be afraid; I have been told that in December 1994, at the start of the war, they were called in separately by the Moscow Mayor's office and the FSK and warned that if any major Chechen terrorist actions took place in Moscow, the entire Chechen community there would be deported, and its leading members would 'disappear' along the way.

As for the Chechen educated classes, and especially the handful of Chechen female professionals, their attitudes and fears were well expressed by a Chechen woman doctor called Natasha (her name of course indicating a certain degree of Russification) with whom I talked privately at the Grozny Military Hospital on 15 December 1994:

> I was born in Kazakhstan, and lived most of my life in Alma Ata, but when the coup happened here in 1991 my family and I came back, because we wanted to live in a Chechen state ... but I have to say that Chechnya in the past three years has not been what I expected. The Chechens here are different from the Chechens living in other republics. They are less educated, and more nationalistic. They did not accept us very well... The educated people here, the doctors, teachers, engineers, have all suffered badly. I for example have not been paid for more than a year. I can only live because my family supports me, and so I can also help some of the other doctors as well. I also feel a growing Islamisation, it is creating a bad atmosphere for educated women...
>
> The truth is, we Chechens should learn to restrain ourselves a bit more. There are too many of our young people who are ready to fly off the handle, and too many leaders who encourage them. That is why we need more educated leaders...
>
> I am not politically active, but to tell you the truth I think that if we

had more educated leaders, it would have been possible to settle this problem with Russia much earlier and without war. I once met Ruslan Khasbulatov, and I think that if he had had more influence, he could have managed things better...

Of course I am proud of our people and their courage, but when I see young kids ready to attack tanks almost with their bare hands, it makes me cry. No one should want this.

Or in the blunter and more prejudiced words of Professor Khasbulatov, 'what we have seen in Chechnya under Dudayev is a peasants' revolt; and you as a historian will know that a peasants' revolt is the ugliest, the most stupid and the most dangerous political phenomenon.'

On top of the alienation of the professional classes, the arrogant and dictatorial style both of Dudayev himself and of his various swaggering hangers on had also infuriated his former political allies, and to this, of course, was added furious resentment at not getting the share of the spoils of office to which they thought themselves entitled. The former Soviet establishment in Chechnya was solidly against Dudayev, and they were increasingly joined by the intelligentsia, angered by the collapse of their wages and worried by the General's increasing moves – in rhetoric at least – towards the establishment of an Islamic state.

Dudayev responded to the protests by dissolving the parliament and crushing the opposition by force. In the subsequent fighting, several dozen people were killed and Grozny town hall, Gantemirov's headquarters, was destroyed. For the parliament, Dudayev substituted hand-picked 'councils of elders' (Mekhel) and 'councils of teip leaders', and in 1994 revived the Chechen National Congress in an effort to bolster his rule.[35] From this time on, Dudayev frequently spoke of the Chechen people having made an 'irrevocable choice' of leader in 1991 – a pretty clear sign that he had no intention of ever facing real elections or surrendering power.

The opposition retreated to the countryside: Gantemirov to his home base of Urus Martan, south of Grozny; the rest of the opposition, based mainly on Doku Zavgayev's political clan and the former Soviet establishment, to Znamenskoye, in north-west Chechnya near the Russian border. This area had come under Russian rule earlier than the rest of Chechnya, and under the Tsars Chechen opponents of Shamil had been resettled there, giving it a certain pro-Russian tradition.

It should be noted that at this time there was no overt Russian military help for the opposition, or even major covert arms supplies, it would seem, since during the clashes in Grozny the opposition used no heavy weapons. It seems likely that the Russian failure to seize this opportunity to try to bring him down was simply due to the fact that with the struggle with the Supreme Soviet in Moscow building to its climax, and the Yeltsin administration's survival at stake, senior officials simply had no attention to spare for what seemed a thoroughly peripheral issue.

However, there is also no reason to doubt that, from the first, the opposition did receive some Russian encouragement. In Nadterechny they set up the Chechen Provisional Council in June 1994, under the chairmanship of former police officer and Zavgayev protégé Umar Avturkhanov, and received Russian backing in arms and money. The latter enabled them to consolidate their hold on this region by paying wages and salaries to its inhabitants.

But as far as many other Chechens were concerned (including many who did not support Dudayev), the Provisional Council leaders' receipt of Russian aid only confirmed their reputation as traitors and Russian stooges. A good many leading Chechen opponents of Dudayev, including Soslambekov, refused to have anything to do with them, and other Chechens who may have been wondering about going into opposition may have been persuaded by Russia's role to go on supporting the President. The waverers, or so it was rumoured at the time, included even Shamil Basayev, after his return to Chechnya following the Abkhaz victory in October 1993. If it is indeed true that in early 1994 even so absolutely a dedicated Chechen nationalist as Basayev had become disillusioned with Dudayev and was wavering, then it suggests even more strongly that if the Yeltsin administration had been prepared to play a waiting game, they would have been rid of their bugbear fairly soon.

Dudayev's Regime

The lack of a real Chechen state under Dudayev was evident in the government's preparations for the war – or rather lack of them, because while the regime drew up some quite detailed military plans, there was no serious attempt either to mobilise or to protect the civilian population. Tens of thousands of Chechens did, of course, at one time and another go to fight for Chechnya, including some women, both as nurses and fighters; but this was the result of spontaneous action from Chechen society, not action by the 'state'.

'A government plan to feed the population if the Russians start a siege, and evacuate children? I don't know about anything like that, but if President Dudayev said so, then of course it is true,' said one official in early December 1994, sitting in his deserted office in the municipal offices of Grozny's central district as the winter twilight deepened outside the dirty windows. 'Anyway, it doesn't matter. We Chechens are such a great, such a unique people that we will succeed in feeding ourselves whatever happens. My responsibility? What do you mean, my responsibility? I'm here in my office, aren't I? Don't you think I'll fight to the death to defend my country?' With this, he gave a loud belch, sending a waft of vodka in our direction, and with his grubby fingers levered a greyish bit of meat out of a glass jar on his lap. This he fed to his cat, a dirty but immensely contented-looking animal, which yawned and went back to stretch out in front of the electric heater. Two weeks later, the Russian armoured push down Pervomaistaya Chaussee was brought to a bloody halt two hundred yards from the ruins of this building.

Men like this official were a principal reason why many of us did not rate very highly the Dudayev regime's potential for stopping such a Russian assault. Another was the nature of Dudayev's 'presidential guard', which in the battles with the opposition in 1994 were the only force actually prepared to fight for Dudayev against other Chechens. I often talked with these men, hanging around the presidential headquarters, and several of them made no secret of the fact that they had formerly been criminals in Russia – indeed, it was a mark of pride. I asked Mansur Kaisarov, formerly a sergeant in the Soviet army , then a 'trader' in Russia, how they were paid in·Chechnya. 'Allah provides,' he said with a giggle.

In late January 1995, when I was travelling in western Chechnya with David Filippov of the *Boston Globe*, we twice in one day had encounters with members of Dudayev's secret police, the DGB. The first was in the town of Achkoi Martan, held by the separatists but with considerable activity by the pro-Russian opposition. With the agreement of the chief doctor, we went to see two Russian prisoners who were being held in the local hospital. Our path was blocked by two DGB men in smartish, shabby suits, one of them with the face of a hoodlum, the other short and slim, with a facetious arrogance. 'You can go to the prefect or hell or wherever you like. I am the authorities here,' he said. A nurse whispered to me,

> The opposition is active here. No one knows what is in anyone else's heart. It looks like the only choice today is for Chechens to fight each other, or to stand aside and be silent... These people came here yesterday, and started throwing their weight about. They won't even tell us their names. We don't know who they are or where their authority comes from, but we know they are dangerous. They talked to the chief doctor, and now he is terrified.

Later that day, we were interviewing Chechen civilians in the village of Sernovodsk when a deep purple-coloured BMW drew up beside us – a striking sight, in that winter landscape of white fields and drab grey and brown houses, with the people in their plain, dark working clothes. Out of it stepped another DGB agent, a Las Vegas cowboy all of five foot four inches tall, in a leather jacket and sharply pointed cowboy boots set with little silver stars, wearing a thick gold chain round his neck, another round his wrist, a gold watch and a huge gold ring with a silver medallion – standard second-rank Russian mafia gear, together with the large automatic pistol stuck casually into his belt – and in this condition, he had driven through two Russian checkpoints. He spoke curtly to the local people, and they scattered, 'because they have no right to speak to you without the permission of the Chechen government'. He said that his name was Rustam, and that he had fought with the Afghan Mujahidin before going to Moscow – 'to work as a bandit', as he said frankly. 'And I'm still a bandit, but now I'm a bandit for my country.' Our Chechen driver was spitting with rage at him as he drove us off. 'That little runt, that whore – if he was ever in Afghanistan, it was only to buy drugs. Please don't think that people like that represent Chechnya.'

In August 1994, I witnessed how these men blocked supporters of Ruslan Khasbulatov from holding a rally near the town of Stary Atagi. Swaggering, beefy and menacing, their eyes hidden by flashy dark glasses with gold rims, they were the very image of Latin American political thugs, and, I thought, probably with about the same degree of real patriotism and stomach for a real fight. In this of course I was quite wrong. Thuggish they were; cowards they most decidedly were not.

The day after the conversation with the official and his cat, I was standing on one of the upper floors of the presidential headquarters, beside one of the cleaning women, a forty-year-old half-Chechen widow named Tamara, formerly a technician in a factory, with a face that would once have been rather attractive, but was now deeply lined. She had 'returned' to Chechnya – where she had never in fact lived – from Omsk in Siberia, after her husband died, and for whatever reason had fallen through the cracks of the normally supportive Chechen family system. She was triply disadvantaged in the Chechnya of Dudayev: that she was poor would not have been such a disadvantage if she had had an extended family, but she had none; and in any case, she was a woman, and therefore of no public account, unfortunately. If this majority of Chechens had actually had a say, things might have gone differently and better for their country.

For while it is true that many Chechen women always supported Dudayev, before the war I also several times had the experience of speaking to groups of women in the market or on the street, and hear them calling for a reasonable compromise with Russia, 'so that our children can live in peace'. Then, inevitably, a large male of the species would stride up, roaring about fighting to the last man, and they would fall silent.

There was a light dusting of snow on the floor of the corridor, and Tamara and I were both of us shivering in the icy wind that blew through the window – already shattered by Russian bombing – and perhaps as well from fear. In the square below, a Chechen religious dance (zikr) went round and round, like a propellor driven by the deep humming, droning, rhythmical engine of the dancers' chant; and indeed, the zikr and the traditions it represented could be called one of the engines of the Chechen resistance.

> Scared? Of course I'm scared. I want to get out before the fighting really starts, but I have three children to feed, and no relatives in the countryside here. It's only in Grozny I can find work – for what that's worth. For five months they haven't paid me for coming to work for their government – the only reason I come is to eat in the canteen. When we ask them for pay, they reply, 'How can you think of money at a time when the nation is in danger?' And then I have to watch them

stuffing themselves with food at their feasts, building palaces for themselves at our expense, and this has been going on for three years. May God punish them! If only the Russians would come! Only they can restore order here, and end all this banditry. I lived well under Russian rule. For 120 roubles a month, I could look after my children properly. Now, look how we live. We were starving anyway, and now we have to live in the cellar for fear of being killed. Oh God, Oh God, what will become of us? How will we survive?

The building in which we were standing was like the set of the last scene of *Aida*, as occupied by the cast of the third act of *Carmen*. Built for the Central Committee of the Communist Party, and it was a typically cold and tomb-like Soviet official structure. The men who were in fact to make this building their tomb, in January 1995, were however anything but Soviet in appearance. When I last visited it before its destruction and capture, these inhabitants had already become troglodytes; with Russian bombs falling all around, they had moved into the cellars, where they were to hold out against repeated attacks for the next month, while the building above them was gradually blasted into ruins. In the dim light, made dimmer by an icy fug of cigarette smoke, and amidst the huge pipes and cables, they looked like something from the war of the end of the world. Wandering among them was a figure from a hallucination, with an enormous white woolly beard, dressed in a tall white woolly hat with a bobble, and black motorcycle boots, and an enormous white woolly beard, and clutching a bundle of books on Chechnya tied up with string. This was Viktor Popkov from Moscow, whose visiting card proudly announced him as a 'Magister' – and he was indeed a bit like my idea of the Master from 'The Master and Margarita'. Standing among the machine guns and crates of ammunition, he said that he was a former Soviet dissident, and that he had come to Chechnya to try to propagate 'non-violent instruments for solving national disputes', and to preach 'spiritual reconciliation between the Chechen and Russian peoples'. The fighters seemed to regard him as something between a saint and a rather shaggy mascot. For me, he symbolised – perhaps unfairly – all the tragic political failure of the democratic strands of the Russian dissident tradition. He is probably one of the best men I've ever met – and one of the most useless.

A much more appropriate figure under the circumstances was a volunteer from the Ukranian extreme nationalist UNA/UNSO movement, called Sashko Bily – a man who looked as if he had been born in a cave. He had a massive face with a forehead sloping straight back from his eyebrows, a jutting jaw and a broken nose, and was wearing an American baseball cap turned back to front and a green Islamic headband. He said that he was there to 'fight against Russian imperialism and help destroy the Russian empire... and then on its ruins, we will build a new, truly great Slavic power, uniting all the Slavs under the leadership of the Ukrainians, the oldest, greatest and purest Slav people.' I was told some months afterwards that he had been killed in action in Grozny.

Bily was one of perhaps twenty Ukrainian volunteers who fought in Chechnya; I met three of them, and also once encountered four Arabs. There may have been several dozen Arabs in all, one of whom, who took the *nom de guerre* of Khatab, reportedly became a local commander and stayed on after the war. I heard of a few Afghan Mujahidin, but never met them, and at one time or another I met perhaps a dozen volunteers from Daghestan, most of them ethnic Chechens. And that was all. So much for all the official Russian talk about '6,000 Islamic mercenaries fighting for Dudayev'.[34]

The Russian Decision to Intervene and the Geopolitics of Oil

The Russian events of September–December 1993 guaranteed the success of the Russian liberal-capitalist revolution of the 1990s, and the survival of the Yeltsin administration in power. It also had fateful results for relations between Russia and Chechnya. For not merely did Yeltsin's defeat of the Communist and nationalist parliamentary opposition free the Russian government to think about its lesser irritations, but the formalisation of a new Russian constitution made Chechnya's refusal to sign a union treaty even more starkly apparent – the more so after Tatarstan finally signed a special treaty in March 1994.

In seeking the origins of the Chechen War, the Dudayev government's refusal to sign some form of federal or confederal treaty must be judged the most important. Without it, though tension and covert Russian attempts to get rid of Dudayev might have continued, there would have been no war. As was already seen in 1991, the Russian armed forces were very unwilling to become involved in another attempt at suppressing a national movement, and in 1994 the advocates of direct intervention were in a small minority in the Russian administration. With regard to Dudayev, Russian ministers were 'willing to wound, but afraid to strike'. For what it is worth, 'defending Russia's unity' was also the first reason for military intervention given by Yeltsin to the Russian people in December 1994.[35]

Nor, as will be seen, is this a regime with a strong martial character or one most of whose members were animated by a strong sense of Russian nationalism – though some of them did think they could appeal to the Russian people in this way. In the end, only an issue as critical as Russian territorial integrity could have brought on an actual invasion of Chechnya. Thus there was no question of a refusal to grant autonomy to Chechnya (though this is sometimes written in the Western press). If in 1993–4 Dudayev had been prepared to negotiate on the same basis as Tatarstan, for broad autonomy or confederation, this would have been accepted by Yeltsin.[36] (Of course, Dudayev was right to fear that this would not necessarily have meant an end to covert Russian attempts to get rid of him personally, and from that point of view his recalcitrance is understandable.)

That said, subsidiary reasons were of course present. Chief among these was the oil pipeline which runs from the oilfields of Azerbaijan through Daghestan and Chechnya to the Russian port of Novorossiisk, and in this context, fear of and rivalry with Turkey and fear of growing Turkish influence. Thus one reason given to me by Russian officials and officers for the impossibility of Russia ever recognising Chechen independence is that if the Turks could set up an embassy in Grozny, they would turn Chechnya into 'a base behind our lines'. This fear of Turkey is rooted in old Russian national anxieties, but also in the new and very uncomfortable awareness that Russian forces around the Black Sea are now very inferior to Turkish ones.[37] (For the history of Russo-Turkish rivalry in the area, and its catastrophic consequences for the peoples living there, see chapter 9.)

The Baku–Novorossiisk pipeline has come to be of major geopolitical importance due to the discovery and planned development of major new oilfields on the Azerbaijani shore of the Caspian, beginning with the Chiragh, Azeri and Guneshli fields, and with the possibility that Kazakh oil may eventually follow the same route.[38] These fields are estimated to contain some 3.5 billion barrels of oil, comparable to the North Sea. At the time of writing their full exploitation has not yet begun, due precisely to uncertainty over the pipeline route, and Russia's arguments over the legal status of the Caspian Sea. Control over access to and shipments from these fields is seen as of great geopolitical importance in Moscow, Ankara and Washington alike. I will not treat the struggle for the pipeline route at greater length here, because it is peripheral to the main themes of this book, and because the situation is a rapidly changing one. It is worth pointing out in passing, however, that the biggest single obstacle to Russian pipelines gaining the principal share of Caspian oil shipments as of the mid-1990s was neither the troubles in Chechnya, nor the geopolitical pressure from the Turks and Americans: it was the purely private thieving by the directors of the Russian state pipeline monopoly, Transneft, which no oil company in its senses would have wanted to trust.

The presence of Chechnya across the existing pipeline route from Baku to the Black Sea has obviously been an impediment to Russian hopes. Under Dudayev, the pipeline was riddled with holes by local people siphoning off the oil, and in 1994 the Russian government estimated that it would take 55 million dollars to repair. The war, of course, wrecked it still further.

As chapter 9 will describe, the Russian strategic imperative in this region remains in many ways the same as it was during the nineteenth-century wars with Shamil; that is to say, it is not that Chechnya is important in itself, but that it lies on the routes to much more important places. However, in my view this factor, though important, was probably still a subordinate one in the Russian decision to step up the pressure against Dudayev, and was largely irrelevant to the December 1994 decision to invade. Apart from anything else, the FSK had warned quite accurately that in this event Chechen attacks would in any case make the pipeline largely inoperable. And finally, the Russians could simply have built (and can still build) a pipeline around Chechnya, through Daghestan and Stavropol.

Catalyst for Intervention

Whatever the background reasons for the Yeltsin administration wishing to bring Chechnya to heel, it is important to remember that the catalyst for the Russian government's renewed pressure on Dudayev was the series of four bus hijackings by Chechen criminals in the Russian North Caucasus. The last three incidents, in May, June and July 1994, all took place in the town of Mineralny Vody, and all, curiously enough, on a Thursday. The hijackers demanded millions of dollars for the release of their hostages.

In the first three cases, the criminals were either seized on Russian soil, or fled to Chechnya, where they were arrested with the help of General Dudayev's forces. In the last case, Dudayev refused to let either the hijackers or the Russian special forces into Chechnya, fearing with some reason that Russia would use this as an excuse to occupy part at least of Chechnya. Russian special forces then stormed the hijackers' helicopter at Mineralny Vody airport, a bungled operation in which four hostages and one Russian soldier were killed.

Strangely enough, in the search for 'deeper' reasons for the Russian decision to invade Chechnya, the hijackings are often forgotten. In fact, whatever the underlying reasons, the timing of the Russian administration's decision to turn against Dudayev was a direct result of the last hijacking; nor should this be hard to understand, if we remember the impact of such small and contingent, but provocative, incidents on Western decision-making processes.[39]

The Dudayev government for its part claimed that the hijackings were carried out by the Chechen opposition with the backing of the Russian secret services, so as to discredit the Chechen government and provide an excuse for intervention. There is nothing very implausible about the Chechen Provisional Council adopting such a strategy, for later in the war anti-Dudayev Chechens were credibly accused of carrying out several crimes in an effort to make peace impossible. However, what seems difficult to believe is that they would have found Chechens willing to risk the strong likelihood of death (for the last set of hijackers were executed) in such a cause. The fact that in the last operation the Russian forces attacked the helicopter and a Russian officer died along with the hostages and a hijacker also makes this theory seem rather unlikely.[40]

As of the spring of 1994, among leaders of the Russian government and Yeltsin's entourage only Sergei Shakhrai, Nationalities Minister, and Doku Zavgayev were calling for direct intervention against Dudayev; they were later joined by Yeltsin's chief of staff, Sergei Filatov. In all three cases, their hard line was probably motivated partly by a desire to regain a prominent role in government, lost in the reshuffles of the past year. In Shakhrai's case, he may also have been inspired, as a descendant of Terek Cossacks, by traditional

Cossack hatred of the Chechens and desire to recover lost Cossack land – or at least, by desire to gain Cossack political support for his own political ambitions.

The rest of the administration did not see Chechnya as high on their list of priorities. Whether this was in part because of bribes distributed by Dudayev's followers, as alleged by Govorukhin and others, is not clear. Given the deep corruption of the Yeltsin administration, the military high command and the Russian bureaucracy, there is nothing inherently implausible about this charge; but as usual, details are lacking.

There is some evidence that the Yeltsin administration thought that a 'small victorious war' would increase their domestic popularity, especially given the sources of ultra-nationalist Vladimir Zhirinovsky in the December 1993 parliamentary elections, when his party gained almost a quarter of the vote. This seemed – wrongly – to indicate a strong current of militant nationalism in Russia. Colonel Sergei Yushenkov, then head of the Duma Defence Committee, says that he was told this in January 1995 by Oleg Lobov, Secretary of the Security Council and a key figure in the 'security clique' around Yeltsin ('The President needs a small victorious war, like the USA had in Haiti'); Lobov asked him therefore 'not to make so much noise' in opposing the war. Andrei Piontkovsky, who knows some of the members of various Russian think-tanks personally, has also told me that they expected the war to be popular and to stimulate Russian national feeling in support of the President. In this they were of course wrong. In Piontkovsky's words, 'They had everything ready for an imperialist strategy – except an imperial people.'[41] Public opposition to the use of force was widespread even before the intervention, and was expressed for example in surveys by Itar Tass, normally so obedient to the prevailing government line, which wrote in early December 1994 that 'Itar Tass reports from all over the country and from some foreign countries show that most Russians and foreigners want the Chechen conflict to be settled by peaceful means.'[42]

In February 1994, Shakhrai inserted a special mention of Chechnya, emphasising the illegal nature of the Dudayev government, into Yeltsin's address to parliament. According to Emil Payin and Arkady Popov, analysts on Yeltsin's staff, he also played a key role in the Duma's adoption the following month of a resolution denouncing Dudayev and calling for negotiations with the Chechen opposition. Either Shakhrai or Filatov was presumably responsible in March 1994 for wrecking the possibility of an invitation to Dudayev to take part in direct talks with Yeltsin on a confederal treaty. Shortly afterwards, the Chechen hijackings led to a conclusive and disastrous deterioration of relations between the Kremlin and Dudayev.[43]

The immediate aftermath of the hijackings in July saw a meeting between Sergei Filatov, Yeltsin's titular chief of staff, and the head of the Chechen Provisional Council, Umar Avturkhanov (a former police major and Zavgayev supporter). On 1 August, the Council declared Dudayev deposed, and announced (quite fictitiously) that it had taken power. On 29 July, the Russian government issued a statement strongly condemning Dudayev, saying he had seized power by a coup d'état. Describing the situation in Chechnya as 'practically out of control', it warned that it would protect citizens of Russia against violence. This was linked in the Russian press to the fighting between Dudayev and Labazanov in Grozny: pictures of the heads of Labazanov's men, displayed in Grozny's main square after they were killed in the fighting, appeared prominently in the Russian media, accompanied with comments on the 'barbarism' of the Dudayev regime. Activity by the FSK in Chechnya increased, and at the end of August a colonel in that service was arrested by Dudayev's forces.

However, at this stage the bulk of the Russian government was still determined to act by arming the Provisional Council, not by direct intervention. Yeltsin's words on television on 11 August were not hypocritical, and reflected the advice he was then receiving:

> Intervention by force is impermissible and must not be done. Were we to apply pressure by force to Chechnya, this would rouse the whole Caucasus, there would be such a commotion, there would be so much blood that nobody would ever forgive us. It is absolutely not possible. However, the situation in Chechnya is now changing. The role of the opposition to Dudayev is increasing. So I would not say that we are not having any influence at all.[44]

According to inside information I received at the time, caution, and above all expert military advice, played a central role in the decision not to attack directly and immediately; Shakhrai's plan for an airborne assault on Grozny to seize Dudayev was turned down by the army and was privately described by Oleg Lobov as 'lunatic' In this context, General Grachev's statement in November about how the capture of Grozny would take 'one airborne regiment and two hours' is to be put down to characteristically empty bragging – even he wasn't that stupid. This was also the public, and I believe the private advice of the Provisional Council opposition at Nadterechny, at least until Dudayev beat them in November. As Bislan Gantemirov told me in Znamenskoye on 10 August: 'I have said and will say again that if there is a Russian intervention, the whole Chechen people will unite against it. It would be a disaster.'

It is important to note that according to government material leaked to the author in August and September 1994, at that stage both Russian intelligence services (military intelligence, the GRU, and the then federal domestic intelligence service, the FSK under Sergei Stepashin) advised strongly against direct military intervention, at least until the Russian army had had much more time to prepare itself and to concentrate the necessary forces on the borders of Chechnya.[45]

This was also the strong advice of the army commanders in the North Caucasian Military Region. They pointed out that as of August 1994, there were barely 10,000 Russian troops in the immediate region, most of them deployed as peacekeepers in Ossetia and Ingushetia – not nearly enough to crush

Dudayev's forces, which they estimated as numbering (counting all the armed Chechens who could be expected to rally to Dudayev in the event of a Russian invasion) at more than 20,000 men. The utterly chaotic nature of the Russian intervention in December 1994 makes no sense unless it is assumed that it was botched together at the last moment – and this was specifically stated by General Eduard Vorobyev, who refused the command of the operation precisely on the grounds that there had been no plan and no preparation.

In a briefing paper for the Russian cabinet of early August, based partly on this military advice, the FSK warned that a military operation to suppress Chechnya would be slow and would involve heavy casualties both among the troops and the civilian population, especially of Grozny. Military intervention would irritate the non-Russian autonomous republics like Tatarstan, would tend to make Dudayev into an anti-Russian symbol, and would stir up the other Caucasian nations and increase the power of the Confederation of Mountain Peoples (in fact, they greatly overestimated this danger). The paper warned of the prospect of a long partisan and terrorist war.

It is precisely the fact that the Russian government and Defence Ministry had good warning of the dangers ahead that makes the initial Russian debacle in Chechnya in December and January so surprising and blameworthy, and has led to such furious criticism of General Grachev and his clique from within the Russian army itself.

In the first ten days of August 1994, the Russian Security Council, the Presidential Commission on Security and the cabinet under Chernomyrdin all met to discuss Chechen policy. As it turned out, however, the Security Council in the end took over all the power to make Chechen policy, as part of a general strengthening of Yeltsin's 'security clique' at the expense of Chernomyrdin's government. A consensus was reached, on the basis of the above advice, not to intervene directly but to give technical, financial and military support to the Provisional Council and the clans which supported it (the faith in the possibility of a successful clan coalition against Dudayev was however itself based on a fundamental anthropological misconception: see chapter 10). On 25 August, the Council was accordingly recognised by Moscow as the sole legitimate government of Chechnya, thereby sidelining both Khasbulatov and the Moscow-based 'Government of National Confidence' set up by former Chechen Prime Minister Yaragi Mamadayev.[46]

According to Emil Payin and Arkady Popov (who as members of the analytical centre in the presidential apparatus were peripheral to the real decision-making circles, but were still in a position to know a certain amount of what was going on):

> The relative successes of the Labazanov and Gantemirov armed formations (including the latter's capture of the Grozny airport for a period of time in early October and issuance of an ultimatum to Dudaev) created a false impression of Dudaev's weakness and, consequently, of the possibility of his removal by an armed opposition. Meanwhile,

Yeltsin's main political enemy at the time, former-Speaker of the Russian Parliament Ruslan Khasbulatov, was busy forming his own militia. Khasbulatov had recently returned to Chechnya and offered his services as a unifying force for the domestic opposition. He was the only leader in Chechnya whose popularity among the people was on par with that enjoyed by Dudaev.

Perhaps it was the threat of a strengthening of Khasbulatov's position that made the Kremlin decide to strengthen significantly the position of Avturkhanov (and Khadjiev, who had joined the latter in early fall) in the opposition alliance. In any event, the Russian government began to provide covert military support, thereby ensuring that the acclaim for expected future military victory over Dudaev, and, consequently, power in Grozny, would not fall into the hands of a hostile Khasbulatov or an unpredictable Gantemirov but, rather, into the hands of 'our people'. Moreover, in an attempt to upgrade the effectiveness of local opposition forces, the Russian leadership approved the delivery of Russian tanks and combat personnel to the region.[47]

The decision once made, the Russian administration stumbled from one bungled approach to another, finding itself progressively drawn in deeper and deeper. There is nothing especially mysterious, or indeed Russian about this: many analogies exist in the histories of other empires and great powers. The Russian-supported, opposition-executed attack on Grozny on 26 November in particular strongly recalls the Bay of Pigs, or to take a British imperial analogy, the Jameson raid of 1896, intended to bring about an internal rebellion to topple the defiant government of the Transvaal.

Russian plans had been complicated when Ruslan Khasbulatov returned to Chechnya in August 1994 in order, he said, to set up a 'peacekeeping group' to disarm both Dudayev's forces and the opposition, but actually to capitalise on his great popularity in Chechnya (thanks to his defiance of Yeltsin in the autumn of 1993) in order to take power from Dudayev himself. He declared that he had a peacekeeping plan 'that has already worked in Europe and Asia', and that 'I am the friend of every person who wants to preserve a human existence in Chechnya.' His supporters made great play with his previous prestige: 'A world-famous economist, and an ex-leader of one of the world's three superpowers', was how he was introduced in the town of Urus Martan.

However, needing a local armed force, Khasbulatov formed an alliance with Labazanov – something about which he was evidently somewhat embarassed. He told me in late August, very disingenuously, that 'I also think that Labazanov is a great bandit, but what can I do? A peacekeeping group has to talk to everyone, both the Gandhis and the bandits. I don't think anyone will blame me for talking with a bandit and telling him not to shoot.' Then on 5 September, Dudayev drove Labazanov from his base at Argun, east of Grozny, after which Labazanov took refuge with his remaining men in Khasbulatov's home-town of Tolstoy Yurt (now given back its original

Chechen name of Deukr Aul). This evidence of Dudayev's capacity for resistance seems to have encouraged the Russians to increase their military aid to the Provisional Council.

Understandably in view of his previous feud with Yeltsin, the Russian administration tried to marginalise Khasbulatov and build up the Provisional Council without him. According to Maria Eismont, Deputy Nationalities Minister Alexander Kotenkov sent Khasbulatov a telegram saying that his presence 'only endangers Russian efforts to help the Chechen opposition'. Payin and Popov, as quoted above, suggest that the whole Russian strategy in the early autumn of 1994 may have been speeded up so as to pre-empt a Khasbulatov success – disastrously for Russia, since the only chance of it working would have been if it had been conducted slowly enough that it built up the opposition without making Russia's hand in the process blindingly obvious.

If the main point was to get rid of Dudayev, then sidelining Khasbulatov was probably a mistake in any case. Khasbulatov's prestige among ordinary Chechens at that time vastly outweighed that of the Provisional Council, since they were seen by most Chechens as Russian stooges and he was not, or not to the same extent.

On 14 September, the Provisional Council appointed Gantemirov commander of its forces, after a political deal reportedly brokered by Moscow. Shortly afterwards, Avturkhanov visited Moscow for talks. On 3 October, Russian helicopter gunships began to operate in support of Chechen opposition forces. Armed clashes between the opposition and Dudayev's forces escalated.

This period saw the first widespread public mention of Colonel Aslan Maskhadov as chief of staff of the Chechen government forces. A Soviet artillery colonel who served in Afghanistan, he had been disgusted by the attempted military intervention in Lithuania in January 1991, which he witnessed, and eventually resigned from the Russian army and returned to Chechnya to organise the Chechen forces against the threat of Russian invasion. This was also the period when Shamil Basayev threw in his lot definitively with the Dudayev government.[48]

On 15–16 October, forces loyal to Labazanov and Gantemirov launched an attack on Grozny, apparently having failed to coordinate this with the Provisional Council and Russia – showing the extreme fissiparousness of the opposition. Avturkhanov at this time openly referred to Labazanov as a bandit.[49] They were beaten off, and Dudayev followed up his victory with unsuccessful assaults on the opposition strongholds of Tolstoy Yurt (27 October), Urus Martan and Nadterechny. During these battles, Russian troops were apparently not directly involved, though Russian military 'advisers' were present. Despite much sound and fury, except in the case of Dudayev's earlier attack on Labazanov's men in Argun, none of these assaults was pushed home with real determination. This led Russian intelligence, and Western journalists, to underestimate the fighting capacity of the separatist forces.

By November, the Russian administration was seemingly committed to getting rid of Dudayev as quickly as possible; on 11 November, Shakhrai declared that the Russian government would hold talks with Grozny only after Dudayev's resignation. With this in mind, and recognising Khasbulatov's influence, the Kremlin had also appparently come round to a limited role for Khasbulatov, who now began to cooperate with the Provisional Council.

On 26 November, the opposition, including Labazanov and Gantemirov, tried again to capture Grozny, this time with the help of forty-seven Russian tanks and armoured personnel carriers, manned by Russian volunteer soldiers. According to a Russian prisoner, Private Andrei Chasov, whom I interviewed in Chechen captivity five days later, these had been recruited from the Russian army (largely from the Kantemir and Taman Guards Motorised Infantry Divisions stationed near Moscow) by the FSK, on a promise of 6 million roubles (1,500 dollars) for their service. In his words, 'They told us nothing about our mission, just that we were going to Chechnya to fight bandits and protect the population. They said everything else was a secret. We didn't know our officers. They didn't give us any maps, and as soon as the fighting started, our Chechen guides ran away, so we were totally lost.' Private Chasov by the way was no hardened professional but a 20-year-old conscript, thin, bewildered and evidently terrified.

This recruitment operation was with the connivance of General Grachev, but without – or so they later claimed, when things had gone badly wrong – the knowledge of the commanders of the divisions concerned. Major-General Polyakov, commanding the Kantemir Division, resigned in protest on 4 December. According to Eismont, the actual recruitment of the Russian soldiers and organisation of the force to attack Grozny was carried out by General Kotenkov, formerly of the Interior Ministry, and an FSK colonel called Khromchenko – in other words by two men with no experience of or training in armoured warfare or indeed serious warfare of any kind.[50]

The opposition forces failed to back up the Russians, and – for this and other reasons which will be set out in the following chapters – the result was another humiliating defeat, the death of around a dozen Russian soldiers, and the capture by Dudayev's forces of nineteen more. In a profoundly foolish but deeply characteristic moment of hysteria, Dudayev then publicly threatened to execute these prisoners as 'mercenaries'.

The threat was shortly afterwards withdrawn, but the Russian government was both humiliated and infuriated. At a meeting of the National Security Council on 29 November, the decision was made to intervene. Yeltsin issued a statement (reminiscent in its mendacity of the Anglo-French declaration at the time of Suez that they were invading Egypt so as to 'separate' the warring Egyptians and Israelis) warning the Dudayev government and the opposition to declare a ceasefire within forty-eight hours:

> If this demand is not met by the set deadline, a state of emergency will be introduced on the territory of the Chechen republic and all the forces and means at the disposal of the state will be used to put a stop

to the bloodshed, to protect the life, rights and freedoms of citizens of Russia and to restore constitutional legality, law, order and peace in the Chechen republic.[51]

Similarly, on 1 December, Russian planes dropped thousands of copies of the following declaration on Grozny:

> In this ancient Caucasian land, an inalienable part of our Fatherland, blood is being shed. Despite all the efforts of the authorities and local elders, Russian and international efforts to end the conflict have not been successful. The two sides are hiring mercenaries, including ones from foreign states.
> Due to the desire of irresponsible politicians to gratify their selfish ambitions, innocent people are perishing, the rights of citizens are being violated, people are becoming refugees…

The declaration gave 'both sides' forty-eight hours to lay down their arms. Otherwise, 'all necessary measures will be taken by the forces of order.'

Small numbers of Russian planes began air strikes on Grozny, but without any clear targets and to no effect except to kill nine civilians, infuriate the Chechens, and begin the process of driving Chechen waverers and enemies of Dudayev into resistance.[52] On 7 December, adopting the formula that the Russian government would use all through the war until the sham peace talks of May 1996, the Security Council declared that there was no conflict between Russia and Chechnya, but only a need to deal with the 'struggle for power by illegal armed formations'. Nikolai Yegorov, former Governor of Krasnodar, was appointed Deputy Prime Minister with responsibility for Chechnya.

Avturkhanov, warned that intervention was imminent but apparently foreseeing the furious Chechen reaction, had declared on 1 December that Russian troops should be brought in, but asked for a delay 'in order to convince the Chechen population that the Russian troops are not hostile'.[53] On 4 December, Khasbulatov quit Chechnya, declaring that

> Russia is bringing in troops, and as you know, I was always against this. I think we can settle the conflict ourselves. My role has become superfluous, the role of an observer of events which I can no longer influence. In these circumstances I must take a very difficult, but in my view the only correct decision – to break off my activity and return to Moscow.[54]

After talks on 6 December with Russian Defence Minister Pavel Grachev and representatives of the Russian parliament, Dudayev returned the prisoners. But Russian military intervention followed anyway, on 11 December 1994. The result was disaster for both Russia and Chechnya.

The Anarchy of Russian Decision-Making

The way in which the Russian state stumbled against its will into this disaster stemmed in large part from the weakness and internal divisions of the Russian central government. In the words of Payin and Popov,

> Nothing, in our view, could be further from the truth than the suggestion that contemporary Russian policy, which is struggling to climb out of the old institutional rubble and ancient prejudices, can in any way be planned or implemented in a conspiratorial spirit. It would be much closer to the truth, and much more productive, to understand Russian decision-making in the more prosaic terms of chaos theory.[55]

This of course is not at all to suggest that there may not be conspiracies *within* the Russian government, and there have been several such in the course of the 1990s. These, however, have been precisely conspiracies aimed at other parts of the administration. It does suggest that the administration as a whole would find it very difficult to mount a secret campaign and follow it through with energy, unity and determination.

The administration strategy which led to the parliamentary armed revolt of October 1993 has sometimes been analysed as a deliberate and well-planned provocation, which achieved its goal.[56] However, even this operation, if it was such, contained numerous elements of incoherence, incompetence and last-minute botching: as indicated above all by the wavering of the troops that Yeltsin needed actually to storm the parliament, and by reports of panic and chaos within the presidential secretariat during the critical period. In fact, the only wholly successful conspiracy from within the administration up to 1997 was probably the 'loans for shares' agreement in the autumn of 1995, which will be analysed at greater length in part II, and the presidential campaign which resulted.

When it comes to the incoherence of Russian policy-making in other fields under Yeltsin, three key reasons for that incoherence must be mentioned. The first is the character, and at certain points also the health of Yeltsin himself. Curiously perhaps for a man who as First Secretary of Sverdlovsk had a reputation as an effective and hands-on administrator, as President he showed little taste for the details of government. As he himself has admitted in his memoirs, when not faced with an immediate challenge he had a tendency to relax and loosen the reins. Worse: not merely did he leave most policy-making to his subordinates, but there is every sign that he actually encouraged them to fight with each other so as to strengthen his own grip on power.

However, it would be unfair to put all the blame on Yeltsin for the failings of Russian government decision-making in this period. A second very important factor was the privatisation of the state, the way in which parts of the administration came in effect to represent private or semi-private economic interests. This is especially striking, of course, in the case of Prime Minister Victor Chernomyrdin, who functioned for long periods in effect not as Premier of Russia, but as representative of Gazprom (and to some extent also the oil sector) in the Russian government. By helping Gazprom avoid taxation, he cost the Russian state billions of dollars in lost revenue and contributed heavily to the fiscal crisis of 1996–7.

Throughout the administration, but especially in the field of security policy, a third critically important reason for the weakness of decision-making has also been the disappearance of the Communist Party and its institutions. For while the central Russian state in 1991 of course inherited both the personnel and most of the administrative apparatus of the Soviet state, this apparatus had been institutionally decapitated by the abolition of the Communist Party, and therefore of the Politburo and the Central Committee. In the words of Charles Fairbanks, 'The end of the Communist state does not leave, as many people still argue, a normal state that is attempting to make a normal transition to democracy, but something closer to the challenge faced by God in creating order out of something that is "without form and void".'[57]

As Fairbanks has argued (drawing on previous work by Seweryn Bialer), the Soviet state was always characterised by a certain 'shapelessness', by bureaucratic cliques and factions, and by a tendency for orders and decisions to be made 'by telephone', that is to say personally and informally rather than by regular, formal and legal means (something which was of critical importance in the run-up to the Chechen War). But the Politburo staff and Central Committee sections worked, however inefficiently, to pull all these informal groupings behind united and agreed strategies and decisions. Moreover, these strategies were based both theoretically and to a considerable degree in reality, on Communist doctrines. These were filtered through the party's 'operational code', which was of especial importance in foreign and security policy. The collapse of the Communist Party and its ideology therefore left the government to a very real degree rudderless when it came to deciding on courses of action in these fields.

As of 1994, nothing had replaced the top Communist institutions when it came to these central decision-making functions. Chernomyrdin and the cabinet had no authority either over the Foreign Minister or over the various 'force' ministers (Defence, Interior and so on), as these reported directly to the President; but the President also gave them no leadership. This was also true of the formulation of an overall policy towards the CIS, or 'near abroad', in the Russian formulation. Aspirations to Russian hegemony existed and still exist; but one would look in vain for any Russian government body, or individual, with the power to formulate such a policy. This is very striking, for example, when compared with the highly centralized formulation of French policy towards her African 'sphere of influence'.

Between 1994 and 1996 an attempt was made to turn the National Security Council into a real policy-making body in these fields, and in 1995 it seemed for a while as if it were indeed becoming a new kind of extraconstitutional quasi-Politburo. But it was hopelessly discredited by the disasters in Chechnya, and its Secretary, Oleg Lobov, had nothing like the intelligence, vision or dynamism needed for such a role. In July 1996, the Security Council was given to Lebed, and his expulsion from power led to its eclipse. Under Ivan Rybkin and Boris Berezovsky, its role became very limited.

The failure of the National Security Council was especially significant because it left real power in the government divided between Chernomyrdin, Chubais and their private backers, and these were men who had never worked in the security field, or had any connection with it. Nor for that matter had Yeltsin himself. Under the highly compartmentalised Soviet administrative system, military, security and foreign policy had been administered quite separately from the rest of the state, with authority concentrated at the top, in the Politburo and Central Committee. Under Soviet rule, this division contributed to the success of the military in extracting huge and unaffordable funds from the state, and Communist foreign policy in committing the state to a variety of costly and dangerous foreign adventures, without the rest of the administration, desperate as it was for funds, being able to hinder this. But after 1991, it has meant that the most powerful men in the state, the ones backed both by private money and by economic reality, have been men who have no experience and indeed no interest in the fields of security policy.[58]

Why Chechnya Fought Alone

However, in one very important regard the consequences of the intervention in Chechnya were actually a great deal less disastrous for Russia than many Russian security experts, including the FSK and the intelligence staff of the North Caucasus Military District, had predicted. For the other North Caucasian autonomous republics did not in fact rise in support of the Chechens; nor did the Georgians and Azeris join in on their side.[59]

The more melodramatic warnings, as issued by General Dudayev's own supporters and a few excitable Russian democrats, had envisaged Turkish intervention and a new world war. And even Shamil Basayev, a much calmer and cooler spirit than Dudayev, was quite convinced in August 1994 that the other Muslim republics in the North Caucasus would at least carry out sabotage and mass demonstrations if the Russians invaded Chechnya. Ethnic civil war in Russia had been one of the grim predictions of the passengers in my train from Baku to Grozny in February 1992 – as well as, of course, of many Western observers at the time; its failure to materialise was another reason why Russians in 1996 felt that things had not been as bad as they might have been, and that they could vote for Yeltsin.

Of considerable importance in limiting the conflict was the fact that by the end of 1994 Moscow had brought all the Transcaucasian republics to a point where their governments were neither willing nor able to mount direct challenges to Russian power in the region. Three years earlier, it might have been a different matter. If the nationalist leader Abulfaz Elchibey had stayed in power in Azerbaijan, and Zviad Gamsakhurdia had still been President of Georgia, these states would at the very least have declared strong support for the Chechens, and might well have gone as far as to provide material support and bases for Chechen guerrillas.

Both of these regimes, however, had long since been overthrown by coups which beyond doubt had strong Russian backing. The subsequent crushing defeat of Eduard Shevardnadze's Georgia in the war against separatist Abkhazia (once again, Russian-backed) left the Georgian regime in no position to resist Russian pressure. In return for military help against resurgent Gamsakhurdia in the autumn of 1993, and some economic aid, Shevardnadze was forced to agree to the long-term stationing of Russian troops in bases on Georgian soil.

This alone made it much less likely that Chechen fighters would be able to use the Georgian mountains as a secure base from which to carry out partisan war. In any case, Shevardnadze was not about to help General Dudayev, who provided a haven for Gamsakhurdia from 1992 to 1993 and strongly backed him in his attempts to return to power in Georgia. As to the Georgian populations along the mountain border with Chechnya, they had memories dating back centuries if not millennia of the Chechens raiding them for cattle and slaves.[60] This tended to diminish their liking for Chechens.

As a highly cautious, cynical and pragmatic former Soviet – indeed Stalinist – bureaucrat, Heidar Aliev of Azerbaijan also had not the slightest sympathy for the nationalist-religious effusions of General Dudayev, whose ideas he regards as a threat to his own regime. By 1996, no strong pro-Chechen movement had emerged in Azerbaijan, partly due to Aliev's tight control, but mainly because the Azeris are tired of war and in any case, as a sedentary people, also harbour ancient dislikes of the Chechens. None the less, it is clear that weapons did continue to flow across the mountains to Chechnya, albeit in relatively small quantities.

The reasons why the Chechen national revolution of 1991–5 remains to date the only independence movement to have taken control of a Russian autonomous republic are rooted partly in historical, anthropological and religious factors which I shall discuss in part III. The passivity of the rest of the North Caucasus in the face of the Russian attack on Chechnya can also be explained by the structure of power in most of the republics. As in Tatarstan, the local Soviet party and managerial elites adopted new political hats and continued in power, but, aware of the economic weakness of their republics and their internal ethnic divisions, rather than negotiate toughly with Moscow like the Tatars, they have rather bowed diplomatically to whatever wind was the latest to blow from Moscow.[61]

Thus in August 1994, the 'Assembly of North Caucasian Democratic Forces' (a front organisation for several of the local regimes) issued a statement denouncing the use of force to solve the Chechen crisis, but also declaring that 'their only wish was to strengthen the united federal state' and calling on Yeltsin to 'protect the Russian Federation's sovereignty in the North Caucasus'. The statement also denounced 'adventurers who do not express the true wishes of the peace-loving peoples', by which they meant Dudayev.[62]

This does not mean that the war in Chechnya was not very unpopular elsewhere in the North Caucasus (except in traditionally pro-Russian and anti-Chechen Ossetia). In particular, there was strong opposition to local units being sent to fight there. In April 1996, the authorities and local parliament in the Adygei Republic protested strongly when the 131st Motorised Infantry Brigade, stationed in Adygea, was ordered to Chechnya.[63] Several of the North Caucasian presidents appealed repeatedly for a negotiated end to the war, though they also strongly denounced Dudayev and especially the raids on Budennovsk and Kizlyar. However, this never came anywhere near really large mass protests, let alone a threat of revolt.

Paradoxically, one reason why local establishments elsewhere in the North Caucasus have been able to retain power has been precisely the persistence of kinship allegiances so often bewailed in the past by Soviet commentators. Although looser and less powerful than in Soviet Central Asia, these 'clan' allegiances in the Caucasus nevertheless proved very durable, and very adaptable to Communist bureaucratic politics. Where in Russia these politics were largely a matter of personal allegiance to a particular boss and his clique, in the Caucasus they were very often defined by membership of a clan or extended family. These bureaucratic groups were in turn linked, once again often directly or indirectly by family, to the black market and 'mafia' groups which had persisted in a small way under Stalin and which grew vastly in wealth and importance under Brezhnev. On the one hand, these features of the Soviet North Caucasian landscape made the ideological pretensions of Communism in the region even more grotesque than they were elsewhere. On the other, it has meant that local former Communist governing groups have often had very deep and enduring roots in their local societies, and this has enabled them to fight off challenges from new would-be politicians basing their appeals on radical nationalism.[64]

And while, as elsewhere in the former Soviet Union, ex-Communist officials in the North Caucasus have themselves adopted nationalist positions in order to stay in power, their natural caution and pragmatism, and their fruitful links to the power elites in Moscow, have held them back from following the dangerous road of full independence. The Yeltsin administration too has treated the native North Caucasian elites with care and consideration, distributing patronage to them and giving them a measure of real or at least potential central power through their positions in the upper house of parliament, the Federation Council.

An indication of how the Yeltsin administration is well aware of its need to woo the North Caucasian leaders is given by its treatment of the Daghestani politician Ramazan Abdullatipov. Despite his having been a strong supporter of the opposition parliament throughout 1993 (though he was careful to withdraw before the final violent denouement in October), there was no attempt to penalise him and administration officials were soon once again seeking his help over North Caucasian issues. This paid off. When the administration moved against Chechnya in the winter of 1994–5, Abdullatipov publicly supported the operation, and helped ensure that anti-Russian agitation among the Chechens in Daghestan would not spread to the other nationalities of the republic.

Yeltsin has also followed a policy of appointing men with North Caucasian experience, such as Sergei Shakhrai and Nikolai Yegorov (former governor and Communist boss in Krasnodar), to take responsibility for 'nationalities' affairs in Russia. While this has been strikingly unsuccessful in terms of Russian policy in Chechnya, it has been another factor ensuring that the (loyal) North Caucasian leaders have had close links to the government in Moscow.

The reasons for caution in the use of ethnic mobilisation by the old regimes, and the lack of success of radical nationalist movements across most of the North Caucasus, are obvious and compelling. They are economic, religious and, most important of all, demographic. Economically, all North Caucasian republics but Chechnya lack significant natural resources of their own and thus count among the Russian regions which depend heavily on Moscow for subsidies. The Adygei Republic, with its oil, used to be an exception, but its reserves are by now almost completely exhausted. The economies of Kabardino-Balkaria and Karachai-Cherkessia in particular used to contain major tourism sectors, but these have largely collapsed along with the Soviet system of mass organized tours. The reputation of the Caucasus for insecurity and crime has ensured that, apart from a few intrepid mountain climbers, these republics have had very little success in attracting Western tourists, while the Russian new rich prefer to go on holiday to the West.

With the exception of Daghestan, on the Caspian Sea, and North Ossetia, lying across the main highway to Georgia, all the North Caucasian republics are also effectively surrounded by Russian territory, with their borders to the south lying across the impassable barrier of the main Caucasus range. This makes them utterly dependent on Russian transport links and thus very vulnerable to Russian blockade in the event of an attempt to separate from Russia.

In terms of religion and culture, the picture of the North Caucasus as uniformly Muslim needs serious qualification. The Muslim nations of the Western and Eastern Caucasus regions have very different religious profiles, and in between lie the mainly Christian Ossetes. The Western Caucasian peoples, whether Circassian (Abkhaz, Kabardin, Adyge, Cherkess, Abazin), or Turkic (Karachai, Balkar), remained until very recent times largely animist by religious practice. In the early Middle Ages, some of them superficially adopted Christianity under the influence first of Byzantium, then of Muscovy, and Kabardin princes intermarried with the Russian nobility.[65]

From the sixteenth century on, these people adopted Sunni Islam under the influence of the Ottoman Turks. But even in the case of the Abkhaz, the Western Caucasian people geographically closest to the Muslim world, Islam has never run very deep.[66] Muslim clerics are respected but wielded only limited social power even before the Soviet period. Their attempts to stamp out the drinking of wine and brandy, a local habit recorded from the most ancient times, never even got off the ground. Religious fanaticism has played a very limited role in this area. The Ossetes, for example, today include Muslims as well as Christians, but compared to Ossete nationalism, religious identity plays almost no role in their politics or even in their social life. In the past, the presence of the Ossetes in the middle of the North Caucasus played an important part in preventing stronger Muslim influence from filtering from east to west, and in stopping Shamil from linking up with Circassian resistance in the west. Today, Chechen or Ingush guerrillas wishing to carry their struggle into the Western Caucasus will have to cross hostile Ossete territory.

The Ingush are ethnically and linguistically very close to the Chechens, but lying further to the west, the Ingush tribes were converted later and less deeply than the Chechens. Since then, their differing religious cultures have helped to divide the two peoples, and the absence of militant Islam was a central reason for Ingush collaboration with Russia during the war with Shamil, something which confirmed the split between the Ingush and Chechens.

Under Soviet rule, the 'official' Muslim clergy became thoroughly subservient to the Soviet state; and moreover, having already been generally badly educated even before the Revolution, they often declined into a pitiful ignorance of Muslim doctrine and thought, beyond a few barely understood prayers. In Chechnya and Daghestan, this was compensated for by the great strength of unofficial Sufi brotherhoods, but these have had little influence elsewhere in the North Caucasus, let alone in Tatarstan or Bashkortostan.

Above all, however, the reason for the lack of movement on the part of the other Caucasian peoples has been demographic: with the exception of the pro-Russian Ossetes, the Chechens at the time of the Soviet collapse were the only 'titular nationality' of an autonomous republic who formed an absolute majority of that republic's population. According to the census of 1989, the total population of the Checheno-Ingush ASSR was 1.29 million, of whom 57 per cent, or 734,500, were Chechens. This is more than twice the number who (officially) returned from exile in 1957, and to this can be added another 300,000 Chechens in the diaspora elsewhere in Russia and other former Soviet republics. The number of Russians was 394,000 (30 per cent), and Ingush, 164,000 (13 per cent).[67] The other peoples simply lack the demographic weight to try to create independent states. The general intermixing of different nationalities in the North Caucasus (known to the medieval Muslim world as 'Language Mountain' for its multiplicity of tongues) creates its own system of checks and balances, and has given governments in Moscow endless opportunities to pursue policies of divide and rule.

Most local establishment politicians, especially in Daghestan, with its thirty-four local nationalities, most with claims on each other's territory, are well aware, and deeply afraid, of the national strife and utter chaos which would result from a bid for independence from Russia; and they are greatly helped in their opposition to radical nationalism by the fact that all the populations of the North Caucasus have by now been exposed to several years of reporting of the suffering and destruction caused by national conflict in neighbouring Transcaucasia. Russian television, which most people in the region watch assiduously, has continuously rubbed home the message.

Thus one reason why the Yeltsin administration tolerated General Dudayev's rule in Chechnya for more than two and a half years was simply because there was no pressing need for the Russian state to take action; there were few signs that the 'Chechen infection', of radical nationalism and demands for full independence, was spreading to other Russian autonomous republics. Dudayev's repeated appeals to the other North Caucasian peoples to rise against Russian rule and form a new Caucasian union had no effect. The General's hoped-for instrument to this end was the Confederation of Mountain Peoples, an umbrella group of nationalist forces in the region. In the heady days of November 1991, this Confederation may indeed have played an important part in dissuading Russia from an attack on Chechnya, thus apparently threatening Moscow with a new Caucasian war. Even more important however was its role – which was sanctioned by the Russian army and worked out very much to Moscow's advantage – in helping the Abkhaz war against Georgia, in which the seven hundred or so North Caucasian volunteers were a key element of the Abkhaz forces. In this case, however, the Confederation troops were fighting a disorganized and badly equipped enemy, and even more important, were doing so with tacit approval of Russia.

When Russia invaded Chechnya, Dudayev appealed to the Confederation and the Caucasian peoples to help Chechnya and rise against both Russia and 'your own cowardly and corrupt leaders'. He declared once again that 'Chechnya is fighting on behalf of all the Caucasian peoples.'[68] But the Confederation restricted itself to verbal protests; after the initial mass protests in Ingushetia and Daghestan only a handful of volunteers went to fight for the Chechens, and the governments of the other North Caucasian republics placed a strict watch on the Confederation's activities.

After 1993, when he broke with Dudayev, Yusup Soslambekov's influence in the Confederation, as chairman of its 'parliament', also played a role in discouraging that body from expressing direct support for the Chechen cause, or mobilising volunteers from other North Caucasian republics to go to fight in Chechnya (though he never joined the Russian-backed administration, and indeed strongly criticised the invasion). As a result, by 1997 its influence and reputation had dwindled to almost nothing. Its failure over Chechnya may be seen as marking the effective end of the Confederation. Its hopes of creating a new independent North Caucasian state were in any case always a chimera: geography, economics, religion and nationalism all stood against it.

3 The Course of the Chechen War

Exchange at a queue for water in Russian-occupied Grozny, May 1995, overheard by the author:
Russian woman (pushing to the front): 'Let me past, we don't have to be afraid of you any more.'
Chechen woman, pushing back: 'Stay in line. We weren't afraid of you then, and we're still not afraid of you.'

War is primarily a sociologic art, and the art of war improves so slowly that Alexander's principles are still standard. The art of changing weapons changes rapidly – the art of handling the men who use them changes much more slowly...

The following chapters will describe the actions of some peoples who relied exclusively on fire weapons and lacked the courage or perspicacity to close with the foe in shock... A fire fight for its own sake is hardly more than an athletic contest. It is not within any true war pattern; it is wasteful of life since it is futile; it can scarcely be called fighting. It is shock or the threat of shock which works one's will on the enemy. The victor of a fire fight is still a long way from his objective. The victor of a shock fight is right there.

Harry Holbert Turney-High, *Primitive War: Its Practice and Concepts*

Bad Planning and Moral Cowardice: The First Three Weeks

The first week of the Chechen War marked one of the most critical moments in the history of the Yeltsin administration and indeed of modern Russia, in some ways comparable in importance to the defeat of the conservative camp of August 1991 and the parliamentary 'rebellion' of October 1993. This is because, for a few days, there seemed to be a real possibility that the unity of the Russian army would crack, and with it the obedience of junior commanders to the Defence Ministry and the military hierarchy. If that had occurred, then Russia would have taken a long step down the road to Latin America not merely in economic and social terms, but in political ones, with coups d'état and military pronunciamentos.

If this had happened, then a key actor in the proceedings would have been

a nose, and indeed not since Cleopatra would a nose have played so important a part in history.[1] The nose belonged to Boris Yeltsin, and was neither as
long nor as beautiful as the legendary Egyptian one. Its role was also passive
rather than active: in the second week of December 1994, the presidential
administration announced that Yeltsin had to enter hospital for a surgical
operation to correct a diverted septum, and for several days he was incom-
municado and issued no statement on the intervention in Chechnya which
began on 11 December. Indeed, he did not make a television address to the
Russian people explaining the intervention until 28 December, two and a half
weeks after it began. Moreover, for the first eighteen months of the war Yeltsin
did not visit the troops in Chechnya, despite the fact that in the course of 1995
he took a holiday at a sanatorium near Pyatigorsk, only a hundred miles away.

The effect of this transparent, ludicrous and contemptible attempt to evade
responsibility in December 1994 (all words that were used to me by Russian
officers at the time) had a terrible effect on morale in the Russian forces
involved in the operation, and contributed to the near mutiny of the western
column commanded by General Ivan Babichev, which had advanced through
Ingushetia. This column had already run into unexpected opposition from
crowds of Ingush civilians, some of them armed, who blocked the road,
surrounded the Russian vehicles, and destroyed some of them. On 13 December, it reached a point near the village of Davidenko on the main road to
Grozny, where it was confronted by a crowd of Chechen women who
performed the zikr on the road and told the Russians that to advance they
would have to drive over them. At this point Babichev, with the backing of an
assembly of officers, announced in my presence that he would not kill civilians and refused to advance any further.

Meanwhile the Eastern column, which was supposed to advance from
Daghestan to Gudermes, never even crossed the border. It was surrounded
by crowds of Daghestani Chechens and brought to a halt. At least two
armoured personnel carriers were taken and reportedly handed over to the
Chechens, and the Russian authorities admitted that forty-seven prisoners
had been taken. After remaining stationary for a fortnight, it was redeployed
north of the River Terek, and joined up with the northern column advancing
from the main Russian base of Mozdok in North Ossetia.

To understand Babichev's action (which I believe from the evidence of my
own eyes and ears to have been very real, and not just a trick, as the Chechens
later thought), it is necessary to keep in mind both the immediate developments within the army in December 1994 and a series of events going back to
1962, when the Soviet army was ordered to fire on demonstrators in the town
of Novocherkassk, and the general in command was dismissed for refusing to
do so. These were summed up for me in an interview with General Alexander
Lebed at his headquarters in Transdniestria in February 1994, ten months
before the war.

Lebed spoke with intense bitterness of all the times in the last years of the
Soviet Union that the army had been ordered to undertake internal policing

tasks – and how, when these had had bloody results and caused a political storm, the military commanders, and the army generally, were left to bear the responsibility alone. He had seen this himself, he said, in Tbilisi in March 1989 and in Baku in January 1990, and had heard about it from comrades who took part in the abortive intervention in Lithuania in January 1991:

> Every time, the orders were explicit, and came from the highest level, the Politburo. And every time, they were by telephone – nothing was written down. And every time, when we had done their dirty work for them, they ran away and left us to take all the blame, and nothing could be proved against them. Believe me, the army will never allow that to happen to it again.

Of course, this is exactly what the army, and more particularly the officers on the ground, did see happening in December 1994; and indeed, at the very start of the Russian intervention, before the real war began, the similarities to Tbilisi or Vilnius seemed all too close. On the afternoon of 13 December, I watched as a Deputy from the democratic bloc in the Federation Council, Viktor Kurochkin (from Chita in eastern Siberia), told General Babichev:

> Don't forget, General, that if you fulfil an illegal order, the law will not protect you. You alone will have to bear the responsibility. I am instructed to tell you to wait here until the Federation Council makes its decision. What is happening in Moscow is a putsch, like in August 1991, and it will also fail.

To back him up, Kurochkin was accompanied by two local Chechen representatives, Salamu Umalatov and Saikhan Barshoyev.

Viewed from the road midway between the Chechens and the Russians, the moral and physical drama of the scene could hardly have been exaggerated. Behind, the crowd of chanting women, some dancing the zikr, others sitting in the road, holding banners with messages like 'Sons! Do not fire on women who could be your own mothers!' Ahead, the squat shapes of a line of Russian tanks, dimly visible against the dark blur of the forest. To the left, attack helicopters drifting across the giant, grim face of the wintry Caucasus.

General Babichev stood in front of his tanks, a bulky figure with a squashed kind of face not unlike Lebed's, very much the Soviet paratrooper. He told Kurochkin and the Chechens that

> The situation is the following: the force involved in this operation is a large one, and I command only one part of it. I have no responsibility for what the others may do. But on my own authority, I have ordered this column to halt for today. And if the other side doesn't open fire, we won't fire either. I have given this order to my officers. If you stay here, I will also try to arrange a meeting with my superiors. But you must tell the people over there not to come any closer...

What we have achieved today is to save the lives of your people and ours. Let's stick to that.

The Chechens told me that General Babichev had actually asked the women to demonstrate on the road, so as to give him the excuse not to advance – though this seems very unlikely.

On the 13th, the officers in the column were very cagey about talking to me, but when I returned on the 17th, they had opened up a lot, and at the time their discipline seemed to me to be disintegrating – though none would give their surnames, which showed a strong residual caution. They were drawn from a mixture of Babichev's own unit, the 76th (Pskov) Airborne Division, an Interior Ministry (MVD) division, and the Taman Guards Motorised Infantry Division. They said that in the meantime they had held an officers' assembly and resolved not to advance any further, because it was not clear to them who had ordered the intervention in Chechnya or what its goal was. 'A mutiny? You could call it that,' a lieutenant-colonel from the motorised infantry told me. 'But we are not going to be made the dupes of the people who cooked up this stew... I don't believe the army will split over this. General Babichev is talking to the other columns, and I don't think they will attack civilians either.'

'We certainly don't want to kill women and children on the orders of those whores in the Kremlin and for the sake of their political games,' one paratroop major told me. 'If it is a question of Chechen bandits, that would be a different matter... But still, I don't know why we are here.' An MVD major told me that 'almost all the officers from my division in this column have written letters of resignation in case they try to make us advance. I have done so today. I saw Yeltsin's appeal to the people of Chechnya and it said that weapons would not be used against civilians. We are certainly not going to do so.'

Most had no strong feelings about keeping Chechnya in Russia. An MVD captain who gave his name as Oleg said, 'Of course, legally it is part of Russia, but when you ask if it is worth fighting to keep the Chechens in against their will, then in my opinion, no... This whole mess has been started by groups in Moscow who want to set the army against the people for their own advantage...I was in the Caucasus before, and three days after we were made to kill innocent people, we sat and looked at each other and asked, My God, what have we done...'

In the background to all this was a general unwillingness of the armed forces to get involved in suppressing domestic unrest, something which was documented in a fascinating opinion poll by the Livermore National Laboratory, the results of which will be described in part II. Specific to Chechnya was the fact that the General Staff and the command of the North Caucasus Military District had not been truly involved in the planning of the operation, leading to a collapse of the normal chain of command and general confusion, and the correct impression that this was essentially a war that had been cooked up by Stepashin and Grachev for their own political reasons.

When, two days later, the Deputy Commander of Ground Forces, General Eduard Vorobyev, was ordered to take up command of the operation (until then, authority on the ground had been exercised by a troika of Grachev, Yerin and Stepashin), he discovered that no plan as such existed, and the troops at his disposal were grossly inadequate for the task. He told Grachev that it would take three months to prepare the forces necessary. Pavel Baev gives the total number of troops assembled by 5 December as 23,800, including 4,800 Interior Ministry troops, and with 80 tanks and 200 APCs.[2] They included elements of the 'elite' Pskov (76th) and Tula (106th) Airborne Divisions. I also met some troops from the Taman Guards Motorised Infantry Division, whom Baev does not list, and by the first week of the operation, the number of tanks involved seems to have increased considerably. Testifying to Duma, Vorobyev later said that he had been worried about evasion of political responsibility for the operation.

Vorobyev's reaction was to refuse the command. He was dismissed from the army, and in January went public with bitter denunciations of Grachev for 'moral cowardice' in not telling Yeltsin that the army was not prepared for intervention. The paratroopers, or at least Babichev himself, would also have been aware of how the Commander of Airborne Forces, General Yevgeny Podkolzin, had been deliberately cut out of the planning of the operation by Grachev, because (so I have been told by officers) he had warned that to be successful, it would need many more men and much more time for preparation.

Even before this happened, some of the most senior and respected generals in the army had come out in open opposition to the war, including deputy defence ministers Boris Gromov and Valery Mironov, General Alexander Lebed and General Georgy Kondratiev. All were forced by Grachev to leave the army (or in the case of Gromov, transferred to a meaningless job in the Foreign Ministry). In all, some 557 officers of all ranks are believed to have been disciplined, sacked or to have left the army voluntarily in protest against the intervention. In January, the commander and entire senior staff of the North Caucasus Military District were also sacked, and I was told that some had already found excuses to leave quietly of their own accord.

What seems to have happened between 16 December, when Vorobyev refused the command, and the assault of 31 December, in which Babichev's column participated, is that the Russian 'Generalitat' and General Staff decided that although they had not wanted this war and looked on it with foreboding, now that the army was involved, it had no choice but to win so as to avoid utter humiliation and the possible disintegration of both army and state. Critically, Yeltsin emerged from hospital and took moral and political responsibility for the operation, thus relieving the generals and officers of the fear that they would be turned into political scapegoats.

With cohesion at the top re-established, Babichev and his officers either fell into line or (in some cases) simply quit the army, which then lurched into battle deeply demoralised and unenthusiastic, but at least on the suface united and disciplined. Their column never did advance down the main road from the west into Grozny, but moved north to link up with the column from Mozdok. Babichev continued as a senior commander, but from then on he did not command a separate force in Chechnya. In April, he was promoted to command the army corps based in Krasnodar.

Apart from the danger of sparking off internal chaos, the reasons why most of the generals felt that once committed they had to fight were probably best summed up by Pavel Felgenhauer, a journalist whose writing has often reflected the views of the *Generalitat*, writing five months later:

> The Chechen recollections of the last Caucasian War [i.e. that in the nineteenth century], however, are very romantic. Apparently, they actually believe that the irresolute Russians will eventually accept defeat and flee when confronted with real Chechen valour. They still do not realise that Russia simply cannot afford to lose this war and grant the Chechen nation its independence, no matter what the final cost may be. The majority of Russian political and military leaders believe that a total withdrawal from Chechnya could facilitate a breakdown of law, order and central government rule in the northern Caucasus. That would grossly undermine vital Russian national interests in this strategically vital, oil-rich region.[3]

As a result, therefore, while military morale in Chechnya never recovered from the incidents at the beginning of the war, by the fourth week of December open protest in the army had been quelled, the military hierarchy had united behind the idea that the war now embarked on had to be won, and the stage was set for the start of the real assault.

In the meantime, as described in chapter 1, Grozny had been subjected to a sporadic but fairly heavy air bombardment which hit no targets of significance (assuming it was even meant to, and was not just intended to terrorise and demoralise the civilian population) but killed hundreds of civilians – most of them Russians – and outraged public opinion in Russia and in the West.

An important role in stirring up condemnation of the war in Russia was played by Sergei Kovalev, a veteran dissident and human rights campaigner from Soviet days, who had spent many years in labour camps. He remained in Grozny through much of the bombing, and his condemnation of the invasion had an important moral effect in Russia. At that stage, Russian independent television (in those days still genuinely independent, before it came under the control of Boris Berezovsky), the great bulk of the newspapers, and even, in a more veiled way, Russian state television were all bitterly critical of the military intervention.

Later, Dr Kovalev's estimate of 25,000 civilians killed in Grozny up to the end of January 1995 received wide circulation – though, with all due respect to him and his great moral and physical courage, it was almost certainly a serious exaggeration. Unfortunately, Russian democrats are not much better than Russian bureaucrats when it comes to care with figures: for example, the estimate of Galina Starovoitova in February 1996 that there were 'about 50,000 killed, 250,000 homeless, and 500,000 refugees' as a result of the Chechen War is as suspiciously rounded a set of figures as one could encounter anywhere.

On the basis of my own investigations in several of the main hospitals at the time (in Urus Martan, Stary Atagi, Shali and Achkoi Martan, as well as in Grozny), and on the usual military assumption of two or three wounded for every person killed, the absolute maximum for civilians killed in the period to the end of January 1995 would be 5,000. The number in the mass and individual graves in Grozny's central cemetery, as I counted them on 25 May 1995, was 737, with 75 more newly buried at the Karpinsky cemetery outside town. I cannot be absolutely sure of the number in the mass graves, because some of the bodies were lying on top of each other and some were in pieces or had disintegrated. None the less, even making allowance for this, the figure would not have been more than 900.

Of course, the full figure would be much higher, because of the Chechen rule of burying people in their ancestral villages, if at all possible; but I visited the cemeteries in a number of towns and villages in May 1995, and while I found a great many new graves, I did not find a figure which if extended to the whole of Chechnya could add up to 25,000, or even a third of that number. (For what it is worth, given the source, in September 1995 the head of the Russian-backed Provisional Government, Salambek Khadjiev, gave the number of civilians killed to that date as between 6,000 and 7,000.)[4]

In January 1997, after the end of the war, Memorial (the organisation founded to recall the crimes and victims of the Soviet era) estimated that 4,379 Russian troops in all had been killed, with 703 missing (partly being held by the Chechens, partly killed) and 703 deserted.

Of course, by the end of the war, after incidents like the killings in Samashki, the bombardment of many towns and villages, and new battles in Grozny and Gudermes, the number of civilian dead might well have exceeded 20,000 – but nothing like the 'hundred thousand' mentioned by Lebed and others. If the latter figure had been correct, it would have suggested that more than a third of the entire population of Chechnya had been killed or wounded, which was manifestly not the case. This is not intended to minimise the extent of the Yeltsin administration's crimes, but a journalist should after all try to be accurate, and not use suspect evidence, even in support of a good cause.

The Storm, January to June 1995

On 31 December, the Russian forces in Chechnya, now united in one group of units north and north-west of Grozny, launched a full-scale ground assault on the city. The choice of that particular date has been alternatively explained by the fact that the Russian media were taking a holiday over the New Year, the expectation that the Chechens would be celebrating, or the fact that it was General Grachev's birthday.

The Russians attacked from only two sides, since their numbers did not permit them to surround and isolate the city. In consequence, throughout the 'siege', which lasted in all some seven weeks, the city was open to the south and east, and the Chechen fighters received continuous reinforcement and resupply, and were eventually able to withdraw from it in good order.

Grachev later claimed that the Chechens had 15,000 well-armed troops in Grozny (probably twice to three times the real number) and General Anatoly Kvashnin, the commander at the time of the attack, gave as an excuse for his failure the suggestion that, based on Second World War experience, he would have needed 50–60,000 troops to capture Grozny. These excuses however were mendacious in their exaggeration both of the numbers and the weapons of the defenders. In the Second World War, the German and Soviet armies had a rough equivalence in heavy weapons; in Grozny, the Russians had total superiority.[5]

The first day's battle was a thoroughly disastrous one for the Russians. Sergei Stepashin later tried to excuse his intelligence department's failure to prepare the army for the resistance they encountered in Grozny by saying that a system of defence installations had been built after 1991, while the only maps the attackers had were made earlier. This excuse was ridiculous even in its own terms, because all those years Grozny was an open city, and it is difficult to understand what the FSK agents were working on there if they were not even able to supply the army with information on the centres of resistance.

But more to the point, there were no such formally organised defences. In fact, the lack of obvious barricades and tank traps made me and other journalists think that the Chechens would put up only a symbolic fight in the city. But as will be seen, they were much better tacticians than that. Barricades would have been blasted to pieces by tank fire from a distance. A Chechen fighter described how the Chechens actually fought as follows:

> The Russian soldiers stayed in their armour, so we just stood on the balconies and dropped grenades on to their vehicles as they drove by underneath. The Russians are cowards. They just can't bear to come out of shelter and fight us man-to-man. They know they are no match for us. That is why we beat them and will always beat them.

Lack of infantry cover was also the explanation for the Russian failure given privately by the Russian General Staff:

> The Russian troops broke through the outer defence perimeter and occupied the left bank of the Sunja River in Grozny. The Chechens wisely retreated. But when our armour entered the city centre, a surprise awaited it. According to the explanations given in the General Staff, the Russian side had a shortage of infantry. The Chechens allowed the tank columns to pass and then surrounded them and attacked.[6]

In traditional American slang, the first stage of the resulting battle would have been called a turkey-shoot. Several hundred Russian soldiers died in the course of a few hours, and complete disaster was only narrowly averted. Ten days later, Valery Kukayev, a nineteen-year-old private from a collective farm in Samara Region, driver of an armoured personnel carrier (BMP, in its Russian version), described from his hospital bed in Chechen captivity what happened to his company of the 65th Motorised Infantry on the night of the 31st and morning of the 1st:

> The commanders gave us no map, no briefing, just told us to follow the BMP in front, but it got lost and ended up following us. By morning, we were completely lost and separated from the other units. I asked our officer where we were, he said he didn't know – somewhere near the railway station. No, he didn't have a map either. We were told to take up defensive positions, but it was hopeless – the Chechens were all around us and firing. There was nowhere to take cover, because they were everywhere.
>
> I asked for orders from our company commander, Lt Chernychenko, and they told me he'd already run for it. Then we tried to escape. That was when I was wounded, by a sniper – I'd got out of the BMP to try to find a way out. My friends put me in another BMP, but it was soon damaged. I saw three BMPs destroyed in all, and I think only five or six of the crews survived. My friends had to leave me behind, they said they couldn't carry me. I don't blame them – two of them were wounded themselves, one in the arm and one in the ear. One of them was captured with me. I don't know if the others made it. I lay there for three or four hours, and then the Chechens found me. They operated on me at a hospital in Grozny, then brought me here. They treated me well, though I was their enemy. I did not want to be their enemy, to come here to kill other farmers. I am a farmer myself. If Yeltsin and Grachev want this war, let them come and fight themselves, not send us to die.[7]

The northern column, advancing towards the centre of the city down Pervomaiskoye Chaussee, was brought to a halt with heavy casualties around half a mile from the presidential headquarters on the main square. On 20 February, by the secondary school on Pervomaiskoye I met a lieutenant-colonel from the 81st Motorised Infantry Regiment, who gave his name as Nikolai Mikhailovich, with half a dozen of his men. Two of them were carrying sacks. Seven weeks after the start of the battle, they were looking for pieces of their comrades, still scattered among the ruins. Around them were shattered, twisted bits of tanks and armoured personnel carriers, obviously hit again and again. Nikolai Mikhailovich cursed the intelligence they had received before the battle: 'If those fools in the FSK had given us any idea of the kind of the kind of resistance we were going to meet, of course we wouldn't have driven into town like that.' He said that the commander of the 81st had been killed and more than half its men killed or wounded. The commander of the 131st Motorised Rifle Brigade was also killed. That brigade, in the western column, reached the area of the railway station, south of the square, but was then surrounded, split up and almost obliterated. The whole attacking group risked being forced to withdraw from the city.

According to the Russian media and military sources, the situation was saved largely thanks to Major-General Lev Rokhlin, a paratroop officer (unusually for the senior ranks of the Soviet and Russian armies, of Jewish origin), who re-established control over the scattered forces, rallied them and broke through to the troops encircled at the station. On the strength of this success he went on to make a political career as a centrist, and after the December 1995 presidential elections became Chairman of the Duma Defence Committee and a leading figure in the contested field of military reform (see chapter 8).

The situation in Grozny then settled down into a grim slogging match, with the Russian forces edging towards the presidential headquarters under cover of one of the most intense bombardments of recent times. In consequence, the centre of Grozny was almost totally destroyed. In the end, rather than storming the Chechen positions, the Russian forces literally blasted the Chechen fighters out of them. The Russian government for its part issued bulletin after bulletin, reporting 'victory', 'an end to the bombing' and 'normalisation', which in their mendacity recalled Soviet days and in their obvious distance from reality served to discredit the state and the official and semi-official media which carried them, and which were scorned by independent Russian newspapers, even those normally sympathetic to the government.[8]

On 19 January, however, after several false claims of capture by the Russians, the presidential headquarters was finally abandoned by its defenders when a penetration bomb pierced the cellars where they had been holding out. Russian military losses were high, although, thanks to the fact that after the first few days they relied much more on artillery than on assault, not apparently as high as some reports at the time suggested. The late General Volkogonov, generally a reliable source, gave the number of deaths in the federal forces up to 24 February as 1,146 men killed, with another 374 missing – most of them also dead.[9]

The attack on Grozny was accompanied by a great deal of looting and attacks on civilians, which have already been sketched in chapter 1. I saw direct evidence of the looting on the morning of 12 January 1995, near the village of Alkhan Yurt on the main road out of Grozny to the west, after the car in which I was travelling towards Grozny was passed at high speed by a Russian armoured personnel carrier tearing wildly down the road in the opposite direction. Shortly before, we had heard a burst of automatic fire from up ahead. Fearing a battle was in process, we went carefully forward, until we came to two Russian trucks with their tyres shot out, one of them lying in the ditch, and surrounded by Chechen fighters.

They invited us to look in the truck. It was full of an assortment of goods that would have done justice to a Russian Sergeant Bilko: an IBM computer; an Epson printer; an air conditioner; a caseful of blank music cassettes; another full of women's underwear. More women's clothes were scattered all over the back of the truck, as if thrown in at random. This was the loot of the captured northern suburbs of Grozny, driven off by Russian troops – including officers – who had left the firing line (with or without the permission of their commanders) to sell it in the bazaars of southern Russia, and who had had the misfortune to take the wrong turning and drive into Chechen-controlled territory.

It is worth pointing out that the first weeks of the Chechen War saw failures by virtually every arm of the Russian armed forces, except for air transport – and as a Western military attaché put it, 'no one was shooting at them.' For example, the contemporary state of the 'elite' Spetsnaz was graphically illustrated for me by an eighteen-year-old junior sergeant of the 22nd Spetsnaz Brigade, Alexander Tupolsky, whose unit was dropped into the Chechen mountains at the end of December to operate as a raiding force behind Chechen lines, presumably in order to hinder the Chechens from regrouping in the mountains for a partisan war (the assumption being, of course, that the Chechen fighters would flee from Grozny as soon as the Russians launched a serious attack). I met Sergeant Tupolsky on January 11 in the hospital of Stary Atagi, after he had been wounded and captured. He told me that,

> We were dropped in by helicopter, about fifty of us in my unit. We were supposed to make contact with other groups, but they were never dropped. When it became obvious that the whole operation was a shambles, after about two days, we should have been pulled out again, but headquarters told us they couldn't send in helicopters because of the cloud and fog. I reckon the pilots were just too scared to try. We called and called for air support, but it only came after we had surrendered, and then they almost bombed us. They missed the Chechen fighters altogether. Maybe they meant to kill us, because we were embarrassing for them. We talked about that among ourselves. God knows – I just don't know what to think any more.
>
> They didn't send in any food or tents or sleeping bags with us, and it was freezing, so we were soon in a bad way... No, I've never had any training in mountain fighting or how to survive in those conditions... For four days we had nothing to eat, and nowhere to sleep, and we were on the move the whole time because of course the Chechens were on to us at once. We were sniped at, and by the time we surrendered we had two killed and two wounded. We couldn't light fires for fear of being seen. In the end we just gave up. Some local Chechens arranged our surrender....
>
> We were never told what we had been sent to do. Our commander wouldn't tell us – maybe he didn't know either – so there was nothing I could tell my lads. All we were told was that we were coming to free the

peaceful Chechen population from Afghan bandits and mercenaries, fighting for Dudayev. But now I think that they tricked us, that this was all some kind of Kremlin game. Every day we see peaceful, ordinary civilians being brought here killed and wounded by bombing. The Chechens have treated us decently – look, we are getting the same treatment as their own wounded. I will never fight them again. If I get out of here, I will go back to my mother and father.[10]

And this, I repeat, was a Spetsnaz group, supposedly the *crème de la crème* of the Russian army.

As for the Russian artillery, its fire was no more accurate than Russian bombing. Thus in late January 1995 I was staying with other correspondents at a house in south Grozny near which the Chechens had established a mortar, which went on firing day after day, apparently from exactly the same position. Once again, repeated Russian attempts to hit it failed. A veteran French war correspondent was utterly bewildered: 'But the Russians have equipment to track where mortars fire from, every modern army has it, that's why you have to keep moving mortars around. What are they playing at?' The old Russia hands present proposed a variety of explanations: that the equipment was defective (due to the lack of replacement spare parts, the greater part of Russian military equipment can only survive by cannibalizing other equipment); that it had all been broken and never repaired; that it had been illegally sold (possibly to Chechen 'businessmen'); that the only men who knew how to use it had left the army and had never been replaced; or finally, that it contained some alcoholic or potentially alcoholic element—in which case no further explanation of its fate was necessary.[11]

But as this last explanation suggests, even many of the military-technical failures come down in the end to a failure of morale, and not just to poor training (since performance did not improve as the war progressed). Russian pilots and gunners who really believed in the Chechen War would have made much more determined efforts to hit their targets, whatever the drawbacks of their equipment; and Russian pilots would have risked the weather and the ground fire and come in low enough to bomb accurately – like the Argentine pilots in the Falklands War, who faced much heavier odds and achieved much greater results.

The Urban Forest

The battles for Grozny also show the extreme difficulty for organised (or 'civilised') armies of operating in the urban terrain, especially without causing enormous damage and civilian casualties. The natural forests of the nineteenth century have been replaced by a modern 'forest' of a different kind, which is spreading all over the world and is likely to make up the chief battleground of the future: the city. The Chechen victory in this war came largely from the fact that just as in the wars of the eighteenth and nineteenth centuries they were masters of the art of forest warfare, in the 1990s they had become 'urban guerrillas' in the truest sense. Moreover, a forest once cut down is useless for defence and ambush; whereas a ruined city is just as good as – or even better than – an intact one for this purpose.

Thus while the Russian lack of maps of Grozny may seem utterly bizarre, it is worth remembering that in many of the vast, unplanned urban sprawls which are growing all over the 'developing world', maps either do not exist or are of very little help on the ground, because there are no street names or they are not marked. This is even more so, of course, after a city has been pounded into rubble.

For a guerrilla-type defensive force, this new urban forest therefore provides many of the same possibilities as the old natural one in terms of opportunities for sniping, mines, booby-traps and ambushes, and of negating the enemy's superiority in cavalry, armour, air-power and artillery. Urban fighting also shows up cruelly the shortcomings of an army used to relying on major units acting together in accordance with a rigid hierarchy of command, because even more than modern warfare in general, it inevitably tends to break units down to section and even subsectional level, throwing tremendous responsibility not just on junior officers and NCOs, but on the individual soldier. It is precisely lack of initiative on the part of junior officers, lack of good NCOs, and rigid reliance on orders from above that have been key weaknesses of the Russian army today, the Soviet army before it, and the Russian army of the nineteenth century.

Finally, even for properly trained, well-led and well-motivated troops, house-to-house fighting is a bloody, hole-and-corner, terrifying business, and exceptionally straining on the nerves. During my whole time in central Grozny in January 1995, whenever I was in the open I imagined the sights of a sniper's rifle zeroing in on my head from some high building half a mile away, and when on the Russian side, every fallen beam and piece of masonry seemed to conceal a booby-trap or unexploded shell, and every ruined building a Chechen ambush.

Parts of Western armies are of course trained for urban warfare in a way that in general the Soviet and then Russian armies before Chechnya were not – strangely, given that the Soviet experience included the three greatest urban battles to date: the defence of Stalingrad, the defence and recapture of Sebastopol, and the assault on Berlin, as well as numerous lesser ones from Rostov to Koenigsberg. The only branches of the old Soviet armed forces to be trained in this way were the troops surrounding West Berlin, and the marine infantry. The latter's special training seems to have been due partly to the fact that they were reformed in the early 1960s with the explicit intention of imitating similar Western units, and partly simply as a matter of regimental tradition, because the marines had played such a distinguished part in the battles of Sebastopol (their Black Sea base) and Stalingrad.

According to General Mikhail Surkov, Deputy Chairman of the Duma Defence Committee,

Street fighting tactics are absent from the manuals of the Russian armed forces. Exercises simulating fighting in urban conditions are conducted rarely, and our army has no relevant experience of the real thing. Such training is practised abroad, and it is often more characteristic of police methods than of army operations. First they use smoke screens and then tear gas to drive out the enemy. Special equipment is used to take buildings by assault, including assault ladders and hooks that are simply non-existent in our military units. Even elementary smoke bombs are in short supply with us. As for artillery, using it in urban conditions is useless. It is like using a cannon to kill sparrows. Tanks and infantry fighting vehicles are also helpless on the streets, something that was confirmed by the first assault on Grozny on New Year's Eve at the very beginning of the war. Vehicles are fired on at point-blank range from grenade launchers, view ports are covered with tarpaulins, vehicles are set on fire – all of these methods have already been honed by the rebels. The communication system in service with Russian units also causes problems in a city; as soon as you go the other side of a building, you can no longer hear anything.[12]

However, there is also no reason for Western complacency in this regard. According to American commentators in 1996, only 4,000 US troops were fully trained in this way. A certain tactical inflexibility, a failure (outside certain elite units) to operate efficiently at squad level, has in past wars frequently been a problem for the US military. Today, American fear of uncoordinated, independent infantry combat has been greatly increased by post-Vietnam fear of casualties – because in warfare of this kind, technological superiority is of limited importance and relatively heavy casualties are almost unavoidable. So, too, of course are heavy civilian casualties.

A US television documentary, showing footage of US marines training for house-to-house fighting at Quantico Base in Virginia, commented grimly, 'if this scenario were real, as many as half these marines would be killed'. In the words of Captain Robert Jones of the Marine Corps,

Most of the fighting is done from a distance of 15–20 feet. The defender has the advantage. This kind of fighting is inherently confusing, even for well-trained soldiers...in limited ways, high technology can improve their chances, but ... in this kind of war, you rely on smart soldiers as much as smart munitions, or even more.

Of course, the US army possesses equipment for urban fighting far superior to anything the Russians possessed. In particular, US soldiers (in limited numbers) have access to night-vision goggles and infra-red technology for fighting at night. However, the efficiency of these weapons will go on being heavily affected by the training – and the courage of the soldiers using them. Morale will therefore be of great importance.

From the point of view of the strategic and tactical lessons of Chechnya, it is also vital to note that the cities of today are enormous in relation to the size of most countries' armed forces – even America's. Grozny before the war had been built for about 400,000 people – not enormous, but large enough to dwarf the initial Russian forces sent into Chechnya. Grozny, like most southern Russian and Caucasian cities, is a sprawling place, with huge suburbs of one-storey houses, and enormous industrial areas, altogether covering more than a hundred square miles. Together with their own timidity and incompetence, this was to make it impossible for the Russian attackers to surround the city and cut off and destroy its defenders.

So while it is legitimate to draw some encouraging lessons from the Gulf War, Western soldiers should also be paying attention to the grim lessons of urban fighting in Mogadishu, and especially the disastrous engagement in which the superbly equipped, supposedly well-trained US Rangers were pinned down for three hours, and suffered eighteen dead and ninety wounded at the hands of an enemy equipped with nothing but kalashnikovs and 'technicals', that is, machine guns mounted on pick-up trucks; not a big debacle compared to that of the Russians in Grozny, but too many casualties for American public opinion and the US administration to bear. US withdrawal followed swiftly.

There are essentially three problems with reliance on long-range bombardment to win battles in heavily populated areas, whether Chechen or Vietnamese. The first, in the words of Colonel James Warner, US Army is that 'the basic reason why we don't use the air force for everything is that we don't want to kill and destroy everything.' Colonel Warner, like many practical soldiers, points out that by developing more effective anti-aircraft guns on the one hand, and mixing up their armed forces and civilians on the other, America's enemies may well be able to go on making both the military and political losses to the USA from its reliance on air bombardment extremely high.

The second, to adapt a saying of Marshal Suvorov, is that 'the bomb is a fool, but the soldier is a clever fellow.' Numerous studies and personal accounts of modern combat have pointed out the extraordinarily low number of military casualties proportionate to the amount of munitions expended, and that has cerainly been my experience in all the wars I've covered. In the case of small-arms fire, one reason is no doubt the long-remarked tendency of most men in battle not to shoot directly at other men, whether because they are too scared to shoot straight, or because of some deep human inhibition. Oddly enough, the advent of automatic rifles has in some ways made this even more true, because it gives the individual infantryman (especially a poorly trained one) the feeling that he can spray the area in front of him with bullets, and stop anything coming at him, without having to expose himself in order to aim. A classic picture from all recent 'militia' wars is of soldiers in a trench or behind a bank, holding their rifles above their heads with both hands and just blazing away in approximately the right direction.

But when it comes to heavy ordnance, the third reason is that the bomb or shell – or even guided missile for the moment at least – is blind to the individual infantryman; it can hit a designated tank or bunker, but it has no personal interest in pursuing men in the vicinity, and indeed cannot do so if they are behind sufficiently thick cover. The men, on the other hand, have a strong personal interest in avoiding the bomb, and fear makes them extremely quick-witted and agile in doing so.

Of course civilians in their homes are a different matter. Trying to win an urban battle by means of bombardment, even given highly sophisticated weapons, means immense damage and numerous civilian casualties on the other side – as with the Russian bombardment of Grozny. The psychological preparation and mood (terror, confusion and extreme physical aggression) and even the combat training of troops engaged in the terrifying business of house-to-house fighting also virtually preclude restraint in the use of force.

Grozny showed, too, that recent technological developments have also given defenders a very significant advantage in the armour-piercing rocket-propelled grenade (RPG) – with a bit of guts behind it, of course. In the hands of brave fighters, this weapon has proved the queen of battles in Chechnya's towns and cities, as well as in mountain ambushes. The classical Chechen three-person squad in this war was composed of a grenadier to knock out the Russian tank or armoured personnel carrier, together with a sniper and a fighter with a light machine-gun, to protect the grenadier and to keep the infantry pinned down in their vehicles.

The RPG, it must be noted, is a great equaliser. Very cheap compared to the tanks it is intended to destroy, it requires only a single operator, and from that man or woman it demands not long training but a good eye and an iron nerve – or the tremendous motivation which gives even the timid person courage, enough to lie still while the tanks pass by or even over the fighter and then to hit them from behind. Given these qualities, and in the right circumstances, above all urban ones, a fighter with an RPG can neutralise many of the advantages of higher technology, and inflict very heavy casualties – more than a sophisticated enemy may be able to bear. The RPG could be called the pike or longbow of our time, the simple weapon which in the right hands can bring the pride of military aristocracies to the dust.[13]

The Chechen Fighters

Idris Dokayev, leader of a small group of Chechen volunteers in the town of Alkhan Yurt, south of Grozny, explained to me in January 1995 how the Chechen forces which used weapons like these were raised. We were looking through the night towards the Russian positions to the north, an immense sea of dark blue spangled with tracers. Every now and then, a beautiful cluster of Russian parachute flares would fall like a golden chandelier spread out across the sky, and his face and those of his men stood out in sharp relief:

You could say that the whole population here is involved in the defence. Every street has provided several groups of four or five volunteers, and they relieve each other on guard duty at the edge of town, at two-hourly intervals, so that someone is on watch the whole time. We worked out among ourselves the times for the reliefs. If they see something suspicious, they fire three shots, and all the armed men in the town will take up position. Of course, there aren't so many, because a lot have gone to defend Grozny, but we could still put up a fight. Behind us, near the crossroads, there is a local staff, made up of men with Soviet military experience. They coordinate what we are doing with the groups in neighbouring villages, and pass on intelligence in both directions. There are no formal commanders here. We just work together... As you see, we are not an army. We are just ordinary people defending our homes. What is better, to live a slave all your life or to die like a hero? Dudayev has said that you can destroy the whole of Chechnya, level the Caucasus, but the desire for freedom will begin again... But I don't want to give the impression that we are fighting for Dudayev. It has gone far beyond Dudayev. We are fighting to defend our homes from barbarians. Russia has never known God. She has always had evil men for a government.

I asked him how a small town could turn out so many armed men. He pointed to a group of fifteen-year-old boys, equipped with pistols and grenades:

You may think those are kids, but they are not. They are strong men. They could defeat any soldiers in the world. Even at fifteen, a boy here is expected to know how to handle weapons. In most families, at that age the father will give his son a pistol, and will teach him how to use it and how to look after it.

Compared to what I have seen of the Afghan Mujahidin, the Georgians, and various other forces, the care and professionalism with which the Chechens handled their weapons was indeed highly impressive (partly no doubt because of Soviet military training). Above all, they didn't wave them around, they didn't fire them in the air for fun, and they kept their safety catches on when not in action. In the words of David Brauchli, a distinguished war photographer now with AP, just arrived in Grozny from Bosnia in January 1995, 'I'm really impressed by the Chechen fighters. They've got so many guns, but you don't see them fooling around with them, showing off and shooting each other by accident. They're really serious soldiers.'

The day before, in Grozny, another Chechen volunteer, Ramzan Selmirzayev, told me that

There are 20 of us here in my group from Vedeno, all relatives or friends. Every group chooses its own commander, or elder. We chose a man who was a sergeant in the Soviet army, because he obviously knows more about what to do. But I wouldn't say he is our commander, exactly. He doesn't order us to fight, he doesn't need to. We all know why we are fighting, and for what.

Our group decides for itself where to fight. We came to Grozny because it is our capital, because this is where we have to fight the Russians, and beat them, let's hope... But of course we listen to the chief commanders. If they said we were desperately needed in Argun, we would go there. On the whole, though, we work things out with the other groups in our area, and we don't have much contact with the high command... This isn't an army. It is the whole Chechen people which is fighting.

This picture was drawn at the very beginning of the war; later, Maskhadov was able to create a more effective central command. None the less, as a picture of how the Chechen forces came into being, it seemed to me entirely accurate.[14]

Russia Loses the Propaganda War

One feature of the Russian military's disorganisation which affected me closely and beneficially was their press policy, or rather lack of it. Throughout the bloody fighting of the first months of the war, it was possible to find a quiet sector of the 'front' and simply drive down main roads, through Russian checkpoints and into Chechen-controlled territory. The soldiers obviously had no orders whatsoever concerning journalists. In the words of a colleague, it was 'the great drive-in war'.

Thereafter, things got more difficult; none the less, throughout the war it was almost always possible to find a sympathetic, or simply relaxed Russian post which would wave you through – in part, once again, because different Russian units appeared to be operating according to completely different sets of instructions. (This bore out something which I and every other war correspondent of my acquaintance has experienced again and again – that unless they have received strict orders to the contrary, or are especially worried about spies and infiltrators, front-line troops tend to be friendly and helpful to visitors.)[15]

Nor was there any serious attempt at organising guided press trips so as to slant the coverage in a favourable direction, except as far as military or government journals like *Krasnaya Zvezda* or *Rossiiskaya Gazeta* were concerned. Independent or Western journalists who dutifully turned up at the official press centre at the military base in Mozdok without a special letter were turned away without even an interview, mainly, it would seem, through sheer bureaucratic rigidity.

This is one of the Russian failures which seems quite inexplicable: after all, Defence Minister Pavel Grachev had already suffered very badly from Russia's free media and their accusations of corruption against him; one would have thought that a desire to keep them from reporting on Chechnya would have come naturally to him. Yet the fact seems to be that, despite ferociously critical and deeply embarrassing coverage by NTV (Russian independent television) and other media, no one in the Russian military even gave this question a thought, or if they did, had the authority to draw up a general policy.

The then head of the FSK (domestic intelligence), and one of the men most responsible for the road to war, Sergei Stepashin, declared in March 1992 that

> Yes, the Russian administration has lost the information war. How brilliantly the Chechen Minister of Information Mauvladi Udugov works, how artfully and easily he releases to the press any distortion, lie, juggling of the facts.... But we push away the journalists; we are not releasing anything anywhere, we are not giving anything! And I myself for a long while did not want to express myself.[16]

When it comes to lies, this is of course the pot calling the kettle black. And it is also striking that far from being 'brilliant', Udugov (later First Deputy Premier under Maskhadov), though a brave and dedicated Chechen nationalist, had a name in the Western press, not only for lies, but for incompetence, unhelpfulness and personal rudeness – and even so, by Stepashin's own admission, he ran rings round his Russian equivalents!

Soon after the war itself began, the Russian official in charge of media coverage, Sergei Gryzunov (informally dubbed 'Minister of the Press'), was removed from his post and sent to head the military information centre at the base in Mozdok. He was replaced by Valentin Sergeyev, head of the cabinet press service. Neither of them, it must be noted, had any previous experience of working with the military, nor is there any evidence of military co-ordination with the government press officials before the actual invasion. For the first few months of the war, the only apparent Russian government and military media and information policy on Chechnya was to tell lies; not in itself an unusual policy on the part of high commands, but rendered absurd – until government pressure on media proprietors in Moscow brought most of them to heel – by the failure to prevent Russian journalists from getting to the front.

The contrast between the optimistic tone of official pronouncements and the real experience of Russian soldiers in Chechnya (reminiscent of the US in Vietnam, but much worse) added to the demoralisation and anger of the troops. Throughout the war, Russian soldiers I spoke with privately said that they believed that their side's losses were between three and five times higher than the official figures being issued. This may not have been true – exaggeration did occur, but not to this degree – but the fact that they believed it was an indication of their morale and their trust in their leaders, and the complete failure of the Russian military to inspire its men to fight.

Certainly the network of former Communist political officers ('zampolits', formerly 'politruks') redeployed after 1991 as 'personnel officers' did not succeed in educating the soldiers in the reasons and justification for the intervention in Chechnya. This is hardly surprising. A soldier who sees a former Communist propagandist now defending Yeltsin is not going to be very impressed whatever he says. Similarly, the ineffectiveness of internal military propaganda is yet another result of the excess of propaganda under Soviet rule, and the gap between rhetoric and reality which became so apparent to the troops in Afghanistan.

Spring 1995

The capture of the ruins of the presidential headquarters on 19 January changed little. The Chechens went on fighting for the rest of the city, though this did not stop the Russian National Security Council from declaring on 25 January that 'the military phase of the operation in Chechnya is over,' and that the task now was to restore order and 'normality' and prepare for 'free elections'. This was only one in a long line of such statements, but it was not without result. By way of giving it substance, the forces in Chechnya were removed from the command of the Defence Ministry and placed under that of the Interior Ministry, with General Anatoly Kulikov, formerly in charge of that ministry's troops as commander in Chechnya and Deputy Interior Minister. The resulting divisions and tensions in the command were to have serious results, above all in August 1996.

The career of General Kulikov also marked another step in the separation of promotion from achievement in the Russian forces and administration: his extremely unimpressive record and that of his troops in Chechnya, and the evidence that as the commander of internal forces before 1995 he had utterly failed to prepare them for serious military operations, did not prevent him from being made Interior Minister in July 1995, when the discredited General Viktor Yerin was finally forced to resign.

The unpreparedness of the internal forces for serious warfare was admitted in February 1995 by two of their commanders, General Stanislav Kavun and General Vladimir Semenov, both of whom said that their troops were not in a position to take part in major fighting and needed army support – a striking admission from Interior Ministry officers, given the rivalry between the two services.[17]

Shortly after the January declaration of returning normality, Nikolai Yegorov was replaced as chief of Russian policy in Chechnya by Nikolai Semenov, before 1991 the First Secretary of the Grozny Communist Party. As head of the 'federal organs of power' in Chechnya, Semenov was placed over the Chechen Provisional Council, with Avturkhanov, Salambek Khadjiev (former Soviet Oil Minister) and Gantemirov (now restored as Mayor of Grozny) as his deputies. Khadjiev was to become Prime Minister of the Russian-backed 'provisional government' until his replacement by Doku Zavgayev in November.

With Grozny more or less secured, the Russian forces moved east and south, but with extreme slowness. There were none of the rapid armoured thrusts that one would have expected both from the Soviet military tradition and from the flat and rolling nature of the country (so suitable for armoured warfare is Chechnya between Grozny and the foothills that the Soviet army had a tank training school near the town of Shali). At this stage, according to Kulikov, the Russians had some 55,000 army and internal troops in Chechnya, outnumbering the Chechen fighters under arms at any one time by almost ten to one (though the reserve of potential fighters was of course very much larger).

Argun, a small town just to the east of Grozny, did not fall to the Russians until 23 March, after a heroic three-month long resistance which left much of the town in ruins. Mid-April saw the start of an even more epic resistance, when the Russians attacked the small town of Bamut in the foothills of eastern Chechnya. They were not to capture it for more than a year, and even then the Chechens only retreated to the hills above the town. (It is near Bamut that in the previous month the well-known American aid-worker, Fred Cuny, is believed to have been killed together with his Russian companions, in circumstances that remain very obscure.) On 19 April, Kulikov made the first of literally dozens of bogus Russian claims that Bamut had fallen.

At the end of March, the Russians had also forced the Chechen forces to withdraw from Shali and Gudermes. The Chechen fighters withdrew towards the foothills, and in a number of towns and villages, elders and notables began to make local agreements with the Russians, recognising the Khadjiev government, handing over arms and promising to expel Chechen fighters from the area. Of course, very often the fighters refused to go, and the resulting Russian impression of Chechen bad faith was often to lead to the bombardment of villages.

An extreme case of what could happen where such agreements were not reached, or where the Russians believed the Chechens had broken their word, was shown in the town of Samashki in western Chechnya on 6–8 April. Chechen fighters in the area had been a major thorn in the Russians' side since the beginning of the war. After the Chechens failed to observe what the Russians claimed was a deal to expel the fighters and hand over arms, Russian forces stormed the town and several dozen local civilians were killed, many of them, according to eye-witnesses, in cold blood. (Local residents claimed 300 dead, Kovalev 211.)

On 17 April, after fairly heavy diplomatic pressure from Western Europe and the USA (heavy that is by the standards of the pressure that the West applies to its friends, like Turkey or Indonesia, not of course by any objective standard), a permanent mission of the Organisation for Security and Co-operation in Europe (OSCE) was allowed by the Russians to begin work in Grozny, under the Hungarian diplomat Sandor Meszaros.[18] Over the next fifteen months, the work of the OSCE was to become very controversial, with its critics alleging that it was not doing enough to raise the issue of atrocities with the Russians, and its defenders saying that its first duty was to try to promote negotiations and a peace settlement.[19]

The arrival of the OSCE coincided with the first Russian peace initiative (or so at least it was presented) since the start of the war, with Chernomyrdin offering a ceasefire without preconditions, and Yeltsin on 26 April ordering a moratorium on further offensive actions by Russian forces until 12 May. Meanwhile, the Russians were making overtures to Maskhadov and other Chechen commanders in an effort to get them to make a separate peace. This period also saw public differences emerging between different Russian leaders, with Grachev declaring that he would not even talk to Maskhadov unless the Chechens first capitulated and handed over their weapons.

These overtures were in any case ignored by the Chechens, whose forces penetrated back into Grozny in small groups and carried out attacks on Russian positions. In an apparent effort to keep open lines of communication to Dudayev, Stepashin declared that this was the work not of the Dudayev government but of Shamil Basayev, and that he had 'escaped from Dudayev's control'. This was in my view a complete fiction, but it was one that was to be valuable on several occasions during the war as a method whereby Russia could denounce the 'terrorist' Basayev while still talking to either Maskhadov or Dudayev. In fact, while differences between these men did exist, they all three worked closely together until the Russians were defeated (or in the case of Dudayev, until his death). Strikingly, although Basayev ran against Maskhadov in the presidential elections of January 1997, after the war, as long as the war lasted he cooperated with him and obeyed his orders – or that was certainly my impression on the occasions I saw them together. In any case, as the OSCE chief in Grozny commented, both sides broke Yeltsin's moratorium repeatedly.

Towards the end of May, the Russians began to put heavy pressure on the Chechen positions in the foothills of the Caucasus, particularly around the villages of Chiri Yurt and Serzhen Yurt. These lie respectively at the mouths of the narrow valleys of the rivers Argun and Khulkhulau, which wind up to the mountain towns of Shatoy and Vedeno. The latter town was one of Shamil's last strongholds during the nineteenth-century war with Russia, and both valleys were the scenes of heavy fighting at that time. The Russians also began to send troops into Chechnya across the high mountain passes from Daghestan, threatening Vedeno from behind.

By May 1995, Shatoy and Vedeno were the last two major Chechen population centres to be wholly in the hands of the separatist forces. When I visited Serzhen Yurt and Vedeno (together with Sebastian Smith of AFP) in that month, we saw considerable evidence that Chechen fortunes were at a low ebb, probably their lowest ebb of the entire war. Ammunition was very short, many of the men were extremely tired and in some cases morale had begun to crack. Basayev admitted later that the Chechens had been close to defeat, and said that as a result he had had unwillingly to adopt the tactic of raids into Russia and the taking of civilian hostages.

The deterioration of the Chechen fighting capacity helps explain why in early June the Russians were able to launch their only really successful operation of the war, which on 4 June captured the town of Vedeno. In the meantime, the Russians had in effect walked out of the OSCE-sponsored peace talks which had begun on 25 May – and Dudayev had also declared that the Russian offensive made it pointless for the talks to continue. He vowed to fight on, but it was beginning to seem as if the Russian strategy of wearing the Chechens down by numbers and firepower was working. On 13 June, the Russians captured Shatoy, and this was acknowledged by the Dudayev government.

The next day, however, came an incident of critical importance in the war, and one which gives Shamil Basayev the right to be regarded as one of the great contemporary Chechen heroes. An armed force under his command, after bluffing or bribing their way through numerous Russian checkpoints, was finally stopped by police just beyond the town Buddenovsk, in Stavropol Region some forty miles from the Chechen border. They thereupon turned back and attacked the town. After storming the police station and briefly holding the town hall, they rounded up several hundred hostages and confined them in the hospital, threatening to kill them if the Russian army did not withdraw from Chechnya. He did in fact reportedly execute several wounded Russian soldiers from the hospital, and some ninety-one people were killed in the Chechen attack, including policemen and local civilians.[20] Basayev was accompanied by Abu Movsayev, a close Dudayev associate and chief of his secret service, the DGB, which suggests strongly that Dudayev knew all about the plan.

Basayev said later that his plan had been to penetrate far deeper into Russia – even if possible to Moscow – but that after spending 25,000 dollars along the way, including around 9,000 dollars in bribes to Russian checkpoints not to examine his lorries, he ran out of money.[21] Dudayev disclaimed responsibility for the raid, and Maskhadov refused to comment on the subject.

On 17 June, Russian special forces made two unsuccessful attempts to storm the hospital, suffering losses and killing a number of hostages and Chechen fighters. An added hazard during the crisis were groups of hysterical and drunken 'Cossacks' who set up checkpoints around the town and harassed local Chechens and Western journalists. A Russian journalist (married to a German correspondent), Tatyana Alyakina, was killed by what seems to have been an accidental or panicky shot by a soldier at a checkpoint.

With Yeltsin absent at the G7 summit in Halifax – typically, having left after the crisis began – Chernomyrdin opened negotiations with Basayev and negotiated an agreement involving an immediate ceasefire by Russian troops, the reopening of negotiations, and transport and a guarantee of safe passage for Basayev and his men to return to separatist-held areas of Chechnya. On the 19th, accompanied by hostages and some courageous volunteers from the Russian media and the Duma, they returned to Chechnya and a hero's welcome.

Although obviously an act of terrorism by the usual definition of that term,

Basayev's was also an act of enormous daring, and may well have saved his cause. The peace negotiations which resulted, and the truce which accompanied them, gave the hard-pressed Chechen forces a critical breathing space of several months before full-scale fighting began again, and during that time they filtered back into most parts of Chechnya and in effect retook them without a fight from under the Russians' noses.

The reason for the Yeltsin administration agreeing to the talks was, I believe, that Budennovsk had shown the very high political price it might have to pay for continuing the fighting, and the Chechens' capacity to inflict severe political humiliation. For while the reaction of the Russian public was inevitably very hostile to Basayev and the Chechens, opinion polls also showed great anger with the incompetence of the Russian authorities and security forces – with television pictures of Yeltsin at Halifax, smiling and toasting world leaders – and the brutality and unconcern for the hostages displayed by the special forces in their attempt to storm the hospital. Both before this date and more recently, the Yeltsin regime has of course shown contempt for Russian public opinion – but Budennovsk happened six months before the date set for parliamentary elections in December 1995, and much more importantly, a year before the presidential ones of June 1996.

In this context, Lee Hockstader, a correspondent for the *Washington Post*, seems to have been mistaken when he commented during the later Pervomaiskoye hostage crisis that an attack was likely because 'over the centuries, Russians have come to expect strength rather than concern for human life from their leaders.'[22] The rise in Chernomyrdin's popularity, and later in Lebed's, shows that the opposite is true of many Russians today.

As for the feeling within the armed forces, a normally cautious columnist for the military paper, *Krasnaya Zvezda*, declared that:

> One has to admit that in spite of all the talk about 'enhancing' and 'strengthening' the security of citizens, the state has proved to be absolutely unprepared to evaluate and deal with such threats. In what other country but Russia could a group of not two or five, but two hundred thugs armed with heavy machine-guns travel for a distance of more than a hundred kilometres? Does this mean that truckloads of killers could appear in Red Square? This whole story testifies to the paralysis that has gripped our security agencies.[23]

Izvestia wrote that Budennovsk proved that 'Russians live in a weak state today,' and accused the government of brutality and incompetence.[24]

Chernomyrdin's popularity rating went up as a result of his negotiations with Basayev, and Yeltsin's dropped to new lows. As a sop to the opposition and public feeling, the Interior Minister, General Yerin, and the FSK chief, Sergei Stepashin, were both removed by Yeltsin. Grachev stayed on for another year, thanks to his loyalty to Yeltsin; despite his share of responsibility for the Chechen debacle, he was in the end removed only as part of the deal whereby Lebed gave his support to Yeltsin in the second round of the presidential elections. Yerin was replaced by Kulikov, who as already noted was equally mired in the Chechen debacle. As throughout the whole Chechen War – and indeed throughout the history of Russia under Yeltsin – no one was brought to real responsibility for what had happened.

Russian Strategy in Chechnya

To reflect on the course of the battle on the ground: once the Russian army was committed, and the great bulk of the Chechen people lined up on the other side, then given the determination of the Chechens to fight to the end, the Russians' only military option if they wanted victory was to pin down the Chechen forces in decisive battle, and destroy them. The Chechens did not have to go so far – they only had to destroy the Russians' will to fight, a task in which, like the Vietcong and the FLN, they eventually succeeded.

The Chechen War therefore raises a fundamental question of military strategy and philosophy. In the wake of the immense European military hecatombs of this century, and of the still greater and indeed final threat of destruction raised by the Cold War and the nuclear arms race, there has been among many military thinkers a deliberate turning away from the doctrines of Carl von Clausewitz (derived in turn from the practice of Napoleon), which had dominated Western military thought and practice in the nineteenth century and the first seven decades of the twentieth century. This change in attitude has also been greatly motivated by the Vietnam War, in which military aims generated by the war itself came to predominate wholly over the original political goals for which it was launched, and military or narrowly strategic arguments became divorced from any serious political analysis either of true American interests or even of the increasingly obvious international strategic reality.[25]

Clausewitz preached the 'true war' (as opposed to the messy inconclusiveness of 'real war'), founded on as complete as possible a mobilisation of national reserves, the deliberate seeking of decisive battle, and the pursuit of the enemy to its complete destruction. In his view, war is the 'continuation of politics with the addition of other means' and he makes allowance for limited forms of conflict, but in general, the victor would be the side which followed the logic of war to its most thorough and ruthless extent. The Chechen War tends to support this view.

In his brilliant work *A History of Warfare*, the British military historian, John Keegan, argues eloquently that in an era of weapons of mass destruction this 'logic' is madness and that there is indeed nothing especially natural or traditional about it. He calls for a return to a much more ancient pattern of warfare, as practised by many 'primitive' peoples: often evasive and indirect, concerned to avoid major direct clashes and the heavy casualties they entail, and wholly or partly influenced by ritual and tradition in its limits on the goals sought, the forces employed and the amount of violence used. (I read this magisterial, deeply felt and deeply moving work while shuttling between the Russian, the Chechen separatist and the Chechen collaborationist sides in December 1995 – a setting which only confirmed for me Dr Keegan's extraordinary grasp of the many different faces and natures of war.)[26]

Western strategists are indeed turning away from the 200-year-old Western tradition of seeking direct and decisive battle, and looking instead at other ways of putting pressure on the enemy, calibrated to match the political ends sought. They are inspired by the politic desire both to avoid suffering heavy casualties themselves and to avoid inflicting them on enemy civilians, thereby stirring up international indignation. Both desires were very much in evidence during the Gulf War. In the case of Chechnya, it would obviously have been very much better for everyone if the Russian government in the autumn of 1994 had stuck with an indirect, semi-covert strategy for toppling Dudayev, and had avoided the direct clash of arms in decisive battle.

But from the point of view of a the standard antitheses of Western/Asiatic, Army/guerrilla, direct battle/evasion, something rather odd, but very easily explainable, happened in Chechnya. After the initial bloody storm of Grozny, the 'modern' Russian army, with its immense superiority in all the weapons needed for a decisive, 'Clausewitzian' battle, usually tried to avoid such battles and proceeded by indirect, evasive means. Above all, the Russians tried to put direct or indirect pressure on local populations to drive out the separatist forces, to make separate truces, and if possible to express formal loyalty to the Russian-installed client 'government' in Grozny.

Bombardment was the principal means of pressure, but generally it was relatively small-scale and selective, except in cases where a decision had been made to punish the local population for a separatist success, as with the destruction of the town of Samashki in November 1995, and that of Novogroznensky in January 1996. On the whole, however, the Russians avoided both direct attacks and massive bombardments intended completely to destroy the town in question. Bombardments were both indiscriminate and discriminate: indiscriminate in that they were intended to kill and terrorise the civilian population, but discriminate in that they were sporadic and limited – most of them were not at all like either the bombardment of December 1994–February 1995 which destroyed central Grozny, the Soviet bombardment of Mujahidin-controlled areas of Afghanistan or the relentless pounding of civilian targets by Western bombers in the Second World War or Korea.

Thus from February to April 1995 the Russians were engaged in a prolonged campaign to drive the separatist forces out of the southern town of Shali, where they had made their headquarters after the fall of central Grozny. To my astonishment however, on visiting Shali again in May 1995, after its 'fall', I found not merely that the town was not much damaged, but that the Russians forces had not garrisoned it and did not control it. Instead they had stationed themselves on the outskirts, and limited themselves to the occasional armoured patrol (but only once or twice a day).

The result was that Sebastian Smith and I were driven around the centre of

a supposedly 'Russian-occupied' town with the local rebel deputy commander, Said Hassan Takayev (though it is true that he had taken the precaution
of shaving off his beard, and when driving past certain houses covered the side
of his face with one hand as if he had toothache). In his words:

> The Russians don't come on foot into Shali. For that matter, they don't
> operate on foot at all. They didn't conquer Shali in any real sense and
> they don't rule it. What they did was to use their armour to conquer the
> land around Shali, and force us to withdraw, but they didn't conquer the
> people. We can come back in whenever we like. We are still in control
> here, because the people support us...
>
> For that matter, if it weren't for the Russian aviation, I could come
> down from the hills, drive the Russians out, and retake the whole area in
> one day. But there's no point. We'd lose a lot of men, and we couldn't
> hold it – their fire is too heavy. But one day, you'll see, we'll do just that.[27]

During the last days of May 1995, Sebastian and I were present in the small
Chechen town of Vedeno, Shamil's old headquarters in the eastern foothills
of the Chechen Caucasus. On the first day we were there, the town was subjected to a series of Russian air strikes, driving us into the cellar of the local
Chechen town commandant's headquarters (during the bombardments that
followed over the next week, this house suffered a direct hit). Over the course
of the previous few weeks, several dozen civilians had been killed and
wounded in Vedeno, though the exact figures were hard to establish.

The raids, however, were by two aircraft at a time, and at very irregular
intervals. During my time in the cellar, and watching subsequent strikes on
Vedeno from the relative safety of nearby hills, I spent part of my time wondering nervously whether the Russians would not send over a squadron or two
of heavy bombers, and simply wipe the whole place off the map. It would have
been very easy to do this, and since Vedeno at that stage was the only major
population centre still firmly in Chechen rebel hands, they could have been
sure of killing many Chechen fighters, and very probably several Chechen
leaders – and as a matter of fact, on the afternoon of the raid Sebastian and I
interviewed both Aslan Maskhadov and Shamil Basayev in a building situated
within the old fort, the most obvious target imaginable.

A few weeks earlier, Russian aircraft, presumably following intelligence
information, had struck a house belonging to Shamil Basayev's family in
Vedeno, killing his sister and ten other members of his family. Of course, during the disintegration of the Soviet Union, Moscow lost much of its conventional heavy bomber forces to Ukraine, but as of 1995 it was still recorded by
Western sources as having 220 Tupolev-22 and Tupolev-26 high altitude
bombers (by 1996, in a striking evidence of decline, this was down to 130) –
and even if most were incapable of flying, they could surely have scraped
together enough to destroy one village.[28]

The principal reason for the Russian reliance on 'evasive' tactics in ground combat was of course the demoralisation of their soldiers and the desire to avoid casualties either in assaults or from ambushes. But when it comes to frontal assaults and massive bombardment, another motive appears to have been that the Russian government genuinely did believe that, with time, it could use a mixture of the so-called 'sword' and the 'samovar' strategies to terrorise, bribe or even persuade a majority of Chechens into 'pacification' and formal acceptance of the Russian-backed government.[29]

During this period, the Russian forces claimed to have signed local truces with more than two-thirds of Chechen settlements, which promised to expel fighters and respect the authority of the Zavgayev government. This was not propaganda – such deals really were an essential part of the Russian strategy, and were achieved in many places, as I discovered during several visits to Chechnya during the war.

Thus on 27 May 1995, I sat with a group of local volunteers outside the village of Mairtup on the edge of the Caucasus foothills. We were watching Russian helicopters and aircraft bombarding the village of Bachi Yurt, four miles away, but Mairtup had made a truce with the Russians, and so these men were no longer involved in the fighting – for the moment. A tough-looking young man called Issa, who said he had fought the Russians earlier in the year, told me that

> We fully support the government of Dudayev, but we have to pay public respect to the government of Khadjiev, though he is a Russian puppet, to put it printably... But for the moment, we have to think of the interests of our village first. We haven't the means to go on fighting Russia. So we made an agreement with the local Russian forces that if we don't attack them, they won't bombard the village. Our women and old people insisted on this, to spare them what has happened in other villages ... But of course, one day we will take up arms again. Russia is in her death agony.

Not all were so spirited. One of his comrades broke in, 'It doesn't look to me as if Russia is going to die so quickly.' Another, an older, bearded man called Daud, who seemed to disagree, added that 'We had to give the Russians thirty automatic rifles, but we know that they will come back and ask for more, which we don't have. Then they will raid us and arrest people, without our being able to do anything about it. But whatever happens, they will not break our spirit.'

As these words indicate, such deals rarely held for long. The situation was complicated from the Russian point of view by the fact that in any given town, there were almost always some elements who did indeed want to make a deal with the Russians – but even if these elements were dominant, that very often did not stop the rebels from also operating quite freely in the area, and relying on local family links for protection. Sometimes, indeed, the rebels seem to have been quite happy that negotiations should proceed, precisely because it did reduce the risk of bombardment and civilian casualties, while doing the resistance no real harm.

A case in point is the mountain town of Shatoy, in the next valley along from Vedeno. As I discovered during visits in December 1994 and January 1995, there was genuine anti-Dudayev sentiment there, as well as a general scepticism about armed resistance dating back perhaps to trouble between local people and Shamil. Negotiations between the Russians and local notables took place throughout the war, and the Russian high command announced on several occasions that it had made peace. This did not stop rebel forces from continuously operating in the area.

None the less, with the image of a gradual process of 'rallyings' in mind, the Russian high command may have been genuinely anxious to avoid driving the whole population into permanent opposition by massive and indiscriminate killings. Restraint was also continuously being urged on them by their own collaborationist Chechens, (the 'pro-Russian' elements I talked to privately were perfectly well aware of how the Russian bombardments and atrocities in the first months of the war had weakened their own position, and of how every successive civilian death was undermining it still further).[30] This factor may also have been responsible for the fact that, unlike the British in the Boer War, the French in Algeria or the Americans in Vietnam, the Russians never adopted the tactic of herding the populations of selected areas into 'protected settlements' to leave the rest of the countryside as a free-fire zone in which anything moving could be killed.[31]

If the Russian army had been capable of fighting better, the strategy of forcing the Chechens to compromise might even have worked, at least for a time (though 'terrorist' attacks would of course have continued). Anyway, whatever the reason, the result was that it was the 'modern' European army which pursued 'Asiatic', evasive methods – and lost – while the Asian guerrilla army repeatedly and successfully sought out occasions for direct and if possible decisive 'Clausewitzian' battle – and conquered.

Maltreatment of Prisoners and the Civilian Population

Atrocities by Russian troops in Chechnya took three forms, familiar enough from both the Algerian and the Vietnam wars. The first was the bombardment of civilian targets, either in the course of military operations (as in Grozny, Gudermes and elsewhere), or to 'punish' villages which supported the separatist fighters, as in Novogroznensky, where around 40 per cent of houses were destroyed. Such bombardments have not in fact traditionally been regarded by Western armies as atrocities. All have used them on occasions, and doubtless will do so again if it ever becomes necessary.

However, as already noted, on one occasion at least in Chechnya, at Samashki, there was also what seems to have been an officially sanctioned near-massacre of several dozen civilians.³² When I asked Salambek Khadjiev, the head of the Russian puppet government, about such incidents in May 1995, he replied that when he asked the Russian generals, 'Sometimes they promise to investigate, but more often they deny anything happened, or just say "war is war."'

Cases of officers presiding over the brutalisation of civilians at checkpoints, or during house searches, were innumerable, and in the first weeks of the war in Grozny, most officers seem either to have participated in beating, vandalism and looting, or at least to have made no effort to restrain their men. The appearance of houses and flats which had been 'searched' by the Russians, and my own experiences at their hands, have been described in my personal memoir. It must be said, however, that from March 1995 on (to judge by what I heard when I returned to Grozny in May), some attempts were made to check this and establish order among the troops with the help of the military police.

I heard a few Chechen allegations of rape by Russian soldiers, but given the nature of Chechen culture, it was very difficult to find out any details, let alone speak to victims, and so I cannot verify any of these accounts. In principle, however, given the nature of the war, and the obvious indiscipline of the Russian soldiers (once again, especially in the first weeks in Grozny), the stories seemed perfectly plausible. Once at least, the crew of an armoured personnel carrier who had raped members of a Chechen family were arrested by their own side, though my informants could not tell me if they had actually been punished, or quietly released again.

I only once heard directly of a Bosnian-style atrocity of this kind, in which Russian officers allegedly ordered the gang-rape and murder of two women captured together with Chechen fighters – but the witness on this occasion was a Russian prisoner with his Chechen captors standing over him, so it might be wrong to attach too much credence to it. There is no sign that rape was used as a deliberately ordered weapon in an effort to break the will of the Chechen people. It is striking that in sharp contrast to reports on most wars of this kind, none of the three reports on human rights abuses in Chechnya that I have read mentions either rape in general or any specific case.

The exact nature and scale of torture and murder of Chechen prisoners by Russian forces is difficult to assess, since both foreign organisations and Russian ones had great difficulty in working. It seems certain that a good many people arrested were later secretly murdered by their captors, and they very likely included many of those who had been most severely tortured. Again and again in Chechnya I heard of young men who had simply disappeared (sometimes while travelling to find other members of their familes who had vanished), months after the heaviest fighting had died down, and the Chechens' assumption was that they had been arrested by the Russians and either beaten to death or shot.

In the estimate of the OSCE mission to Grozny, the number of men detained from the beginning of the war to March 1996 totalled some 2,000, with 500–1,000 still in custody at the latter date. (The separatist side at the same time was estimated by the OSCE to hold 200-400 Russian military and civilian prisoners.) At that time, a list of Chechens who had disappeared contained 1,266 names; by the same period, 416 previously unidentified bodies had been returned to relatives, and 540 remained unidentified.[33] Curiously, there are no recorded cases that I know of women being detained, and female members of Dudayev's family lived peaceably in Grozny throughout the war.

Of the missing, it is assumed that some were killed accidentally during fighting or by Russian soldiers shooting at transport, either at checkpoints or from the air (I heard innumerable examples of this, and some of them are listed in a Médecins sans Frontières report of April 1996); however, it is assumed that many others – several hundred at least – were arrested and subsequently executed by their Russian captors. (Although this is a considerable figure, it should be compared, for instance, with the figure of some 3,000 Algerians illicitly executed by the French forces in the city and district of Algiers in 1955–7, with a population comparable to the Chechen population of Chechnya of 1 million and in a time frame comparable to the Chechen War).

For example, in the town of Shali in May 1995, I was told of a local man named Ruslan Nanakhayev (aged twenty-eight), who in February had gone with two other men in a car to buy food. One of them had a document with Dudayev's name on it. They were arrested at a checkpoint and presumably taken to a 'filtration point'. Several weeks later his body was found by the side of a road, with many broken bones. As of May, there was no word of the others. Ruslan Nanakhayev's elder brother, Aslan, went to look for him and also disappeared; he was found in a mass grave in Grozny, with his skull beaten in. I also heard of another case in Shali where three Chechens in a car had disappeared and were presumed to have been arrested.

To judge by anecdotal evidence, the great majority of Chechens arrested were physically maltreated to a greater or lesser degree, and this also took place regularly during Russian raids for weapons and fighters, and at Russian checkpoints. In the words of a report by a Chechen human rights group (attested as reliable by Western diplomats in Grozny):

> Searches are accompanied by the beating of those being searched. Subsequent to detention, evidence of criminal activity is falsified; weapons and narcotics are planted on those being searched. Up to the start of the SOC's work [the Russian Special Observers' Commission], unlawfully detained persons were released after action by the Main Department (General Headquarters) of the Russian Interior Ministry, but now it is practically impossible to achieve this.[34]

The Médecins sans Frontières (MSF) report contains the following passage:

> As the Russian offensive pushes south-west and south-east, village after village is encircled by the troops. Interviews with refugees from different villages all report the same sequence of incidents:

- A peace ultimatum is issued by the troops to the villagers to 'give up the fighters and weapons'.
- Even if the villagers sign a local peace agreement, it is rarely respected. That night or the following morning, the villages are bombed and villagers are indiscriminately shot at.
- The population has to pay the military for a so-called 'humanitarian corridor'. Prices vary between 50 and 60 million roubles ($5,000–6,000) for two or three hours passage.
- The corridor is often not respected, and villagers leaving with their few belongings are shot at.
- Men and women are separated. Many of the males aged twelve years and older are arrested and no one knows what happens to them or where they are taken.
- Villagers are not allowed to take the dead with them.
- Tanks and armoured vehicles enter the villages. MSF has gathered reliable reports of men, women and children put on the tanks as human shields. Women and children are pushed in front of soldiers as they enter the houses to loot, shoot and pillage. Cattle are also shot or taken away.
- Military trucks take away the looted goods.
- When the pillaging and burning of houses is over, villagers can go back to collect what is left. Many arbitrary arrests have occurred at this stage.[35]

On the second point, it seems only fair to note however that, as the OSCE report states, the separatist fighters also rarely respected such truces, and like all guerrillas, in effect used the civilian population as a shield.

As already described in my personal account of Grozny, I witnessed enormous and indeed universal evidence of casual brutality, looting and wanton vandalism by Russian troops during the period of the battle for the city in January–February 1995. This is unfortunately not untypical for wars of this kind, although the scale and openness of the looting was striking, and very often got in the way of efficiency. In the words of the OSCE report:

Simple extortion is a major factor in the current 'flow' of new arrests by Federal Forces at checkpoints. We have heard many accounts of troops arresting Chechens on trivial or non-specific charges, then exacting payment for their release. Under these circumstances, the borderline between political detention and pure criminality becomes more and more blurred.

What is relatively unusual is the randomness and disorganisation of much of the process, especially concerning the treatment of prisoners. Several former prisoners who had subsequently been released told me that instead of regular interrogation, there was simply random beatings by the soldiers, most of the time without even any questions being asked. It was simply an opportunity for the troops to amuse themselves. Thus in February 1995 I interviewed a Chechen called Zelimkhan, who was arrested by Russian troops on suspicion of being a fighter, and spent two weeks at a 'filtration point' (he was eventually released on the intercession of a Russian neighbour). He was still covered with bruises:

> What did they want to know? God knows. They didn't ask me any questions. They just kept saying that we were mercenaries fighting for Dudayev, and beating and kicking us. When we denied it, they'd beat us again, until they got tired... There were thirty of us kept in a small room of the bus garage in the Zavodsky Region, which they were using as a filtration point. Every day, they would come in and beat some of us, at random – just for fun, I think... Some of us were sent to Mozdok. Maybe they were questioned there, but how they chose whom to send, I don't know. No one has heard what has become of the people sent to Mozdok. I suppose if Sasha hadn't come to get me, I'd either have been sent there myself, or just taken out and shot in the head. We've heard there's been a lot of that.

In other words, this was a 'filtration point' which was simply not doing any efficient filtering.

The Chechens by contrast appear only rarely to have shot their prisoners in cold blood, and then only after grave Russian provocation (for example, in January 1995 I was informed by Chechen fighters in central Grozny that they had executed several Russian prisoners (the numbers given differed from one informant to another) after discovering, during a counter-attack, the bodies of several of their own men with their hands tied and shot in the head, evidently after capture.

As to torture and mutilation by the Chechens, some of this may perhaps have occurred, but neither I nor any other journalist saw any evidence of it. The Russian authorities alleged it again and again, but never produced a single body, witness, photograph, or other proof. On the whole, it cannot be emphasised too strongly that with rare and understandable exceptions (like the hostage-taking in the raids on Budennovsk and Kizlyar) the Chechens in this war fought more 'honourably' than the Russians. According to the OSCE report, in contrast to the Russian brutalisation of prisoners,

> There is some sign that the treatment by the Chechens of their detainees is more 'humane' than that of Chechens in federal hands. AG members have personally seen various federal soldiers held, or in the process of being released, by Chechen captors. All looked in good physical shape. Russian mothers who have been allowed to visit their soldier-sons held prisoner report the same.

I can confirm this from my own meetings with Russian prisoners in Chechen hands, and it does the Chechens great honour.

The Truce, June to December 1995

Since the purpose of this chapter is not to present a full history of the Chechen War, I shall not describe all the twists and turns of the peace negotiations which began in June 1995. The essential problem was set out by the chief Russian negotiator, Vyacheslav Mikhailov, on 17 July, when he said that Chechnya should have a special status which would not contradict two conditions: the integrity of the Russian Federation and the principle of self-determination. The problem of course is that since most Chechens, and certainly the vast majority of those doing the fighting, wanted to use self-determination in order to leave the Russian Federation, these two principles flatly contradicted each other.

That is not to say that a peace could not have been patched up, along the lines actually was achieved after August 1996: in other words, that the Chechens should be left to run their own affairs and the whole question of full independence simply shelved for future decision (or more probably non-decision). But for this, an absolutely essential precondition was that Russian troops withdraw from Chechnya, or at least out of close contact with the Chechen fighters.

Not only was this the key condition set throughout by the Chechen side, but it also involved a very practical point: the Chechens being the kind of people they are, as long as Russian soldiers were in Chechnya, then ceasefire or no ceasefire, and orders to the contrary notwithstanding, Chechen fighters would attack them. This is what happened through all the period of the truce.

Throughout this period – and indeed from May 1995 – another extraordinary sign of the Chechen spirit was that Grozny saw an almost continuous series of Chechen separatist demonstrations, under the very noses of the Russian army and the Zavgayev regime. On Chechen Independence Day, 6 September 1995, some 3,000 Chechens gathered in the square before the site of the former presidential headquarters, carrying placards denouncing Russia and supporting Dudayev. Almost every day during the talks in the OSCE compound in Grozny, Russian generals had to run the gauntlet of booing and chanting demonstrators. For reasons that are not clear, the Russian army made very little attempt to stop these rallies or arrest those responsible.[36]

At this stage, the Russian forces could have pulled back north of the Terek and held that line, thereby keeping a strong bargaining position. However, for them to have done this would have meant abandoning Grozny and their 'provisional government'. In the end, they were forced to do this willy nilly in the autumn of 1996, under the sketchiest of fig leaves provided by a 'neutral' transitional administration. In 1995, however, they went on hammering away at the idea that Dudayev's government should sit down and negotiate with Khadjiev's, something that Dudayev of course adamantly refused to do.

None the less, at first the peace talks seemed to go well. On 30 July, the Russian and Chechen side reached an agreement on military issues, by which the two sides agreed to pull back 2–4 kilometres from each other, and the Russians promised to reduce their forces by stages to two brigades, in return for a step by step disarmament of the Chechen forces.[37] The two commanders, General Anatoly Romanov for the Russians and Maskhadov for the Chechens, both ordered their men to stop fighting from 1 August.

Clashes however continued between Russian and Chechen forces, with each accusing the other of having started them. The most common reason seems to have been that small groups of Chechen fighters – or even sometimes individual snipers – started the incidents by firing on Russian posts, and the Russians then replied both by blasting away in all directions and on numerous occasions by deliberately bombarding local settlements by way of 'punishing' them for having 'harboured the terrorists'. The result of course was that the fighters tended to slip away, and it was local civilians who were killed – though as always in wars of this kind, the Russian soldiers had a point when they said that it was usually impossible to tell the difference between a Chechen fighter and a civilian, and that Chechen tactics made the distinction meaningless.

Then, on 6 October, a car bomb in Grozny critically wounded General Romanov. Though the finger of responsibility for this would seem automatically to point to the separatist side or at least to some separatist commander, the matter is not altogether clear. Maskhadov at least gave every sign of wishing to work with Romanov. Moreover, even at the time there were rumours on the Russian side that Bislan Gantemirov might have been responsible. He had an obvious interest in stopping any peace deal, and had shown his hostility to the peace process at the end of September by closing down the OSCE mission in Grozny, accusing it of helping Dudayev (though it has also been suggested that he may only have been supporting the OSCE's landlord, a client of his, in an attempt to extort more rent). On the other hand, it has been suggested that Romanov may have been personally targeted by the separatists, or some of them, as a matter of revenge, because he had been in overall charge of the attack on Samashki in April.[38]

It is not likely that this question will ever be cleared up. The results however were obvious and immediate. On 9 October, the Russian government announced that it was suspending the implementation of the 30 July agreement. On 24 October, evidently on Russian orders, Khadjiev resigned as Prime Minister and was replaced by Zavgayev – a sign that the Russians had given up on the hope of peace with Dudayev and were going to try to consolidate 'their' Chechen regime. This was confirmed later in the month when Zavgayev announced presidential and assembly elections in Chechnya to coincide with those for the Russian parliament on 17 December.

The separatist forces promptly announced that any Chechen who took part in the elections would be punished, and attempts were made to assassinate both Zavgayev and Lobov, Secretary of the Security Council. By late November, incidents of firing on Russian positions, mining of roads, sabotage of bridges, ambushes and Russian artillery strikes were running at several dozen every night. On 24 November, by way of a demonstration of how they could carry out terrorism in Moscow if they wanted to, Shamil Basayev's men planted a package of low-level radioactive caesium in a Moscow park, and then told Russian journalists where to find it.[39] In December, a series of car bombs exploded in Grozny.

On 8 December 1996, Zavgayev and Chernomyrdin signed an agreement as a basis for a Russian–Chechen federation treaty which would give Chechnya broad autonomy along the lines of that between Russia and Tatarstan, and which also stole the main points of Khasbulatov's proposal (Yeltsin declared that he was 'not afraid to give Chechnya a maximum of autonomy, more than any other republic').[40]

On 14 December 1995, with the intention of discrediting the coming elections, some 600 Chechen fighters attacked Russian positions in Chechnya's second city, Gudermes, and held the centre of town for ten days in the face of Russian counter-attacks before slipping away again. Other forces attacked Russian positions in Urus Martan and Achkoi Martan. This was the first of the three major urban counter-attacks which over the next eight months were to wear down and finally defeat the Russian army.[41] From 14 to 17 December 'voting' was said by the Zavgayev government to have taken place in Chechnya, with a 64.5 per cent turnout and Zavgayev elected by 93 percent. Western and Russian journalists on the spot described these figures as ludicrous, and said that even in Grozny, only a small minority of listed voting stations were even open.

Victory and Defeat, January 1996 to January 1997

Probably in consequence of the successful Chechen attack on Gudermes, the first day of January 1996 saw another change of Russian commander in Chechnya, one of eight that were to take place during the war, with all that this meant for efficiency and morale. An army general, Vyacheslav Tikhomirov, replaced Lt-General Anatoly Shkirko of the Interior Ministry troops. As usual, no attempt was made to bring Shkirko to book for the humiliation in Gudermes, and he was in fact promoted, to Deputy Interior Minister and commander of internal troops. Tikhomirov displayed his own grasp of the situation in a TV interview on 7 January, in which he predicted that the war would soon end because the separatist forces were only 'small groups of fanatics'.

On 9 January, a Chechen raiding party calling themselves the 'Lone Wolves' and led by Salman Raduyev attacked a Russian military airfield near the town of Kizlyar in northern Daghestan. He was beaten off, and then entered the town and, imitating Basayev, took some 2,000 hostages and herded them into the local hospital. Some twenty-five Daghestanis were killed, along with two

Russian soldiers and (so the Russians claimed) seventeen Chechen fighters. Raduyev initially declared that he and his men would fight to the death as 'kamikazes', and told Russian television that 'we can easily turn this city to hell and ashes.'[42]

The fact that the dead and the hostages included local Muslims and thirty-seven members of a Daghestani special police unit as well as local Russians did not increase the love of the Daghestanis for the Chechens. The following day, the presidents of all the North Caucasian autonomous republics with the exception of Ingushetia issued a statement calling on the Russian government to take strong action against 'Dudayevist bandits'. The Daghestani National-ities Minister declared that 'relations with Chechens will have to be reviewed.'

One motive for Raduyev's action was said to be the desire to avenge his brother, killed in the fighting in Gudermes the previous month. However, Raduyev is also married to Dudayev's niece, and there is good reason to sup-pose that the idea for this raid was cooked up between them partly as a way of trying to restore Dudayev's prestige, cast into the shade by the achieve-ments of Maskhadov and Basayev. Maskhadov and Basayev are known to have disapproved of the raid on both military and political grounds, and resented the fact that they had to commit their men to extract Raduyev and his group from the trap they had entered. In March, it was reported in the Russian press that Raduyev had been ambushed and killed by other Chechen fighters. This was furiously denied by the Chechens, who said that he had only been wounded in a Russian air attack – and he did indeed turn up several months later.[43]

On the same day, 9 January, Raduyev's group left Kizlyar for Chechnya with 160 hostages. On the tenth, despite promises of safe passage, Russian troops and helicopter gunships opened fire on them near the Daghestani village of Pervomaiskoye on the Chechen border. Extraordinarily, the Chechens were able to leave the convoy and take refuge in the village, adding some of its inhabitants to their hostages.

On 15 January, the Russian forces launched a full-scale attack on Pervo-maiskoye, including artillery and helicopter gunships, and without any regard for the safety of the hostages, between thirteen and eighteen of whom were killed in the fighting along with twenty-six Russian soldiers. Despite the fact that Pervomaiskoye is a small village with fewer than a hundred houses and was surrounded by thousands of Russian troops, Raduyev's force held out for three days; and then most of them, including Raduyev himself, succeeded in slipping away into Chechnya, crossing the Aksai, a medium-sized river in the process – though the Chechen casualties are said to have been unusually heavy, perhaps as many as half of the fighters involved.

According to Pavel Felgenhauer, a Russian journalist with, as noted, extremely good contacts in the Russian high command (though possibly as a result biased against the Interior Ministry), internal troops at Pervomaiskoye believed that the head of Russian counter-intelligence, General Mikhail Barsukov (formerly the chief of the presidential guard), who had taken personal command of the operation, was 'deliberately sending Interior Ministry officers to certain death'. An aide to Barsukov tried to justify his commander's performance by saying that the general personally led an assault in order to rally the troops, but as Felgenhauer comments, 'If a full general of the army was in fact desperate enough personally to lead an unsuccessful infantry attack, the morale of Russian troops at Pervomaiskoye must have been very near the breaking point'.[44]

The escape of Raduyev's men from such an exposed position – even with such high losses – is another testimony to the deep unwillingness of Russian troops in the war to risk their lives, even with the enemy at their mercy.[45] It was also helped by attacks from forces led by Maskhadov and Basayev, based in the nearby town of Novogroznensky. These also took hostage twenty-nine Russian workers from a power station near Grozny.

More distant support during the Pervomaiskoye siege came from Chechen separatists in Turkey; with the help of Turkish sympathisers, they seized a Turkish ferry, the *Avrasya*, which operates between Trebizond and the Russian resort of Sochi, and threatened to destroy it unless the Russians allowed the Chechens in Pervomaiskoye to leave. The incident was eventually resolved without bloodshed, and the Turkish security forces succeeded in warding off any further such attacks.

On 6 March, the separatists, numbering by Russian estimates 1,800 men, launched the second of their major counter-attacks into urban areas, occupying much of the centre of Grozny and surrounding Russian positions. They pulled out again after three days, leaving more than 150 Russian troops dead. One of the Chechen commanders, Ruslan Believ, later explained to *Obshchaya Gazeta* why the Chechens had been able to escape from encirclement on this and other occasions: 'it was easy to escape from Grozny because they gave the Russian troops the chance to retreat. This caused around 50 per cent of Russian troops to refuse to obey orders and to reach agreements with the Chechens not to open fire on each other. This allowed the fighters free movement all over the city.'[46]

The end of March saw another peace initiative from the Russian side, with an announcement by Yeltsin of another ceasefire and an offer of talks with Dudayev, together with a package of proposals based apparently on ones previously drawn up by Tatar President, Mintimer Shaimiyev.[47] This time, the evidence suggests that the initiative was a complete sham, and that the Yeltsin administration had no intention of pursuing it for more than a few necessary weeks. Presidential elections were due in Russia on 16 June, and Yeltsin himself made the surprising public admission at this time that his re-election depended on ending the war in Chechnya. Following the separatists' brief capture of central Grozny in March and the heavy casualties among the Russian troops, an opinion poll in Russia for the first time showed a majority as in favour of an unconditional pull-out of Russian forces from Chechnya – an admission of defeat, in other words.[48]

The figure in this poll was 52 per cent in favour of withdrawal. Two weeks later, a poll by the National Centre for Public Opinion showed 57 per cent of respondents in favour of direct talks between Yeltsin and Dudayev, and only 28 per cent against, even after eighteen months of government propaganda about 'terrorists' and 'bandits'.

Yeltsin's offer was completely ignored by the separatists: 31 March saw a major attack on Russian forces near Vedeno in which twenty-eight Russian soldiers were killed and seventy-five wounded. On 7 April, the Russian radio station Ekho Moskvy reported that Dudayev's response had been a counter-offer proposing the arrest of leading Russian generals and the dismissal of the Chernomyrdin government. On the 16th, a Russian convoy of the 245th Motorised Rifle Regiment was ambushed near Shatoy by Chechen fighters under a local commander, Ruslan Gelayev, and effectively destroyed. According even to the Russian high command itself, twenty-three out of twenty-seven vehicles were destroyed, seventy-three men killed and fifty-two wounded – a severe defeat in which the Chechens employed their old nineteenth-century tactics of forest ambush.

But on the evening of 21–22 April, the Russians scored their only real and permanent success in the whole war: the death of President Dzhokhar Dudayev, killed by a Russian rocket from an aircraft which homed in on the satellite telephone that he was using in the village of Gekhi-Chu. He was replaced by Vice-President Zelimkhan Yandarbiyev, to whom Maskhadov, Basayev and other commanders promptly vowed obedience.[49]

Hard-hearted though it may seem to say it, Dudayev's death did contribute to the later peace in Chechnya. On past form, it is very difficult to see him either being able to negotiate successfully with Lebed in August, or allowing Maskhadov to do so – let alone agreeing to stand in a free election after the peace. It is also difficult to see him maintaining the self-discipline shown by Yandarbiyev and Maskhadov (and indeed Basayev) during the period of the Russian withdrawal, studiously avoiding crowing over the defeated Russians and reining in their own forces. The elimination of Dudayev, who had been taunting them for so long, also made it psychologically easier for the Russian to admit defeat.

A new approach from the Chechen side was evident on 1 May, when Yandarbiyev offered new talks with Moscow. This was not, or so I was told at the time, because the separatist leaders were fooled by the Russian initiative; they perfectly understood its motives. However, they probably reckoned they had nothing to lose (the previous ceasefire, as noted, had served their military purposes very well) and that, in any case, to help a Communist victory over Yeltsin in the presidential elections would certainly not be to their advantage.[50]

The OSCE now began once again to play a useful part, under the very able and committed Swiss diplomat Tim Guldimann. (The OSCE's mission to Chechnya, though obviously less important than the Chechen military to the final peace settlement, was none the less in many ways a model of patient, stubborn mediation. It played a very valuable 'enabling' role, and I am sorry that I cannot give more space to it). On 27 May, both sides announced a three-day ceasefire, and Yandarbiyev travelled to Moscow with a delegation. After a brief and irritable meeting with Yeltsin which was reportedly saved from breaking down by the intervention of Guldimann, Yandarbiyev and Chernomyrdin signed a new ceasefire agreement. In the words of Maria Eismont, 'not only observers, but even members of the Chechen delegation were surprised that the Russian side was willing to give up so much' – something which can only be explained by the insincerity of the offers being made.

On 28 May, Yeltsin visited Chechnya for the first time during the war – now that it was relatively safe to do so, and as part of his election campaign, as was bitterly noted by Russian soldiers. His visit was restricted to the Russian military airfield north of Grozny, and lasted less than two hours. He told the soldiers that 'the war is over, and you have won.' They were not convinced.

This time, the ceasefire was relatively successful, with attacks on Russian troops and Russian bombardments kept to a minimum. At the same time, peace talks continued in the Ingush capital Nazran. The separatists, however, vowed to prevent the 16 June elections for the Russian presidency and for a Chechen parliament, and in Chechnya these barely took place.

The very day after the final results of the Russian presidential elections were announced, the Russian forces resumed large-scale attacks on separatist positions all over Chechnya. The resulting fighting lasted until Russia's day of nemesis, 6 August. This was the day of Yeltsin's inauguration for his second term as President, and it was a day of humiliation for Russia. In Moscow a puffy, bloated, obviously very sick old man, unable to speak for more than one minute, who had been re-elected only as a result of a media conspiracy to disguise the real state of his health, shuffled up to the microphone to celebrate his victory. The whole affair was acutely reminiscent of old pictures of Brezhnev, Andropov and Chernenko in their last years.

In Chechnya – even though this was a day on which the Russian forces must surely have been expecting some form of attack – separatist forces simultaneously entered Grozny, Argun and Gudermes in the largest Chechen offensive of the war. In Grozny, they rapidly occupied the centre of town, capturing the Zavgayev government headquarters, overrunning or surrounding Russian military posts and forcing others to be evacuated. They won this victory despite the fact that according to a later estimate by the Russian National Security Council, Russian troops in Grozny alone numbered 12,000 and outnumbered their attackers by around three to one. Two-thirds of these were the relatively badly equipped internal troops, but the rest were army, and thousands more army troops were stationed around Grozny, for example at the main Russian base and airfield of Khan Qala, seven miles to the north-west. The Russians also had 207 armoured vehicles, whereas at the beginning of their offensive the Chechens appear to have had none at all – the later ones seen in Chechen hands had all been captured.

One reason for the extraordinary Russian lack of preparedness appears to have been the division in command between the Interior Ministry and Defence Ministry troops. The Defence Ministry in Moscow was at that time in turmoil as a result of the dismissal of Grachev and the swift action of Lebed in dismissing a number of senior generals belonging to Grachev's clique. Shortly before the Chechen assault, the local command had been handed over from the army to the Interior Ministry, and the army later claimed that the internal troops had made no preparations to take over – though this may be just an attempt to evade responsibility. In any case, there can be no excuse for what happened, since the Chechens had after all carried out in March a smaller-scale dress rehearsal of the same operation – from which the Russians as usual appear to have learned nothing.[51]

By the evening of the second day, most of the Russian forces around Grozny were back to the positions they had occupied before the first Russian assault in December 1994, twenty months before. The Chechens also occupied the centres of Gudermes and Argun. Some 494 Russian soldiers were killed in the August battle in Grozny alone, with 1,407 wounded and 182 missing or captured – figures which recall the worst days of the initial storm in January 1995. Eighteen tanks and 69 armoured personnel carriers were destroyed or captured.[52] This very signal defeat presented Russians with the choice of either starting the whole war over again, beginning with a new and bloody storm of Grozny, or of effectively surrendering in return for peace.

As the next few weeks were to show, a large majority of Russians by now wanted peace at almost any price – and the man who was to give it to them, General Alexander Lebed, realised this. On 18 June, he had been appointed as head of the National Security Council and political supremo in the security field after the first round of elections, in which he came third, as part of a deal (almost certainly worked out several weeks previously) by which he agreed to support Yeltsin in the second round.

On 12 August, Lebed travelled to Daghestan and over the next two weeks, in a series of meetings at the border town of Khasavyurt, forged with Maskhadov the basis for Russian withdrawal from Chechnya. The question of Chechnya's constitutional status was to be shelved until the year 2001. This was an act of considerable moral as well as physical courage on Lebed's part. Above all, he prevented some of the generals from launching a new counter-offensive in Grozny, something which could have prolonged the war for months or years. He did this with absolutely no support from Yeltsin, who according to his usual pattern tried to distance himself both from the bloodshed and from the moves to end it.[53]

However, although there can be no question of Lebed's genuine opposition to the Chechen War, which he had opposed from the beginning (after also strongly opposing the military intervention in Tajikistan), it is no doubt also true that he would not have embarked on his Chechen peace mission unless he had thought it would bring him political advantage – which it did, as the opinion polls I will quote in chapter 5 demonstrate.

This was also in line with Lebed's strategy during the Russian election campaign, which was to portray himself as a tough and patriotic soldier, but one who opposed military adventures and the loss of Russian lives. 'Others start wars, he ends them' was the slogan, and it had great resonance with Russian voters. Also of considerable importance is the rapport that Lebed was able to establish with Maskhadov, another rather dour ex-Soviet officer. The two men seem to have recognised in each other a kindred spirit. It is very difficult to imagine that Lebed would have been able to establish such a relationship with the histrionic, capricious and arrogant Dudayev.

But with all due respect to Lebed, it is also vital to remember that this peace agreement came about only because the Chechens had won a great victory, and because the Russians realised that to reverse this would take more years of warfare and thousands of lives – and they simply did not have the stomach for it. Within the army, commanders realised that their men were simply not willing to fight any more. As with the French conscripts in Algeria or the Americans in Vietnam – but to an even greater degree – Russians were just tired of war. This spirit was also amply reflected in Russian public opinion polls concerning the Khasavyurt agreements.[54]

This mood, and the recognition of it by Russia's rulers, is why the apparently intense criticism of Lebed's peace deal from many of the figures on the Russian political scene and in the Russian media in the end had no effects on the peace process – because it was not meant to. The infamous change to support for the war on the part of so-called liberals like the editor of *Nezavisimaya Gazeta*, Vitaly Tretyakov, had little to do with Chechnya and the peace deal, and everything to do with trying to undermine the prestige and authority of Lebed and keep him from succeeding Yeltsin. This was either because the journalists concerned were genuinely afraid of Lebed, or because they had been so instructed by their proprietors – in Vitaly Tretyakov's case, Boris Berezovsky. This process also involved strengthening Interior Minister Anatoly Kulikov against Lebed, despite the fact that Kulikov's role in Chechnya had been simultaneously hawkish, immoral and incompetent.

There is no space here to detail the political struggles in Moscow between August and October which eventually led to Lebed's dismissal by Yeltsin on 17 October something which Lebed's open attempts to take effective power from the ailing President had made inevitable. The real issue during this period was not Chechnya but the state of Yeltsin's health, and the attempts of different groups either to take power from the President or exercise it in his name. Chubais, Kulikov and Lebed's other enemies in the administration and the elites all tried to use the Khasavyurt accord against Lebed; but the important thing to note is that when Lebed was dismissed and Berezovsky himself became deputy chief of the National Security Council (under the ineffectual Ivan Rybkin), the peace deal and the Russian policy of withdrawal continued unchanged – simply because the politicians concerned realised that to resume the war would be extremely costly and, more to the point, extremely unpopular.

Berezovsky began to meet Chechen leaders to negotiate on restarting the oil pipeline across Chechnya from Daghestan (a personal approach possibly not wholly unconnected with the fact that earlier in the year he had gained control of Sibneft, Russia's sixth largest oil company, which was believed to be trying for a stake in the Caspian oilfields).[55] For two months, the Russian government tried to stick to its previous position that one army and one Interior Ministry brigade should remain stationed in Chechnya, but in the face of an adamant and united stand by Yandarbiyev and Maskhadov, they eventually backed down. On 23 November, Viktor Chernomyrdin effectively set the seal on Lebed's work by signing an agreement with Maskhadov agreeing to withdraw Russian troops from Chechnya completely ahead of Chechen presidential elections scheduled for the end of January 1997. Not even the line along the Terek River giving Russian protection to the old Cossack lands to the north was to be held. The Communists and Zhirinovsky's extreme nationalist LDPR made noises of mock-outrage about 'treason', but in point of fact none of them when pressed by journalists was prepared to come out in favour of restarting the war. Yeltsin's press secretary declared that, 'this decree is a new confirmation of the President's view that there is no military way of solving the Chechen problem,' and that 'the Chechen people have been given the opportunity to make their choice not at machine-gun point'.[56] Six weeks later, the last Russian troops did in fact quit Chechnya, bringing to an end – at least for the present, and probably for many years to come – a Cossack and Russian military presence going back some four hundred years.[57]

Although the war came to an end because in Clausewitz's phrase, the Chechen fighters had 'imposed their will' upon their enemies, some important factors, or the Russian government's perception of them, also had their effect. First of all, Dudayev was dead, and the Kremlin had decided, in the course of negotiations with him over more than a year, that Aslan Maskhadov was a man they could work with. They also had good reason to think that unlike Dudayev, Maskhadov would neither embarrass Moscow with histrionic insults, nor seek to stir up revolt elsewhere in Russia. Secondly, it had also become obvious that Moscow did not in fact have to fear a 'spread of the Chechen infection', and a 'breakdown of law, order and central government rule in the northern Caucasus'.

Thirdly, it had become clear, and it had been expressly promised by Maskhadov, that a rational Chechen government would share Russia's interest in seeing the oil and gas pipelines from the Caspian running safely through Chechnya and the North Caucasus on their way to the Black Sea, both for its own sake and in return for Chechens being allowed to travel and trade freely in Russia.

Finally, there is the question of Chechnya's formal political independence from Russia, which according to the agreements reached by Lebed and Chernomyrdin was simply shelved for five years. The reason why it was possible for both sides to agree to this is quite simply that the Russian government realized that as long as no foreign country is going to recognise Chechnya as independent, the whole issue is highly theoretical, with the decision over recognition lying firmly in Moscow's hands, and very little that the Chechens can do about it.[59] (This is not to say, however, that men like Raduyev may not in fact try to use this issue, and perhaps once again resort to violence in pursuit of this goal and their own ambitions.)

In Chechnya, presidential elections in January 1997 resulted in the victory of Maskhadov over eight other candidates, including Yandarbiyev, Basayev and Udugov. Apart from his prestige as a commander, Maskhadov seems to have held the balance successfully between the desire of many rural Chechens for an Islamically based state and the desire of many from the towns for a more modern and secular order. He also won the votes of the remaining Russians in Chechnya. His victory was overwhelming, with 64.8 per cent of the votes to Basayev's 22.7 per cent and Yandarbiyev's 10.2. The OSCE declared that the elections had been free and fair.

Maskhadov promised the restoration of internal peace and stability, and the reconstruction of the economy in cooperation with Russia. Up to mid-1997, however, he had only very limited success in reaching these goals. These months saw a spate of kidnappings of Western and Russian journalists and aid workers (some allegedly with the connivance of members of the Chechen government), and bomb attacks in neighbouring regions of Russia, for some of which Raduyev claimed responsibility. Banditry in Chechnya had of course been increased by the war, along with the numbers of heavily armed, unemployed young ex-fighters wandering about.

Although in the last stages of the election campaign, Basayev had described Maskhadov and Yandarbiyev as 'crooks', he entered Maskhadov's government for several months as a deputy prime minister. He resigned in July, for reasons which were somewhat obscure. I was told that in part, he was frustrated by his inability to bring about the release of the kidnap victims. Maskhadov's staff, largely drawn from the Soviet professional classes, were also uncongenial to him.

Salman Raduyev claimed responsibility in April for some of the bombings in Russia, claiming that they formed part of a continuing struggle for full independence by his 'Army of General Dudayev'. He claimed that Dudayev was still alive, and that he was his representative – so that in a way, the dead general continued to play a baleful role.

In the first eight months of 1997, there were several attacks on Russian policemen and border guards in neighbouring Daghestan, apparently in retaliation for Russian attempts to control smuggling through Chechnya. Feuding between warlords also led to a number of attacks and assassinations. Meanwhile Chechnya's dubious legal status and reputation as a centre for smuggling was drawing an extremely fishy collection of international businessmen to Grozny.

On 12 May, Maskhadov and Yeltsin signed a peace accord in Moscow, leaving the future status of Chechnya open but recognising Maskhadov as legally elected President of the 'Chechen Republic of Ichkeria'. He was received with honours, and the accord was accompanied by a separate agreement signed by Chernomyrdin opening the way for Russian economic relief. This remained a dead letter, but more important was an agreement between the chiefs of the

Russian and Chechen central banks. This stipulated that the Chechen currency would continue to be the rouble, but the Chechen government would have authority over regulating non-cash transactions and commercial banks in the republic – one can only wish it luck, because it will need it! – and would not be subject to the authority of the Russian Central Bank. They also agreed on a customs union and the reopening of Grozny airport.[59] The following months saw repeated disputes, over issues ranging from Russian permission for Chechen official flights to Chechen public executions of criminals according to the Shaiah. However, there was no suggestion of a resumption of hostilities.

Maskhadov also committed his government to restoring the oil pipeline across Chechnya, and protecting Russian and other foreign workers, though the credibility of this promise was badly compromised by the kidnap of several Slovak construction workers. The Chechen President signed an agreement to this effect with both Russia and Azerbaijan. On 11 July, the Chechens, Russians and Azeris signed a deal on the transport of oil from Baku via Grozny to Novorossiisk, with repair to the pipeline beginning immediately.[60]

Agreement on the pipeline was endangered by the kidnappings and Maskhadov's demands for compensation for war damage, but in the end, the Russian government called Maskhadov's bluff by threatening to build a new stretch of pipeline through northern Daghestan and Stavropol. At this, Maskhadov gave in, and the restored pipeline through Chechnya is set to go ahead. Though they were as far apart as ever on independence, they did at least treat each other with mutual respect, and made appropriate noises about national reconciliation – another example of what a good thing it was that Dudayev had gone, and been replaced by Maskhadov.[61]

As of mid-1997, therefore, the prospects for the Chechen state looked mixed. Maskhadov was doing his best to create effective institutions and combat crime and terrorism, but there were strong indications that Chechen traditions of independence and resistance to higher authority – and of brigandage – would prove too much for him. In neighbouring Georgia, Eduard Shevardnadze by 1997 had been able to restore much of the Georgian state's authority, even though that had looked a hopeless task in 1993 and Shevardnadze had been responsible for a lost, not a victorious, war. On the other hand, Georgian Soviet state institutions had fared better than those of Chechnya did under Dudayev and during the war, and Shevardnadze as a former First Secretary knew much more about controlling them. At the time of the conclusion of this book, therefore, the question of whether the Chechens can do as much to create an effective modern state remains open. What one can say is that if Maskhadov cannot succeed in this, it is unlikely that anyone can.

Part II: The Russian Defeat

Ivan Vasilich the Terrible with his valiant retinue is feasting tirelessly near Mother Moscow.

A row of tables glitters with golden jugs; the dissolute oprichniki are sitting at the tables.

From Vespers onwards wines flow onto the Tsar's carpets, from midnight spirited minstrels sing to him;

They sing of the joys of war, of the battles of olden times, of the capture of Kazan and the conquest of Astrakhan.

But the voice of former glory does not gladden the Tsar; he bids his cupbearer hand him a mask.

'Long live my officers, my oprichniki! And you bards, you nightingales, pluck the strings more loudly!

Let each of you, my friends, choose himself a mask; I will lead off the gay dance myself!'

From Alexei Tolstoy, 'Prince Mikhail Repnin'

The different chapters in this part of the book deal in succession with the background to Russia's defeat in Chechnya. Since this defeat was the product both of a systemic crisis and a long process of change in the Russian state, Russian society and indeed Russian culture, explaining its different aspects necessarily involves covering a good deal of ground. Basically however the explanation is twofold: the weakness of the contemporary Russian state, and the failure of Russian society to generate forces which would in some way compensate for that weakness. In the context of the defeat in Chechnya and the mobilisation of Russian power for external domination, this means in the first instance forces of popular nationalism.

The chapters therefore take the following pattern: chapter 4 examines the hollowing-out of the Russian state by its new elites, and draws analogies between Russia and other weak, corrupt states produced by the liberal revolutions of the past two hundred years; chapter 5 analyses the transformation of Russian society and public attitudes – above all, towards the military – in the context of modernisation and social, cultural and above especially demographic change; chapter 6 takes a particular example, that of the

Cossacks, and through them examines the general failure of Russia to generate forces of paramilitary radical nationalism, *à la Serbe*, in part because of specific historical features of Russian 'nationalism', which is a very weak plant by European standards; chapter 7 extends this to an analysis of the political weakness of the 'Russian diasporas', with particular reference to Moldova, Crimea and Eastern Ukraine; and chapter 8 looks at the particular problems of the Russian armed forces in the 1990s.

The wider implications of my arguments concerning the condition of Russia in the 1990s are twofold. On the one hand, I believe Russia is an example of how liberal capitalism can reduce tendencies to militarism and foreign war. On the other, one reason why this is so in the case of Russia is that the sort of liberal capitalism which has predominated there, at least as of 1997, has been of a kind that no sane person would want to risk his or her life to fight for. I believe that this will go on being the case even if the Russian economy begins to recover. In the autumn of 1997 there seemed finally to be some signs of this. The appalling fiscal crisis of the previous year had led to the introduction of a new tax code and attempts to raise revenue by finally trying to sell state property for a fair price (though one senior regional official who tried to do this, Deputy Mayor Mikhail Manevich of St Petersburg, was killed for it, and Deputy Premier Boris Nemtsov was threatened). There was also a boom (possibly short lived) in foreign investment, amid signs that some of the new Russian capitalists at least have come to recognise their need for this, and are willing to play by certain international rules in order to get it – though whether that would extend to surrendering their own autocratic control of particular enterprises is a very different matter.

However, when it comes to Russia's capacity for serious warfare – the main question raised by this book – none of this makes much difference. Not merely are the new Russian capitalists opposed to dangerous military adventures (except perhaps on a very small scale and when they are sure it would bring them profit) but, as chapter 5 will argue, mutual trust is the foundation of all successful military mobilisation – and mutual trust in Russian society has by 1997 reached such a low level that economic progress alone would do little to restore it.

Trust could only be restored if the new Russian elites showed real signs of a willingness to spread any new wealth throughout society; and outside Moscow, there is very little sign of this – just as foreign investment and stock market booms in a number of developing countries have done little to raise the living standards of the poor of many of the regions distant from the national metropolis. Moreover, even if economic gains were to be more widely distributed, the factors contributing to demilitarisation in Russia would continue or even get stronger as Russia moved closer to the West. I believe therefore that for Russia once again to become a military force that could threaten the peace and stability of Europe, a very new kind of Russian nationalism and national identity would have to appear, against a new international and domestic background. The question of how far this may be possible will be raised in the conclusion to the book.

The Russian economy may well improve, but whether enough to turn it into a stable and prosperous democracy seems very doubtful.

4 The Masque of Democracy: Russia's Liberal Capitalist Revolution and the Collapse of State Power

They were aiming at the creation of a modern state, and they created a bastard.

Gramsci, *Prison Notebooks*

Lorsque les principes du gouvernement sont une fois corrompus, les meilleurs lois deviennent mauvaises et se tournent contre l'état. [Once the principles of government are corrupted, even the best laws become bad and turn against the state.]

Montesquieu, *De l'Esprit des Lois*

The Russia that went to war in Chechnya in December 1994 was both a weak state and one in the throes of a liberal capitalist revolution – part of the second great wave of such revolutions that the world has seen over the past two hundred years.[1] The first wave, in the nineteenth century, shattered the old ruling trinity of monarchy, church and nobility (while also coopting elements of all three), and also destroyed or severely undermined the social and economic forms and traditions of the peasantry and the urban artisanate.

That was the true modernising revolution of the modern era, and it has been repeated in our own time in the active or passive revolutions against Communism: in China since 1979 by a state-led process, and in the former Soviet bloc since 1989 by a mixture of elite-led changes and upsurges from below. However, it is quite clear that the first wave of liberal revolutions had very different results for different countries and cultures, and different regions within the same country. The striking economic success stories usually occurred either where existing social and cultural trends strongly favoured this, or – as in Russia from 1894 to 1914 and China in the 1980s – where a strong state threw its power behind reform.

Elsewhere – in much of Italy and Spain, and most of Latin America – liberal economics for most of the past 150 years has produced only weak, unstable and unbalanced economic growth, and social and political progress. Most of the world in the 1990s, after all, lives neither under totalitarianism nor under a prosperous Western-style capitalist democracy. Most people live under political systems more akin to the anarchic quasi-feudalism – with political and criminal 'clans', including armed retainers, following particular magnates or bosses – incisively described by Vladimir Shlapentokh.[2]

However, rather than the medieval feudalism Shlapentokh uses as a model – which was at its height a formal, recognised system enshrined in law, contract, religion and culture – a closer historical analogy might be the 'cacique' system of liberal Spain and much of Latin America in the later nineteenth and early twentieth centuries. It was a time when Spain's governments never ceased to trumpet their allegiance to constitutionalism, law and enlightened progress, but in which real power on the ground was held by corrupt local political chieftains (*cacique* comes from the Caribbean Indian word for a chief), who distributed patronage and government contracts, fixed or 'made' elections on behalf of their patrons in Madrid, and occasionally bumped off inconvenient political opponents, critical journalists, trade unionists and so on. The key difference between feudalism and the cacique system, all too applicable to Russia today, was incisively remarked on by Gerald Brenan: 'The defects of the Spanish upper classes are sometimes put down to their having a feudal mentality. I do not think this word has been well chosen: feudalism implies a sense of mutual obligations that has long been entirely lacking in Spain.'[3]

Systems of the cacique type can prove remarkably stable and long-lasting, and even generate considerable economic growth. To their better-off inhabitants, and those with some form of 'protection', they offer major personal freedoms and opportunities. They also however tend to be characterised by very high levels of organised crime, personal insecurity, atrocious public health, bad public education, rampant bureaucracy and bureaucratic corruption, and vicious exploitation of the poor and the environment. Their states are generally too weak and corrupt to enforce the law, honestly and equitably, raise taxes efficiently and fairly or to protect the weaker sections of society. In extreme cases, like Columbia and to an increasing extent Mexico in the 1990s, the state itself may be largely taken over by criminal forces.[4]

What happens when such a state sends its army against a brave and well-motivated enemy, however small, was shown at Anual in Morocco in June 1921, perhaps the closest parallel in this century to what happened in Chechnya. An army of demoralised and hungry Spanish conscripts, drawn from a Spanish population which was either indifferent to the Spanish colonial war in Morocco or actively hated it, was attacked by a much smaller and less well armed force of Berber tribesmen under the proto-nationalist leader Abd-el-Krim. The result was a crushing Spanish defeat, with the loss of 10,000 killed and 4,000 prisoners and all the artillery taken.

While in recent decades some of these countries have escaped from these syndromes, a good many others have remained to a considerable extent stuck in them. Even periods of 'miraculous' economic growth, as in Mexico, have not been enough to raise the bulk of society to a high, stable and secure economic plane – if only because of the way that economic distribution was skewed.

The truth of this for the modern world was brought out in a sober and perceptive series in the *Washington Post* at the turn of 1996–7, entitled 'For

Richer, For Poorer'. With regard to Mexico – a country which in recent years has carried out a full programme of economic reforms and attracted vastly more foreign investment than Russia – Molly Moore wrote:

> Now, Mexico stands as a prime case study for critics who argue that globalisation … is proving not to be a reliable mechanism for raising the Third World out of poverty… Billions of dollars of capital flowed into Mexico during the past 10 years… But Mexico, like many of its Latin American neighbours, has two almost separate economies, divided by geography, technology and by ethnicity – and only one of them has benefited from the new money. [The] proportion of Mexicans considered 'extremely poor' has increased sharply.[5]

It is typical in such cases that the wealth generated is disproportionately concentrated in the capital and one or two other great commercial centres. Where Russia is concerned, Moscow's economy is estimated to have grown by 10 per cent or more in the mid-1990s, even while the economy as a whole was declining precipitously, and Moscow may now account for as much as 35 per cent of Russian GDP – something which also facilitates the concentration of political power in the hands of a metropolitan oligarchy.[6]

Privatisation as Enclosure of the Common Land

Leaving aside the absence of mass violence and the links between liberalism and nationalism, in another respect there is rather a close parallel between the Russia of today and Italy – and other liberal-ruled states – of the nineteenth century. This link lies in one of the processes by which the new elites acquired their wealth: in Russia, through privatisation of state property; in Italy, Spain, Mexico and elsewhere through 'land reform'; and in both cases, with the help of massive corruption and under the ideological umbrella of a triumphalist liberal capitalism. We have seen all this before.

The land reforms which in Italy, Spain, Mexico and elsewhere redistributed the lands of the church, of the village communes, and of some of the great feudal landowners have a very familiar ring to anyone who knows Russian privatisation. They were supposed to be equitably and justly conducted, to lead to the creation of a class of small but efficient capitalist peasant farmers, to break the power of the church and other anti-liberal forces, and to help the peasants themselves escape from the twin traps – as seen by the urban liberals – of traditional peasant culture and traditional peasant agriculture.

That is what was supposed to happen – and in a few places did happen. In England, the dissolution of the monasteries and the enclosure of the commons (much older processes, of course, than the nineteenth century liberal land reforms) undoubtedly contributed greatly to the eventual development of efficient modern agriculture in England, though they were socially deeply unjust, destructive of ancient communities and traditions, destructive of the environment and hated by the poorer peasantry.

What happened elsewhere can be summed up in a few examples. In Mexico, for instance, the liberal reformers, the so-called 'cientificos' (because of the positivist claim of these US-trained Mexican economists to represent 'scientific' solutions to Mexico's problems – very reminiscent of Gaidar, Chubais et al.) set out to break up the lands of the church and the common lands of the Indian villages in the name of economic efficiency and progress.

An initial limit of 2,500 hectares was supposed to prevent the accumulation of new vast haciendas (great estates), but this was ignored from the start. As a result, 'the 1880s and 1890s witnessed a land grab of unprecedented proportions.' By 1910 more than half of rural Mexicans lived on haciendas. Local magnates, political bosses or military men, with links to the regime, simply used the law to seize the land of the peasants, after declaring that they were *baldio*, or lacking private title. Where the Indios and peasants resisted, they were shot down and driven off by the army, the police or privately hired pistoleros. A million acres of Yaqui Indian land went to the Torres family alone.

In a majority of cases, the improvement in economic efficiency was very limited (inevitably, on estates of such an unmanageable size and given the lack of new capital), and certainly did not begin to offset the resulting immiseration of large sections of the peasantry and especially the indigenous Indian population. Moreover, thanks to the weakness and corruption of the Mexican state, as with privatisation in Russia, the state treasury received only a derisory proportion of the money that the land being privatised was actually worth. In Benito Juarez's sale of 'vacant lands' in the 1860s, for example, the state received about 100,000 dollars for 4.5 million acres, or about two and a half cents per acre. Under Porfirio Diaz, a fifth of the country was given away for three and a half cents an acre, compared to a market price which averaged two dollars.[7]

The social, political and economic consequences are with us to this day in Chiapas and other regions. And as in the case of Russia in recent years, both local reformers and their foreign backers and advisers resolutely turned their eyes from the reality of what was happening, and justified privatisation not for any goods it was producing, but as an absolute good in itself.[8] This was coupled with an obsession with the stability of the currency and the government's credit rating – and Mexico under Diaz was in fact judged a very good bet by international financiers, as will be Russia in the late 1990s if the success of the June 1997 Eurobond issue is anything to go by.[9]

In southern Italy, where the regimes of Joseph Bonaparte and Joachim Murat introduced legislation to end feudalism and break up the great latifundias, the result was the same. Most of the peasants were effectively excluded from participation by legal chicanery and high registration fees, and were also stripped of the common village land which they had held under the great estates. The result was that the great bulk of the land was acquired by a small number of great magnates, whether the old feudatories themselves or new bourgeois proprietors – often civil servants of the Bonapartist government, like the two greatest owners in Calabria, who between them gained control of almost half the province.[10] Once again, this very notoriously did absolutely nothing to improve agricultural efficiency, let alone the general well-being of the population, which in many areas declined sharply as a result.

In other words, there is nothing very new about the way in which Russian public property was grabbed in the course of 'privatisation'. It is exactly what has always happened over the past two hundred years when a ruthless liberal capitalist ideology combines with a corrupt bureaucracy and a weak legal order, and is prepared to justify almost anything in the name of 'progress'.

For to be fair to Chubais, it would be wrong to see personal corruption as the root of his approach to privatisation. He did receive a 3 million dollar, five-year interest-free loan from Alexander Smolensky's Stolichny Bank (part of the 'semibankirshchina' or 'group of seven') even while that bank was acquiring enormous Russian state assets at a knockdown price,[11] but he is by all accounts absolutely and genuinely convinced of the rightness of his cause. In his interviews, Berezovsky too presents himself articulately as a force for economic and even moral progress – an 'ideologist for cash', perhaps, as Ostap Bender described himself.[12]

One factor which is connected to this and very reminiscent of the nineteenth-century liberal movements is the contempt of the 'cientifico' liberal reformers and the New Russians for their poorer, older and less dynamic compatriots. This attitude is composed of two elements: a general progressive and 'scientific' contempt for their backward culture – in the past, peasant and Catholic, today Soviet and 'Communist' – and a personal contempt for their 'cowardice' and lack of dynamism.

This attitude was summed up in the words of a Siberian entrepreneur middleman in December 1996 about the miners of Kemerovo, who were protesting that their wages were three months in arrears and that their families were hungry: 'They don't do anything at work, but it saves them from being at home with their wives. The world is divided into those who get up and do something and those who don't.'[13] Or in the words of David Remnick, 'The new oligarchs, both within and outside the Kremlin, see themselves as undeniably lucky, but worthy as well. They righteously insist that the fortunes will spawn a middle class, property rights, and democratic values. No matter that the Kremlin lets them acquire an industrial giant like the Norilsk nickel works for a thief's price; they claim to be building a new Russia, and rationalize the rest.'[14] This contempt for the masses in Russia is increased by the fact that the new businessmen are risk-takers in the physical as well as the economic sense.

The story of Russian privatisation thus forms part of a pattern in the history of the past two hundred years. And when it comes to improved efficiency – the ultimate stated goal of privatisation as of nineteenth-century 'land reform' – as of the end of 1996 the only possible answer was given by Professor Igor Birman:

I am certainly not against wealth, but … to provide for the economic independence of citizens, privatisation must:

- minimize the economic role of the state;
- stimulate the producer to work for himself;
- inspire him with competition.

None of this has been achieved: the economic role of the state remains immense; producers are stimulated more to steal from the state than to produce; monopolies in the sphere of production have not been overcome.

It would be wrong to rule out the possibility that in future, privatisation will lead to increased efficiency and stable economic growth benefiting the mass of the population – but it would also be difficult to argue that this had happened as of 1997.

The Russian population is well aware of the injustices of the privatisation process. The way in which public property has been shared out under Yeltsin, though it has not led to revolt or a desire to return to Communism, has created what I would call a deep moral wound, an offence against the moral economy of ordinary Russians. In the words of David Satter:

The reformers (all of whom are former Communists) have acted as if the building of capitalism in Russia supersedes the requirements of morality and they have made little effort to establish a state based on law. The result is that the majority of the population has seen its living standards decline without the compensation of a system which protects the individual's basic integrity…

It is important both for the Russian reformers and for the West to understand that the drive to create a market economy, however necessary it may be in the long run, is not sufficient to give the reform process moral legitimacy in Russia. The psychological power of communism derived from the fact that it claimed to connect the social system to certain ultimate values. During the perestroika period, the 'class values' of the Communist system were discredited, creating a moral and emotional vacuum. Russians will not forgive the reformers for betraying the universal values, expressed in respect for law, that were supposed to have taken their place.[15]

If this feeling is combined with economic misery for the mass of the population over a long period of time, this may eventually lead to serious long-term consequences for the legitimacy of the new Russian order – akin to the feelings of Spanish, Italian and Mexican peasants about the new liberal order in the nineteenth century.

The Privatisation of the Russian State

In between the two waves of liberal revolution of the past two hundred years came the reactions against liberal capitalism of the early and mid-twentieth century: Communist revolutions, and a great range of national-socialist (or national-populist) semi-revolutions, which were, or claimed to be, popular reactions against both Liberalism and Communism.

The Communist regimes and ideologies which took power as a result of the catastrophes of 1914–45 then pursued their own version of modernisation, but in a manner both much more savage and much more incompetent than the liberal societies. Meanwhile the latter, in part because of the external threat of Communism and the internal one of Marxist-inspired socialism, introduced systems of social welfare, and were enabled to do this by the long years of economic growth after 1945.

The result was societies which appeared to people in Communist states so materially – and to a lesser extent spiritually – appealing that, combined with the Communist systems' own manifest failings and present and past evils, they convinced many ordinary inhabitants, and above all large sections of the ruling elites (especially the younger ones), that a major change of course was necessary. The motivation could be either patriotism, or simply a desire to gain personal access to Western material culture, or repulsion at Communist corruption, or loathing of Communist oppression and a desire for more freedom, or, more often, some combination of all four.[16]

I remember vividly my first sight of the living standards of the Communist elites in Eastern Europe, when during the Romanian Revolution of 1989 I was shown the flat left behind by an escaped Securitate colonel. The Romanians who took me there were full of fury at its 'disgusting luxury', but in fact, it was furnished and equipped like an ordinary British working-class home. This struck me again and again in 1990 and 1991 when I visited the offices and on rare occasions the homes of members of the Soviet elite. Of course, the colonel's flat was far above the homes of the vast majority of ordinary Romanians; but what the colonel's more astute colleagues across the former Soviet bloc had already begun to discover was that if they abandoned Communism and used their state positions to privatise state resources into their own pockets, they could live not like British workers, but like British millionaires.

The privatisation of the Soviet Russian state had however begun several decades earlier and was indeed probably implicit in the entire Communist–autocratic (or Marxist–Leninist) experiment – but it accelerated enormously, of course, under Gorbachev and reached its apogee under Yeltsin. As already indicated, this process involved not just the transfer of state property, but also to a considerable degree control over the state itself, reflected in the ability to evade taxes and tariffs, extract subsidies and flout the law in various ways.

The moral tone for the privatisation of the state was set by the privileges of senior Communist officials, which began in the earliest days of Communist rule and was later institutionalised in the Fourth Department of the party. This however was not privatisation; these privileges were given by the party and could be – and were – withdrawn by it. Real privatisation of the state by its own officials began under Brezhnev. It was helped by the inevitable tendency of the Communist Party and the state bureaucracy to clientelism, to the politics of leaders and their followings or cliques and the creation of bureau-cratic/managerial clans (especially of course where, as in Central Asia and parts of the Caucasus, traditional clan loyalties in the strict sense also still persisted).[17]

The process of the privatisation of the Soviet state has been charted best by Arkady Vaksberg, who as a Soviet lawyer and *Izvestia* correspondent con-nected to and protected by sections of the Soviet internal security apparatus was in a position to learn a great deal about what was happening.[18] There appear to have been two linked but separate developments, one centred on southern Russia and the Caucasus, the other on Central Asia. Of these, the Central Asian variant was the more straightforward, and in some of its essentials was not even specifically Soviet. It formed part of the implicit Brezhnevite deal whereby, in return for absolute public loyalty to the system and the General Secretary, republican first secretaries and their bureaucratic followers were given a considerable degree of freedom by the centre – includ-ing most notably freedom from anti-corruption investigation by the KGB.

In the cotton-growing republics of Central Asia, this translated into the notorious system by which the local leaderships, in collusion perhaps with Brezhnev himself, certainly with members of his family, faked the figures for raw cotton that their republics were supplying to the central Soviet ministries, and pocketed the difference. I say that aspects of this were not specifically Soviet because the syndrome whereby local satraps, bound to provide their imperial ruler with taxes in kind, take an increasing amount of them for them-selves is probably as old as the empire of Sargon; as is the tendency of a weak imperial ruler to look the other way so as to avoid provoking revolt in far-flung provinces.

Developments elsewhere were more specifically Soviet, in that they stemmed from the Soviet Communist attempt, unprecedented in recorded history (except for a few local and small-scale religious experiments) entirely to suppress private trade, ownership and profit. A state philosophy and strat-egy so totally opposed to human nature could be imposed only by mass terror, and was bound to be progressively, if slowly, undermined once that terror was lifted after Stalin's death. (There were occasional attempts by the KGB to crack down again, above all associated with the name of Andropov, but these were only temporarily and locally effective).

In the Soviet Union, this process predictably began in areas of surplus food production – notably the North Caucasus and the Transcaucasus. These also happened to be the areas closely linked to the world of the Black Sea, with its ancient commercial traditions; and they contained peoples whose languages, ethnic and religious traditions, and family structures allowed them to develop limited commercial and criminal networks (for the orthodox Communists, of course, these words were one and the same) while resisting penetration by the KGB. Concerned above all with providing foodstuffs and alcohol to the black market in Moscow and the other great Russian and Ukrainian cities, the growth of these 'mafias' was naturally and inextricably intertwined with state corruption, which can also be described as the covert privatisation of parts of the state apparatus by the officials who ran it. Other rewards and bribes were provided by the state tourism apparatus, also centred on the Black Sea–Caucasus region.

The classic example of this was the Moscow food distribution network under First Secretary Viktor Grishin, as described in the 'revelations' which were used by Gorbachev to get rid of him; but essentially the same system was at work in every food shop in every one of Russia's cities, and involved everyone from the salesgirl to senior figures in the party and state. This process involved some of the criminal figures who have emerged to prominence in the business world under Yeltsin, and it pointed directly both to the privatisation of the state and the inextricable intertwining of 'criminal' and 'legitimate' business in the 1990s. These links took some time to develop, and owed much to the Caucasian mafias. The old-style Russian criminal bosses, or 'thieves in law' (*vory v zakone*), had a strict code of non-involvement with the state or state officials, which they gave up only with some difficulty in the 1970s and 1980s. In fact, these older godfathers seem to have lost much of their power in recent years.

There is no space here for a full discussion of the nature and extent of Russian organised crime in the 1990s (for a portrait of the Chechen mafia, see chapter 10). In the context of the general development of the Russian state and society, however, it should be said that Western analysis of this factor has often suffered from one or other of two misconceptions. The first is to exaggerate the structured and united nature of the organised criminal groups, and the extent to which they are descended either from the old thieves in law or the Communist bureaucracy.[19] In fact, while both these groups obviously played a part, it would be closer to the truth to see post-Soviet organised crime as a multiplicity of groups, which, although internally structured, have no real 'all-Russian' structures (unlike the Sicilian Mafia and the Triads, at least at certain points in their history), and which have grown up in response to the amazing new opportunities of the post-Soviet period.[20]

However, this does not make the power of organised crime any less dangerous to Russia – contrary to the second preconception. Some of those who have sought to play down the extent of Russia's state and social crisis have pointed out that mafias often substitute for a corrupt and chaotic bureaucracy and legal system when it comes to resolving commercial disputes and enforcing contracts – a role often played by the Sicilian Mafia and its various Mediterranean analogues. In the Russian expression, they act as 'roofs' for legitimate business.[21]

Thus a Russian friend working for a private pharmaceuticals company in St Petersburg described to me in 1994 how the local bureaucratic agency responsible for regulating the medicine trade suddenly tried to close them down on the basis of a newly introduced local rule about imported medicines:

> Our boss did some investigation, and he discovered that the head of the state committee involved was closely linked to our main local rivals. So going to the authorities would have been pointless. What to do? Naturally, he went to our 'roof'. They negotiated with the 'roof' of our rivals, and sorted out the whole thing between them. We didn't even have to pay anything extra – they said it was covered by our regular payment, that's what it was for. Generous of them, you could say …Without question the state committee head is also under a 'roof'. Who are our roof? I couldn't tell you. I try not to get too close to these things.

So the mafia does indeed substitute for corrupt and useless state authorities. But this is the whole point. A country in which a business can only get its debtors to pay by having some of them killed as an example, in which hostile takeovers are paid for with bullets, in which 'judges' have sidelines in drug-smuggling and prostitution is a country in the most desperate trouble.

As Louise Shelley has pointed out, the domination of organised crime is also a terrible obstacle to the growth of civil society and a true and open democratic system, suppressing free debate and protest with a leaden fist.[22] Furthermore, the evidence suggests that when organised crime has come to play this quasi-legal role in society, it will be exceptionally difficult to get rid of it again. It took Fascist rule in Italy to suppress the Mafia, and then only for twenty years; the same is true of the Communists in South China and the Triads.

While the enormous role of strictly criminal groups in the Russian economy is probably by far the biggest threat to the West from Russia today (because of the smuggling of arms, drugs and illegal immigrants), within the country it is less the criminal groups as such than 'legitimate' big businessmen in alliance with them who have played the most striking role, and it is their control of Russia's raw materials which may be the biggest threat to the country's economic future.

The line between crime and legitimate business in Russia is, however, not at all easy to draw. Thus in September 1996 the *Washington Post*, in an article based on interviews with FBI officials, described how Russian banks were setting up on Caribbean islands like Antigua (with 'one room and a computer' apiece), allegedly for the purposes of money laundering and links with the Latin American drugs cartels. One these was the EUB Bank, set up in Antigua in July 1994 by one Alexander Konanykhin, wanted in Russia on charges of embezzling 8.1 million dollars from the Exchange Bank in 1992.

The article states that EUB was set up as an offshore subsidiary of the Menatep Bank of Mikhail Khodorkovsky. He denies this, but the *Post* quoted a 'senior US official' as saying that Menatep had a 'horrible reputation for involvement with organised crime'. Menatep is one of the largest Russian banks and has control of important industries including Russia's second biggest oil company, thanks to 'loans for shares' in 1995–6, and Mikhail Khodorkovsky was one of the 'group of seven' big bankers ('semibankirshchina') who financed and organised Boris Yeltsin's re-election in 1996. So if the *Post* is correct, it would be hard indeed to regard organised crime as in some way peripheral to the Russian economy under Yeltsin.[23] Similar accusations have been levelled at many other leading business figures with links to the administration.[24]

The forces of order look like a broken reed in this respect – as evidenced both by an almost endless series of stories about police and legal corruption (in part I, I have described the hopeless corruption of the police and troops reponsible for enforcing the 'blockade' against Chechnya) and by the notorious incident in July 1997 when the Justice Minister, Valentin Kovalev, was sacked by Yeltsin after being photographed by a newspaper with prostitutes in a sauna known to be frequented by criminal bosses. In 1995, Chief Procurator Alexei Ilyushenko was removed for illegal business dealings – but in fact as a political concession to parliament – and was repeatedly accused of links to organised crime. It might seem all to the good that Kovalev was actually sacked, but he was replaced with the discredited Sergei Stepashin.

Apart from the general cost of organised crime to society and social morale, the tolls paid to the 'mafia' by businesses of every kind have also had a very negative effect in practical, day-to-day terms, especially on raising prices of food and consumer goods. In 1994, the Russian government's Analytical Centre for Social and Economic Policies estimated that around three-quarters of private enterprises in that year were forced to pay between 10 and 20 per cent of their earnings in extortion.[25] Mafias and monopolies between them have made Moscow the third most expensive city in the world for foreign businesspeople to live in, and so the confidence of foreign investors has also been hit. Thus in October 1996, a report by the international corporate consultants Merchant International Group declared Russia the riskiest of all the more popular 'emerging markets' in which to do business, above all due to 'widespread crime, extortion, a thriving black economy and the possibility of a political vacuum'.[26]

A tremendous boost to these developments was given by Gorbachev's anti-alcohol campaign of 1985–6: by shutting down much of the state alcohol sector and harrying private trade, it at a stroke transferred much of the most lucrative state monopoly into private and often criminal hands (a process with some analogies to Prohibition in the USA).[27] Even worse was the granting of independent decision-making powers to enterprise directors without freeing prices or introducing other free market restraints on behaviour: this was simply an invitation to them to steal the products of their factories, mines or oil-wells, sell them on the black market or abroad, and pocket the difference.[28] Since in 1991 the fixed domestic price of Soviet oil was less than one-fiftieth of its price on the world market, one need look no further for the origins of most of the great Russian fortunes of today.

Yeltsin put it very well in a speech of October 1991, on the need for a privatisation programme:

> For impermissibly long, we have discussed whether private property is necessary. In the meantime, the party-state elite have actively engaged in their personal privatisation. The scale, the enterprise, and the hypocrisy are staggering. The privatisation of Russia has gone on [for a long time] but wildly, spontaneously, and often on a criminal basis. Today it is necessary to seize the initiative, and we are intent on doing so.[29]

But it has been under Yeltsin that the criminal privatisation of Russia has in fact reached its full-blown form.

Given the nature of Communist ideology, the massive entry of organised crime into business may well have been unavoidable; for it would seem to stand to reason that if the state criminalises all forms of business activity, then when it eventually changes its mind and legalises business, it will find that the businessmen are by origin and nature criminals. To take a broader overview of the process going back to the years after the 1917 Russian Revolution, what began to happen under Brezhnev can be described as a resumption of a natural tendency, which began under the New Economic Policy (NEP) in the 1920s, and was then savagely interrupted by Stalin and the Communists: that is to say, the reabsorption of the Communist Party and state by society. The danger – indeed the certainty – of NEP's restoration of market ownerships was a key reason why the bulk of the old Bolsheviks enthusiastically supported Stalin in what was in fact a second revolution: the end of NEP and the smashing of the peasantry by collectivisation. They realised that otherwise Soviet Russia would eventually be a state and society dominated by the big peasant landholders. The Communists thereby implicated themselves in a monstrous crime which also led directly to their own deaths.[30]

Collectivisation, the Five Year Plans and the Terror were to destroy the oldest and deepest Russian class, tradition and social institution – the peasantry, its community organisation of mir and the Orthodox Church in the villages; then the surviving (and under the first years of NEP, burgeoning) merchants and shopkeepers; then the remnants of the old intelligentsia; and finally, the autonomy, institutions and personnel of the Bolshevik Party itself. It was this revolution, more even than that of 1917-21, which was to tear Russian and Soviet society away from the general path of the rest of the world, and set (for a few decades) a new paradigm. It wrecked both Russian society and the Russian tradition.

In one sense the Communist state did indeed find itself being taken over by 'society' in the 1930s, as a flood of new men from the proletariat and peasantry,[31] without Bolshevik background and imbued with Russian chauvinist attitudes, flooded into the party, executing or imprisoning the Old Bolsheviks. But in another sense, because the old structures of Russian society had been destroyed, this absorption took place very much on terms set by the Stalinist state itself. Not social groups, classes or institutions, but only a mass of dera-cinated individuals were to enter the party, and if they transformed it into something very different from what Lenin and the Old Bolsheviks had envis-aged, it also transformed them into people of an utterly different character from that of their parents twenty years before.

Russia's Passive Revolution

Thus in the long run, Stalin's terror paradoxically contributed to the ease with which the state he created was privatised into a relatively small number of deep pockets in the 1990s. It is because Stalin shattered and atomised Rus-sian society (and that of most of the other Soviet republics) that in our time it has proved largely incapable of generating mass democratic politics of a kind which might have put some check on the thieving of the elites.

Unlike in Eastern Europe or the Baltic States, the processes within Russia that contributed to the destruction of the Communist system and the Soviet Union were predominantly elite-led and dominated. The masses were of course not wholly absent, and at critical moments their disgust with the old Communist order played a critical role: above all in the elections of 1989, 1990, 1991 and 1996, and the referendum of March 1993 on support for Yeltsin and the idea of reforms. (On the other hand, in Gorbachev's referen-dum of March 1991 a large majority also voted to preserve the Soviet Union, thus demonstrating the critical distinction, among several of the Soviet peoples, between Communist and Soviet loyalty.)

With rare exceptions, however, the events of this time were not a revolution mainly powered by spontaneous upheaval from below – and those exceptions, in the Baltic States and the Transcaucasus, were motivated overwhelmingly by nationalism rather than anti-Communism as such. Major demonstrations were few and far between compared to previous revolutions, they were entirely peaceful, and almost entirely confined to a handful of larger cities. Even in Moscow, the crowds which helped frustrate the attempted Soviet counter-revolution of August 1991 were fairly small in comparison to the size of the city, and were mainly composed of educated elements.

Most striking of all was the relative absence of youth, something commented on sadly by middle-aged former dissidents at the time. Even before the Soviet Union fell, Russian youth was showing strong signs of that political apathy and cynicism, the concentration on the private and personal, which has continued up to the present, and which was demonstrated in their lack of public response – either negative or positive – to the Chechen War, in which a good many of them were killed. The processes initiated by Gorbachev and Yeltsin have indeed led to a great liberation of energy (both positive and negative) among

Russian youth, but it has been directed overwhelmingly into economic channels; and in many cases, the new freedom has meant freedom to emigrate.[32]

Can events in Russia therefore be described as a 'passive revolution', in the sense formulated by Antonio Gramsci? And if so, does it also make sense to apply to Russia other Gramscian concepts like 'trasformismo' and above all, 'hegemony'?[33]

In my view, the Russian revolution of the 1990s was a 'passive revolution' in that the masses were largely absent. This may have contributed to the fact that the process was far more peaceful than might have been expected; but it also meant that democratic politics have not become rooted in Russian society, above all at the level of local government, which is in some ways less democratic and responsive to the needs of the population than it was in Soviet days. On the other hand, in one key Gramscian sense the latest Russian revolution was certainly not a passive one, because it has led to a complete transformation of Russian property relations and the power that stems from them.

With regard to Risorgimento Italy, Gramsci used 'passive revolution' to indicate a process of 'revolution without revolution' whereby apparently radical changes took place both in the distribution of power among the elites and in the structures of power themselves, without however transforming the basic structures of the economy, or the property relations upon which real power in Italy rested or the ways in which their power was exercised – indeed, in many cases the whole process contained a strong element of masquerade.

The political and economic elite of unified Italy, rather than being a new class, was largely made up of the old elites, with some additions, and continued the economic behaviour of its predecessors, thus prolonging the factors responsible for Italy's economic and social backwardness. In the words of John Davis, which would appear at first sight to have great relevance for contemporary Russia:

> The 'passive revolution' had meant that Italy remained trapped in a framework in which capitalist and pre-capitalist groups co-existed side by side in mutual interdependence. Unlike America, Italian society contained large parasitic and non-productive groups, superfluous bureaucrats and professionals, whom Gramsci described with a characteristic flourish as 'pensioners of economic history.'[34]

Or in Gramsci's own words about the Moderates during the Risorgimento, 'They were aiming at the creation of a modern state, and they created a bastard.'[35]

The masses either took no part in this revolution, were mobilised by one side or another to fight for causes in which they had no genuine interest, or when they did try to defend their own interests, were promptly and ruthlessly suppressed. More radical political and military leaders of the Risorgimento were coopted or marginalised – and when safely dead, were canonised.

Gramsci's concept has proved enormously influential, and while it has been criticised by some contemporary scholars with reference to the Risorgimento, it has been extended by others to take in cases like that of the Mexican Revolution.

Superficially, the attractions of this framework of analysis for Russia and several of the other Soviet republics in the Gorbachev and Yeltsin period are obvious. Indeed, the anti-Soviet revolution in these areas may seem even more 'passive' than the revolutions in Italy or Mexico, since unlike those cases, it did not even involve serious fighting, either in terms of internal war or of international struggle. Even if the suppression of the Azerbaijani nationalists in January 1990 is to be included, the total number of lives directly lost in the overthrow of the Soviet Union was less than two hundred. The attempted counter-revolution of August 1991 cost three lives in Moscow; the independence of Ukraine cost none at all. Yeltsin's suppression of the parliament in October 1993 cost around two hundred more. Of course, the tens of thousands of deaths in Chechnya and the wars in the Transcaucasus and Tajikistan, were also a consequence of the collapse of the Soviet Union, but they were not a direct part of the overthrow of Soviet rule in the Soviet heartland.

To understand why the Soviet state could collapse with such lack of violence, it is important to remember that (*pace* Brzezinski and others),[36] since the death of Stalin, while it remained a police state and did its best to be a totalitarian one, it was not 'terrorist' in the full sense. This is true whether by terrorist we mean the Stalinist totalitarian model or the more chaotic and spontaneous methods of regime and elite self-defence characteristic of Central America. The main reason for this change was of course that Stalin had given the Communist elites themselves a frightful lesson in how terror could get out of hand and threaten everybody.

Thereafter, 'socialist legality', while a myth, was not wholly without content when it came to restraining regime behaviour. For example, in the memoirs of Soviet dissidents such as Petro Grigorenko and Irina Ratushinskaya,[37] it is made obvious how the KGB regularly breaks Soviet law and the Soviet constitution in its persecution of enemies of Communist rule; but what is also striking, by comparison with Stalinist times and indeed parts of the capitalist world, is the extraordinary lengths to which the police and even the KGB go in order to pretend – sometimes it seems almost to themselves – that the rules are in fact being followed. This tendency became even stronger after the Soviet Union signed the Helsinki Human Rights Agreement in 1975, thereby forcing the KGB to perform yet more contortions in an effort to show that Soviet behaviour was really in line with Soviet legal commitments, and giving added legitimacy to domestic criticisms of regime illegality and hypocrisy.[38]

A critical period in this regard was 1962–4. June 1962 saw the last occasion on which Soviet forces opened fire on civilians in the Soviet heartland, when workers protesting against wage cuts were dispersed by army gunfire in Novocherkassk. The wavering of some officers on that occasion – General Matvei Shaposhnikov was dismissed in disgrace for refusing to open fire –

persuaded the regime that it was simply too dangerous to risk mass protest. The lesson was rubbed home by the fall of Khrushchev. His Politburo enemies were backed not just by the armed forces, angry at military cuts, but by the leadership (Communist, bureaucratic and completely Soviet loyalist, of course) of the miners and certain other 'elite' industrial sectors, furious at attempts to shut worn-out pits and reduce benefits. Thereafter, the Soviet regime gave up trying to challenge major institutionalised groups within the Soviet state, even while it cracked down on smaller groups like the liberal or nationalist dissidents. As will be noted in part III, in the 1970s it even compromised, albeit to a very limited extent, with mass nationalist protest in Georgia and Chechnya.

If despite this wariness about using force, Soviet rule was able to continue for another generation, this is partly because for a decade or so the economy went on growing, and then for another decade, the rise in world oil prices bolstered the Soviet treasury. Even more important, however, was the fact that Stalin had done his work too well. Not merely had he established a memory of unspeakable and indiscriminate terror which for decades made people glad of whatever limited security and freedom they enjoyed (in 1990 and 1991, I frequently heard the question put to supporters of radical change, 'Do you want Stalinism to come back? Aren't we better off as we are?'), but he had smashed into atoms any mass social and political forces which could have organised revolt – something which remains of vital importance to this day. Revolution, when it came, had therefore to come from the Soviet elites themselves, but could be conducted without force.

As chapters 6 and 7 will emphasise, in the latest Russian revolution there has therefore been no need for a Garibaldi, no romantic paramilitary radical to set an example of charismatic national leadership and establish a cult of action by an unelected national vanguard – a factor which has already been of immense importance for Russia, and which we should hope will go on being the case.

Something like the concept of 'passive revolution' has been implicit in many interpretations of what has happened in Russia and other former Soviet republics, which often speak of a 'reproduction' or 'circulation' of the old Communist elite into the new post-Soviet ones. In the words of Lilia Shevtsova, 'it is the extent of elite continuity that distinguishes Russia's political transformation.' Françoise Thom developed the theory of a 'second echelon' of younger, more dynamic elements of the Communist nomenklatura who engineered perestroika and glasnost (a more extreme version of this would claim the entire democratic transformation) in order to displace the Brezhnevite old guard and take power themselves, while at the same time gaining access to the full range of Western luxuries and experiences.

On the other hand, a cynical desire to maintain their own power and position against Gorbachev's reforms and the processes they unleashed – and especially to escape implication in the collapse of the August 1991 conservative coup – has been widely held to be responsible for the swing of large parts of the Ukrainian Communist leadership to nationalist positions in 1989–91.

Finally, the continuity of much of the personnel in the fields of political leadership, bureaucracy, and economic management (and military command) has been held responsible for many of the ills of Russia today, from an allegedly Soviet imperial or 'great power complex' to a lack of real commitment to democracy on the part of the Yeltsin administration, to conservatism and corruption on the part of industrial managers.

A good deal of this makes sense; in the case of Boris Yeltsin, for example, it is clear that we were very naive in 1991–3 to think that a sixty year-old Communist Party First Secretary had somehow shed the habits of a lifetime and been reborn a true democrat, simply because in the late 1980s and early 1990s he was for his own reasons opposed to the rule of Gorbachev and the Communist Party.[39]

It is also clear that in Yeltsin's Russia, a tremendous share of economic wealth and power remains in the hands of the old managerial elites. The greater part of manufacturing industry, for example, has in effect become the private property of its former state managers, who have used a wide variety of means – including not infrequently murder – to prevent 'outsiders' (whether Russian or foreign) from gaining an important stake, let alone control. They have also maintained or reforged very close links with the new/old political elites, especially in the great industrial centres in the Russian provinces.[40]

Nomenklatura privatisation has been especially dominant in the regions, but at national level too, the biggest single company in Russia, Gazprom, is also a textbook case, as are Lukoil and Surgutneft. It has been calculated that overall, some 61 per cent of the richest Russians are drawn from the ranks of the former nomenklatura,[41] or senior cadres of the Party and State. Moreover, many of the most powerful private banks, though ostensibly independent, are in fact very dependent on soft loans from the state, and could be ruined overnight if those loans were withdrawn. A great part of the greatest Russian fortunes also originated in the system of state licences and quotas, as described by Pyotr Aven, who ought to know, having been Foreign Trade Minister in the Gaidar government (on the strength of which he himself became one of the great comprador bankers): 'One fine day, your insignificant bank is authorised to conduct operations with budgetary funds, for instance. Or quotas for the export of oil, timber and gas are generously allotted to your company, which is in no way connected with production. In other words, you are appointed a millionaire.'[42]

However, this picture needs to be heavily qualified by three facts. The first is that as the events of 1996 made clear, there are also many among the richest and most powerful men in the Russia of the later 1990s who are not from the old nomenklatura. They are new men who have made their own way to great wealth. Thus the authors of a recent book on Russian privatisation, *Kremlin Capitalism*, write of the 'loans for shares' deal (see below) that 'one new propertied class in Russia, the bankers, had finally succeeded in pushing the government to design a privatisation scheme that did not uniformly favour insiders.'[43] By this they mean the old Soviet management insiders – what this deal did was to consolidate the economic power of a new group of economic 'insiders', those allied to one part or another of the Yeltsin regime, and notably with privatisation chief Anatoly Chubais.

Moreover, a good many even of the 'nomenklatura' elements – like both Vladimir Potanin and Mikhail Khodorkovsky, later head of Menatep bank and one of the chief Yeltsin-created compradors – were from the Komsomol, the Communist Party youth wing. They were young opportunists who had joined the Komsomol in the first place with no belief in Communism, but simply to get ahead. They had not achieved senior state positions, and were too young to have been thoroughly steeped in nomenklatura culture. Under Gorbachev, they used their influence to gain the extraordinary decree of 1988 which gave the Komsomol the first right to set up cooperatives – and went straight into private business.

It is doubtful therefore to what extent these very new men can really be described as part of the 'old elite'. The continuity line also ignores the very major differences between the Communist Party elite, which ruled the country, and the state elite, which managed the economy (and has benefited the most from privatisation). This was not a monolithic or united force.

The critical part in the revolutionary process from 1988 to 1993 was played by the Soviet intellectual elites, which for several decades had been growing in importance as a result of the modernisation and urbanisation of Soviet society. Many of the figures who took leading roles were either from the Communist elite, like Alexander Yakovlev, were children of it, like Yegor Gaidar, or were aspiring to join it, like Sergei Stankevich, Sergei Stepashin, Ruslan Khasbulatov and other opportunist and ambitious young intellectuals. And if Soviet rule had continued for decades, many of these figures would no doubt have risen to the top of the state. But as David Lane points out, such men decided that they could 'realise their intellectual capital in monetary terms' by smashing and completely replacing the Communist system. The element of economic continuity in their thinking was small.[44]

Certainly it would be a mistake to see the old party structures as the organisational base of the new economic elites, who soon freed themselves from any reliance on such a base even when they had formerly belonged to it. It is true that the old Central Committee and its staff continues to be the point of origin of many senior bureaucrats in the Yeltsin administration – but these bureaucrats are clearly less powerful than, and often dependent on, the business magnates. It is these men who wield power, and also set the pattern of social desires and aspirations.

Vladimir Potanin, controller of Oneximbank, from 1995 of Norilsk Nickel, and from 1996–7 Deputy Prime Minister, appears to fit the model of a 'nomenklatura' capitalist. He seems to have had some kind of family connections – at least, he studied at the Moscow Institute of International Relations (very much for the sons of elite, training for prestigious and comfortable foreign assignments).[45] From there he went to the Ministry of Foreign Trade, working in the

metals section. On the basis of this, under Gorbachev, Potanin set up a coop-
erative and went into private metals trading, using his contacts among state
managers, whom he presumably helped to become rich by illegally selling the
products of their mines for their own profits. On the strength of his own profits and contacts in the former Soviet foreign trade bank, Vneshtorgbank,
Potanin founded Oneximbank in 1993. In 1995, he acquired control of the
giant Norilsk nickel-cobalt plant in the 'loans for shares' deal, which he
allegedly worked out personally with privatisation minister Anatoly Chubais.

However, it is important to note that while Potanin's job in the Foreign
Trade Ministry was typical for the nomenklatura capitalists, that was because
of the unique opportunities this job gave both to discover export opportunities in the West, and then to export personally as the Communist system
collapsed. It was by no means a standard 'nomenklatura' job in the sense of
being a senior one in the party or state administration.

Of the other members of the so-called 'group of seven' bankers, four (or
possibly five) were almost by definition semi-outsiders in terms of the old
Communist state, being Jews; and this is also true of many of the rest of the
new businessmen.[46] Of these, Vladimir Gusinsky worked in theatre management, and Boris Berezovsky as a junior planner in the Soviet car industry –
neither of them in nomenklatura positions.

The origins of Vladimir Gusinsky's rise are not clear. In Boris Berezovsky's
case, it seems to have been contacts in the USA and Israel which first allowed
him to begin importing luxury Western cars, while his bureaucratic links (or
simple bribes) allowed him to evade import tariffs on them.[47] The other members of the 'group of seven' (Mikhail Khodorkovsky, Pyotr Aven, Mikhail
Friedman and Alexander Smolensky) all rose through different parts of the
state management system, but an analyst in the mid-1980s would not have
considered any of them to have been part of the nomenklatura in the strict
sense.[48]

The second qualification to the picture of continuity from the old party and
state elite is that when it comes to the partial financial dependence of these
men's businesses on state money, the question is 'Who Whom?' Of course on
the one hand their need for this money virtually forces any major Russian
business or banking figure to seek allies in the administration. But in today's
Russia, rather than this being a sign of state strength, the ability of private
business interests to plunder the state coffers for their private gain is surely a
sign of state weakness, of the manipulation and hollowing-out of the state by
private forces, and above all of course of the corruption of the bureaucracy.[49]

Finally, while much of the membership of the Russian elites may have
stayed the same since Soviet rule, the nature and basis of their power has
changed out of all recognition. The power, the status, even the personal com-
forts of the old elites were given and taken away by the party and state.
Today's oligarchical elites control their own wealth, spend it where they will –
including most notably outside Russia – and will defend it to the death.
Individual tall poppies like Berezovsky may well be cut down by future admin-

istrations, but the wealth of the new Russians as a class could not be taken away from them without a real and violent counter-revolution.

In other words, as far as the elites are concerned, it is Gramsci's passive revolution turned on its head: in Russia, while many of the personnel have stayed the same, the basic economic relations in society have been utterly transformed. There is an echo rather of one of the key phrases of the 'passive revolution' in the Risorgimento spoken by a fictional character a hundred years after the event: the Sicilian nobleman Count Tancredi Falconieri in Lampedusa's *The Leopard*. He tells his uncle that he and his class should support Italian unification so as to secure their own dominance, because 'for everything to stay the same, everything will have to change'. But one of the points of the book is that while this may work for individuals like Tancredi, who make their way into the new Italian liberal national elite, the old feudal world of his uncle is indeed irredeemably doomed.

Russia as a Weak State and a Weak Society

Sometimes, if a state is weak, it is because society is very strong, too strong to be disciplined by state power. While this can give the appearance of anarchy, it can also provide great underlying strengths, at least in the face of particular challenges – something which is exemplified by Chechnya, as part III will describe. Russia by contrast represents one of those cases where a weak state is combined with a weak society. One key result of this has been the failure of Russian society to generate effective democratic political parties as a check on the government and the elites. As of 1997, the Communists remained the only real mass political party in Russia.[50]

The weakness of the Russian state and of Russian society are intimately linked. Under Lenin and Stalin, Russian society was dissolved and atomised to a far greater extent than in any non-Communist country, or even in the Communist ones where Stalinism or Maoism did not operate with full force. For all the (in any case relatively weak) social institutions and traditions of Russia were substituted only the Communist Party and the Soviet state.[51]

Russian society was of course (at least since the fall to the Mongols of Kievan Rus) always underdeveloped by Western European standards. In the – very un-Leninist – words of Gramsci:

> In Russia the state was everything and civil society was primordial and gelatinous: in the West there was a proper relation between the state and civil society, and when the state trembled the sturdy section of civil society was at once revealed. The state was only an outer ditch, behind which was a powerful system of fortresses and earthworks.[52]

Both society and Russian national feeling were therefore much more closely tied to the state than elsewhere, a phenomenon which was vastly increased by

Communist rule. It is hardly surprising therefore that when the Communist Party and the Soviet state collapsed, Russia should be left in such a 'pitiable' condition.

It is also especially important to emphasise the moral dimension. Just as the Communist Party supplanted traditional social forms, so Communist 'morality' supplanted traditional morality, and when it collapsed – as of course it had begun to do decades before Communist rule and the Soviet Union disintegrated – it left moral anarchy. As a result, there is no reason truly enshrined in established social, cultural or state tradition, let alone in the behaviour of the rulers, why Russians today should not steal or take bribes; and there is certainly no reason why they should die in battle.

The level of corruption of the early and mid-1990s, when combined with sheer state disorganisation and the undefined division of powers between the centre and the regions, meant that a great many of the innumerable decrees issued by Yeltsin and Chernomyrdin in recent years were simply never implemented – and quite possibly were never intended to be. An example in the mid-1990s was the repeated decrees granting tax breaks to direct foreign investment, most of which were either simply ignored by the tax authorities, or were contradicted by other laws and decrees. In many cases, the only object of these decrees seems to have been to impress the IMF. The spirit of much of the post-Soviet Russian bureaucracy is summed up in the phrase used by Spanish colonial bureaucrats in replying to orders from Madrid that were against their interests or that they viewed as impossible to enforce: 'obedesco pero no cumplo' – 'I obey but I do not comply.' There is no need for bureaucracies, or local 'parties of power', to break out in open revolt against Moscow in order for them to be able to frustrate state policies which they dislike.

Up to 1998 at least the weakness of the Russian state was such that much of the time it didn't matter a damn what laws were passed in Moscow. Corruption, crime and disobedience are not simply aspects of the new Russian state, as the analysis of some Western economists suggests – they lie at its heart.[53]

A key aspect of this was the collapse of revenue collection, both from taxes and tariffs.[54] In 1992, revenue amounted to 44.2 per cent of GDP, but by 1996 the figure was only 29 per cent. In 1996, the state was able to collect only between 60 and 71 per cent (by some accounts, very much less) of the taxes owed to it – the classic and ancient sign of a failing state (arrears of wages in the same period equalled 7.5 billion dollars).[55] According to the State Revenue Service, one-third of Russian businesses paid no taxes in 1996, another 49 per cent only sporadically.

Tax inspectors who did try to do their jobs could be in mortal danger: twenty-six were killed and seventy-four wounded in 1996 alone.[56] Moreover, while some of these were honourable and indeed heroic servants of the state, others were killed because they had become embroiled in private feuds. As a Chechen mafia leader in Moscow told me,

Much of the tax apparatus here works for us. We tell them who to tax. That means we can protect our business friends, and it also means that we can hit our enemies, quite legally – we just loose the taxmen on them. We also make sure that our friends in the tax inspectorate are safe from any kind of bureaucratic discipline.[57]

In this recent period, there were essentially two aspects to this failure. The first was the involuntary reduction in revenue due to massive evasion and the corruption and sheer disorganisation and contradictions of the tax authorities and the tax codes. Thus in 1996 only 2.8 million people even filed their tax forms, out of an adult population of around 100 million. Russia in 1997 had no computerised database of taxpayers, and indeed many tax offices lacked computers altogether. Even more importantly, Russia's 35,000 junior tax inspectors are officially paid less than an equivalent of 100 dollars a month.[58] In these circumstances, it is hopeless to expect that many taxes will be collected from people who have the wealth to bribe their way out of them. Instead, the tax inspectors are reduced to the ancient habit of taxing not those who can pay, but those who have no defences – in Russia's case, salaried workers and above all foreigners, whose high visibility, lack of local political defence, and more transparent business practices make them easy targets. And even then, much of the money collected never reaches the Treasury. Thus in a typical case, a Western newspaper colleague of mine was asked by the tax inspectors to prove that his office in Moscow was not conducting business – and pending this, his bank account in Moscow was frozen. For 'proof', he was told he would have to have an audit – and the tax inspector just happened to know a Russian auditor who would do the job for 6,000 dollars. When my friend tried to choose his own auditor, this was rejected.

The financial damage to the state is colossal. In 1996, the authorities in the port of Vladivostok estimated that half the goods passing through the port were paying no duties of any kind, nor were their owners paying taxes on their profits.[59] All over Russia, powerful businessmen were using their grip on politics and the bureaucracy to extract tax concessions – thus Potanin used his power over the Yeltsin administration to gain more than 500 million dollars (by some accounts, up to 1.3 billion) in tax exemptions for his Norilsk Nickel, extracted from the state under 'loans for shares' (though the concession was withdrawn in 1997 as the fiscal crisis worsened).

The second development, which took place at the end of 1995 and in the first half of 1996, was the entirely voluntary renunciation by the Yeltsin administration of enormous sums in revenue, by way of giving a bribe to influential sectors of the economy to support Yeltsin in the presidential election of 1996. The most outrageous single example of deliberate exemption from taxes was the National Sports Foundation, directed by Yeltsin's tennis coach and personal friend (and later Sports Minister) Shamil Tarpishchev.

Russian Compradors

Post-Soviet Russia has suffered an added burden because of the comprador nature of its new elites: that is, businessmen, bankers and the officials who are their clients and allies, people who are overwhelmingly dependent for their wealth on the export of raw materials, and only to an extremely limited extent on manufacturing, or on 'adding value' in some way to Russia's products. This perhaps is inevitable, given the intense wastefulness and incompetence of Soviet industry, many of whose sectors, as is now notorious, were actually value-reducing – that is to say that the raw materials would have earned more if sold on international markets than the shoddy and useless finished product.

None the less, dependence on the export of raw materials could well represent a trap for Russia, of a kind that has closed around many other countries in the past. It enables the Russian state to support basic services and buy off significant parts of the population without having to conduct truly deep reforms. More importantly, it allows many Russian big businessmen and officials to become fantastically wealthy simply by using existing Soviet equipment to extract various substances from the ground, without having to reinvest a kopek in the new kinds of production and plant that the country will desperately need in the longer term.

Thus the move of Boris Berezovsky from the motor industry first to banking and then to oil extraction (not by founding a new company, but by using state connections to seize an existing state one) is both typical and from his own financial point of view, entirely logical. It is not, however, in any way beneficial for Russia. Equally important is the way in which a business world concentrated on the struggle for control of strategic raw materials will tend to resist or ignore the new mentalities, business practices and legal norms so crucial to true economic progress. By their nature, oil and minerals can also be controlled by a small number of people or of big corporations – which can create the political domination of a narrow, corrupt and unproductive oligarchy, as Latin America found for so many decades.[60]

The comprador nature of the Russian oligarchy under Yeltsin is at its most glaringly visible in Vladivostok in the Russian Far East.[61] This is an area which for several years has been undergoing an acute economic crisis, due to the collapse of local industries and the cost of shipping fuel and materials from Russia. In terms of infrastructure and manufacturing, it makes a pitiful comparison with the East Asian states (except of course for North Korea). The Far East has been the scene of some of the most dreadful stories of contemporary Russian poverty and hunger, and in the winter of 1996–7, thousands of local workers were on strike because their wages were up to six months in arrears. Yet the crumbling, potholed roads of Vladivostok, where most of the street lights have long since failed or been turned off to save electricity, are jammed with second-hand Japanese cars (many of them admittedly originally stolen), and the casinos and night clubs are crammed with very prosperous-looking types and their women. The wealth to buy these comes purely from the export of raw materials – timber, fish, oil, gold, metals, even tiger skins. As long as these last – and the tigers and the trees are admittedly going pretty fast – and there is anything of the old Soviet pie to carve up, the local elites will have no interest in manufacturing, let alone outside investment. In the bitter words of a local journalist, 'Why should they care about any of that? Half the wealth of Siberia passes through their hands!'

This is one key difference from the American robber barons of the nineteenth century, or indeed the pioneering Russian capitalists of the same period, the Morozovs and Putilovs. These were true pioneers, who built from scratch. With extremely rare exceptions, the contemporary Russians of the early and mid-1990s exploited existing Soviet plant.

Equally importantly, the gains made by the great American magnates were mostly ploughed straight back into American production, or were at least spent at home. They were not sent out of America on a massive scale to Swiss or other bank accounts. In Russia, by contrast, capital flight was estimated by Western experts to have reached a total of between 60 billion and 73 billion dollars between 1992 and 1996, though by 1997 there were signs that some was returning.

Moreover, with rare exceptions, the new Russian compradors up to mid 1997 at least were deeply hostile to outside strategic investment – for after all, what could Western control of companies bring them but extra competition? This hostility has been especially clear and overt in the case of the banks, but in a more muted way it is true of the extraction industries as well. For example, most Russian owners in this field supported the rule which bars non-Russian companies from owning more than 15 per cent of oil companies; and the privatisation process could then be rigged so that the blocks of shares auctioned at any one time were more than 15 per cent, thereby excluding Western participation altogether.[62] This, on top of the general insecurity of the investment climate, the contempt for contractual obligations and the dreadful tax situation, kept new direct foreign investment between 1989 and 1996 to a mere 5.3 billion dollars, a third of that in Hungary which has one-fifteenth of Russia's population.[63]

The possession of abundant raw materials can thus prove a curse rather than a blessing; first, because they spare both the state and many of its people from having to make hard choices and take real risks until it is too late; secondly, because it encourages the creation of small, wealthy but unproductive elites; thirdly, because the interests of these elites lie far more in keeping their foreign markets open than they do in stimulating domestic consumption or investment; and finally, because the raw materials eventually run out – and if a state, or its businesspeople, have not reinvested the profits from them in some form of other production or infrastructure, then the country will eventually find that from all this it has gained precisely nothing.

While evidence of reinvestment at home is therefore slight, so far, while evidence of wasteful conspicuous consumption is overwhelming. Newspaper articles over Christmas and the New Year 1996–7 described the New Russians and their families queuing up at Sadko's Arcade in Moscow to spend hundreds – sometimes thousands – of dollars apiece on artificial Christmas trees from the West, in a country with the largest number of fir trees on earth, and while hungry workers and their children in the Far East had been reduced to a diet of stray dog. According to a reliable source, in 1995 one of the 'group of seven' spent 35,000 dollars in one evening at the new Hotel National in Moscow, on a birthday party for his seven-year old son.

Some kind of record in such behaviour was set by Chernomyrdin on his notorious Yaroslavl bear hunt of January 1997. Not merely did he break Russia's hunting laws by shooting a she-bear and her two cubs, but in order to hunt in comfort he spent up to 500,000 dollars of the state's money to clear a helicopter landing strip, build two kilometres of new road through the forest, and fly in a small army of hunters and beaters.[64] Despite having been so well defended, Chernomyrdin replied to later criticism by bragging in macho terms about the danger that he had been in, and offered no apology whatsoever. It is not easy to speak of real 'democracy' in a country in which the Prime Minister can brazenly ignore both the law and public opinion in this way.

The contrast with the plight of much of the population is all too clear. In the words of Joseph Blasi and his colleagues, all of them in principle strong supporters of the privatisation process,

> the government as a whole has exhibited an unfortunate lack of concern for the plight of old people, the sick, the unemployed, and its soldiers while it has paid close attention to the demands for subsidies, favours and insider deals by powerful directors of big enterprises and other people with political connections… The IMF and World Bank have repeatedly stipulated that the government must make a social safety-net a priority to aid the weakest citizens during the transition. The government has ignored this injunction.[65]

Thus funding of health care has dropped by almost 50 per cent, not just in absolute terms but as a proportion of the budget: from 3.4 per cent of the Soviet budget under Gorbachev to only 1.8 per cent in 1996.[66]

The merging of the top ranks of the financial, industrial and comprador elites, and their achievement of supreme power over the state, was a culmination of the Russian privatisation process, involving as it did the disposal of some of the most important and above all profitable state properties. The way that privatisation has been conducted in Russia is by now pretty well known, but it bears repeating because there is still a strong tendency in the West to hail it as the greatest success story of the 'economic reforms'.[67] In terms of shops and small businesses, this is fair enough; the problem lies above all in the extraction industries, where the great comprador profits are to be made.

The privatisation programme introduced by the Russian government in

1992 allowed for the purchase of state property by the Russian people by means of vouchers worth 10,000 roubles each, one of which was given to every member of the population. This amounted to only a small fraction of the total value of the Russian state economy (and also only a tiny fraction of the savings of ordinary Russian people in savings banks, which were wiped out by inflation). In other words, an element of fraud was present from the start. However, this was unavoidable. To have distributed freely tradable vouchers with a worth really equivalent to that of the state property for privatisation would have triggered an unstoppable hyperinflation – which apart from anything else would itself soon have nullified the vouchers' value.

According to official figures, around 39 per cent of Russians simply sold or gave away their vouchers; 8 per cent said that they used their vouchers to buy shares in the enterprises where they worked; and 9 per cent bought shares in other enterprises, mostly famous national or local ones.[68] Another 30 per cent put their vouchers into investment funds, many of which simply stole them, passed them on, and then vanished into thin air. As for the people who bought shares in companies, very few have seen any dividends, while shareholder control remains almost completely absent. Workers' shares generally became a means of consolidating management control, in an implicit deal whereby the workers allowed the management to run the companies as their own property in return for the managers guaranteeing the workers their jobs – albeit frequently without paying them. In the perhaps unduly contemptuous words of Albert Speransky,

> The worker's most dangerous enemies are his own fearfulness, passivity, readiness to give way before stronger, more powerful people, and his complete legal and economic illiteracy. At the beginning of privatization, he elected people whom he never considered his friends, to represent his interests. They, in turn, sold him out and made him a hostage of the directors, and made him still more miserable and dependent... Hired workers today have absolutely no idea what is going on with property, where the country is headed, or where they are being driven like a herd of sheep.[69]

The failure of privatisation to create anything like real mass shareholding, let alone control and restructuring of enterprises, is hardly surprising. Even the far better regulated, more democratic, and economically mature Czech Republic suffered innumerable problems both during and as a result of its own mass voucher privatisation, as the economic crisis of the spring of 1997 revealed.

The distribution of what could be called the 'commanding heights' of the Russian economy, and the creation of a new class of great compradors, however took place largely separate from mass privatisation. Chubais's argument in defence of what has happened, which has been taken up and parroted by his Western allies, has been summed up and criticised by Andrei Piontkovsky, head of the Moscow Centre for Strategic Studies (not, it must be emphasised a reactionary or left-leaning figure, and a great admirer of another reformer, Boris Nemtsov):

> Like many reformers, Chubais believes that it is not important how property is distributed, as long as property owners are created. After they have had their share of thievery, so the argument goes, they will start to turn their efforts to raising productivity. But Russia has experienced not so much the privatisation of control over property as the privatisation of control over the state, over financial flows and budget resources. The reformers have created a Frankenstein reform, and those who have got a taste of this fabulous means of enrichment are like addicts who will never get off the needle of budget money.[70]

Sergei Kovalev, the former dissident and leading democrat, reported that Chubais had told him in 1994 that the new businessmen 'steal and steal. They are stealing absolutely everything and it is impossible to stop them. But let them steal and take their property. They will then become owners and decent administrators of this property.' Mr Kovalev commented that 'from my point of view this is economic romanticism. There is a view that the country will become a market economy and everything good will follow. Then there will be democracy. In my view it is a very dangerous mistake.' Yegor Gaidar, the original father of Russia's free market reforms, has also warned against the way in which the new economic oligarchy, with its close ties to the state, was restricting the free market and 'creating the basis for enormous corruption'.[71]

The consummation of Chubais's privatisation and of the seizure of the most valuable assets of the Russian state was the 'loans for shares' scheme implemented in the autumn of 1995. This was presented as a response to the state's fiscal crisis, already looming in 1995. The idea was that in return for large loans from the biggest private Russian banks, the state would *temporarily* give them controlling shares in some of Russia's main companies in the extraction field.[72] The greatest of these industries, Gazprom, (with a market capitalisation – for various reasons very undervalued – of 8.2 billion dollars in 1996), had effectively already been privatised into the hands of its management, notably Prime Minister and former Gazprom general director Chernomyrdin, while retaining its monopoly; thereby allegedly making Chernomyrdin the richest man in Russia (though of course he denies this).[73]

In return for these industries, the beneficiary millionaires promised to support Yeltsin, and not some other and healthier anti-Communist candidate, in the upcoming 1996 presidential elections. They financed the campaign, and directed their respective newspapers and television stations to propagandise on behalf of the President.[74] Boris Berezovsky had acquired an 8 per cent, but in effect dominant, stake in the central state television company, ORT, in 1994, allegedly with Chubais's help, and became its deputy general director (as of 1997, ORT remains 51 per cent state-owned). He also controls the leading daily *Nezavisimaya Gazeta*. Gusinsky controls NTV, the newspaper *Segodnya* and the news magazine *Itogi*.[75] All over Russia in these years, big companies were doing the same in their own areas. Thus in Vologda region, the giant Severstal steel-making plant had by 1997 gained control of a radio station, four local TV stations and two newspapers, which it used to support favoured candidates in local and national elections.[76] In 1997, after the 'group of seven' had broken up, Berezovsky and Gusinsky used their media quite openly to attack Potanin, as a weapon in the battle to sieze the remaining state extraction industries. Potanin hit back with his own media, notably *Komsomskaya Pravda*. So much for media 'independence'.

Following the loans for shares deal, these men's chief representative and benefactor, former privatisation chief Anatoly Chubais, was reappointed to the government first as presidential chief of staff with responsibility for organising the electoral campaign, and then as Deputy Premier, and two of these men, Potanin and Berezovsky, later joined the government themselves. On top of loans for shares, Chubais has also sought to increase the power of the banks by shaping the development of the stock market in the direction of the German model, where a few great banks play the leading role in investment. Of course, this is not in itself illegitimate, but in Russia's circumstances it looks very like another attempt to both strengthen and justify the new status quo. In the words of Joel Bismuth, Vice-President of Unibest Bank and a critic of this tendency, 'This gives incredible power to the banks. They will hold the reins of the securities market and will have a strong influence on the pricing of shares. An oligarchy of banks will gain predominance.'[77]

In an interview with the *Financial Times* in October 1996, Berezovsky himself was extremely frank, not to say boastful, about what they had done and the power and wealth they had achieved. He said that the businessmen concerned – himself, Potanin, Vladimir Gusinsky of the Most group, Mikhail Khodorkovsky of Menatep, Alexander Smolensky of Stolichny Bank and Pyotr Aven and Mikhail Friedman of Alpha Bank – had decided that it was vital at all costs to defeat the threat of a Communist victory in the June 1996 presidential elections, and that they engineered the appointment of Chubais as campaign organiser, and first the alliance with General Lebed and then his dismissal. He said in particular that the Jewish members of the group feared a nationalist and anti-semitic backlash in Russia.[78] (Berezovsky himself from 1993 to 1996 had Israeli dual citizenship; he took it, he explained later, not because of identification with Israel, but because in 1993 there were powerful people in Russia out to get him and he wanted an escape hatch for himself and his family.)[79]

Above all, he said, he and Vladimir Gusinsky 'were the first who realised how the mass media could assist the different steps we wanted to take'. He said that apart from using the media, he and his associates had paid 3 million dollars to a special election committee headed by Chubais and including Yeltsin's daughter Tatiana Dyachenko because 'she is the most effective channel to inform the President.'[80] Chubais is closely linked to Tatyana

Dyachenko – Moscow rumours say that she is his mistress – who has been playing an increasingly important role and in June 1997 was made an official aide to the President.[81]

In fact, in this interview Berezovsky exaggerated both the power and the cohesion of this new oligarchy: despite their enormous wealth, it seems unlikely that, as he claimed, they control between them more than 50 per cent of Russia's GNP, and by the next spring, various members of the group were once again rivals – but his words were an accurate reflection of their colossal arrogance and self-confidence.

Under 'loans for shares', the stakes in the oil, mining and transport companies concerned were supposed to be auctioned off to the bank which offered the biggest loans – but in fact, the auctions gave every sign of having been rigged in advance in favour of chosen banking groups, and the sums of money raised were pitiful, if only because foreign bids were as usual excluded. In all, the state received barely 1 billion dollars in 1995–6 for handing over controlling stakes in a large part of Russia's most profitable sectors and in some cases (notably nickel) of the world production of the commodities involved.

After one year, according to the deal, the state could buy back these shares at a relatively modest rate of interest. If the state could not find the money the banks would have to put the shares up for auction; but auctions managed by *themselves*. In fact – and this was transparently obvious from the start – in no case has the state been able to buy back the shares, and 1996–7 has seen a series of rigged auctions whereby control of these companies has passed permanently to the banks concerned at prices which almost invariably were barely above the starting level.[82]

Several fights developed as a result between the old state managements and the new political insiders over control of some companies – for example the giant Novolipetsk steelworks. Oneximbank acquired a 15 per cent stake as part of 'loans for shares', and then faced a determined counter-attack by the management. Western investors faced off on different sides, with two investment funds backing the MFK Bank, and Transworld Metals backing the management.[83]

But this share in Novolipetsk was the least of the assets acquired by Potanin's Oneximbank under loans for shares. He also gained a controlling stake in the giant oil company Sidanko and the North West shipping line (the latter for a derisory 7 million dollars), and most importantly, a 38 per cent (and effectively controlling) share in the Norilsk Group, which owns the rights to 35 per cent of the world's estimated nickel reserves, 20 per cent of the platinum and 10 per cent of the copper. The total price was less than 300 million dollars (170 million dollars for Norilsk) – perhaps one-fifteenth of their market value. However, due to the cost of supporting the over-large population of the Arctic city of Norilsk, 300,000 strong, after the steep rise in fuel and transport costs of recent years, for the time being this may have been something of a poisoned gain for Potanin. By the spring of 1997 the group was deep in debt and the workers were on strike because their pay was months in arrears.[84] It is also only fair to add that while the oil and gas producing companies have all evaded taxes on a massive scale, they have also suffered from non-payment by their own domestic consumers. In the case of Gazprom, this became worse in 1996 because as part of its inducement to industrial forces to support Yeltsin in the elections, the government forbade the gas giant to cut off supplies for non-payment.

In May 1997, Berezovsky moved to take full control of Russia's seventh largest oil company, Sibneft, which he had provisionally acquired under loans for shares. By then, the original 'group of seven' had fallen out again, and Potanin, who had been removed from the government in March,[85] tried to cut in with a bid from KM Bank, an offshoot of his Oneximbank.[86] He then found turned against him exactly the same tactics he had used himself in the past. Berezovsky's MFK Bank, which had received 51 per cent of the Sibneft shares in 1995, was also responsible for auctioning them. KM Bank was informed that the documents it submitted for the bid were not in order – on the eve of the auction, so that there could be no chance of rectification or appeal. Foreign bidders were completely excluded. Sibneft was eventually 'sold' to a hitherto completely unknown company called FNK (Finantsovaya Neftyanaya Kompaniya), which was universally assumed to be a barely camouflaged front for Berezovsky' s MFK itself. The price paid was 110 million dollars: only 9 million above the starting price, and around one-sixth of Sibneft's estimated market value. The *Moscow Times* commented,

> The outcome may be poetic, but it is not justice. Once again, the government has let prize assets go for a fraction of their market value, and shown that it cares little for the idea of transparency. The notion that an anonymous buyer could gain the rights to such a major company would be cause for outrage if it were not so patently false [false that is that FNK really existed].[87]

As for Russia's second biggest oil company, Yukos, Dow Jones (which can hardly be accused of lack of sympathy for the reform process) reported in December 1996 that the Russian Federal Property Fund (Chubais's former domain), in a rigged auction, had sold a controlling share to a front company for the bank Menatep – which was also charged with organising the auction. In the words of an analyst with a Moscow brokerage, 'This whole auction was planned, and it came out just the way everyone expected. The winner is just acting for Menatep.' The front company had paid 160.1 million dollars for a 33 per cent share – just 100,000 dollars above the required minimum bid, and less than half the market value of the shares as assessed by independent experts.[88]

In February 1997, a 40 per cent stake in another of Russia's huge oil concerns, Surgutneftegas, was sold for 73.5 million dollars (415 billion roubles) to a 'pensions fund' created and controlled by the company's existing management. Once again, competitors (above all foreigners) were excluded and the price was less than 100,000 dollars above the starting price. The estimated market capitalisation of Surgutneftegas in May 1997 by contrast was 4.7 *billion* dollars.[89] In this case, however, the outcome was typical of the insider privatisation by the existing managements which had formed so large a part of privatisation in general, and not of 'loans for shares'.[90]

The losses to the state exchequer from corrupt privatisation and especially loans for shares have been enormous. The 1996 state budget forecast 12.3 trillion roubles in revenue from privatisation in that year. The figure collected was barely 2.5 trillion, most of it from one relatively honest sale, of a stake in the telecommunications giant UES, in December, after the fiscal crisis had become so grave as to threaten the stability of the state and its access to international loans.

Although, as already noted, the group of seven soon broke up again, and in 1997 the state was forced to make greater efforts to raise revenue from the compradors, in my view the ascendancy of this oligarchy, or a new one composed of different individuals but the same essential elements, is fairly secure. It will almost certainly survive changes in the political leadership in Moscow, simply because the profits from the extraction and export of raw materials are so great, and the government's ability to tax and control them so slight, that they have become by far the single most powerful factor in Russian politics – more so than the presidency, much more so than the parliament.

The presence of these raw materials is indeed the key to the whole nature of the Russian polity as it has developed in the 1990s, and as I believe it will remain for a considerable time to come. The new Russian elites, whether drawn from the former Communist managerial elites, like Viktor Chernomyrdin and the managers of Lukoil and Surgutneft, or junior officials turned entrepreneurs, like Potanin or Berezovsky, are basically compradors; the great bulk of their wealth, whether directly (as with Chernomyrdin and Potanin) or indirectly, through a banking sector heavily dependent on export profits (as with Gusinsky), comes ultimately from the export of raw materials, and to a lesser extent from the import of goods which are ultimately paid for by these exports. The same is true, of course, of several other former Soviet republics, notably Kazakhstan, Azerbaijan and eastern Ukraine.

This is hardly a matter of doubt: the official figures speak for themselves, and are likely to be if anything a severe understatement of the real position, given the obvious interest of Russian companies in under-reporting the amounts that they are exporting. Thus according to the World Bank's figures for 1995, Russian exports of all kinds totalled $79.8 billion. Of this figure, by far the largest share was provided by non-metallic mineral products (principally oil and natural gas), which accounted for $33.3 billion. Next came base metals, with $15.5 billion. Precious stones accounted for $5.3 billion; wood and paper products (but mainly raw timber, plywood and pulp), $4.1 billion. Altogether then raw materials amounted to $58.2 billion, or 73 per cent of total exports. As against this, the much vaunted Russian armaments industry, together with exports of civilian planes and vehicles, amounted to only $4.7

billion, chemical products (including unprocessed ones), $6.2 billion, and machinery $3.8 billion.[91]

As of 1993, Russia was the world's largest producer of natural gas, with 27 per cent of world ouput, and of nickel; the second largest producer of diamonds, aluminium and platinum; the third largest of oil; and the fourth largest of gold, copper, steel, coal and cereals. No other country produces such a range of commodities on such a scale.[92] It was the export of these commodities, and above all oil and gas, which were chiefly responsible for sustaining Communist rule and the Soviet Union in the 1970s and 80s, and for funding the expansion of the Soviet armed forces, the Soviet space programme and the geopolitical challenge to the West in Africa, Central America and elsewhere. They now lie in the hands of a few dozen great compradors and their followers and some thousands of smaller businessmen. It is hardly surprising not just that they are doing very well, but that they are able to support a significant part of the rest of society, thereby creating the appearance of a 'middle class' in Moscow and a few other cities.[93]

The importance of raw material exports is equally striking when compared to the value of domestic industrial production.[94] Meanwhile, Russia's greatest long-term asset, its highly educated population, has been wasting away. With highly trained scientists reduced to repairing TV sets for a living, school-teachers unpaid for months on end, money both for universities and for scientific research projects reduced to derisory levels, and student entries into even the most prestigious Russian universities dropping radically, the signs in this field are hardly encouraging (an exception is in the field of computer software, where the Russians are proving real wizards – but often, unfortunately, in the criminal wing of the industry).

The question of whether Russia can break out of this trap leads inexorably to the question of whether the world economy of the early twenty-first century will actually need Russia as anything other than a source of raw materials and their profits. To this it is obviously impossible at present to give any categorical answer, but the signs are not very encouraging. There seems to be a real danger of Russia becoming (or rather remaining) an economically dependent *Nebenland*, peripheral to the major developments of the world economy and of human civilisation.

Ruinous But Probably Stable

This picture is the reality behind what journalists, pundits, economists and governments have all called 'Russian economic reform' – in many ways a most misleading phrase. For while legal changes and policies by the Gorbachev and Yeltsin administrations played a part in unlocking the gates, what has followed this liberation has been far less a process of state-led reform than a tremendous explosion of chaotic energy and initiative from below – with results both good and bad, but certainly unplanned.

Up to 1996, the good results in the economic field have been above all in the release of entrepreneurial initiative and energy in the field of small business, retail and services, and in the vastly increased range of services and goods available to those Russians with high or medium incomes, compared to the miserable situation under Soviet rule. The main bad results were the creation of an economic oligarchy whose grip on the state is helping to cripple revenue collection and foreign direct investment; the entrenchment of organised crime in both the economy and the administration; and the creation of an extreme dependence on imported consumer goods and foodstuffs. If this continues, it will destroy any possibility of building up Russian agriculture or a domestic consumer industry.

And it seems likely to continue. In principle, of course there might be strong arguments for a moderate and selective policy of protective tariffs, as practised by the United States, for example, during the period of its industrial development in the later nineteenth century. However, not merely is the whole weight of the West, and Western-dominated international financial institutions, directed against protection on the part of Russia; equally or more importantly, as the example of large parts of nineteenth-century Latin America demonstrates, a comprador elite which depends on exports of commodities and raw materials for its wealth and power is very unlikely to allow a policy that might provoke Western retaliation against those exports – especially since the sectors of the Russian economy to benefit would be ones in which the dominant oligarchy has little stake.[95]

However, on the positive side, this also means that even if the Russian armed forces were in any condition to mount major operations beyond Russia's borders (which for the foreseeable future they clearly are not), such operations would be very unlikely. So, while Russia might perhaps be drawn into an intervention in Kazakhstan, for example, an invasion of the Baltic States, or even of Ukraine, would be out of the question – even if rhetoric by members of the regime might sometimes suggest otherwise. Moreover, this will be true of all these men's successors in power, so long as they go on representing the same economic interests. So the new Russian order is unlikely to be destabilised by international war.

The way in which the control of Russia's natural resources was privatised into a small number of hands might have been expected to produce violent resistance – especially since (as, for instance, the London property market shows)[96] so much of this wealth has been invested abroad, or simply spent on foreign luxuries. That serious protest has not happened is partly due to Russia's demographic structure (see following chapter) and partly to the absence in the world today of any serious ideology of revolution – indeed, any really powerful ideological alternative whatsoever to liberal capitalism; of this more later.

However, also of great importance is the simple fact that thanks to its enormous size, Russia has so many natural resources to go around. Siberia, largest and second oldest (after Spanish America) of all the European territorial conquests, continues to pay dividends. Of course, per head of population,

Russia's mineral and other wealth cannot compare to Saudi Arabia's or Kuwait's; but there is certainly enough to satisfy both key sections of the former elites and the more dynamic sections of the younger generation. In the cynical words of Sir Robert Walpole concerning official patronage and early eighteenth-century British politicians, 'there is enough pasture for all the sheep'. Moreover, there has still been something left over to stabilise the currency and maintain services for the population at large. This, at least as much as faster Russian reform, has been responsible for Russia's economic lead over Ukraine, for example.

Equally importantly, natural economic processes, in Russia as elsewhere, ensure that a disproportionate amount of the wealth generated will concentrate in the capital, Moscow. In the long run, this may create imbalances and resentments with serious consequences; for the moment, however, the result has been that whoever is in power has no need to fear serious social unrest, let alone revolution, on the Kremlin's doorstep. On the contrary: both the parliamentary election of 1995 and the presidential one of 1996 produced large majorities in Moscow for the status quo.[97]

Finally, as a cause both of Russian state weakness and of Russian stability, there is Russian federalism, which combined with the weakness of the central administration under Yeltsin has allowed a tremendous leaching away of power to the regions and republics. However, while this has in turn contributed mightily to the weakness of the central state and the erosion of its revenue base, it has proved very effective in defusing moves for secession from most of Russia's ethnic minorities.

As noted in part I, the Chechen example of revolt has failed to spread to other autonomous republics.[98] Their rulers are generally from the old elites, long accustomed to carry out an elaborate political dance with the central authorities in order to extract subsidies and concessions from the centre, and more than happy that the new weakness of the central state allows them to extract such concessions on a previously undreamed-of scale.[99] The sheer anarchy of the Russian constitutional order and tax code also means that they are able to evade paying many of the taxes they owe to the central state, and Yeltsin's bribes in 1996 as part of his election campaign have strengthened the position of the regional elites still further.

Liberal Capitalist Hegemony in Russia

My judgement would be therefore that for the medium to long term the new ruling comprador elites are now quite firmly in power. There may well be violent changes of government, and a number of individuals will certainly be replaced if a new regime comes to power – and may very well be subjected to show trials if they do not get out of the country quickly enough – but the basic nature of the system will remain unchanged. There are essentially four reasons for this: the openness of the new elites to entry from below; the ability of the new elites peacefully to fix elections; their willingness to fight, and use repression, if peaceful measures fail; and the hegemony of liberal capitalist consciousness in Russia and throughout today's world.

The ascendancy of the 'group of seven' in 1996 suggested that the Russian political and economic systems had both fallen under closed oligarchical control of a very narrow kind. If this had continued to be the case, it would sooner or later have provoked a really serious explosion led by all the excluded groups, notably of course businesspeople shut out from their share of government loans and contracts.

In neighbouring Ukraine that year, the dominance of the 'Dnipropetrovsk mafia', brought to power by President Kuchma and Prime Minister Pavlo Lazarenko, and its greedy monopolisation of the fruits of office, was beginning to cause serious discontent among the elites of other regions of Ukraine, and ultimately led to Lazarenko's dismissal in June 1997 – though only after vehement protests from the USA and international financial institutions.

In Russia however, by the summer of 1997 the 'group of seven' had clearly broken up again, and there seems little reason to doubt that in the eventual battle to succeed Yeltsin they will be found on different sides – unless there seems a real possibility of a Communist victory, in which case they may campaign again. In any case, Moscow is not the whole of Russia: in the eighty-nine regions and autonomous republics, though local 'parties of power' can close their ranks to exclude outsiders, it would be impossible for any group of Moscow-based magnates to achieve a general monopoly, so there will always be opportunities for new people to make their way.

In the winning of elections the first asset is the sheer amount of wealth that has been accumulated by the new elites, and which they can use in politics to defend their position and to 'make elections', in the old Spanish phrase. Compared to liberal regimes of the nineteenth and early twentieth centuries, their capacity to fix or make elections has suffered a major setback, but also gained a tremendous asset. The loss is the introduction of universal suffrage, which has obviously complicated matters enormously compared to the days of electorates with high property qualifications. Moreover, to judge by opinion polls, while very sceptical about most of the other results of the 1990s revolution, ordinary Russians are deeply and genuinely attached to the idea of free and fair elections, and would be angered by too gross and public an infringement of this principle. A minor additional hazard is the presence of international observers.

Against these drawbacks, however, must be set television as a force for shaping and manipulating public opinion, whether in the hands of the state or of private business. Moreover, the use of television in this way, and its control by a small and decreasing number of great media magnates, is coming to seem perfectly natural in the West as well, as is demonstrated both by the ascendancy of Rupert Murdoch, and the increasing domination of American election campaigns by purchases of TV advertising. Rather than an anti-democratic scandal, the manipulation of television in Russia thus comes to appear to the Russians themselves as a natural part of a global trend.

Another reason why the present order in Russia seems likely to endure is the ruthlessness and courage of the comprador magnates who dominate it. Detestable though many of them are, one must give them this: there is nothing wrong with their nerves. Moral or physical cowards, or men with many scruples, did not become successful businessmen in Russia in the early 1990s. They have already proved that they are willing to risk death, and to kill each other to gain wealth; there can be little doubt that they will kill anyone else who threatens them, so long as they think they can get away with it. In Pareto's terminology, they are not foxes but lions, willing to use violence to acquire and keep power. (Though, as noted, this does not mean that any government in Moscow could succeed in imposing an effective authoritarian regime on the whole of Russia, given the very genuine federal or even confederal nature of the Russian state today.)

Another question of course is whether anyone else will fight for them. On this it is impossible to give a definitive answer at present. My impression of the men in SOBR (who presumably would be in the forefront of the defence of the administration against serious public unrest) was that, as they themselves said, they would be very unwilling to defend the Yeltsin administration against any repetition of October 1993; and certainly that they would be utterly unwilling to fire into crowds of demonstrators. They might however be willing to engage in battle with the armed retainers of the political rivals of their immediate employer.

The great magnates of course now have their own small private armies of security guards, but whether they would be effective in keeping public order remains to be seen. Faced with really serious public protests, therefore, a Russian administration might collapse with surprising speed.

However, it seems doubtful whether Russian society today is actually capable of generating mass social and political protest, and also, if for example the Yeltsin administration – or a succeeding one of the same stripe – were brought down, whether whatever followed would be essentially different. In today's climate, a method of rule which exploits the levers of power of a liberal capitalist hegemony seems altogether more feasible than a regime invoking any kind of faith – or, of course, in spite of the gesture of elections, than any kind of genuine democracy.

5 'Who Would Be a Soldier If You Could Work in a Bank?': Social and Cultural Roots of the Russian Defeat

War is a trial of moral and physical forces by means of the latter... One might say that the physical seem little more than the wooden hilt, while the moral factors are the precious metal, the real weapon, the finely-honed blade.

Clausewitz, *On War*, p. 185

In war, the moral is to the physical as ten to one.

Napoleon Bonaparte, attributed

There was always opposition to the state among the people; owing to the excessive geographical space, however, it was expressed in flight and the shunning of obligations which the state imposed on the people, but not by effective opposition and not by struggle.

Nikolai Kostomarov, 1817-85, Russian–Ukrainian historian

In this chapter I shall analyse the different underlying social, cultural and psychological reasons for the Russian defeat in Chechnya, and the overall weakness of Russian society today when it comes to the waging of war and the pursuit of imperial goals. This weakness will remain even if the Russian economy improves somewhat over the years to come, for economic growth alone will guarantee neither that the Russian state will be able to mobilise greater national wealth for its own purposes, nor that it will find enough Russian soldiers willing to risk their lives to support these purposes. Russia's weakness in this regard has specific features, but also reflects wider trends in the modern world.

Overall, Russia's importance in the world will almost certainly go on declining. First of all, it should be remembered that Russia is quite simply not among the real heavyweights any more in terms of population or economic power: at 147.5 million (1996 figure) the Russian population is barely half that of the former Soviet Union and will soon be less than half that of the USA. It ranks sixth in the world, less than Indonesia (187 million) and Brazil (162 million) and not much bigger than Pakistan and Japan.[1] Russia's relative decline will become more and more evident in the years to come, for the Russian population is dropping fast (by almost 3 million, or 2 per cent, since

1989), whereas those of 'developing' states in Asia continue to increase. The population drop would have been even steeper, to around 145 million, were it not for the influx of Russian and other migrants from other republics of the former Union. If the population decline of 1990–6 continues, then it is projected that by the year 2015 the Russian population will have dropped to only 115 million.[2]

This of course would not matter much if the Russian economy were successful and growing; but in fact it is in steep decline. This is likely to continue relative to other states even if the Russian economy recovers somewhat. Thus by 1997, Russian GNP was barely twice that of Mexico. By the year 2000, if present trends continue, Russian GNP will be only twice that of Poland, which renders absurd the idea that Russia could once more in the foreseeable future dominate Central Europe. Most important of all, by 1997 Russian GNP was already barely a quarter that of China, which has therefore emerged as by far the leading economic force in continental Asia, and the obvious senior in any future Sino-Russian alliance.

This does not mean of course that Russia will not go on being the most important state within the former Soviet region, and of major significance for those states and regions directly adjoining it – notably Europe; but it is already apparent that for the United States, a global and oceanic power, Russia is becoming of less and less importance.

Demographic Change: The Engine of Expansion Goes Into Reverse

Underlying the reduced population, and the whole changed nature of Russian power at the end of the twentieth century, has been a historic shift in demographic patterns – part of a general shift in the industrialised nations, but with specific post-Soviet features. This shift has implications for the Russian state and its political and military condition in three main fields: Russia's relations with its various neighbours, especially in Asia; for the political behaviour of the Russian population; and the Russian armed forces in their social and economic context.

From the mid-eighteenth century until the 1960s, the Russian population grew appreciably faster than that of most of Russia's neighbours, quadrupling in the century to 1850, and then growing by two and a half times to 1914. It was the resulting rural overpopulation which sent millions of Russian peasants to settle in the steppes of Central Asia and the North Caucasus, the forests of Siberia and the Far East, and the great factories of Ukraine and the Baltic States. This movement, however, continued a process of migration which had been underway for much longer. In the words of Richard Pipes,

> A major secular process in progress for four hundred years has been carrying the Russian population outward from the central forest zone,

mostly towards the east and south, causing them to inundate areas inhabited by nations of other races and cultures, and producing serious demographic dislocations in the path of their movement.[3]

Two other factors put Russians at a further advantage. One was the massacre or forced expulsion under Tsarism of selected enemy populations in the North Caucasus and Central Asia (analogous to the behaviour of the Americans towards the Red Indians and the British to certain primitive peoples), followed by Stalin's decimation of the Ukrainians and Kazakhs during collectivisation in the 1930s. The second was the willingness of many Russian peasants to move far from home, to seek new lands to farm and then, from the later nineteenth century, to seek work in the new industrial cities. The fact that for several decades, Russian peasants were much more ready to move to Ukrainian and Central Asian cities to work than were the Ukrainian and Central Asian peasants themselves was of crucial importance in creating huge Russian minorities in these regions, with consequences that are with us to this day.

By the 1970s, however, it was clear that this engine was going into reverse (just in time to save the Latvians and Estonians from being completely swamped by Slavic immigration), and following the collapse of the Soviet Union, Russia's population decline has become precipitous. In the last three decades of Soviet rule, the key reason for the slowing down was the decline in the Russian birth-rate. In part, this was a Russian (and Ukrainian and Balt) reflection of general world trends following on urbanisation, industrialisation, general 'modernisation' of attitudes, huge growth in the divorce rate and so on. To this were added more specifically Soviet features of shortage of housing and consumer goods.

Since the late 1980s, the birth-rate has plunged still further, from 13.4 live births per thousand of population in 1990 to 9.3 in 1994, among the lowest in the world. The figure for 1994 compares to 13.2 in Britain, 15.7 in the USA, 17.9 for China, and 31.2 for Mexico. To this has been added an appalling rise in the death-rate, from 11.2 to 15 per thousand – by far the highest of any industrial or post-Communist country (with comparable age structures, Britain has 10, Poland 10.1).[4] In the first half of 1996 alone, 1.7 million more Russians died than were born.

This is due to a mixture of malnourishment, the decline in health services, a growth in alcoholism – in the first six months of 1996, 19,000 Russians died from alcoholic poisoning – an increasing number of accidents, the return of epidemic diseases, the growth of crime, and above all, psychological stress.[5]

The growth in malnutrition shows that there is nothing illusory (as some Western observers have argued) about the deep decline in the living standards of many Russians. In October 1996, Deputy Prime Minister (and former chief of staff and close friend of Yeltsin) Viktor Ilyushin declared that 'however deplorable it is, we have to acknowledge that mass poverty has arisen and the number of citizens with incomes below the subsistence minimum is a quarter of the whole population of Russia.' He admitted that the Health Ministry actually received a bare 60 per cent of the funds it was allocated in the 1996 budget.

From the mid-1970s, the growth of the Muslim populations of the Soviet Union *vis-à-vis* the Slavic ones, thanks to the high birth-rate among the former and the steep drop in births among the latter, began to cause serious concern to Soviet officials, and became a major theme of debate among Western observers.[6] In Chechnya, as will be seen, the higher Chechen birth-rate (in part for traditional cultural reasons, in part quite deliberately encouraged by Chechen society so as to recover from the terrible losses of deportation and to outnumber the Russians) was of key importance in the Chechen recovery of local dominance after their return from exile in 1957. By the 1980s, Muslim birth-rates began to drop in many areas as a result of urbanisation and modernisation (with later marriage and so on), but remained well above those of the Soviet Slavic peoples.[7]

From the 1960s, the central Soviet state under Brezhnev allowed the elites of various republican nationalities to increase their power, tolerating (or indeed participating in) their autocracy and corruption so long as things were kept quiet. An unintended result however was to allow growing, though discreet displays of hostility towards the local Russians. With many of their previous employment opportunities also cut off as a result both of the new power balance and of Muslim urbanisation, these began to leave. The broader, century-old pattern of migration went into reverse. Thus whereas in the period 1961–70, the balance of migration in the case of Uzbekistan, for example, was 257,000 in favour of the immigrants (mainly Russian), in the decade 1979–89, 507,000 more people left than came in.[8]

This tendency has of course increased exponentially since the end of the Soviet Union, to the extent that today the Kirghiz and Turkmen governments in particular are trying hard to check the flow so as to keep their Russian and other specialist workers. They are failing, however, because they cannot regulate the feelings of their own people and the tendency of the latter to put pressure on the Russians to leave, and because the new language laws have inevitably hit Russian employment. Between 1990 and 1994 1.14 million 'Russians' left Central Asia for Russia. In a survey of 1992, 43 per cent of the 'Russians' in Uzbekistan said that they wished to leave (up from 25 per cent the previous year), and only 18 per cent definitely wanted to stay, and in Kyrgyzstan, 36 per cent said that they were determined to go.

Incidentally, the fact that *even under Soviet rule* the tendency of many Russians outside Russia, when faced with local national assertiveness, was to pack up and leave rather than stand and fight (by appealing to the central authorities, or discreetly and informally consolidating their own defences within the local parties, something the Armenians and Abkhaz for example were experts at) says something about the background to the present passivity of the Russian diaspora. In other words, as a Russian 'fifth column', these populations are a broken reed.[9]

The change has been especially dramatic, and especially threatening for the Russians, in Kazakhstan. As a result first of massive Russian immigration, then of the Kazakh demographic backlash, and because of the cultural differences between the two nationalities, this is one of the very few areas in the former Soviet Union where there could be a serious danger of future ethnic conflict involving Russians. Thanks to a much higher birth-rate, the Kazakhs in the population soared from 2,795,000 in 1959 (30 per cent of the population) to 6,531,921, or 40 per cent in 1989. The Russians and Ukrainians increased from 4,736,200 to 7,122,364, but this was mainly due to immigration during the 'Virgin Lands' development in the 1960s, and overall the Slavic proportion dropped from 47 to 43 per cent. (The remainder of the population is made up of Germans, Uzbeks and other groups.) Since 1989, the Kazakhs have become the largest group.

The social, economic and political tensions which it was expected would ultimately result from this shift in the demographic balance were given by Hélène Carrère d'Encausse, for example, as a reason for her prediction that the break-up of the Soviet Union would begin in Central Asia.[11] This of course did not come to pass, but Russian fear of being swamped by growing numbers of Asiatics both on the old territory of the Soviet Union and from China remains a deep element in the contemporary Russian psyche. I am therefore convinced that faced with the implications of living again in a state which might one day have a Muslim majority, most Russians would back off.

In these demographic changes, and their implications, the Russians are not on the whole following a special path of their own. The expansion of the West European empires, and indeed the American movement westwards, were all largely carried along by the nineteenth-century European demographic explosion. Khrushchev's 'Virgin Lands' project, by which millions of Russian and Ukrainian collective farmers were settled in the arid Kazakh steppe, can be seen as the last gasp of a centuries-old process which had taken white colonists to the Dakotas at one extremity and New Zealand at another. Today, as in Russia, this process has gone into reverse, and the former European colonisers everywhere find themselves threatened by immigration from their former empires.

There are special features for Russia, however. In the first place, Russia is on the same continent as the areas it conquered, which makes it in principle much more threatened by the former colonised, from whom it is not separated by the protecting seas. On the other hand, the proximity has had the effect of diminishing the cultural contrast between Russians and the conquered peoples. With the exception of the Caucasians, whom they dislike for specific reasons (citing 'mafia' activity, though they also refer to the alleged success of Caucasians with Russian women, a classic symptom of suspicion), Russians have no strong feelings of hostility to the ethnic minorities within Russia, Muslim or otherwise. As will be discussed below, with the partial exception of the extreme nationalist Zhirinovsky, there has been no serious attempt to mobilise feeling against Tatars or Yakuts. On the other hand, there is also no desire greatly to increase their numbers – a perfectly understandable combination of attitudes, reflected in the views of many liberals in the West concerning minorities and immigration.

The second feature is the various strands of 'Eurasianism': the belief that unlike the other European nations, Russia has a special affinity with and understanding of the 'Asiatics', and that Russia's special destiny lies in creating a bridge between Europe and Asia, uniting the northern Eurasian continent in one union of peoples. This sentiment remains powerful to this day, in part because it simply reflects the geographical reality of Russia's position, and in part because it gives the Russians an escape hatch from their permanent position of being poorer and more backward Europeans. It has on occasions been evoked by Russian statesmen, whether as a mask for Russian imperial expansion (as in the famous memorandum of General Kuropatkin, before the First World War, on the need to create a huge new Russian territory out of Chinese Mongolia and Tatarstan), or as an appeal for friendship and cooperation with the Asian nations, as in Mikhail Gorbachev's talk of a 'common Asiatic home'.[12]

However, it is my view – based on numerous personal conversations with ordinary Russians – that these various Eurasian philosophies are essentially intellectual constructs, designed from the mid-nineteenth century on to meet essentially intellectual or political dilemmas – to do with the desire to find a special imperial and cultural role and identity for Russia, different from her inferior one in Europe. Fear of Asian demography, 'swamping' and invasion has long had much deeper and more powerful roots in the psyche of ordinary Russians.

An interesting example is that of popular attitudes to China in Soviet times. In the 1950s, the official rhetoric about Russian–Chinese friendship and world communist alliance did not seem to strike any very deep chord; conversely in the 1960s, the growing tension with China and the clashes on the border led to an upsurge of visceral fear of the Chinese, reflected both in the Russian masses, and in the work of intellectuals like the film director Andrei Tarkovsky and the dissident Andrei Amalrik. Strikingly, in his furious attack on Yeltsin's military policy in July 1997 (see chapter 8), General Lev Rokhlin referred not only to the threat from 'America and her allies' but also – albeit in veiled terms – to the danger that the Russian Far East might fall into the hands of China.

Concerning the Russian–Muslim relationship, I once tried out on a group of St Petersburg students the ideas of the pre-1914 Eurasianist Prince Nikolai Trubetskoy about the affinities between Orthodox Christianity and Islam, especially as practised by the nomadic Turkic peoples of Central Asia. They were horrified and furious, and I think some of them suspected me of making it up, as another insulting Western reference to 'Russian barbarism'.[13]

Distrust of 'internal Asiatics' is also true of the Russian military. From the early 1970s, Soviet generals were becoming increasingly concerned both by the growth in the number of Muslim conscripts relative to Slavic ones, and by the Muslims' supposed unreliability, low education and, above all, lack of knowledge of the Russian language – especially as the army became more technical, and military manuals more complicated. Thus Dr Georgy Derluguian, in the early 1980s an officer in the 'elite' Kantemir Guards Motorised Infantry Division, told me that, on the one hand, large numbers of Central Asian conscripts were sent to serve in armoured units like his because they were physically smaller, and so could fit more easily into the appallingly cramped and uncomfortable spaces of Soviet armoured vehicles; on the other hand, the officers openly despised the Central Asian troops, despaired of ever turning them into 'proper soldiers', were frightened by their lack of understanding of the weapons they were using, and referred to them as 'internal Afghans'.

When I visited the border guards in Tajikistan – the rank and file of which are now almost entirely local Tajiks, transferred from Tajikistan's army – their Russian officers also gave me the very strong impression of distrusting their men. They had not bothered to learn their language, and were well aware that they did not know what they were thinking or what local links and allegiances they might have. In the words of Senior Lieutenant Igor Danilov, commanding a very lonely Russian border post at Karaul-Tyube, on the Oxus, in April 1995, with the mountains of Afghanistan looming in the distance across the dusty plain:

> Ninety per cent of my soldiers are Tajiks, and with many of them I have to speak through an interpreter. Even the Tajik officers and sergeants can barely make themselves understood in Russian, and they are supposed to do three months training, with Russian lessons every day… Yes, I'm afraid there may be opposition elements among them, but what can I do? I don't decide who they send me as soldiers…I don't believe that in a real fight, my Tajik troops will fire on people who might be their relatives – perhaps the ones who have served here for a year or so, but certainly not the new drafts. So you could say we are in a trap here. We might be shot in the back, perhaps even by our own men.

As we spoke, Lieutenant Danilov's three-year-old son, also called Igor, dressed in a sort of miniature military bush-hat, wheeled his tricycle around us, with the Tajik soldiers smiling at him. A French journalist present, Laure Mandeville, created a bond with the Russians by describing her father's experiences as a lieutenant with the Tirailleurs Algeriens in the Aures during the Algerian War: 'he wasn't sure what they were thinking, either.'[14]

Lieutenant Danilov continued:

> But for the moment, a more important problem is that many of the Tajik conscripts they send us are so feeble, because of malnutrition and disease, that they should be in hospital, not the army. The police just sweep them off the streets. They are not even given a chance to tell their fam-

ilies where they have been sent. They've never been to school, so they can't write, often don't even know their own addresses. So we have to write to their families, and then of course their mothers will turn up, begging us to give them back. Meanwhile the better-off have bought their way out of conscription... Anyway, thank God there's a unit of the 201st [the Russian army division stationed in Tajikistan, and the backbone of the Tajik government's defences] close to here. They'll back us up if there's ever a real crisis, at least I hope so.[15]

Lieutenant Danilov was not a happy imperialist.

It is important to realise therefore that while Russian officers would certainly like to see guaranteed Russian military hegemony within the former Soviet region, and a strong Russian role in the armies of the other republics, those who have given serious thought to this question emphatically do not want to see the recreation of either the Soviet army or some new Russian imperial army, in the sense of combining soldiers from all the different republics in common units. This is especially true in terms of the acute shortage of funds, the plans for severe force reductions and the need for deep military reforms.

An Aged and Weary Population

The character of the Russian population as a consequence of demographic change also has implications for domestic Russian political stability. For one major point in which Russia today departs from the parallel with weak 'developing' states like Mexico is the fact that the population is declining and not growing. So Russia is not faced with the problem of millions of unemployable youths coming on to an inadequate job market every year, and this is of critical importance in limiting social tensions and pressures for political protest, unrest and revolution. Instead, Russia has a largely and increasingly aged population – and however angry and miserable they may be, old age pensioners are not the stuff of which revolutions are made.

(A striking contrast in this respect is contemporary Chechnya, whose people have a higher birth-rate both because of their traditions, and because, as noted above, they seem to have made a quite conscious decision some decades ago to outnumber the Russians. The result is a very large number of unemployed Chechen youths, whose role in radicalising the Chechen political situation in 1991, in carrying out the Chechen national revolution and, of course, in filling the ranks of the Chechen fighters in 1994–6 has been very obvious.)

The age structure of Russia's population conditions its political attitudes to a question of great importance for the survival of the prevailing order, the widespread desire for the restoration of the Soviet Union. This takes the form of a deep yearning for stability and order, which is exactly what one would expect from an elderly population. It is in terms of a nostalgia for this past security, rather than a desire for national conquests, power and glory, that Soviet restorationist feeling in Russia should be mainly seen.

Confirming this view is both the evidence of numerous opinion polls, and the fact that this nostalgia for the Soviet Union is also extremely widespread in many of the other former Soviet republics, including among peoples like the Georgians, who can hardly be accused of sympathy for Russian imperialism. Soviet nostalgia is likely to diminish as the older generation dies off and the age structure of society assumes a less top-heavy form (this is already happening, as surveys of opinion among youth clearly show) – and there are few indications that it will be replaced among younger voters by a new and deeply felt (as opposed to superficial and rhetorical) Russian imperial nationalism.

The people who express this opinion are nostalgic for the pre-Gorbachev Soviet Union because it was after all their whole world, because for whatever reason – but most often age, lack of education, geographical location, or sheer absence of jobs – they have not been able to take advantage of the new economic opportunities offered by capitalism. As they conjure them up now, in Soviet days they lived better and more securely; they were not afraid of crime, of ethnic strife or of unemployment; they could afford holidays to the Black Sea; they could travel freely across the whole Soviet space without harassment and extortion by corrupt and greedy border guards; and the sins of their rulers were decently veiled, rather than being paraded with vulgar ostentation before the eyes of the hungry and the betrayed.

However, the lack of real will and determination which underlies the desire for a Soviet restoration is reflected in the fact that according to opinion polls, in the years from 1992 to 1996 a desire to return to the Soviet Union grew steadily (in eastern and southern Ukraine as well as in Russia); but in the latter part of that period, so too did the belief that such a restoration was in fact impossible. Thus a poll by the Russian magazine *Itogi* (linked to the news show on NTV) in December 1996 showed only 11 per cent of respondents saying that the Byelovezhskaya Pushcha agreement ending the Soviet Union had been good for Russia, and 65 per cent saying it had been harmful (24 per cent could not commit themselves one way or the other); but a plurality of 46 per cent saying that the Union could not now be restored.[16] This mass attitude exactly supports a saying common among the Moscow intelligentsia: 'Whoever does not want to restore the Soviet Union has no heart. Whoever thinks it is possible to restore it has no brain.' (As will be seen below, a majority of Russian officers also share this view.)

With regard to specifically Russian national goals, a poll during the December 1993 parliamentary election campaign (the high point of Zhirinovsky's popularity, as it turned out) by members of the universities of Keele and Glasgow showed 49 per cent of Russians believing that some parts of neighbouring republics – such as Crimea and northern Kazakhstan – should in principle belong to Russia, but only 25 per cent being willing to threaten military action to defend the rights of Russians in these areas.[17]

Even more strikingly, when a number of opinion polls on the Russian involvement in Tajikistan were taken in the summer of 1993, after a Russian outpost had been wiped out in an opposition attack, large majorities of those polled spoke in favour of Russian withdrawal – even though both the Yeltsin administration and the parliamentary opposition, and indeed every major Russian politician (with the exception of Alexander Lebed) was speaking of the absolute need for a continued Russian involvement, so as to defend Russia's vital interests in Central Asia.

Fourteen months later, in a poll of April 1995 (after the start of the Chechen War, and at the time of the Ukrainian moves drastically to restrict Crimean autonomy), only 9.6 per cent of respondents were willing to support the use of the Black Sea Fleet or the army to 'defend the Russians of Crimea' – even though a full 40.6 per cent had agreed that 'Russia should work for the return of Crimea to the Russian Federation,' and 23.8 per cent had said that Russia should 'guarantee the rights of the Russians in Crimea', and though eighteen months later, in September 1996, 70.4 per cent agreed with Yuri Luzhkov that 'Sebastopol is not part of the Ukrainian state'.

To judge by my own informal polls (what journalists call 'vox pop') in Moscow, St Petersburg, Novgorod, Vladivostok, Tula, Rostov-on-Don and Novocherkassk during the election campaigns of December 1995 and June 1996, I should also judge that under 10 per cent of Russians at that time supported the use of force in the 'near abroad' – though it should be said firstly that these 'polls' were very small scale (fewer than two hundred respondents in all), and secondly that a majority of respondents said that 'of course' Russia should act if Russians in other republics came under physical attack and were in danger of massacre.

Curiously enough, even Vladimir Zhirinovsky gives some evidence of ambiguity in his attitude to war, or at least war in the sense of real Russian military sacrifice – partly because he has never troubled himself in the slightest about ideological, moral or even logical consistency, but also because for all his hateful foolery, he has often shown a very acute sense of what many ordinary Russians feel in their guts. Thus his book *A Last Bid for the South* has been compared to *Mein Kampf*, which may perhaps be true of its literary style. A close reading however reveals a very different spirit. When Hitler spoke of the need for war, there could be no doubt that he meant what he said, if only because he had himself been a soldier in the First World War; a 'Darwinian struggle for existence' between nations was central to the entire Nazi philosophy, and the whole nature of what Hitler thought the Aryan superior race was and should be about. Peace was not even the ultimate goal or dream. This is also true of some of the ideology of the Russian fascists such as Alexander Barkashov.

But while Zhirinovsky sometimes speaks in pseudo-Hitlerite terms of purging Russia of the West's 'satanic contagion', of Russians engaging in a struggle from which 'we will emerge as hard as tempered steel,' he also – crazily, in view of what he has just said – declares that 'we need pluralism, openness and peace', that:

We will understand one another because every family will have the home that it wants – be it in a large or small town, in a village in Central Asia or the Caucasus, in the tropics, in the forest or on a mountainside. We will live peacefully, with no dominant ideology... All this will become possible only when Russia finds a national as opposed to an international identity. This is not so that Russians can rise up and subjugate other peoples, but rather so that, having risen up herself, Russia can raise up other peoples living beside her... The sound of Orthodox church bells on the shores of the Indian Ocean would proclaim peace to the peoples of the region, brotherhood to the nations, prosperity, happiness...the end of wars and inter-ethnic strife. Some day there will be no more passports.

Rather than serious fascism, this looks like a pathetic, romanticised, vulgarised and openly nationalised version of the old Soviet official dream. Even his words about the Indian Ocean are suggestive:

A last bid for the South. How I long to see Russian soldiers wash their boots in the warm waters of the Indian Ocean and wear summer uniform all the year round. Light boots, light trousers, short-sleeved shirts, no tie, and open collar, light caps. And a small Russian submachine-gun produced in Izhevsk...

Is this a description of the Afrika Korps at Tobruk, or – leaving aside the machine-gun – an advertisement for a Soviet package holiday in Sukhumi or Yalta, now barred to ordinary Russian holidaymakers by the collapse of the Soviet Union?[18]

An interesting and very important example of the gap between Soviet nostalgia and the desire for a militant programme of Soviet restorationism was the public response to the Communist-led vote in the Russian Duma in March 1996 declaring the Byelovezhskaya Pushcha agreement illegal and calling for the restoration of the Soviet Union. The Communists obviously reckoned that this would gain them additional support – but nothing of the sort happened. On the contrary, the barrage of criticism and alarm from Russia's neighbours seems to have convinced a good many wavering voters that a Communist victory would bring a danger of war – something relentlessly repeated by Yeltsin's propaganda. In consequence, they voted for Yeltsin or Lebed, or stayed at home. Incidentally, Yeltsin himself may have made a similar mistake in launching the Chechen War, if, as has been reported, his staff thought that a victorious war against the hated Chechens would increase his popularity. In fact, in a poll of 16–20 December 1994 – before even Russian casualties began to mount – only 30 per cent of respondents favoured 'decisive measures to restore order in Chechnya', whereas 36 per cent were for a peaceful solution and 23 per cent for an immediate withdrawal of the Russian army. The following month, January 1995, no less than 77 per cent of respondents to an opinion poll said that they opposed the bombardment of Grozny, with only 12 per cent in favour; and 53.8 per cent were now claiming that they had *always* been against sending in the army.

The only signs of Russian majority enthusiasm for the war came in the immediate aftermath of the hostage-taking in Budennovsk in June 1995 (viewed by most Russians, understandably enough, as terrorism). By February 1996, 46 per cent of Russians were agreeing with the Chechen separatist demand that Russian troops should be withdrawn immediately, with only 33 per cent saying that they should be withdrawn only after the 'restoration of order', and by March 1996, 52 per cent were in favour of immediate withdrawal (according to an opinion poll by Yuri Levada's Centre for Research on Public Opinion).[19]

According to another poll, of April 1996, after Yeltsin announced peace talks with Dudayev in March 1996, only 5 per cent of respondents said that they were against talks with Dudayev. (A year earlier, only 3 per cent had been against talks and for a 'forceful solution', 22 per cent had been for a 'reasonable compromise', while 50 per cent had said that they would like a compromise, but doubted it was possible.) Also in April 1996, 15 per cent said that they were wholly in favour of peace, and 20 per cent expressed support for the statement, 'I am not convinced that this is the best path, but it is still better than a bloody war'; 30 per cent replied that they did not believe Yeltsin's plan was sincere (rightly, of course), while 11 per cent knew nothing about the subject.

By September 1996, after the defeat that August and the Lebed–Maskhadov peace agreement, 39 per cent of respondents gave their approval to the proposition that the Russian government should ensure full compliance with the agreed ceasefire, 32 per cent that Russia should agree to free elections in Chechnya, and 46 per cent that Russian officials responsible for starting the war should be punished. Only 14 per cent said that the Russian army should recapture Grozny, and 11 per cent that under no circumstances should the Russian government allow Chechen independence.

By November 1996, 33 per cent were agreeing that the Chechens should be left to make their own decisions, and 26 per cent that they should have independence if they wished. On the other hand, 23 per cent were for establishing strict border controls, and 22 per cent for keeping Chechnya in the Russian Federation.

These figures hardly show a population obsessed with Russian prestige or even territorial integrity, let alone imperial glory, when faced with real costs. It is important, therefore, not to take what either Russian politicians or ordinary people say too seriously on the score of empire-building. Not every American reader of *Soldier of Fortune* magazine would have made a good US Marine on Okinawa; and not all the Russians who roar about how Ukraine is really part of Russia would be willing to go there to kill and perhaps die – or send their sons to do so – to back up their claims.

A very representative figure in Russia today is the woman who, after expressing a range of aggressively chauvinist opinions, admits that she would do anything to save her son from serving in the army, both because of the risk from the Chechens and, more importantly, because the army itself is such a notoriously brutal, brutalizing and dangerous institution for its conscripts. Or in the words of a student at Moscow State University, speaking about relations with Ukraine and the question of Sebastopol: 'Look at how many magnificent lands the Ukrainians have taken from us, and then Sebastopol on top of that. Instead of making so much anti-Russian noise, they should be thankful for what they've got, and sit as quiet as mice.' But, she added,

> No one in Russia actually wants to fight Ukraine, and send their sons to die there, for Sevastopol or anywhere else. We don't hate the Ukraini-ans. They're just annoying, that's all... And all this Russian talk of Ukraine not really existing, that the Ukrainians say they're so worried about – yes, it exists, but it's just kitchen-table talk. In practice, every Russian with any sense knows that Ukraine is independent, and will stay independent. They know that to take away that independence they'd have to fight, and no one wants to fight, on the contrary most Russians want good relations with Ukraine, that's the whole point. The bitterness is over particular issues, like Sevastopol. If we could solve these, rela-tions and attitudes would get much better, I'm sure.

The gap between rhetoric and real feelings is greater in Russia than else-where, for obvious reasons. The whole Brezhnev era was one long education in the meaninglessness of public statements, as made by everybody from the General Secretary to the humblest 'citizen', something which was felt to a greater or lesser degree by a majority of inhabitants of Soviet Russia, as revealed in innumerable anecdotes.

Only such a past could have produced a figure like Vladimir Zhirinovsky, for whom public rhetoric is everything—but also exactly nothing. Even in his own mind, it probably has little connection to reality, and his ordinary follow-ers vote for him not because of his 'programme', but because the noises he makes cheer them up. It is all in the strictest sense a political circus, and Zhirinovsky is more like one of those traditional Russian village idiots, licensed by tradition to go around dressed in women's clothes, mixing in their language absurdity and the expression of the ordinary people's true feelings, than he is like the leader of a modern mass party.

The results of the 1996 presidential election also showed that although most Russians are pretty unhappy with many of the developments of the past few years, a majority have no desire whatsoever for political upheavals and the risk of civil strife. In keeping with the proportion of older people in the pop-ulation, the great mass of ordinary Russians have a deep yearning for stability and order, which in one way or another was reflected in the votes for all the three leading candidates, Gennady Zyuganov, Boris Yeltsin and Alexander Lebed.

The Communist vote – 40 per cent of the total, but overwhelmingly from the older part of the population – certainly reflected nostalgia for the Soviet Union, but it was nostalgia for the peace, order and above all economic security of Soviet days. These are very understandable sentiments given the way that older people in particular have suffered in recent years, and are at heart hardly revolutionary. Western commentators were not wrong to take worried note of Zyuganov's increasing ideological borrowings from nineteenth-century Russian messianic nationalism – but they would be very wrong to think that they were why sixty-five-year-old Maria Ivanovna of Ufa, for instance, would vote for him. Moreover, Communism in Russia is fading fast, if only because, for biological reasons, its electorate is fading too.[20]

I say this without any great feeling of satisfaction. This is after all the Soviet generation which at the cost of immense sacrifice saved the Soviet peoples and the world from Nazism, and for its pains has been betrayed twice: by Stalin and his regime after 1945, when instead of using victory to seek reconciliation between state and society, they exploited it to strengthen their own tyranny; and by Russia's present rulers, who have fattened themselves at their expense and left them to starve in their old age.

Part of the vote for Yeltsin, especially in Moscow and St Petersburg, was undoubtedly in favour of change and economic reform, as reflected in the fact that his voters were on average some fifteen years younger than Zyuganov's. The result showed that basic principles of private ownership and free economic activity have now been accepted by most of the population; but to a great extent his vote also reflected fear of instability.

This is because, thanks to the compliance of the Russian media, Yeltsin had been able to convince most Russians of two things: first, that Communist victory would mean a new revolution and massive upheaval. This line was hammered home by endless television clips showing the gulag, the famine of the 1930s, Stalin's show trials and so on. Apart from the sheer amount of this propaganda, it drew its force from its essential truth – all these past Communist crimes were after all very real and very terrible, and Zyuganov's Communists had wholly failed to come to serious terms with them. In emphasising this, Yeltsin's camp could draw on the wholly sincere, unbought support of many of the most famous names in the Russian liberal intelligentsia. And here it must be noted that for Russians (and indeed some of the other post-Soviet peoples) the Soviet Union and Communist rule are held to be quite different things: nostalgia for one does not necessarily imply nostalgia for the other.

But a second belief of critical importance – held by a majority of voters whom I interviewed – was that even if he lost, Yeltsin would not surrender power, which might mean civil war. There was ample support for this view in some of the statements of Yeltsin's aides, especially before March 1996, when the arguments of the faction in the leadership, led by General Korzhakov, which favoured cancelling the elections and carrying out a form of 'coup from above' were defeated by the alliance of Anatoly Chubais and Yeltsin's daughter Tatyana. However, on the eve of the first round of the elections, Yeltsin himself declared that he 'would not play the role of a President Hindenburg' – which was taken to mean that he would not hand over power to the Communists even if they won the elections. In other words, Yeltsin's victory also in part emerged from a gut fear of disorder, political violence and potential civil strife.

As for Lebed, his programme was explicitly devoted to calling for peace, order and a crackdown on organised crime. His campaign – with or without covert help from Yeltsin's team – was a very clever one, simultaneously using his image as a tough, patriotic soldier, stressing his opposition to military 'adventures' like Chechnya and Tajikistan, and referring to his successful 'peacemaking' campaign in Transdniestria in 1992: 'Others start wars, he ends them' was the slogan. Another was 'Yeltsin: freedom without order. Zyuganov, order without freedom. Lebed – order *and* freedom.'[21]

Now it is quite true of course that a Moldovan might have some hard words to say about Lebed's role in 1992 as commander of the 14th Army, but the point is that in his appeal to the Russian public, he portrayed himself as a tough peacemaker, not an aggressive conqueror. And it must be said that in his peacemaking role in Chechnya during his brief period as national security chief, he justified the faith of his electorate – albeit only in the wake of the Chechen victory in August – and according to opinion polls, the Russian people responded with overwhelming approval of his peace deal. On NATO expansion and relations with the CIS, he has more recently taken a studiedly moderate and pragmatic line.

Social Change, Culture and Demilitarisation

For the West, and indeed much of the world, an enormous sociological literature has long existed describing and analysing the effects of urbanisation and 'modernisation' on social and demographic behaviour, and how that behaviour in turn has determined social and economic development. But because of Communist control of Soviet study and isolation from Western study, scholarship on these changes within the Soviet Union has lagged far behind. This is one of the reasons why a 'primordial' view of Russian national characteristics among many Westerners who regard themselves as experts has been able to maintain itself for so long. Another reason is that social change in the Soviet Union has not been fully recognised as modernisation, which it was – albeit of a particularly brutal, ruthless and economically inefficient kind.

In the context of the defeat in Chechnya, an important aspect of modernisation in Russia has been the demilitarisation of social attitudes which has been characteristic sooner or later of almost all modern urban societies: the growing unwillingness to perform military service and contemplate military casualties. The case of contemporary Russia tends to support the trend of thought going back to Veblen and Schumpeter (or even to Adam Smith) which sees the development of modern societies and economies as naturally reducing tendencies to war and militarism. As elsewhere, one fundamental reason for this is the drop in family size. Bluntly put, parents in the past – from whatever country – were more willing to contemplate losing a son in battle when they had several sons than they are today when they are quite likely to have only one. One of the heartbreaking things about the mothers whom I met in Chechnya looking for their sons was that very often they were their only sons, or even their only child. With modernization, too, there may have been a shift, also noted elsewhere, from economically based traditional peasant family groups to 'affectionate' modern ones. Other features more specific to the post-Soviet military – for example, the hateful practice of *dyedovshchina* – will be examined in chapter 8.

To understand Russian attitudes today, and their implications for 'Russian imperialism' and for the Russian army, you have to listen to what Russians – and especially Russian young people, since they both represent the future and are the ones who have to do the actual fighting in places like Chechnya – are saying in discos, cinemas and workplaces. These days the ordinary thinking and feeling human being – the *homme (et femme) moyen sensuel* – tends in their present Russian incarnation, to be very *sensuel* indeed, and not at all *ideologique*. When I first arrived in Russia, I also went looking for budding Dostoyevskies, Lenins and Kornilovs among the younger generation – and didn't find them. There are of course small groups of fascists, or of hooligans who decorate themselves with the name – but you find such groups all over the West; they do not reflect society as a whole and they *do not make good soldiers*.

Desire to avoid military service, and a positively encyclopaedic knowledge of the various medical and legal ploys involved, were literally universal among my acquaintances in Moscow's educated youth.[22] This is hardly surprising, both because educated youths everywhere in the world tend to think they have better things to do than serve in the military in peacetime, and because 'intellectuals' among the conscripts were so often picked out for beating and harassment by their fellows.

But Western observers who have gone among the workers report the same attitudes among them. Strikingly, even male adolescents from backgrounds in which in the early 1980s their predecessors would still have taken a pride in military service, so as to 'become tough', 'become a man' and so on, have begun to avoid it in increasing numbers – something which began during the Afghan War.[23]

The first public sign of a deep public unwillingness to see conscripts serve in danger areas came in January 1990 with the mass protests of women in Krasnodar against local reservists being sent to Azerbaijan to suppress the nationalist uprising there (protests which actually led to the cancellation of the mobilisation order). This incident was one episode in the genesis of the Committee of Soldiers' Mothers, which has led the fight against *dyedovshchina* and also played a leading part in protests against the Chechen War.

Most ordinary Russian youths however protested against conscription not collectively but individually, either by faking illness or by simply not turning up. The collapse of conscription has been partially redressed by the military authorities since its nadir in 1992, but evasion is still extremely widespread. As with the US army in Vietnam, the perception by rural and provincial youth that educated and wealthy youths can cheat or, increasingly, bribe their way out of service does nothing for morale – or relations between them when they do serve. In 1996, 31,000 youths listed for conscription simply failed to turn up, and because of the unpopularity of military service in the population, and because of low pay and demoralisation in the police, the latter made no great effort to find and punish them: 18,000 were booked, but only 500 were charged and a mere 60 sentenced – not much of a threat.

Speaking with my wife's friends from Moscow State University (MGU), I have gone to the very brink of the journalistically permissible in trying to provoke them into uttering strongly nationalist opinions on questions like Sebastopol – in getting them to express any strong political opinions at all, for that matter – usually without the slightest success.

Incidentally, it is important in this context not to confuse nationalism with either ethnic dislike or with a certain authoritarianism. Many people in Russia have a great desire for a 'strong hand' – like Lebed's – but that is mainly out of fear of crime, hatred of corruption and a desire that the state should pay wages on time; it is internally, not externally directed.

There is also an important difference, in Russia and elsewhere, between what might be called 'skinhead' politics and violence on the one hand and old-style militant nationalism on the other. Thus in Germany in the 1990s, many observers saw the growth of anti-immigrant youth gangs as an ominous sign of a new wave of German nationalist extremism – and these gangs did often employ Nazi symbolism, just as do their Russian or British equivalents. They also of course very often have the sympathy of many policemen, from Moscow to Los Angeles.

None the less, these movements are essentially internally directed and very often strictly local. They are motivated partly by sheer thuggery, and partly by a desire to 'repel intruders', to defend working class jobs, to maintain 'pure neighbourhoods' and to support national football teams. The old nationalist obsessions, of recovering lost territory, recreating 'historic borders' and conquering other countries so as to achieve national hegemony may be mentioned, but are in fact very far from their real concerns, and still further from those of the broader sections of society who may condone them (for example, the Germans who felt that 'something had to be done' about the wave of immigrants in the early 1990s).

German skinheads may beat up Polish immigrants in the street, but they would be very unlikely to volunteer to go and fight for the reconquest of Danzig. Of course, where historically hostile ethno-cultural groups live cheek by jowl, as in the former Yugoslavia and Northern Ireland, the distinction between 'skinhead violence' and nationalist-inspired war may become blurred. None the less, it should be kept in mind. Beating up Chechens in Moscow is one thing; travelling a thousand miles to fight them in Chechnya is another.

The Russian Cossacks, who will be analysed in the following chapter, are an interesting example of this distinction. They are usually seen, and often rightly, as a force for Russian nationalism and anti-minority feeling. However, much of the Cossack violence in the North Caucasus has been directed not against 'Russia's enemies', the Chechens, but against Armenian immigrants. Local Cossacks often hate the Armenians for their economic success, and fear their increasing numbers, just as English skinheads look on British Asians. This is despite the fact that at a national and strategic level, the Armenians are Russia's closest allies in the region!

According to Dr Taylor Dark, an American temporary lecturer at MGU, despite some nationalist rhetoric,

> Russian nationalism didn't seem to have very deep roots among my students, a fact that clearly reflects Russia's history as a predominantly illiterate peasant-populated multinational empire with a diverse mix of identities. When I told one student about my discomfort with handing out applications for a NATO-sponsored student conference, which included a free trip to Brussels and a tour of NATO headquarters, she agreed that such activities might appear compromising for an academic organisation working in Russia, and were probably propagandist in character. But her very next question was: 'How can I get to go?' The West was far more likely to be viewed as an almost magical source of great treasures and entertainment than as a threat to any unique Russian identity.[24]

Numerous opinion polls have shown a majority of Russians as contemplating emigration (if possible) or at least not sure that they wanted to stay in Russia.[25] An interesting opinion poll in the summer of 1996 showed almost 75 per cent of those questioned saying that Russia should follow her own 'special' path of development – but a similar proportion, when asked in detail what this should be, gave one or other of a range of Western variants, and not Soviet, mystical nationalist, or collectivist ones.[26]

The political apathy of Russian youth is something which is complained of bitterly by more committed older Russians, and ironically, I have heard both former dissidents and Communists bewail the 'cynicism' of the young. Even at the funeral in November 1994 of the twenty-eight-year-old journalist Dmitri Kholodov, murdered because of his investigations into military corruption – a hero figure for educated Moscow youth, one would have thought – the number of young people, though considerable, was greatly outweighed by their elders, several of whom talked to me in depressed terms of the way in which their generation of Russian intellectuals felt betrayed not just by Yeltsin and the new elites, but even by their own children.

Concerning Chechnya, though according to all the polls very unenthusiastic about the war, Moscow youth – and youth all over Russia – has not demonstrated either for or against. They just don't demonstrate. They think they have better things to do. Today, Russian youth culture is overwhelmingly non-militarist and indifferent or hostile to the idea of self-sacrifice and military discipline. The admired figures among most young Russians today are some version or other of the 'New Russians'—bankers or mafia-type 'businessmen', with their luxury cars, ostentatious lifestyle and strings of 'girlfriends'. Poor old Captain Maxim Maximovich doing his duty in the Caucasus simply doesn't get a look in.

These attitudes are not simply the result of the transformations of the past few years; they grew slowly through the last four decades of Soviet life. For after all, the separation of parts of Soviet urban youth at least from official culture and dogma has been going on since the time of the *stiliagi* of the 1950s – not in the form of a political revolt as such, but out of boredom with and scepticism about official and parental values, just as in the West.

The lack of underlying militarism in a society as cynical and would-be materialist as that of Russia today should not be surprising. The Soviet Union was a society that, in principle and state rhetoric and education at least, was in a state of permanent mobilization, economic, ideological, and with the possibility of military mobilisation always present. When that state and its controlling ideology collapsed, society and culture swung ineluctably to the opposite extreme. This effect was apparent, long before the Soviet Union fell, in the steadily diminishing psychological returns, especially among Russian youth, from the endless flow of patriotic material on the Second World War emitted by the state in the Brezhnev years, and from the extreme disillusionment resulting from the losses and futility of the Afghan War.[27]

Soviet propaganda concerning the memory of the 'Great Patriotic War' also contained its own central flaw from the point of view of maintaining a militarist spirit in society. The constant repetition of Russia's immense sacrifices and suffering in that war was intended to strengthen national pride; but '20 million dead' is not a figure calculated to encourage an eager attitude to warfare – especially when backed up by the memory of losses in one's own family, and the testimony of survivors.

Soviet films set in the Second World War, though they glorify the heroism of the Soviet troops, also show a great deal more real suffering and death among the protagonists than do American films, and this is true to a considerable degree of standard products as well of more artistic and sophisticated ones like *The Cranes are Flying*, or masterpieces like Tarkovsky's *Ivan's Childhood*.[28]

During the Afghan War, by contrast, the regime was careful to conceal the number of Soviet casualties – to the extent that it both multiplied rumours, and contributed to demoralising the troops, who had to see their comrades shipped home in unmarked coffins, and buried without official honours.

Afghanistan, and the unvarnished accounts of the Soviet soldiers' experience there, published and shown very widely in the late perestroika years, had a very real effect as the 'Soviet Vietnam' in diminishing any romantic vision of war. In the words of Zhenya, a conscript I spoke with in Grozny, 'I knew what to expect here, more or less, because I had talked to some of my older brother's friends who came back from Afghanistan, and I also saw a film about it. Most of us knew. So why didn't those bastards know what they were sending us into?' – those bastards being the Russian government and high command.

As a matter of fact, some of them did know. Just as the Vietnam War worked permanent changes in the psychology and attitude to war, casualties and public opinion among officers who served there like General Colin Powell, so Afghanistan changed the attitudes of Soviet officers like generals Alexander Lebed and Boris Gromov (the last Soviet commander in Afghanistan), both of whom opposed the war in Chechnya. Lebed's opposition to the Chechen War did not therefore seem feigned or inconsistent, and he expressed it from the beginning. When I first interviewed him at the headquarters of the 14th Army in Tiraspol in February 1994, ten months before the intervention in Chechnya, he declared that

> The way that they sent the Soviet army into Afghanistan was simply a crime. They had no idea of what they were getting us into, they knew nothing of the country or its people. It seems to me that they didn't even have a real strategic plan. They should have studied British history – you fought there for a hundred years and achieved nothing, the same as us. We had no real idea why we were there, or what we were dying and killing for. And when our boys had done their 'internationalist duty' and came back invalids or psychologically disturbed, and went to the government for help, they found some bureaucrat behind a desk saying, 'It's not our business, we didn't send you there'. I don't love my own profession, at least in its main purpose. War gives nothing. You fight for a hundred years and then have to make peace in the end, and then those who have destroyed everything have to build it up again, if they can.[29]

During that interview, he also strongly opposed the Russian military presence in Tajikistan, on the same grounds.

Since the Soviet collapse, Russian television has contributed, partly unwittingly, to spreading fear and hatred of war. Concerning Chechnya, by the end of 1995 most Russian channels had become agencies of state propaganda in what they said: the fixed characterization of the Chechen forces as 'bandit formations', the admiring interviews with Russian troops and the reporting without comment of the most outrageously false official statements. But what they *showed* was different.

Most Western TV stations, at least since Vietnam, have presented a relatively edited and sanitized visual version of war, and Western armed forces have tried to keep them as far as possible from the firing line. Not so Russian TV. Whether because of basic honesty, courage, sensationalism – or sheer insensibility – it tends to show the unvarnished truth, and several years of looking at piles of brains, charred bodies, and severed limbs on the evening news about Karabakh, Tajikistan, Abkhazia, and finally Chechnya has not left Russian viewers with many romantic illusions about warfare. Chechnya therefore may be said to have provided a fresh argument to those Western journalists who argue that really forthright, even gruesome, coverage of war is in fact a force for peace.

Television – which is now available to the great majority of Russia's population – also has a much wider impact in the context of demilitarisation than simply showing the horrors of war, as in Chechnya and Vietnam. Above all, it has to a considerable extent rescued the masses from boredom. This deadly ennui was one of the dominant features of peasant and proletarian life in previous generations, and was a very important factor in sending young men off to join the army, simply for a change from the repetitive tedium of the conveyor belt and the plough.

It has a similar effect in keeping young men away from revolutionary movements and political violence. In Pakistan in 1988–9 – in those days a society the mass of whose population had no TV sets – I was struck by the way in which political rallies, and still better riots, were good fun for a large part of local male youth. Access to television would I believe have greatly diminished this factor in political instability.

Urbanisation, Economic Development and the Attempts to 'Catch Up'

Of central importance in the context of cultural demilitarisation has been the shift from a mainly rural to a mainly urban population, and from a collective social world to an individualist one. Numerous military experts of my acquaintance have told me that the idea that traditional peasants make better natural soldiers is a myth, that a good army can take anyone and make him or her into a soldier. I've listened to them carefully – and I don't believe a word of it. Or rather, you can of course turn an urban youth into a fine soldier, but you have to spend a good deal more time and money – which Russia does not have – both on training and on creating a military spirit.

All the empirical evidence from past wars suggests that peasants – especially from formidable climates like that of Russia – just are tougher, less squeamish, more obedient and above all better at standing up to prolonged exposure to the elements. The problem for modern armies is not simply that there are not enough peasants, but also that peasant societies tend to lack technically educated cadres.

In this sense, the Soviet military victory in the Second World may be understood as the consequence of an unusually favourable combination of historical and technological circumstances. A crippling weakness of the old Russian imperial army, with its illiterate peasant troops and dilettante officers, had been the lack of technically educated personnel. By 1941, however, thanks both to the scale and the nature of the Soviet education drive, the

Soviet army could mobilise huge numbers of technically educated people, educated moreover very much in the appropriate technical fields; yet it could also still call on a mainly peasant population to provide the physically and emotionally tough cannon fodder, and a totalitarian state and party to provide the ideological and organizational backbone. The result was – briefly – one of the greatest armies the world has ever seen.

The official Soviet naming of the war of 1941-45 as the 'Second Great Patriotic War' was of course intended to draw an artificial parallel with the 'First Great Patriotic War' of 1812. But in important ways, the parallel was also a real one. Firstly, these wars came at the summit of a particular epoch of Russian modernisation and particularly of military development, whereby the Russian state by a herculean effort over several decades had made its military economy (which in the Soviet case meant the whole economy) and army capable of taking on any state in Europe.

By 1812 – thanks to the development of the Urals metallurgical industry begun by Peter the Great – Russian artillery was among the best in the world, and Russian drill and discipline, in large part introduced by West European mercenary officers, was also of the highest quality.[30] Together with Russian peasant stoicism, and the courage of Russian noble officers, this created the army of which Frederick the Great said admiringly that 'it is not enough to kill a Russian soldier; he will remain standing until you knock him to the ground.' The smashing Russian victories in 1812–14 mesmerised Europe for a generation and created a myth of overwhelming Russian power; in England, this was also stoked by Russophobe elements who, for whatever reason (support for Turkey or Poland, fear for India), were determined to create an image of a dire Russian threat to British interests.[31]

What happened in the meantime was that because of the nature of the Russian state, society and economy, Russia missed out on the industrial, educational and railway revolution of the mid-nineteenth century – with the result that when the Crimean War broke out in 1854, Russian soldiers found that their old-style cannon were being outranged by modern British rifles. Faced with another near-humiliation in 1877–8, and the growth of German industrial power, from the 1890s the state made another convulsive attempt to catch up. The resulting social strains contributed greatly to the revolutions of 1917 and an appalling economic setback; but after 1929, militarised industrialisation resumed at breakneck speed and with a ruthlessness never seen before. The result was a Soviet Union which by 1941, from a military point of view, was well up with the essential elements of the early to mid-twentieth-century industrial revolution: metallurgy, railways, chemicals, radios, aircraft and motor vehicles.

Then the same thing happened as after 1812. For a variety of reasons mainly related to Communism, the Soviet Union failed to keep up with the next technological revolution, in computers and electronics; but to an even greater extent than before, this was masked from the West by the closed nature of Soviet society, by the genuinely impressive victories and above all capacity for suffering of the Soviet army in the Second World War, and by groups in the West who for whatever reason dedicated themselves to exaggerating Soviet power.

A key question for the future therefore is whether, as before, the military-economic nadir in which Russia now finds itself will lead to another convulsive and ultimately successful attempt to 'catch up'. The answer, which has been suggested in the previous chapter and will be examined later, is: at some stage in future, perhaps; but only after the dawning of a new historical age, and the radical transformation of the existing Russian political, social and economic order. In other words, not any time soon.

Why Modern Peoples Fight

The other, and deliberately emphasised parallel between the two 'patriotic wars' was of course the fact that both began with the Russian and Soviet armies defending their own territory against invasion, and retreating into the very heart of Russia before being able to counter-attack. One has to be a little careful in approaching this theme – that the Russian soldier achieves his true spirit when defending his country – because the views of Leo Tolstoy, Soviet propaganda and indeed of J. J. Rousseau cast a long shadow.[32]

None the less, it cannot be stressed too strongly that whatever the ambitions of Stalin and his regime, and whatever the ideology of the Communist Party, for the overwhelming majority of ordinary Russian soldiers, the Second World War was neither a war of Russian imperial conquest nor a war to spread Communism. Every soldier's and observer's memoir, whether officially sanctioned or dissident, brings out the fact that the war was seen by the great majority of soldiers – and rightly – as a war of self-defence against an enemy who was intent on the merciless subjugation and enslavement of the Slavic peoples.

Western commentators who wish to deny the evidence of Russian military decline point out – as an example of rapid Russian military regeneration – that in 1939 the Soviet army was thoroughly beaten by the tiny Finns, but went on barely two years later to crush the mighty Germans. This misses the whole point. Even in the first five months of the war in 1941, the Soviet army suffered defeat after defeat, because of unpreparedness, poor leadership, but above all because of lack of morale (and of course because the Finns, fighting in defence of their homes and homeland, conducted themselves so magnificently). This has been documented by a striking new Western study by Roger R. Reese. He describes Soviet soldiers on their way to the Finnish campaign deserting in droves (240 from one division!), openly threatening to shoot their own officers, and singing songs about their unwillingness to fight.[33] Nor was this at all surprising, given that most of the conscripts were peasants who over the previous ten years had been subjected to collectivisation, forced requisition, sporadic terror and mass impoverishment.

If from October 1941 on, Soviet and especially Russian soldiers began to fight back with formidable courage and determination, then it was not Stalin or his commanders who were responsible – it was Hitler and the Nazis, and the evidence they showed (in their treatment of prisoners of war and civilians) of their savage intentions. As I wrote in an article for the *National Interest* in May 1996: 'If, today, NATO were to invade Russia and attack Moscow, then, after the usual confusion and slaughter, the end result would probably be the Russian battle-ensign flying over Paris and Berlin. But none of this is going to happen.'

Exactly the same applies to the other post-Soviet armies – which is why the fact that they are in an even worse mess than the Russians would not matter so much to them in a future war, so long as it is Russia which *attacks them and is seen to attack them*. Thus in the words of a Ukrainian captain, Vadim (speaking off the record), with whom I talked in August 1995:

> Only a tiny minority of officers, even in our Officers' Union, actually want to fight Russia. Most would agree with Lebed. It's quite true that we are closely related: I served for much of my career in Russia, and of course many of my closest friends are Russians. I come from a military family, my wife is Russian, my sister is married to a Russian officer and they are stationed in Leningrad [*sic*] now...
>
> As to how the Ukrainian army would fight in a war with Russia – and a war really isn't likely, thank God – to be honest, I think that would depend on how the war started. If it seemed as though a nationalist Ukrainian government had gone out of its way to provoke the Russians, and if at the same time they were ramming Ukrainianisation down our throats and sacking good officers so as to appoint nationalists and political time-servers, and at the same time paying us a pittance – like what happened in 1992 and 1993, say, but even worse – then I think the army might just fall to pieces if it was asked to fight. But if on the other hand it was obviously Russia that was attacking us, say if some madman like Zhirinovsky came to power and started threatening us and demanding or invading Ukrainian territory, maybe trying to throw us out of Crimea by force – then I think Ukrainians would be so angry they would fight very hard. I would, certainly – after all, Ukraine is my home. I won't allow anyone to disturb its peace, to kill its people. But we really don't want to fight Russia, and I'm convinced the vast majority of Russians don't want to fight us either...

The importance for morale of soldiers fighting against an invasion of their homeland must be about the oldest cliché in military writing – but that does not make it any the less accurate. Of great importance also is *distance* from their homes. Even in such small countries as Georgia and Azerbaijan, during the wars there in the early 1990s, it was striking how detached people in the national capitals, Tbilisi and Baku, were from the fighting in Abkhazia and

Tbilisi, and how few metropolitan youths felt moved to go and fight there – despite all the ferocious nationalist rhetoric that these same youths were often fond of uttering (a high proportion of the Georgian and Azerbaijani soldiers I met were from the areas under direct attack). By contrast, no Abkhaz or Karabakh Armenian could possibly have been any doubt that he or she were in the front line, pinned in a tiny territory with no possibility of retreat – and this was also true of the Chechens. For a Russian soldier from St Petersburg – let alone Novosibirsk – hundreds or thousands of miles from Chechnya, the idea of a direct Chechen military threat to his home was obviously absurd.

In fact, whatever the myth of Russian 'genetic imperialism' (a phrase used in my presence by the Estonian Social Democrat leader Marju Lauristin), over the past hundred years or so, Russian conscript soldiers have never fought very hard (though often of course much harder than in Chechnya) in wars which have started outside Russia's territory. In *Anna Karenina*, Tolstoy satirised the vast gap between the high-flown Pan-Slav rhetoric of the intelligentsia in support of 'our Serbian and Bulgarian brothers' before the war of 1878, and the utter indifference of the mass of the peasantry.[34] In that same war, Vsevolod Garshin, who served as a volunteer infantryman, described the level of Pan-Slav commitment among the troops:

> Only rarely, and reluctantly, did the men speak about the future. They had only the vaguest idea why they were going to war, despite the fact that they had been stationed in Kishinev for a whole six months, ready for the campaign. That was surely the time when the meaning of the war could have been explained to the men, but this had evidently been considered unnecessary. One soldier, I remember, once asked me.
>
> 'What do you think, Mikhailich, will it be long before we get to the land of Bokhara?'
>
> I thought at first that I had misheard, but when he repeated his question, I replied that there were two seas between us and the land of Bokhara, which was 4,000 versts away, and that we should not be likely ever to go there.
>
> 'No, Mikhailich, you're wrong there. The clerk told me, he said once we've crossed the Danube we'll be in the land of Bokhara.'
>
> 'But that's not Bokhara, it's Bulgaria!'
>
> 'Ah well, Burgaria, Bukharia – whatever you call it. It's all the same, isn't it?' He fell silent, obviously annoyed.
>
> All we knew was that we were on our way to fight the Turk, because he had shed so much blood. We really did want to fight him, but not because of all that blood he had shed – we hadn't the faintest idea whose – but because he had caused so much trouble to so many people, so that we had to endure this long and gruelling march ('We've had to slog God knows how many thousands of versts – all because of him, the dirty heathen!')[35]

(Incidentally, his picture of the failure of the Russian army to give its men a sense of why they were fighting – indeed, its lack of any interest in doing so – was repeated in Chechnya. What is slightly suprising however is that the factor of taking out on the enemy 'all the trouble he had caused' did not operate more strongly in motivating the Russians in Chechnya to fight hard, especially given the general Russian dislike of the Chechens.)

The ordinary soldiers' lack of 'national awareness' in the later nineteenth century was a result of the backwardness of Russian society, and above all, the lack of a widespread state education system dedicated to turning 'peasants into Russians', to adapt Eugen Weber's famous phrase. This was also of crucial importance in the failure of the Russian soldiers to last out the rigours of the First World War, the collapse of the imperial army, and the Revolution. Very significant in this context is the fact that Russian soldiers in that war did not see the areas where the fighting was taking place – the Baltic provinces, Byelorussia, the western Ukraine – as part of Russia, even though they were part of the Russian empire. For them, they were either 'Poland' or 'Germany'.

However, in their indifference to 'colonial' wars far from home the Russians have been by no means unique. Historians who stress the importance of colonial rivalry in the deteriorating relationship in the late nineteenth century between Germany on the one hand and Britain and France on the other are not wrong; but they are wrong to think that these powers would ever have gone to war over this issue. The striking thing is that in the forty years before 1914 the European powers had repeated opportunities to fight each other over colonies – and they always backed off, whether over Egypt in 1882, at Fashoda in 1898, over Afghanistan in the 1880s and 1890s, Venezuela in the late 1890s or Morocco in 1906 and 1911.

One reason is of course that even for the most crazed French imperialist, it did not seem worth risking a European war for the sake of the southern Sudan. But more importantly, they did not think their peoples would follow them; and an age reared on the doctrines of Clausewitz and still under the shadow of the French revolutionary and Napoleonic victories (reinforced by memories of the Franco-Prussian War) did not need to be reminded of the importance for victory of the highly motivated 'people in arms'.

More specifically, the Socialist and Social Democrat parties which in August 1914 voted for war credits did so out of a visceral sense that their national territory was or was about to come under direct attack (and in the case of Britain, that the German invasion of Belgium violated both a moral principle and the oldest, most consistent and most important national security interest). The German Social Democrats have often been held to have disgraced themselves by voting in support of the war, but they did so because they believed that Russia was about to attack Austria as a prelude to an attack on the whole German world. They would never, ever, have voted for war in support of the Kaiser's imperial ambitions in Morocco or South Africa – and this is something of which the German government was very well aware.

In consequence, with extremely rare exceptions European governments did not fight colonial wars with conscript troops; under the laws of the French Republics after 1870, this was explicitly ruled out – and the key force in French colonial expansion, the Foreign Legion, was a mercenary unit recruited from foreigners (this was also largely true of the Portuguese colonial forces in the 1960s and early 1970s). The exceptions prove the rule: the European governments which did use conscripts in colonial or colonial-style ventures were either autocratic ones which thought they could ignore the feelings of their people, or ones which claimed to be defending not imperial but national territory, or to be combating not a colonial enemy but a global ideological threat – and anyway, they *always lost*, usually because the conscripts, or their relatives (the electorate at home), or both, lost the will to go on fighting.[36]

The Russians lost in Manchuria in 1904–5 in large part because of the bewilderment of the ordinary muzhik soldier as to what he was doing fighting Japanese in the middle of China. The French conscripts in Algeria – like the Russians in Chechnya – were fighting in what according to the constitution was supposed to be an integral part of France. French governments tried to use both the world Muslim and the world Communist threat to motivate public support – 'Jamais la marine sovietique à Mers el Kebir!' – but with mixed success. The Soviet Union (another autocratic power) in Afghanistan, and the Americans in Vietnam, both went to war as part of an ideological struggle. In both cases, this soon failed to inspire their troops, and in the US case, domestic support also crumbled.

The British imperial army was of course almost always a regular one. Only during and immediately after the two world wars were British conscripts employed for imperial tasks; and after 1945, a subsidiary reason for the precipitate British withdrawal from India was the bitter domestic unpopularity of using conscripts for colonial policing there.

Patriotism and the Private Soldier

When it comes to the state of Russia as a military power, and the calibre of the armed forces, another question which must be considered is that of social morality. The new social values of capitalism and materialism, and the general atmosphere of corruption in Russia have two main effects on the armed forces. The first is the armed forces themselves are infected with corruption. Russia has by now reached a state which also struck me very forcibly in Pakistan, whereby corruption is so all-pervasive that social and official (as opposed to personal) honesty becomes simply irrational, irrelevant, unpraised and unrespected, like chastity at the Court of Naples. With Chernomyrdin as Prime Minister, Potanin as Deputy Prime Minister and Berezovsky as Deputy Security Chief, for someone to go to a Russian captain or sergeant and tell him that for him, on his salary, to sell military equipment or fuel is wrong – *morally wrong* – becomes morally impossible and an insult to the intelligence.

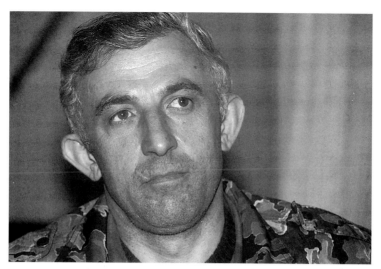

General Aslan Maskhadov

General Dzhokhar Dudayev

Shamil Basayev

Lieutenant Ponomarev (in scarf) of SOBR with comrade
in Grozny, February 1995

Russian soldiers in front of ruins of mosque in Grozny

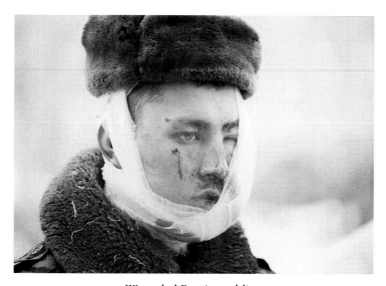

Wounded Russian soldier

Chechen fighter with wreck of Russian armoured personnel carrier
in Grozny, January 1995

Russian marine infantry and ruins of presidential headquarters,
February 1995

Russian soldiers in Chechen captivity

Grozny after the storm

Grozny 1995

At prayer in the mountains

Preparing to be warriors

Russian soldiers in camp

Russian dugout

Russian mother looking for her son

The other effect of course is on the soldier's willingness to risk his life and health for his country. I say 'of course', but it is remarkable how many military analyses of the Russian and other armies regard ordinary soldiers like pawns who can be moved around at will without reference to the state of their feelings. The question of individual morale has of course always been crucial in war, but it is even more so today, because the nature of modern infantry fighting gives great autonomy to the individual soldier or small group. We are no longer in the days of Frederick the Great, or even the First World War, when masses of soldiers could be led or driven forward by sufficiently ruthless and determined officers and NCOs. At the same time, technically trained soldiers – not easily driven peasants – have become vital to modern armies.

This all seems evident enough; but it is extraordinary how pervasive an image the blind but overwhelming Russian 'steamroller' remains among many Western experts. For example, a study in 1995 from the US National Defence University compared the position of the Baltic States today to that of South Korea in 1950[37] – the argument being that if NATO does not give them an explicit security guarantee, Russia may take this as an invitation to attack, on the analogy of Dean Acheson's failure explicitly to include Seoul under the American security umbrella (this is also a favourite analogy with the Balts).

Now, if pressed, no doubt the authors would qualify their remarks and point out that there may be other means of pressure short of outright invasion, which is quite true. None the less, the mental image at the heart of the Korean parallel is not hard to perceive: it is that of hundreds of thousands of infantry pouring across the border, driven by a fanatical ideology and iron-willed leaders; cut down in their thousands, they continue to advance, charging with the bayonet, climbing over the bodies of their fallen comrades. This is a powerful image, with deep roots in traditional Western fears of the Russians and the 'East' in general. It is also grotesquely far from the reality not just of the Russian army today but of any army that could conceivably be created on the basis of contemporary Russian society – unless Russia itself were to be invaded.

A Russian opinion poll of October 1994 – two months before the outbreak of the Chechen War – showed 95 per cent of respondents believing that real power in Russia lay in the hands of the 'mafia'. My private talks with ordinary Russian soldiers in Chechnya showed the vast majority of them believing the same – and what sane man is going to risk having his legs torn off and his guts ripped out for the mafia without even being paid for it?

It is often argued, and not wrongly, that a critical role in the soldier's behaviour is played by loyalty to his small group, or section – the desire 'not to let down his mates'. This is true, but it only pushes the question to a different level. If the army, or even the regiment as a whole is imbued with a reasonably high commitment to its cause, and a willingness to fight, then the mood of the small group will act on the frightened or indifferent so as to keep them in the line. If the army or regiment as a whole is demoralised and lacks belief, then on the contrary the mood in the group will act against the remaining individuals who are brave and determined, to convince them that their bravery is pointless and is only bringing their mates into danger against their will.

This specifically military problem highlights the character of the country's leaders to whom soldiers are expected to give their allegiance.

Late nineteenth-century America may have been dominated by robber barons, but it was already a mature constitutional democracy, which proved capable by democratic means of bringing to power forces which eventually reined in these barons, and under President Theodore Roosevelt introduced the beginnings of a modern system of state regulation. It may be that Russian democracy in future will be able to achieve this without violent upheaval, but this seems very questionable.

Moreover, the robber barons did not establish the moral and cultural code for the whole of society: other, and immensely influential models remained present; above all of course from religious sources, but also from a political tradition of honest service to the community. The new Russia has no such founding models. In the words of Professor Igor Kon (by no means a Communist sympathiser):

> Ironically, there is more corruption and cynicism in Russia in post-Soviet Russia than under Brezhnev's rule, when officialdom paid some homage to appearances and feared losing its privileges. Before 1985, the Soviet Union was the most hypocritical country in the world, now it is the most cynical... The moral lesson young people are likely to learn these days is every man for himself, or, as Ilf and Petrov put it long ago, 'Rescuing a drowning man is the task of the drowning man himself.' As a survival strategy in times of cataclysm, this is better than learned helplessness, but it hardly qualifies as a moral imperative.[38]

Or in the words of a St Petersburg rock-poet,

> The only problem is that 'smart' and 'corrupt' and 'honest' and 'stupid' have come to be thought of as synonyms. Smart equals corrupt, and vice versa. Honest is stupid. So you opt to join money like you used to join the Communist Party, giving up any pretence of personal morality. It's simply the smart thing to do. Honest people are peasants, clodhoppers. So it's all right to deceive them and steal from them.[39]

There were indeed nineteenth-century countries whose whole political tradition could be described in similar terms – but they were not the USA, they were in Latin America.

Reforms, discipline, even leadership can only do so much. To a very great extent, the spirit of an army has to be generated spontaneously and from within, on the basis of a mixture – in one proportion or another – of national loyalty, general social, moral and cultural values, and particular regimental or even 'clan' loyalties. This is illustrated rather well by two quotes by outside observers about the German and Soviet armies in the Second World War, which help illustrate why the clash between them was of such an appallingly bloody, dogged and prolonged nature. The first, surprisingly enough, is by Milovan Djilas, then a leader of the Yugoslav Communist partisans, about German soldiers he encountered during a parley in 1943:

> What surprised me more than anything during all these negotiations was how little of the Nazi ideology and mentality was evident in the German army, which did not seem at all like an unthinking automated machine. Officer–soldier relations seemed less disciplined and more cordial than in other armies. The junior officers ate out of the soldiers' kettle, at least here on the battlefield. Moreover, their army did not appear particularly organised or blindly obedient. Its militancy and homogeneity sprang from vital national sources rather than from Nazi discipline. Like any other men, they were unhappy that events had embroiled them in a war, but once embroiled they were resolved to win, to avoid a new and worse defeat and shame.[40]

This is echoed in a passage by Primo Levi about the Soviet army at the end of the Second World War (allowance must be made in his remarks about the Germans for the fact that he had seen the SS, not the army; and in those about the Russians, for gratitude for the fact that they had saved him from Auschwitz and certain death):

> For the most part they lived together with friendly simplicity, like a large temporary family, without military formalism... And yet, under their slovenly and anarchical appearance, it was easy to see in them, in each of these rough and open faces, the fine soldiers of the Red Army, the valiant men of the old and new Russia, gentle in peace and fierce in war, strong from an inner discipline born from concord, from reciprocal love and love of their country; a stronger discipline, because it came from the spirit, than the servile and mechanical discipline of the Germans. It was easy to understand, living among them, why this former discipline, and not the latter, had finally triumphed.[41]

In this context, of immense importance are Igor Kon's words above about Russia today being in a state of 'every man for himself'. This view is confirmed by a survey carried out in 1996 by the Centre for Research on Public Opinion (directed by Professor Yuri Levada) in Moscow, which asked how people were trying to respond to the social and economic problems facing them, wage arrears, the threat of unemployment and so on, and how they would respond to an even greater catastrophe. The reply favoured by 70 per cent replied that 'I rely on myself and try to do the best for myself and my family.' Only seven per cent took the view that they tried to act collectively and cooperate with others, and only 4.6 per cent that 'I help others.'[42] Despite the numbers who replied that 'our present existence is unbearable', Levada said that 'all the indications are that the social patience of the population remains relatively high and steady.'

This has the most important implications for every kind of collective political activity or protest, for the growth of democracy and for labour organisation; but it also has severe negative consequences for the military and its chances of regeneration. One anthropological definition of warfare is 'organised and directed friendship'.[43] If we accept this version, then it would seem to follow automatically that a society as atomised, cynical, individualistic (in the worst sense) and mutually distrustful as Russia in the 1990s would find it almost impossible to give birth to an army with the capacity for spontaneous discipline and solidarity remarked on in the passages from Djilas and Levi – unless the nation as a whole were to come under an immediate, obvious, direct and mortal outside threat, of a kind which is hardly likely to face Russia in the foreseeable future.

Of course, the difficulties modern individualistic societies have in generating effective armed forces are not restricted to Russia, though for a variety of reasons they have taken especially extreme forms there; the unwillingness of people in such countries to risk their lives for their country or for any other cause has been repeatedly commented upon and analysed. The reaction of modern Western professional armies – but relying of course upon very ancient military traditions – has been to some extent to wall themselves off from society and social culture at large, and to inspire their members with a culture and a set of loyalties drawn above all from within the military itself.

In the words of the *Wall Street Journal*'s Pentagon correspondent, Thomas E. Ricks, about some newly recruited US Marines,

> I was stunned to see, when they went home for postgraduate leave, how alienated they felt from their old lives. At various times, each of these new marines seemed to feel a moment of private loathing for public America. They were repulsed by the physical unfitness of civilians, by the uncouth behaviour they witnessed, and by what they saw as pervasive selfishness and consumerism. Many found themselves avoiding old friends, and some experienced difficulty even in communicating with their families.[44]

The classic example of an army with its own culture is of course the British army, with its loyalties and morale based largely on a form of clan – the regiment – with origins and traditions going back hundreds of years.[45]

In relation to Russia, this leads to the question of whether, in a deeply corrupt society, the military can be to some extent 'walled off' from this corruption. Sometimes this is possible. Listed in recent reports as one of the most corrupt states on earth, Pakistan's military however gives the impression of being a relatively dedicated, honest and highly motivated force (internally – not when soldiers go into politics). This is partly because Pakistan's successive military rulers transferred to the military as a whole enormous quantities of property, which was then organised into companies (by local standards efficiently and honestly run) which have been exploited to support the living standards of serving soldiers and to provide employment for retired ones. Something of the same sort exists in China.

The second factor however is that the Pakistani army has a strong sense of a particular and mortal enemy – India – and also a strong and not unjustified sense of itself as the very heart and foundation of the state; as if without the army, Pakistan itself would not exist, which is probably quite true. For all these reasons soldiers in Pakistan (who are also still very much drawn from particular 'martial races', as the British used to call them, with strong warrior traditions of their own) feel themselves very superior to their society in general.

It is not easy to see how anything like this spirit could be created in the Russian army today. And of course, if it were, it could have very mixed consequences, both for Russia's neighbours and for Russia itself. For the West, it would probably on balance be a good thing, because the danger of nuclear smuggling by hungry and disaffected officers would diminish – and nuclear terrorism is by far the biggest direct threat to the West today. But a Russian army which was proud, well motivated, patriotic and internally cohesive would not long tolerate the kind of civilian government we have seen in Russia over the past few years – and for that matter, the Russian people themselves would welcome their intervention to 'clean up that brothel in the Kremlin'.[46]

In this context, an opinion poll in May–July 1995 among 600 Russian field-grade army, navy and strategic missile forces officers commissioned by the Livermore National Laboratory (USA), and organised by Deborah Yarsike Ball, provided really fascinating evidence of military opinion and the effects on it of the war in Chechnya, even when that war was only five months old (the poll was carried out by Russian pollsters, and the respondents were not told of the American involvement).

Asked whether authoritarian rule was needed to solve Russia's problems, 38 per cent agreed or 'somewhat agreed', but 62.2 per cent wholly or partially disagreed. Asked about freedom of the press, 82 per cent said it was good for Russia. The overwhelming majority were against military involvement in politics and other 'non-military tasks': 80 per cent said that they would in no circumstances whatsoever fire on peaceful demonstrators. On the other hand, 98 per cent said that they would fight to protect the Kurile islands from an attack by Japan.

Concerning the fall of the Soviet Union, 73.6 per cent agreed wholly or partially with the proposition that its collapse was 'a catastrophe for our country', but only 42.5 per cent said that this collapse should have been prevented by all means, including military ones, while 57.5 per cent disagreed.[47]

Even more striking – indeed astonishing – were their responses when asked if force should be used to suppress a separatist rebellion. Not merely were 68 per cent against this (up from 59 per cent even before the war, in 1994, according to a poll by the Friedrich Ebert Stiftung), but 39 per cent said that they would definitely or probably disobey such an order if given. Now, as the example of General Babichev in December 1994 shows, it is one thing for an officer to say that, quite another to do it in practice. But it is astonishing that it should even be said. It is impossible to conceive of more than a tiny fraction of French or British, let alone Turkish or Indian officers replying to this effect. As Dr Ball said, 'for field-grade officers to say this is evidence of an extraordinary breakdown of discipline and morale.'[48] It is impossible not to agree with her – and, I would add, this is true not just for the armed forces, but for the Russian nation as a whole.

6   Failure of the Serbian Option, 1: The Collapse of the 'Cossacks'

> The family fell apart before Pantelei Prokofievich's eyes. He and his old woman were left alone. Kindred ties were destroyed unexpectedly and quickly, the warmth of mutual relations was lost, and and more and more often notes of irritation and alienation crept into their conversations. They no longer sat round the communal table as a single and harmonious family, but rather as though they had accidentally gathered together.
>
> Mikhail Sholokhov, 'The Quiet Don'

The Serbian Option

The 'Serbian option', in a Russian context, could also be called the 'neo-Cossack option'. It is a combination of three factors, all to be seen in embryonic form in some of the Russian areas of the former Soviet Union, and in fully fledged and deeply evil form in the former Yugoslavia. These factors are: the move by major sections of the Communist ruling elite to radical nationalist positions in an effort to preserve their own power, with resulting attempts by state forces to whip up national fear and terror, especially among members of a given nationality living beyond the state borders; the mobilisation of local ethnic groups, above all from such diasporas, partly as a result of 'manipulation' and partly on the basis of real historically based fears and hatreds and local fighting traditions; and the exploitation of the resulting conflicts by criminal gangs and warlords posing more or less sincerely as nationalist militias.

These factors came together on a large scale in the creation of the Transdniestrian Republic out of Moldova – the nearest thing in the former Soviet Union to the Bosnian Serb Republic or the Serbian Republic of Kraina from 1991 to 1995, and a development in which 'Cossacks' played a leading part. So far, however, this model has not spread in the Russian diaspora in the former Soviet Union (the Abkhaz, South Ossete and Nagorno-Karabakh states were not founded by ethnic Russians, and the Crimean moves in a Transdniestrian direction failed, for reasons which will be explored below).

In the context of the end of the Soviet army and the failure of the Russian army, the question is whether such militias may arise to substitute for that army, but also perhaps by their actions to draw Russia into fresh conflicts within or beyond its borders. In Georgia, Azerbaijan and for a briefer period in Armenia, all these factors have been strongly present. In Russia and in the Russian diasporas, these three factors come together in the 'Cossacks', who have formed the bulk of Russian forces of this kind. I have put 'Cossacks' in inverted commas, because a great many – perhaps a majority – of the people now calling themselves Cossacks have only the most tenuous link to the Cossack tradition. Dr Georgy Derluguian has suggested that they should rather be called 'neo-Cossacks', because their distance from the pre-revolutionary Cossack tradition, after seventy years of Soviet rule, is extremely great.[1]

Rather, the Cossacks in some areas have become a general rallying force of paramilitary Russian nationalism, or at least (in Kazakhstan) of Russian protest and mobilisation – and also, very often, for the gathering of a variety of hooligans, gangsters, racketeers, unemployed ex-officers, and politically ambitious figures excluded from local ruling establishments (or 'parties of power', as they are known in the former USSR). In the Cossacks' own rallying words,

> Everything for which Russia was great, with its lands from the Dniester to the Kurile Islands, its powerful economy, splendid culture, military glory – all that until recent times made the world consider us a great power – this is the merit of the multinational Russian people. Much of this, Cossacks, was achieved by our ancestors, by their blood, sweat and intellect.[2]

As will be seen, among the Russians these forces have, however, played a very much weaker role than many well-informed observers feared a few years ago. They have not emerged as a popular force to supplement, aid or substitute for the crumbling army,[3] and in Chechnya they have been wholly peripheral. There have been three essential reasons for this: the fracturing of the Cossacks' own traditions; the very weak mobilising potential of contemporary Russian society, whether for national or economic causes; and the fact that, unlike the Serbian state under Slobodan Milosevic, the Russian state under Boris Yeltsin has given only limited encouragement and help to the Cossacks and other paramilitaries to play a radical nationalist role either within or beyond Russia's borders, and on occasions have acted to rein them in.

In Chechnya, there was very little attempt to use them to supplement the army. A key reason for this was that by mid-1994, before the war began, relevant individuals and groups in the Yeltsin administration had already decided that the Cossacks were a weak, divided and unreliable force – had indeed developed a certain contempt for them. This feeling was increased by a murky episode in the summer of 1994, when the chief Don Cossack Ataman, Nikolai Kozitsyn (a former prison guard), signed a 'treaty' with the Dudayev government which provided that Dudayev would protect the Cossack communities in Chechnya, in return for which the Don Cossacks would not allow forces hostile to Chechnya to cross their territory or use it as a base.[4] Interpreted at the time as a promise to block Russian troops headed for Chechnya (which would have been vastly beyond Kozitsyn's strength even had he dared to take such a politically risky position), it was just a promise, as Kozitsyn later explained to me, not to allow Don Cossack groups to go to fight in Chechnya, as they had in Transdniestria and to a lesser extent Abkhazia.[5] This may very well be true. What he did not say, but is generally believed by observers of the Cossack and Chechen scene, is that money played a major part – apart from the possibility of direct bribes, there were very important business dealings, especially in the field of construction, between the Rostov-on-Don region (of which the old Don Cossack territory is now part) and Chechnya.

By the spring of 1996, Kozitsyn had made his peace with the Yeltsin administration, and was campaigning hard among 'his' Cossacks for Yeltsin's re-election; but an obvious legacy of mistrust remained. Government attitudes were echoed in the senior ranks of the army, where the Cossacks were regarded as shambolic and worthless irregulars whose commanders gave themselves airs as 'generals', ranks which they had not merited.[6] For example, when in 1992 Ataman Viktor Ratiyev, leader of one of the all-Russian unions of Cossacks, offered his organisation's help to General Lebed, the latter replied contemptuously that he had nothing to say to 'police lieutenants calling themselves Lieutenants-General'. Ratiyev, who is indeed a former policeman, had been appointed General by the Yeltsin administration as part of its efforts to woo Cossack support in its struggle with the opposition-dominated parliament. This must have been singularly galling to Lebed, himself still only a major-general at the time; but more importantly, according to one of his staff with whom I talked the next year, he already despised the Cossacks as a fighting force, and was irritated with their links to organised crime – despite his mother being of Cossack ancestry.

Interestingly enough, four years later, when Lebed was running for president, like Yeltsin and Zyuganov he made assiduous attempts to woo the Cossacks – but this is a testimony to their voting potential, not to their fighting potential. It also demonstrates the fact that Cossack 'identity' today is entirely optional – it can be put on and taken off again like a Cossack hat, according to circumstances. Within the Yeltsin regime, for example, both Sergei Shakhrai and Oleg Lobov are of Cossack descent. Shakhrai made great play with this in an attempt to strengthen his political base in some Russian regions; Lobov, whose base was in the old bureaucracy and the military industrial complex, as far as I know hardly ever even mentioned it in public.

The weakness of the Cossacks was demonstrated for example at a meeting of Cossack leaders in Stavropol on 20–21 January 1997, when they demanded yet again that the Cossacks be turned into units within the Russian army, and sent to Chechnya to protect the old Cossack territories in northern Chechnya and their Russian populations, and partition these from the rest of the country (as they had been before 1957). The meeting was provoked by the Russian military withdrawal from Chechnya, and the murder of some twenty-six Cossack civilians in villages in northern Chechnya in the week that followed.

(The attackers are unknown. They could have been pure bandits, but it also seems likely that they were acting for pro-Moscow Chechens, anxious to destabilise Chechnya and worsen relations between the new Chechen authorities and Moscow.) One Terek Cossack representative, Viktor Zaitsev, declared that 'we will never agree to the loss of the left bank of the Terek. We will fight for it just as the Chechens have fought for land that they regard as their own.'

The Russian government found the Cossacks sufficiently important to send the powerful Boris Berezovsky to the meeting, where he pretended to adopt their most radical demands (whether to neutralise them, or out of pure personal opportunism, it is impossible to say), and declared that 'the federal authorities have proved unable to protect those who live in areas adjacent to Chechnya. In this case, I think it necessary to give these people the same possibilities which the opposite side has. That is to say, to give them arms on legal grounds.'[7] It is difficult to say however who was being more cynical on this occasion: Mr Berezovsky, who almost certainly had no intention whatsoever of pressing the government for any such policy; or the pro-government Cossack leaders, who listened to him with a straight face. Their ancestors of course would have hung him in pieces from a tree.

Earlier that month, a draft law to create armed Cossack units within the army was introduced in parliament by the government and was defeated, because, I was told privately, the government had let it be known that it had no real desire for it to succeed. As for the Cossacks themselves, it is striking that after six years in which the Chechens had displayed the possibilities of spontaneous military organisation and the acquisition of arms, the Cossacks were still asking the Russian state and army to do this for them. They were not about to go to Chechnya and fight on their own; nor had they spent their money on trying to circumvent the Yeltsin administration and the army and buy really serious weapons stocks on the black market. It was not in this spirit that the Cossack chieftain Yermak set out to conquer Siberia for Stroganov, God and the Tsar.

The only place other than Transdniestria where the Cossacks have played a major role in their own right has been in North Ossetia, where in 1993 they sided with the Ossetes in their brief but bloody clash with the Ingush over ownership of the Prigorodny District.[8] In part, this was a reflection of the traditional Ossete–Russian and Ossete–Cossack alliance (the Terek Cossacks in the eighteenth and nineteenth centuries actually came to include a considerable number of Christian Ossete communities). It was also of course due to the fact that the Cossacks had profited along with the Ingush from land taken from the Ingush when they were deported by Stalin in 1944. However, it is important to note that this Cossack role in Ossetia is very much due to the support and protection of the North Ossetian government; in other words, it is not a reflection either of their own spontaneously developed strength or of support from Moscow.

The Yeltsin administration has played its part in restraining the Cossacks, in Chechnya as elsewhere. In Chechnya, the reason appears to have been that up to August 1996 Moscow was still hoping that enough Chechens could be bullied, bribed or persuaded into accepting the rule of the Russian-backed Chechen governments of Aslanbek Khadjiev and Doku Zavgayev. The chances of this would have been diminished still further if Cossack units had been allowed to participate in the war on a large scale, stoking local ethnic conflict between Russians and Chechens and almost certainly indulging in looting and mayhem. After August 1996, in the face of overwhelming evidence of the war's unpopularity and the popularity of Lebed's peace moves, the Yeltsin administration's desire was simply to get out as quickly as possible – and to hell with the Cossacks and their 'historic lands'.

Moreover, a Cossack involvement would indeed have risked spreading the war to other areas of the Russian North Caucasus – and it is vital to remember that while under Yeltsin, Russia has to some extent played the role of a discontented, unsatisfied or radical power in its desire to restore Russian hegemony over the former Soviet Union (albeit to a much lesser degree than has been alleged by Western Russophobes), in its relations with its own ethnic minorities or autonomies it is in the position of a conservative power, frightened of change.

Or to put it another way: it may be true, as someone wrote, that Russia feels the loss of the Soviet empire as a man feels the itching in an amputated leg; the question is, however, whether for the sake of an attempt to get back her lost leg, Russia would be prepared to risk the loss of her remaining leg. That consists of the maintenance of the exisiting Russian state without the loss of more terrritory, on the basis of internal ethnic peace, a relatively stable currency and a central government grudgingly accepted as legitimate. Almost all the evidence of the past five years suggests that Russian leaders – and, at heart, the great majority of ordinary Russians – know that it is not sensible to put this at risk, and this is also reflected in the Yeltsin administration's Cossack policy.

Thus in March 1995, a Kuban Cossack Ataman at the Russian military base of Mozdok in North Ossetia (original headquarters for the Chechen operation), Grigory Pogrebnoi, told Agence France Presse that 'my assigned role here is actually to hold back intervention by our [Cossack] brothers in the fighting... Of course individual Cossacks try to come to fight here, but we stop them, by force too if needed.' (Instead the really enthusiastic ones were allowed to sign up as *kontraktniki* with the army or Interior Ministry troops, but only on an individual basis.)[9] Ataman Pogrebnoi did not say who had 'assigned' him this task, but as an ex-officer serving at the Russian military base, we may assume that the Russian government and army had a hand in it.

However, in giving the impression that Cossacks were 'volunteering by thousands for the Chechen War', and that it was sometimes necessary to use force to restrain them, the Ataman was leading the correspondent concerned astray. Russian correspondents were also guilty of this; thus in the same month, Igor Rotar of *Nezavisimaya Gazeta* wrote that '12,000 well-trained and well-armed Cossacks are ready to go to Chechnya.'[10]

Now for some of us who know the contemporary Cossacks, the very idea of a 'well-trained Cossack' may seem a contradiction in terms. That may be unkind, but it is highly doubtful that in the whole of Russia there are 12,000 well-armed, well-trained and organised Cossack fighters, or even a quarter as many.[11] Nothing I've seen of the Cossacks has suggested that they could generate in their units the superb spontaneous discipline, tactical skill and fighting spirit of the Chechens. More to the point, neither I nor the other more experienced Western and Russian correspondents in Chechnya during the war saw many signs of the desire to fight claimed by these correspondents' informants, and very few of us ever saw any fighting Cossack troops at all.

In April 1996 the Russian independent television channel NTV reported that a unit of Cossacks had been formed to fight in Chechnya, and had been named after the nineteenth-century Russian commander Alexei Yermolov. But the report added that after suffering casualties, 200 of the Cossacks involved had asked to go home, after just two weeks' service.

Cossacks were not wholly absent. In December 1996, shortly after the outbreak of war, the chief Ataman of the Terek Cossacks, Alexander Starodubtsev, was killed by a Chechen mine while visiting Cossack communities in northern Chechnya. However, in a sign of the acute internal divisions among the Terek Cossacks, Starodubtsev had been declared deposed by a dissident assembly in Stavropol the previous August, which also practically established the Stavropol Cossacks as a separate organisation and thus weakened the 'Terek Host' still further as an effective force. Starodubtsev's ill-fated visit to Chechnya was in part an attempt to rebuild his prestige.

I may be biased as a result of one particular encounter. In February 1995, behind the Russian lines, after the Russian army had stormed central Grozny, demolishing much of it in the process and killing thousands of its mostly Russian inhabitants, I encountered a group of lightly armed Terek Cossacks from Pyatigorsk – once most of the city was safely in Russian hands, they had come to give 'humanitarian aid' to Russian civilians in Grozny. Stinking of alcohol, filthy and unshaven, they bragged of how Grozny was a Cossack city, of how the Chechens should be herded on to reservations, and if any Chechens rejected this fate, 'we will ram pork fat down their throats with our bayonets, the same as the Cossacks have always done... Stalin should have finished the job in 1944.' Even the Russian conscripts looked at them with disdain, and I was told later that the military command had insisted on their removal.

Yet over the previous three years, the Cossacks and Russians in Chechnya could often have done with some help. Russian state propaganda concerning Chechen atrocities against Cossack villages in Chechnya and Russian civilians in general was grossly exaggerated, but it is true that Dudayev's government was incapable of preventing Chechen criminals from preying on anyone who was unprotected. In the words of Georgy Galkhin, Ataman of the 'Grozny Cossacks', who stayed in Chechnya throughout Dudayev's rule and the first year of the Russian occupation, and did his best to cooperate with Dudayev,

Our position under Dudayev got worse and worse. I don't think he himself had anything against us, but he couldn't control the criminal elements. No one gave an order to drive us out, but banditism was an everyday thing – plus insults, threats, rapes, the seizure of flats … my young nephew, for example, was continually bullied in school by the Chechen kids. They knew he was the nephew of the Cossack Ataman, and they would follow him home, beat him, rob him, curse him. The fact that I was officially at least an adviser to Dudayev on minority affairs, and under his protection, made no difference to them.

Russians with some links of family, business, friendship or even good neighbourliness to Chechen society *were* however often protected, in accordance with Chechen tradition, as many of them admitted. The Lazanya Restaurant in Grozny, refuge of journalists until it was destroyed by Russian bombardment, was run by a very amiable extended family of Chechens and their Russian wives and mistresses, who had obviously fitted in very well. The business links between Grozny and the Don helped produce the Don-Cossack-Chechen 'treaty' of August 1994. But others, whether Russian villagers raided by bandits, or Russian women in Grozny harassed by Chechen youths, could be very vulnerable – a major reason why around two-fifths (180,000) of the Russian population, including many Cossacks, fled from Chechnya under Dudayev's rule up to December 1994.

In March 1994, Cossack villagers in the Naurskaya District of northern Chechnya told Reuters that they had been subjected to repeated Chechen banditry, with the Chechen authorities refusing to take any action. A local Ataman, Vladimir Kashlyunov, declared that the local Cossacks were ready to take up arms, and if that happened, 'then the entire North Caucasus will blow up. The Cossacks will come here from the whole region, and all of Russia will be involved in the war.'[12]

In retrospect, this sounds like not a threat but a desperate appeal for help; for during all this time up to the beginning of the war, I never heard of a single organised Cossack group actually entering Chechnya to defend these Russians. Already in 1992, Cossacks with whom I spoke in Grozny and northern Chechnya were expressing extreme scepticism about whether fellow Cossacks would come to help them; by December 1995, two-thirds of the way through the war, this had turned to open contempt and anger, directed at the Cossack movement, the Russian army and the Yeltsin government. In Ataman Galkhin's words, as we sat in the Russian headquarters in Grozny (the next day, shrapnel from a car bomb tore across that same room),

How could the Cossacks help us? They are scattered among a dozen different subjects of the Federation, and they have no serious weapons. Why not? Better ask them… The army is not giving us arms, and we have not asked for them, because we are law-abiding people, and we also know that in the long run we have to live together with the

Chechens... All this talk of partitioning Chechnya, of a Cossack region here, of exterminating and deporting the Chechens is just talk by people sitting safely hundreds of miles away, I don't care if they call themselves Cossacks, they can call themselves what they like for all I care, I know what I call them...

The Chechens now, they are a strong people, physically and spiritually. The deportation of 1944 made the Chechen nation more healthy, because the weak died and only the strong survived. When there is danger, the Chechens all rush together to the danger point. They fear nothing. And then, unlike us, every Chechen family has so many sons that it can afford to lose a few.[13]

These views were echoed in the same month by Cossack leaders living north of the Terek – who interestingly enough also rejected the idea of partitioning Chechnya along the Terek; they cursed the Russian army and government, and declared that the goal must be coexistence with the Chechens. Again and again I noticed that the closer Cossacks got to the Chechens, the more moderate they became – though in fairness, one should say that in other parts of the North Caucasus too, some had always emphasised ethnic harmony. Thus Yuri Antonov, the Deputy Ataman of the Kuban Cossacks (and a retired Soviet major-general), told me in October 1994, with war in Chechnya already looming,

We are dead against any military intervention in Chechnya. It will only cause unnecessary bloodshed, turn Dudayev into a hero, and make the Cossacks in Chechnya into hostages. And we have no intention of starting a war ourselves. Our role in the Caucasus should be as peacemakers. After all, we are no colonists, we also are an ancient Caucasian nationality, and we had *kunachestvo* with many of the other nationalities, and intermarried with them. We are only partly Russian...

It is true there were Cossacks serving in Abkhazia, but they served as individuals, not as organised Kuban units, and we issued a statement disapproving of their activities. It's not that I approve of Georgian policy, after all it was the Georgians who started the war. But it wasn't our business.[14]

Also very striking was the almost complete failure of the Russian army in Chechnya to mobilise the Cossacks to support them, to seek contacts with the local Russian population, or even (when it came to indiscriminate firing and damage to property, though not of course to arrests) to make any distinction between local Russians and Chechens. As Pyotr Tolokonnikov, deputy head of the district administration in Naurskaya, told me, 'God knows why the army came here. To protect Boris Yeltsin, to keep the pipeline from the Caspian, to line someone's pockets – only not for us, that's clear.'[15]

The Terek Cossacks from outside Chechnya meanwhile limited themselves to patrolling the roads leading to Chechnya, ostensibly to 'search for arms', and in the immediate run-up to the war in the autumn of 1994, to 'impose a blockade'. In the event, this was turned into an excuse simply to extort money and goods from Chechen and other traders; and the corruption of the Cossack and other Russian 'forces of order' entrusted with this task are one reason why the idea of isolating and ignoring Chechnya, advocated by Solzhenitsyn and on occasions by Lebed, was never a viable option. As a Chechen trader called Bauddin, selling cigarettes, chocolates and beer ('beer is our main international aid,' he said cheerfully) told me in November 1994,

> Whatever the Russian blockade may be, we'll either get around it or bribe our way through. Don't you worry, unless they blow it to pieces, this bazaar will always stay open. These Russian guards and soldiers, they can all be bought – though they do force up prices. For example, last week I went to Krasnodar on a bus with people most of them going to buy, and of course we came back packed with goods. Every Russian police checkpoint would ask 40,000 or 50,000 roubles from each of us – not too much. They're not fools, you know – they want to keep the trade going, not to choke it off.
>
> Then we came to a military one, and they asked for 200,000 roubles. We said to them, 'Look, be human – why do you want so much more than the others?' They threatened us – 'All right, you can stay here till the commander comes, then he will take everything.' But it was bluff – we haggled for an hour, and they let us go for 100,000 roubles... They're greedier than the police, because they're not in the army forever, they know they're not going to have the opportunity for long...
>
> The conscripts are worse than the police, the regular troops [kontraktniki] are worse than the conscripts, but worst of all are the Cossacks. They are simply drunken brutes, they swear at you, threaten to kill you, sometimes they steal everything.

The most visible activity of the Cossacks during the Chechen War was during the seizure of the hospital and several hundred hostages in the Russian town of Budennovsk (Stavropol Region) by Shamil Basayev's raiders in June 1995. Cossacks set up roadblocks around the town and harassed local Chechens, Western and Russian journalists, and travellers in general.[16] They threatened to take hostage all Chechen civilians – men, women and children – living in the Budennovsk region and to kill them if the hostages in the hospital were not released.[17] This threat was never carried out, was not approved by the Russian military or civilian authorities, and was probably just another piece of empty talk; none the less, it gives a certain flavour of the Cossack spirit, and why the Yeltsin administration has been so very sensible not to use them in Chechnya or encourage them to act elsewhere.

In April of the next year, during the presidential election campaign, Boris Yeltsin visited Budennovsk and made various promises of state money to the

Cossacks. He flattered them to the skies, declaring that the Cossacks fighting in Chechnya had 'thrown the Chechen fighters into a panic... They have to understand that you don't mess with Cossacks.' But this was mere campaign rhetoric.[18] It was fortunate that this paramilitary mobilisation failed – because if such groups had emerged on a large scale along Russia's frontiers and in the Russian diasporas, they might have spread war and chaos across much of Eurasia.

The Nature of the 'Cossack Revival'

I first met Cossack volunteers on their way to fight in Transdniestria at a meeting (*Krug*, or 'circle') of Terek Cossacks in Vladikavkaz in February 1992, when they voted to restore the united Terek Host of Tsarist days.[19] As with so many other declarations by and about the Cossacks, this has in practice come to nothing, and as of 1996 the Terck Cossacks were even more divided than the other Cossack 'hosts', with several different leaders and local centres.[20]

The Cossack movement as a whole is extremely disunited (in part still aligned by whose ancestors fought on which side in the Civil War), and attempts by the Yeltsin administration to unite it under state control have come to very little. At the national level, there are two Cossack bodies – they can hardly be called 'organisations': the Union of Cossack Hosts of Russia and Abroad, led by Viktor Ratiyev, and the Union of Russian Cossacks, of Alexander Martynov. Martynov's group stemmed largely from the Soviet Cossack establishment (in so far as such a thing existed), made up of those Cossacks whose ancestors had fought on the Red side in the Civil War. As its name suggests, Ratiyev's grouping was originally formed from those Cossacks whose ancestors had fought on the White side in the Civil War.[21]

During the troubles of the 1990s, Ratiyev's group established links with the surviving White Cossack groups in exile, from whom much was hoped. But of course the original White émigré generation was long dead, and the whole émigré tradition is by now so attenuated as to be virtually worthless from a financial, political or even cultural point of view, let alone a military one. This is in the sharpest contrast to the help given by the Baltic, Armenian and Ukrainian emigrations to their respective countries of origin, and the failure of the Russian emigration to generate effective institutions and perpetuate itself over the generations is an interesting footnote to the general theme of the weakness of Russian political traditions.

Of more importance than their origins is the fact that in 1990–3 Ratiyev forged links with Yeltsin, whereas Martynov tended towards first the Soviet government and then the Communist-nationalist opposition. However, among ordinary Cossacks on the ground neither of the two bodies has any real influence, and many Cossacks told me that they cannot tell them apart. There is really no such thing as a Cossack 'movement', or for that matter of a 'host' in any real sense, whether on the Don, Kuban or Terek.

At the time, however, the Terek Cossack assembly of February 1992 did look rather impressive and frightening to me, and seemed to have most of the elements that were already causing mayhem in Yugoslavia. First, there was the heavy presence of men from the Soviet army (as it still was then, although the Union had been dissolved two months before), some recently retired, others it seemed to me still serving and deliberately sent to help turn the Cossacks into a fighting force. Only a few kalashnikovs were visible, but I assumed that major arms supplies would soon be on the way – if only because, as I had seen in Chechnya the previous week, the Soviet army was in a state of disintegration and its soldiers were selling off its arms. The Combined Arms Military School in Vladikavkaz (where the second Terek Ataman, Colonel Alexander Starodubtsev, was a senior instructor) acted as a training school for Cossack cadres.

Added to this was the evident encouragement and help from the local government of North Ossetia – though they had their own reasons for this, to gain Cossack help in their dispute with the neighbouring Ingush. But most alarming at the assembly in Vladikavkaz was the evident hatred of the Chechens, the lurid talk of Chechen atrocities, and of most of Chechnya being 'ancient Terek Cossack land', for which 'we must fight to the last Cossack, after the glorious example of our ancestors' – all very Yugoslav.

This was three months after the Chechen declaration of independence and the humiliating retreat of the Russian forces sent in by Boris Yeltsin to crush the uprising, and one Cossack declared that 'it is for us now to step forward and fight beside our glorious army, which the Democrats are destroying, for the sake of the historic Russian Caucasus.' As was to appear over the next four years, however, the real Cossack desire or ability to take their place in the line of battle was very slight. The then Terek Ataman, Vassily Konyakhin – an elderly former major in the Soviet air force who derived his prestige from his Second World War record as a Hero of the Soviet Union – was well on the mark when he opposed the wild talk of some of the other Atamans at the Vladikavkaz *krug*, telling them, 'Don't fool yourselves. We are not yet anything like a real military force.'

The Cossack Tradition and its Destruction

In the North Caucasus, despite the breaking of the traditions, the feebleness of the Cossack revival is all the same rather surprising, because the Cossacks have been there for a very long time – longer than the Protestants in Ulster, longer for that matter than the ancestors of any white person in North America.

Cossacks have lived to the north of the Caucasus for some five hundred years, intermittently fighting with the mountaineers for land, cattle and dominion, and trading and intermarrying with them (and indeed adopting their dress and many of their customs). During the first two hundred years of their stay, the Cossacks appear to have generally fitted themselves into the interstices of the complicated North Caucasian ethnic and economic mosaic, rather than carving out a major dominion by conquest.

The Cossack tradition was therefore a long one: as part of their disputes with the local peoples over territory and autonomy, and of their demand to be officially included among the 'repressed peoples' – those also singled out for deportation under Soviet rule – the Cossacks indeed now claim to be an 'indigenous people of the region'. But of course the truly indigenous Caucasian peoples, like the Chechens, have been there far longer, in some cases for thousands of years. The exact date of the Cossacks' first arrival is debatable, with some Russian, and especially Cossack historians trying to make it as early as possible, and Caucasian ones to make it later. General Antonov in conversation with me tried to portray the Cossacks as a pre-Russian ethnic amalgam, embracing 'Scythians, Myotokasari Slavs, Tanais tribes and other nations of this region. We only adopted Russian much later.'[22] (He however used this not as an argument for Cossack land claims, but for autonomy.)

Be that as it may, up to the later eighteenth century the Cossacks pursued an uneasy relationship, of cooperation interspersed with rebellion, with the Russian state, which had arrived to the north of the region with Ivan the Terrible's conquest of Astrakhan in 1556. In 1594, Ivan's successor, Fyodor Ivanovich, adopted the titles 'Lord of the Iberian Land, of the Tsars of Georgia and of Kabarda, of the Cherkess and Mountain Princes', though there was at that date no reality to back up this grandiose and presumptuous claim.

The first Cossacks of the region were known as Grebentsi, from *greben*, a ridge, because they lived among the hills to the south of the Terek river, north of the formerly forested plain that slopes into the foothills of the Caucasus. It seems that at that point the settled habitations of the Chechens were in the mountains, the forests and their fertile clearings, and that the bare hills and semi-steppe of what is now northern Chechnya were inhabited by Nogai Turkic nomads, who were then partially supplanted by the Cossacks, before these were in turn driven back by Chechens migrating northwards.

It is striking evidence of the comprehensiveness of the latest Russian defeat in Chechnya that in January 1997, despite this long Cossack historical presence north of the Terek, and the fact that before 1957 these districts had been part of Russia proper (Stavropol Krai), and despite appeals from the local population, on the orders of the Russian government Russian troops quit this region. The Yeltsin administration, after vilifying General Lebed for his 'betrayal of Russian interests' in his August peace agreement, thereby went beyond what even Lebed had promised, and abandoned territory which had in some sense been Russian for more than four hundred years.

The key reasons for the weakness of the contemporary Cossack movement, and for the general weakness of Russians today in the field of national and political mobilisation, were given to me by a descendant of Terek Cossacks from Grozny, Dr Ilya Grinchenko, now a political scientist in Vladivostok. I had asked him how the Chechens, despite returning home from exile in 1957 with almost nothing, and despite the acute distrust of them by the Soviet state, had so soon been able to achieve a local ascendancy over the Russians:

> The reason is that from the Revolution on, the whole policy of the Communists was to destroy national traditions and any capacity for independent social and political organisation. Not just among Russians, of course – everywhere. But it succeeded much better with the Russians, because other peoples, like the Chechens, were protected by many rings of defence: an incomprehensible language; close clan links and loyalties; secret religious traditions and groups which no outsider, no non-Chechen official or KGB man could penetrate.
>
> So the Chechens were able to resist Communism taking over their national identity, and they kept a capacity for autonomous action. The Russians lost it, and became completely dependent on the state and the party. So that is why one can say that in some ways the Russian people suffered the greatest loss from Communist rule. We lost more of our soul, and all capacity for self-help and spontaneous action. Unlike the Chechens, the Soviet state became our state. We were afraid not of outsiders, foreigners against whom we could combine to defend ourselves. We were afraid of ourselves.[23]

The Cossacks suffered especially badly from Soviet rule, because of the key role that many of them had played in the White anti-Bolshevik forces during the Civil War. Indeed, until the deportations of the Chechens and other nations in the 1940s, the Cossacks probably suffered worse than any other section of the Soviet population but the Kazakhs and the Ukrainians. Like the latter, they were singled out for particularly harsh treatment during Stalin's collectivisation in 1929–33, in which tens and possibly hundreds of thousands of them died of starvation; but from the beginning of 'Soviet power' under Lenin they had also been the target of particularly repressive measures.

The first mass deportation in Soviet history was in fact of Terek Cossacks; in the first months of 1921, following the final Communist victory over the White army of General Wrangel in the Crimea, some 70,000 Terek Cossacks were deported to Kazakhstan.[24] They were followed by tens of thousands more from all the Cossack regions through the 1920s and during collectivisation. Many others were massacred by the Red Army (including Red Cossacks), and tens of thousands more perished in the famines of 1921–2 and 1933. Up to half a million meanwhile had fled to the West following the White defeat, and their descendants are now scattered from Courbevoie to Canada. Relentless Soviet persecution of the Cossacks continued until the late 1930s.

During the Second World War, as part of Stalin's general strategy of reviving Russian traditions to strengthen the war effort, there was a brief and symbolic reinstatement of the Cossack military tradition. Two Cossack divisions were formed (or rather perhaps – as at present – symbolically dubbed 'Cossack', because it is not at all clear that they were really formed on the basis of Cossack communities), and Cossack war songs were belted out by Soviet choirs. As soon as the war was over, however, the units were dissolved, and – though the songs remained as part of the official Soviet Russian folk music repertoire – no further official recognition was given to the Cossacks as a group until the later Gorbachev years.

This suggests two things. The first is the extent of the distrust of the Cossacks on the part of Stalin and the Soviet regime. To some extent, this continues to this day, though mainly in the form of concern on the part of the local authorities about the Cossacks' tendency to crime, hooliganism and the stirring up of ethnic hostility. Secondly, it indicates the very limited, constrained and directed nature of the Soviet state's exploitation of the Russian tradition during and after the Second World War.

The Soviet Union did not simply become a 'Russian empire', as Ukrainian and other nationalists like to allege. While the Communist state did become more imbued with Russian national feeling, its main drive was rather to exploit, direct and feed off that sentiment, and certain Russian traditions, for its own ends, like a vampire sucking blood. The Communist state thereby strengthened itself – for a few decades – but, as the quotation from Dr Grinchenko suggests, it left those Russian traditions debauched, sucked dry and exhausted.

As for the Cossacks, lacking any Soviet state institutions of their own, they had no possibility of defending their traditions, not even the limited opportunities given to ethnic minorities in Russia by the possession of their own autonomous republics.[25] The shattering of autonomous social formations is of course especially important when it comes to the potential of the Russians along Russia's frontiers and in the diaspora for mobilising their own paramilitary groups. In reading the memoirs of Milovan Djilas about Montenegro and Bosnia during the two world wars, it is very apparent that Serbian partisan groups, whether Chetnik or Communist, were in many areas formed on the basis of existing clan traditions, allegiances and feuds.[26] Albeit to a greatly reduced extent, this also seems to have remained true in our own day. Nothing quite like this has ever existed in most of Russia, least of all after the shattering, crushing and atomising effects of seventy years of Soviet rule.

As so often with things Russian, the importance of the Cossacks today has been exaggerated both by their admirers and by those who fear and hate them. In the West, their odious role under Tsarism in anti-semitic pogroms has gained them an enduring place in infamy, which many Cossacks today have burnished with their own anti-semitic remarks. At the same time, the Cossacks' romantic and sinister past, instant name recognition and colourful traditional uniforms also make them excellent media copy for both Russian and Western journalists, seeking to give the impression of the contemporary recovery of a timeless and undifferentiated Cossack tradition, powerful and menacing.[27]

It is true that the demands of various Cossack groups in the North Caucasus – if they had the ability to put them into effect themselves, without

Russian state support – would indeed represent a serious threat to peace in the region. This applies not just to the Cossack territorial claims on Chechnya, but also in Karachai-Cherkessia and other North Caucasian republics, where local Cossack groups have been demanding their own autonomous areas. But these are demands which are fully supported only by small groups of Russians and Cossacks actually living in these republics. When it comes to the major Cossack centres of southern Russia, their support for these movements has been rhetorical, but as of 1997 nothing more, and this is also true of their attitude to the complaints and grievances of the Russians and 'Cossacks' of Kazakhstan.

The Cossacks and the 'Invention of Tradition'

The Cossack trappings at the *krug* in Vladikavkaz in 1992 seemed authentic enough – the uniforms, the sabres, even the hard, sunburned faces under the woolly caps. Characteristic too was the extreme variety of racial types, the result of the Cossacks' long history of intermarriage with some of the North Caucasian peoples. Sitting next to each other on the platform was one Ata-man who could have been a Finn, an almost albino blond, and another who could have been an Assyrian, with dark face, hooked nose and curling beard.

But there was one discordant note – literally discordant. The previous evening at dinner, my Cossack hosts had been belting out 'Katyusha' and other old Soviet military favourites. The next day, at the start of the meeting, prayers were said – part of the much-stressed revival of pre-revolutionary traditions. But the choir which stepped forward to sing traditional Cossack hymns consisted of four very old women, whose feeble, quavering voices and impoverished Soviet farmers' clothes made a strange contrast with the vigor-ous young soldiers and the splendid uniforms all around. These were evidently the only people they could find who could actually remember any of the old hymns.

It is also of some significance that while the religious trappings of this meet-ing were Orthodox, this is not in fact the original tradition of the Terek Cossacks. For many of their ancestors, the reason why they moved to the North Caucasus in the seventeenth and eighteenth centuries was precisely because they were 'Old Believers', who were trying to get away from perse-cution by the Russian Orthodox state (their special religious identity, and the extra distance this places between them and the Russians, emerges strongly from Tolstoy's novella *The Cossacks*, drawn from his own experiences when living among the Cossacks of the Terek Line as a Russian officer). Only in the later nineteenth century did the Russian state succeed in officially converting the Terek Cossack host to Orthodoxy – and thereby of course weakening their identity. Together with the other Tsarist moves to subordinate, standardise and regulate the Cossacks, this could be called the first alienation of the Terek Cossacks from their own traditions – to be followed by another, much more savage and radical one under Soviet rule. Together, these two processes add up almost to a paradigm of why Russians today find it so hard to generate from below political institutions or political movements.

The 'circle' at Vladikavkaz was my first inkling of the extent to which the Cossack – and beyond that, the Russian – tradition had been broken. It may be possible to 'invent' individual and specific 'traditions' – in the phrase of the famous collection of essays, *The Invention of Tradition*[28] – but for these to achieve power in their own right, the invention has to be on the basis of some really existent and continuous traditions and memories, of real sentiment (especially religious sentiment), and in the context of the right social and historical moment.[29] The Cossacks therefore provide an interesting footnote to the great debate between 'constructionists' and 'primordialists' with regard to the origins of nationalism, of 'tradition', and indeed of human culture, which I shall comment on with regard to the Chechens in chapter 9.[30]

The member of the constructionist camp who has developed the most brilliant insights concerning the cultural creation of modern nationalisms and national identities in the European empires in Asia has been Benedict Anderson in his *Imagined Communities* (though one may well have reservations about his application of some of the lessons of the Dutch East Indies, for example, to small and ethnically homogeneous peoples in Eastern Europe).[31] One thing that makes his work so valuable is his sense of the way in which, rather than being consciously 'constructed', new ways of nationalist thinking emerged from numerous creative imaginations in response to new historical and social circumstances. These were especially the creation for the first time of 'monoglot mass reading publics' by the action of capitalism, the printing press and the new education systems; and of course the creation of new 'intelligentsias', often badly paid, socially marginal, but desperately aspiring to power and glory, to serve these new masters and audiences.

On this score, Anderson has levelled some cogent criticism at the late Sir Ernest Gellner, who wrote that 'nationalism is not the awakening of nations to self-consciousness; it invents nations where they do not exist.'[32] In Anderson's words: 'Gellner is so anxious to show us that nationalism masquerades under false pretences that he assimilates "invention" to "fabrication" and "falsity", rather than to "imagining" and "creation".'[33] (It is only fair to say that Gellner's bald formulation in this instance is hardly typical of that deep and subtle mind. Elsewhere, he himself has written that while nationalism is a created phenomenon, under the historical circumstances of modern times, 'nationalism does become a natural phenomenon, one flowing fairly inescapably from the general situation.') This criticism could also be levelled at the phrase 'the invention of tradition'. I believe that the word 'invention' in this context is utterly mistaken, implying as it does a sudden and radical break with the past, a mechanistic and artificial creation and an act of conscious human will. It makes more sense to speak of the 'generation' of new traditions by older ones, and their 'cultivation' by particular states, movements and individuals.

Or to take another metaphor. Criticising the related notion, now very popular in anthropology, that 'human worlds are culturally constructed', Tim Ingold has written that:

> Perception is a mode of engagement with the world, not a mode of construction of it. This contrast between construction and engagement might be more simply represented as one between building and dwelling. It is by being dwelt-in, not by being constructed, that some portion of the real world becomes an environment for people … building is encompassed within dwelling rather than vice versa. Real life has no authors save the persons who are living it, and these persons, if they would build, must *already* dwell. Thus every act of building is but a moment in a continuous process of dwelling. This process … is one in which persons and their environments are reciprocally constituted, each in relation to the other. (emphasis in the original)

To adapt the metaphor to the Cossack case, one may say that it has been so long since anyone 'dwelt' culturally in the Cossack tradition that it no longer really feels like home to those who now claim to occupy it, and they cannot really pretend that it does.

A musical example of the generation of a tradition is that of the great Latvian and Estonian song festivals organised from the later nineteenth century to the present day. These were quite new, and played a key part in the creation of the modern Baltic national identities. But it seems quite clear from the evidence that not merely were the songs themselves the product of a continuous tradition of great antiquity, but so too was a sense of ethnic (though not 'national') identification and common hostility to non-Estonians and non-Latvians. Never, in the whole modern history of the Baltic States, not even in the depths of Soviet rule, would you have found a situation where the only people able to remember some of the greatest old songs and hymns were a handful of old women.

A Journey to the Cossack Lands, June 1996

The nature and limitations of the Cossack movement in Russia became fully clear to me during a tour I made of Cossack areas to look at the support for General Alexander Lebed during the presidential election campaign of June 1996. My first stop was Novocherkassk, the former Don Cossack capital where General Lebed was born.

While there, I interviewed Ataman Viktor Ratiyev, who was working at the time for the Yeltsin re-election campaign. Our conversation took place in a historic building, once the base of the former local Communist Party Central Headquarters, and before that the headquarters of the Don Cossack Ataman and his staff. In this building, in February 1918, the Ataman and White commander General Alexei Kaledin, abandoned by his Cossack followers and with the Red forces advancing on the town, retired into a private room and put a pistol to his head.

In the pleasant square outside, in June 1962, Soviet troops opened fire on workers protesting about price rises and cuts in bonuses – the only occasion in the last three decades of Soviet rule that the regime fired upon its Russian subjects, one of the very rare occasions between the Stalin era and Gorbachev that the army (as opposed to NKVD, KGB, or Interior Ministry troops) was used to quell internal dissent, and an incident which helped to determine the economic and social caution of the Brezhnev era. (General Lebed as a boy watched the demonstration and the shooting from a tree in the square.)[35]

Ratiyev reiterated the Cossack demand for the restoration of Cossack autonomous areas on the territories of the old Cossack hosts. He argued, not altogether unfairly, that the fact that Cossacks were now a minority in these areas was not in itself a bar, as in a majority of Russian autonomous republics the 'titular nationality' is in fact a minority; but, as he said, these republics still play an essential role in safeguarding these peoples' language, identity and traditions. 'Any other people will still be able to live on the Don, as they have always done, so long as they respect Cossack traditions and customs.'[36]

But the social, economic and demographic make-up of the Don region (now mainly part of Rostov-on-Don Oblast) makes the establishment of Ratiyev's vision most unlikely. For the result of Soviet repression of the Cossacks under Lenin and Stalin was that the Cossack areas became partly depopulated, and the Cossacks were replaced by new Russian settlers moving down from the north (part of a process which had been going on for more than half a century under Tsarist rule, and which helps explain why the Cossack regions did not fight more unitedly and effectively for the Whites). Meanwhile, a great many Cossack farmers, or their children, abandoned their villages, either from hunger or to escape from the deadly label of 'kulak', and swelled the urban proletariat. Traditional Cossack centres, like Krasnodar and Novocherkassk, grew enormously in size and became industrial centres.[37]

The result is that today, Cossacks (even if you count as a Cossack all those, like General Lebed, who are of partially Cossack ancestry) are only a small minority in many of their traditional areas – and the rest of the population, not surprisingly, does not take kindly to their demands for special privileges and status. This was true even in 1917-20; by the Revolution Cossacks were only 47 per cent of the population of their territory, and the resentment of the non-Cossacks, or *innorodtsi*, at Cossack privileges impelled many of them into the arms of the Reds. By 1996, only 28 per cent of the population of Rostov Region (including most of the old Cossack territory and its capital, Novocherkassk) was 'Cossack' even by the loosest use of that term.

Of twenty-five people whom I interviewed on the street in Novocherkassk in June 1996, only four expressed support for a state or military role for the Cossacks, or even sympathy for them, whereas thirteen were more or less critical (the rest said they had no opinion). Interestingly, critics of the Cossacks included voters for all three presidential candidates, and all three of the soldiers in my sample (a conscript, an officer teaching at the local military academy, and an officer cadet) were hostile to them. The cadet said resentfully that

> When Yeltsin came here a few weeks ago, we all had to work like dogs preparing for him, cleaning and polishing, and then he didn't come to our school at all, he went to the Cossacks. These days everyone is flattering them, God knows why. They may have had a great tradition once, but you can't put a broken cup back together again and in my personal opinion, there's no point trying... They're not soldiers, that's for sure. How could they be? In a modern army, who needs weekend soldiers in fancy uniforms? What we need is good professionals and technical experts, and for that we have to be able to pay them... In my opinion, all this concern for the Cossacks by the government is just a game to win votes, and as for the Cossacks themselves, they're a commercial racket.

Some local people interviewed were even less polite. In the words of one middle-aged housewife, 'These so-called Cossacks aren't real Cossacks any more. Any kid who doesn't want to work, he goes to the Cossacks, dresses in a pretty uniform and goes to the market to extort money... Them, fight in Chechnya? Not likely!' Or according to a former plumber, a pensioner and Communist voter, 'I never saw such a mob in all my life. What, give them a republic of their own here and the right to rule over the rest of us? Why not just hand over the whole place to the mafia and have done with it!'

The Cossack autonomy demand has been generally unpopular among most Russians (outside Karachai–Cherkessia, where there is a much closer identification of the local Russian population with the Cossacks, in part in reaction to Karachai nationalism and in part because more local people genuinely are of Cossack descent). However, it has been above all the growing perception of the Cossacks as a force for organised crime and disorder which has diminished their prestige both with local people and the local authorities. In their own self-image, the Cossacks are patrolling the markets and the roads to crack down on organised crime, especially by 'blacks', as they tend to call the non-Russian Caucasians – but more and more Russians see the Cossacks themselves as 'just a second racket'.[38] In early 1993, an opinion poll in the Rostov region showed 41 per cent of local people as viewing the Cossacks favourably and only 15 per cent negatively, but since then the figures appear to have reversed themselves (and even in 1993, only 10 per cent of local people said that they would support a Cossack-based political party, while a large majority were against local rule by the 'Atamans').[39]

The existing regional governments are obviously not at all happy with the Cossack autonomy demand. As a Rostov official told Reuters: 'We are sick to death of people coming down here and asking us about the bloody Cossacks. There are more important things to be getting on with.'[40] On the other hand, in Kuban successive governors have thought the Cossacks sufficiently politically important at least to claim (whether truthfully or not is difficult to say) to be of Cossack descent themselves.

From Novocherkassk, I went on to another former Cossack centre, where I was the guest of a junior Ataman, a local businessman and politician, candidate for mayor, and the local campaign organiser for Lebed. Since he was an exceptionally generous and thoughtful host, I shall leave him anonymous. He seemed to me the kind of local figure who a couple of years earlier would probably have been a Zhirinovsky supporter, not because he was especially chauvinist, or had any sympathy for Zhirinovsky's antics – he made some mildly racist remarks, but on the other hand his chief bodyguard was an Armenian, whereas elsewhere the Cossacks have been bitterly hostile to Armenian immigration from the Transcaucasus – but because he came very much from the background of local Zhirinovsky organisers whom I met in 1993–4.

That is to say, he was an aspiring local businessman who had never been a Communist Party official, manager or military officer, and for this and other reasons was therefore an 'outsider', excluded both from the local political and business establishment (dominated by former officials and the directors of regional banks), and from the Cossack establishment as represented by the now pro-Yeltsin regional Ataman, a protégé of Viktor Ratiyev. My friend, therefore, together with other 'outsiders', was supporting an ostensibly anti-establishment political movement to muscle his way into local dominance. This was also probably the reason why he had sought the title of 'Ataman'. It undoubtedly had some sentimental importance for him personally, but it also brought him a measure of local prestige, and possibly bit of extra armed support in case of trouble.[41]

Born in 1953, he is a former martial arts instructor and the owner of a sports stadium, a casino and night-club, a sauna, and a chain of shops and petrol stations – a typical medium-sized Russian provincial businessman (outside the oil and raw materials producing areas, where he would have had different priorities). He began by producing leather goods when Gorbachev first allowed the formation of cooperatives, then moved into petrol during the big shortages of the early 1990s, and moved on from there.

Typically, he is a determined and physically brave individual, as you have to be in that world, with a boxer's nose and hands, and a tough, cynical, humorous face which does not soften when it looks at women – but acquires a mildly sentimental cast when framed by a Cossack cap. He had his own little medieval or indeed oriental court, with a uniformed Cossack guard, a court bard – a local journalist and detective story writer; a court chronicler – a local historian; and a small but quite dazzlingly beautiful harem, to the members of which he has reportedly shown a princely generosity.

In his way therefore a legitimate descendant of the real Atamans of old – who often mixed legitimate trade with piracy – but a very different figure from the Ataman of Russian or Western military myth, and a completely urban figure, with no real connection to the Cossack countryside of today, let alone that of myth. Religion was probably always of limited importance for the Cos-sacks – it is certainly so in his case and that of most of the Cossacks of today, though at the opening of his new night-club I was treated to the sight of a priest sprinking holy water over the assembled staff. Since most of these were effectively dressed in bathing costumes, it did not seem to worry them one way or the other... The fact that he invited the priest shows a respect for moral tradition – firmly in the service of contemporary sin.

He may have the character and proclivities of the old Cossacks, but the basis for his power, the nature of his operations and his ambitions, the social, economic, political and even ideological context for his activities – all of these are as different as could be from the position seventy years ago, just as that was totally different from the situation three hundred years before. This is truly not a Cossack but a neo-Cossack, a new type of man in a new world. In the words of his court bard, the journalist,

> He is a unique character, a New Russian in the best sense. And he is also like the old Atamans, back in the sixteenth century – he is not afraid of anything or anyone, he is decisive, he has made his own way and estab-lished his own authority without any help from above, and men follow him because he is a natural leader, not because of his rank.

Or in his own words (he likes to speak of himself in the third person, like Robert Dole or Julius Caesar), 'there was never a goal he set himself that he did not achieve. He is that kind of man.'

The Ataman himself was fairly frank about his business activities, and very frank about his priorities for himself and the Cossacks. He described his rela-tions with organised crime:

> Yes, I've been threatened by those people. They're not businessmen, not sophisticated you know – they rely only on physical force. But I'm quite forceful myself ... I can rely on my friends from the Sports Club, and I can call on about 300 men from the Cossack movement here if I really need to. For that matter, old friends of mine from the sports world are now in Israel, the USA – they'll put in a word for me if necessary...
>
> One time, a criminal group from outside our area wanted to take over my stadium, and started threatening me. So I fixed a time for a meeting with them, and then lined up all my friends. They took a look, said OK, OK, we are not looking for trouble, you know we respect you and so on... There was no need for a fight. And actually it's true – many people in these mafia groups were my students when I was head of the sports club, and they do respect me. They don't give me any trouble, and I don't bother them... It's the government mafia, the 'party of power' that really gives me trouble, and to any businessman who's not part of their circle, especially if he has political ambitions. Look at the way they carried out the privatisation process here. You can't even call

it doubtful, because there's no doubt about it – they grabbed the lot for themselves and their friends... They can hit you with so many legal weapons, what they call legal – taxes, permits, inspections – and there's nothing you can do about it, except bribe them of course, or try to get a share of political power yourself.[42]

On the Cossack movement, he declared that

> I am very much against emphasising a military role for the Cossacks. It is not our main goal today, and it can get us a bad name. The Cossacks should be military reservists, with our own special units; but they shouldn't have their own units in the regular army – it's pointless. How can someone serve in a modern army and work at the same time? What we need to concentrate on now is strengthening the Cossacks as an economic, social and political force. That's why I'm supporting Alexander Ivanich [Lebed], for his own sake, because he is a good man with a good programme, and to stop the Communists coming back and reimposing totalitarianism and a state economy.

His words on this were echoed by Ratiyev, a man for whom he had no respect – and they seem in fact to be becoming the new orthodoxy among many more practical Cossack figures, so many of whom are after all now in some form or other of 'business':

> In the opinion of my organisation, and in the history of the Cossacks, we never had a purely military role. We served and defended the Motherland, but we also traded and worked in the fields. That is why we are now supporting Yeltsin, so that totalitarianism should not be restored – and it is thanks to us Cossacks that the Yeltsin vote in this area has been so large... I have pointed this out to Yeltsin in person, the decisive political role the Cossacks can play, and I think he agrees with me, and will make sure that his latest decrees are implemented.[43]

The Yeltsin Regime and the Cossacks

In examining Yeltsin administration policy towards the Cossacks it is also vital to distinguish between rhetoric and reality; as one Cossack declared to me, 'I've heard what seem to be millions of these decrees of Yeltsin's about the Cossacks. It would be nice to see something actually come of them.'

There have in fact been a series of such decrees since the first one of October 1993 which created ('in principle', as the Russians say) Cossack units within the army. The date is interesting; this was apparently a reward to Ratiyev's Cossacks for not backing the parliamentary opposition; but it also came at a time when the real Cossack path had just been defeated.[44] Not surprisingly, nothing real came of it, beyond the symbolic renaming of two army divisions and vague promises to create a role for the Cossacks in the border troops.

Little more was heard from Yeltsin himself until the winter of 1996, when, in view of the election, he began to issue a new stream of decrees concerning the establishment of Cossack units.[45] As of the end of 1996, these had also not been implemented, and probably could not be, given the acute limits on military spending and the deep anti-Cossack feelings of the army's high command. By then the extent of official Cossack military action was that they had on occasions been used officially to supplement the police (and had usually performed extremely poorly). In the words of Ataman Vasily Kaledin of the Don Cossacks in April 1996, 'the revival process is going very slowly, hardly moving at all. There are great anti-Cossack forces at work. The present organs of power are either being too slow to solve our problems or are resisting us.'

There have been two aspects to the response of the Yeltsin administration to the Cossack revival, and both have parallels in the past. The first is an attempt to take over the Cossack movements, appoint their leaders, exploit their political potential to strengthen the Yeltsin administration and restrain their excesses at least in so far as they threaten to disturb state policy. This is an approach with many parallels in the policy of the Tsars towards the Cossacks from the sixteenth century on; for of course the Cossacks were by no means always the Tsarist gendarmerie of pre-revolutionary fame; earlier, different Cossack regions had thrown up successive waves of revolt, most notably those of Stepan Razin on the Don and of Yemelyan Pugachev on the Yaik (Ural).

Breaking in the Cossacks was a process which took centuries. At the heart of it, then and now, was the push by the central government to appoint the Cossack Atamans, replacing the original system of free election by the Cossacks themselves. This was a change that cut the heart out of Cossack independence and to a degree out of the whole original Cossack tradition. By the later nineteenth century, it had been so successfully imposed that the Russian government was able to appoint as Atamans Russian generals with no personal connection whatsoever to the Cossacks – like General Grabbe, the last imperially appointed Don Cossack Ataman, whose German origin was obvious.[46]

As so often, the result of this policy for Tsarism was Janus-faced. On the one hand, the Cossacks were turned into obedient and disciplined military servants of the Russian state, useful both for guarding the borders and for suppressing protest at home. But on the other, it is only superficially paradoxical that the damage done to the Cossacks' own traditions, the destruction of Cossack democracy and the imposition of military-bureaucratic commanders from outside, culturally separated from their men, helped cripple the White Cossacks as an anti-Communist force during the Russian Civil War.

The second aspect of Yeltsin administration policy towards the Cossacks harks back to that of Stalin's regime during the Second World War. As then – though of course for quite different reasons – there is today a real pressure to be seen to restore 'Russian traditions', in the military field as more generally, and the Cossacks are certainly seen by most Russians as in some way an important and integral part of the national tradition.

So matters stood as of 1996. It is of course possible that in future some Russian population, either within Russia or in another republic (such as Kazakhstan), will generate effective paramilitary forces of their own, and that these will call themselves 'Cossacks'; but to win their fight, these would have to be organised along very different lines, and to have a quite different spirit, from any modern Cossacks we have seen so far.

For that matter, they would have to be rather different even from most of the pre-revolutionary Cossacks. For the repeated journalistic descriptions of the pre-revolutionary Cossacks as 'elite troops' is wide of the mark. Nothing about the Cossacks recalled the British, Prussian or indeed Russian Guards. The whole point about them – for which they were despised by professional soldiers like Clausewitz, and have been accorded some approval by John Keegan – is that rather than charging home, or standing their ground in the face of attack, they followed an 'asiatic' tradition of cavalry warfare. This involved avoiding direct clashes with the enemy's major forces – indeed, very often simply running away when directly attacked – and falling upon them where they were weak (and plundering them whenever possible), as during the harrowing of the French on their retreat from Moscow.[47] At Balaclava, faced with a charge of genuine elite troops – the British cavalry – the Cossacks turned and tried to hack their way through the Russian lines in order to escape.

Of course, as in 1812, such evasive tactics can sometimes be very useful. If they cannot win a battle, they can help to win a war. On the other hand, as I have already pointed out, if the enemy sets everything on a pitched battle, and if the enemy is of a kind that presents no loopholes for Cossack-type fighting, then troops like the Cossacks were, are and will always be worse than useless, not merely unreliable in themselves, but a recipe for spreading all their bad habits to the rest of the army.

7   Failure of the Serbian Option, 2: The Weakness of the Russian Diasporas

The [Communist Party] membership at large has been exercised only in the practices of iron discipline and obedience and not in the arts of compromise and accommodation. And if disunity were to seize and paralyse the Party, the chaos and weakness of Russian society would be revealed in forms beyond description... Soviet power is only a crust concealing an amorphous mass of human beings among whom no organisational structure is tolerated. In Russia there is not even such a thing as local government. The present generation of Russians have never known spontaneity of collective action. If, consequently, anything were ever done to disrupt the unity and efficacy of the Party as a political instrument, Soviet Russia might be changed overnight from one of the strongest to one of the weakest and most pitiable of national societies.

George Kennan, 1947

The Transdniestrian Path

The weakness of the Cossacks and of Russian radical nationalism today therefore has deep roots in Soviet and even Russian imperial history, but one could also attach a single date, symbolically and to a degree in reality, to the blocking of this course of Russian development in the immediate post-Soviet period: 3–4 October 1993, when pro-Yeltsin forces first defeated an attempt by armed supporters of the parliamentary opposition to take over key points in Moscow, and then went on to shell the parliament itself, and force its surviving defenders to surrender. As a result, Yeltsin was able to impose a strongly 'presidential' constitution, and get it passed by an (almost certainly rigged) referendum in December of that year.

Prominent among the defenders of the 'White House' were groups of Cossacks, whose virulently anti-Western and anti-semitic language did much to strengthen the already strong pro-Yeltsin bias of the Western media at that time.[1] Although our bias in retrospect is an embarrassment, and Yeltsin's victory was certainly no triumph for democracy, we were probably not wrong – *sub specie aeternitatis* – to take the line we did. By simultaneously weakening the power of the central state, increasing Russian radical nationalism inside Russia and in the Russian diasporas, and spreading the power and influence of armed Russian paramilitary groups, a victory for the parliamentary opposition at that time could have had really disastrous consequences for the whole region.

Although from a Russian nationalist point of view the growth of such paramilitaries might have seemed a good substitute for the end of the Soviet army and the failure to create an effective new Russian army out of its ruins, in fact, like the Serbian forces in Croatia and Bosnia, they would almost certainly have ended by bringing disaster to the populations they set out to 'defend'. By contrast, the Yeltsin administration, though it has issued much rhetoric about defending the position of Russians outside Russia, has not given support to Russian radicals, or would-be Russian paramilitary groups, in other republics – or at least, there is no evidence of it having done so. This caution has been especially evident in the case of Crimea in 1994, where the Russian government held the separatist movement of Yuri Meshkov at a long distance, and strongly urged him in private to moderate his position in relations with Kiev (see below).

One reason for this may be, of course, precisely that the Russian paramilitary groups which did emerge in the early 1990s were mostly bitterly hostile to Yeltsin. Among those in Moscow in October 1993 were fighters sent by several of the Cossack and nationalist groups from the separatist Russian-speaking Moldovan region of Transdniestria – 150 men in all, according to the Moldovan authorities. Over the previous three years the region had effectively seceded from Moldova in protest against local Moldovan nationalist moves, and in May–June of 1992 had fought a brief but bloody war against a Moldovan attempt to reconquer the region.

Cossack volunteers from Russia had played a prominent part in the fighting (indeed, Transdniestria has been the Cossacks' only real campaign to date. Cossack mercenaries fought in Abkhazia, but when I met Russians as tank drivers and gunners in the Abkhaz front line in 1993, I had the strong impression that though some of them called themselves Cossacks, they were actually Russian professional soldiers deliberately sent by the Russian army to help the Abkhaz. The real Cossacks in Abkhazia numbered around two hundred, and had volunteered individually and for pay, not as part of organised Cossack groups.[2]

There were strong suggestions that in September 1993, the decision of some of the Transdniestria Cossacks to go to Moscow to defend the parliament was supported by the Transdniestrian government, which in its composition – local Communist bosses and Soviet loyalists turned virulent Russian nationalists – was itself very close to the forces making up the backbone of the parliamentary opposition to Yeltsin at that time. The Transdniestria forces included remnants of the odious OMON units from the Baltic States, who had harassed and in some cases murdered Baltic policemen and border guards in 1990–1.[3] When I visited Transdniestria for the second time, Colonel Mikhail Bergman, military commandant of Tiraspol, presented me with strong evidence that these men had forged strong links with local Ukrainian and Russian armed criminal groups.

Bergman's chief, General Alexander Lebed, commanding the 14th Army in Transdniestria, took a very strong stand against these groups and refused adamantly to let them have any of his force's weapons. After the October events, he called for the dismissal of the Transdniestrian officials responsible, and resigned his seat as a local deputy in protest. Lebed claimed that eight men from the Transdniestria batallion had been killed in the defence of the White House, though as far as I know the exact figure was never established.[4] Lebed's stand on this issue, which contributed to an acrimonious falling-out between him and the Transdniestrian government, strengthened his credit with the Yeltsin administration and in particular with security chief Alexander Korzhakov. This enabled him to keep his post in Tiraspol for another two years, despite the ambiguity of his position and the growing hostility of Defence Minister Pavel Grachev.

He was also strongly supported both by the local population and by his own troops, which by 1994 were mainly (around 85 per cent) themselves natives of Transdniestria, as the army had been enormously reduced in size (to a mere 6,000 men) and most of the others had gone home.[5] Some of the Russian soldiers I saw were very much at home, almost like Roman legionaries on some forgotten frontier in the declining years of the empire. They had a chicken-hutch in the corner of their yard – 'Well, military food is not very nourishing,' as their officer said sheepishly.

Lebed's stand against crime and military corruption also won him high praise from the Moldovan authorities, who previously had had no reason to love him. When I interviewed Moldovan President Mircea Snegur in September 1994, he said that

> This may surprise you, but when the Russian Defence Ministry recently began to move to replace Lebed, I sent a message to the Russian government asking that he should stay. Lebed has played a negative role for us in that he has helped the separatists, but a positive one in that he has genuinely struggled against corruption and the theft and leakage of the 14th Army's weapons, which if they fall into the hands of the Transdniestrian separatists will be a menace not just for this region but for the whole of Europe. He is a disciplined and honest commander, and he keeps good order in his forces.[6]

The threat from a mixture of criminals and extremists was very real. Transdniestria in fact represents the closest that Russians (or rather 'Russian-speakers') have come to adopting the Serbian option and creating a sort of Republic of Kraina or a Bosnian Serb Republic – indeed, small numbers of Cossack and other volunteers who came from or had served in Transdniestria actually went to support their 'Serbian brothers' in Bosnia, though it is not clear that they actually saw any fighting there. Crimea could have gone in the same direction but did not, for reasons that I will examine.

In the split between Transdniestria and Moldova, a key role seems to have been played by conflict within the Communist Party and state elites. Since Moldova was annexed from Romania by Stalin in 1940, and Transdniestria was joined to it, officials from mainly Slavic Transdniestria had dominated the Moldovan SSR party leadership and government. In the 1980s, this began to change, with Communist officials like Mircea Snegur (later President) reaching the top, and causing corresponding resentment among cadres on the other side of the Dniester.[7]

Since the fall of the Soviet Union, such elite conflicts have been exacerbated by disputes over privatisation and the control of state-backed commercial monopolies. This factor played a part in the Crimean independence movement, and in 1996 it also contributed to a major rift between Kiev and the Russian-speaking Donbas, with the Donetsk elite (including commercial and criminal groups) furiously resentful about the way in which the 'Dnipropetrovsk mafia' around Prime Minister Pavlo Lazarenko was centralising control of immensely profitable commercial monopolies (notably in the field of natural gas) in its own hands.[8] (In November 1996 the degree of Ukrainian government corruption under Lazarenko even drew a very unusual public rebuke from the World Bank.)

In Moldova, to bureaucratic rivalry in the late 1980s was added the rise of pro-Romanian nationalism in Moldova, in favour of a new union between Moldova and Romania. Although this later proved to be a relatively weak force, for a time it seemed very strong and perhaps unstoppable, and some of the rhetoric was extremely chauvinist and anti-Russian.[9] In 1989, a new language law established Moldovan (a branch of Romanian) as the state language and returned it from the cyrillic alphabet (in fact, the original Romanian alphabet, used in Romanian from the fourteenth until the mid-nineteenth century), reimposed under Soviet rule, to the Romanian Latin alphabet.[10] The language and education laws were seen as especially menacing, even though they were less rigorous, and much less sternly enforced than in the Baltic States, for example.

In 1989, the 'International Front' called a general strike by Russian-speakers against the law, which drew a massive response in Transdniestria and laid the basis for the moves towards separation. Most frightening of all for the Russian-speakers was the Moldovan Popular Front's growing and public commitment to union with Romania.[11]

In the mid-1990s, however, most Slavs in Moldova continued live happily enough on the west bank of the Dniester, in other words under Moldovan rule, and with their state-supported Russian-language schools, newspapers and so on. Moreover, all residents of the republic have been given citizenship, whether or not they immigrated under Soviet rule, another clear difference from Latvian and Estonian policies. This inclusive policy prevailed because from 1992 on, forces based on the former Communist establishment, relatively friendly to the Russians and Moscow, had prevailed over the nationalists. If the Popular Front had consolidated its power things might have been very different.

In Transdniestria, Ukrainians (mainly Russian-speaking) and Russians together make up 60 per cent of the population, although Moldovans are the largest single group, with 39 per cent. The Transdniestrian republic, though it is a very odd shape – a long ribbon along the east bank of the Dnieper – and covers only 4,163 square kilometres, has a relatively large population of 712,000, or just over a sixth of the Moldovan total of 4.3 million. It is also the heart of the Moldovan Soviet economy, with most of the republic's heavy industry. From 1989 on, Communist officials, industrial managers and leaders of the official trade unions began a campaign to turn the region into an autonomous republic within Moldova (under the banner, however, not of Russian nationalism but of 'Soviet internationalism', just as in the Baltic republics at that time); after the Moldovan declaration of independence on 27 August 1991 this turned into a movement for outright secession – although the Transdniestrian government has not ruled out a confederal relationship with Moldova, and the official title of the Transdniestrian state remains the Dniestria Moldovan Republic.

The strong element of Soviet loyalism (as opposed to Russian nationalism) in the Transdniestrian movement meant that ethnic loyalties were initially at least somewhat blurred. Thus the first Transdniestrian Defence Minister and the Chairman of the Supreme Soviet were both ethnic Moldovans; while on the other side an ethnic Russian from an Old Believer background commanded the Moldovan police in the fighting in Bender (see below).[12]

With the help of weapons given covertly by the Soviet 14th Army (whose then commander, General Gennady Yakovlev, later joined the Transdniestrian government) the Transdniestrian leadership built up its own forces, supplemented by Cossack and other volunteers from Russia.[13] In large part, these were mercenaries, though their pay of 5,000 roubles (then 300 dollars) per month was hardly high by international standards.[14] As the Soviet government of Mikhail Gorbachev crumbled, these forces took over Moldovan administrative buildings in Transdniestria and expelled Moldovan officials. In December 1991, a referendum allegedly produced a 97.7 per cent vote (on a 78 per cent turnout) for Transdniestrian independence. Though there is good reason to be sceptical of this, it seems likely that a smaller majority of Transdniestrians did in fact vote yes.

In March 1992, the Moldovan government declared a state of emergency, fighting flared up along the Dniester River, and in May the Moldovan forces launched a major attack on the Transdniestrian positions in the city of Bender (Tighina), on the right or Moldovan bank of the Dniester. The resulting clashes left at least six hundred dead.[15]

The Moldovan forces were getting the upper hand when in June the war was brought to an abrupt halt by the new 14th Army commander, General Alexander Lebed, who after a short but intense bombardment of Moldovan positions, issued an ultimatum to both sides (but in fact, to the Moldovans) to stop fighting or face attack by his forces. A Russian peacekeeping force was established, which continues to be responsible for peacekeeping in Bender.[16]

Meanwhile another national movement in Moldova, that of the Turkic (but Christian Orthodox) Gagauz, after flaring up in the early 1990s, in January 1995 settled for autonomy within Moldova.

From 1992 on, the power of the pro-Romanian forces in Moldova declined greatly, and the government and parliament passed laws abandoning the Romanian national anthem as the state hymn and strengthening the idea of Moldovan as a separate language. It emerged after the brief euphoria of 1989–91 – a reaction against forty-five years of Soviet rule and the denial of any Romanian affiliation – that the idea of unity with Romania was not really very popular among Moldovans, who have sour memories of Romanian rule in the 1920s and 1930s. A quasi-referendum in March 1994 produced a 90 per cent vote for Moldova as an independent state, and a law now decrees that any change in Moldova's national status – in other words union with Romania – requires a national referendum, thereby giving the Transdniestrians in effect the right to secede should this happen (pan-Romanian nationalists in Romania would in any case be happy enough to let Transdniestria go in return for union).

However, pro-Romanian sentiment remains, especially in the Moldovan intelligentsia, and could well revive if Romania were to join NATO and draw far ahead of Moldova economically. On the question of whether Moldovan is a separate language (it isn't, according to linguists) the debate in Moldova, and state policy, has swung back and forth.[17] Romania for its part has shown strong support for Moldova, but has stopped well short of direct involvement in the Transdniestrian dispute.[18]

Meanwhile Transdniestria has remained as a cross between a last relic of the Soviet Union (it uses a variant of the Soviet Moldovan flag, its currency is the Soviet one with a stamp of Marshal Suvorov, who conquered the region from the Turks, and its press and political parties are tightly controlled)[19] and a giant smugglers' camp with certain analogies to criminalised Caribbean islands like Aruba. In particular, it became an entrepot for arms flowing between the former Soviet Union and the wars in Yugoslavia and the Caucasus.

The highly criminalised nature of the Transdniestrian government and its forces contributed to the hostility to them of General Lebed, who strongly resented their attempts to bribe his own men into selling off the 14th Army's weapons and fuel. General Lebed denounced the Transdniestrian leadership as 'thieves and protectors of thieves'.[20] Colonel Bergman went even further, saying of Transdniestrian President Igor Smirnov, 'he is not just black through and through, he has horns and a tail.'[21]

Yeltsin administration officials were not responsible for helping to set up the Transdniestrian government – that was the work of Soviet loyalist forces in the last years of Gorbachev – and in principle have no love for them, because of their past role in supporting the Russian opposition. On the other hand, Moscow as of 1997 appears determined to keep the 14th Army in Transdniestria (which violates the Moldovan constitution), both as a bargaining chip against NATO expansion, and to prevent any conceivable future possibility of the region being incorporated into Romania. Indirectly, therefore, Russia went on supporting the Transdniestrian state, and this will probably go on being true, whoever succeeds Yeltsin as President.

In understanding what happened in Transdniestria, and the similarities – or more importantly, in my view, the differences – between this and other regions of the Russian diaspora, it is necessary to keep four things in mind. The first two demonstrate that the Russian-speakers in Transdniestria did have a genuine mobilising grievance and a stronger position of their own as a basis for revolt and resistance; the other two however show that they also relied on help and encouragement from Moscow to a far greater degree than other peoples who have carried out revolts or national mobilisations in the former Soviet Union, and to a far greater degree than can be hoped for by Russian minorities elsewhere, especially in the aftermath of the Russian defeat in Chechnya.[22]

Firstly, ordinary Russians and Ukrainians (but mainly Russian-speaking) of Transdniestria had in 1990–2 a real fear and at least the rudiments of a real legal and moral case for separatism.[23] The fear was of a Moldovan union with Romania. This prospect has now greatly receded and may no longer be a serious possibility at all – though the Transdniestrian authorities of course base their whole propaganda on continuing to exaggerate it. In 1990–2 however, it seemed real enough, and it certainly was and is the dream of important nationalist groups in Moldova.

This moral, emotional and historical aspect is tremendously important in contrasting the behaviour of the Transdniestrian Russian-speakers with those in the Baltic States; for in the Baltic, not merely did the Russian liberal intelligentsia (backed by their fellows in Russia) recognise that the Balts had been genuinely independent, and had close ties with Scandinavia and Europe, but even among ordinary Russians there has always been a gut, if grudging acceptance that the Balts have a higher civic culture. To this, since 1991, has been added the tremendously important perception that the Balts are advancing economically far faster than Russia. A Russian would find it much more difficult to say any of these things about Romania.

It is important to stress the very different popular Russian attitudes to the different peoples of the former Soviet Union, because one of the themes of Russophobe literature in the West is that Russians regard the whole of the former Soviet Union as simply 'Russian land'. In any clear-cut sense, this is only true of a very limited number of areas, like northern Kazakhstan. Between the grudging Russian admiration for the Balts and the attitude of complete superiority to the Tajiks, there is a world of difference, and indeed a whole range of nuances along the way.

Similarly, no Russian thinks of Samarkand as 'Russian land', any more than at the height of British imperialism, an Englishman thought of Benares as part of England. Even in Crimea, while Sebastopol is seen as indubitably Russian, a Russian standing in the old Tatar palace in Bakhchiserai does not feel he or she is in Russia. The fact that Russian soldiers in Chechnya did not in fact feel – whatever the Russian constitution and their own government said – that they were on Russian soil was of the most critical importance in determining the level of their fighting spirit.

Moreover, the Transdniestrians also had the point that their area had been a region of Slavic settlement for more than 1200 years (though many of the Russians had in fact moved there under Soviet rule); had not been part of Romanian Moldova from 1918 to 1940, or even of the Tsarist Russian province of Bessarabia before 1918, but since its conquest from the Turks in the later eighteenth century had always been part of Russia (or from 1920 to 1940, of Soviet Ukraine); and that, like Crimea, Nagorno-Karabakh and other areas, it was allocated to another republic by Soviet fiat, without its population being consulted. National fears, and legal, historical or moral arguments for secession, do of course exist in other areas inhabited by the Russian diaspora, but not in nearly as strong a configuration as in Transdniestria. History therefore gave the Slavs in Transdniestria a well-defined area both legally and historically. Geography made it easily defensible, along the Dniester River.

The contrast with the Soviet loyalist movements in the Baltic States is an interesting one. These 'international fronts' were organised along very similar lines, and both gave strong support to the attempted Soviet counter-revolution of August 1991; but in the Baltic States, the failure of the Moscow coup led to the collapse of the Soviet loyalists virtually overnight. One reason for this was the Baltic Russians' lack of a territorial base. The only usable one would have been Narva, in north-eastern Estonia – but this area is a good deal smaller than Transdniestria, and in any case the recognition of Baltic independence by the West, and indeed by Russia and the Soviet Union in August–September 1991, would have made the establishment of such a secession extremely difficult.

The third feature of the Transdniestrian secession is the fact that its bases were all laid while the Soviet Union still existed, and therefore so did the Communist Party and the Soviet state bureaucracy. In particular, the official Communist trade unions (as in the Baltic States) played a key part in bringing out the workers behind the strike of 1989. The subsequent near-collapse of the official trade unions all over the former Soviet Union and the almost universal (except to a degree among the miners) failure of new independent trade unions to replace them have been factors of the most crucial importance in limiting economic and social protest and allowing what we are compelled to call economic 'reform'. Paul Kubicek has described the Federation of Ukrainian Trade Unions (FPU), successor to the old Communist unions, as a 'sheep in wolf's clothing, unable or unwilling to make life difficult for the state elite'.[24]

Less widely recognised has been the fact that the absence of such trade unions, along with most of the other attributes of modern civil society, has also been of vast importance in limiting the capacity for national mobilisation of the various Russian diasporas; for as so often in the past, elsewhere in the world, if these mainly working-class diasporas could have organised for economic protest, then this might very well have taken on a national form. In a way, this failure could be seen to parallel the failure of the Cossacks. A people's militia has not appeared to replace the old Soviet army; popular trade unions have not been generated to replace the old trade unions. (In a 1994 opinion poll, 9.2 per cent of Ukrainians said they trusted trade unions, compared to 92.6 per cent who said they relied on themselves, 89.2 per cent on their families, and 63.5 per cent on God.)[25]

The fact that the Transdniestrian mobilisation took place under Soviet rule also meant that hardline officials in Moscow had direct points of bureaucratic contact with and even control over local officials and managers in Transdniestria – and of course powers of patronage and official reward (something which was very apparent in the creation and direction of the 'interfronts' in the Baltic States). In other words, the possibilities for the manipulation by Moscow of local power structures and politicians, and through them the local population, were vastly greater than they have become since the Soviet Union's disintegration.

In contrast, by 1995, when I spent several weeks travelling in the Russian-speaking areas of eastern Ukraine, both local observers and local officials themselves emphasised that the lines of command and patronage now ran to the Ukrainian government in Kiev; that Moscow's influence over the region was therefore for this and other reasons extremely limited; and that as long as Kiev did not try to remove local Russians from their jobs and replace them with Ukrainians from the centre, most local bosses were content enough that this should be so – because they were bigger fishes in the relatively small political world of Ukraine than they would ever be in Moscow.

The fact that the Transdniestrian revolt began under Soviet rule is also of great importance because it meant that for a critical period it was protected from police and military retaliation by the Moldovan government. In future, by contrast, if the Russians of northern Kazakhstan, Crimea, the Donbas or Narva wish to try to secede, they will have to do so in the face of an immediate and possibly overwhelming response by the national governments of the states concerned.

Connected to this is another factor, the critical role of the 14th Army. Transdniestrians are well aware of this, and when I visited the region in February and September 1994, I found the vast majority of local people supporting Lebed ('our saviour') rather than their own government, and declaring that it was to the 14th Army, not the Transdniestrian forces, let alone the Cossacks, that they looked for protection. There was a good deal of discreet and not-so-discreet criticism of the Cossacks for their criminal activities and 'hooliganism'.

Of course, Russian forces are stationed in other Russian-speaking areas outside Russia's borders, most notably Sebastopol; but nowhere are they in a position of such total military superiority as in Transdniestria, and in many areas (notably the Baltic States) they are not present at all, and could not be introduced without an international war. After Chechnya, I believe that it is inconceivable for the foreseeable future that any Russian government or military command would want deliberately to risk another war – although they might of course stumble into one by mistake.

It is interesting to note, especially in the context of the post-imperial and post-revolutionary experiences of other countries, that Transdniestria is the only post-Soviet conflict involving Russia that has thrown up a general as an important political figure – or so he seems for the moment at least – in the form of General Lebed. This is partly because Lebed's intervention in Trans-dniestria remains to date the only one where the Russian army has been victorious at minimal cost. The only general to emerge with credit from Chechnya, Lev Rokhlin (who extricated the forces in Grozny from complete disaster in the first week of January 1995) became the chairman of the Duma Defence Committee after the elections of December 1995, but for the time being anyway his further rise has been blocked, if only because his criticisms of regime neglect of the army have made him bitterly unpopular among Yeltsin's aides.

The 'Manipulation' of National Conflict

It is also important to keep the special features of the Transdniestrian experi-ence in mind because a widespread prejudice in the West holds Moscow responsible for creating virtually all the ethnic and national conflicts in the for-mer Soviet Union (just as the Indian nationalists have long held the British to have been responsible for creating a separate Muslim political identity, lead-ing to Pakistan). Moscow certainly has made use of ethnic friction. Thus while Soviet and Russian manipulation played a very secondary role in the Karabakh conflict, it played an undeniably important one in another Caucasian war, that of Abkhazia – though even there, only on the basis of previously existing and deeply felt conflicting claims. In no case did Moscow or the Communists suc-ceed in 'creating' or 'inventing' a dispute.

While it is reasonable therefore to see similar elements at work across much of the former Soviet bloc, there is no reason to assume that these will com-bine in very similar mixtures irrespective of location and local history. As a journalist in the former Soviet Union between 1990 and 1996 (for much of the period, stationed in the Baltic States and the Transcaucasus), I observed half a dozen different ethnic disputes and conflicts, and while manipulation was present in each case, in each one its importance, and the local response, were different.

The Baltic States, for example, present interesting examples of determined attempts at provoking ethnic conflict that failed to work, despite all the nec-essary flammable material apparently being at hand. I witnessed myself in 1990 to 1991 how Soviet loyalists and Communist hardliners went round the great factories of Tallinn and Riga, trying to convince the Russian-speaking workers that the Baltic national movements were making preparations to massacre them, and that they should take up arms in self-defence. In Riga, I witnessed how a crowd made up overwhelmingly of Soviet military aviation cadets masquerading as local Russian civilians tried to start a riot with the Latvian police. None of these efforts succeeded, because the mass of local Russians stayed aloof and the local authorities and Baltic nationalists did not overreact. They could have succeeded – but only if many more local Russians, and the police had reacted by opening fire, which was what happened at the beginning of the nationalist demonstrations and counter-demonstrations in Karabakh in 1988.[27]

In Lithuania, I saw attempts by both Soviet loyalists and Lithuanian nationalists to stir up renewed hostility between Lithuanians and Poles. The Soviet loyalists tried to get the Polish minority to demand its own autonomous region, with a view to separating from Lithuania if Lithuania achieved independence. Vytautas Landsbergis and some of his supporters for their part convinced themselves of a continued Polish threat to Lithuania and tried to persuade Lithuanian voters that they too should fear this and vote for the nationalist parties. Once again, this failed to work.

The reasons why in each particular case national conflict took fire or failed to do so are immensely varied. Contemporary Estonians, Hungarians, Kazakhs and Chechens all have their own nationalisms, with specific features which are not peripheral and decorative but of central importance.

First of all, there are behavioural norms. Beginning at opposite ends of the spectrum, take the Estonians and the Azeris. It is impossible to spend any length of time in Estonia without being impressed by the extreme emotional coolness and self-restraint with which most Estonians relate in public, coupled with an avoidance of physical contact. My own strongest arguments with Estonians have been conducted by them in terms of icy politeness.

However, it is impossible to stay for long in Azerbaijan without being struck by the excitability of many Azeris, the tendency of many people to fly off the handle and for arguments to become hysterical and end in kicks and punches. Similarly, the Georgians, with strong cultural traditions of individualism, machismo and the cult of weapons, differ a very great deal from the peaceable, gloomy and obedient inhabitants of the cities of eastern and southern Ukraine. It is not hard to see why, all other things being equal, an ethnic dispute in Azerbaijan or Georgia would be more likely to turn extreme and violent than would be the case in Estonia or Ukraine. Of critical importance therefore in the Baltic States – and something which does the very greatest credit to the Baltic peoples and their national movements – was the fact that the Russian minorities knew that they did not have to fear physical attack. The minority peoples in the Transcaucasus would have been very foolish indeed to make this assumption.

Moreover, you do have to consider history and the results of history for present circumstances. In the Transcaucasus, it would be misguided to approach contemporary Armenian nationalism without reference to the genocide of 1915. In the Baltic States, and other areas of the former Soviet Union containing large Russian-speaking minorities, a knowledge of the historical background is essential to understand why, with the exception of Moldova, these populations have remained so politically passive and why the feared *pied noir* style uprisings have failed to materialise. In the case of Lithuania, to understand the present you also have to know a twentieth-century history which has involved the murder or removal, between 1939 and 1945, of the greater part of the country's traditional Polish and Jewish minorities.

However, even where very real national hatreds and grievances have existed in the past, there is nothing to say that these cannot be changed, modified and soothed by historical change and new political and international circumstances. Hungary and Romania give a very encouraging example of how disputes that at one stage seemed very menacing, can start to dissolve. In the past, it would have seemed that Hungarian bitterness over the loss of more than two-thirds of Hungarian territory after the First World War was an immutable issue which lay at the heart of Hungarian politics and which was bound to flare up again as soon as the restraining bonds of Communism were removed. Moreover, in 1990 and to a lesser extent the following two years, there were blatant attempts by the new Romanian regime of President Iliescu, made up of former Communists who had jumped ship from the Ceausescu dictatorship, to inflame Romanian fear and hatred of Hungary and the Hungarian minority so as to consolidate their own hold on power.

But, as it has turned out, while the Hungarians undoubtedly still feel bitter over their loss, the character of the Hungarian nation has changed over the years. Above all, if only because of the disastrous example of Yugoslavia on their doorstep, they have not been willing to risk war over this issue – not even to recover Hungarian land from Serbia, which they could have attacked between 1992 and 1994 with the applause of much of the West. Instead, Budapest has acted with great restraint, and as a result of this and changes in Romanian attitudes, in 1996 Romania and Hungary signed a state treaty, and the new, anti-Communist Romanian administration elected in November 1996 has made ethnic harmony a central part of its programme.

However, this outcome is not simply due to the fact that much of the heat has gone out of Hungarian and to a lesser extent Romanian nationalism. It also owes a good deal to contingent factors, for example the fact that, unlike the various national groups in Yugoslavia or the Transcaucasus, the Hungarian minority in Romania no longer possessed its own autonomous area (as it had in the 1950s), in which it might have established a base for secession and resistance. This also meant that the Romanians had less to fear than did the Serbs, the Georgians or the Azeris.

Also of great importance have been international circumstances. The Hungarians had good reason to hope that, given their record of economic reform and democracy, they stood a very real chance of entering NATO and much more importantly the European Union. They were also left in no doubt that if they were to subvert or attack Romania, this would have dealt a fatal blow to their hopes in this regard. Meanwhile, the sight of the Hungarians accelerating past them in the race to join these institutions also inspired the Romanians to act more responsibly in ethnic relations.

But for such Western moral pressure to have worked, the hopes had to be well founded. No one is going to persuade the Abkhaz to compromise with the Georgians by arguing that if they do, they will one day be admitted to the European Union. Similarly, the Balts have been influenced in the direction of peaceful and legal methods by their own traditions, but also by those of their Scandinavian neighbours, and the influence they have exerted. No one is going to influence the Georgians in the direction of peaceful and legal methods by pointing to the example of the Turks, the Russians or the Armenians. Once again, the success or failure of outside manipulation, whether benign or malignant, is wholly contingent on local circumstances and histories.

The Crimean Path

The example of Crimea has a lot to say about the capacity for national mobilisation of the Russian diaspora. For while Crimea is the only part of Russian-speaking Ukraine to have generated a serious Russian nationalist movement, aiming at secession from Ukraine and confederation with Russia, the real ability of the Crimean Russian population to struggle for their national cause has proved in the end very limited.

The reasons for their greater radicalism compared to other areas of Ukraine (such as Kharkov or Odessa) are fourfold: the fact that Crimea is the only area of Ukraine with an absolute majority of Russians (67 per cent, with the 20 per cent Ukrainian population also overwhelmingly Russian-speaking), thanks to state-encouraged immigration both under the Tsars and during Soviet rule; bitter and understandable resentment at the way that Crimea was transferred to Ukraine from Russia by Khrushchev in 1954, without the local population being consulted; strong ties to Russia, both because much of the population immigrated from Russia after the Second World War, and because the Crimean economy was critically dependent on the tourist trade from Russia and has been very badly hurt by the disintegration of the Soviet Union; and anger at the authorities in Kiev over economic decline.

In January 1991, these sentiments led to a referendum, with a 93 per cent vote for restoring Crimean autonomy and for making it a full union republic (in other words separate from both Ukraine and Russia). The Ukrainian parliament agreed to make Crimea an autonomous republic, the only one in Ukraine (though people in both Transcarpathia, in the extreme west, and Donetsk, in the east, have occasionally made the same demand). The call for 'union' status was ignored.

In the next two years, as the economic situation and differences between the Ukrainian and Russian states worsened, sentiment increased for a complete break from Ukraine and union with Russia – though this was not completely clear-cut Russian nationalism, for it was also mixed up with a desire for the restoration of the Soviet Union as a whole. Phrases often used were that 'Crimea should be a bridge between Ukraine and Russia', and that 'Crimea should be the foundation stone of a new Union.' Local pro-Russian feeling, especially in Sebastopol, was encouraged by the dispute between Russia and Ukraine over the division and basing of the Black Sea Fleet, which the overwhelming majority of local people believed should be completely Russian and remain based in the peninsula. A belief in Russian support was encouraged by the vote of the Russian Supreme Soviet on 9 July 1993 declaring Sebastopol part of Russia – a declaration, however, promptly denounced as illegal by President Yeltsin and the Russian Foreign Ministry.

By the end of 1993, these sentiments had led to strong support in Crimea for separation from Ukraine and either independence or union with Russia, and a series of votes by the Crimean parliament strengthening Crimean sovereignty (denounced as illegal by Kiev). In January 1994, Crimean presidential elections led to the victory (with 73 per cent of the vote) of a pro-Russian and pro-independence candidate, Yuri Meshkov, as President of Crimea.[28] In March, a referendum produced a 78.4 per cent vote for a vaguely-defined 'sovereignty', and 82 per cent for the establishment of joint Russian-Ukrainian citizenship. At that stage, the Crimean Russian movement looked both unstoppable and a very real threat to Russian–Ukrainian relations and therefore to peace.[29]

Within a very few months however – a much shorter time than it took for other post-Soviet presidents – Yuri Meshkov was at daggers drawn with the Crimean parliament, over the extent of his powers and of economic reform. His authority was also badly shaken by his failure to gain any support from the Russian government, which instead continued to pursue negotiations with Kiev on the division of the Black Sea Fleet (apparently using the Crimean Russian movement as an extra lever). Even the 'Cossacks' in Crimea were taking a studiously moderate line, and above all were not waving their guns about (if indeed they had any) after the manner of the Transdniestrians. Their Ataman, Viktor Melnikov, a veteran of Transdniestria, emphasised his desire that this experience should not be repeated, and that Russia and should seek 'brotherly relations', because 'our principle is that Russia, Ukraine and Belarus are one nation, but they must come together again peacefully. No one should talk of violence or coercion.' In his words to me:

> Above all, we do not want to create a military psychosis here, and start a panic on either side. That is why we are not accepting volunteers from outside Crimea, though many would like to come – we are very anxious not to inflame the situation. We only take people whose roots are in Crimea... Well, it's true that our roots are not Cossack. I for example only became a Cossack when I had to leave the army, because the new Ukrainian government wanted me to swear an oath to Ukraine. But that's the way it always was – any man could become a Cossack if he

honoured the Cossack tradition...As to the Crimeans, you mustn't think that anyone wants a revolution or a war. They just want to live in their own way. Actually, all they want to do is sit by the sea.[30]

In September 1994, President Meshkov declared the parliament suspended, and a majority of deputies responded by suspending the President's authority. The result was a stand-off which effectively paralysed the Crimean government and shattered the pro-independence forces. Not surprisingly, in March 1995, with Moscow's attention distracted by the war in Chechnya, the Ukrainian government stepped in, removed Meshkov and appointed a pro-Ukrainian government under Anatoly Franchuk (a relative of President Kuchma), while the Ukrainian parliament passed a law abolishing the Crimean presidency and severely curtailing Crimean sovereignty. Once again, the Cossacks held back, with Ataman Ratiyev arriving in Crimea, almost certainly on the orders of the Russian government, to urge restraint – in striking contrast to the tone taken in Moldova three years before. Only small public demonstrations occurred in Crimea, though subsequent opinion polls suggested that support for independence remained high.

There are several reasons for this surprisingly rapid and complete collapse of a movement which undoubtedly enjoyed, and probably still does in principle enjoy, the support of a majority of inhabitants of Crimea. The first, very important to note, is that it received no support from the Yeltsin administration, or from the Russian armed forces attached to the Black Sea Fleet in Crimea. It is possible that there was some support from Russian secret services (Meshkov, a former state prosecutor, was widely thought to have worked with the KGB in the 1980s) but if so these were wildcat actions.

Nor was this due to distraction by Chechnya, because when President Meshkov went to Moscow in June 1994, soon after his election (and six months before the Russian intervention in Chechnya) to seek help against Ukraine, he was not officially received, and in private was told very firmly to act with restraint and not to hope for Russian support for any moves that would risk conflict with Kiev. His 'Prime Minister', former Soviet Deputy Prime Minister Yevgeny Saburov, who came from Moscow and was widely thought to be acting partly at least on Russian instructions, also took a studiedly moderate line. Politicians and groups in the Russian Duma gave rhetorical support, but that was all (and in the case of Russia's Communists, their rhetoric was also moderated by the urgent desire to stay on good terms with the Ukrainian Communists, who do not favour Crimean secession).

However, even more important were internal political factors in the Russian population of Crimea (also, it must be said, heavily intermarried with Ukrainians, though not to the same degree as in the great industrial cities of eastern and southern Ukraine). The old Soviet managerial elites, who dominated the Crimean parliament, proved far more interested in fighting with Saburov over the privatisation of state property (which of course they wanted themselves) than in risking a real showdown with Kiev, especially of course without Moscow's support; this was and is also the interest of the immensely powerful Crimean mafia groups, who are closely linked to the local elites.

Meshkov himself proved an extremely, indeed almost comically incompetent leader and administrator. In many ways, both in his behaviour and in his relations with Moscow, Meshkov recalled the President of Belarus, Alexander Lukashenko. (Of course, Moscow was much politer to Lukashenko, as leader of a large, strategically vital and internationally recognised state.) But the Russian government also proved completely unwilling, or unable, to consolidate his friendship by giving him the subsidies he kept asking for. Most important of all, however, was the fact that in the end the mass of the Russian population, though it had voted for independence, did not mobilise in support of it – unlike the Balts or the Ukrainian nationalists. If the Crimean parliament had been regularly surrounded by crowds of tens of thousands of people ready to die in its defence, then the Ukrainian government would not have been able to intervene without risking serious bloodshed and consequent Russian state intervention. In fact, pro-independence demonstrations even at the height of the movement never amounted to more than 10,000 people at the most, and only very rarely numbered more than a thousand.

At the same time the negotiations between Russia and Ukraine over the vital Sebastopol issue continued and in June 1997 succeeded in placing the question on ice for twenty years by the Ukrainian–Russian Treaty of June 1997. This allowed the Russians to lease most (but not all) of the base for this period, in return for an annual rental of 100 million dollars to be written off against Ukraine's huge oil and gas debt for Russia.

However, at the end of that period, the issue could surface again, perhaps more dangerously than ever. For the great bulk of Ukrainian officials say that at the end of that time, the Russian fleet must leave; and the treaty now gives them an international legal basis to demand this. Russian naval officers, the great majority of Sebastopol's population, and the whole Russian political establishment are equally emphatic that they will not leave. So this question has been shelved, not solved.

The behaviour of the Russian diaspora in Crimea is in striking contrast to the mobilising capacity of the Crimean Tatars. The Tatars are led by dedicated, determined and honest leaders, steeled by years in Soviet prison camps. Because of the searing experience of deportation, the long campaign to return home and overwhelming unity on the most important national questions, the Tatar community as a whole has an extremely impressive capacity for political mobilisation.

There is a clear parallel here with the Chechen capacity for mobilisation, and for one of the same reasons – the experience of deportation in 1944. However, while in the Chechen case this has strengthened their capacity for spontaneous military mobilisation, up to 1997 at least it had all too obviously done little to create a capacity for modern, united political activity in the peaceful pursuit of common goals – and it remains to be seen whether after the terrible experience of 1994–6, the Chechens will manage their affairs better in future.

The reasons for the difference are that in the first place, for thirty years after the Chechens were allowed to return home, the Crimean Tatars had to struggle to do so; and under Soviet rule, that struggle could only be by means of peaceful protest. Secondly, the Tatars, in part because of their close contacts with the highly developed Volga Tatars, were already involved in a degree of political organisation and protest during the last decades of Tsarism (through the Jadids, the various socialist movements, and to a lesser extent pan-Turkism), whereas the Chechens came from a background that was much more pre-modern and isolated, and Chechen protest after the defeat of Shamil took a mainly religious form.

Over the past five years, demonstrations of up to a hundred thousand Tatars have taken place in Crimea on several occasions, and on the fiftieth anniversary of the deportation, on 18 May 1994, some two hundred thousand, or 80 per cent of the entire Tatar population, turned out in the regional capital of Simferopol. A Crimean Tatar demonstration has also been responsible for the only instance of mass violence in Crimea since independence, when in June 1995 Tatars protesting against the extortions of Russian gangsters from Tatar shopkeepers launched attacks on Russian-owned shops and businesses thought to be mafia controlled, and clashed with police. Two Tatars were killed when the police opened fire.[31]

And here, perhaps, lies a danger for the future, quite possibly the only serious danger of ethnic strife in the whole of Ukraine, because while no ethnic hostility exists between the Russians and the Ukrainians with whom they live, there certainly is hostility between the Russians and the Tatars.[32] On the Tatar side, this is rooted in bitterness against the people who first conquered their country and then stole their land and homes. On the Russian side, it is founded in a mixture of fear and a bad conscience. Fear may seem an absurd emotion under the circumstances, given that the Russians in Crimea outnumber the Tatars by more than six to one. But the Russians know of Tatar ambitions to turn Crimea once again into a Tatar Autonomous Republic (as it was before 1941) with special ethnic rights for the Tatars; they fear that this would mean that the Tatars sooner or later would come to evict them from the homes they now own; they believe that the Tatars are backed by an increasingly powerful Turkey, even as Russian power declines; and above all they have seen with their own eyes the Tatar capacity for mobilisation and ethnic solidarity. The risk is of course that at some stage, it will be precisely this Tatar example – and not hostility to Kiev – which will lead the Russians to counter-mobilise.

The Nature of the 'Russian Diasporas'

The failure of the Russian national movement in Crimea reflects the political weakness and lack of mobilisation of all the 'Russian' populations living beyond Russia's borders. This failure can be explained partly by the fact that the very words 'Russian diaspora' are in fact a misnomer, which I only use for want of anything better. In fact, these populations are neither truly Russian, in an ethnic or nationally conscious sense, nor are they a diaspora, in the classical sense of the Jews and Armenians, or even of some more recent peoples like the Balts and the Galician Ukrainians. They lack most of the historically derived and spontaneously supported religious, cultural, educational, leisure and charitable institutions which have marked out such diasporas; they have very few effective political organisations; and both for this reason and deeper ones to do with the nature of Russia and Russian nationalism, they have a very weak identification with the 'old country', Russia.[33]

Nor has the Russian state so far done anything to create or subsidise such bodies among the Russians outside Russia – in sharp contrast to the attitude of the Hungarian state to the Hungarian diaspora, for example, which involves very substantial open and covert subsidies in order to support schools, newspapers and cultural institutions. I could find no evidence of this whatsoever in eastern Ukraine, and there is indeed evidence to the contrary, in the evident poverty of the institutions which do exist.

In eastern and southern Ukraine, neither the 'Russians' nor the very large number of Russian-speaking Ukrainians feel any great loyalty to *the Russian state*, and they are gradually developing a genuine allegiance to Ukraine. What they do feel is a real attachment to *the Russian people*, and a strong desire therefore to maintain close and friendly, but also equal relations with Russia. The Russian language, and the historic separation of state from ethnicity in Russia, give Russians in Ukraine an opportunity to express this clearly in a phrase their spokesmen often use: 'my Russkiye, no my nye Rossiyane', that is, 'we are (ethnic) Russians, but we are not Russian citizens' – or perhaps, since citizenship is a concept which has had little meaning in most of Russian history, 'we do not belong to the Russian state'.

Of great importance in this regard is the fact that the Russian state was never a Russian national state as such, and Russian loyalties were focused on institutions which, although they embodied large elements of Russiannness, were not purely Russian: the Orthodox religion, the Tsar, Marxism, the Communist Party, the Soviet Union.

The weak national feeling and mobilising capacity of local Russian populations outside Russia is of vast importance for the future of the whole region. It suggests that even if Moscow were to develop a strategy of trying to mobilise these populations, it would have little success *unless* local people had major local grievances to stir them up, and not just 'Russian nationalism'. So far, *all* the major 'Russian' populations outside Russia, with the exception of Transdniestria and Crimea, have been remarkable for their political passivity. Some of the reasons, as we have seen, differ. In Latvia and Estonia, the failure of the local Russians to react to their wide-ranging exclusion from local power owes much to a respect for the success of the Baltic economies, and for Baltic civic culture, and a belief that if they sit still, the Russians may find themselves in the European Union before too long. In Ukraine, by contrast, the mollifying factor is exactly the opposite – not economic success, but the ease of assimilation and the free entry of local Russians into the Ukrainian elites. But even in Kazakhstan, where neither of these factors applies, the Russian population has so far shown very few signs of serious organisation to counter 'Kazakhisation' and its progressive loss of political power.

The lack of mass protest in eastern Ukraine since independence, and the lack of the development of an articulated pro-Russian identity, is partly due to contemporary factors, but it has deeper roots in the nature of the population of this and other areas of the Russian diaspora, of the supposed 'Russification' process which took place under Soviet rule, and indeed of the nature of Russian nationalism and the Russian nation, a subject to which I shall return in the conclusion to this book.

The first point is that rather than a 'Russian diaspora', these populations are in fact mainly by origin *Soviet* migrants, drawn mainly from Russia but also from many of the other ethnic groups of the former Union. They are not Russian, but Russian-speaking – a different thing. In Ukraine especially, they also embrace many 'Russified' elements of the local indigenous population, who help make the attitudes of the local 'Russian' population both to Russia and to Ukraine even more complicated, ambiguous and non-national in any clear-cut sense of the word. Even the ethnic Russians among them are usually by origin peasants, whose ancestors in Russia had a relatively weak sense (by European standards) of a specifically Russian national identity. This was true both because of the diffusion of this identity into other loyalties, mentioned above, but also and predominantly because of the relatively undeveloped nature of Russian society and of mass education before 1917.

As Eugen Weber has noted in his famous work *Peasants into Frenchmen*, even in France most French peasants at the start of the nineteenth century had a pretty weak sense of French national identity, and it took a hundred years of intensive and almost universal national education to produce the voluntary hecatomb of 1914–18. In most rural areas of imperial Russia, the schools could not turn 'peasants into Russians' – because there were no schools. The Russian equivalent of the nineteenth-century spread of mass education in France took place in the twentieth century under Soviet rule. As a result, the loyalty and identity of the newly literate were once again – but to an even stronger degree than in imperial times – not focused directly and immediately on the Russian nation as such, but on Russia as part of a wider, and in this case explicitly ideological schema. The entire modern education and cultural shaping of these newly urbanised populations therefore took place in a Soviet context. They were truly, in the Communist phrase 'cooked in the workers' pot'.

This Soviet education of previously illiterate peasants is especially important for understanding the Russian diasporas, because these are mostly of relatively recent origin. Although, of course, some Russians have been present in many areas outside Russia's borders for centuries, in most cases the major movement of population began only a hundred years ago or so (of workers to the Ukrainian cities, and peasants to the Kazakh steppes). In other words, these are in many ways still immigrant populations. Even in Moldova, where the East Slav presence is some 1200 years old, a very large proportion of the present Ukrainian and Russian populations are first generation: 36 per cent of the Moldovan Russians were born in Russia, and 29 per cent of Ukrainians were born in Ukraine. If to this you add second generation immigrants, whose parents were born elsewhere, these figures become a majority. So these are still relatively recent societies, with not much time to settle down and develop a new identity of their own out of the various additional nationalities of which they are composed.

As to the other national elements from which these Russian-speaking populations are composed, the key to understanding the Russification process and its results among them is that it was in fact only to a very limited extent *Russification*, in the sense of attaching people to a specifically Russian national, cultural and historical identity. It was rather *Soviet modernisation*, expressed through the medium of the Russian language. This is of course of particular importance in Ukraine, where a very large proportion of people listed as ethnic Ukrainians are Russian-speaking. (The 'ethnic' designation in many Ukrainian cities in fact makes very little sense. Given the degree to which Russians and Ukrainians are intermarried, the choice of nationality on the passport was often almost completely arbitrary. In the eastern Ukrainian cities, my informal polls revealed that more than 90 per cent of Russian respondents have a close Ukrainian relative and vice versa.)

A distant analogy may be drawn to the process by which European immigrants to the USA over the past century shed many aspects of their previous peasant identities and became Americans, usually through a process which also involved them changing from being farmers to being some form of urban worker. This process, stretched over two generations, also generally involved their children forgetting their native language and adopting English for use at home as well as at work. But of course this did not mean in the very slightest that as a result they started identifying with the specific culture of the original settler populations. They became modern Americans, not Anglo-Americans.

The analogy is especially apt in the case of the mining centre of Donetsk, because workers for this area were drawn from all over the former Union – I have met people with Tatar, Caucasian and Belarus backgrounds among the miners, but all of them now speaking Russian, and many, through intermarriage, entered as 'Russian' in their passports. The same is true to a lesser extent of the other major cities of the region, but at least they in some cases do have the elements of a local historic identity

Of course, compared to the Soviet Union, the American process of assimilation was a more voluntary one – but in the Soviet Union too, a considerable number of people from small or 'backward' linguistic nationalities voluntarily abandoned their own languages in favour of Russian, as a passport not to Russian nationality but to modern education and career opportunity, without renouncing their own nationality or coming to think of themselves as Russian.

The lack of peasant commitment to Ukrainian nationalism has often been given as a reason for the failure of the Ukrainian national independence movement between 1917 and 1921; but it can equally well be used to explain why Russia's peasant conscript army was beaten by Japan in 1904–5, and failed to endure the test of the First World War, a test as much of national loyalty and determination as it was of strategy, tactics or even supply.

Soviet, as opposed to Russian education, was of course especially dominant in the case of those who made their careers in the Communist Party, and especially in the first three decades of Soviet rule, when Communist ideology was at its strongest and least mixed with Russian or other national elements. A striking case is that of Nikita Khrushchev, Soviet leader from 1953 to 1964, as revealed through his memoirs. Khrushchev, born in 1894 in a Ukrainian-Russian village, came from an absolutely typical, uneducated Russian peasant family which moved to work in the industries of Hughesovka (Donetsk), where he joined the Revolution. It is clear from his memoirs that Khrushchev did have certain Russian national and indeed imperial attitudes; but above all, the impression is of a man whose entire culture and view of the world had been shaped by a specifically Soviet and Communist education, so that this formidable, highly intelligent, not altogether inhumane, and by nature highly independent individual was almost incapable of stepping even partly outside that education and looking at the world through clearer eyes, even after his fall from power and alienation from the new Soviet leadership.[34]

The first thing that strikes a visitor to the great cities of eastern Ukraine today is that these are still *Soviet* cities, in architecture, in culture and in spirit. There is of course a growing overlay of Western commercial culture, advertising and so on, but most people's basic culture and identity remains Soviet. In large parts of this area, this is indeed the response of many ordinary people when you ask them to identify themselves by nationality. As a miner in Donetsk told me, 'In my passport I am an ethnic Russian, but my grandfather was an Armenian and my wife is a Ukrainian. I was a Soviet citizen. Now what am I?' Many others reply quite simply and seriously, 'I am a miner' – and fifteen hundred feet below the earth's surface, in the horrible and desperately dangerous conditions of a clapped-out post-Soviet mine, it did seem to me that nationality was not a rational priority. In any case, everyone was black. Worn-out equipment, lax safety rules and deeper digging for exhausted seams has made Donbas coal the most expensive in Europe in terms of lives lost per million tonnes mined – in 1995, 4.7 lives, to be precise. During that year, 345 Donbas miners were killed and another 6,700 injured.[35] I myself reached the coal-face at the Tenth Capitolina mine in March 1994 by crawling for some two hundred yards on my hands and knees, and this is by no means the oldest and most decrepit mine.[36]

In many ways, Donetsk never was a city in any sense that would have been understood in previous ages: like some former industrial cities in North America, the place is simply a temporary encampment of the nomadic forces of the industrial revolution. Today, it is, economically, a Soviet ghost town, but still inhabited by a million live people. In the words of Leonid Savonov, of the 21st Petrovskaya mine, 'our region is dying fast, but we have somehow to go on living.'

As a child of the Soviet Union, the Donbas could be accused of complicity in parricide – a tragic irony of which the miners themselves are well aware. Although founded by a Welsh mining entrepreneur, John Hughes, in the 1870s (on land owned by a Baltic German nobleman), Donetsk was really created and shaped under Soviet rule. Soviet identity was the only identity its people ever had; and in 1989 and 1991, it was strikes by the Donbas miners which did much to undermine the rule of Gorbachev and destroy the Soviet Union.[37]

Moreover, Andrew Wilson has written that many Ukrainians could still be plausibly described in a pre-national, peasant sense as *tuteshni* ('people from here'), that is to say as people whose primary identification is with their local- ity rather than with their state or 'nation' – and that is also true of the Russians in Ukraine.[38] As Grigory Nemiria told me about the Donbas,

> For the Donbas, the real economic and political centre was the Soviet one, in Moscow. Kiev was just the regional administrative centre, not of great importance. So when we became independent, there had to be a major and very difficult re-evaluation of which centre to look to. It was made even more complicated by the fact that for us here, regional iden- tity was always more important than national identity. The fact that you came from the Donbas was more important than that you were Russian or Ukrainian; so of course the break-up of the Soviet Union also meant a raising of this regional identity and loyalty...In any case, most people here honestly couldn't say what they are ethnically, because most families, like mine, are mixed.[39]

People in Donetsk are still much more defined by their pride in the 'all-union boiler-room' (the Soviet eulogy to Donetsk) than they are by a sense of more general identities, and the Miners Day' celebrations I attended in August 1995 dwarfed both the tiny official celebrations of Ukrainian Independence Day and the equally tiny counter-demonstrations by Russian nationalists and Communist Soviet loyalists in the city.

These then are what might be called potential societies in the national sense, neither Russian nor Ukrainian, and with the potential to become either, or, just conceivably, to develop into something new and individual of their own. This ambivalence is closely related to the fact that these Russian-speaking popula- tions outside Russia are not *civil societies*. The Soviet system notoriously involved the destruction of all existing forms of spontaneous and independent political, economic, religious, literary, social, cultural or even sporting organi- sation and mobilisation; and this atomisation of society bore particularly hard on the new working-class cities of eastern Ukraine, with their in any case largely immigrant – and therefore naturally more atomised – populations.

As the distinguished historian of the pre-1917 and revolutionary Donbas,

Theodore H. Friedgut, has pointed out, this lack of a civil society in the new industrial areas of Ukraine was also very much a feature of their first decades, in Tsarist times:

> It was of great importance to the region's development that those immigrants who came to seek work found themselves in newly established settlements lacking any previously formed social structure or local institutions...[Thereafter] perhaps the most significant feature of Iusovka's development was the inhibition of any participatory institutions that might have given the population both the appetite for self-government and the experience necessary for its success.[40]

As in Russia, every opinion poll in Ukraine – among both Ukrainians and Russians – in the mid-1990s showed an extreme scepticism about the possibility of changing anything through collective activity or mass protest. Asked if they could do anything against a decision by the Ukrainian government that hurt the interests of the people, 65.6 per cent of Ukrainians (including Ukrainian Russians) replied no. Asked about specific means of protest, 16.7 per cent named demonstrations, 15.6 per cent voting in elections, 7.9 per cent strikes, and only 3.6 per cent armed resistance or occupying buildings. Compare the 32.1 per cent who said that nothing would do any good, and the 30 per cent who found it impossible to answer, (more than one answer was allowed, so the figures add up to more than 100 per cent). They also expressed utter scepticism about the possibility of changing anything through appeals to their elected representatives, whether on a national scale or concerning local or personal problems. Ordinary people throughout Russia and Ukraine have often complained to me that when it came to practical difficulties like dealing with public services, local Communist Party officials in the past were actually considerably more responsive to complaints and appeals than the 'democratic' ones of today.[41]

Though much lamented by well-meaning Westerners, this lack of a civil society has been helpful for Russia, Ukraine and some of the other former Communist states over the past decade in trying to bring about 'free market' economic reform. Had these populations contained large groups with the capacity and the institutions for political and social mobilisation, it is impossible that the wrenching, deeply painful economic, national, cultural and psychological changes of recent years could have taken place with so little mass unrest and resistance.[42] In this context, the past five years have seen more mass protest against budget cuts in France than in Russia or Ukraine, where the suffering has been incomparably worse. And given Ukraine's national configuration, if such social protest had occurred, it might have gone on to take nationalist forms deeply threatening to the Ukrainian state.[43]

Also very important in Ukraine is the extreme degree of Russian–Ukrainian intermarriage among the urban populations of the east and south, so that it is quite often impossible to tell who is in fact a Ukrainian and who is a Russian.

The nationality entered in a Soviet citizen's passport was that of the father, unless the holder specified otherwise; but given the number both of mixed marriages and of divorces, it is quite common to find people who are officially 'Russian' but who have been brought up by Ukrainian mothers to consider themselves Ukrainian – and vice versa. An example is the first and strongly nationalist Ukrainian Defence Minister, General Kostiantyn Morozov. Officially an ethnic Russian, he was in fact brought up by his Ukrainian mother very much as a Ukrainian, although – another very common twist – in a Russian-speaking environment. On the other hand, a politician closely identified with the Russian and Russian-speaking camp is former presidential candidate and close Kuchma ally Vladimir Grinev (Hrynyov), from Kharkiv. His mother was also Ukrainian, and he too feels a strong sense of Ukrainian identity, though one very different from that of Morozov. Many such 'Russians' will very likely at the next, independent Ukrainian census redefine themselves as 'Ukrainians'.

Informal polls on the streets of Kharkiv, Dnipropetrovsk and Donetsk revealed more than 90 per cent of 'Russian' respondents having a close relative (mother, wife or close relation by marriage) who was Ukrainian, and the reverse for almost 90 per cent of the Ukrainians questioned. This gives the families involved a very strong stake in opposing the spread of hostility along national or ethnic lines, and indeed I found the vast majority of people in this region to be strongly opposed both to anti-Russian Ukrainian politicians (not just the 'ethnicist' radical nationalists, but also more moderate ones who preached hostility not to Russians but to Russia) and to Russian politicians preaching hostility to Ukraine. When asked to take a firm stand on one or other side of a Russian–Ukrainian issue, many showed extreme discomfort and took refuge in soothing platitudes on the need for agreement and compromise. This was particularly true of course in the numerous cases where a mixed couple was interviewed together.

This level of intermarriage, much higher than in the Baltic States and the Caucasus, let alone in Central Asia, is of course made possible by the linguistic and cultural closeness of the peoples concerned. In the past, this helped 'Russification'; today, in a perfectly natural twist of fate, it is working for 'Ukrainianisation'. Just as in the past most Ukrainians from the east and south did not feel a really bitter sense of loss at adopting the Russian language and elements of Russian culture, so today many Russians do not feel a terrible threat from gradually learning to read and speak in Ukrainian, at least for official purposes, and taking on aspects of a Ukrainian identity and loyalty to the Ukrainian state.

Of course, much depends on how and in what form this prospect is presented to them. If the Ukrainian state were to swing in future towards a more ethnicist and 'Galician' version of Ukrainian nationalism, and adopt a more determined programme of 'Ukrainianising' the east and south of the country, then in the long run this might very well lead to a counter-movement by the Russians in Ukraine, and a hardening of their own ethnic identity. It is also of critical importance that nationalist Galicia on the one hand, and the Russian-speaking areas on the other, are at opposite ends of the country; for in their case hate-filled myths really do exist about each other which have some analogies to those of Yugoslavia (above all, concerning what happened in the Second World War). A local Russian businessman and politician in Dnipropetrovsk, Gennady Balashov, told me in 1995:

> Despite all the wrong actions of the nationalists, there are no ethnic divisions or tensions here as yet. [But] if the central government here goes on with forced Ukrainianisation, then there could one day be a problem. The population here is peaceful, but then up to now, no one has tried to mobilise them, to stir them up. Russia itself has shown no interest in this. But if the day came, then Moscow might well be able to create some kind of movement in East Ukraine with money and support, because many people here are really fed up, and find a new Bogdan Khmelnitsky to lead it.[44]

There are some elements in the Ukrainian government (and above all of course in the nationalist opposition and the Ukrainian emigration in the West) who would like to adopt a more radical nationalist programme; but under President Leonid Kuchma the Ukrainian state has taken a different course, and defined Ukrainian national identity in 'civic' and inclusive terms. Some of the history being presented in the schools is deeply alienating to Russians, but on the other hand during the anniversary celebrations of the end of the Second World War in 1995, the Ukrainian government emphasised the common myth of Ukrainian–Russian heroism in the Soviet army during the liberation of Ukraine – which was deeply irritating to the Galician nationalists.[45]

It is sometimes suggested that the lack of ethnic tension in Ukraine proves nothing, because there was also very heavy intermarriage between urban Croats and Serbs in Yugoslavia, but this did not stop the persistence of deep hatreds and fears leading ultimately to bloody civil war. This however seems to me to be mistaken. In the first place, the proportion of mixed marriages in the Russian-speaking parts of Ukraine appears a good deal higher than in urban Yugoslavia; and the great cities of Ukraine provide both a much larger share of the population than those of Croatia, Serbia and Bosnia, and dominate society and culture to a greater extent. It is sadly apparent that in the villages and small towns of Yugoslavia, hate-filled traditions continued to fester, untouched by the superficially cosmopolitan and Yugoslav culture of the handful of cities. This is true in Galicia, and in some ethnically mixed parts of Russia, but not in eastern and southern Ukraine.

But more importantly, such an analysis misses the key importance of history and historical culture. Croats and Serbs come from very clearly delineated, strongly held and sharply opposed and indeed hostile religious-cultural traditions (Catholic and Orthodox) whose differences go back almost a thousand years. Over the past six hundred years, Croatia and Serbia have had very different historical experiences, with Serbia falling under the cruel and retrogressive rule of the Ottomans, while Croatia under Habsburg rule became part of Central Europe. This of course has given the Croats a strong sense of superiority, allied to the well-founded belief in Yugoslav days that they would be much more prosperous if freed from the link to Serbia. Ukraine and Russia have a quite different and much more closely linked and amicable historical relationship.

Most importantly of all, most Croats and most Serbs fought on opposite sides in the two world wars; and in the Second World War, the Croatian forces of the pro-Nazi Croat state committed massive atrocities against Serbian civilians, which the Serbian Chetniks, and to a lesser extent the mainly Serb Communist partisans, repaid against Croat civilians on numerous occasions.

An element of this kind does exist in Ukrainian history. The OUN, or nationalist partisan forces of Stepan Bandera, as well as Ukrainian units serving the Nazis, did carry out atrocities against ethnic Russians (and Soviet Russian prisoners of war) during the war, and after the Soviet reconquest, the Soviet army and NKVD also carried out atrocities in Western Ukraine.[46] However, both the area of recruitment and the sphere of action of these forces was largely confined to western Ukraine; and Nazi atrocities in Ukraine were not restricted mainly to ethnic minorities, as was the case in Yugoslavia, but fell very heavily on ethnic Ukrainians as well.

To create a parallel for the Yugoslav case, one would have to imagine Galicia and Volhynia expanding to cover two-thirds of the country and to control the Ukrainian government. In this case, civil war would have been not just possible but very likely, for many ordinary Russians and Russian-speaking Ukrainians in Ukraine do genuinely hate and fear the 'Banderovtsi', as they call the West Ukrainian nationalists, and of course this hatred is repaid with interest. Fortunately, as already pointed out, Ukraine is configured in such a way that these two populations rarely come into contact; Croatia and Bosnia of course are much smaller, with a great deal less space in which to feel secure.

Mutual hatred may develop and be cultivated over time; but as of 1996, we must recognise again that so far things have gone far better than could reasonably have been predicted a few years ago. Far from displaying the obsession with imperial identity and power portrayed by Richard Pipes and others, the 'Russian diaspora' so far has displayed less of this spirit than any other European former imperial nation – if only because it is in its origins and nature neither wholly European, nor really imperial, nor even truly part of a nation.

8 'A Fish Rots from the Head': Military Roots of the Russian Defeat

> Your rulers have forgotten that the Russian people and the Russian army are not the same as they were. There is no longer twenty-five years' military service, as in the time of the Tsars, when the soldier was isolated from society. Today, the soldier can no longer be sent hither and thither by his commanders without knowing the reason why.
>
> Major-General Dzhokhar Dudayev, Grozny, 17 December 1994

By September of 1996 the Russian army was mired in one of the most disastrous situations it had ever experienced. Of course, this was neither as bloody as the defeats of 1941, nor as chaotic as the disintegration of 1917. The difference is, however, that in those years the forces and motives for a revolutionary and triumphant regeneration were present under the surface, and rapidly showed themselves. In 1996 there seemed no way out at all, and no ideology that could restore to the armed forces a pride and faith in what they were doing. In the words that month of the new Defence Minister, General Igor Rodionov,

> Russia may lose its armed forces as an integral and viable state structure, with all the consequences this may have.
>
> The armed forces are experiencing the deepest crisis… The families of many servicemen are in dire straits and have to get engaged in doubtful business, to the detriment of their direct duties. This may lead to extremely undesirable and uncontrolled processes…When the army starts falling apart, people will just stop going to work. Instead they will start making money or selling what they guard – ammunition depots. These are in great demand today.

In the same month, the liberal politician, ex-Finance Minister and Duma Deputy Boris Fyodorov, wrote that:

> The actual result of our [Chechnya] policy is quite obvious. The Russian armed forces and special services have proved incapable of fighting; huge human, financial and material resources have been wasted; Russia's territorial integrity is in greater danger now than before. Russia has, in effect, capitulated, suffering humiliating military and political defeat.

This can please only separatists and morally degraded people who hate the words 'patriotism' and 'statehood'... One thing is clear, it is not the end of the tragedy. The Russian state is still in danger.[1]

An Unparalleled Defeat

The disgraceful failure of the Russian army of the 1990s in Chechnya, and what it says about the general state of the Russian armed forces, should hardly need emphasising. It has been the stuff of literally thousands of articles and despatches by Western correspondents actually on the ground. However, a considerable number of Western analysts and commentators played down this aspect of things until the last possible moment, and amazingly, some of them continued to do so even after the Chechen victory of August 1996 made their arguments manifestly untenable.

Along these lines, it was suggested that the military's problems are contingent, temporary and not especially deep, related to poor leadership and shortage of funds rather than to a crisis of the entire system. Thus professors Stephen Blank and Earl Tilford, of the US Strategic Studies Institute, in a report for the US Army War College of January 1995 wrote that:

> although this invasion may seem to show that the Russian armed forces are strategically and tactically incompetent, Western analysts need to be cautious in assessing the performance of Russian forces in Chechnya. It is not advisable to extrapolate too much from the seemingly poor performance of Russian troops fighting in an unpopular war against their own citizens. The tendency might be for the West to assume that a seemingly substandard performance in Chechnya might mean that Russian forces could not adequately defend the nation's interests under different circumstances elsewhere.[2]

As already stressed, even by January 1995 it was clear that there could be no talk of a 'seemingly' poor performance by Russian forces in Chechnya. And in addition the argument about Russian troops' motivation in relation to their own citizens is as back-to-front as it is possible to be. As is well known to anyone who has lived in Russia, long before the war broke out the Chechens, for historical reasons but also because of their prominence in the Russian mafia, were by far the most hated national group in Russia.

This hatred was reflected in the brutality with which Russian troops frequently treated Chechen civilians. It was not expressed however in a fierce determination to fight and win against Chechen warriors; and if Russian troops will not fight willingly and well against the Chechens, how likely is it that they will do so against Ukrainians, whom they regard as erring younger brothers, or against Poles, about whom they hardly think at all?

Moreover, the Chechen War could plausibly be presented as a war to defend Russian territorial integrity – a principle which elsewhere in the former Communist world has inspired soldiers to fight with the grimmest determination. In so far as the Russian high command made any effort to inspire its men with propaganda, this was indeed one of the arguments used, and repeated by those few Russian officers with whom I've talked who argued in favour of the war. The point however is that it seems to have had almost no effect; and if ordinary Russians will not fight hard even to defend their existing borders, what reason is there to think that they would fight hard to extend them?

In June of the next year Dr Richard L. Kugler of the RAND Corporation wrote concerning the Russian military performance in Chechnya that

> too much should not be made of this single case. The units committed to Chechnya were hardly the cream of the Russian army, and reserve-component forces of other countries have often shown weak performance in trying to quell civil disturbances... As the conflict dragged on, the performance of Russian forces improved markedly.[3]

This observation has been repeated by General William Odom, and by officials I have spoken with in both the Pentagon and the intelligence community – and it is nonsense.[4]

If the Pskov Paratroop Division, the Kantemir Guards Motorised Infantry Division, the Marine Infantry and the various Defence and Interior Ministry 'Spetsnaz' units, like the Special Rapid Reaction Forces (SOBR), all deployed during the war, were not elite units, then it is clear that Russia does not possess any forces which can be called 'elite' by serious international standards – which is indeed the case. How can the Kantemir Division, for example, be an elite force when in 1996 its soldiers spent much of the time working on farms around Moscow in order to eat? (Yet the Kantemir Division is also one of the units of the so-called 'iron ring' of troops around Moscow, supposedly especially well paid and treated so as to consolidate their loyalty to the regime.)

Moreover, far from 'improving markedly' with time, the end of 1995 and the first eight months of 1996 were marked by renewed and shameful failures: the failure to destroy or capture the Chechen forces which occupied Gudermes in December 1995; the failure to destroy the raiders at Pervomaiskoye (though these were in a tiny village supposedly entirely surrounded by Russian troops), and the failure to destroy the Chechen forces in Novogroznensky; the failure to prevent the Chechen forces in March 1996 from re-entering Grozny, holding the centre of town for several days, and killing hundreds of Russian troops – and so on. Lastly and most crushingly came the separatist offensive begun on 6 August 1996, when the Chechens recaptured not just central Grozny, but effective control of the towns of Gudermes and Argun as well, and won the war. The August 1996 assault was timed to embarrass Yeltsin during his presidential inauguration, a time when the Russians should have been at the highest state of alert.

The reason, very often, has been that Russian troops, when confronted with heavily armed and determined Chechens, have simply stood aside – something I saw with my own eyes in December 1995. The Russians' excuse was often that a 'local truce' was in effect, but this is the whole point: a few miles away, heavy fighting was raging, and the Chechens at the time were launching regular attacks on Grozny – but these particular Russian troops had made a separate peace.[5]

Rebuilding the armed forces from such a foundation is an expensive proposition. It is impossible to create a well-motivated officer corps unless you can pay them. Switching from a conscript to a professional army is more expensive still, even if the resulting forces are much smaller than the previous ones. In the case of the USA, it was only by creating well-paid professional armed forces, to some extent walled off culturally from the rest of society, that the country was able to place its morally battered forces on a firm footing again after the Vietnam debacle.

Although Pavel Grachev, the General Staff and most older generals have been vehemently in favour of keeping conscription, General Lebed, General Rodionov and most of the younger and more intelligent senior officers in the Russian army (including generals Gromov and Rokhlin) agree that such a shift is desirable in principle. Some of the conservatives do have reasonable arguments, however. In the words of General Vorobyev (in September 1994 – he may have changed his mind after Chechnya):

> We are very short of money – and the Russian soldier is the cheapest in the world. We also have the longest land frontiers in the world, which means that our army simply has to be bigger than that of the USA, for example. So our armed forces should be a combination of regulars and conscripts, with the regulars providing the NCOs, and the conscripts the rank-and-file. I am absolutely against a move to a fully professional army.[6]

In May 1996, just before the presidential elections, Yeltsin promised to abolish conscription and move to a wholly professional force by the year 2000.[7] Apart from such a change being quite impossible in four years, given the financial situation, this reversed his own and the administration's line of the previous year. Then it allowed the Defence Ministry to persuade the Federation Council (the upper house of parliament) to pass a law in April 1995 extending the length of conscription from eighteen months to two years, and abolishing many exemptions for students and others. In February 1997, Defence Council chief Yuri Baturin reversed presidential course once again, declaring on television that the 2000 date was unrealistic, and that the army 'would not survive' if conscription were abolished.[8]

Incidentally, it is a measure of the chaos and incompetence, as well as the conservatism, of the Russian legislative process that the April 1995 conscription bill contained no provision for conscientious objection; and although this is theoretically enshrined in the Russian constitution of December 1993, no procedure has been established. The result is that many genuine objectors are swept up by the draft, often to be savagely bullied or killed (see below), while many others are exempted by sympathetic or bribed judges, and thus end up doing no service whatsoever.[9]

Meanwhile, as the social prestige and economic rewards of a military career shrink, and the opportunities for the working class and the peasantry in many parts of Russia also shrink, the officer corps is being drawn more and more from the proletariat. The resulting social and cultural alienation of the officer corps from an economic and hence political elite which, unlike in Soviet times, is more and more dominated by the educated classes could be a potent source of danger for the Russian state in future. One should not forget the example of many Latin American countries, where for generations the economy and politics were dominated by small groups of comprador and landowning families. As a result, the only real means of advancement open to the lower middle classes was service as military officers, which the elites shunned. Of course, in the end, the officer corps also entered into politics – by force majeure.

The increase in length of service in 1995 was a measure so unpopular that even the Duma tried to amend it; and the change in government policy the next year was not of course due to any new analysis of what would be best for the army or Russia, but simply to win votes for Yeltsin – successfully as it turned out. Yeltsin's statement on a wholly professional force contained no indication of how such a change could be paid for, and neither Lebed, Rodionov nor any of the other advocates of reform have given any concrete proposals for this. Baturin's remarks in 1997 suggested that the reformers have had to give up professionalisation as hopeless in view of the financial situation (the reforms announced in July 1997 will be discussed below).

The trend on the ground was in the opposite direction. Due to lack of money, instead of a planned 280,000 'contract servicemen' (or 'regulars') by 1996, the army in reality recruited only 180,000, with no plans for any more. So low was the pay being offered to the *kontraktniki*, and so often was it in arrears, that malnutrition was a problem. Of the new recruits, around 100,000 were women, overwhelmingly the wives of officers and NCOs, given a variety of auxiliary jobs by the army so that they could earn enough to keep their families alive. This was not a sign of a move to a 'professional army'.[10]

A Systemic Crisis

The reasons for the Russian defeat are manifold, beginning with the special qualities of the Chechens, to be described in part III. The deep-seated social, cultural and moral changes in Russia, following on those in the West, and dating back several decades, have already been examined. In the more recent past there was the legacy of the Afghan War, comparable in its effects to those of Vietnam on the US army. But whereas for the US armed forces, the

Vietnam War was followed by a long period of general peace and relative prosperity, during which it was possible to carry out a thoroughgoing military reform, in Russia withdrawal from Afghanistan was immediately followed by one of the most drastic political, strategic, cultural and economic transformations in all its history.

The Soviet collapse also involved the chaotic division of the Soviet armed forces. This should have been followed by a complete restructuring of the new Russian forces, but the nature of the crisis simply left no breathing space for major reforms. Like the other armies of the former Union (with the exception of those of the Baltic States), Russia therefore still has a fragment of the Soviet armed forces – albeit by far the largest one – rather than a new, truly Russian army. The Russian army also inherited all the vices of the Soviet army, and by the outbreak of the Chechen War had developed no truly new spirit of its own.

There was, as we have seen, a collapse both of morale and of morality in the armed forces. The growing perception of Communism's failure by ordinary Russians over the last decades of the Soviet Union contrasted with the official rhetoric and resulted in a growth of cynicism and corruption. This became vastly worse with the complete collapse of Communism and the end of the Soviet Union, to which Russian officers had sworn allegiance. The impoverishment and social humiliation of the officer corps was made more acute by the spectacle of a new political elite dedicated above all to self-enrichment.

Specific problems of military organisation played their part as well, above all Yeltsin's apparent policy of building up the Interior Ministry and border forces against the army; and the lack of a solid corps of non-commissioned officers. This latter failing allowed brutality among the rank-and-file to flourish unchecked, which did much to destroy the internal cohesion and esprit de corps of Russian units. An acute shortage of funds, consequent on the Soviet collapse, led to extremely poor maintenance of equipment, failure to order new equipment, and above all, cutbacks in training. These exacerbated the inherited drawbacks of Soviet military training. It is to these issues that we now turn.

Shortage of Training and Equipment

Poor training has been apparent throughout the Chechen War. As noted, the lack of urban warfare training, despite the historical legacy of Stalingrad, was especially damaging. This was already visible in the Soviet Afghan intervention which began fifteen years earlier. In both Kandahar (which I saw from the Mujahidin side) and Herat (which I visited on the government side, after the Soviet withdrawal) the Mujahidin had retained control of major suburbs throughout the war – in the case of Herat, extending right up to the walls of the ancient citadel, the Arg-e-Herat. Instead of sending troops in to flush them out, and then hold the area, the Soviet forces had simply kept their distance and blasted these areas to pieces with planes and artillery, with the

Mujahidin intermittently sniping back at them; and this went on for *nine years*. In the case of the southern suburbs of Kandahar, the resulting destruction was even more complete than in central Grozny – houses had been hit and then hit again, shattered not into ruins, but jagged, unrecognisable fragments.

The only Soviet troops trained in urban fighting were those stationed around West Berlin, and the marines – the latter partly because this arm was reconstructed at the beginning of the 1960s along deliberately innovative lines, and partly because of regimental tradition, due to the glorious role they played in the defence of Sebastopol and later Stalingrad. I was told this by soldiers of the marine brigade which had fought to capture the presidential headquarters in Grozny, one of the very few Russian units to have performed creditably in the course of the war.

It seems extraordinary that other Soviet troops were not trained in urban fighting, given that Warsaw Plan strategy for an attack on NATO dictated an offensive through West Germany, one of the most heavily urbanised countries in the world; but the assumption was that the cities could be bypassed by armoured forces, cut off and surrounded, and any NATO troops trapped in them would sooner or later meekly surrender. The analogy was drawn from what supposedly happened during the Soviet drive westwards in 1943–5 – oddly, because these offensives in reality involved several major urban battles resulting in literally millions of casualties, most notably Budapest, Koenigsberg and Berlin.

Soviet training also proved poor in the periodic attempts to destroy the Afghan resistance in the mountains and plains: the lessons of the Soviet anti-partisan campaigns of the 1920s against Russian peasants and the Basmachi guerrillas of Central Asia, and of the 1940s and early 1950s against Ukrainian and Baltic nationalists, seemed to have been completely forgotten. One key reason for this was doubtless, as Geoffrey Jukes has written, that it was forbidden on ideological grounds to recall that in the fairly recent past major Soviet nationalities had been in revolt against the Soviet Union. (A link could be drawn here with Mikhail Gorbachev's extraordinary failure to predict the nationalist upsurges in parts of the Soviet Union in the late 1980s. It may be that like most Soviet people, he had simply never been told what had really happened in these places decades before.)

Nor had Soviet troops participated directly in the Soviet-sponsored but Cuban-fought campaigns of the 1970s in Africa. As a result, in Dr Jukes's words, 'the Soviet forces which entered Afghanistan in the closing days of 1979 lacked not only experience in counter-insurgency, but also other prerequisites, from a doctrine for subconventional war down to training manuals for small-unit actions. They were forces trained and configured for "Big War".'[11]

This remained true of the army as a whole even after official military interest in the war increased after 1986. And as far as the Interior Ministry forces were concerned, they were not involved in the Afghan War and seemed to draw no lessons from it at all. The failure to learn from Afghanistan in the years following the Soviet withdrawal seems odd, given that so many 'Afghan generals', including Defence Minister Pavel Grachev and Deputy Minister Boris Gromov, were subsequently appointed to top positions, and given that official discussions and public presentations from 1991 to 1994 stressed repeatedly the new military priority of fighting and containing small local wars.

However, few Afghan veterans were appointed to the General Staff, which continued to be dominated by General Mikhail Kolesnikov and other 'Germans' – in other words officers who had served throughout their careers in East Germany and elsewhere in Europe, preparing for the big push against NATO. Russian military journals dealing with tactical questions remained into 1996 dominated by highly theoretical articles about large-scale campaigns and battles, fantastically removed from what was happening on the ground in Chechnya.

According to officers with whom I have spoken, some of these members of the military establishment are by now well aware of the deficiencies of their own military education; but in the second place, they also suffered from the added factor that, whatever was being said in public, the wrenching disruptions of 1991–4 simply left the army no time and resources to think seriously about refiguring its tactical doctrine. With the exception of the presidential security adviser, Yuri Baturin (from October 1996, secretary and effective head of the newly formed presidential Defence Council),[12] the Yeltsin administration paid no attention to this question until 1996, and then only for reasons of its own political advantage. In the words of General Eduard Vorobyev, 'the state has distanced itself from military reform, simply leaving it up to the military themselves; but only Baron Münchausen could pull himself out of a bog by his hair.' He said at the start of 1995 that reform of the army should simply be abandoned, 'postponed until better days', until new material and technological conditions for reform could be created.[13]

Until the arrival at the top of generals Lebed and Rodionov in the summer of 1996, that was pretty much what happened. As regards the former man at the top, General Grachev, he appears throughout this period to have been obsessed with only two things: personal financial gain, and personal political survival, which he associated with the survival of Yeltsin. Under his ministry, the General Staff in 1992 drew up a plan for reducing the armed forces to 1.5 million by the year 1995, and in the third phase of reform, to the year 2000, merging the air defence forces and rocket forces – integration of different forces was to be improved and staff overlaps were to be reduced by abolishing the system of military districts and instead creating four to six regional strategic commands. There was also a proposal – as of 1997 not implemented or even begun – to change the existing bulky Soviet regiment-division structure for ground troops to a more flexible British-style battalion-brigade one.

However, as Pavel Baev notes, the fairly long time frame – as it then appeared – was essentially used by the armed forces and especially the General Staff as a breathing space, during which they waited in the hope that funding would improve, and occupied themselves with the admittedly horrendously difficult task of moving the Soviet forces and infrastructure back from Eastern Europe and the Baltic States and dividing them between Russia and the other former Soviet republics. They excused the slowness of reform both by lack of money and by the lack of a new strategic doctrine which would tell the armed forces whom they were now supposed to be defending Russia against. An additional complicating factor was the restrictions placed on Russia by the Conventional Forces in Europe (CFE) Treaty, though in fact the Russian armed forces to a great extent ignored these as far as deployment in the Caucasus was concerned.

Meanwhile Grachev occupied himself with establishing political control over the army in the name of the administration – something which was of course of critical importance during the battle with the parliament in October 1993, when the Officers' Union led by the reactionary Colonel Stanislav Terekhov joined the parliamentary opposition, and when for several critical days the generals hesitated about whether to support the Yeltsin administration. Yeltsin rewarded Grachev for his loyalty by keeping him in his job for nineteen months after the Chechen debacle had rendered him politically and morally bankrupt.[14]

To soothe public opinion, impress the West and cover up what was really happening, Grachev indulged in empty boasting about the progress of reform, the resumption of a full training system and the high morale of the troops.[15] In fact, in 1995, the army allocated only 300 million roubles (60,000 dollars) to the latest kind of computer-based combat training, and even this paltry sum was not in the end spent.[16]

And in any case, lack of funds meant that training of every kind largely collapsed from 1991 on. To the best of my knowledge, the Russian army has held no field exercises above battalion level since that date, and very few small-scale exercises either.[17] Lack of training was commented on bitterly by Russian officers and NCOs I met in Chechen captivity, and affected 'elite' units just as much as 'line' ones.

The failure to use heliborne assault troops effectively in Chechnya – indeed, the almost complete failure to use them at all (a partial exception was during the successful drive into the mountains around Vedeno in May 1995, one of the very few well-coordinated and competent Russian operations) – marks a drastic change from the Afghan War, where such forces were used frequently, and on occasions very successfully.[18]

More generally, Afghanistan showed up the poor quality of much Soviet equipment. This was admittedly due in part to the surprising lack of priority given to Afghanistan by the Soviet General Staff (in spite of what many Westerners alleged at the time, the Soviet 'limited contingent' really was limited, and so was official Soviet military interest). John Gunston, a British officer turned war photographer who travelled with the Mujahidin in the early 1980s told me of his astonishment – after being told so often when serving with the British Army of the Rhine of the supposedly powerful, superbly armed Soviet colossus facing them – at seeing Soviet companies and platoons signalling to each other with flags, apparently for the lack of walkie-talkies (and thereby of course immediately betraying their positions).

By the time of the Chechen War, the decline in the quality of equipment had become very much worse. On occasions, the Chechens with their modern radio-telephones even outclassed the Russians in efficiency of communication. Even after the Chechen War began, the entire air force in 1995 received only ten new fighters and bombers (the figure for 1993 and 1994 together was twenty-three). In 1996, the year the Chechen War ended (in part because of the inefficient and inadequate use of Russian air-power), the Russian air force purchased not one – not one! – new plane or helicopter, and the proportion of combat-ready planes dropped to 53 per cent.[19] However in a sign both that Russia was still capable of producing internationally competitive weapons, and that Russian military industries and their government sponsors were now thoroughly focused not on patriotism but on profit (or perhaps, one should more fairly say, commercial survival), Russia made deals worth several billion dollars to sell military aircraft to China, India, Malaysia and other countries.

The armoured forces in these years received only a few dozen new battle tanks. To keep its armoured forces at their existing level, the army should have received 300 new tanks in 1995; it got forty, a pattern which, if continued, will mean that by the year 2005 the effective Russian armoured forces will be a small fraction of their present numbers. In September 1996, General Rodionov declared that barely 30 per cent of the weapon systems in the army were of the latest design, and that many of the rest were already completely obsolete.

All services have been reduced to cannibalisation in order to keep at least some of their equipment operative. During my various visits to the Russian lines in Chechnya, I saw literally dozens of examples of lorries and BTR armoured personnel carriers standing immobilised, their tyres or wheels removed as replacements for those of other vehicles.[20]

In the years leading up the Chechen War, senior Russian officers warned repeatedly that lack of funds for training as well as equipment replacement was having disastrous effects on their units' combat readiness, and they were entirely correct. This was most striking in the case of the air force, an area where the Russians had total superiority over the Chechens and – unlike in Afghanistan – did not even have to fear many ground-to-air missiles. I did see one Soviet SAM missile-launcher, in the hands of one of Dudayev's guards, but there do not seem to have been many; most of the helicopters at least that were shot down fell victim to fire from heavy machine-guns. In some of these cases, especially in the mountains, the planes may also have crashed because of poor handling – also a result of inadequate training – and then been claimed by the Chechens as 'kills'. As to Russian claims that the Chechens had American Stingers, supplied by the Afghan Mujahedin, these seem pure fabrication.

On several occasions before the war, the Russian air force commander, General Pyotr Deinekin, warned that due to budget cuts some of his combat pilots were down to ten hours practice flying time a year. This may be an exaggeration, but the reality does seem to be that up to the Chechen War, and up to 1997 in units unconnected with that war, the average has been less than twenty-five hours' flying time per year for combat pilots, compared to between 180 and 240 hours for NATO pilots.[21]

This is of course far too little to maintain efficiency. The extreme inaccuracy of Russian bombing during the Chechen War cost thousands of Chechen and Russian civilians their lives, as well as hundreds of Russian troops killed by their own bombs (something of which Russian troops in Chechnya complained bitterly and repeatedly). Incredible as it sounds, it took the Russian air force more than two weeks from the beginning of the war even to score a direct hit on the government headquarters in Grozny. So poor was the quality of most of the pilots that according to Western military sources, the air force was reduced at the end of December 1994 to creating special combat squadrons out of test pilots and aerobatics display teams.[22]

Shortage of Men

Part of the reason for the failure of the Russian army is that even numerically it is not nearly as strong as it looks. From the beginning of the Chechen War, it repeatedly proved incapable of launching two major local offensives simultaneously even in such a tiny area as Chechnya. This may seem absurd for a force with a paper strength of 1.7 million men, but the actual planned strength of the armed forces, according to figures released in the summer of 1996, was only 1.47 million, and the number of men in effective combat units of course very much lower – indeed, General Rodionov said publicly after taking over the Defence Ministry in August 1996 that Russia had no units capable of being rapidly deployed into action. This is hardly surprising, given that in that year even 'elite' paratroop units were being used to dig for potatoes and cabbages, not as in the past to 'help the national economy', but to earn money, or even simply for a share of the food. One such unit was the 119 Paratroop Brigade of the Tula Division, General Lebed's old command (its commander, Colonel Vladimir Glebov, said that many of his officers had resigned in fury when the Defence Ministry informed them that it had no money to strike medals for courage that they had earned in Chechnya).[23]

According to Western estimates at the start of 1996, the Russian Defence Ministry (as opposed to the Interior Ministry forces) had only seven divisions which it even pretended were 'battle-ready'. With many units going unpaid, in October 1996 General Rodionov announced a plan to reduce the armed forces to 1.2 million by the middle of the following year – but this led to violent disagreement with General Lebed and airborne forces commanders over proposals to reduce the paratroops.[24]

In fact, by that stage the army's real (as opposed to paper) manpower had probably already dropped *below* 1.2 million – a point worth emphasising. Since all the reforms discussed both by the Yeltsin administration and its critics have involved reducing the army to this figure, it may be asked what all the fuss was about. The reason of course is that the dispute over the cuts involved not the ordinary soldiers, but the fate of the professional officers and staffs: the sore point is a reduction of the number of units, not the number of men.

Because of massive draft evasion (up to 75 per cent in some areas of Russia in 1992–4, though by 1996 the situation had improved somewhat) and corruption in the army's record-keeping, it has been very difficult to say just how many soldiers are in fact serving – something which seems to have been of key importance in the near-collapse of the Russian military effort in the first weeks of the Chechen War. According to a report of September 1995, on average army units contained only 65 per cent of their supposed number of troops (according to Russian military doctrine, a unit must be staffed to at least 75 per cent if it is to be considered combat-ready). The real figure, for the reasons given above, was probably very much lower.[25]

As Chechnya glaringly demonstrated, several of these 'elite' divisions were also greatly under strength. Thus, according to their official strength the Russian forces that moved into Chechnya (including formations from supposedly elite, 'battle-ready' units like the Kantemir Motorised Infantry Division and the Pskov Paratroop Division) should have numbered some 70,000 men. According to General Eduard Vorobyev, appointed to command the Chechen operation in mid-December 1994, the real figure was only 12,000 to 15,000, and this number also includes auxiliaries and rear units. The number of servicemen available for combat actions was considerably less, and was obviously insufficient.[26]

It was on the grounds of lack of sufficient manpower and general unpreparedness that two days after arriving in Chechnya General Vorobyev refused the command. On the basis of my own observations, I would put the numbers involved in all three columns of the initial operation at slightly higher but not more than 20,000 at the most – which accords with the assessment of NATO military attachés in Moscow.

I have heard it privately suggested by Russian soldiers that Russian divisional and regimental commanders may also have been to blame, because of the corrupt practice widespread among commanders either of exaggerating the number of men in a unit in order to pocket the pay of these non-existent 'dead souls', or of sending men away on private construction and transport work, and sharing the proceeds. When actually called on to go to Chechnya, of course, such commanders could not have explained that their units were even further under strength than their official reports had stated.

The genesis of the intervention in Chechnya, and its near collapse in the first fortnight, says a lot about the internal state of the Russian army at that time. As already described, in August 1994 the commanders of the North Caucasus military district had advised strongly against an intervention, saying that they were simply not prepared and did not have the right troops and equipment in sufficient numbers; and at the time, their warnings were heeded.

In December, the evidence suggests that not merely were they overruled by General Grachev and the security clique in Moscow, but the conduct of the operation was taken out of their hands altogether. Most of the units involved and the commanders were sent in from elsewhere in Russia in the fortnight between the defeat of the Chechen opposition on 26 November and the intervention on 11 December. Indeed, when the operation began it had no supreme commander at all, with this function apparently being discharged by the Defence Minister in person, with the assistance of Interior Minister Viktor Yerin and domestic intelligence (FSK) chief Sergei Stepashin. General Vorobyev was only sent to Chechnya three days after the operation began, took a look at it, and resigned again. It is no wonder therefore that the first three weeks of the operation presented such a strange spectacle. The lack of leadership at this time contributed greatly to the near-mutiny of General Babichev's Western column, described in part I.

Shortage of Money

As indicated, the armed forces commanders have blamed all these failings on the cuts in the military budget. In the words of the then Chief of the General Staff, General Mikhail Kolesnikov, in September 1995: 'To speak of the financing of military reorganisation is extremely difficult. It would be more accurate to speak of the continued existence of the armed forces.'[27]

In the same month, the National Security Council under Lebed privately prepared a document declaring that 'national defence cannot be financed with the existing taxation system,' and pointing out that:

> Given the present economic situation half the federal budget needs to be spent on defence, which is impossible. In this connection, the Security Council proposes increasing budget revenues by reimposing an export duty on natural gas, enforcement of a law on state control over turnover of ethyl alcohol and hard liquors and also by better management of state-owned property.
>
> As additional measures the Security Council proposes a special tax on imported foreign currency and total and final abolition of all import preferences.

'In view of the persistent inability of the Russian government to solve the tax collection problem,' noted the source, 'the authors of the document consider it necessary to put the Security Council in charge of tax and custom authorities.'[28]

This of course would have amounted to military direction of state financing. It would have been a mortal threat to the economic interests of Russia's comprador elites and especially the 'group of seven' around Anatoly Chubais – and something probably impossible to achieve without a military coup, for which the Russian armed forces in September 1996 were wholly unprepared, even if they had been prepared to follow Lebed.

Reduction in spending has indeed been catastrophic for the armed forces.

By 1996, at 83.5 trillion roubles (roughly 17 billion dollars) the Russian military budget for that year was less than one-fourteenth that of the USA, for armed forces which, on paper at least, still outnumbered America's (Russia also has to pay for the upkeep of most of the former Soviet military infrastructure and nuclear forces). The Russian military budget for 1997 was first planned at around 18.5 billion dollars (that of the USA was 250 billion dollars), but the fiscal crisis in 1996 meant that it was then slashed to 15.3 billion dollars, or 88 trillion roubles. In July 1997, as part of the government's reaction to criticism, Chubais promised to raise it again – but since by that month, the armed forces had in fact received only 22 trillion roubles, or a quarter of their budget allocation, there must be serious doubts as to whether this promise can be kept, or was indeed meant to be kept.[29]

From 1991 to 1996, weapons procurement was reduced fifteen times over, with results that were very obvious in Chechnya. By September 1996 the state owed the army alone some 25 trillion roubles (around 5 billion dollars) in funds budgeted for but never paid. Of this, 5 trillion roubles was in unpaid wages. The armed forces as a whole in turn owed around 12 trillion roubles (2.4 billion dollars) to local authorities in unpaid bills for electricity, water and gas.

The Russian military has repeatedly blamed its failures in Chechnya on this lack of funds (and on Islamic aid, foreign mercenaries, domestic traitors and so on). In the words of a Russian journalist close to the General Staff, Pavel Felgenhauer of *Segodnya*, 'financing is at such a low level that the Russian army is really only capable of guarding its own arms dumps.'

General Rodionov, arguing for higher military spending in the 1997 budget, said that

> We obtained 39 per cent of all required appropriations throughout 1995. And the 1996 situation has deteriorated still further...
>
> This problem has been becoming ever more painful and acute during the last few years. See for yourself. A total of 147,000 officers received their leaving papers over the last two and a half years. Eighty per cent of this number were discharged ahead of schedule. Officers aged under thirty, as well as officers in the 34–40 age bracket, make up the majority of all demobbed personnel in this category (approximately 35 and 46 per cent, respectively). The number of young officers who have been discharged from the armed forces is almost equal to the annual number of our new lieutenants being graduated by Russian military schools. As a result, we don't have enough officers to fill 64,000 vacant positions (despite the fact that the Russian army and navy have been pruned for several consecutive years). Lack of platoon and company commanders is particularly acute.[30]

Shortage of Honesty

However, if all the money allocated had actually reached the military, it would have been enough at least to keep things ticking over – and at 88 trillion roubles, the military allocations in the 1996 draft budget were clearly pushing the upper limits of what the state could afford, given that the total proposed budget was only 511 trillion.[31] Moreover, to the military budget can be added spending equal to more than 15 billion dollars on the Interior Ministry forces and border troops, as well as billions more in subsidies to military industries. Even more importantly, on average the pay of Russian officers, NCOs and regular soldiers is less than a sixth that of their American counterparts. On the whole therefore, and even given an expenditure of some 4 billion dollars on the war in Chechnya in 1995, the Russian military budget today ought to be sufficient to maintain the Russian armed forces at a level sufficient, not of course to launch a really major war like the invasion of the Ukraine, but at the very least to crush the Chechens.

The problem is that so much of it is either not being handed over by the government, or simply being stolen, either by the financial bureaucracy or the military command. Sheer corruption underlies many or most of the problems the Russian troops have faced in Chechnya, from poor morale to poor training and equipment. As a Russian conscript back from Chechnya told me in the headquarters town of Mozdok, 'our commanders are all thieves, from top to bottom.' 'A fish rots from the head' is the extremely apt proverb quoted to me by no fewer than three different Russian soldiers when describing the state of their army.

Of great importance in undermining military morale was the scandal in the autumn of 1994 concerning General Matvei Burlakov, a close associate of Defence Minister Pavel Grachev and former commander of the Western Group of Forces, stationed in East Germany during and after German unification. General Burlakov and his staff were accused, with compelling evidence, of massive corruption and the private sale of immense quantities of military equipment. A state commission formed to investigate was dismissed on Yeltsin's orders. In November 1994, an investigative journalist for *Moskovsky Komsomolets*, Dmitri Kholodov, was killed by a bomb planted in a briefcase while following up the Burlakov affair.

This occurred on the eve of the intervention in Chechnya, and did not contribute to the morale of the troops there. Of five ordinary conscript soldiers whom I interviewed privately in the headquarters town of Mozdok in January 1995, four said that they believed that Burlakov and Grachev had been behind this murder to cover up their corruption, and three said that they suspected that Grachev had also launched the Chechen War to distract people from his crimes. In the words of one of them, 'Valery', an Interior Ministry forces conscript,

Mistake? This is more than a mistake, it's stupid, it's a disaster, it's a complete ******** shambles. We've lost an enormous number of men, for no reason at all... The Chechens are fighting well because they're fighting to defend their homes. I'm not saying I like the Chechens, and there are plenty of bandits among them, but basically, that's the way it is. They're fighting for their homes, and we're fighting because our commanders tell us to fight. And who are our commanders? Thieves who steal from us then send us to die to cover up their own political mistakes.[32]

Among regular officers, NCOs and *kontraktniki*, the most bitter and frequent complaint concerning corruption has been that their wages often arrive after a delay of weeks or even months, and even when they are fighting in Chechnya. They are convinced – and with good reason – that the reason is that officers in the payments department, with the connivance of senior commanders, are 'borrowing' the money to invest in trade deals and in banks, where the rate of interest can be up to 30 per cent a month. Meanwhile, of course, the men for whom the pay is destined are losing through inflation.

This is an old military habit in Russia (and elsewhere as well). In *The Brothers Karamazov*, the father of Yekaterina Ivanovna, a lieutenant-colonel, is caught out doing just this with his men's pay.[33] In the contemporary Russian security forces, however, it has reached epidemic proportions. In the autumn of 1995, even the Foreign Intelligence Service (the former external wing of the KGB, and a body which ought to have been in a position either to protect or to purge itself) found that its pay was arriving weeks late. By the summer of 1997, Defence Ministry troops were owed 8.1 trillion roubles (1.4 billion dollars) in unpaid wages. Pavel Felgenhauer, defence correspondent of *Segodnya*, has alleged that part of the reason for the arrears was a conscious decision by Grachev and his staff to divert pay into spending on essential military services and research and development, which would otherwise have gone completely unfunded but sheer theft seems to have been the usual motive.

In a truly bizarre sign of the extent of the crisis, in August 1996, the Moscow Military District Procuracy (legal office), backed by the Defence Ministry and the Russian Federal General Procuracy, filed a court case against the Defence Ministry's Main Military Budget and Finance Directorate and the Russian Finance Ministry in an effort to force them by law to pay the arrears of servicemen's wages. By January 1997, the court had spent five months simply sitting on the case, allegedly under pressure from the government, which feared an avalanche of such cases.[35]

The result of all this was that by 1996 the great majority of officers were doing part-time jobs – some of them two or three. One lieutenant-general was reduced to sewing to keep alive; other officers became porters, hawkers or security guards (with their service weapons), strengthening still further the links between the armed forces, commerce and organised crime.

On 6 June 1996 at the military base near the town of Engels on the Volga, and on 26 July in the town of Kursk, the wives of officers and NCOs of the air defence forces stationed there held demonstrations and blocked the military airstrips because their husbands' wages were months in arrears and their children were going hungry. By the same month, even the wages of staff officers of the Russian Defence Ministry, were in arrears and the new Minister, Igor Rodionov, announced that he himself would not draw his pay until his soldiers had received theirs – not an idea that had ever occurred to General Grachev. He also, amazingly, urged workers in defence plants to picket the Russian government to demand state payment of their wages and for goods delivered.[36] It was statements like this which helped bring about his dismissal in May 1997.

As already pointed out, both for this reason and because of the general moral atmosphere in Russia today, officers and men alike compensate themselves by doing thieving of their own, exacerbated in the case of the troops in Chechnya by sheer terror of the Chechens. In the bitter words of Maria Eismont, a Russian expert on Chechnya and correspondent for the Russian newspaper *Segodnya*,

> In spite of the frequent statements of the Russian military command that rebel arms caches have been discovered and destroyed, the rebel fighters experience no shortage of arms: they continue to buy small arms and ammunition from the Russian soldiers themselves for money, food, or even a promise that the Russian unit won't be attacked; it is slightly harder for the Chechens to get armoured vehicles – they have to wait until the next Russian armoured column is defeated.[37]

Or in the words of the Chechen separatist deputy commander in Shali, Said Hassan, whom I have quoted elsewhere, in answer to my question about whether the Russians might not be able to cut off corridors for the supply of arms to Chechnya,

> Don't you worry about that. There will always be a 'corridor', because the Russian soldiers here sell us their own guns and ammunition in return for money or vodka. As long as Ivan is here, there will also be guns for us to shoot at him! Sometimes even commanders bribe us not to shoot at their units, to shoot at their comrades somewhere else instead.

The condition of units based on *kontraktniki* during the Chechen War is summed up by Thomas Goltz, one of the bravest and most dedicated of the Western journalists covering the Chechen War, who played a key part in exposing the Russian massacre of civilians in the town of Samashki in November 1995. Earlier that autumn he spent a hair-raising time with a unit of military police. In his words,

Even worse than dealing with the youthful deserters was dealing with the nayomniki, the mercenaries. These men often were former convicts or even provincial policemen who had volunteered for action in Chechnya in exchange for hard cash. And they had the bad habit of temporary dereliction of duty: on a whim, they might disappear from their positions to wander through 'liberated' Chechen towns...using their weapons to shake down people for food, cash and vodka.

But the Chechens often were only too happy to oblige. [When the soldiers became completely drunk] the Chechens either bought or stole from them everything from hand grenades to anti-tank mines. Acquired from Russians one day, they would be used against their former owners the next.[38]

This picture was confirmed for me both by Chechens and by some Russian soldiers with whom I talked privately – though the scale of such transactions was never clear. In the words of a Chechen woman in the mountain town of Shatoy,

> You almost have to feel sorry for these Russian conscripts, they are so hungry and miserable. I blame Yeltsin and the Russian generals, the evil men who sent them here, and of course the professional killers. The conscripts just want to eat – and drink of course, being Russians They bring us everything – petrol, spare parts, weapons when they think they can get away with it, and we give them food, vodka, money. Their officers are in it too, of course, and we hear stories about high-level deals and sales involving huge amounts of weapons and dollars. It's not surprising Russia is losing this war.

There has thus developed at all levels a culture of outright theft of military funds, equipment, fuel, and of misuse of military transport for commercial purposes. I witnessed this myself when in May 1995 I travelled back from Tajikistan to Moscow on a military transport aircraft carrying wounded and soldiers going home on leave. It was diverted via the Black Sea resort of Anapa so as to pick up several thousand bottles of red champagne. Ostensibly this was for the celebrations of 'Border Guards Day', but as a Russian colleague on the flight remarked, 'Even Russian border guards couldn't drink that much in a day. Of course, most of it will end up on sale in kiosks.'

Shortage of Unity

Another key reason for the Russian failure in Chechnya has been sheer disorganisation and internal divisions at all levels. The most important and damaging aspect of this has been the split between the Defence Ministry and Interior Ministry troops, and the build-up of the latter at the expense of the army, not just in Chechnya but generally as a result of Russian government policy in the years from 1991 to 1996. The Border Guards, the Presidential Guards (numbering by 1996 40,000 men, at least on paper) and the forces of the new Ministry for Emergencies were also strengthened at the expense of the army. And as Chechnya conclusively showed, the Interior Ministry forces are neither equipped nor trained for large-scale warfare, in part because no one in Russia has yet decided whether they should be, or whether they are in fact a kind of gendarmerie, which seems their obvious role. They were good enough at 'controlling' the situation in South Ossetia in 1990–1, and North Ossetia/Ingushetia in 1993, but the Chechens have been altogether too much for them. As for the Interior Ministry special forces (OMON and SOBR) some of these were real professionals, but they were few in number and essentially trained for crowd control and anti-mafia raids (see below). This made them useful enough for conducting anti-partisan sweeps in urban areas 'controlled' by the Russian forces, but completely useless for serious fighting in the mountains or the countryside.

In part, the strengthening of the Interior Ministry and other forces could be seen as a logical step given Russia's changed geopolitical circumstances – no longer facing NATO or the Chinese, but with a real risk of internal disorder and secession. Similarly, the strengthening of the border forces seems to make sense given the growing threat of smuggling and infiltration, as well as the Russian government's desire to use the stationing of these troops on the former Soviet borders (under 'cooperation' treaties with other republics) as part of its strategy of trying to reintegrate the former Soviet republics as one security space. In the words of the Baturin draft national security policy document:

> The particular features of the present foreign political situation, where there is no large-scale external military threat, permit Russia to mobilise efforts [for domestic reform and development]…
>
> In present conditions an important threat to national security is regional and national separatism…
>
> The main challenge to the country's security stems from the unfinished nature and instability of democratic institutions of administration and power…[39]

However, by 1995 the end result was that instead of one set of integrated armed forces, Russia had an eccentric, quarrelling and dissolute family of forces consisting of about a third of an army, a quarter of an army, an eighth of an army, a tenth of an army and a strange hermaphrodite offspring – the troops of the Ministry for Emergencies – of dubious parentage, poor education and uncertain purpose, but which by the summer of 1996 controlled 120,000 men, and was angling for another 20,000. The Interior Ministry troops had been increased to 270,000 men.[40]

Army officers have pointed out that getting the Interior Ministry involved in internal combat operations and endlessly strengthening the number of its armed divisions, riot police and security guards also weakens its efficiency as a crime-fighting force. In the words of Colonel Valery Borisenko:

> Previously two-thirds of Interior Ministry employees were involved in pure law-enforcement tasks. This has decreased to one-sixth today. Naturally, this force cannot stem the rise of crime. The remainder serve as a reserve in the case of mass disturbances, and also for protecting the government...
>
> Interior Ministry troops are well armed; they have everything but nuclear weapons, missiles, and tactical and strategic aircraft. The rest of the equipment is almost the same as in the regular army.

The latter is not entirely true; one of the great drawbacks of the Interior Ministry forces in Chechnya is precisely that they did not have integrated armoured units including heavy tanks. However Colonel Borisenko continued that the reason for this was plain: 'They joke at military headquarters that the Interior troops and the police will be the chief electorate of the regime, if the presidential elections are cancelled.'[41]

According to General Lev Rokhlin,

> The lack of funding is making it impossible not only to implement the army reform but even to carry out a simple reduction of the troops for economy reasons. At the same time other power structures are expanding unchecked.
>
> In terms of numerical strength the Internal Troops are as large as the Ground Forces. In the Border Guard Troops the number of generals or, in simple terms, those who 'look after number one', has doubled... The Ministry for Affairs of Civil Defence, Emergency Situations, and Elimination of Natural Disasters is trying to increase its staff by 20,000. All these departments are pursuing their own narrow interests. There is no single administrative organ over them which could counter certain leaders' ambitions. There is no common security concept for the country which would delineate the limits of the powers and responsibilities of each power structure. And all this is taking place despite the state's poverty and the growing discontent in the army.[42]

An amusing symptom of a very unfunny situation was that by 1996, representatives of the different armed forces were placing articles in the newspapers declaring how efficient and well led they were by comparison with all the others. One, an interview with the Chief of Staff of the Border Forces, General Timko, had the simple title, 'It's Worth Investing Money in Our Service'.[43]

Things were of course made much worse because, due to the collapse of leadership from Yeltsin and more generally, coordination even between the commanders of these troops was extremely poor, while junior officers and men came increasingly to loathe and despise each other. The different services at all levels blamed each other for every defeat and difficulty; and after every new defeat in Chechnya, the commander there would be replaced, adding to the general confusion.

The fragmented state of the security forces has also played a role in preventing reform. In the words of Yevgeni Kozhokin, director of the Institute for Strategic Studies, 'to achieve anything, you have to negotiate with half a dozen "power ministries" in this country. Military reform can't be done inside the Defence Ministry alone.'

Russian army officers with whom I have spoken are convinced that the build-up of the other services, and the difficulties between them, did not just reflect the general disorganisation, lack of leadership and internal divisions of the Russian government. They believe, and with good evidence, that they also reflected a strategy of 'divide and rule' on Yeltsin's part, designed to set the different security forces against each other and reduce the possibility of any threat to his rule from this quarter.

As is evident from the way that the Chechen War was planned and begun in the first place, however, these problems also stem to a considerable extent from a personal failing of Yeltsin's, his chronic failure to exercise any close, 'hands-on' control over the Russian government, and in the absence of any major crisis to slip into apathy, laziness, drunkenness and depression – a feature of his character and behaviour which was there from the beginning of his rule, but became worse as his health and stamina deteriorated. Instead, in the manner of many other leaders with little taste for administrative detail and faced with squabbling deputies, rather than take the lead himself on a particular issue – other than ones which directly threatened his personal survival, like the parliamentary resistance of 1993 – Yeltsin has usually preferred to play his various leading followers off against each other, allowing him to act as the ultimate arbiter. Meanwhile, although the Russian armed forces as a whole remained determined to keep out of politics, the events of 1991 and 1993 had inexorably drawn senior generals into politics, or at least bureaucratic factionalism.

Throughout 1994 and 1995, until the threat of defeat in the next presidential elections briefly galvanised him again, Yeltsin's presidency often appeared more like a vague suzerainty over a pack of squabbling vassals than the leadership of an administration, and the Russian ship of state simply drifted along, with different members of the crew cursing each other and pulling on opposing ropes.

For example, the Russian debacle in Chechnya of August 1996 (like previous more minor disasters) was apparently made possible in part by the fact that the previous two months had seen the dismissal of Defence Minister Pavel Grachev and his closest associates in the high command, as well as the progressive removal or demotion of the entire team which had taken Russia into the Chechen War. Grachev's place was left unfilled for more than a month while Yeltsin weighed different options.

Meanwhile the appointment of General Lebed as security supremo had set off ferocious infighting within the Yeltsin administration, as Lebed sought to turn his rather undefined and theoretical powers (as Secretary of the National Security Council) into real ones and Premier Chernomyrdin and Yeltsin's new chief of staff, Anatoly Chubais, sought to clip his wings. A key aspect of this was Lebed's attempts to gain real control over the Interior Ministry, against the resistance of Interior Minister Anatoly Kulikov. Such splits inevitably added to the divisions and demoralisation of the Russian troops on the ground.

Dyedovshchina, the Abuse of Servicemen and the Lack of NCOs

The most striking and evil aspect of divisions in the Russian military at ground level, however, long predates the Yeltsin administration and became entrenched over the last three decades of the Soviet Union. This is the practice of *dyedovshchina* ('granddadism'), meaning the exploitation, frequently with loathsome cruelty, of the newly joined conscripts by the 'grandfathers', the older conscripts and the volunteer soldiers. This practice has been principally responsible for the almost unbelievable numbers of murders (whether from beatings as part of *dyedovshchina*, or in retaliations against it by junior soldiers driven to desperation), suicides and nervous and physical breakdowns in the Soviet and Russian armed forces, which has exacted a toll in peacetime casualties *each year* which has been considerably greater than all the allied armies together suffered in the Gulf War. In 1995, according to the Military Procuracy's own figures, 423 soldiers committed suicide, mainly because of *dyedovshchina*, and in 1996 543 did so. This does not, of course, count cases where suicide (or murder) was covered up and described as 'accidental death'. In 1996, an almost incredible figure of 1,071 soldiers were murdered, mostly by other soldiers.[44]

Dyedovshchina, it should be noted, is not 'hazing', which is usually taken to describe a fairly ritualised abuse intended either to initiate new soldiers into a self-styled military elite, or informally to punish infractions of a group code. Nor is this bullying by NCOs as part of training. Both of these are familiar enough in Western armies today, and in the records of armies and warrior groups throughout much of history and anthropology, from the warrior societies of the Mandan Indians to the contemporary Canadian army. Such traditions can be extremely nasty, but they have some purpose in creating group solidarity – even if this is only unity in hatred of the sergeant-major. *Dyedovshchina* is something quite different. It humiliates men, weakens them physically, breaks them down without 'building them up', without giving them new pride, identity or self-confidence: it is a Hobbesian anarchy unregulated by ritual or tradition, a general war of the stronger against the weak.

The result of *dyedovshchina* is units riven and wrecked by internal hatreds and the desire for revenge – and if the frequent peacetime reports of bullied soldiers turning on their persecutors and killing them are anything to go by, then a good many Soviet and Russian soldier 'granddads' in Afghanistan and Chechnya must have died in action from a bullet in the back. 'Fragging' in the Russian army – according to anecdotal evidence – seems to be directed as often against other soldiers as against officers or NCOs (unlike for example the pattern in the US army during the Vietnam War).[45] Nothing has done more to destroy the pride of ordinary Russian soldiers in their service, and to undermine military morale.

Ethnic minorities, and especially those identified as historical 'traitors', have suffered especially badly. A story from my Chechen host in the town of Shali, Musa Damayev, about his time as an eighteen-year-old conscript in the Soviet army in East Germany in the early 1980s illustrates the natures both of *dyedovshchina* and of the Chechen spirit. If I had heard this story before the war, I might have dismissed a good part of it as hot air. Not any longer:

> If there were several Chechens in a unit, then they usually left us alone, however much they outnumbered us; but I was the only Chechen in an engineering unit of 2,000 men. Of course the 'granddads' picked on me from the first day. They cursed me as a savage, a traitor, a bandit, what have you...They ordered me to clean their shoes, make their beds, bring their food, but I refused. So every evening they beat me with their fists, with belts – my ribs were black and blue. But when the officers asked me where the bruises were from, I told them I'd fallen over. I held on.
>
> Then after about six months, they woke me in the middle of the night, about twenty of them, and started beating me. They pushed me back to the end of the room where a clock was standing, with the sentry's bayonet in its sheath hanging from it. I grabbed it and went for them, and they scattered, all twenty of them.
>
> I spent fifteen days in the cooler for that, and the guards beat us. I held on.
>
> When I came out, the others in my company didn't beat me again, they kept a safe distance...
>
> Later, of course, I became a 'granddad' myself; but I treated the younger soldiers decently, I didn't beat them or take their money or force them to do things for me. And so I gradually gained a certain authority, first in the platoon, then the company, then the regiment.
>
> The 'granddads' forced the younger soldiers to buy useless things from them, hand over all their pay – and 20 marks a month was all we got. One young soldier in my squad had had to give most of his pay for a broken clock. I took it to the 'granddad', asked him, 'Why did you sell him this?' He cursed me. Now we Chechens don't lightly curse each other – for us, this is a serious business. I broke the clock over his head. I got another three days in the cooler for that...But I never complained to the officers, I always stuck up for myself and I respected the principle of solidarity among the soldiers, even if no one else did.

That is the difference between the Russians and the Chechens. The Russians have no principles, or rules or traditions. Nothing is sacred for them, not even their own families. Look at the way they swear the whole time, foully insulting each other's mothers and sisters. If a Chechen did that to another Chechen, he'd be dead. That sums up why we are superior to the Russians.[46]

The practice of *dyedovshchina* says a good deal about the symbiotic relationship, especially in the Soviet Union, between tyranny and anarchy. It is an example of how an ultra-strong state cripples society and its rules and restraints. The lack of these in turn undermines the state order, leaving only a veneer of autocratic but in fact largely powerless authority over a pit of chaos, corruption and a host of private tyrannies. In the military case, the lack of any redress, either by law or through the media, for abused or murdered soldiers and their families allowed more and more abuse, until finally the spirit of the magnificent army which marched from Stalingrad to Berlin was destroyed from within. The spiritual roots of *dyedovshchina* presumably lie in the traditional brutality – and drunkennness – of much Russian working-class and peasant life, exacerbated by Soviet contempt for the individual and by traditional Russian and Soviet military indifference to casualties and human suffering.

It has been encouraged by the violence of many Soviet officers towards their men; what in the British or American armies would be a court-martial offence is accepted in Russia as a matter of course. The tendency of Russian officers to hit their men (and indeed each other) appears several times, for example, in the memoirs of General Alexander Lebed.[47]

However, even where officers have had the will to try to stop this practice, they have often lacked the means. This is above all because of the lack in the Soviet and Russian armies of a really good corps of non-commissioned officers (NCOs). This is something which Russian military thinkers before 1917 repeatedly lamented, and to which indeed some of them later attributed the failure of the army to survive the First World War and resist Bolshevik infiltration (it was linked with the absence of a patriotic, property-owning and relatively well-educated peasantry, the class from which most French and German NCOs were apparently drawn).

It seems odd on the face of it that the supposedly 'egalitarian' Red Army should have failed to remedy this failing. However, throughout its early decades, the Soviet forces were always critically short of good officers, first because the officers were Tsarist, then because the army grew so much in the 1930s, then because so many officers were purged under Stalin, then because of the massive casualties and massive recruitment of the Second World War. The result was that any sergeant who could read and write and showed a glimmer of leadership tended to be quickly promoted to lieutenant, creating an immensely high turnover of NCOs.

This syndrome persisted in peacetime. Those privates who were promoted from the ranks tended to stay a very short time as NCOs before becoming officers; and most NCOs, rather than being long-service regulars as in Western conscript armies, were until recently, and remain to some extent today, conscripts themselves. The description of his capture by Junior Sergeant Alexander Tupolsky of the 22nd Spetsnaz Brigade has already been quoted in chapter 3 to illustrate the decay of Russia's 'elite' forces. Perhaps most striking of all, though, was his own rank. What serious elite force, anywhere in the world, makes an eighteen year old conscript with six months' service into a sergeant?

More thoughtful Russian generals are perfectly well aware of the failure of their NCO system. A few have even overcome their pride sufficiently to express an interest in learning from the American system. In September 1994 General Vorobyev told me that,

> The weakest element in our army is the sergeants. They should be professional soldiers, the rest conscripts. Say we were both born in 1975; we studied together, were conscripted into the army together. Then after six months service, I am a private, and you have become a sergeant. How am I going to respect you? Maybe at school and as privates it was me who was the leader and whom people respected more. There is a natural psychological resistance among the soldiers to obeying sergeants who are the same as them. So that is why we now think sergeants should be older, more experienced and educated, and obvious and proven professionals. His first encounter with the private should inspire respect. This is what we are now planning and thinking about – a return to the kind of sergeants we had in the Great Patriotic War [Second World War]. But we are hindered by lack of money.

General Vorobyev went on, however, to say that

> As for morale, I am convinced that it is very high among our conscripts, because they serve out of conviction, not for pay. In the Russian army, material questions always came second. First came the moral one. As in the Second World War, when the Motherland called, they went. There is not a single country in the world with such solid moral foundations for its defence forces as Russia.[48]

As these words of General Vorobyev suggest, there is a deeply rooted reluctance to admit any problem and seek an outside solution. The preference is generally to look backwards, to Russian or Soviet models. A key question for the years to come will be whether the defeat in Chechnya has been enough of a shock and humiliation to jolt the Russian generals out of such attitudes.

The Struggle Over Military Reform, 1996–1997

To judge by conversations with Russian officers, the general hope – or rather vague dream – seems to be in the long run to make the Russian army something like the French, with conscripts serving in 'garrison' troops, performing guard duties and acting as a reserve, and a smaller number of professional units acting as mobile, heavily armed 'intervention forces'. Both General Rodionov and most of the other senior officers agreed that the army would have to be considerably smaller. Rodionov has spoken of an army of sixteen divisions;[49] General Lebed, during his time as national security chief, said that it might even be advisable – if the divisions were to be really effective fighting units – to reduce the number to twelve.

If, as up to now, these divisions were not in fact fully manned, this could put the Russian army (not counting missile troops, Interior Ministry forces and so on) barely ahead of the Turks in terms of real effectives – a horrifying thought for many Russians. In 1996, even on paper there were only 670,000 men serving in the Russian ground forces (as opposed to the missile troops and so on), and the number of real effectives was a good deal lower. As a result of the reforms announced in 1997, the number of men in fighting units could drop to 200,000. In 1996, there were around 400,000 in the Turkish army, and according to military experts, these are genuinely effective effectives. It is very important to remember, therefore, that if the 1997 plans for reductions in the numbers of troops are carried out without a general reform of force structures, then the result could be an army with very many fewer than the planned 1.2 million men.[50]

Military reform was virtually stalled for almost a year from the defeat in Chechnya in August 1996 to the declaration of a new plan for reform by Yeltsin in July 1997 (and at the time of writing, it is not at all clear that this reform will actually be implemented).

Much of the Western press attributed this delay to resistance to reform by General Rodionov, allegedly representing the conservative top brass who did not want the number of troops to be cut and were still obsessed with the NATO threat. Those journalists who saw Yeltsin as a sincere military reformer[51] – which up to July 1997 at least was simply not the case – therefore applauded him for dismissing Rodionov in May 1997, and replacing him with the more compliant General Igor Sergeyev. As commander of the strategic missile forces, it was assumed that Sergeyev would have less of the mentality of the old General Staff and ground forces officers, and also less support in the officer corps.

There is some truth in these accusations against Rodionov;[52] but it is also true that he was sacked because he had told Yeltsin a number of uncomfortable truths, and had defended the rights of his subordinates – notably, the right to be paid – in a way that was no more than his clear duty. A fairer apportioning of blame for the delay in reform was suggested by an editorial in the *Moscow Times* of May 1997:

Igor Rodionov certainly did little to distinguish himself in his brief tenure as defence minister, but it is President Boris Yeltsin and not the former general who is to blame for the impasse over military reform.

Rodionov never really had a clear mandate from Yeltsin. He was chosen as a neutral compromise candidate who was acceptable to Alexander Lebed during Lebed's short-lived heyday as Yeltsin's right-hand man on security issues.

In an army riddled with corruption the veteran general was honest, and his commitment to reforming the army after the debacle in Chechnya was undoubted.

Rodionov was always a military man of the old school with a commitment to the traditions of the Soviet army. His idea of reform was bringing back the good old days.

Yet his responsibility for the year that has been lost is clearly secondary to that of Yeltsin, who has made shrill calls for military reform but has failed to say exactly what he means. Yeltsin's only contribution to the debate has been an unfeasible call for a volunteer army, clearly designed to win votes from youngsters afraid of conscription [in the run-up to the presidential election].

Without some real direction from the top on the big question of what the ultimate geopolitical role of the Russian army will be in the twenty-first century, Rodionov could only tread water.[53]

The key problems with military reform – other than corruption and a general lack of state interest – are twofold: money, and where the cuts are to be made. Ironically, military cuts require more, not less money in the short term, if officers are not to be simply thrown on to the street and weapons raffled off. This was not so in the 1920s, when following the Russian Civil War the Red Army under Mikhail Frunze reduced itself in the course of three years from over 5 million men to 650,000 – but of course the circumstances were totally different: the infantry and cavalry units of those days were relatively simple affairs whose weapons did not require expensive decommissioning or storage; and much more importantly, the men could be reabsorbed into the rural and industrial economies, and the officers found endless jobs in the Communist Party and its affiliate organisations. This was also true, to a lesser extent, during Khrushchev's great reduction at the end of the 1950s – though even so, the resulting military discontent was one of the factors which brought him down.

Today, according to General Rodionov (and Western experts with whom I have spoken find this realistic), to reduce the paper strength of the army to 1.2 million men – by abolishing units – and to begin to upgrade the reduced forces would require another 40 trillion roubles, on top of a total defence budget for 1997 of only 104.3 trillion. The President's staff, and senior Russian economic officials, reportedly met this proposal with mockery, as absolutely unthinkable in present fiscal circumstances. As we have seen, for most of the Yeltsin administration, at least until the summer of 1997, an effective military has been very low on their list of priorities. By the end of 1996, even the supposedly 'hardline' Duma was also refusing to ask for more money for the military. Of course, given Russia's situation, the argument that Russia's real needs are elsewhere is a perfectly valid one – but the Yeltsin administration record makes nonsense of the persistent Western myth that it is passionately committed to Russian imperialism.

Also involved in the furious and complicated battle over reform in the second half of 1996 and the first half of 1997 was Yuri Baturin and his Defence Council. The Defence Council seems to have been formed in the summer of 1996 principally as a counterweight to Lebed within the administration (it did not even meet until October), but under its ambitious and hardworking secretary, it was soon closely involved in the details of military change.

One critical aspect of this was the issue of reductions in the five 'elite' paratroop divisions, two of which, as already noted, despite their (relatively speaking) high numbers and huge expenses, had so signally failed in Chechnya.[54] Rodionov's original plan involved reducing the number of divisions to three, and bringing the remainder under the command of the respective military districts where they are stationed, thus reducing their separate command staffs. This plan set off reverberations which will be very familiar to anyone who has followed Western military cutbacks in recent years. To this was added, however, the political instability of Russia, with politicians in both the government and opposition reckoning uneasily that if the succession to Yeltsin were to turn nasty, they might well need the support of these troops at some point in the future. Thus Rodionov's order (of 24 September 1996) created a serious breach between him and General Lebed (at that time still chief of national security, and himself a former paratrooper). In principle, Lebed is for perhaps even deeper cuts than Rodionov – anywhere but in the paratroops. He described the plan as a 'criminal scheme'. At the start of October, the paratroops commander, Colonel General Yevgeny Podkolzin, was sacked, allegedly for lining up with Lebed.[55]

Even after Lebed's dismissal, the internal battle rumbled on, and contributed in November to the dismissal (initially blocked by elements in the Kremlin, supposedly led by Chubais) of the ground forces commander, General Vladimir Semenov.[56] In December, a provisional compromise was reportedly reached under pressure from the presidential staff, which seems to have been the worst possible from the point of view of real reform. The paratroops were to be reduced, as planned, by 14,500 men, to 48,500. However, all five divisions were to be retained, and the paratroops were to remain a separate service with their own command.[57]

If this plan had been followed, a reform intended to produce a force with a smaller number of fully manned divisions would therefore have resulted in the same number of divisions even worse manned than before, but – surprise, surprise – all the generals and most of the officers would have kept their jobs (if the two divisions had been disbanded, 2,872 officers would have been dismissed).[58] In the summer of 1997, following Rodionov's dismissal, his successor, General Sergeyev, and Baturin revived the original plan to put the paratroops under the army, as part of a general plan to reduce the armed forces as a whole from twelve to only three arms (army, navy and air force). But at the time of writing, it is still not entirely clear that the regime will in fact dare to anger key military units in this way; shortly before his dismissal, Rodionov himself once again proposed that the number of paratroop units should be cut, and Yeltsin promptly vetoed it.[59]

In May–July 1997, the struggle over reform peaked with four events: the dismissal of General Rodionov; the appointment of Chubais to control military financing; a public protest by General Rokhlin against the administration's approach; and the announcement of a new reform programme by Yeltsin. The personal intervention of the President, after such a long period of evading responsibility, should be seen above all as a response to Rokhlin's attack on him, which seemed to threaten a real movement of protest within the army itself. General Rodionov, as already noted, was dismissed on 22 May 1997 after his public protests against underfunding of the military had also provoked fears that military resistance might begin to coalesce into a serious threat.[60]

On 6 June, Yeltsin reinforced the administration's victory by making Chubais head of a new commission in control of the financing of all the armed forces, including the Border Guards and Interior Ministry troops. Chubais was also put in overall charge of drafting the new military reform plan.[61] As usual in Yeltsin's administration, however, spheres of authority clashed, because both Baturin and Chernomyrdin (placed in charge of a new commission for military restructuring) were also given responsibility in this field.[62] The appointment of Chubais was utterly infuriating to many in the military, above all because until this appointment neither he nor his staff had ever shown the slightest real interest in or commitment to the armed forces – and this applied to Chernomyrdin too.

In Chubais's case, this reflects his ideological concern with the market to the exclusion of anything else. It also, to be fair, reflects the immense economic problems with which such figures are wrestling, which take their full attention. It may also in part be a reflection of the highly compartmentalised nature of Soviet, and post-Soviet Russian government, in which Soviet officials in non-military industries, and state economists, would have had absolutely nothing to do with the army.[63]

It is true that Yuri Baturin is said by Russian experts to be genuinely committed to the creation of effective armed forces, and in the summer of 1997 was reportedly sleeping only five hours a night as he worked frantically to draw up new draft reforms.[64] In the words of one ex-colonel, 'He's not one of the free marketeers who just say to the military, this is the market. Sink or swim. He does understand that Russia needs an army and needs to do something for the army.' But Baturin is not a figure who carries much real weight within the administration, let alone with the regime's business backers or masters.

Reacting against Chubais's appointment, General Lev Rokhlin, in an open letter which he read to the Duma on 24 June, launched a furious attack on Baturin's plans and on Yeltsin's personal responsibility for the state of the military. In particular, he warned that the missile forces were 'facing extinction' for lack of funds. He fiercely criticised Yeltsin:

> You bear a personal responsibility for unleashing the war in Chechnya; and having made the decision to use troops, you then abandoned the army... Against mercenaries and trained fighters, you threw into battle eighteen-year-olds, boys who had never held guns in their hands... The army is being destroyed catastrophically quickly. Pilots don't fly, tank drivers don't drive military vehicles and the infantry don't have shooting practice.

Rokhlin called for a movement to support the army and oppose government policy: 'There is only one way left – the influence of society. I suggest the organisation of a public, non-political "All-Russian Movement of Support for the Armed Forces, Military Science and the Defence Industry", involving a wide spectrum of Russian society... Its main task will be to strengthen the army and the social protection of military personnel.' To the officers he said, 'Organise yourselves. Choose leaders to preside over officers' meetings. Demand fulfilment of your legal rights. Do not hope that someone else will do it for you...Otherwise the army will die.' He specified that the movement he proposed should include serving officers and veterans as well as representatives of society in general.[65]

It must be stressed that General Rokhlin was not protesting against reforms as such, of which he has in fact been a leading advocate. He was demanding that rather than simply cutting the number of troops and throwing the officers out of work, money must be found to retrain officers made unemployed and to improve conditions for the officers and troops who remained. He said that the army could be cut to 1.2 million men, but only if this were accompanied by 'a broad assessment of the country's strategic and military requirements. In fact, it is being driven only by a short-term desire to save money.'[66]

Rokhlin's letter caused an immense stir precisely because he had not previously been seen as an opponent of the administration. His public image as a military hero (not undeserved) had indeed been deliberately built up by the administration in 1995 both to save face over Chechnya and to provide itself with a popular military candidate in the 1995 parliamentary elections. Rokhlin stood for Viktor Chernomyrdin's 'Our Home is Russia' bloc in the Duma and became a leading member. His protest attracted great support across the political spectrum, including from Lebed, the Communists and leading members of 'Our Home', including its parliamentary chairman, Sergei Belyayev.[67]

More to the point, there were certain signs that the officer corps might heed Rokhlin's words to organise – though one of his own aides was sceptical on this score: 'Like Western journalists say, Russia has the most obedient army in the world. We grumble a bit, and then we follow the orders coming from the top.' It is also worth noting the wooden-tongued language of Rokhlin's statement ('The All-Russian Movement of Support for the Armed Forces, Military Science and the Defence Industry' is not exactly a title to set hearts ablaze). None the less, the threat appears to have been taken seriously by the administration.[68] In response, on 16 July Yeltsin himself finally took a strong stand on the military reform issue, backing up changes already proposed by Sergeyev and announcing some new ones. This was also apparently intended to pre-empt the Defence Ministry's own plan, which was due to be presented on 25 July.

In his speech, Yeltsin said that the number of troops would be cut to 1.2 million; but much more importantly, he said that the generals would be cut by around 900 to 2,300, and he supported Sergeyev's plans for the abolition of the autonomous command structures, which were to be reduced from twelve to three. This included the abolition of the autonomous railway troops and air defence commands. Most importantly of all, the President announced that the Ground Forces Command, once the most important and prestigious in all the armed forces (and the source of most of the General Staff), would be abolished and merged with the army. The staff of the Defence Ministry would be cut to 1,200, or 1.5 per cent of the total military strength.[69]

Although these last two moves look like not just a reform but also an attempt to dissolve a potential focus of military opposition, these changes if implemented would have a real and positive effect on the armed forces, above all by reducing the number of generals and staff officers proportionate to fighting troops, and simplifying the command structure as a whole. In a clear response to Rokhlin's attack, Yeltsin also promised that 'great attention will be paid to the needs of servicemen who are discharged.' He said that the state would build 50,000 new flats for them and that the regions would be asked to provide another 50,000. In order to pay for the reforms, Chubais for his part announced that in 1998, military spending would rise by 3.4 per cent of GDP.[70]

At the time of writing, it is still unclear what will actually happen, and past experience gives good grounds for pessimism. Chubais's promise looks quite unbelievable, since it would mean more than doubling the 1997 figure of 3.26 per cent of GDP (around 7 per cent for all the security forces) – and we have heard such promises before from the Yeltsin administration. On past form, the money for new housing, and indeed for the reforms in general, may in any case very well be stolen either by officials or generals. And it has to be clearly stated once again that reforms of this kind on their own – even if successful in their own terms – will not create a new army: a new spirit is also needed.

Part III: The Chechen Victory

In the name of God, the Compassionate, the Merciful:
We have given you a glorious victory, so that God may forgive you your
past and future sins, and perfect his goodness to you; that He may guide
you to a straight path and bestow on you His mighty help...

It was He who sent down tranquillity into the hearts of the faithful,
so that their faith might grow stronger (God's are the legions of the
heavens and the earth. God is all-knowing and wise); that He may bring
the believers, both men and women, into gardens watered by running
streams, there to abide forever.

From the Forty-Eighth Shura, 'Victory', of the Koran

The Chechens' struggle in 1994–6 was the latest in a series of anti-colonial
wars throughout the world, of which the past two generations have seen a
whole series, from Indochina through Algeria and Portuguese Africa to
Afghanistan. In one important respect, however, the success of the Chechens
and their commanders is even more striking than this parallel would suggest,
and is indeed highly unusual – perhaps unique – in the modern history of war.
This is that the Chechens won not just without the support of a real state but
without the help of any formal military or even political organisation, on the
basis of the strengths of their society and its traditions – albeit equipped with
Soviet weapons and military training.

This marks the Chechens out from the major communist and nationalist-
led armed rebellions of the second half of the twentieth century, all of which
were organised and led by modern cadre parties (and even the Zulus, in their
brief victory over the British in 1879, had the advantage of a superbly disciplined system of regiments under the control of a ruthlessly effective military
autocracy). The Afghan Mujahidin of course were also mostly without serious
party or military organisation – but then, though they wore the Soviet army
down, they certainly did not win outright, as the Chechens did.

In Chechnya, the Dudayev regime never succeeded in creating anything
like a cadre party, and the formal Chechen armed forces when the war began
numbered fewer than two thousand men. The vast majority of Chechen fighters joined up after the war started, and not in formal military units, but in

spontaneously formed groups of relatives, friends and neighbours. Further-more, while individual operations were superbly planned by General Maskhadov and an informal staff of commanders, Maskhadov never had the kind of overall control of the Chechen forces exercised by General Giap, over the Vietcong.

To explain why the Chechen fight has taken such an extremely radical, resilient and victorious form, it is necessary to examine three interlinked fac-tors: the Chechens' particular and very unusual pre-Islamic social and cultural traditions; the impact of Sufi Islam as adopted by and adapted to this traditional culture; and the effect of the experiences, memories and myths experienced and generated over the past two hundred years – above all, of course, those related to conflict with and oppression by the Russian empire and the Soviet Union.

The three chapters of part III therefore examine, in order, Chechen history, society and religion. The first chapter also necessarily includes some analysis of the history of Russian power in the Caucasus.

9 The Two Hundred Years' War: The History and Context of the Russian–Chechen Conflict

Russians have for all practical purposes forgotten the Great Caucasian War. And so they made and are making many of the same tactical and strategic mistakes they made 150 years ago… The soldiers marched into the conflict as unprepared and ignorant of the task ahead of them as were their nineteenth-century predecessors. But the Chechens forgot nothing.

Pavel Felgenhauer, defence correspondent of *Segodnya*

Today, the Bolsheviks fear the dead Shamil more than the Vorontsovs and Bariatinskys feared him as a live, but honourable enemy.

Svobodny Kavkaz, 1952

Shamil's Legacy

In early February 1995, I interviewed Umar Avturkhanov, Chairman of the Russian-backed 'Provisional Council' in the north-western Chechen town of Znamenskoye. The council was at that time engaged in setting up a 'government' to attempt to run Chechnya on behalf of Moscow. Outside the office in the former Communist Party headquarters of this bleak, shabby, dusty town of the North Caucasus steppe stood row on row of Russian military transport, waiting to transport the 'Chechen provisional authorities' to the ruins of Grozny on the back of the Russian military machine.

I asked him whether this destruction, as well as the Chechens' historical traditions of fighting the Russians and resisting Russian conquest, would not make it impossible for his side ever to achieve real legitimacy and authority in Chechnya. He responded by cursing both Dudayev and the Russian army, Dudayev for his 'crazed tyranny – this war was provoked by him to rally the people behind him and stay in power', and the Russians for their 'hamfistedness'. In his words, 'Grozny could have been taken quickly and without bombardment, but that wasn't enough for them. All they have done is to create new enemies everywhere.'

But Umar Avturkhanov's most bitter criticism was reserved for Imam Shamil:

> They talk about the tradition of Shamil, but what did Shamil do for Chechnya in fact? He brought us only decades of unnecessary war, the ruin of the country and the death of half its people. And he wasn't even a Chechen. He came here from Daghestan, preaching his crazy religious fanaticism, hatred of the Russians and holy war, and we Chechens behaved like fools as usual, and followed him, to our destruction.

It seems odd on the face of it for Avturkhanov to speak about Shamil as of his greatest personal enemy, when Shamil has been dead for 120 years; but he wasn't wrong. Shamil's image is alive and well in Chechnya. His religious legacy has been greatly weakened, but the myth he helped create, of stubborn resistance against the Russians, remains at the heart of the present Chechen struggle, and that struggle is in turn – and quite rightly – becoming part of the heroic national myth. By February 1995, with Chechen volunteers still slogging it out in southern Grozny against overwhelming odds, it was already much too late for Avturkhanov and his allies to subtract from that myth.

For the entire period from 1785 to the present in the Eastern Caucasus has been essentially one long struggle by the Chechens against Russian domination, interspersed with unstable truces and periods of sullen and unwilling submission. Regularly suppressed, the Chechens just as regularly rose up again whenever Russian or Soviet power faltered or oppression became too acute to bear. In our own century, this has been true in 1905 (albeit the disturbances in that year were limited and easily put down), in 1917–21, in 1929, in 1937, in 1942, in 1957 (the return from exile), and now from 1991 onwards.[1]

In our time, General Dudayev and other leaders of the Chechen independence forces have repeatedly stressed that Chechens never formally submitted to Russia, never signed any document of surrender or accession, and therefore have full legal and moral right to independence. This is true – though of course it would be equally true of many other subordinated peoples throughout the world. It is also true that in these wars the Russians have always found a significant number of Chechen native collaborators, even if these have been almost always outnumbered by the anti-Russian fighters.

These wars have shown some remarkable similarities over the centuries but have also developed some crucial differences: most notably, that the Chechen War of the 1990s has been far more national, in the modern sense, and far less religious, than those from 1785 to 1921, which it has already however equalled both in bloodshed and in historical importance.

The Russian Wars Against the Mountaineers

The first recorded contacts between Chechens and Russians came with the arrival of the Cossacks in the Terek region in the early sixteenth century (there doubtless were much older contacts, but these have not been set down). The Cossacks established settlements south of the river, where they lived for several decades. The Chechens had already lived in the area for some thousands of years. At that stage, they were still mainly confined to the mountains and forests, leaving the Terek steppe to the various Turkic nomads, and open to Cossack settlement.

In 1604, however, a Russian army was badly defeated in Daghestan, and there followed a general movement of the Cossacks back across the Terek. The same thing happened after another Russian defeat at the start of the seventeenth century. Under increasing pressure from Chechen clans moving northwards, the Greben Cossacks retired to the north bank of the Terek, under Russian protection, where they became part of what was later officially designated the 'Terek Cossack Host'.

It was almost a hundred years before the Cossacks crossed the Terek again in force, this time as armed colonists in the service of the Russian Imperial Army. As part of the same process, 'loyal' Chechen groups who came over to the Russians in the fight against Sheikh Mansur and Shamil were given lands north of the Terek, safe from the revenge of the 'rebel' Chechens, while hostile villages were sometimes deported there en masse.[2] It was this, according to many Cossacks today, which led to ethnic Russians being eventually outnumbered by Chechens in this area. And in the meantime, the passivity of the Russians in the region for most of the 150 years up to 1783 allowed Islam deeply to penetrate the Eastern Caucasus, and to establish a presence which has been a gall for the Russian state ever since.[3]

Moreover, thanks to the isolation and natural protection of their mountains and forests, the Chechens remained right up until the early modern period – and even, to a limited extent, until the present – a clan-based society of a strikingly archaic and egalitarian cast, without rulers, feudal lords, a military or merchant caste, or a formal clergy. Until the 1920s, the Chechen language also lacked a written script (the tiny number of literate Chechens were religious figures literate in Arabic, the language of the Koran; Avar, or Azerbaijani Turkic were used as lingua franca for communication between the Chechens and other linguistic groups in the region).[4] This naturally makes their earlier history obscure, except where it touched upon the histories of the literate civilisations – Arabic, Persian, Turkish or Russian.[5]

The early Chechen–Cossack contacts consisted both of intermittently friendly interchanges, and of the raiding and cattle-reiving which was endemic to both parties. On several occasions, outright war ocurred, and the Cossacks tended to get the worse of it, until in the later eighteenth century, under Catherine the Great, the Russian army established a permanent military presence in the North Caucasus for the first time (other than their brief occupations of the Daghestan coastline on the Caspian Sea, from the tenth century onwards) and began the effort to bring the mountain peoples under Russian imperial rule. The result of this pressure was the 1785 'revolt' of Sheikh Mansur Ushurma – called a 'revolt' by Russian historiography, though the

Chechens at least can hardly be called rebels, since they had never acknowledged the slightest Russian sovereignty.

Sheikh Mansur led his Chechen, Daghestani, Kumyk and Kabardin Mountaineer followers to victory by ambush over a Russian column in the Chechen
forests, but he failed to unite them, and after only a few defeats they melted
away. Fighting continued however for six years, after which Sheikh Mansur fled
to the Western Caucasus and the Ottoman fortress of Anapa on the Black Sea.
In 1791, he was captured when this fortress fell to the Russians, and died in
Russian captivity. The capture of Anapa (repeated conclusively in 1828) marked
part of the process by which the Russians advanced south along the Black Sea
coast, gradually cutting the Muslim North Caucasians off from Turkish help.

The years from 1791 to 1818 were ones of uneasy peace in the north-eastern Caucasus, though a peace continually disturbed by Mountaineer raids and
Russian retaliations – and indeed by Russian raids and Mountaineer retaliations – and by intrigues among and between the various Daghestani khans
who now owed formal allegiance to the Tsar. Russia's attentions in the region
were mainly concentrated on extending and consolidating its empire in the
Transcaucasus, which had been formalised with the annexation of Georgia in
1801 – and of course, after 1792 a powerful Western distraction also
appeared, in the form first of the French Revolution, and then of Napoleon.

But with the final victory over Napoleon, the year 1816 saw the appointment of General Alexei Yermolov as Commander-in-Chief in the Caucasus
and the resumption of a 'forward policy' aimed at ending raids by the Mountaineers into Russian territory, and bringing the khans and tribes of the region
to a state of full submission. It was this policy, pursued by Yermolov with
extreme brutality – even a fellow Russian general wrote of him that 'he was at
least as cruel as the natives themselves' – which led to a revolt of the Chechens
in 1824, followed in 1829 by the revolt of Qazi Mullah, the spread of war to
the whole region, and the continuation of the struggle by his disciple, Imam
Shamil, for no less than thirty years. The Chechens remember Yermolov with
hatred to this day, attributing to him the sentiment that 'the only good
Chechen is a dead Chechen' – some fifty years before General Philip Sheri-
dan said the same thing about the Red Indians.[6]

Very frequently, of course, these punitive expeditions, and any attacks on
Chechen mountain villages (auls), also became the occasions for Russian
soldiers to indulge in rape and pillage on their own account.[7] This was freely
admitted by Russian generals, who later in the war made some attempt to
check these excesses. Yermolov's methods were not universally accepted in
the Russian army, and what was known as the 'sword or samovar' controversy
– that is, the argument between those favouring military solutions as against
those for peaceful persuasion and assimilation – continued to the end of the
Caucasian war, and has been revived in our own day.

The nineteenth-century Chechens for their part were not over-gentle to any
Russians they captured. Sometimes they massacred them in reprisal for Russian attacks and atrocities, though they generally kept them alive to exchange

for their own men captured by the Russians – something which has also been true in the latest war. They also abducted Russian, Cossack and Georgian women on frequent occasions, as was their tradition. Shamil for his part behaved with extreme ruthlessness towards his Chechen and Daghestani rivals and towards any 'backsliders', which helps explain his mixed reputation among some Chechens today.[8]

As to the Russians, it is important not to read back into the behaviour of nineteenth-century Russia the exceptional totalitarian ferocity which characterised the Soviet, and especially Stalinist regimes in our own century. Regrettably, there was little that was unique to Russia about its methods of colonial 'pacification' in the nineteenth century: the French in Algeria and Senegal, the British in the suppression of the Indian Mutiny and the Matabele Revolt, and the Americans of the Western frontier were no gentler. Charles Callwell, Victorian soldier and author of the standard late nineteenth-century British study of anti-guerrilla operations, makes no distinction between the behaviour of the various European colonial armies. While stressing the desirability of a 'samovar' (or maybe teapot) strategy when dealing with 'civilised' enemies, he also writes that:

> In South Africa in 1851–52, in 1877, and again in 1896, rigorous treatment was meted out to the enemy in crushing out disaffection, and with good results; the Kaffir villages and Matabili kraals were burnt, their crops destroyed, their cattle carried off. The French in Algeria, regardless of the maxim 'Les représailles sont toujours inutiles', dealt very severely with the smouldering disaffection of the conquered territory for years after Abd el kader's power was gone, and their procedure succeeded. A system adapted to La Vendée is out of place among fanatics and savages, who must be thoroughly brought to book and cowed, or they will rise again.[9]

Or in the words of Baddeley,

> From a Christian and moral point of view, there is no justification of such a ruthless policy as Yermolov's, in reference to which, however, let it be emphatically repeated that, while individually any man may have the right to condemn it, collectively, as nations, it is a case of glass houses all round.[10]

In 1969, an attempt was made to blow up the monument to Yermolov in Grozny – (a sign both of how hatred of Yermolov had endured and of how the spirit of resistance continued to simmer throughout Soviet rule; Soviet and Chechen anecdote in fact says that the monument was blown up several times in the 1970s and 1980s, but I have been unable to establish whether or not this was true). Its destruction was one of the first acts of the Chechen national revolution in 1991.[11]

A striking feature of Shamil's wars, which has also been replicated in our own time, was the extreme tenacity of the resistance and above all, its astonishing capacity to recover from what seemed like crushing defeats; this also marked a crucial difference from the earlier failure of Sheikh Mansur to hold on to his followers in the face of adversity. Twice the Russians thought they had won a final victory: in 1832, Qazi Mullah was killed when the Russians stormed Gimri in Daghestan, but Shamil, though badly wounded, escaped by a miracle and in 1834 was himself proclaimed Imam. Then in 1839, the Russians stormed his stronghold of Akhulgo and wiped out many of his closest followers; but Shamil once again escaped, wounded and with his youngest son on his back, the eldest having been given to the Russians as a hostage. Once again his followers rallied and he resumed the fight.

A young Russian officer of the time, Dmitry Miliutin (later Minister of War) described with reluctant admiration the suicidal defence of one village (in Daghestan, however, not Chechnya) by Shamil's Murids (disciples or followers) in terms which have been repeated again and again in Grozny over the past two years:

> At 9 a.m. our troops were already in occupation of the greater part of the village, and even of the flat roofs of the houses where the Murids still defended themselves, but the bloodshed continued the whole day through until dark. The only way to drive the Murids out of the dwellings was to break holes in the roofs and throw down burning substances, and so set fire to the beams. Even then, they remained many hours in the houses. Sometimes they found means to break through and secretly pass from one dwelling to another, but many bodies were found completely charred. In spite of their disadvantageous position...the most fanatic among them were satisfied if they could destroy even some of the infidels.[12]

The Crimean War (1854–6) in which Britain and France supported Turkey against Russia, seemed at last to promise the Western and Ottoman help the Caucasians had been dreaming of for so long; but the incompetence of allied commanders, the stubborn and heroic resistance of the Russian defenders of Sebastopol, and Russian victory over the Turks at Kars in the Transcaucasus brought this to nothing. With this disappointment, and sheer exhaustion after thirty years of war, the heart seemed to go out of the Mountaineers. Shamil's followers abandoned him, and he himself, surrounded and hopelessly outnumbered, was forced in 1859 to surrender at the aul of Gunib in Daghestan. Treated with honour, he was eventually permitted to go on a pilgrimage to Mecca, and died at Medina in 1871.

Shamil's achievement was not just to fight for so long against overwhelming odds, and to set an example of resistance which has strengthened the resolve of many Muslims and some Christians. It was not even that he to a considerable extent created the 'mythomoteur' and national identity of the modern Chechen nation (without of course having any such object in mind). Shamil was the first person to introduce state institutions – as part of his war effort – into Chechnya. He himself said later, after his surrender, that it was only this that had allowed the Russians later to rule Chechnya in relative peace, because he had accustomed the Chechens to government – and there may be some truth in this.

Basing his rule theologically on Islamic law, and practically on the ability of his Murid-led forces to terrorise backsliders and traitors, Shamil did his best to create a functioning Islamic administration, through a system of 'naibs', or local governors, ruling on the basis of the Shariah. From first to last, however, Shamil's rule remained intensely personal, and he was plagued by the dubious loyalty of many of the regions and clans following him. Often, control could only be maintained by savage reprisals and hostage-taking – for example, in his relations with the Avar khans, which involved numerous murders and led to the ultimate defection of his ally, Haji Murat. This seems to have borne especially hard on the Chechens, who had never had rulers or a native aristocracy of any kind and strongly resented some of the naibs Shamil set over them, and especially his land grants to them.[13]

This heritage may partly explain the adherence to Russia of certain Chechen groups today, and the unpopularity of Shamil's name among them. The measures taken by Shamil, like those of his contemporary Abd al-Qadir in Algeria, were exploited by their Russian and French enemies to brand them as 'despots' and 'savages'.[14]

It must also be emphasised that while Shamil certainly practised a form of tyranny over the Chechens, his rule was still closer to Chechen traditions of egalitarianism than was that of Dudayev, because Shamil's domination over other men was justified by his own absolute, slave-like *submission* before God and the rules of Sufi Islam. This aspect of his leadership emerges from various stories and anecdotes – for example, the occasion on which, to shame into submission Chechens who wished to surrender to the Russians and had used his mother to intercede with him, he had himself publicly flogged to atone for their sins.

Such appeals and examples however are hardly relevant or effective in the context of modern Chechnya (and it is hardly possible to imagine General Maskhadov asking to be publicly flogged, or that it would have anything but a disastrous effect on his prestige in contemporary Chechnya if he did). For some time to come therefore it will remain an open question whether the superb military discipline and cooperation displayed by the Chechens in the latest war can be carried over into peacetime.

There is little need to repeat in detail here the stories of the earlier wars; there already exist in English two excellent military histories, by John Baddeley (1908) and Moshe Gammer (1994), as well as Lesley Blanch's more famous, and more highly coloured *The Sabres of Paradise*, and a shorter study by Robert F. Baumann.[15] In Russian of course there is an encyclopaedic literature;[16] in Chechen, unfortunately, the accounts seem so far to be largely mythological in tone. In the sections that follow, I will rather suggest some comparisons between the earlier wars and those of the present, and between the Russian wars in the Caucasus and other colonial wars of the period, which may contribute to a better general understanding of the region.

Just before that, however, it is important to note that one of the things that has changed radically is the aspect of Chechnya one would have expected to change the least: the terrain. Until the mid-nineteenth century, most of Chechnya was covered with thick primeval forests of beech, oak and nut. On the ground, it was a war more reminiscent of Vietnam, and Russian tactics more reminiscent of the American use of Agent Orange to defoliate South Vietnamese jungles and strip the Vietcong of their cover, than of the British wars in the bare mountains of Afghanistan – or indeed the Russian wars in the equally bare mountains of neighbouring Daghestan. As Baddeley writes,

> The forest, composed as to nine tenths of giant beech trees, was their [the Chechens'] sure refuge in distress; their chief safeguard against the advancing Russian. To it the Tchechens owed much of all that went to distinguish them from their neighbours of the Koumuik plain and the Daghestan plateau – and just as it constituted the chief natural feature of their country, so did it mainly determine the nature and duration of the war for their subjugation. As long as the forest stood they were unconquerable. The Russians made no impression on them save when and where they cut the beech-trees down; and it is literally the fact that they were beaten in the long run not by the sword but by the axe.[17]

Most of the fighting of the nineteenth century, and most of the Chechen victories, were in forests and took the form of forest ambushes, until the Russian army steadily cut down the woods. On some Chechen roads, like that leading from the plains to the gorge of the river Argun, you can still see where Russian troops cut the trees back to a straight line, a long musket shot from the road.

A Tragic Geopolitical Location

In comparing Russia's Caucasian wars, then and now, with other colonial and neo-colonial struggles, the first question which suggests itself is: why did the Russians bother? In our own time, this question is perhaps easier to answer, after a recent history which has included the French struggles in Indo-China and Algeria, and numerous wars to defend 'territorial integrity'. The Russian war against Shamil was, however, a war of conquest, and on the whole, the nineteenth-century experience was that European powers rarely wanted to expend really massive amounts of men and materiel for the sake of colonial conquest.

It is instructive in this context to compare the Russian experience in the

North Caucasus with that of the British in Afghanistan during the same period. Even at the anecdotal level, there are many parallels, with the murder of General Prince Pavel Tsitsianov (Tsitsishvili) at a parley outside Baku in 1806 matching that of Sir William Macnaghten in similar circumstances outside Kabul in 1841, and the massacre of the Russian mission to Teheran under Griboyedov in 1829 looking forward to the massacres of the British missions to Kabul in 1841 and 1879. The events of 1841 in Kabul were followed by the annihilation of the British expeditionary force in Afghanistan as it struggled back through the passes to India, a fate which occurred to several smaller Russian detachments in the Caucasus.

Thereafter, however, British policy towards Afghanistan and Russian policy towards the Caucasus diverged sharply. The British sent fresh expeditions to avenge the slaughter of their missions, but after 1842 they had learned their lesson: they made no further attempt to conquer Afghanistan and turn it into a fully subject 'princely state' like those of the British empire of India, let alone into a British province. Instead, the British reverted to a variety of methods intended to keep Afghanistan within their 'sphere of influence', or at least out of Russia's; notably bribes to Afghan rulers, khans, and tribes, and when these failed, punitive expeditions, whether to avenge an act of banditry, deal with a menacing outbreak of Sufi 'religious fanaticism' or warn against a movement towards alliance with Russia. But these expeditions were of limited scale and intent. As Kipling makes his British commander-in-chief say on launching one of them: 'I don't think we need keep the ladies waiting any longer. We can settle the rest over the cigars. It's punishment – not war.'[18]

The Russians by contrast went on battering away at Chechnya and Daghestan for more than thirty years, employing literally hundreds of thousands of troops to this end, and weakening their army correspondingly in other areas. Tens of thousands of lives and hundreds of millions of roubles were expended to conquer an area only a fraction the size of Afghanistan. In the 1840s, the number of Russian troops was increased to some 200,000, or almost a third of the entire effective army; the final defeat of Shamil by Bariatinsky took around 300,000 men. This is five times the largest total number of British (as opposed to Indian Army) troops ever deployed in the whole of British India before 1941 – and Britain's military establishment in India was by far the largest colonial force of any of the West European empires.[19]

Was this simply innate Russian brutality and bull-headed expansionism? In the case of Yermolov, perhaps; but Nicholas I showed in his dealings with the Turks, Persians and Central Asians that he knew very well when not to press his luck, and when to carry out a tactical retreat. Moreover, many of his subordinates also knew very well what they were facing in the Caucasus, and that its conquest would take many years. In the words of a famous memorandum of 1828 by Yermolov's chief-of-staff, General Veliaminov:

> The Caucasus may be likened to a mighty fortress, strong by nature, artificially protected by military works, and defended by a numerous

garrison. Only thoughtless men would attempt to take such a strong-hold by storm. A wise commander would see the necessity of having recourse to military art, and would lay his parallels, advance by sap and mine, and so master the place.[20]

The reasons why the Russians felt they had to take Daghestan and Chechnya are threefold, and in different forms, all are applicable today. The first is that they had in fact tried sphere-of-influence tactics and they had broken down. This has recurred again and again in Western dealings with the Muslim world, most notably in our own time. The various Russian client rulers in Daghestan, largely deprived of the low-level warfare which had been their principal *raison d'être*, and simultaneously introduced to a variety of hitherto unknown infidel luxuries, notably alcohol, rapidly became so disgustingly decadent that they lost the respect of their subjects – whom they also had to tax more heavily than ever to pay for those luxuries. The result sooner or later was religious revolt.

Today, corruption as such is not the issue, since it would be very difficult to say whether 'pro-Russian' regimes in the CIS are, or are not, more corrupt than the various nationalist ones have been; but the fact that an overtly pro-Russian regime is apt to lose the respect of its subjects has of course been of key importance in pushing former Communist regimes in a nationalist direction and undermining Russian hopes of hegemony.

The second reason is 'banditry', in this context not a crime, but both a social tradition and social obligation for younger males and a form of social and national resistance: the client rulers of the Eastern Caucasus (in Daghestan; the Chechens had no khans) before the1820s often could not have prevented their unruly subjects from raiding into Russian territory even if they had tried. The key role this factor played in imperial expansion, at least as an excuse, was set out forty years later by the Russian Foreign Minister, Prince Alexander Gorchakov, in his famous circular of 1864 to European governments concerning Russian expansion in Central Asia – a circular whose language was deliberately intended to appeal to the experience and the imperial and racial prejudices of his British and French counterparts. They themselves had indeed frequently used similar language, as had the Americans of his day, when hunting for excuses to suppress the American Indians of the Western frontier and take their land. In all these cases, an element of genuine justification was mixed with a large quantity of hypocrisy, greed and opportunism:

> The position of Russia in Central Asia is that of all civilised states which are brought into contact with half-savage, nomad populations, possessing no fixed social organisation.
>
> In such cases, it always happens that the more civilised State is forced, in the interests of the security of its frontier and its commercial relations, to exercise a certain ascendancy over those whom their

turbulent and unsettled character make most undesirable neighbours.

First there are raids and acts of pillage to put down. To put a stop to them, the tribes on the frontier have to be reduced to a state of more or less perfect submission… It is a peculiarity of Asiatics to respect nothing but visible and palpable force…

Such has been the fate of every country which has found itself in a similar position. The United States in America, France in Algeria, Holland in her colonies, England in India – all have been irresistibly forced, less by ambition than by imperious necessity, into this onward movement where the greatest difficulty is to know where to stop…[21]

Tolstoy, writing in a very different spirit, agreed only in placing Russia's crimes in the Caucasus in a general context of European military imperialism. In his words, what happened there was

what always happens when a state, having large-scale military strength, enters into relations with primitive, small peoples, living their own independent life. Under the pretext of self-defence (even though attacks are always provoked by the powerful neighbour), or the pretext of civilising the ways of a savage people (even though that savage people is living a life incomparably better and more peacable than the 'civilisers'), or else under some other pretext, the servants of large military states commit all sorts of villainy against small peoples, while maintaining that one cannot deal with them otherwise.

That was the situation in the Caucasus … when Russian military commanders, seeking to win distinction for themselves and appropriate the spoils of war, invaded peaceful lands, ravaged villages, killed hundreds of people, raped women, rustled thousands of cattle, and then blamed the tribesmen for their attacks on Russian possessions.[22]

The factor of banditry from the Chechen side did, however, genuinely play an important role in our own time. As noted in part I, the precipitating factor, in the escalating indirect Russian intervention in Chechnya which began in July 1994, and led to the military invasion of December, was the series of bus hijackings by Chechen armed criminals in the preceding months. If these had not occurred, then a Russian invasion would not have happened when and as it did, and conceivably would not have occurred at all.

But in the 1820s as in 1994, a third factor was also present: a vital geopolitical and strategic interest, or what was seen as one. It was also this that distinguished the Russian dilemmas over the Caucasus from those of the British over Afghanistan. The latter country lay on the periphery of the British empire and was backed by no major Muslim power. As a number of studies have suggested, India throughout the nineteenth century was surprisingly peripheral to the strategic thinking of most British governments, and the 'Russian threat' to India was generally taken with a pinch of salt in Whitehall. The

Eastern Caucasus by contrast lay on the edge of Russia's two main lines of communication to the Transcaucasus, the Caspian coastal road via Derbent to Baku, and the Georgian Military Highway from Vladikavkaz to Tiflis (Tbilisi).

Moreover, the Russians knew well that in any future war with Turkey (Persia ceased to be even a regional great power after the 1820s), the Chechens and Daghestanis would undoubtedly strike at Russia's rear at the first sign of an Ottoman victory. With Russia either on the military offensive against Turkey, as in the nineteenth century, or on the defensive, as today (in a general geopolitical sense, of course, rather than a directly military one), the position of the Eastern Caucasus becomes of key concern to Moscow.

Today, the issue also remains lines of communication; with Chechnya fully independent, the geographical connection of Daghestan to the Russian Federation would become thoroughly eccentric. But even more important of course is the fate of the oil pipeline from Azerbaijan through Chechnya north to the Russian port of Novorossiisk, the rival to which is the plan for a new pipeline through Georgia to Turkey. The chief regional protagonists are the same as they were 150 years ago: Russia and Turkey, the latter however now backed by the USA rather than the British empire. And seen from Moscow, the ultimate issue is the same: hegemony over the Caucasus.

Four Hundred Years of Deportation and Ethnic Cleansing

During the decades of Shamil's war, an equally fierce and equally geo-politically vital struggle was being waged against Russian conquest by the Circassian and Turkic peoples of the north-western Caucasus, the results of which were to be tragic for them and to have important results for our own day. Their wars are much less known in the West than those of Shamil, mainly because the lack of a strong Sufi movement in the western Caucasus meant also that there was never a single leader or unifying force. Each clan or group of clans tended to fight separately, despite the efforts of semi-official British agents to unite them against the Russians.[23]

Final Russian victory in the western Caucasus in the 1860s brought a different and crueller fate to its peoples than was the case in the east. In Chechnya and Daghestan, after the surrender of Shamil there was no attempt to drive most of the local peoples from their homes. In the western Caucasus, by contrast, the Tsarist authorities launched a campaign of harassment, destruction, confiscation and intermittent massacre which by the end of the 1860s had driven the greater part of its indigenous peoples into exile in the Ottoman empire, where many died of disease in refugee camps. The Russian military authorities gave the Mountaineers the choice of leaving or of moving to the North Caucasus steppes where they could be easily supervised, taxed and conscripted. Most chose flight.

It has been estimated that up to 1.2 million Circassians and Turkic

Caucasians (Karachai and others) left, to be replaced by Russian, Cossack, Georgian and to a lesser extent Armenian settlers. The Circassian peoples, together with a smaller number of Chechens, are today to be found all over Turkey and the Middle East. They play an especially distinguished role in Jordan, where they comprise the royal guard and many of the senior ranks of the army (two Jordanian Chechens became the 'foreign ministers' of Dzhokhar Dudayev). The number of Abkhaz is estimated to have dropped by more than half in the 1860s.[24]

The 'ethnic cleansing' of the Circassians, Abkhaz, Shapsugs and others forms part of a tragic sequence of such events in the region, by which the great powers (Turkey and Russia or the Soviet Union) on either side suppressed, expelled or physically eliminated minorities whom they feared might act as fifth columns for their enemies.

The first such event in modern history was in the early sixteenth century, when the Ottomans under Bayezid and Selim I defeated the Turkic Shias rebels, including the famous Qizilbash, who had fought with the Turkic Safavids of Iran in their wars with the Ottoman empire. Many of the Shia Turkic tribesmen of eastern Anatolia were massacred, and tens of thousands of others were expelled or fled from the Ottoman lands to Iran and the Moghul empire (I met some of their descendants among the present-day great landowners of the Pakistani Punjab).

The process continued with the Russian conquest of the Transcaucasus in the early nineteenth century, after which tens of thousands of Muslim Turks and Kurds moved or were expelled west into the Ottoman territories, to be replaced by Armenians moving east to the protection of the Christian Tsar. In the 1860s, the Russians drove out the West Caucasians largely (though not only)[25] because they were the ones close to the Turks and therefore the greatest strategic danger. The Chechens and Daghestanis, now separated from potential Turkish aid by a broad band of secure Russian territory, presented no such strategic threat, and could be left in relative peace.

The single bloodiest episode in this ghastly game of tit for tat was of course the Armenian genocide of 1915, when the Ottoman government, fearing Armenian revolt behind their lines as the Russian armies advanced, and determined to make eastern Anatolia a purely Turkish region, fell upon its Armenian subjects. Up to 1.5 million were killed or starved to death in the resulting massacres and deportations.

Even then, 'ethnic cleansing' in the region was far from over. It culminated in Stalin's deportations of 1944 – and, as we have seen, it continues among the peoples of the Transcaucasus in our own day.

The North Caucasus Under Soviet Rule

As noted earlier, the first major Soviet deportation from the Caucasus, with attendant massacres, came under Lenin, and was of ethnic Russians: the

Kuban and Terek Cossacks who had played a key role in the White armies in the Russian Civil War. Stalin's deportations of the Chechens, Ingush, Karachai, Balkars, Meskhetian Turks and Crimean Tatars in 1943 and 1944 also claimed hundreds of thousands of victims, executed or dead of hunger, exhaustion and disease. The official reason given for the deportations was 'collaboration with the Nazis', but it seems likely that in fact Stalin, with his innate savagery and Communist ruthlessness, and his own roots in the Caucasus, was both taking revenge for past revolts and was looking forward to the next planned move against Turkey.

Pressure on Turkey, with the threat of war clearly in the background, was initiated by Stalin even before the Second World War was over, with demands for territorial concessions (Kars and Ardahan, taken by Russia in 1878, surrendered by Lenin in 1921) and Soviet rights over the Bosphorus. This policy was pressed until the USA, succeeding an exhausted Britain as the great power of the region, in 1946 threw its weight behind Turkey and made it clear to Moscow that it would back Turkey against Soviet atttack.[26]

It would have seemed perfectly natural to Stalin to prepare for this by removing all the peoples who might have helped the Turks in the event of war (the Karachai, Balkars, Kalmyks, Tatars and Meskhetians all being Turkic peoples, while the Chechens were old Turkish allies with a strong, loyal and bitterly anti-Soviet diaspora in Turkey); just as on the other side, he assiduously wooed the Armenian diaspora in these years and encouraged its leaders to think that he would reconquer their ancient Anatolian homelands for Soviet Armenia.

The argument for an anti-Turkish strategy applies with particular force to the 125,000 Ahiska, or 'Meskhetian Turks' of Georgia. These had had no contact with the Nazis whatsoever – but they did live right up against the post-1921 Turkish border. Meanwhile, of course, Stalin was also trying to undermine Turkey from within by encouraging Kurdish revolt. This strategy was followed by the Soviet Union in subsequent decade. It was a major contributing factor to the Kurdish revolt against Turkey, and reportedly helped make the reputation of the then NKVD (later KGB) General Heidar Aliev, now President of Azerbaijan.

Active and Passive Resistance, 1859–1944

The surrender of Shamil at Gunib in 1859 ended large scale armed resistance in the Eastern Caucasus for fifty-eight years, but unlike the reaction of the Azeris, the Chechens' will to resist was not broken. Disturbances took place throughout 1862 and 1863, and in 1864, after the arrest of Kunta Haji, a meeting of his adherents at the village of Shali (notable in the war of the 1990s as a centre of Chechen resistance) was broken up by Russian troops, leaving some two hundred dead. Some five thousand Murids and their families were deported to Turkey.

In 1877–8, the war between Russia and the Ottoman empire led to a new rising in Chechnya and Daghestan, which was brutally suppressed, leading to fresh deportations and emigration. After this, both the Naqshbandis and the Qadiris turned from open work to clandestine organisation and spiritual purification of their societies – but, it would seem, with the goal of ultimate revolt and independence always in mind. In 1905, the revolution throughout Russia led to more disturbances and arrests in Chechnya. Finally, in 1917–21, the collapse of the Tsarist regime and the Bolshevik seizure of power led to the last common struggle for Islam and independence which united Chechens and Daghestanis behind the banners of Naqshbandi Sufism. The two inspirers of the revolt were two Naqshbandi Sufi sheikhs, Najmuddin of Hotso, an Avar from Daghestan, and Ujun Haji, a Chechen. The nominal chief of the revolt was a great-grandson of Shamil, Said Beg, who returned from Turkey to take up his ancestor's banner.[27]

The anti-Bolshevik uprising of August 1920 followed three years in which the Mountaineers had usually been allied with the Red Army against the Russian White forces which controlled most of the North Caucasus lowlands and the main towns of the region. In May 1918, the Chechens and Daghestanis had set up a North Caucasus Republic, recognised by the Central Powers, which fought against the White armies. The attempts of General Denikin's forces to suppress the Mountaineers (which included numerous atrocities) diverted the Whites from their struggle with the Bolsheviks, and contributed to their defeat.

By the summer of 1920, the Whites had been driven from the region and were approaching their final defeat. In April 1920, the Red Army, having occupied coastal Daghestan, entered Azerbaijan and overthrew the independent government there, cutting the Mountaineers off from potential aid from the south. A year too late, the Sufis of the mountains turned their attention to the Bolshevik threat, which was represented not just by the Red Russian forces, but also at this time by a small but distinguished group of Caucasian national Communists like Najmuddin Samursky, who fought hard to bring the Caucasus into the Soviet Union (the great majority of them were to be executed later under Stalin). In setting up Bolshevik rule in the region, they benefited both from local hatred of the Whites and from the Communist repression of the White Cossacks, which included confiscating some of their land and 'returning' it to the Chechens and other peoples.

The mutual hatred of the new intelligentsia and the traditionalists was however bitter: as witness Ujun Haji's words, 'I am weaving a rope to hang engineers, students, and in general all those who write from left to right' (in Russian, not Arabic). It has endured to this day in the loathing of the present Soviet-educated Chechen liberal intelligentsia (what there is of it) for the Islamising tendencies of the Dudayev regime and its successors.[28]

The full-scale war which resulted lasted for nine months; several Red units were completely destroyed, and in a historical irony, a Communist force stood a long siege in Shamil's old stronghold of Gunib. In May 1921, the last rebel auls were stormed by the Red Army with the help of modern artillery and aeroplanes. Najmuddin of Hotso, however, remained at large in the mountains until 1925, when he was captured and executed. In the view of some analysts, this war, perhaps the fiercest local struggle in the whole complex of conflicts which made up the Russian Civil War, may have prevented the Red Army from launching planned incursions into Iran and the Middle East, with unpredictable consequences.

Meanwhile, in 1921 the Soviet government, with Stalin as its local representative, had set up a Soviet Mountain Republic embracing the Chechens, Ingush, Ossetes, Karachai and Balkars, but omitting the Daghestanis, who were organised separately. In 1924, this was broken up and separate autonomous regions were organised. In 1936, the Chechen–Ingush region was raised to the status of a republic. Tragically, however, it became an Autonomous Republic and was kept as part of the Russian Federation, rather than being given status as a full Union Republic like Azerbaijan and Georgia – something which would probably not have prevented Russian interference in Chechnya after 1991, but by avoiding the later threat from the Chechens to 'Russian territorial integrity' would almost certainly have avoided the invasion and full-scale war which began three years later.

In 1929, renewed disturbances broke out in Chechnya and elsewhere in the Caucasus in protest against agricultural collectivisation, the suppression of which required the deployment of tens of thousands of Soviet troops. Small-scale guerrilla (or, as the Russians and Soviets have always called it, 'bandit') activity continued until 1935, and after a brief period of quiescence, flared up again in 1937 after an NKVD operation in which thousands of suspected Chechen oppositionists were arrested and executed.

The revolt of the Chechens is striking when compared to the passivity of many of the other peoples in the Soviet Union in the face of Stalinist terror. It is also great interest that this was the first revolt to be led not by traditional religious or clan figures like Ujun Haji, but by new secular leaders – indeed, by leading members of the Chechen Communist Party, who fifteen years earlier had played a major part in Ujun Haji's defeat. These included Mayrbek Sheripov, former General Procurator and from a distinguished Bolshevik background.

The point is that they had acted then out of a genuine hatred of Muslim obscurantism, and a belief in Soviet progress and egalitarianism, but also, and most importantly, in a belief that Lenin's promises concerning the genuine autonomy of the non-Russian peoples, and respect for them by the Russians, would be honoured. In this of course they were no different from many other pro-Soviet secular Muslim intellectuals from other nationalities (Sultan Galiev being the most famous), who were later to be cruelly betrayed and massacred by Stalin. However, the Chechen Communists did not wait passively to be massacred; when they saw that Stalin intended to oppress them, they followed their ancestors and took to the hills.

In January 1940, a former leading Chechen Communist intellectual, Hassan Israilov, led a rising in the Chechen mountains, which gathered pace after the German invasion of the Soviet Union in June 1941. The Germans, however, were stopped by the Soviet army west of Grozny, which they bombed. A few dozen or hundred (figures differ) Chechen fighters were able to make their way across the front lines and join the Germans. These included the later distinguished Chechen émigré historian and writer Abdurrahman Avtorkhanov.

The surrender at Stalingrad in February 1943 began the German withdrawal from the North Caucasus; and eight months later, with most of the area firmly in Soviet hands and the Chechen rebels driven from their remaining strongholds, Stalin launched the operation to deport the entire Chechen, Ingush, Kalmyk, Karachai and Balkar peoples, beginning with the Karachai in November 1943 (the Pontic Greeks had already been deported in 1939, followed by the Volga Germans in August 1941). On 22 February 1944, tens of thousands of NKVD troops assembled and deported at one hour's notice the vast majority of the indigenous Chechen and Ingush populations. This time, 'pacification' was supposed to be final. The nationalities involved were struck out of all Soviet official documents, and vanished from the 'Great Soviet Encyclopaedia', as if they had never been.[29]

According to the most credible figures, 478,479 Chechens and Ingush were loaded on to trains in February 1944; when Khrushchev publicly revealed what had happened, 400,478 were later officially reported as having been deported – which is a strong suggestion that the other 78,000 died en route or soon after they were unloaded, freezing and starving, in the Kazakh steppe. Thousands never made it to the trains at all. In half a dozen mountain villages, from where it was difficult to move the population in mid-winter, the NKVD troops herded them into mosques and barns and killed them all. Patients in hospitals were also killed. A few Chechen rebel bands held on in the mountains, attacking Russian troops and settlers, and preventing the latter from establishing themselves in the mountain regions.

The report from Colonel Gveshiani, the NKVD officer responsible for the massacre of the people of Khaibakh, to his ultimate boss, Beria, reads simply, 'In view of the impossibility of transportation and the necessity of fulfilling on schedule the goals of operation "Mountaineer", it was necessary to liquidate more than 700 inhabitants of the village of Khaibakh.' In return, Beria wrote to Gveshiani announcing his decoration and promotion. Stalin for his part officially congratulated the NKVD on its 'successful fulfilment of state tasks in the North Caucasus'.[30] (It is worth pointing out that all three men were ethnic Georgians and convinced Soviet Communists, since the Chechens, and some of their Western sympathisers, have got into the habit of calling the deportations a 'Russian atrocity'. Russia has been responsible for numerous other atrocities in the Caucasus – but this particular one was not among them. It was a Soviet and Stalinist, not a specifically Russian action.)

Murad Nashkoyev, an elderly Chechen journalist, described to me how his younger brother, then a baby, was picked up by a Soviet soldier and thrown

into a truck beside his mother in February 1944. His father had been killed
the previous year, fighting with the Chechen rebels.

> In my cattle-truck, half of us died during the journey. There was no
> toilet – we had to cut a hole in the floor, and that was also how we got
> rid of the corpses. I suppose we could have escaped that way, but
> the men did not want to leave their families. When we arrived in
> Kazakhstan, the ground was frozen hard, and we thought we would all
> die. It was the German exiles who helped us to survive – they had
> already been there for several years...
>
> From the moment we arrived, people were writing to the Central Com-
> mittee in Moscow, saying that we had been deported unjustly, and from
> 1953 – Stalin's death – we began to send back individual men, who came
> to Chechnya secretly, with false papers, and acted as scouts. Of course,
> some were caught, and at first, they were severely punished; later, not.
>
> In 1956, when they opened the camps, there was a big push to return
> – some families assembled in Akmolinsk by arrangement, just bought
> tickets and went – thirteen wagons full, with five or seven families in
> each... Of course it wasn't that simple – we'd planned it carefully, col-
> lected money from the whole Chechen community, and we paid huge
> bribes to the police, the KGB and the railway authorities. We were act-
> ing as an advance guard for the rest of the nation.
>
> They didn't finally stop us till we got to Mozdok [in North Ossetia,
> about fifty miles from Chechnya]. They held us there for several weeks,
> then by order of Khrushchev, they let us go, and the next year the rest
> of the people followed. You have to grant it to Khrushchev, he didn't fol-
> low the old Russian policy of force, there was a real move at that time
> to get rid of the memory of Stalin, and we exploited that.[31]

The stark monument to the deportations dedicated by the Dudayev gov-
ernment on their fiftieth anniversary, in 1994, and largely destroyed during the
Russian assault on Grozny less than a year later, was made up chiefly of old
Chechen gravestones from cemeteries demolished after 1944 and used by the
Soviet authorities and Russian settlers to pave roads and build houses (as they
were doing in Latvia at about this time with the tombstones of my own Baltic
German ancestors).

On the surrounding walls, tablets showed the villages and places where
massacres took place – Khaibakh, 700 killed; Urus Martan hospital, 62 killed
– and the Beria documents quoted above. In the centre, beside an open stone
Koran, a huge concrete fist held an upraised sword – forgiveness for past
wrongs not playing a major part in the the Chechen tradition. The inscription
read: 'We will not weep; we will not weaken; we will not forget.'

Return from Exile

T. E. Lawrence once described life in the desert as 'the deepest and most biting of all social disciplines'. For the Chechens, the years of exile from 1944 to 1957 tempered in them that steely national discipline which became apparent in the war of 1994–6. More even than the wars of Shamil in the nineteenth century, the memory of the deportation became the central defining event in modern Chechen history. One reason for its continuing impact is that, as Murad Naskoyev's account implies, it involved not just intense suffering but intense *humiliation*, of a people who must surely count among the proudest in the world. Another reason is simply that it is comparatively recent. Almost all older Chechens lived through it; almost all middle-aged ones, including the entire present generation of Chechen leaders, were either taken to Central Asia as small children or were born there.

The way in which the Chechens preserved their culture, language, identity and especially spirit of independence in exile and the camps is deeply impressive. Solzhenitsyn, who witnessed it during his own exile, paid tribute to it in a famous passage of the *Gulag Archipelago* (which will be quoted below). Ethnic solidarity and kinship-based mutual support, as well as a sheer determination to survive and a very high birth-rate, meant that extraordinarily, despite the terrible losses of 1944, more Chechens came back from exile than were deported.

Most impressive, too, was the way in which, after Stalin's death in 1953, the Chechens organised their own return. As described above by Mr Nashkoyev, they and other deported peoples effectively forced the Soviet government's hand over the issue. Unlike the Crimean Tatars and the Meskhetian Turks, most of whose land and homes had already been occupied by Russian, Ukrainian and Georgian settlers, all the deported North Caucasian people were in the end allowed back. This was possible in part because such new colonists as there were in their lands had mainly stuck to the cities and lowlands.

A sixty-seven-year-old Russian woman in Grozny, Lydia Leonidovna, whom I interviewed in a cellar in Grozny during the bombing of December 1994, described what it was like in the city after the Chechens had been deported:

> Before the war, we Russians who lived in Grozny had nothing against the Chechens – on the contrary, it was thanks to them that we were spared hunger in the 1930s, when so much of Russia, and especially the Cossack areas, were starving...
>
> I was here for the first part of the war – so you see, this is the second time I've been bombed – though the first time by my own government, for heaven's sake... My family were eventually evacuated from here, and only returned in 1946. With the Chechens gone, the city was eerie – it was boring, empty, frightening, without people – like a desert. And we had been used to a lively life. Then after that, masses of new people

322 The Chechen Victory

arrived, from Russia, Ukraine – they were simply thrown together from everywhere. No one knew anyone else. Grozny was a depressing place, compared to how it had been before.

In my conversation with Haji Mahomet (Willi Weisserth), he described his return to his village:

> When we came back in 1958, all the villages were empty or Russian-occupied. The village here used to be on a hill, with a hot spring. When the Chechens were deported, they put Russians, or rather Ukrainians, there…
>
> In the old cemetery, there was a small shrine, the mausoleum of a saint. The new settlers destroyed it, and dug two metres into the ground underneath it, looking for treasure. They destroyed all the graves…
>
> The Russians began to leave as soon as we came back. They seemed to be afraid of us, and perhaps they even had a bad conscience. Most slipped away in the night, and the local authorities lent them lorries. Within a few months, they had all gone.[32]

Lydia Leonidovna's words about how the new Russian population in Chechnya was thrown together also suggests one reason why they left so easily. For not less remarkable than the way they forced their own return was the Chechen success, through what can only be called an exercise in sheer national will power, in gaining the psychological, economic and finally even political ascendancy over the Russian population in the region. This was despite the fact that in 1957 the Russian-speakers had outnumbered them – as well, of course, as possessing a complete monopoly of local political power and the backing of the Soviet state and army. Moreover, in 1957, in what seems to have been an attempt to play at 'divide and rule' and dilute Chechnya ethnically, two traditionally Cossack (or until the eighteenth century, mainly Nogai Tatar) districts were detached from Stavropol Region and added to the Checheno-Ingush ASSR.

Although for ten years after their return from exile, the highest job they had been able to aspire to had been that of collective farm chairman, by the advent of Gorbachev, the Chechens in most fields were effectively in control. An important event in this context was the mass demonstrations of 1973, which began in support of the Ingush demands for the return of land by the Ossetes, but rapidly came to include demands – which were largely granted – for a bigger share of local official positions. And this in the depths of the 'era of stagnation'! The Chechen victory was not absolute, however, and it was not until 1989 that a Chechen, Doku Zavgayev, became First Secretary of the republican Communist Party. Moreover, the possibilities for the Chechens of achieving a formal and official (as opposed to unofficial, informal and in large part illegal) expression of their culture and local dominance had remained of course highly restricted.[33]

As to numbers, though by the late 1940s the sufferings of the deportation had reduced them to barely 400,000, by the census of 1989 there were 775,980 Chechens living in the Chechen-Ingush Autonomous Republic (58 per cent of the population), with more than 300,000 living elsewhere in the then Soviet Union. In the 1970s and 1980s, the Chechen birth-rate per thousand had been between 31 and 40, while the Russian had dropped to 12. Their proportion of the urban population in Chechnya increased from a mere 9 per cent in 1959 to 42.1 per cent in 1989.[34]

Dr Ilya Grinchenko, today a liberal sociologist in Vladivostok, but in the 1950s a Russian child of Cossack ancestry in Grozny, gave me another picture of the Chechens' return, describing how the local Russians attempted to prevent it: in July 1958 there was even a Russian riot in Grozny in which the railway station was occupied (to block the trains bringing the Chechens back), the regional Communist Party headquarters was sacked, Chechen returnees were attacked, and the army had to be sent in to restore order,

> But by the 1970s, the Chechens got the upper hand. We had always been frightened of them – in school, they always stuck together and made us feel like foreigners. Unlike us Russians, they have tremendously strong family and clan links. Every Chechen is a member of a clan (teip), it helps him and he is completely loyal to it. Also, they soon began to outnumber us. For Chechens in those days, it was common to have six or more children – we heard that their elders went round encouraging them to do this – whereas for Russians, to have more than three was already uncommon, and since then of course it has dropped even further.
>
> But what really gave the Chechens their chance was the decay of the Soviet organs of power. As the Soviet state became more and more corrupt under Brezhnev, and the police got weaker, the Chechens moved into the cracks. Soon several powerful Chechen criminal clans had a very strong presence in Moscow, with influence on central ministries, and after that there was nothing anyone locally could do to stop them. When I returned home to Grozny in 1974 from my military service, I saw how powerful the Chechens had become, and I decided to leave. It was already clear that there was nothing there for Russians.[35]

10 'We are Free and Equal like Wolves': Social and Cultural Roots of the Chechen Victory

> One of them asked me what they had really come to achieve in Sicily, these Italian volunteers. 'They are coming to teach us good manners,' I replied, 'but they won't succeed, for we are gods.' I don't think he understood me, but he smiled and went on his way. So I reply to you as well, my dear Chevalley: the Sicilians will never wish to change, for the simple reason that they believe they are perfect.
>
> Giuseppe Tomasi di Lampedusa, *The Leopard*

> God made man – Colt made him equal.
>
> Saying in the American West

Writing at a Chechen headquarters in southern Grozny on 18 January 1995, I entered as an aside in my notebook: 'Those thugs in the Presidential Guard, who I always thought a mixture of the brutish, the sinister, and the mildly ridiculous, are looking awfully good today. I always thought they were like the Georgian paramilitaries. They're not that way at all.'

A key reason why I, most other observers, and of course more importantly, the Russian government, underestimated the Chechen capacity for resistance was precisely that the Dudayev regime had looked so ramshackle, its 'troops' so criminalised, unimpressive and disliked by the mass of the Chechen population. In appearance, Dudayev's guards had indeed looked just like the Georgian National Guards and 'Mkhedrioni' who had put up such a deeply unimpressive fight in Abkhazia, and the rag-tag private armies in Azerbaijan which in 1991–4 were regularly scattered by the Armenians.

What we missed were the deep underlying strengths of Chechen society and the Chechen tradition, as tempered and hardened by the historical experiences of the past two hundred years. Unfortunately, these have not helped the Chechens to create the institutions of a modern, let alone a democratic state; indeed they have worked against it. But they have given this people the most formidable capacity for national armed resistance – made them in fact one of the great martial peoples of modern history. The true face of Chechnya was not the presidential guard – which was unfortunately very much the way I described it – but a small column of Chechen volunteers I encountered in the ruins of central Grozny in January 1995, marching towards the roar of the guns, into a battle against apparently hopeless odds, cheering as they went past us. One old man raised his fist and cried 'No Pasaran!' – the kind of soldiers of whom most commanders can only dream.[1]

A small Chechen volunteer group, made up of friends and neighbours with no regular military training, surrounded, cut off from its fellows and its superior officers (even assuming that such officers in the usual sense existed among the Chechens), hopelessly outnumbered and outgunned, under intense fire, fought on to the end essentially for three reasons: complete solidarity and mutual reliance among its fighters; a conviction of their own superiority ('one Chechen is worth ten Russian tanks or a hundred Russian soldiers'); and a belief in the absolute national and moral justification for their fight.

What makes the Chechen victory of such striking interest from the point of view of military history is the way in which the Chechens have combined the best qualities of both 'primitive' and 'civilised' armed forces (with no connotations of either insult or praise, but simply in terms of traditional classifications).

The Chechen forces in the latest war have been 'primitive' in the sense that the great majority of them have been spontaneously generated on the basis of informal social groups and traditions, and not through action by the state; that they lack a military hierarchy and organisation, formal training, formal commanders and tactical doctrine, and also lack most of what are considered essential arms for modern war – air-power, armour, heavy artillery, electronic intelligence. In terms of their lack of capacity for state military organisation and mobilisation, one would almost have described the Chechens of 1994 as a semi-tribal, loosely 'anarchistic' people, and therefore, to use a phrase coined by Professor Turney-High, 'below the military horizon'.[2]

Indeed the spirit in which the Dudayev forces and the Russian-backed Chechen opposition approached their battles with each other between 1993 and 1994 (for example the 'assault' of the Dudayev troops on the opposition centre of Znamenskoye in September 1994, which was beaten off very easily) did show some of the features associated with the warfare of many primitive tribes, more about display than actual fighting. (As for example, 'the militarist displays in the "nothing fights" of the Tiwi or the Dani, which may be better described as mobilised confrontation than as combat'.)[3] There was a strong unwillingness to come to close quarters and either inflict or suffer heavy casualties, and instead a desire to intimidate the enemy by a show of determination and numbers, with the hope of getting them to withdraw or persuading their allies to abandon them. The ineffectiveness of the Dudayev fighters in these operations led me to underrate them very badly – and no doubt had the same effect on Russian military planners.

For of course the whole point was that the unwillingness and restraint shown was an unwillingness to kill *other Chechens*, because for reasons both historical and anthropological (the blood-feud) there are extremely deep inhibitions against Chechen killing Chechen, except in the semi-formalised context of the 'blood feud'. In the words of Professor A. Vachargayev in September 1994, 'neither side wants to fire first, because whichever is the first to shed Chechen blood will lose prestige and support.'[4]

It is interesting in this connection that after the Chechens reconquered Grozny in August 1996, while there certainly were revenge killings of Chechens for collaborating with the Russians, there were not nearly as many as the bloodiness of the previous conflict, or analogies with other such conflicts, would have suggested. One reason of course may have been that many of these people had been in some sense sitting on the fence, and passing information or protection to the separatist side.

To take three examples from my visit to both sides of the lines in May 1995. In the headquarters of the Russian-backed government in Grozny, a Chechen youth who was a supporter of that government and a relative of the then Prime Minister, Salambek Khadjiev, told me that his family in Gudermes had given shelter to several relatives and even friends of relatives who had fought for the separatists and were in danger of arrest by the Russian army. On the other side, my host in the mountain village of Haji Yurt in the same month, Islam Dunayev, who had been a very brave and determined fighter on the separatist side in the defence of Argun in January and February, later joined the pro-Russian side, for reasons that are not clear.[5] By December 1996, at least, nothing had happened to him as a result – I hope that this has stayed the case. Finally, there are the words of the separatist deputy commander in Shali, Said Hassan, when I asked him whether it wasn't terribly dangerous for him to go on living at home even after the Russians had (formally at least) 'occupied' the town, since there were surely Chechen informers in Shali who knew him and could betray him to the Russians. He replied,

> Everyone knows who the FSK [Russian intelligence] man here is, and he knows that we know. He wouldn't dare betray someone from his own town. On the other hand, we won't kill him, as long as he doesn't harm us – we don't want to quarrel with his family if there's no need. So what does he tell his masters? Maybe he betrays people from other villages, maybe he just makes things up. I couldn't say.

The exception that proved this rule of the reluctance of Chechen to kill Chechen was the determined and successful attack of the Dudayev forces on those of Ruslan Labazanov in Argun in October 1994, because Labazanov, by himself killing members of the presidential guard and their relatives, had established a blood-feud between himself and the presidential forces. This was then fought out for essentially traditional Chechen motives rather than those of a modern ideological 'civil war'.

The invasion of the hated Russians provoked an utterly different set of responses, and it was not only the motive that changed but the mode of fighting. According to the classical patterns of war, one would have expected such forces as the Chechens to avoid direct confrontations with a superior enemy, relying instead on 'evasive' tactics of ambush, withdrawal and concealment. Instead, despite their overwhelming inferiority in heavy weaponry, the

Chechen separatists repeatedly sought out occasions to confront the enemy in head-on battle – and eventually triumphed, thanks not only to vastly higher morale and courage, but also to some really superb staff-work and planning. They have also stood their ground and fought for weeks and months on end under intense bombardment, have managed complicated operations involving regimental-size forces, and have kept considerable numbers of men permanently in the field – all of them achievements very uncharacteristic of primitive warfare.

As the reference to staff-work suggests, one reason for the Chechen success was that a good many of them had previously had some training in a modern army, that of the Soviet Union, and had learned something about modern weapons and tactics. This was above all true of the Chechen forces' chief-of-staff, Colonel Aslan Maskhadov, formerly a Soviet artillery officer, who became a commander of genius (just as many of the leaders of tribal revolts against imperial Rome had previously served with the Roman auxiliaries and several FLN commandos in Algeria had fought with the French Army in Vietnam.)

However, when it comes to lesser commanders, and the bulk of the ordinary fighters, the factor of Soviet experience should not be exaggerated. For example, the other best-known and most effective Chechen commander, Shamil Basayev, had also served in the Soviet army, but as a fireman, and he told me that he had received no real military training as such at all when he led the Abkhaz volunteers to Abkhazia in 1992. Nor had most of the Chechen fighters I met during the war served in Soviet front-line units, in part of course because the Soviet army regarded the Chechens as unreliable.

The most surprising thing, however, was the way in which a society that had seemed before 11 December 1994 to be deeply divided – with the bulk of the population sullenly resentful of the 'government' and 'President' – put up such a magnificently united and resilient fight against invasion.

Aeneas with the RPG

A number of Russian anthropologists, including Dr Sergei Arutiunov and Dr Georgy Derluguian, have compared Chechen society to classical Hellas, in terms of a culture and ethnos which seemed and indeed was extremely divided and even anarchic, but which because of its underlying social structures and traditions proved capable of uniting formidably for war when threatened from outside. Dr Derluguian emphasises that like the classical Greeks (at least of Athens), the Chechens had long since got rid of their great aristocrats (who had not in any case been ethnic Chechens), and that also like them, the Chechens in time of peace have become a highly entrepreneurial people, very successful at their own kind of commerce (largely criminal, of course), and therefore not in fact 'primitive' in the popular sense of the word.[6] This analysis in part recalls analogies made by Robert Montagne and other

French anthropologists between classical Greece and the world of the Berbers.

As the event has proved, there is much truth in this analogy. However, at the time – and lacking deeper anthropological insights – Chechnya in the years 1992–4 suggested to me and other journalists rather a growing kind of 'bastard feudalism', in which the previous Soviet state and indeed social institutions were collapsing and people were seeking protection from mafia bosses and bandit chiefs in official uniform – except that the Chechen state could not even provide any 'uniforms'. This of course is not incompatible with successful private commerce, as long as certain rules and restraints are observed (as for example in mid-fifteenth-century England), but it does not suggest a society that could easily organise for united resistance.

This superficial view missed the deeper sources of Chechen solidarity and morale – but it was not entirely false, and if the Dudayev regime had gone on ruling for a few more years and Moscow had adopted a slower, more cautious and restrained policy, then it is entirely possible that a demoralised, exhausted and cynical Chechen population would have fallen back into Russia's arms, and settled for autonomy within the Russian Federation.

What actually happened when the Russians invaded is perhaps best summed up in a passage by Professor Anthony Wallace, in an essay entitled 'Psychological Preparations for War':

> All human societies, and the societies of many of the higher primates below man, are observed to exist alternately in two states. [Thus among the American Indians, Cherokee society had formally recognised structural poses of peace and war, while the Cheyenne recognised two main forms of social existence, peace and buffalo hunting.] In order for a society to shift from the relaxed to the mobilised state, the population must recognise a releasing stimulus, in response to which everyone promptly disposes of himself in accordance with a plan…
>
> The releasing stimulus is therefore apt to be – particularly in the case of mobilisation for war – a report that a certain kind of event has occurred to which a people with that character type will respond with anger, determination, fear or whatever affective state is desired by the communicating group.[7]

Or to quote Robert Montagne on the Berber tribal alliances of Morocco,

> Even if the confederation has, strictly speaking, no specific institutions other than a uniform body of customary law by which all members are bound, its solidarity is assured by the strength of the powerful feelings of unity and mutual obligation which emerge in times of conflict. Our [the French] military officers in the Middle Atlas have recognised this for a long time past. 'When you wish to pacify them,' Maurice Le Glay makes one of his heroes say in a novel, 'you will find before you a

scatter of humanity. You have to chase after each tent in order to talk to the head of each small family, and to establish any sort of control over them takes years. If you face them in battle though they fall upon you all at once and in vast numbers, and you wonder how you can possibly extricate yourself.[8]

Finally, there is a sriking passage by the Russian anthropologist Sergei Arutiunov about the Chechens:

> Chechnya was and is a society of military democracy. Chechnya never had any kings, emirs, princes or barons. Unlike other Caucasian nations, there was never feudalism in Chechnya. Traditionally, it was governed by a council of elders on the basis of consensus, but like all military democracies – like the Iroquois in America or the Zulu in southern Africa – Chechens retain the institution of military chief. In peacetime, they recognise no sovereign authority and may be fragmented into a hundred rival clans. However, in time of danger, when faced with aggression, the rival clans unite and elect a military leader. This leader may be known to everyone as an unpleasant personality, but is elected nonetheless for being a good general. While the war is on, this leader is obeyed.[9]

The Russian invasion of December 1994 was of course just such a 'releasing stimulus', sure to strike the most sensitive nerves of Chechen history and indeed of the personal memories of all those older Chechens who had experienced the deportation of 1944. And it only emphasises the tremendous power of these historical factors as a stimulus when one remembers that the other elements of Professor Wallace's equation are missing: given the weakness, the ineffectiveness and the incoherence of the Dudayev regime, there was in Chechnya no serious 'plan' for the mobilisation of the population, and no effective 'communicating group' to stir up the population to war. The Chechen war effort was overwhelmingly spontaneously generated by Chechen society.

At first sight, many younger Chechen fighters appear – and would certainly like to appear – as Homeric heroes, Achilles with a rocket-propelled grenade. It shows in their love of personal display – especially in clothes – their boasting and general swagger, their impatience with formal discipline. There is a Homeric aspect, too, to the tradition of the *djigit* common to most of the North Caucasian peoples and adopted by the Cossacks. Originally, this meant a showy piece of horsemanship, a form of dressage, in which the horse would be made to prance with its tail lifted and hooves held high off the ground. It was taken into the Russian language by the Cossacks and Russian imperial forces in the Caucasus, and came to have the general meaning of a 'hero', 'champion', or simply fine fellow. The Russians were especially impressed with the way that during actions Chechen horsemen would ride out and perform showy displays of horsemanship in front of the Russian lines and under Russian fire.

The visual aspect of this bravado was expressed perfectly in a photo-report on the Chechen War which appeared in *Paris-Match* in 1995, based on a series of portraits of Chechen fighters. Much criticised at the time for glamorising its subjects and placing them in carefully designed 'warrior' poses, it seemed to me accurate and valuable in that it portrayed its subjects exactly as they themselves would have wished to be portrayed. This element of archaic championship has indeed done much to add dash and élan to the Chechen fight, but it is of course only a small part of the story; for after all, a notorious aspect of most of Homer's heroes, as of many such archaic and 'primitive' warriors, is their willingness to turn and run when circumstances demand it; and what has been most notable about the Chechens has been their willingness to stand and fight. Moreover – and critically – Homer's heroes were kings and noblemen; the Chechens are by tradition an egalitarian people.

The Chechens then are archaic warriors schooled and trained in centuries-long influences of ethnic and/or tribal solidarity and duty, to which over the past two hundred years have also been added religious unity and national suffering and resistance. Rather than as the vainglorious, individualistic, aristocratic and unreliable Achilles, they have appeared as Hector, dying in defence of his family and homeland – or even more aptly as Aeneas, a hero adopted by Virgil, given a set of Roman virtues of fortitude and stoicism, and sent out into an epic of duty, carrying his father on his back like the burden of his national tradition and its iron demands. Rather than archaic Greek heroes, the Chechens are classical Greek hoplites, held in the line of battle not just by loyalty to the *polis*, but by ties of family and neighbourhood to the next man in the line – and held there very firmly indeed.[10]

The Chechens: A Primordial Ethnic Nation?

An obvious comparison of the experience of the north-eastern Caucasus over the past two hundred years is with the Maghreb. The elements of similarity are clear: both were conquered in the same decades of the nineteenth century by European imperialist powers; both generated resistances inspired by Sufi Islam and led by Sufi religious figures who showed considerable similarity in their approach to government. Both were defeated and subjected not just to alien rule but to colonisation by settlers. Both revolted again in the early 1920s, and finally and successfully a few decades later. The two histories come together strikingly in the victory of the Chechens over the Russians at Grozny in 1996, and of Abd al-Krim's Berbers over the Spanish at Anual in 1921, also one of the most crushing victories ever won by a 'disorganised', tribal people over a modern European army which both outgunned and heavily outnumbered them.[11]

Moreover, when it comes to an attempt to analyse both Chechen ethnic traditions and the nature of Chechen political society in the 1990s, the work of anthropologists on the Berber tribes of Morocco is of great interest. Robert Montagne, already quoted above, developed two concepts which are absolutely central to understanding contemporary Chechnya: that of 'oscillation' between a loose tribal democracy and an unstable personal autocracy; and that of 'ordered anarchy', whereby a society which appears to an outsider to be utterly chaotic and riven by internal feuds in fact obeys extremely strict rules and restraints in its behaviour, and most importantly, in its capacity to mobilise against a common enemy. (The idea of 'ordered anarchy' was also developed more or less simultaneously by E. E. Evans-Pritchard with regard to the Nuer and other African tribal peoples.[12] However, Montagne's analysis has stood up to criticism better – and is certainly more applicable to Chechnya – because it is not so 'static'; it leaves more room for the changes wrought in the very ancient and conservative cultures he studies by a whole series of outside influences.)[13]

Before employing these concepts in Chechnya, however, it is also very important to notice why Berbers and Chechens are unalike, because this is one key to the resilience of the latter. The first major difference goes back to a feature of Berber society which forms the heart of the social theory of Ibn Khaldun: the process by which tough Berber (or Arab) tribes, united and disciplined by close ties of kinship, would sweep down from the mountains and out of the desert to overthrow decadent kingdoms, and found new and more vigorous kingdoms of their own, like the Almohads – until these in turn became decadent, and the process repeated itself.[14]

Moreover, as Montagne pointed out, even the Berber tribes which remained in the mountains – in the land of *siba*, freedom or dissidence – saw their ancient traditions gradually transformed by the influence of the land of *Makhzen*, or government, down in the plains, and of course by Islam.

Now the Chechens, like the Berbers, are a people who archaeological evidence suggests have been settled in the same place for an immensely long period (up to 4,000 years), and have a very ancient language, perhaps originating in Upper Mesopotamia (Urartu). However, unlike the Berbers – unlike indeed any other major Muslim or Christian people of Europe, the Mediterranean littoral or the Middle East – before the arrival of the infidel Russians the Chechens had never had any close contact at all with any major or serious state.[15] (The French in North Africa found it much easier to conquer the 'Bled el-Makhzen', or tribal areas strongly influenced by government, than they did the completely free tribes – and the similar effect of Shamil's role in bringing institutions to Chechnya has already been noted in chapter 9.)

To the south, the Caucasus separated the Chechens from the Kingdom of Georgia and the various great Muslim empires of the Middle East; to the north, they looked out as if from a rocky island over a sea of grass, across which passed various nomad peoples who never set up a stable or effective state. Nor did the Chechens themselves descend from their mountains to try to create such an empire themselves. In other words, Ibn Khaldun would have added, they remained uncorrupted by government and by civilisation; and, he would have said, retained in consequence their primitive purity and vigour and, above all, their capacity to fight. And it has been strikingly obvious over the past few years that while certain aspects of the ancient Chechen tradition have been vastly modified under Soviet rule, important elements of others still remain.[16]

Moreover, unlike the Berbers and the great majority of other Muslim tribal peoples – even in the Caucasus – the Chechens neither developed an aristocracy of their own, nor submitted permanently to one imposed from outside, nor created one by giving land to hereditary descendants of religious saints (Marabouts or Pirs) – though the latter developments might well have occurred in the long run if Shamil had won, and had it not been for Russian and Soviet power.[17] One reason for the growing discontent with Shamil's rule in Chechnya may have been his grant to his 'naibs', or commanders, of land confiscated from rebels against his rule and collaborators with the Russians. If continued for a long period, this would have for the first time created a native landowning aristocracy, of military and service origin, in Chechnya. Islam however had come very late to Chechnya, and took deep root there only in the context of resistance to Russian conquest, so that there was no time for a wealthy hereditary sainthood to appear there either.

In other words, to a remarkable extent for a people living on the fringes both of geographical Europe and the Middle East, the Chechens really did remain until the modern era a tribal, egalitarian, economically undifferentiated ethnos of a strikingly primitive cast. But if the mountains kept out government and feudalism, they did not keep out military technology: rather than confronting African tribesmen armed with spears and arrows, the Russians at the end of the eighteenth century encountered tribesmen who had been crack shots with the musket for a hundred years and more.

Can Chechnya then be described as a 'primordial ethnic nation'?[18] In one sense, obviously not. It is perfectly clear that while certain primordial traits have survived to a greater extent than elsewhere, Chechnya's modern identity and self-consciousness as a nation have also been overwhelmingly shaped by two factors, both of them originating outside Chechnya. The first was conquest first by the Russians and then by the Soviet Union (viewed by the Chechens as simply Russia in a new guise). The second, and intimately connected with Russian conquest and the resistance to it was the adoption of Sufi Islam, which then for several decades became both the inspirer and the organiser of Chechen resistance. The wars of Shamil – not a Chechen, and acting in the name of a form of Islam which in Chechnya was really only a few years old – have become another central part of the modern 'national myth', indeed probably the greatest element in the national 'mythomoteur', to use Anthony Smith's phrase.[19] It could be said, therefore, that it was Russia that was the catalyst which set off the chemical reaction out of which ultimately developed the contemporary Chechen national identity: by trying to conquer the Chechens it thereby encouraged them to resist, and adopt institutions and strategies of resistance.

Of key importance is historical memory, partly of Shamil's fight, but more importantly of a period well within the memory of most older Chechens: their deportation to Central Asia from 1944 to 1957. This not only helps to explain Chechen hatred and fear of the Russians, but conversely it contributes greatly to the national solidarity which in Chechnya underlies the apparently bitter divisions between Chechen politicians, and the chaos of the Chechen political system.[20]

By far the greater part of the Chechen cultural 'border guards' (in John Armstrong's phrase), or the conscious national 'myths, memories, and symbols' (in Anthony Smith's) are therefore the product of the past two hundred years – though they are not on the whole the kinds of processes described either by Eric Hobsbawm and others for Europe or by Benedict Anderson for South East Asia.

One example that would support the idea of Anderson's 'imagined communities' is that of the role of Tolstoy's *Haji Murat*. In many ways, this would seem a very ambiguous work from the point of view of a Chechen nationalist. First of all, neither Haji Murat nor his arch-rival Shamil was a Chechen. Both were Avars, in Murat's case of princely blood. Secondly, in the story as in reality Murat allows his feud with Shamil to lead him into a brief and personally disastrous alliance with the Russians. Thirdly, Shamil is portrayed as certainly more honourable than the odious Nicholas I, but still as ruthless, vindictive and capable of great cruelty. And finally, of course, Tolstoy was not a Chechen!

None the less, so powerful is Tolstoy's idealisation of Haji Murat's mountain virtue, and so lacking are other widely known literary celebrations of the mountaineers' struggle, that the Chechens have adopted *Haji Murat* almost as their own (one old Chechen is on record as having suggested to a Western visitor that it must have been written by a Chechen and stolen by Tolstoy), and refer to it repeatedly in conversations with outsiders. However, a note of caution may be needed. They may refer to *Haji Murat* in speaking with Western or Russian scholars and journalists because they reckon that we will know it, or know of it; a Chechen oral or religious tradition would need more explaining. That said, the fame of *Haji Murat* among the Chechens themselves derives from the modern Soviet school system, and literacy in Russian.

So far, so 'modern', or created. On the other hand, however, it is also perfectly clear that the Chechens are not an 'imagined community' in the sense of the communities examined by Benedict Anderson elsewhere.[21] Russia may have in some sense created Chechnya; it did not create Chechens. Long before the coming of Islam or the Russians, the Chechens had a common name for themselves and their language, a set of clans embraced within one clan system (however loose), and a set of social rules which – although often closely related to those of their neighbours – were seen by the Chechens as unique to themselves. They adopted Sufi Islam as part of their fight to preserve these.[22] (It has been suggested by Jan Chesnov and others that originally the Chechens were one single undifferentiated people, or one clan not subdivided into smaller clans or clan alliances, and that these were a response to attempts at subjugation by Kabardin and Kumyk princes. The evidence for this is so obscure, however – in part because Chechen was until this century not a written language – that such speculation remains just that.)

When it comes to the nation, the creation of a written alphabet for Chechen under Soviet rule (replacing Arabic, which was accessible only to a tiny minority of religious figures) was a significant step. Out of it came a small intelligentsia writing in Chechen, a necessity for what one might call the codification of modern Chechen nationalism, which, as the next chapter will demonstrate, is very different from the religious ideology of Shamil. But there was never anything resembling a real Chechen 'bourgeoisie', as there was for example among the Volga Tatars, the Azeris and so on, so there was no question in Chechnya of a 'new middle-class intelligentsia of nationalism' using its wealth, position and cultural hegemony to 'invite the masses into history', to use Tom Nairn's phrase.[23]

The tiny national-communist elite of the 1920s might have come with time to play such a role – but Stalin did not give it time. The new Chechen millionaires are certainly not fulfilling that role, of which they have and could have no conception. Analyses based on state strategies also fail with regard to Chechnya, because, except to a very limited extent under Shamil, the Chechens did not participate in any state whose bureaucrats could have adopted nationalism as a means to 'bind the people to itself'. The vigour with which so many Chechens from the beginning continually and openly rejected Soviet culture in the name of their own Chechen culture suggests that something pretty solid, pre-modern and well defined was already present as a basis.

One thing which is enormously striking about the Chechens under Russian and Soviet rule is how very few of them ever displayed the 'cultural cringe' towards their masters so characteristic of semi-Westernised, semi-elite elements of other colonised peoples, and described so painfully in so much colonial literature. The Chechens really did always behave as if they were gods – helped of course by the fact that, unlike the British, the French, the Spanish or even the Persians, the Russians never really felt themselves to be heaven-sent in terms of civic or material culture, because the briefest visit to London, Paris or Berlin (or even Tallinn) would remind them that in the 'cultural superiority' stakes, they were always in a very insecure position.[24]

Finally, while elements of the Soviet-created Chechen intelligentsia and administrative classes have played key parts in the Chechen national struggle (generals Dudayev and Maskhadov being obvious examples), the great majority of these Soviet classes have in fact been very opposed to more radical Chechen nationalism over the past five years, for reasons both of economic interest and of cultural allegiance to modern secularism. A study of the individuals who have played leading roles in Chechen nationalism and the Chechen resistance in the 1990s reveals an extremely wide range of occupations, often (as with Shamil Basayev) very ordinary ones. So it is not possible to portray modern Chechen nationalism as the creation of disappointed Soviet administrative and cultural cadres.

To sum up, Chechen society and the Chechen fighters in the latest war may be compared to a Japanese officer's sword earlier in this century: a weapon whose basic form is of immense antiquity, but which is tempered and retempered in the fires of the modern age, and placed in the hands of men who combine extremely archaic values and virtues with modern military skills of the highest order. Very old, very new, and very effective.

The Russian Intervention: An Error of Colonial Ethnography

In steering this course of qualified primordialism, one should watch out for rocks. In the context of Chechnya, two are especially important. On each of them sits a savage. One is a Tolstoyan noble savage, the other the 'wicked Chechen' of Lermontov's 'Cossack Lullaby', the bandit of Russian colonial and popular prejudice. Both images suggest a Chechen who is primordial and essentially unchanging, and it is striking how both have endured through all the vicissitudes of Soviet ideology, and are still very much alive today.

The first is represented for example by the following Edenic passage:

> Turning to the peculiarities of Vainakh civilisation, we will note certain historical facts. For example, before the epoch of the Caucasian War, Chechnya represented a country that was wonderfully cared for. There were forest reserves, where hunting for beasts was prohibited. Gardens and fields were watered with complex irrigation systems. It produced so much wheat that it fed neighbouring Daghestan and exported it even to Iran. The shepherd did not drive his flock at a run, in order that their little hooves would not push too deeply into thin soil of the mountain pasture. All of these are aspects of a high ecologically developed civilisation.[25]

This is by Jan Chesnov, undoubtedly a fine anthropologist, and one who has done irreplaceable work on the structures of Chechen traditional society, but with a certain tendency to idealise his subject. It is a charming picture, with deep echoes of religious and environmentalist versions of paradise, but it does not contain 'historical facts'. Rather, it forms part of an extremely widespread (and culturally and ideologically positive) world movement of reaction against modern civilisation, as represented by the Soviet Union in an especially crude and environmentally destructive form. In the process, the less peaceful and admirable (by modern standards) aspects of the noble savages in question are shaded over.[26]

This 'blind eye' is also typical of those critics of military attitudes in their own society (even appearing as out-and-out pacifists), who tend to ignore or even praise the military spirit of their country's enemies, at least if these are the underdog. This was very apparent in the attitudes of some American opponents of the Vietnam War, and it occurred in Russia during the Chechen War as well.

Of course, far more evil and tragic in its consequences is the other Russian stereotype of the Chechens. Gut racial hatred of the 'Chechen bandits' does appear to have played its part in the Russian decision to intervene, and in Russian atrocities thereafter. But there is also a more complex aspect in terms of anthropological analyses of Chechnya, for this decision was based on an underestimation of the enemy very characteristic of some colonial approaches to ethnography – and in an equally common pattern, this was related to a view of the enemy society as not just primitive but also static.[27] Though not surprising historically speaking, this is somewhat unexpected in this specific case, because after all the attack on Chechnya came only six years after the Soviet withdrawal from Afghanistan, an experience that should have taught the Russians not to underestimate 'primitive' opponents. In the words of General Lebed, 'Russia has, for the second time, stepped on the same rake.'[28]

As a matter of fact, however, the Russians thought that they *had* learned the lessons not just of Afghanistan but also of the civil war in Tajikistan, in which the Russian army had also become involved. The Russian domestic intelligence service (FSK) thought that it had done its anthropological homework. Though its policy, as accepted by the Yeltsin administration in general, led directly to the catastrophic war in Chechnya, it was meant to avoid precisely this eventuality. Their thinking was revealed to me in a government briefing paper to which I was given access in August 1994, and which at the time impressed me with its sophistication. I was told that the policy it delineated was meant to answer two concerns: the great unwillingness of the army to launch a direct intervention in Chechnya, something which the commanders both of the North Caucasus Military District and the Military Intelligence Service (GRU) were strongly against; and the desire of the FSK, and its director Sergei Stepashin, to take over Chechen policy and score a notable success.

The FSK analysis assumed that, as in much of Central Asia, the key to understanding Chechen politics and society was the Chechen system of clans, or teips. In the FSK paper, these were treated as largely closed, internally cohesive and mutually exclusive building blocks, which take hidden but mainly united political decisions, and which give their allegiances as teips to different political causes and leaders. It was in these terms that the FSK analysed the Chechen national revolution of 1991, seeing it above all as a revolt of excluded teips against the 'Tyerekhskoi' clan, which under Communist Party First Secretary Doku Zavgayev had come to dominate the local Communist and state structures. This 'clan' has a history of 'pro-Russian' behaviour going back to conquest by and cooperation with Russia in the eighteenth and nineteenth centuries – indeed, some elements of this 'clan' had been members of completely different 'teips' which had fled from the mountains to get away from Shamil, and had placed themselves under Russian protection.

In particular, the Tyerekhskois' domination of the oil industry and the illegal profits from it had, in the FSK's portrait (and to some extent in reality), caused burning resentment among other groups. In this analysis, General Dzhokhar Dudayev was chosen as leader by the Chechen National Congress partly because of his fiery rhetoric and the prestige of his military rank, but also because both as an outsider who had not lived in Chechnya for many years, and as a member of the small Ertskhoi teip, he represented a compromise between the larger clans and interest groups in Chechnya.

The FSK paper portrayed the subsequent political struggles within Chechnya as the unravelling of this compromise between the clans, as a new teip coalition under Dudayev (dominated by his allies in the powerful Myalkhi teip) themselves tried to monopolise government and the oil industry, and in turn drove other clans into opposition. Dudayev's mobilisation of radical nationalist youth also alienated the established clan leaderships. Meanwhile the ousted Tyerekhskoi also rallied for a return to power, basing their strength mainly on the profits they had made from government and oil in the last years of Soviet rule, and which had been invested in various kinds of private 'business', and to a lesser extent on their prominent position in the small Chechen educated elite. In the FSK view, these anti-Dudayev clan interests had come together in the opposition movement of April–June 1993 in Grozny, which had ended with Dudayev's forces defeating the opposition and driving them from Grozny.

At that time, the internal political preoccupations of the Yeltsin administration – its struggle against the Russian Supreme Soviet, which was to culminate in October with the storming of the parliament in Moscow – had prevented Moscow from fully exploiting General Dudayev's difficulties, though arms and money had been supplied to the Chechen opposition. But in the summer of 1994, with the Kremlin's hands untied, and anti-Dudayev feeling running high, the time seemed ripe for a continuation and intensification of this policy. The FSK therefore recommended that the Russian government increase the supply of arms and money to the opposition 'Provisional Council', founded on the Tyerekhskoi *tukhum* (group of teips, or clans) and based in their home area in north-western Chechnya; but that Russian agents also work by bribes and mediation to establish a solid clan alliance against Dudayev, with prior agreements on how to share out the spoils in the event of victory.

One of the reasons why this advice impressed me at the time was not just that it seemed to be based on an acute and sophisticated knowledge of Chechen society and anthropology (and tied in with what Chechen oppositionists like Yusup Soslambekov were saying), but also because it had a genuine awareness of how difficult and bloody a direct Russian military intervention in Chechnya would be, and advised strongly against it.

The strategy set out – of increased backing for the Chechen opposition – seemed by contrast to have a very good hope of success. It was apparent to me when I visited Chechnya in August and September 1994 that Dudayev was extremely unpopular with much of the population, that ordinary people in Grozny were infuriated by the collapse of wages, public services and public order, and that his support was now largely based on the more conservative mountain areas, and on his own presidential guard. The return of Ruslan Khasbulatov to Chechnya in that month had attracted major demonstrations of support, and my own informal opinion polls suggested that he was at that time more popular than Dudayev (especially among Chechen women – not that anyone ever asked their opinion). It was also obvious that 'clan' links in some sense do play a very important role in Chechen political behaviour. It seemed to me therefore at that time that this Russian strategy might well succeed.

Part of the reason why this policy failed and provoked the very military option it was meant to avoid was that the FSK was in too much of a hurry, mainly for domestic political reasons. More importantly, however, it was based on a set of fundamental misconceptions about the nature of the Chechen clan system, about how it works today, and about the importance of other factors in Chechen society. The FSK also – as so often in colonial history – seem to have been led astray by their own informants from the Chechen opposition, who were naturally anxious to stress the limited nature of Dudayev's support and the inward-looking base of his government, and to argue that he was motivated by narrow clan feeling and not by nationalism.[29]

What was missed, in the first place, was how for centuries teip loyalties have been cut across by other ties – to relations by marriage, to neighbours from other clans, to wider clan alliances, to religious brotherhoods, and finally of course to Islam itself. Teips were never therefore rigid vertical divisions in Chechen society. Secondly, the whole teip system was greatly weakened by the immense disruption caused by Soviet rule and especially the deportation of 1944. Finally, of course, the FSK picture completely ignored the immense uniting power of Chechen nationalism, too modern-sounding a phenomenon to fit into its 'tribal' scheme – and perhaps too ideologically uncomfortable for men raised in the Soviet school of support for 'national liberation movements', since it suggested that the Chechens had right on their side and Russia was playing an imperial role. It was much more convenient – and of course wholly in tune with old Russian prejudices – to portray them as a prenational, primitive, tribal and bandit people.[30]

Instead, the FSK generalised from Central Asia and Afghanistan to assume that the Chechen teip retained the central political importance of Kazakh 'hordes' or Tajik tribes. This is an exaggeration even for parts of Central Asia (in the Tajik civil war, regional links and loyalties seem to have been more important than clan or tribal links as such).[31] In Afghanistan, however, the Soviet strategy of divide and rule among the various Pashtun tribes had had considerable success in splitting the Mujahidin and attracting some of them (particularly from among the Durrani of Kandahar) to make a truce with the Najibullah government in the period 1987–9. The GRU (military intelligence) – which had great experience of this in Afghanistan – reportedly advised the FSK over its teip policy in Chechnya.

A fatal misinterpretation where Chechnya was concerned, this kind of approach – exaggerating the 'timelessness' and the 'traditionalism' of the

'Asiatic' society under examination, rendering internal divisions as fixed and unchangeable rather than fluid and adaptable – has a long history in the approaches of European ethnography to various colonised societies. It is often based on an unstated and indeed often unconscious contrast between 'our' society – modern, rational, organised and dynamic – and 'theirs', traditional, irrational, divided, static and inflexible. It also reflects a very natural desire to simplify, categorise, understand – and therefore control – what is actually an informal, highly complicated and very opaque set of relationships operating on alien principles. In the FSK case, to this seems to have been added a mixture of characteristically Soviet and characteristically secret police attitudes: that no political developments happen for obvious reasons, or by themselves; that there is always some underlying, secret set of factors and forces which can be manipulated if you have the right key and can design the right conspiracy – a 'magical' view of the world, in Derluguian's phrase. Rarely however have the results been so disastrous for the imperialists as the Chechen intervention has been for Russia.

Tribal Warrior Egalitarianism: Teip, Vird and Adat

There is no space here for a lengthy discussion of the origins and historical nature of the teip system, a subject in any case in much dispute among Russian anthropologists. Three of the leading ones, Mahomet Mamakayev, Jan Chesnov and Viktor Chasiev, take opposing positions on their origins, with Mamakayev arguing that they are ancient tribal sub-ethnoses, and Chasiev and Jan Chesnov arguing for their origins in a struggle some four hundred years ago by the poorer Chechen tribesmen (or 'peasants') for collective land ownership and against feudal and especially non-Chechen (Kabardin, Kumyk and Avar) landowning nobles.

We know that, as already noted, traditional Chechen society had strikingly egalitarian features compared to the Chechens' neighbours, that from the sixteenth century on the Chechens expelled their native and non-Chechen overlords, and that this has played a crucial part in their history of resistance to invasion. Chechen folklore also retains memories of the struggle against the lords, in the form of stories about the fortified towers belonging to them, the ruins of which are still to be seen in Chechnya. Thus the tower Tsoi-Pkheda is associated with the story of a Prince Sepa, who tried to enforce *droit de seigneur* on the girls of his village, and was killed by one of their brothers. The struggle against these lords presumably strengthened still further the warlike characteristics of the ordinary, non-noble Chechen. Both aspects are summed up in the ancient Chechen proverb, 'we are free and equal as the wolves.'[32]

There seems at all events no reason to doubt that in the prehistoric period (which for the study of Chechnya means until the early eighteenth century, that is, before the first significant written historical descriptions of them are to be found), teips did indeed play a crucial part in Chechen society and in the shaping of the preconditions for the modern Chechen nation. In traditional Chechnya, according to Mamakayev, writing in 1973 (that is, in the depths of Soviet rule, and long before the latest war),

> At the heart of Chechen life were the ideals of the hearth, strong and healthy male heirs, and the flourishing of the kinship group. Individual death was not considered an evil, because it was inevitable and sent by the supreme God, or *Dela*. But if there was a danger of the extinction of the teip, that was thought a most terrible misfortune. This attitude opened the way for the adoption of outsiders into the teip, after which they had the same rights as the existing members of the teip... Such adoptions were attended with great celebrations, including the ritual sacrifice of a bull. This has led to the continued Chechen saying, when men from different families swear friendship and alliance, or make up differences, that 'they have slaughtered the bull'.[33]

The continued Chechen use of the ancient Chechen word *Dela*, not the Arabic and Islamic 'Allah', in contexts of Chechen social rules and traditions shows the pre-Islamic origins of most of these. Dela appears to have been the highest god of an animist pantheon. Suppressed in Chechnya by Sufi Islam, strong elements of this ancient polytheism are still observable in the folklore of neighbouring Ingushetia. It is also interesting to note that the ancient Chechens took a stoical but rather comfortless view of death as inevitable, but without the later Islamic promise of paradise for the believer and especially the martyr. In the latest war, I heard many Chechens express an Islamic willingness to die, because, as they said, 'We know that Allah has promised paradise to every martyr (*Shahid*) for religion and nation' (not quite what Allah actually said to Muhammad, but never mind).

On the whole, however, I had the impression that the older, less conceptu- alised but perhaps more deeply felt Chechen attitude to death was more important in the willingness of so many not very religious Chechens to fight and die. As one fighter said to me, 'Of course I don't want to die, but for a Chechen, death is not important. What is important is to have lived and died for your family and your people' (*narod* – we were speaking Russian).

The former importance of the teip is summed up in the traditional Chechen saying, 'the teip is the fortress of Adat', Adat being ancestral custom. Tradi- tional Chechen folklore also had numerous sayings attributing particular hereditary characteristics to the people of particular teips, with some regarded as 'noble', some as 'unreliable' – especially those that in the nineteenth century made an early peace with the Russians, like the Tyerekhskoi, or were originally formed from members of non-Chechen ethnic groups. For it is a sign of the attractiveness of the Chechen lifestyle, and of the Chechen teips' ability to offer physical protection against attack from outside, that according to legend, in the sixteenth and seventeenth centuries, even some Cossacks were adopted into Chechen teips (along with Nogai and other nomads), as the Chechens expanded from the mountains into the Terek plains.

In particular, the tribal and egalitarian form of traditional Chechen society has in more recent times contributed greatly to the Chechen ability both to resist conquest and assimilation and (as stressed by both Mamakayev and Chesnov) to maintain ethnic numbers by coopting members of neighbouring ethnic groups. The Chechens have been much less likely than their neighbours (notably the Azeris and Daghestanis) to be demoralised by the destruction or cooption of their elites, for the simple reason that in the past four centuries they never really had any, whether secular or religious.

Leadership among Chechens seems at least from the seventeenth century to have been principally a matter of personal achievement and prestige, not heredity, with the council of elders of a teip choosing its leader (*Khalakancha*, sometimes rendered by the Chechens themselves as *Tamada* – literally 'chairman' – now a widespread word for various kinds of leadership among Caucasian peoples, but drawn originally from the famous Georgian institution of toastmaster and peacemaker). If the leader was too old to command in warfare and raiding, the council would also choose a war-leader (*Byachcha*), analogous to the Scottish 'captain of the clan' but strictly non-hereditary. A closer parallel might be to the elected 'war-chiefs' of some of the Plains Indians tribes, whose authority was strictly limited to wars and raids, or to Sparta's elected kings.

But when it comes to the specific role of the teip (as analysed by the FSK), it must be noted that even in the traditional Chechen order, the dominance of the teip as a focus of hereditary allegiance was qualified by other loyalties: to the 'tukum', or territorial grouping of several different teips, to the extended family, to the lineage group, and to the Sufi brotherhood or 'vird', itself an increasingly hereditary institution. In the time of Shamil, his religious war and the military institutions it generated – the first state or quasi-state structures Chechnya had ever known – united Chechens across teip lines, as nationalism does today. As Chesnov points out, since the wars of the nineteenth century at least (and especially of course during and after the deportation of 1944), the teip has been losing its connection to a particular territory, greatly weakening it as a force for ethnic division.[34]

The extended family has been of particular importance as an alternative, and in some cases rival, source of identity and focus of loyalty; because for several centuries at least Chechen teips have mostly been exogamous, and (in contrast to many other Islamic societies, but with analogies to the ancient Anglo-Saxons and other groups) the mother's family is of great importance to Chechen men, with the mother's elder brother in particular having a strong role, sanctioned by tradition, in the upbringing of male children. It may be noted that Chechen blood-feuds, both today and it would seem in the past, have been conducted not between teips but between families or extended families.

The exact role of the teip in present Chechen society is extremely difficult to establish. Less educated Chechens from rural and conservative back-

grounds, who have remained closest to such traditions, have a great unwillingness to talk about them; there seems to be a conscious or unconscious
feeling that this would be to betray national secrets. As far as more educated
and urban Chechens are concerned, these often seem motivated by the desire
to play down the importance of the teips, the Sufi tradition and so on, out of
an obscure feeling that their survival would brand the Chechens as 'backward'
and 'primitive'. Many Chechens today are moreover quite simply ignorant of
what the teip is or used to be, and of how the teip system is or was structured.
Twice, for example, I have been confidently informed by Chechen intellectuals that the tukum is a subdivision of the teip, rather than a grouping of teips
– a mistake which itself of course indicates how little importance this whole
tradition had for my interlocutors (unless it was a deliberate attempt to
deceive – but the context made this most unlikely).

The present situation appears broadly speaking to be the following: as a
matter of personal identity and family tradition, the teip has a varying significance for Chechens, depending on the degree of their 'modernisation', their
urbanisation, their education, their place of habitation (the mountains being
much more traditionalist in this regard than the plains) and indeed their
degree of ideological nationalism or religious commitment – I have heard a
few Chechen nationalists, especially ones of a religious cast, declare that the
teip tradition should really be done away with, because all that matters is the
nation and God. However, as with so many such traditions in the period of
their long decomposition, the teip continues to play a role in 'rites of passage',
and most especially in burials.

As an element of the national tradition, the teip (like Islam) is regarded by
most Chechens, more or less vaguely, as something which ought to be cher-
ished and preserved. As a force for political mobilisation and organisation,
however, the teip today plays only a very limited part in determining
Chechens' political behaviour.

This combination of attitudes was perfectly displayed in the teip policy of
the Dudayev regime. On the one hand, General Dudayev made a great show
of recognising and restoring the teips, and frequently called public meetings
of elders from the different teips, paying them ostentatious public respect.
This formed part of a general public revival of the teips in the period 1990–3,
a natural consequence of having being prevented from expressing this part of
the Chechen identity. Chechen politicians – Dudayev chief amongst them –
tried to exploit this revival for their own ends. In the words of Soslambekov,

> Some politicians in 1992 organised teip congresses, hoping by this to
> use the argument of the number of members of their teip to strengthen
> their influence and gain places in the government. The organisers of
> these congresses of course kept their real motives secret, talking instead
> of the need to unite the Chechen people, to revive ancestral traditions
> and so on.[35]

After the dissolution of the Chechen parliament by Dudayev forces in May 1993, a succession of hand-picked Chechen national councils and congresses, made up largely of such elders, were used by Dudayev to maintain a façade of democracy and consultation – in preparation, so the opposition alleged, for a declaration of his presidency for life. On occasions, they legitimized his taking of more powers. Dudayev also used them to carry out more or less fake 'peacemaking' missions to the Chechen opposition. Whenever I visited Chechen government headquarters between 1992 and 1994, I could be sure of coming across some group of these people sitting and peering about them, their white beards wagging gently away as they talked, usually to each other. It was just the same with the Chechen opposition forces; Khasbulatov in particular assembled gatherings of elders wherever he went.

But this of course was the whole point: these elders and their teips had some symbolic value, but no real power. As Dudayev himself is reported to have said on one occasion to a group of elders who dared to criticise him,

> I called you together to serve the nation, not to split it. You are here because of me. If you serve the nation, you can stay and help me. If not, you can go home. You are not the government, you are not a parliament, you are nothing. Mind your own business. I didn't ask you here to tell me what to do.[36]

After the outbreak of the war, these figures largely faded from sight, and when I attended meetings of local notables to discuss various questions, they tended to be made up of middle-aged, much more dynamic men, with a sprinkling of young military commanders, and perhaps one or two old men as a symbolic presence.

In the words of Professor Vachargayev, speaking of the Sufi religious brotherhoods, which are by now largely hereditary and closely linked to kinship groups,

> All the virds have their own meetings of elders, and they do have some real influence, through religion. They can't order people to do anything, to attend meetings or reach a compromise, but they can influence the situation. And if they go to an area where there is fighting, no one will actually shoot at them, and no one will say, 'go to hell.' Chechen tradition and customs demand that you have to be polite to them, and they can use that to play the role of diplomats, moderating and mediating.[37]

This is also true of the teip elders, the two being very closely linked, when not identical.

Particular vird traditions do affect political behaviour today. Thus I was told that members of the vird of the late nineteenth- and early twentieth-century preacher Doku Sheikh, concentrated in his home-town of Tolstoy Yurt,[38] are still influenced by his pacific teaching, and that is one reason why many local people rallied around Khasbulatov in September 1994. I was also told that the Arsanov vird, founded by Saint Din-i-Baharuddin Arsanov, has similarly always been in favour of compromise with Russia, and that its present head, Bauddin Arsanov, is a KGB colonel – his brother was a Soviet Deputy, and his father had also been a senior Soviet official. Another member became chief Mufti of Chechnya in the last years of Soviet rule.[39] Sazhi Umulatova, the notorious Chechen Stalinist politician, comes from an Arsanov background, and I met Bauddin's grandson, Ilyes Arsanov, with Ruslan Labazanov in December 1994, presumably acting as some kind of go-between.

And while the teip may be to a great extent politically moribund, the 'clan' in a much looser sense continues to characterise Chechen politics. One reason why lineage links have remained so important in Chechen society is that they provided various forms of assistance and roles to the large number of Chechen young men who could not find adequate and equally important *respectable* (according to Chechen criteria) employment in the Soviet economy. Closely linked to this has been the role of such connections in forming a basis for particular Chechen criminal groups – though once again, not in any formal sense of teips or tukums.

Such 'clans' – like the one which came to dominate the leadership of the Communist Party under the leadership of Doku Zavgayev – are partly based upon the teip, but they also combine many other elements: from links through and between extended families to bureaucratic cliques and alignments, economic and regional interest groups, business and mafia links and so on.

The spirit of the teip – in the sense of an emotional and moral legitimation of a new political grouping through appeals to some form of common ancestry or older familial and local links – may however still be important; thus when he returned to Chechnya in August 1994 in an effort to take over from Dudayev (or in his words, to play the role of a 'mediator and peacemaker'), Ruslan Khasbulatov tried in a sense to gather a new 'clan' around him, with numerous and public meetings with elders of teips and leading members of virds, and references to various teip traditions. This seemed not just a practical strategy to create a political base, but also a moral one to legitimize the re-entry into Chechen political society of a man who had spent almost his entire life elsewhere, spoke the Chechen language badly, and had made his political name by his activity in Russia.

These links were therefore not irrelevant, but as much as anything else they functioned to perform a kind of blessing over a process which was taking place for other reasons. Incipient bastard feudals, one might say, were given the appearance of legitimate descendants of Chechen tradition with the help of references to the teip.

Several months before the war began, a Chechen mafia leader in Moscow gave me some insights into how Chechen society works today. I asked him if Chechen mafia groups were recruited on the basis of particular teips or virds. He replied that the system is not so formal:

What matters is that someone has to be recommended to us by people whom we know and respect. They may be our relatives, or they may be connected to us in some other way. We Chechens are a small people – we all know each other, we know who is respected and who isn't. The point is that when someone joins us, then his family and his backers, the men who recommended him, are also responsible for his behaviour. If he were to betray us or let us down – and that happens very rarely – then they would be ashamed, they would lose respect. They themselves would bring him to task, and make him apologise or make things good in some way. We wouldn't have to do anything. That is why you very rarely find Chechens killing each other, unlike the Russians and other groups. We don't need to. We have our traditions, and they are very strong.

'It is Hard to Be a Chechen'

It was on the basis of a mixture of the neighbourhood and the extended family that most of the volunteer units which formed after the Russian invasion were spontaneously generated, and their commanders chosen. In the words of a Chechen religious elder,

> The teip is much too large a unit, and much too dispersed, to exercise any direct control over individuals any more. What matters is the family group, including the mother's family. That is the unit which is going to decide whether a youth goes to fight or not – unless he's already decided for himself, of course. If his father, or the most respected adult in the wider family, says fight, the young men will fight. And if he says 'don't fight', they will at least listen attentively.

In a large number of cases a role was also played by the family-linked vird.

In the absence of formal military discipline (at least until the rise of Shariat punishments as the war progressed), the men in these units were kept in the ranks mainly by an unforced discipline of honour and shame related above all to the desire to keep the respect of their relatives and neighbours. These units are therefore quite literally 'bands of brothers'. Of course, in modern armies, and probably most armies through history, the desire 'not to let down your mates' in the section or platoon has played a very important role in keeping men in the front line; this motive is enormously strengthened when to run away would also mean disgracing yourself before your immediate family, and your family before your extended family and all its connections, in a tradition in which courage, respect and 'name' are the most honoured of all male attributes. It would take a very morally brave man to be a coward in these circumstances.

A striking example of the role of family and tradition in inspiring the Chechen struggle is the tremendous efforts the Chechen fighters made to recover the bodies of their fallen comrades so that they could be returned to their families for burial. This stemmed not only from a desire to show respect to the families of the dead, but more particularly from the tremendous importance the Chechen tradition attaches to being buried in the ancestral village of your family or clan, beside your ancestors (one of the things which has made assessing the number of casualties from the war extremely difficult).[40]

During the assault on Grozny I was told of literally Homeric combats fought by groups of Chechens in order to recover and carry away just one dead comrade. In the words of a Chechen fighter, 'it may seem senseless to you to risk our own lives to bring back someone who is already dead and doesn't care about it one way or the other. But you see to the family of the dead it is very important indeed. If we didn't do our best to bring him back, we would be ashamed before them and before our own families... This is our tradition.' The separation from their ancestral cemeteries, and their desecration by NKVD troops and Russian settlers, was one of the most bitterly felt aspects of the Chechens' deportation to Central Asia, and when they returned they were careful to bring back with them handfuls of earth from the graves of those who had died in exile, so that these could at least symbolically be laid to rest beside their ancestors.

The willingness of Chechen fighters to risk, and often lose their own lives to recover the bodies of their comrades expresses the spirit of a Chechen proverb, now well known to many Russians: 'it is hard to be a Chechen.' This feeling of having been born into a heavy and harsh, but immensely noble and glorious set of duties, rituals and responsibilities is one which to some degree or other affects the great majority of Chechens, at least those who remain connected to Chechen society. Once again, it is something that calls up the image of Aeneas and his father. Many of the younger generation may fail to live up to these demands, but none can altogether ignore them or are wholly unaware of them – unlike for example many Azeris, who have no specific social tradition or code.

The tremendous, almost terrifying morale and moral toughness this gives the Chechens has been recognised even by otherwise not very sympathetic Russian observers. They themselves love to quote the following passage by Solzhenitsyn about the behaviour of the Chechen people in the labour camps and in exile – though only the first few lines! It reflects a rather classical mixture of genuine admiration and self-criticism in the cultural mirror held up by the Chechens, but with patronisation and fear. It is a mixture characteristic not just of the nineteenth-century Russian attitude to the Mountaineers but of a number of Western colonial peoples towards various 'noble savages'.

Despite these reservations, it cannot be dismissed out of hand. Apart from Solzhenitsyn's general honesty as a witness, this passage is borne out by my own experience of the contemporary Chechens, and does help to illuminate a great deal about them: both their spectacular military victories against overwhelming odds and their equally striking successes over the past two decades in the world of the 'mafia' and illegal business. The only quality not mentioned by Solzhenitsyn is the iron law of Chechen hospitality, a tradition quite as ancient as the blood-feud or banditry:

> There was one nation which would not give in, would not acquire the mental habits of submission – and not just individual rebels among them, but the whole nation to a man. These were the Chechens...
>
> I would say that of all the special settlers, the Chechens alone showed themselves zeks in spirit. They had been treacherously snatched from their home, and from that day they believed in nothing...
>
> The Chechens never sought to please, to ingratiate themselves with the bosses; their attitude was always haughty and indeed openly hostile. They treated the laws on universal education and the state curriculum with contempt, and to save them from corruption would not send their little girls to school, nor indeed all of their boys...
>
> They tried whenever possible to find themselves jobs as drivers: looking after an engine was not degrading, their passion for rough riding found an outlet in the constant movement of a motor vehicle, and their passion for thieving in the opportunities drivers enjoy. This last passion, however, they also gratified directly. 'We've been robbed', 'we've been cleaned out' were concepts which they introduced to peaceful, honest, sleepy Kazakhstan. They were capable of rustling cattle, robbing a house, or sometimes taking what they wanted by force. As far as they were concerned, the local inhabitants, and those exiles who submitted so readily, belonged more or less to the same breed as the bosses. They respected only rebels.
>
> And here is an extraordinary thing – everyone was afraid of them. No-one could stop them from living as they did. The regime which had ruled the land for thirty years could not force them to respect its laws.

Solzhenitsyn goes on to describe an occasion when the Chechens in his settlement in Kazakhstan pursued an open blood-feud. All the local Soviet authorities were aware of this, and did nothing: 'a savage and ancient law had breathed on them – and all at once there was no Soviet power in Kok-Terek.' The feud was resolved in the end not by the authorities but by Chechen elders, who – as is their tradition – imposed a compromise.

Solzhenitsyn continues in words that echo some of the Chechens' own unflattering opinions about the Russians:

> We Europeans, at home and at school, read and pronounce only words of lofty disdain for this savage law, this cruel and senseless butchery. But the butchery is perhaps not so senseless after all. It does not sap the mountain peoples, but strengthens them. Not so very many fall victim to the law of vendetta – but what power the fear of it has all around. With this law in mind, no highlander will casually insult another, as we insult each other in drink, from lack of self-control or just for the hell of

it. Still less will any *non*-Chechen look for trouble with a Chechen...
The Chechens walk the Kazakh land with insolence in their eyes,
shouldering people aside, and the 'masters of the land' and non-masters
alike respectfully make way for them...

'Strike your neighbours, that strangers may fear you!' The ancestors
of the highlanders in remote antiquity could have found no stronger
hoop to gird their people.

Has the socialist state offered them anything better?[41]

These words curiously enough are almost identical to ones used in my
presence by Dzhokhar Dudayev in early December 1994, in declaring that
internal disputes in Chechnya were of no real importance and that the
Chechen people would fight as one against Russian invasion (the closeness of
the very words may perhaps be, of course, because Dudayev had read
Solzhenitsyn, and was consciously or semi-consciously quoting him back to
the Russian journalists present).

We would have done well to listen more carefully to Dudayev; but his
pronouncements were so rhetorical, and the true and sensible were so mixed
with the histrionic and the grossly exaggerated, that it was difficult to take him
seriously. On the other hand, it must also be said that this arrogance of the
Chechens, though it contributed enormously to their own morale and fighting
spirit, was also one reason why their North Caucasian neighbours were not
more anxious to help them after the Russian intervention began. For obvious
reasons, they are not much loved in their neighbourhood.

Typical was an exchange I heard between an older and younger Chechen
fighter, whom I had asked about the relationship between the Chechens and
the Ingush. The older man gave a standard official Chechen line, that the two
peoples are brothers whom the wicked Russians have divided. The younger
one broke in with a burst of vituperative-sounding Chechen, ending scorn-
fully in Russian: 'yes of course we're related – like the lion and the hyena.'

Anarchy and Autocracy

It is of course all too apparent from many parts of the world that Chechen-
style societies with traditions of 'ordered anarchy' have often had extreme
difficulty in developing effective modern forms of government, especially of
course government by formal and regulated consensus. Afghanistan is one
tragic example: the system of local shuras or councils, which I saw at work
several times, reconciling local differences, and promoting local military
cooperation between different commanders and their groups, proved
untranslatable to Kabul and the government of the whole country.[42]

For reasons already sketched, it seems unlikely that Chechnya could ever
fall into the near-chaos (as opposed to anarchy, a very different thing) and terrible internecine bloodletting of Afghanistan or Somalia – especially since the

latest war has served as another great forge of national unity. In General Aslan Maskhadov, the Chechens in January 1997 elected as president a man of truly great and admirable qualities, by world standards and not those of Chechnya alone. Never the less, as of the Summer of 1997, the picture was far from encouraging.

From 1991 to 1994, under the rule of General Dudayev, the Chechen state and political society presented a most unfortunate picture. The institutions of the Soviet state in Chechnya progressively collapsed – in my portrait of Grozny from my three visits between 1992 and 1994, I have already noted the rapid decay of most public services – and the Dudayev regime and indeed Chechen society almost completely failed to generate effective new ones. In 1993, political consensus broke down, democracy was effectively abolished, and a considerable number of political leaders, backed by Moscow, went into armed opposition.[43]

The Chechen forces were not entirely united even during the war. The lack of centralised command and control of them was one reason for the break-down of the first armistice in the autumn of 1995, because with the best will in the world, generals Dudayev and Maskhadov could not prevent individual Chechen groups from taking a crack at the Russians. Crucially important for the future will be whether any central Chechen government will be able to prevent the growth of anti-Russian terrorism or banditry by individual groups, and consequent Russian reprisals against Chechnya.

Two observations of Robert Montagne's about the Berber tradition which are worth noting in reference to Chechnya in the 1990s. The first, already noted, is that Berber society, unable to generate or tolerate stable and effective government whether by ordered bureaucracy or by consensus, has tended to oscillate between long periods of tribal 'anarchy' and briefer, but often very tyrannical periods of personal despotism. Connected to this is his perception that the more prolonged and deeper a period of despotic rule over the Berber, the more unruly and violent is the subsequent outburst of *siba* – which leads in turn to another round of despotism.[44] As of mid-1997, the government of Maskhadov was making only limited progress in breaking this unhappy cycle in Chechnya.

If the Chechens cannot create stable mechanisms for achieving peacetime legitimate government with an effective monopoly of armed force, then Chechnya is likely in the long run to remain unstable, poor and in effect part of Russia – for the simple reason that Russian governments will always be able to play one Chechen leader off against another. The Chechens' best hope of course is that given the weaknesses of the Russian state and political society, they in turn will be able to do exactly the same to the Russians.

The 'Bandit' Tradition and the 'Chechen Mafia'

The question of the 'bandit' tradition in Chechnya is an extremely delicate one, because it has so often been used by Russian governments and spokesmen as an excuse to conquer and oppress the Chechens, inflicting in the process cruelties worse than any bandit could have conceived of. Thus the Russian domestic intelligence chief, General Nikolai Barsukov, said early in the war that 'one local man told me that a Chechen can only be a robber or a killer, and if not this, then he will be prepared for some other kind of crime.' Public opinion polls have shown that large proportions of Russians put the Chechens first among the groups held responsible for the rise in crime.

Where old Chechnya is concerned, before the Russian conquest, one should perhaps rather refer to a social institution of 'raiding', because 'banditry' has connotations of criminality which were certainly not felt by any Chechen either then or now. 'Raiding' has a different flavour. Cattle-raiding, horse-theft, abduction and piracy have inspired a number of classics of world literature, and at various times and places have formed an integral, respectable and indeed central part of many societies and cultures, from the Danes to the Dinkas and from Munster to Malakand.

As for banditry as a form of social protest, the work of Hobsbawm and his successors has made this seem almost legitimate – except, of course, to the victims. Banditry as a form of indirect ethnic or regional protest against alien rule has been less studied, but was and is extremely common in a great many areas. Ireland of the eighteenth century is one example, southern Italy in the 1860s another, Georgia under Russian and Soviet rule yet another. All over the Caucasus, the *abrek*, or bandit of honour, is a hero of both oral and written traditions.

Raiding in Chechnya, as elsewhere, was for obvious reasons generally a function of young men, and a task through which they passed to full manhood. Older men had and have other responsibilities, above all the care of their immediate families and the playing of a sober and worthy role in their wider lineages.

Whatever its roots, banditry in Chechnya over the past 250 years or so has not been a static phenomenon. In particular, the later eighteenth century may – it is difficult to speak with any certainty – have seen two major changes, both of which find echoes in the present day. The first is that it has been suggested that the introduction of corn-growing to the mountains allowed a rapid growth of population, with consequent social and economic pressures to increase raiding. The second is that instead of their traditional neighbours, the Chechens increasingly came into contact first with Cossacks and then with the Russian empire – and at a time when the growing influence of Islam among the Chechens was increasing the perception of the Russians not just as succulent targets, but as religious enemies. This may have been important if, as elsewhere, traditional Chechen raiding observed certain restraints and limitations, because with regard to the heretical and alien Russians these restrictions would not have applied.

Baddeley, a very balanced and neutral observer who visited the region in the 1890s, when the memory of the old days was still very much alive, commented on the relationship between banditry and Chechen honour:

Cattle-lifting, highway robbery, and murder were, in this strange code, counted deeds of honour; they were openly instigated by the village maiden – often, by the way, remarkably pretty – who scorned any pretender having no such claims to her favour; and these, together with fighting against any foe, but especially the hated Russian, were the only pursuits deemed worthy of a grown man.[46]

For many young men, raiding was used as the only way to become a family man, because it was the only way to capture or to acquire the money to buy a wife. Since the latest war, according to Georgy Derluguian, the abduction of educated Chechen girls by Chechen youths – with the goal of marriage – has reportedly increased drastically, not because the youths have no money, but because having missed out on most of their schooling through war or truancy, they cannot impress educated women (who having nothing else to do stay in school) and therefore claim them by kidnap.[47]

Among contemporary Chechens, the raiding tradition has perpetuated itself both in terms of unusual success in the world of organised crime, and in brigandage pure and simple. This is not to follow Russian chauvinists who try to make the Chechens and others responsible for all or most of Russian organised crime; the vast majority of criminal groups in Russia are made up of ethnic Russians, and Russian organised crime today is a social, not an ethnic phenomenon, affecting most of society. It's just that the Chechens appear to be more skilful at it.

Brigandage has been and threatens to go on being wholly bad in its effects on Chechnya itself. The attacks on Russian trains crossing Chechnya on their way to and from Daghestan and Azerbaijan, and the endless private tapping of the oil pipeline from Baku, helped to destroy Russian confidence in the Chechen government as a negotiating partner, to undermine the usefulness of Chechnya to Russia as a communications route, and indeed to lose it the revenues that the Chechen state could have levied on that route. The threat of Chechen banditry to peace, security and economic development in Chechnya and the whole north Caucasus has continued after the Chechen victory of 1996, especially in the form of repeated kidnappings which Maskhadov seems powerless to stop.

Organised crime on the other hand has had both negative and positive effects on contemporary Chechen society. On the negative side, it has increased the hostility of the Chechens' neighbours – mainly the Russians, but also fellow Caucasians, who resent the Chechens' dominance over their own mafias; it has crippled still further any chance of creating an effective modern Chechen state; it greatly strengthens tendencies to 'bastard feudalism' and rule by armed followings of particular chieftains at the expense both of democracy and of lineage rules; it has thrown up some evil individuals, like the late Ruslan Labazanov and Bislan Gantemirov, to play a quasi-feudal role; and in the period 1991–4, clashes between criminal groups contributed to a major return of the blood-feud, which Soviet rule had suppressed.

Even more seriously, organised crime and the profits it generates (together with other aspects of social and economic change) may well destroy the essential unity of Chechen society by creating, for the first time in Chechnya, glaring differences betwen the very rich and the mass of the population, thereby ending the egalitarianism which has been at the core of the special Chechen identity; and it is beginning, especially among youth and the Chechen diaspora, to undermine those Chechen rules of conduct which have done so much to keep Chechnya an 'ordered anarchy' and not a Hobbesian chaos – as well as forming the backbone of Chechen fighting resistance.

On the other hand, to put it bluntly, the 'mafia' has brought in an awful lot of money, without which Chechnya's position even before the war would have been desperate, and which may provide the only real chance of postwar reconstruction. Before the war, this money was immediately visible in the great mosques and palatial residences built by the 'businessmen' from Moscow and elsewhere. Conversations with ordinary Chechens soon brought out the fact that a large part of the population was being helped, even if only at second or third hand, by rich relatives somewhere in their extended families.

The decay of the Soviet state and of checks on the black market under Brezhnev – especially in the Caucasus region – gave the first opportunities to Chechen businessmen. They seem to have been unusually favoured not just by social traditions and the impenetrability of their society but also by the fact that the deportation had had the effect of spreading them all over the former Soviet Union. The Chechens are possessed of great self-confidence in this field. As my mafia acquaintance, quoted above, told me, in words vaguely reminiscent of those I could imagine a Sicilian Mafia leader having used about Irish gangs earlier this century,

> We Chechens keep our secrets, and none of our people will ever talk about them to an outsider. We are also united. But even more important is the fact that we are disciplined and self-restrained. Unlike the Russians, we don't go round killing people or smashing things for fun or because we got drunk. We only use force when really necessary; but if we give a warning, everyone knows we mean it and they'd better listen. That is why all the other groups, the Russians, the Azeris, the Georgians and whoever – they all have to pay rent to us, and respect our territory.

This does not seem to be an exaggeration. For example, when in November 1988 a crowd of Azeri traders at a Moscow market killed a Chechen gangster who had been extorting money from them, the Chechens united to launch a series of retaliatory beatings of every Azeri they could find, leaving more than a hundred people badly injured.

It must be said that in accordance with his self-image, my mafia contact was a small man with a modest, unassuming manner, who did not throw his weight around – though on the other hand he hardly needed to, since he was accompanied by an exceptionally large and ferocious-looking bodyguard, who no doubt threw the weight – when 'really necessary'. According to his portrait, the Chechens are what in Elizabethan England would have been called the 'upright men' of the criminal world; that is certainly what they would call themselves. A profile of the different Moscow mafia groups by *Nezavisimaya Gazeta* in 1996 said that 'no expert could name a single location in Moscow without a Chechen mafia patron,' and that in that year the Chechens, together with the Russian Solntsevo gang, were the two most powerful criminal groups in the city.[48] Nikolai Modestov has written that:

> The Chechens were the first, having developed a perfect mastery of the art of making a 'roof' for businessmen and putting a tax on trade, to switch over to the manufacture of counterfeit letters of advice – a type of crime that for a long time had been ignored by the law-enforcement agencies and that cost the state, even according to the most modest estimates, tens of trillions of roubles.[49]

Chechen mafia power in Moscow, however, reportedly diminished greatly in the course of the Chechen War, with the police backing other criminal groups in cutting them down to size. What will happen next is hard to say. On the one hand, the tension between Russians and Chechens should ease; on the other, the influence of the criminals' allies in the ranks of the Russian-backed Chechen opposition has obviously also been radically reduced – though it could rise again if Russia resumes covert attempts at influence in Chechnya.

The opportunities given to criminals of every kind by the Soviet collapse and privatisation have already been noted. In the Chechen case, they were undoubtedly helped by the national revolution of 1991. This is not simply a Russian accusation; several of these men told me so themselves.

Chechens are in fact usually remarkably frank and open in talking about their criminal activities with outsiders – 'admitting' would not be the right word, for there is no implication of guilt or apology. For example, I once asked a Chechen fighter whom I met during the fighting in Serzhen Yurt in May 1995 what his prewar occupation had been. 'Oh, I was a racketeer in Moscow,' he replied – adding cheerfully 'And I suppose when this is all over, *insh'allah*, I shall go back to my racket. Come and be my guest when I'm mayor of Moscow!'

The reasons for this approach seem threefold: in the first place, as noted, it is a respectable part of their tradition; secondly, Chechens do not in the end give a damn what anyone else, or any other people thinks about them; and thirdly and most importantly, after their experiences of the past two centuries, there is an underlying feeling that they owe no moral obligation to any other people, state or set of laws – and with the Russians, of course, they have on the contrary a long score of their own to settle.

From this point of view, the Chechens might be called a nightmare for the modern Western liberal's views and ideals. They are a nationality with no identification with the state and the society in which they live, and no motivation whatsoever to conform with its laws; equipped with ancient traditions which are in contradiction to those of 'enlightened', 'pluralist' and 'progressive' liberalism; with social forms which make them opaque to outside investigation; internally cohesive, and remarkably efficient and ruthless in pursuit of their aims; and in a country in which a mixture of poorly institutionalised 'democracy', social disintegration, state weakness and state corruption have opened up the most enormous opportunities and spaces for organised criminal activity. One might almost say, to adapt a phrase of Robert Musil's, that if the modern Western bourgoisie could dream, it would dream Chechens.

11 'The Prayers of Slaves Are Not Heard in Heaven': Chechnya and Islam, a Religious Nation or a National Religion?

In the Name of God, the Compassionate, the Merciful:
Believers, why is is that when you are told: 'March in the cause of God', you linger slothfully in the land? Are you content with this life over the life to come? Few indeed are the blessings of this life, compared to those of the life to come.
If you do not go to war, He will punish you sternly, and replace you with other men...'

From the Ninth Shura, 'Repentance', of the Koran

The prayers of slaves are not heard in Heaven.

Teaching of al-Yaraghi, Naqshbandi leader in Chechnya and Daghestan, 1820s

Religion and Nationalism

In explaining the unique fighting morale of the Chechens it is impossible to ignore the role of religion, but also important not to exaggerate its political importance for the present day – something which Russian propagandists do all the time. At one level, the gut, often unformulated belief that the Chechens are a people especially chosen by God remains of tremendous importance, and is intimately tied to the belief, already emphasised, that Chechen traditions, or Adat, supposedly sanctioned by Islam (though often in fact long predating Islam, or even in direct contradiction to Islamic precepts), give Chechen life and behaviour a particular nobility, dignity and beauty.[1]

Above all, Islam is held to as something that makes the Chechens different from the Russians, and – in so far as they are convinced that they are better Muslims than any of the other supposedly Muslim peoples of the Caucasus – superior to their other neighbours. There are many examples among both Muslim and Christian nations for religion acting in this way. The process develops over time and goes something like the following:

Some form of ethnos, and of ethno-cultural identity, usually with one formal religious allegiance, emerges over the centuries (though this formal religious alignment may well, as in sixteen-century Ireland, the Dutch East

Indies or the eighteenth-century Caucasus, cover a host of what are in effect pagan beliefs and practices). This ethnos then comes under attack from an empire, or national group, with another religion. The threatened ethnos develops a stronger and stronger allegiance to its own religion and, in particular, to those forms of it which will help strengthen its military and/or cultural powers of resistance. In the struggle, it may also generate new religious forms and institutions. For long periods, it may appear – and it may even to an extent be true – that the struggle is a religiously inspired and not an ethnic or proto-national one. Then, in the modern era, the specifically religious identity and forms of resistance are supplanted by those of secular nationalism – but a nationalism whose symbols and rhetoric are thoroughly permeated with religious metaphors and language.

How far the new nationalists will feel committed to the religion as such will depend essentially on two things: the conservatism (or 'backwardness') of their society and class; and the degree to which their national culture appears threatened either by assimilation or destruction by outside cultural influences. In cases like Ireland (or to a lesser extent Ukraine) where even the national language has either disappeared or seems in danger of being overwhelmed by the 'imperial' language, then even nationalists who in terms of their basic ideology ought to be secularists or even anti-clerics may cling with catatonic strength to their 'national religion' as the last anchor of national cultural separateness.

Even if the threat is not so great, some nationalists may stick closely to religion if the process of homogenising modernisation in their societies has been both especially wrenching, ruthless and bleak, and closely associated with the outside imperial power and culture. Only in very rare cases of a few clear-headed nationalist intellectuals and/or politicians are these conscious strategic choices. Most people of course turn in one or other direction instinctively or as a result of general cultural transformations which they themselves never analyse.

Finally, a nation and its members who have fought many wars and expect to fight many more may well keep a stronger religious sense than a nation long at peace. We all pray when under fire.

Islam in the War of Shamil and the War of Dudayev

During the latest war, the word 'atheists' (or rather 'godless') was often used by Chechens as a term of contempt for the Russians, not really in its strict sense, but to suggest that by contrast with the Chechens, the Russians had no personal or national dignity, and none of the real or alleged codes of behaviour which – according to the Chechen self-image – govern Chechen life and society. And, as the passage from Solzhenitsyn quoted in the previous chapter suggests, this self-image really has been active not just in maintaining a fighting spirit, but also in restraining personal behaviour in what from a 'modern' point of view seems a very lawless society.

For its part, the Russian exaggeration of the political role of religion in con-temporary Chechnya is an effort to brand the Chechen separatists as 'Muslim fundamentalists'. The intention (very close to the propaganda of the French against the FLN during the Algerian War) has generally been threefold: to appeal to Western audiences with the line that the war has been a sort of West-ern crusade against a common Islamic enemy; to argue that the Chechens are too 'primitive' to have developed a modern nationalism and sense of national identity; and to suggest that as simple, primitive people, they have been mis-led by religious propaganda into acting contrary to their own best interests.[2]

From my own observations, I would say on the contrary that the Chechen struggle of the 1990s has been overwhelmingly a national or nationalist one. In so far as it has taken on a religious colouring, this was mainly because Islam is seen, even by irreligious Chechens, as an integral part of the national tradi-tion and of the nation's past struggles against Russian domination. As Soviet officers, neither General Dudayev nor Colonel Maskhadov can have previ-ously been regularly practising Muslims; and even Shamil Basayev, while always a convinced Muslim, did not give me the impression before the war of being a particularly strict one. Islam seems less of a motive force in itself than something which has been adopted both by the Dudayev regime and by indi-vidual Chechen fighters as a spiritual clothing for their national struggle.

By contrast, from 1829 to 1921, in the Chechens' wars and revolts against the Russians, religion was undoubtedly a prime source of inspiration. These struggles were also religious wars, 'ghazavats', taking place under the banner of Islam and under the leadership of members of the Naqshbandi order of Muslim Sufism. The difference is summed up in the following two songs or anthems, the first from the time of Shamil, the second the most famous national fighting song of the 1990s.

Psalm of Shamil
Oh servants of God, people of God!
Help us, in the name of God,
Give us your help.
Maybe we shall succeed by the mercy of God.

For the sake of Allah, servants of God,
Help us for the sake of God.

For the sake of Ta-Ha, the Sovereign of the Worlds,
For the sake of Ali the Most Holy:
You, the light of the eyes of truth,
Lead us to the wished-for end.
For the sake of Allah etc.

Make bare the sword, oh people!
Come to our help:

Bid farewell to sleep and quietness,
I call you in the name of God!
For the sake of Allah etc.

Zaynul-Abidin is in your midst,
Lo, he stands at the door.
He shivers on account of your want of steadfastness,
And prays to God the Only One.
For the sake of Allah etc.

You are the Gates to Allah,
Come, save, make haste,
Those who have strayed, who have fallen away,
Have fallen away from the people of God.
For the sake of Allah etc.

Zaynul-Abidin inspires you,
He stands at your doors.
God preserve us from backsliding.
On, comrades in the cause of God!

Freedom or Death [Sung in Russian]
We were born at night when the she-wolf whelped,
In the morning to the roar of lions we were given our names.
In eagles' nests our mothers nursed us.
To tame wild bulls our fathers taught us.

There is no God but Allah. [in Arabic]

Our Mothers pledged us to our people and our homeland.
And if they need us – we know how to fight hard.
With the eagles of the mountains we grew up free together.
With dignity we have overcome every obstacle in our way.

There is no God but Allah.

Granite rocks will sooner fuse like lead,
Than we will lose our dignity in life and struggle.
The earth will sooner be consumed by the fire of the sun,
Than we will face the world, having lost our honour.

There is no God but Allah.

We will never submit to any man or any force.
Freedom or Death – for us that is the only choice.
Our sisters heal our wounds with their songs.
The eyes of our beloved inspire us to feats of arms.

There is no God but Allah.

If hunger torments us – we will eat the roots of trees.
If thirst troubles us – we will drink dew from the grass.
For we were born at night when the she-wolf whelped.
And to God, people and homeland,
We owe alone our lives and our duty.

There is no God but Allah.[4]

The language of the first is purely religious, and contains mystical references, like those to Ta Ha (a mystical name for God) and Imam Zayn ul-Abidin, which the great majority of Chechens of today – including most members of Sufi orders – would find utterly obscure. The second is overwhelmingly nationalist, almost at times unwittingly animist in its imagery, with the refrain 'There is No God but Allah' (the Koranic declaration of faith, in Arabic) tacked on almost as an afterthought. The language differs from the common run of such appeals in its greater use of natural imagery, in its stronger appeal to traditional family links – and in the fact that unlike most of the peoples who sing such songs, the Chechens have actually lived up to their own heroic self-image.

Sufism in Chechnya

It was in the early nineteenth century that radical Sufism among the Chechens made rapid strides, precisely due to the fact that it preached resistance to the Russians, who were beginning to press harder and harder on the mountain tribes. Defence of Islam and defence of the Mountaineers' ethnic traditions, societies and (largely pre-Islamic) way of life ran together from the start, and though the feelings of the Mountaineers at that time could not be described as 'nationalist' in the modern sense, they might be called pre- or proto-nationalist.

The ascetic traditions of the original Sufi mystics, however compromised by their later descendants in much of the Muslim world, were and are also of course admirably suited to the needs of a military order fighting against heavy odds. There is also a possibility that the attractiveness of Muridism to the Chechens stemmed in part from older, pre-Islamic traditions of voluntary 'warrior brotherhoods' among Chechen youth, with analogies to the warrior lodges of the North American plains Indians.

It also seems likely that just as the unrelenting spirit of resistance to the infidel in Sufism appealed to the passionate Chechen desire to defend their freedom and way of life against the Russians, so the 'brotherly', non-hierarchical aspect of the Sufis appealed to the lack of hierarchy and monarchical authority in the Chechen tribal traditions (something in which Chechnya sharply differed from neighbouring Daghestan, with its Khans and its traditional 'Shamkal' overlords, who maintained a tenuous hegemony over the region until the later seventeenth century). In the words of an old Chechen saying, 'there are no intermediaries between a Chechen and his God.'

By virtue of the fact that their revolt was not just against the Russians but also against the Russians' local clients among the khans of Daghestan, the war of Qazi Mullah and his successor Shamil took on some aspects of an anti-elite struggle – though Shamil also of course made willing use of any members of royal families who were willing to support him. The two leaders themselves came from notable families, but neither royal nor distinguished by religious achievement. Thus Shamil's father was a notorious wine drinker (until Shamil disciplined his erring parent by threatening to commit suicide). Nor, unlike Abd al-Qadir in Algeria or the great hereditary pirs of the Middle East, Afghanistan and South Asia, did either of them claim descent from the Prophet (Abd al-Qadir was the descendant of an important lineage of marabouts). Both Qazi Mullah and Shamil appear to have achieved leadership in the first instance not through hereditary prestige but through sheer force of character, charisma, physical and moral courage, and public displays of piety and ruthless religious self-discipline, according to the Naqshbandi code. Thus a key moment in the beginning of their uprising was when they publicly and savagely flogged each other in their ancestral village for having in the past sinned by drinking wine.

'Miraculous' elements also played their part. Thus one characteristic of a Sufi leader, regularly displayed by Shamil (as by Abd al-Qadir), was his ability to know in advance when someone was coming to see him – the 'miracle' in this case no doubt consisting in a good system of sentinels. Like Abd al-Qadir, Shamil also experienced (or staged – though the distinction would doubtless not have been clear even in their own minds) religious trances, in which he would receive instructions from the Prophet.[5]

The Sufi 'movement' has over the past centuries stimulated resistance to infidel rule over much of the Muslim world. In Afghanistan, Sufi hereditary 'saints', or pirs, played a major role in beginning resistance to Communist revolution and Soviet invasion, though they were soon overshadowed by more modern Islamic radicals. These radicals themselves, however, often drew on older Sufi traditions of asceticism, of resistance, and indeed of organisation.

Sufism is a very old tendency within Islam. Its name is thought to derive from the Arabic for 'wool', after the simple woollen clothes that its adepts wore as a symbol of their simplicity and indifference to the world (in the manner of various orders of Catholic monks). One of the founders of the Sufi tradition in the eight century AD was a woman, Rabia al-Adawia, and women in Chechnya today have their own Sufi groups as part of the wider orders, and on occasion perform the sung zikr in public – as they did on the road to Grozny in order to stop the advancing Russian troops in the first days of the war.

From as early as the twelfth century, when the Christian crusades in the Middle East marked the first real infidel counter-attack against the hitherto continuous expansion of Islam, Sufi orders in different places and at different times have also been strongly marked by a combination of the defence of the faith in arms against external enemies, and its strengthening from within by the purging of un-Islamic practices among the faithful. Certainly in the Sufism of the North Caucasus there has been little of the free-ranging, often hetero- dox mystical speculation that used to mark the Sufis of the Middle East, Iran and the Moghul empire of India. Members of Chechen virds today seem to be in principle perfectly orthodox Sunni Muslims, distinguished from those outside the Soviet Union only by their relative ignorance of Muslim traditions, natural in people who have lived for so long under Soviet rule and therefore without an educated Islamic clergy. In fact, ever since Sufism arrived among them in the eighteenth century, the Chechens have had more immediate things to think about than mystical speculation.

In our own time, and elsewhere in the Islamic world, Sufi traditions have by contrast been bitterly attacked by radical Islamic reformers for their unde- mocratic, 'aristocratic' and therefore decadent aspects, as well as for their 'impure', un-Islamic borrowings from local tradition (animist, Hindu or other). The attacks have focused above all on the cults of hereditary Sufi saints, in North Africa called 'marabouts' (as rendered in the French transla- tion), and in South Asia, pirs. Because of the wealth they accumulated, and their established position, these pirs and marabouts later had a tendency to accept colonial rule and oppose radical attempts to overthrow it, whether from a nationalist or an Islamist direction.[6]

Both aspects of hereditary pirdom in its decadence were classically dis- played by the family of Pir Ahmed Gailani of Afghanistan, with whose largely ineffective Mujahidin forces I travelled to Kandahar in January 1989. His simple fighters would regale me around the tea-kettle with tales of the Pir compelling the worship of snakes, taming earthquakes, and bringing down supernatural vengeance on the wicked (one story had the Pir holding up a col- lapsing house by his will).

This was rather hard for me to imagine. The Pir himself, his family and lead- ing suppporters were known in the press corps as 'the Gucci guerrillas' for their lavish international lifestyle – unkindly, perhaps, since many of us had bene- fited from his courtesy and hospitality – and the closest some of them got to military activity was the wearing of tastefully camouflaged crocodile-skin shoes (I was acutely reminded of them at my first meeting with the Georgian 'militia' leader Djaba Yosseliani, who had a camouflaged gold fountain pen). They were of course cordially hated by Afghan radical Islamists of every stamp, even when these also loathed each other. The radical Islamists of our time have stamped out traditional pirdom wherever they have had the power to do so.

It is interesting to note that the modern secular Turkish state was also for a long time also strongly hostile to the Sufi orders, because all three main tendencies in Sufism appeared to threaten it and its goals. Ataturk and his dis-ciples hated the Sufis on the one hand because in the form of the 'dervishes', with their public performances and their association with drugs and ecstatic dancing, they represented decadent 'superstition', hostile to the modern, rational, nationalist Turkey of the Kemalist dream; on the other hand, in their role as defenders of the orthodox faith, they threatened the secular Turkish state with a return of the divinely sanctioned Ottoman order. Finally, because of their capacity to create clandestine brotherhoods, they represented a gen-eral threat to state authority and police control. In consequence, until the 1980s most Sufi orders were strictly banned in republican Turkey.

Sufism historically has been in some ways virtually coterminous with Islam in Chechnya, in that, under an Islamic veneer, most of the population remained largely animist in its beliefs and behaviour until the arrival of Sufi missionaries of the Naqshbandi order in the later eighteenth century. The Ingush, to the West, were already under Russian control, in many cases fought on the Russian side, and were not really converted from their traditional pagan animism (by missionaries of the Qadirya order) until the later nineteenth century, and then not to nearly the same extent as the Chechens. Baddeley describes how in 1897, Sufi Muslims suppressed an Ingush festival still dedicated to two traditional pagan demi-gods.[7] This difference, more than that between the related Chechen and Ingush languages, explains the politi-cal, cultural and social differences between the Ingush and Chechen peoples today.

The fact that in the 1780s, the Naqshbandis had not had time to strike deep roots in the north-eastern Caucasus is undoubtedly a major reason for Sheikh Mansur's failure to bring unity and stamina to his forces. Sheikh Mansur him-self was a leader of the Naqshbandis, but his followers were made up of mostly barely Islamic tribesmen with little to unite them (the Kabardins, in particular, in the Middle Ages alternated between a formal and superficial Orthodox Christianity and an equally formal Islam, and today, though they are nominally Islamic, religion plays little part in their culture). In conse-quence, his followers melted away after the first defeats, whereas most of Shamil's remained loyal – a testimony first and foremost to the discipline and spirit of his Naqshbandi Murids. It is also a notable testimony to the power of religion that although Qazi Mullah and Shamil were both Avars from Daghestan, not Chechens (and even Sheikh Mansur's ethnic provenance is doubtful), that did not prevent the bulk of Chechens from rallying to their cause.

The same was true in the war of 1920–1, which was led by Naqshbandi sheikhs. The key importance of Sufism is also demonstrated by the disunity of the anti-Russian resistance of the Western Caucasus, where the tribes had no Sufi ideology and brotherhoods to unite them. Indeed, this difference between the two regions persisted under Soviet rule and has up to the present day, and is one reason (together with the depopulation of the Circassians and Turkic peoples in the 1860s and 1940s) for the failure of the Chechen example of revolt in the 1990s to spread to the Western Caucasus.

Islam and Politics in Contemporary Chechnya and the North Caucasus

Today, the relative importance of religion and nationality has been reversed. Of course, some members of General Dudayev's regime may well have been genuinely devout Muslims; and certainly, as the spontaneous wave of mosque-building mentioned above indicates, Islam retained a major role in Chechen society. However, for many Chechens in lowland and urban Chechnya this role had during Soviet rule become largely ceremonial, in a characteristically modern way; that is to say, a matter for rites of passage, for circumcisions, marriages, burials and – after Gorbachev's liberalisation began to allow this – for public and national occasions. For many leading figures, and certainly for Dudayev, it had essentially become an aspect of Chechen national tradition and national pride, rather than the central motivating force in its own right. To judge by various conversations with him, I should even say that this was true to a considerable extent of Shamil Basayev, though he was more Muslim by culture and came from a more conservative background, in the mountain area of Vedeno.

For the first two years after he came to power, Dudayev explicitly ruled out the creation of an 'Islamic republic' – at least when speaking to Russian and Western journalists. In his words, 'Where any religion prevails over the secular constitutional organisation of the state, either the Spanish Inquisition or Islamic fundamentalism will emerge.'[8] It is striking that in his pre-election programme of October 1991 there is almost nothing about Islam or even about religion in general, let alone any indications of radical Islamism. On the contrary, even the section headed 'The Spiritual Sphere' is entirely filled with the language of human rights, pluralism and democracy – in other words the discourse which was then dominant throughout Russia, especially in the wake of the defeat of the August coup: 'To guarantee to every citizen of the republic the defence of their freedom, honour, conscience and personal dignity, and the development of their culture, faith, language and national traditions…'[9]

Dudayev really began to shift on this in 1993, as his regime came under heavy internal pressure, and as he dissolved parliament and came to rely instead on 'traditional', religiously sanctioned 'councils of elders' to provide a façade of democracy and popular legitimacy. However, it was only with the autumn of 1994, and the imminent threat of war, that the rhetoric of political Islam became insistent – and even then, it was I felt overwhelmingly a symbol and expression of national feeling rather than a detailed programme in its own right.

President Yandarbiyev, Dudayev's ally and successor, is generally held to be the man who on the general's return to Chechnya in 1990 introduced him to the symbolic possibilities of political Islam. How far Yandarbiyev himself was acting opportunistically rather than from conviction I wouldn't like to say. His memoir/propaganda work, published in 1994, has very little on Islam – possibly, of course, because it was written in Russian and intended to influence a Russian audience (he even quotes a Russian philosopher, Lev Shestov, on freedom, rather than any Muslim work).[10] I heard that to visitors from the Muslim world he set out a very different line, but certainly the language, style and indeed contents of his book are extremely Soviet.

His enemies portray him as an unsuccessful minor poet, one of the legions of semi-employed Soviet provincial intellectuals, who latched on to Islam as a way of making a name for himself; but this does not of itself preclude conviction, and it is in any case a testimony to the continued power of religion in Chechnya that he should have seen a future in this (it is not a thought that would come to an ambitious intellectual in Azerbaijan, for example).

On the other hand, an example of the relative weakness of Islam as a possible tool for building political support, and its general irrelevance to the political process in 1991–4 is the case of Bislan Gantemirov. A former police sergeant turned used-car dealer and minor mafia boss in Moscow, he returned to Chechnya in 1990 and went into politics, becoming Mayor of Grozny from 1991–3, and then joining the opposition and returning as Mayor under the Russian occupation, forming the 'Islamic Path' party. When I interviewed him in February 1992, I therefore dutifully asked him all the proper questions about Islamic politics and social reform, Islam and pluralism, and links to Iran – and his answers of course were vague, not to say embarrassed – in fact, just like those of someone who has gate-crashed a party.[11]

Concerning the Chechen Information Minister, Mauvladi Udugov, when I first interviewed him in January 1992 he was quite obviously playing on fears of Islam simply to try to gain his real goal, which was Western support, and I detected no serious Islamic feeling whatsoever in his conversation:

> The task the Dudayev government has set itself is to create a democratic constitutional government, and so far the people support this. But if Moscow creates terrorist acts and blames it on Dudayev, and this leads to civil war, then this could lead to a victory of the Muslim fundamentalists and an Afghan situation here. This would not be in anyone's interest, ours Russia's or the West's. So it is in the interests of the international community to support Dudayev as the leader of a democratic secular state, on the model of Turkey, not Iran.[12]

Dudayev himself also explicitly used the 'Islamic threat' to try to deter Russian attack in 1994. Speaking to the 'council of elders' in November 1994, he said that 'one way to fight against Russian aggression' would be to introduce the Shariat, but that 'if the Russians will stop the aggression, we will take away this Islamic constitution.' There could hardly be a more obvious and open attempt to use Islam for a political and national end rather than for its own sake.[13]

The growth of Shariat courts and punishments in the separatist-held areas of the mountains from the spring of 1995 onwards reflected partly the greater conservatism of these areas, but it also appeared to spread chiefly from the Chechen fighting groups, and to have been motivated above all by military considerations. This was partly a matter of individual psychology: men who have been under continual bombardment for months on end and have seen their comrades fall around them one by one may well seek comfort in religion and in the belief that their struggle is divinely inspired. But in forces with no military organisation and no other formal code, the need for military discipline also played a part (something I have also seen in Afghanistan). As the war progressed, and war weariness and the temptation to give up and go home grew among the fighters, the Shariat was called in as an extra means of discipline, to join the existing ones of familial loyalty and social shame. Such informal, 'spontaneous' sources of discipline have been both crucial and strikingly successful.

This decline in the religious factor and rise in the national one is especially important in explaining the failure of Daghestan today to rise in support of the Chechens. For Daghestan, divided and subdivided by its high ridges and deep valleys, is the very core of 'Language Mountain' (as the Arabs called the Caucasus). Twenty-six 'official' languages were registered there under Soviet rule, with at least a dozen more mutually incomprehensible dialects.[14] In the past, it was religious culture that held this area together as a sort of unity, with the educated classes (who were by definition also the religious elite) communicating in Arabic, the language of the Koran, and others using Persian of Avar as a sort of lingua franca. Today, the dependence of the region on Russia is emphasised by the fact that to understand each other at all, the different nationalities of the region have to communicate in Russian.

Under Soviet rule, the separate consciousness of these 'nationalities' was assiduously fostered – 'divide and rule', as usual – even as the state pressed down hard on both organised and informal religion. The attempt to destroy religion completely has failed, but the fostering of nationality has been strikingly successful (though not always in ways Moscow would have wished!), if only because, as with so many Soviet trends, it was not unique but formed a particular and peculiar aspect of a general world process of 'modernisation'. After all, in the modern world in general, Islam – and Christianity – have had only mixed success in the mobilisation of political movements across national or ethnic borders. Islamic allegiance in India was strong enough to split Pakistan from 'Hindu' India, but has not done too well in keeping it united thereafter.

After the fall of the Soviet Union, therefore, several of Daghestan's main national groups have developed territorial claims against each other and are watching each other with intense wariness. The ex-Communist rulers of the Autonomous Republic – and indeed, any politically aware Daghestani – know that any attempt to follow the Chechen example would lead not to collective revolt but to a whole series of local ethnic wars, which would be assiduously fanned by Moscow, and would lead to disaster for the region.

In terms of unity against Russia, the influence of Sufism in Chechnya in the nineteenth century was also to an extent Janus-faced. While it was, as already argued, essential for the discipline and unity of the Mountaineers' struggle, in its Caucasian variant as a force of Koranic, puritan and reformist Islam, it also ran up against many of the Mountaineers' ancient customs, embodied in the codes of the Adat. Shamil's state was formally based on the Shariat, or Islamic law. He made determined efforts to stamp out smoking and drinking – the latter, in particular, a deeply-rooted tradition among all the Caucasian peoples – as un-Islamic. Above all, he concentrated on those aspects of tradition which tended to sow division and weaken the war effort, most notably the blood-feud.[15]

In our own time, this tension between Shariat and Adat was mentioned by several of my Chechen acquaintances, who said for example that to beat a man in public for a crime, according to the Shariat, was against Chechen tradition, because it humiliated him: 'his name will never recover.' Even more importantly, 'to punish a woman is the business of her own family, not of strangers.' In Daghestan in 1997, the increasing preaching of strict Koranic Islam by Wahabi-influenced missionaries was beginning to lead to violent clashes with defenders of the old local traditions, which they called Sufi but which were often in fact pre-Islamic.

Resentment at this Islamic pressure on traditional and peasant customs probably added to the resentment of Shamil which was also motivated partly by the Chechen resentment of all authority, and partly by sheer war-weariness (a combination of factors which has also been present in Chechnya in the 1990s). Bitterness with Shamil and the Naqshbandis over the long and in the end futile struggle was widespread in the wake of the surrender of 1859, when many of the Naqshbandis fled or were deported to the Ottoman empire. So strongly embedded had Sufism become, however, so appropriate was it to the organisation of resistance, and so deeply did the Chechens hate Russian – and later Soviet – rule that, rather than abandoning Sufism altogether, many Chechens switched from the Naqshbandi to new local branches of the Qadiriya, the other great Sufi tradition. Most notably they followed the local saint and preacher Kunta Haji, a contemporary rival of Shamil and by origin a Kumyk from Daghestan living in Chechnya. Though he was arrested by the Russians in 1864 for allegedly plotting revolt, and died three years later in Russian captivity, Kunta Haji had preached a more contemplative form of Islam, which appealed to people for whom active resistance to the Russians was temporarily at least impossible.

Unlike the Naqshbandis, who worship in silence, the Qadiris practise ecstatic public rituals, sometimes ending in religious trances. In Chechnya, this took the form of the 'loud zikr' – zikr, or dhikr, meaning 'remembrance', as in remembrance of God, and indicating collective prayer and the repetitive chanting of the ninety-nine names of God (from the command in the Koran to 'remember God often'). I was told by Mahomet-Haji Dolkayev, one of the main leaders and organisers of the zikrs in the main square of Grozny at the start of the war, that the circular motion of the dance is meant to imitate both the passage of worshippers round the Kabala in Mecca, and also the movement of the universe, as well as bringing the dancers into a state of religious ecstasy. The dancing and chanting circles of Chechen men (and occasionally of women, for female orders, though relatively rare, do exist in the contemporary Chechen Qadirya), which have become a symbol of Chechen mass resistance, belong to this tradition.

In recent times, I have heard some supporters of the pro-Russian forces in Chechnya give their membership of the Kunta Haji Qadiri tradition as a 'principled' reason for their position. For example, in the words of a Mullah who had declared his support for the pro-Russian 'government' of Salambek Khadjiev, and gave his name simply as Mahomet,

> Kunta Haji was for peace with Russia and all countries. He opposed Shamil and was imprisoned by him. He preached only the duty of every man to obey God's law and set a good example. Shamil, on the contrary, used to rob the whole people to pay for his endless wars. He allowed his Murids to steal whatever they liked. Kunta Haji would not agree to this. That is why Shamil drove him out. He wanted to kill him, but he was too holy and respected... We are following his teaching today.[16]

This may however be pure hypocrisy, and in general the majority of Chechen adherents of the Kunta Haji tradition today are just as committed to armed resistance as are those of the Naqshbandi orders. Mahomet-Haji Dolkayev, mentioned above, a descendant of Sheikh Mansur, a repeatedly imprisoned Soviet religious dissident, and Kunta-Haji member, is a strong supporter of Dudayev – and for that matter the family of Dudayev himself came from this background.

Because of its potential for inspiring resistance, the loud zikr of the Qadirya was strictly banned by the Tsarist authorities – the US authorities were led in the same period to launch a severe repression against the 'Ghost Dancers' of the Sioux, leading to the battle and massacre at Wounded Knee. The ban on the loud zikr was of course enforced even more strictly under Soviet rule, and from the early 1970s the Sufis were recognised by the KGB, and by Communist scholars, as a major threat to Soviet rule and Communist ideology in the region. A considerable Soviet literature grew up on the theme, much of it admittedly grossly inaccurate.[17]

A Sufi Evening

I had a brief but solemn and deeply moving experience of Chechen Sufism during a visit to common prayers of a Kunta-Haji vird (sub-sect of the Qadirya) in a small working-class flat in Grozny in February 1992. It was entirely made up of close relatives, brothers, nephews and cousins, which tends to confirm a point made by Alexandre Bennigsen and Enders Wimbush (relying on Soviet sources) that membership in a vird under Soviet rule became increasingly the automatic result of belonging to a particular lineage, or even extended family, and that becoming a member is one of the passages to adulthood and to a recognised role as an adult male within the family.

On the one hand, this has weakened the purely religious aspect of Sufism in Chechnya, and drawn it away from both mysticism and religious asceticism; on the other hand, it has woven it still more deeply into the social fabric of the country. As already noted, this interweaving of the virds and the lineages has been analogous to the process of Chechen military recruitment and unit formation during the war, and has also itself contributed to unit cohesion and morale. These groups are very Chechen in that the only authority within them is informal and stems from family relationships and personal prestige without any role for official clergy.

Another point of these authors which my hosts confirmed was that under Soviet rule it was considered no mortal sin by Chechen Sufis to deny membership of the vird if interrogated by the Soviet authorities, and to eat pork and drink vodka when there was no other choice, as during military service. 'God does not expect us to commit suicide for no good reason' was the way one of them put it. He spoke of the vital role which the virds had played during the deportation, in holding the Chechen people together and preserving their traditions.

The prayer-chants themselves were wonderfully beautiful and impressive, and also as far as I know specific to the north-eastern Caucasus – certainly completely unlike the 'Qawali' mystical Sufi music of Pakistan and the Middle East: this was a deep, droning bass chant, rising and falling, as if the earth were humming to itself. The nine men accompanied this by beating their hands softly on the table, a massively heavy Soviet contraption, so that the whole flat shook gently.

Such a gathering of course would have been quite impossible to keep 'secret' in any real sense; but as one member said, 'among Chechens, neighbour does not betray neighbour. Two of us here were members of the Communist Party, you had to be. That didn't stop us being Chechens and Muslims. It didn't mean we were betraying Chechnya.'

In spite of its solemnity, the evening did have a lighter note. Early on, my host, an elderly, grizzled truck driver, showed me an old, hilt-less sword and a *kinjal* (long dagger) on the wall, telling me that they had belonged to his grandfather, had been buried during the deportation and dug up when his family returned. His son confided to me later that his father had bought them two years before in return for a used car. A high price to pay, and therefore a testimony to the power of Chechen tradition – though also evidence that, like most traditions, while organic, it is not necessarily immemorial, and is capable of creative cultivation and regeneration over time.

Conclusion

In the centre of the Spanish position in the fields before Rocroy there stands today a little modern monument, an unassuming grey monolith: the gravestone of the Spanish army; almost, one might say, the gravestone of Spanish greatness.

C. V. Wedgwood, *The Thirty Years War*

By way of conclusion, I would like to examine the question of whether the new order of things in the Russia of the 1990s is stable: first, whether the new social, political and economic order is liable to change radically; secondly, whether Russian nationalism could in the foreseeable future take forms dangerous to the peace of Europe.

The Hegemony of the New Order

Concerning the internal situation, there seem few reasons to fear a new revolution, which is what would be needed in order to replace the new elites and transform the nature of the state and economy. This is both because of their own power, and because of the tremendous cultural and ideological support which they receive from the outside world. Simply put, the liberal capitalist model of society is not just overwhelmingly dominant ideologically in the world today, but in global terms it holds sole sway, now that the Communist model has collapsed and the social democratic one is failing.

Unable to confront liberal capitalism in general ideological battle, its opponents have been driven to the periphery, where they justify their positions in terms not of general principles, but of particularist ones, national, cultural or religious (in other words, not that liberal capitalism is wrong *per se*, but that it is wrong *for us*). Associated with this model is, of course, that of 'democracy'; not necessarily the reality, but at least the appearance. In this sense at least, Francis Fukuyama, in his famous or notorious *End of History*, was entirely correct.[1]

Thus numerous governments and elites around the world operate under conditions and in political circumstances where the legislative and judicial branches are emasculated, and the executive all powerful. These executives rig, manage, guide or buy elections, and truly free and fair ones are still in the minority (and for that matter, who can say if even those of the USA today are truly free and fair, given the power of television and the immense money tributes it demands). Relatively few governments however still have the courage, the gall or the desperation to do without elections altogether.

The following passage concerning liberal Mexico in the early twentieth-century, under Porfirio Diaz, could well describe Russia for many years to come – as in many ways it still describes Mexico today:

> The regime's neglect of constitutional requirements...was even clearer in the operations of Mexico's supposedly representative democracy. Diaz's Mexico was thus a member of that great tribe of 'artificial democracies', states in which political practice diverged radically from imposed, liberal theory. Mexican politics were shot through with fraud, graft and nepotism; vices in the eyes of the regime's critics, but sources of strength to Porfirian rulers, complementing brute force, and so deeply entrenched that they easily survived the overthrow of the Porfirian system. It was expected that men in power, nationally and locally, would protect and advance their families and compadres, that political and judicial decisions would be influenced by considerations of personal gain, that concessions and contracts would be awarded according to criteria other than the purely economic. The *mordida* – the 'bite', or bribe – was an integral part of business and politics.[2]

Thanks to the disappearance of the ideological alternatives, even more common are elections without real ideological choices, in which the campaign issues are reduced essentially to those of personalities, honesty and competence in management. This characterises several Western countries. In Russia, at least since the Communist defeat of June 1996, the system seems increasingly to resemble *trasformismo* in liberal Italy (before the introduction of universal suffrage), where the lack of real mass parties and real ideological divisions gave endless possibilities of coopting opposition elements, and members of a government, on losing power, tended simply to flow into the next.

Russia's federal system also gives many opportunities for formerly radical oppositionists to achieve local power, and then to be drawn into working within the system, and together with the economic elites. As the behaviour of the Communists and other 'opposition' groups in the Russian Duma shows, there are already signs of this in Russia. A striking individual example is General Alexander Rutskoy, who in October 1993 tried to bring Yeltsin down by force, and by January 1997, as newly elected Governor of Kursk, was vowing to shun ideology, attract Western investment, and work with the administration and within the system.

As of mid-1997, this also seems true of the Communist Party, at least as led by Gennady Zyuganov. After failing in the 1996 elections (which included the failure of its appeal to Soviet loyalty), it has almost completely passed up opportunities to try to stir up mass protest against the Yeltsin regime – if only because it realises the extreme difficulty of mobilising such protests, at least anywhere close to the seat of power in Moscow. In October 1997, the Communist-led parliament backed off yet again from a vote of no-confidence in the government. In the words of Zyuganov's close adviser, Alexei Podberyozkin, 'Under a constitution which gives parliament limited scope for putting pressure on the government, cooperation is the only pragmatic option... We act according to the real, objective possibilities given us.'³ (Podberyozkin is not a member of the Communist Party – and is head of the American-Russian University!). The most popular and charismatic Communist leader, Aman Tuleyev, joined the Russian government in 1996 – though he left the next year to become Governor of Kemavno.

Or in the words of Oleg Shchedrov in July 1997,

> Yeltsin's main election rival, Communist leader Gennady Zyuganov, and maverick ultra-nationalist Vladimir Zhirinovsky ... control opposition parties but are widely regarded as new members of the elite club. Yeltsin, who vowed not to let the Communists return to power during his election campaign, said after his victory that he was ready to work with all major political forces as long as they play the game. Zyuganov and Zhirinovsky certainly do. They wage a war of words with Yeltsin. Their political groups, which dominate the State Duma, reject some government bills. But when it comes to voting on crucial programmes, such as the budget or the new tax code, the communist and ultra-nationalist deputies have generally preferred under-the-carpet bargaining, and, perhaps surprisingly, often emerged on the Kremlin's side when it mattered most... Rejecting proposals to try to oust the government, Zyuganov said this month, 'We are the responsible opposition.⁴

While therefore, it cannot be excluded that the 'Communists' will win a future Presidential election, this will only happen if they have dropped much of their ideology and done a deal with part of the new capitalist elite.

The security of the new order does not necessarily exclude military coups and demonstrations or some pretty bloody local protests: but while these might change the composition of a particular ruling oligarchy – and would certainly cause momentary panic in the West – they would not lead to an overthrow of the domination of the elites, or a change in the economy. In consequence, they would also not lead to a fundamental change in Russian foreign policy, in so far as this reflects the interests of the new elites in the export of raw materials to the West.

In many Latin American countries in past decades, repeated military coups and military protests have passed as it were over the surface of the state and society, and even caused some ferocious-seeming storms, but never stirred their depths. So it will probably be in Russia, even if the exasperation of the armed forces were one day to boil over into outright mutiny.

Future Revolutions

The present dominance of liberal capitalism in Russia may be compared to the situation in the Italy and Spain of the later nineteenth century, after the defeat of the anciens régimes and before the rise of the Marxist and socialist mass parties – when for many years, some form of the British parliamentary and capitalist model, as represented in theory by the ideology of local liberal elites, seemed self-evidently valid in principle to the great majority of educated opinion, and certainly to its younger and more dynamic elements.[5]

A difference is that on this occasion, the dominance seems even greater and more secure. In the nineteenth century, the Catholic conservative and monarchist forces – unlike the Communists – did not collapse on their own, under the weight of their failures; they had to be defeated by force of arms. And even so, the Church proved to have moral, cultural, ideological and indeed organisational reserves and possibilities far greater than those of Communism, which allowed it in a couple of generations to generate a new ideology ('Social Catholicism') and new mass parties like the Italian Popolari.

In Russia today, the appeal of Communism has definitively collapsed as far as younger, educated and dynamic people are concerned – after all, they do know it pretty well – and nothing has emerged to provide a new ideology of protest. In this sense, there is simply no theoretical alternative to liberal capitalism, and the argument can only be about how efficiently, honestly and justly it is administered (with a great many Russians believing that to expect any of this from politicians is in any case futile). This means that the many discontents with the new order cannot in a sense be formulated, and whatever social, economic and political protests occur in future will find it very difficult to acquire an ideology, and a unifying banner, let alone a party discipline.

Among the later nineteenth-century Spanish and Italian peasantries, following the suppression of the Carlist and the pro-Bourbon 'bandit' revolts, these feelings of moral outrage also did not generally express themselves in terms of mass movements in support of the old royal, clerical and peasant order. The peasants were too inarticulate, impoverished and disorganised for that, the new bourgeois rulers were too militarily and intellectually dominant, and the Catholic Church was either coopted or too cautious and conservative to lead a popular revolt.

But just because discontent cannot be articulated or organised does not mean that it will simply go away; and just because ordinary Italian peasants then or Russian workers now cannot formulate an alternative to the existing order does not mean that they will learn to love it – unless the Russian economy does not just begin to grow, but also to distribute the fruits of that growth throughout society, and the Russian state recovers enough power to act as an agency of elementary social justice.

In Italy and Spain, the bitter resentment of the peasantry at the theft of the common land did not disappear, it simply went underground, where it remained latent, and appeared decades later in new and unpredictable forms: extreme reactionary Catholicism and modern Social Catholicism, but also anarchism, communism, even fascism, united only in their common hatred of the liberal bourgeois order. These movements were never simply generated out of local or national history – the world was already too interlinked for that. Rather, these societies proved especially receptive to infection by various extreme ideologies which were floating around Europe as a result of general socio-economic changes, which they then developed in local and especially virulent forms.

A new Russian revolutionary ideology, if it appears, is also unlikely to be originally home-grown. For the past three centuries, all the various 'Russian ideas', from the new imperial thinking of the seventeenth century through Peter the Great's reforms to Slavophilism, Populism and Communism, have had their intellectual origins outside Russia, although it has often been in Russia that they have taken their most extreme forms. For example, even the most supposedly Russian of all Russian political, cultural and intellectual movements, Slavophil nationalism, in its reaction against the Westernising legacy of Peter the Great, derived intellectually from Herder and from German romantic nationalism. The Bolshevik Revolution would have had neither its intense self-confidence nor its widespread intellectual support in Russia if it had not been seen as part and peak of a general European revolutionary movement, and for that matter, even Lenin would have shrunk from attempting it. In other words, for a new revolutionary wave in Russia we shall have to wait for a new age not just in Russia, but of the world.

But that such a new age will come is beyond question. Our liberal capitalist assumptions will one day surely falter as a result of changes in the economic, ethnic, environmental or even biological balance of the world and of human society. Social problems and strains resulting from economic globalisation are already apparent and could one day lead to reactions against the global economy and immigration. The danger of a global crisis resulting from environmental destruction and climate change is plausible, though as yet not proven. If such a crisis assumed really dramatic proportions, it would demand answers which liberal capitalism and Western-style pluralist democracy by their very nature would find it impossible to give, since the mobilisation of resources necessary to combat them would require greatly increased social discipline, an end to growing prosperity for Western society and an end to capital accumulation for Western business. Such a crisis could be expected to provoke new revolutionary movements. Venturing into the realms of science fiction – but by no means beyond the bounds of the possible, given developments in science which are already occurring – one might speculate about growing movements against increasing physical differences between rich and poor produced by medical developments and genetic engineering, along the lines of a quasi-religious, racial and egalitarian revolt to defend the 'true image' of man. Even in America, your average Joe Morlock doesn't much like James Eloi III as it is. It seems unlikely that his faith in the free market could survive a situation in which Mr and Mrs Eloi are seven feet tall and living to be 120, especially if the health of the mass of the population has gone into decline as a result of new or medicine-proof diseases. This may seem idle fantasising – but it is simply intended as a reminder that there are innumerable (and nasty) possibilities which cannot possibly be accommodated in Fukuyama's complacent dreams.

Two things, however, do already seem predictable: that if such revolutionary ideologies do emerge, they will as in the past find an especially fertile soil in Russia; and, on the other hand, that they will not make a serious appearance for many years to come. History has not ended, as Fukuyama suggested, but it does indeed seem to have reached a kind of plateau, doubtless insignificant in terms of the whole span of human history, but reassuring to us, the temporary dwellers on its relatively peaceful and fruitful plains. It may well be therefore that with all the new Russian order's many problems, inequities, crimes and weaknesses, it will for a long time be able to stumble on, until we all fall down together.

The Exhaustion of Russian Idealism

But of course, short of a new revolution, there are other possibilities for changes in Russia which could have grave consequences for Russia's neighbours and Russia itself. These relate above all to the question of Russian nationalism and the Russian national identity, leading to a greater capacity for national mobilisation and for the inspiration of an aggressive fighting spirit in Russia's soldiers. They should be considered, if only because there are things that the West could do which might risk pushing Russia in this direction.

It should be clear from the whole of this book that I do not think that this is at all probable. Such a change would not be possible without a considerable measure of cultural change and the growth of a new idealism (however misplaced) in Russian society – and chapter 5 analysed the way in which the betrayal and exhaustion of the messianic promises of Communism have worn out the messianic and idealist tradition in Russia, not just the tradition of Communism, but the whole tradition of a belief in Russia's unique spiritual role and mission, which appeared in the works of so many thinkers and writers throughout the last decades of the nineteenth century.

The indifference both of most Russians and of the people who dominate contemporary Russian intellectual life (and much more importantly, Russian television), to thinking about Russia's identity and historic role is shown by the comprehensive sidelining of Russia's most serious and morally prestigious thinker on these themes, Alexander Solzhenitsyn. As Stanislav Kondrashev has written, there is today 'no strength, no will, and no messianic zeal with which to nurture the will to restore today's Russia to its previous status.'[6]

The problem is that precisely because the national identity of ordinary Russians was so weak before the creation of the Soviet Union, and then became so bound up with the Soviet Union and to an extent with the Soviet vision, its disappearance has left the Russians with no clear national identity and indeed without a strong sense of national solidarity. This has negative consequences both social and spiritual. As Regis Debray has written:

> The nation, with its stress on a beginning and a flow in time, and a delimitation in space, raises barriers to the flood of meaninglessness and absurdity that might otherwise engulf human beings. It tells them that they belong to ancient associations of 'their kind', with definite boundaries in time and space, and this gives their otherwise ambiguous and precarious lives a degree of certainty and purpose.[7]

Russian leaders are aware of this gap, but their attempts to fill it have inevitably been pathetic. One aspect of this was Yeltsin's call in the summer of 1996 for the creation of a Russian National Idea – and a state committee promptly got working to create one.[8] Another is Mayor Yuri Luzhkov's attempt to symbolise the Russian identity in a set of monumental buildings in Moscow. With the exception of two reconstructed gems on Red Square (the church of Our Lady of Kazan and the Iversky Gate), the results have been both spiritually empty and aesthetically ridiculous. This is especially true of the giant gonorrhoeic phallus erected on Poklonny Hill to celebrate the 50th anniversary of 1945.

The anniversary celebrations of victory in World War II, in May 1995 included one moment which was highly symbolic for the state of the Russian identity today (I am indebted to my brother, Professor D. C. B. Lieven, for drawing my attention to it). The ceremonies needed a musical climax – but what to play? The International, the Soviet hymn of the wartime period, was obviously out, and so was the Soviet anthem, composed in honour of the victory. The Soviet Russian anthem had been abandoned. The new Russian anthem, a melody from Glinka, was unknown during the war, and has no words as yet (and is also a pretty tinny tune, compared to its imposing predecessors). Desperate, the organisers resorted to Tchaikovsky's '1812'. But even here there was a problem: the climax is of course the old Russian imperial anthem, 'God Save the Tsar', hardly something to play in honour of men who died fighting under Soviet banners. So they played the '1812' – with the climax left out.

It has widely been assumed among Western commentators that the best way of filling this spiritual vacuum, and ending the dangers stemming from Russia's past, would be if Russians moved from their previous Soviet or 'imperial' identity to a 'normal' one as members of a modern nation-state. In the words of Martin Malia, 'Russia surely needs remaking as a cohesive nation state in order to wean her from a now anachronistic imperial heritage.'[9]

Perhaps. But modern nation-states come in many shapes and sizes, and not all are pleasant to live either in or next to. In the case of Russia, any attempt to create a new and narrower version of the Russian national identity runs into two questions: 'What is a Russian?' and 'Where do the borders of the Russian nation lie?'

The Nature of Russian Nationalism

Up to now, the question 'What is a Russian?' has not been at all easy to answer. For while the evil results of Russia's imperial and expansionist identity are obvious, it also had one positive side-effect, which has not been so much commented on: it gave the Russians a very weak sense of themselves as an ethnos, and to a considerable extent it divorced Russian national identity from ethnicity. This was true for reasons both ideological and practical. Ideological, because the claim to be the Third Rome and leader of the Orthodox world precluded the development of a narrow ethnic or national version of loyalty; practical, because from the fifteenth century, Russia conquered and absorbed many other ethnic groups, and in many cases assimilated their elites – as witnessed by the large proportion of Tatar and Circassian names among those of the 'Russian' nobility.

From Peter the Great onwards, the Russian empire also enlisted very large numbers of Germans and others from the West, and at least in the case of the Baltic Germans, these retained their own religion and culture. From Peter up to the later nineteenth century, the Russian emperors – themselves increasingly of German blood – were above all *emperors*, even if they employed Russian symbolism and professed the Orthodox religion. Catherine the Great, like her contemporaries Joseph II and Frederick the Great, was no nationalist, but a centralising moderniser and militarist. Her own culture was purely European.[10] The state slogan coined by Count Uvarov for Nicholas I was 'Pravoslavie, Samoderzhavie, Narodnost', which is usually translated into English as 'Orthodoxy, Autocracy, Nationalism' – but *narodnost* does not mean nationalism, at least not in a modern or ethnic sense.

The imperial regime only swung towards a narrower, more ethnically based version of Russian nationalism in the later nineteenth century, partly in response to the growth of nationalism elsewhere, partly in a desperate attempt to appeal to the masses in the face of the growing revolutionary threat. This distinction between imperial and ethnic loyalty may seem irrelevant today to Poles or others who have suffered from Russian imperialism without living side by side with Russian populations, but as chapter 7 suggested, it certainly ought to matter both to Russia's ethnic minorities and to her neighbours which contain Russian minorities, because it is a key factor in the weak capacity for national mobilisation of the contemporary Russian diaspora, and the general willingness of ordinary Russians to live peaceably with local ethnic majorities. In the words of Vadim Ryzhkov, a Russian historian and journalist from Dnipropetrovsk in Ukraine,

> Russians are not nationalists in the Baltic or Galician sense. For one thing, they have absorbed so many other ethnic groups over the centuries that they really have become a kind of 'super-ethnos', and then the Soviet state sucked away all their national feeling into itself. They

have a very weak national consciousness, but have – or had – a very strong state or imperial consciousness. That is why when their state is taken away they are so incapable of acting or organising themselves to defend their interests – and then of course the local parties of power are taking good care that *no* popular parties of any kind should appear, because that would threaten them and their exploitation of the state.[11]

It should be said that in having in the past owed allegiance to an ideological rather than an ethnic construct, the Russians are far from unique – and even the special nature of Russian national idealism has been somewhat exaggerated by historians like Pipes. Looking round the world, today and in the past, it is the 'classic', 'normal', self-contained ethnic nation which is the one that looks abnormal, at least among the greater powers.

Thus France, America, the Ottoman empire, China, India and Britain all in their different ways developed at some stage in their histories self-definitions which were distanced from ethnicity and which to a greater or lesser extent were open to members of different ethnoses. Such an openness and capacity to attract and assimilate other ethnoses was in fact a condition of their growth. This is also true by their very nature of the new colonially founded states of Africa, into which the imperial powers indiscriminately lumped together different tribes and ethnoses – though how successful these states have been in assimilating these different groups and creating new identities is of course a different matter.

In the case of the British empire, if it is to be seen as originally the *English* empire, then that empire can be said to have swallowed the ethnic identity of its founders. So totally did English nationalism become confused with British imperial patriotism that today it finds tremendous difficulty in even giving itself a name, and survives in public only in strange disguises like 'Euro-scepticism' – not altogether unlike the way in which Russian nationalism was subsumed by the Soviet Union. With the last major colony, Hong Kong, now gone, and Scotland about to become autonomous, it will be very interesting to see how British identities now develop. There is a fruitful comparison to be drawn, fascinating in both the similarities and the differences that it reveals, between the Anglo-Scottish and the Russian-Ukrainian historical relationship.[12]

The lack of a clear Russian sense of ethnic identity has thus been of the most critical importance in the avoidance of ethnic conflict not just in neighbours with large Russian minorities, like Russia and Kazakhstan, but also in Russian autonomous republics where titular nationalities have asserted themselves and gained a measure of statehood, like Tatarstan and Yakutia. There have of course been ethnic tensions in these places, but remarkably slight when compared with the experiences of other post-imperial regions, or some of the doom laden predictions of 1992.

None of the major Russian parties today (with the partial exception of Zhirinovsky's, now fortunately in eclipse) espouses a narrowly ethnicist version of Russian nationalism – and in the elections of 1995–6, all sought support from the rulers of the Russian ethnic republics. Instead, the image, derived from Soviet culture, is that of the Russians 'leading' a voluntary alliance of other peoples. General Alexander Lebed, and other Russian politicians dubbed 'nationalist' (or even 'ultra-nationalist') in the West, have spoken repeatedly of the Russian Federation as a 'multinational' state, and General Lebed – and indeed the Russian government – have spoken of Islam and Buddhism, along with Orthodox Christianity, as Russia's 'traditional' religions, which the state should foster and support.[13] (This does not, however, necessarily imply democracy, and is quite compatible with a more or less benevolent dictatorship.) The Duma's law of June 1997 limiting proselytisation by foreign religious groups also established Judaism, Islam and mainstream Buddhism as official state-supported religions in Russia.

The argument of many critics of the Soviet Union, and especially of nationalists belonging to former subject ethnic groups like the Ukrainians, is that the Soviet Union was simply a version of the Russian empire, and Russian-Soviet and Russian-Communist loyalty was simply a cover for Russian national ambition and aggrandisement. While this view contains certain elements of truth, it is a great oversimplification. It is simply not the case, for example, that 'in the prevailing view of Russians, the whole of the USSR was the real Russia', or at least not in a spiritual and cultural sense.[14] And at a gut level, a Chechen mountain does not feel like a Russian birch forest, and most of the Russian soldiers whom I talked to privately in Chechnya admitted that in fact this was not 'Russian land'.

As to the other lands, different attitudes swirl around in the Russian psyche, sometimes mixing, sometimes not: ambition and fear of bloodshed and financial sacrifice; desire for a new federation and fear of Islam; a feeling of 'Eurasian' identity and a feeling of European superiority to the 'Asiatics'. In Ukraine, Russians think that a Russian naval base in Sebastopol is definitely Russian; a baroque square in Lviv is definitely not. What exactly is Kiev? Russians themselves are not at all clear.

Of course, there were strong Russian imperial elements in the Soviet Russian identity, especially during and after the Second World War, when the Communists exploited Russian symbols and traditions. However, these Russian national elements coexisted with Communist ones, and with a quite genuine belief that the Soviet Union was a voluntary union of peoples. Even the 'Great Patriotic War' was not presented to Russians as a simply Russian struggle, even if Russians were the leaders. In the words of a letter from a former Soviet army nurse (with a Ukrainian name) to *Izvestia* in 1991, lamenting the growth of ethnic violence in the Caucasus:

> I was a participant in the war and from 1941 to 1945 I helped the wounded. They were all dear to me. I was with the 223rd Azerbaijani Division defending the Caucasus. And it never came into my head to think about which of my friends were Azerbaijani, and which ones were

Armenian or Georgian...Let the memory of the war, the friendship of peoples tempered in its fires, be an example for our conscience today.[15]

In this context, it should be remembered that much of Soviet propaganda was devoted to preaching this belief in voluntary association. As Lowell Tillett wrote of the Soviet Union in the 1960s, 'Efforts are being redoubled to indoctrinate the Soviet citizen to the concept that he belongs to a commonwealth of people with a long record of good relations...'[16] This propaganda has usually been studied as something directed towards the non-Russian nationalities. Less studied, but more important, was its effect on the Russians themselves. The poem 'Felitsa' in praise of Catherine the Great, by the eighteenth-century poet Gavriil Derzhavin, also spoke of other nations placing themselves voluntarily under the Empress's rule. Andrei Sinyavsky wrote of it that: 'This of course is just pseudo-internationalism and pseudo-freedom of nationalities living under the wing of a great empire. But if the empire wants to preserve itself, it must profess a relative "internationalism". It must pretend that all the enslaved peoples have come to it voluntarily.' But he continued,

> Not that Soviet Communist internationalism was always a fraud or a means of restoring the old Russian empire. The continued annexation of new territories proceeded from the idea of world revolution and a single, universal socialist state. In fact, this was imperialism of a new type, aimed not at one nation's predominance but at a pan-national fraternity under socialism's wing...
>
> And Russian national sentiment assumed with the revolution and the International a messianic character; for many, the Party hymn, 'The International' was virtually the Russian national hymn. This was one precondition for the degeneration of internationalism into great-power nationalism. But in the twenties, the International played a different role: one of its missions was to restore among the small peoples of the USSR their confidence in the Russian centre and in unification within the framework of an integral State.[17]

The way in which the Soviet Union collapsed is only comprehensible if it is recognised that most Russians did not in fact consciously see it as a Russian empire. Above all, this is true of Mikhail Gorbachev. His extraordinary blindness to the danger presented to Soviet rule by nationalism can only be explained by the fact that he had been truly convinced by Soviet propaganda about the 'friendship of the peoples'. As for Yeltsin and his supporters, as long as Gorbachev and the Soviet government were their enemies, they showed a complete indifference to Russia's stake in the survival of the union. Indeed, an essential role in Yeltsin's victory was also played by the fact that so many Russians saw the union not as a Russian empire, but as a means by which other republics battened on Russia for subsidies and cheap raw materials.

As to the Russian people, this Soviet-inspired belief in the voluntary nature of the union explains both why so many of the Russians of Russia, and of Ukraine (notably the miners), helped the Soviet *state* to collapse, and also why they were so surprised that some form of Soviet *union* did not survive. In this way, Russian attitudes could perhaps be compared to some of the more naive and optimistic hopes of British people (especially Labourites like Gaitskell) in the 1940s and 1950s about the future of the British Commonwealth as a truly effective but voluntary association of free states under British leadership; it was not a mistake that the tougher-minded French were ever likely to make. Today, the necessarily voluntary nature of any reintegration of the former Soviet republics is stressed by all the mainstream Russian parties, including the Communists; and if this is dictated above all by contemporary Russian weakness, ideology also plays a certain part.

In this connection, Russian ambitions for leadership or hegemony within the former Soviet Union have a very important impact both on popular attitudes and on state policy. For as noted, such a hegemony cannot today or for the foreseeable future be based mainly on coercion; it has to have a genuine element of consent and mutual interest. It would be impossible for a Russian government on the one hand to have such a programme, and on the other hand to take up an ethnic chauvinist position at home, and foster a narrowly ethnicist version of the Russian identity.

Moreover, while the Russian state can play with 'ethnic' Russian protest as a lever to put pressure on neighbouring states, so long as it hopes for any kind of general hegemony across the territory of the former Union, it cannot go very far in this direction – and in fact, it has been very careful not to go far. In the case of eastern Ukraine, Alexei Nestnov of the BBC Ukrainian Service told me,

> If a civil society here does develop, it will have to come from within and from the new business classes... So far, Russian influence has played no role – there are no new Russian-backed associations, even cultural ones, no organised attempts to maintain links. If I were in the Russian government and had their ambitions towards Ukraine, I would play this card much more wisely and thoroughly. It's extraordinary – they haven't even bothered to open a consulate here, though they promised long ago. They won't even pay for Ostankino, which is by far their biggest source of influence here. In the economic field, they simply seem to be pursuing Russian interests. There is no industrial policy towards this region, no attempt to retain ties to Russia and affection for Russia by encouraging exports to Russia from the Kharkiv-based factories, for example.[18]

In the case of Kazakhstan, up to 1997 there has been almost no evidence that the Russian state has been encouraging the Cossacks in their attempts to orchestrate Russian opposition to Nazarbayev. Rhetorical commitment to 'defend our compatriots beyond Russia's borders' should not be mistaken for practical help, let alone support for local military revolt. The Russian government realises that if they encouraged such groups against the Kazakh government in an effort to make the latter more responsive to Russian demands, there would be a serious risk that this could get out of hand, split Kazakhstan, involve Russia in another war, and destroy the whole Russian position in Central Asia. The risks in Ukraine are obviously much greater still, given the size of that country and the West's interest in it.

For in the end, Russia can have a general hegemony over Central Asia, *or* it can expand Russia's ethnic borders to include northern Kazakhstan, and lose the rest of the region. It can seek influence over the whole of Ukraine, *or* it can mobilise ethnic Russian nationalism and seek to separate Crimea and perhaps the Donbas. It cannot do both; and if the Russian state were seriously to support ethnic Russian movements in the other republics, it might find itself forced towards a choice which it is very unwilling to have to make.

A number of such gambits have been advanced in imperial and post-imperial history, and they have often led to tragedy. Thus the British Unionists' mobilisation of the Northern Ireland Protestants (descended from Anglo-Scottish colonists) against the native Irish nationalist movement for Home Rule in the later nineteenth century is part of the same syndrome, resulted from some of the same choices, and led to tragic results for both Britain and Ireland, which are with us to this day. Up to 1997, the Russian government has taken a more benign course.

This must be emphasised again and again: in the end, ethnic Russian nationalism, carried to its logical conclusion, and hegemony over the other former Soviet republics are incompatible, even if Russia were to become much more powerful. In so far as the Cossacks, for example, are a force for ethnic chauvinism, and in so far as the Yeltsin administration is committed to seeking influence over Russia's neighbours, it *and any other Russian government with such a commitment* will be forced to rein in the Cossacks.

The Future of Russian Nationalism

The trend of my argument should by now be apparent. If Russians were to abandon their hegemonic ambitions and traditions while retaining a broad and open sense of what it is to be a Russian, well and good; but there are other and more dangerous possibilities. One of these has been sketched by Professor G. M. Tamas in a brilliant and terrifying essay.[19] Writing of the wars in Yugoslavia, and of certain tendencies elsewhere, he has remarked how the older tradition of liberal, idealist European nationalism, in which nationalists believed that their nations possessed uniquely good but also universal values, and were examples to other nations, has been replaced in Yugoslavia and some other areas by a spirit of purely ethnic allegiance, in which values as such have no place. He takes a number of the old liberal nationalist beliefs, and gives the new ethnicist answers:

Belonging to a political community is defined apart from the aleatoric accident of birth, by what you do and think. No, they say, cads and traitors are also members, provided that they are not of alien origin.

It is a good thing if our country is glorious, victorious, admirable. No, they say, this is immaterial: there are no universal criteria according to which a winner can be declared. Admiration is illusion, no foreigner understands Us.

High culture and religion are good for the well-being of the political community. No, they say, these are again necessarily contaminated by strangeness and alien influence; what we need is merely the celebration of identity.

Or in the words of Professor Charles Fairbanks,

There is something new and alarming going on. There is a kind of nationalism very different from nineteenth-century nationalism in that it is not imperialistic and does not build up the state. Even in the case of Serbia what the Serbs want is not at all that Serbs should rule Croatia or Slovenia. They simply want to have a greater Serbia which is their own – a kind of isolated, autarkic community. In order to do that they think they must kill or drive out people who don't fit into that vision.[20]

Tamas sees this as part of a 'revolt against transcendence' – and since the Soviet Union was of all states the most 'transcendent' in its claims (apart from the Vatican), it might be logical to that it could sooner or later be succeeded by an exceptionally earthbound, brutal and nihilist national ideology – especially since the current state of Russian society and social morals is an obvious breeding ground for moral nihilism.

The danger then is that if Russia were in fact forced to abandon her present very weak and qualified 'imperial' identity, it might swing to something very much worse. This would be especially true if Russia were to be simultaneously excluded from Western institutions and surrounded by a ring of Western-backed states with strong and strongly anti-Russian official national identities and programmes – which is in effect Henry Kissinger's programme. It would also be the case if ethnic Russians beyond Russia's border came under physical attack on a large scale. The fact that this has not happened so far has been of critical importance in limiting the growth of a radical and ethnicist Russian nationalism – and we must hope that it stays that way.

There is a historical model for how Russia might react in these circumstances, and strangely enough, it is one which has been advanced by some Western commentators as a *positive* model for Russia: this is Turkey as reshaped by Mustapha Kemal 'Ataturk'[21]. The reasons why this is seen as a positive model in the West are threefold: that Ataturk's Turkey gave up the Ottoman empire's pretensions to lead the Muslim world (through the caliphate) and rule over huge areas beyond Turkey's ethnic borders; that

Ataturk and his successors have crushed both conservative and radical Islam in the name of Western-inspired modern secularism; and that they have aligned themselves with the West geopolitically, first by refusing to ally with Germany in the Second World War, then by joining NATO in the Cold War, then by lining up alongside the USA and Israel in the Middle East.

The possible parallels with contemporary Russia look clear enough, and it is probably only traditional Russian contempt for the Turks which has prevented them being picked up by Russian thinkers. By the early twentieth-century, the Ottoman empire had experienced decades of repeated humiliation at the hands of the West, and of failed reforms. The multinational empire itself and its claims to leadership of the Muslim world were fading fast. With defeat in 1918, they disappeared altogether, and former subject peoples advanced towards the heart of ethnic Turkish territory itself.

In these circumstances, younger and more radical elements of the Turkish elites, and especially the military, decided to rebuild and strengthen their state on the basis of Turkish ethnic nationalism. Hitherto, this had been almost completely lacking in the Ottoman elite's ideology and culture. 'Turk' had been almost a term of abuse, implying a coarse and uneducated Anatolian peasant. In terms of blood, the elites (and most probably Ataturk himself) were overwhelmingly non-Turkish.

It was in reaction to all this that Ataturk launched the slogan, 'Be proud to be a Turk', and launched a brutal attack on religious tradition in the name of modernisation. In part because of the strength of the traditions he had to overcome, and in part because of the Turkish military's traditions (and its Wilhelmine German models), the state that he founded embodied very strong authoritarian, military and chauvinist elements. As James Pettifer has written, to this day external and internal enemies are seen everywhere: 'It is very diffi-cult to be Turkish. In the loyal bureaucrats' view great national discipline is necessary to surmount these ever-present threats.'[22]

Kemalist Turkey also had quasi-absolutist claims to total cultural control over the entire population within Turkey's new and much reduced borders, something which had also been lacking in the intermittently savage, but gen-erally lazy and pluralist governing philosophy of the Ottoman empire. Despite the fact that by the early nineteenth century, the Turks had been written off by many European (and some Turkish) commentators as hopelessly decadent and incapable of reform and regeneration, the result of the Kemalist national revolution was in fact – or seemed to be for many years – a relatively success-ful experiment in modern state-building and development. However, it is one which has been a disaster for Turkey's ethnic minorities, Armenians, Greeks and Kurds, who were respectively subjected to genocide, massacre and expul-sion, and an attempt at complete suppression of their language and cultural identity (though the Turks reply, with considerable justice, that this was no worse than the fate with which these enemies were threatening them).

Later of course this state philosophy also threatened intervention in neigh-bouring states harbouring ethnic Turkish minorities, like Cyprus – for while

Kemalist nationalism had abandoned claims to rule over non-ethnic Turks beyond Turkey's borders, it certainly did not imply the abandonment of claims to protect ethnic Turks; and in this context, it needs to be emphasised that *no* Russian state – even a liberal, capitalist and democratic one – is ever going to be able to abandon all claim to a right of protection over ethnic Russians outside Russia, at least against actual physical attack. This may also be true of the Russian stake in Sebastopol.

The parallels to Russia's position could hardly be clearer; and the advocates of a Kemalist path have not thought through the implications of their arguments, or what a true Ataturk and his programme, with a capacity for mobilising and inspiring the Russian army and people, would mean for Europe today. Apart from anything else, just as it would in part be a reaction against the ethnicist nationalism of neighbouring states, so it would in turn produce further reactions in this direction among Russia's neighbours (and of course its own minorities), risking a downward spiral of hatred, oppression, unrest and ultimately war. As I hope this book has made clear, such an outcome is not at all probable. All the same, we should not do anything to encourage it.

Notes

Introduction

Epigraph from Desmond Bagley, *Landslide* (Collins, London, 1967), p. 240.

1. See Svetlana Kovaleva, 'Desperate Russian Nuclear Scientist Commits Suicide', Reuters, Moscow, 31 Oct. 1996; Grigory Yavlinsky, 'A Chain of Calamities', *Financial Times*, 31 Jan. 1997; the report on Chelyabinsk-70 by Arina Slabko on the *Segodnya* programme of NTV, 27 Dec. 1996 (reprinted in *Johnson's Russia List*); and Andrei Vaganov, 'Nuclear Facilities Slip out of Control', *Nezavisimaya Gazeta*, 30 Nov. 1996. For the situation in the Northern Fleet, see *Izvestia*, 16 July 1997.

2. Colonel C. E. Callwell, Royal Artillery, *Small Wars: Their Principles and Practice* (General Staff-War Office, 1899; rep. EP Publishing, Wakefield, 1976).

3. Richard Pipes, 'Russia's Past, Russia's Future', *Commentary* (June 1996). See also his article 'A Nation with One Foot Stuck in the Past', *Sunday Times*, 20 Oct. 1996. For a similar historicist view, see for example Mark Galeotti, *The Age of Anxiety: Security and Politics in Soviet and Post-Soviet Russia* (Longman, 1995), esp. pp. 3–24.

4. Ariel Cohen, 'What is the Future of Russia?', *Washington Times*, 16 Dec. 1996. See also 'Making the World Safe for America' by Ariel Cohen, Thomas Moore, John Hillen, John Sweeney, James Phillips and James Przystup in *Issues '96: the Candidate's Briefing Book* (Heritage Foundation, Washington DC). (*Issues '96* is intended as a handbook for conservative candidates of all parties seeking national office in the USA.)

5. See 'The CIA and the Soviet Union: the Politics of Getting It Wrong', by Melvin A. Goodman, National War College.

6. George Will, 'Eastward-Ho – and Soon', *Washington Post*, 13 June 1996.

7. Peter Rodman, 'Four More for NATO', *Washington Post*, 13 Dec. 1994.

8. Pipes, 'Russia's Past, Russia's Future'.

9. See the polls quoted in part II, ch. 5.

10. See Anatol Lieven, *The Baltic Revolution: Estonia, Latvia, Lithuania and the Path to Independence* (Yale University Press, 1993), esp. ch. 7, and the preface to the paperback edition (1994) written after the success of Zhirinovsky in the December 1993 parliamentary elections.

11. Richard Layard and John Parker, *The Coming Russian Boom: a Guide to the New Markets and Politics* (Free Press, London, 1996), p.11.

12. See Francis Fukuyama, *The End of History and the Last Man* (Macmillan, New York, 1992).

13. David Hoffman, in 'After Grim Times, Armenia Lightens Up'. *Washington Post*, 18 Sept. 1996.

14. An enormous literature exists for example on how the Japanese state manages its economy – and successive US administrations have recognised this by abandoning free market arguments in their trade negotiations with Japan in favour of managed quotas. See Karel van Wolferen. 'Market? What Market?' *World Link*, Jan.–Feb. 1996.

Part I: The War

Epigraph from Leo Tolstoy, 'Christianity and Patriotism', in *War–Patriotism–Peace*, ed. Scott Nearing (Garland, New York, 1973), pp. 30, 34.

1. Quoted in Pavel Baev, *The Russian Army in a Time of Troubles* (Sage, London, 1996), p. 104 n 2.
2. See Lee Hockstader, 'American Advisers Work Quietly in Moscow', *Washington Post*, 1 July 1996.
3. See Lee Hockstader and David Hoffman, 'Yeltsin Campaign Rose from Tears to Triumph: Money, Advertising Turned Fortunes Around', *Washington Post*, 7 July 1996.
4. See *Kommersant Daily*, 28 Feb. 1996, and Victoria Clarke in the *Observer*, 5 May 1996.

1   A Personal Memoir of Grozny and the Chechen War

Epigraph from *Mikhail Lermontov: Major Poetical Works*, ed. and trans. Anatoly Liberman (University of Minnesota Press), p. 305. The battle of Valerik, in which Lermontov participated as a Russian officer, was fought on 11 July 1840. Lermontov distinguished himself by his courage in this engagement, but the tone is very different from his earlier patriotic poetry (cf. 'Borodino'), and the last two lines show his scepticism about official promises of an early victory; in fact, of course, the war had still nineteen years to run.

1. All this chapter is compiled from my own notebooks, accumulated during nine visits to Chechnya between 1992 and 1996.
2. Many of the Russian fortresses of the North Caucasus were named like warships, either with names like 'Defiant' and 'Vigilant', or after Tsars or local commanders. A greater curiosity of the Russian borderlands, and especially the North Caucasus, is the 'gender' relations between the different settlements. This is because of the Russian bureaucratic habit of grading them in order of importance. Thus Grozny began as a female, Groznaya, because a fortress (*krepost'*) in Russian is female, as is a Cossack village or *stanitsa*. A village is neuter (*selo*), as is a fort (*ukreplenie*). But when a place was promoted by the government to be a town (*gorod*), it inevitably became masculine.
3. John F. Baddeley, '*The Rugged Flanks of the Caucasus*' (Arno Press, New York, 1973; first pub. 1940), part 1, p. 54.
4. After the Chechen victory, Grozny was renamed after Dudayev, but so far the name does not appear to be sticking.
5. Interview with the author, 3 Dec. 1994.
6. This trip was arranged by Sebastian Smith of Agence France Presse (AFP), to whom I am very grateful.
7. Interview with the author, 3 Dec. 1995.
8. See my article in *The Tablet*, 27 Aug. 1994.
9. In *Goodbye to All That*.
10. See my article, 'Trading Spirit and Clan Networks Keep Grozny Refugees In Fighting Form', *The Times*, 26 Jan. 1996.
11. The market is now working again, though reportedly not quite at its pre-1995 level.
12. *The Times*, 29 Dec. 1994.
13. Interview with the author and Heidi Bradner, 26 Feb. 1995.
14. Besides myself, our group was made up of Victoria Clarke of the *Observer*, and Heidi Bradner and Ellen Binder, both photocorrespondents.
15. As I pointed out at the time, for my part I have a beard and do not wear tights, white or otherwise. 'Ah, but you might have been in disguise,' replied one of our captors with a grin. For a Russian newspaper report on the supposed White Tights in Chechnya, see *Izvestia*, 17 Jan. 1995.
16. If this seems odd behaviour on our part after what happened, the answer may be that war correspon-

dents are odd people, and ones who have some understanding and sympathy for how even decent men may behave when under prolonged fear and strain.

2 Russia and Chechnya, 1991–1994

Epigraph: Mulay Ahmed er-Raisuli quoted in D. S. Woolman, *Rebels in the Rif: Abd al-Krim and the Rif Rebellion* (Oxford University Press, Oxford, 1969), p. 59.

1. For the protests of 1973, see *Nezavisimaya Gazeta*, 2 Dec. 1992. According to this article, Chechen members of the local KGB refused to investigate the demonstrations, citing pressure from their clans.

2. The best and most objective sources that I know for Checheno-Ingushetia in the period of the overthrow of Soviet rule are Timur Musayev and Zurab Todua, *Novaya Checheno-Ingushetia* (Information Group Panorama, Moscow, 1992), and a book by Dr Georgy Derluguian, which he was kind enough to let me read in manuscript, contrasting Chechnya and Tatarstan during this period: *Chechnya and Tataria* (United States Institute of Peace, Washington DC, 1997). For a portrait of Checheno-Ingushetia in the 1980s (with many useful statistics), and a useful though hostile picture of Chechnya under Dudayev's rule, see Valery Tishkov and A. S. Orlov (eds), *Chechensky Krisis* (Moscow, 1995).

   For Chechen accounts, from radically different standpoints, see Zelimkhan Yandarbiyev, *V Preddvery Nezavisimosti* (Grozny, 1994); Yusup Soslambekov, *Chechnya (Nokhchichob) – Vzglyad Iznutri* (Moscow, 1996); Ruslan Khasbulatov, *Chechnya: Mnye Ne Dali Ostanovit Voinu* (Moscow, 1995).

   For short accounts in English, see the chapter on Chechnya in Suzanne Goldenberg, *Pride of Small Nations* (Zed Books, London,

1993), Marie Broxup's essay in Broxup (ed.), *The North Caucasus Barrier: The Russian Advance towards the Muslim World* (New York, 1992) (a pro-separatist account); and for the Russian reaction to the 1991 events in Grozny, see Flemming Splidsboel-Hansen, 'The 1991 Chechen Revolution: The Response of Moscow', *Central Asia Survey* 13:3 (1994); Pavel Baev, 'Russia's Policy in the North Caucasus and the War in Chechnya', Royal Institute of International Affairs Briefing Paper, London, Mar. 1995; and Emil Payin and Arkady Popov, 'Chechnya', in Emil Payin and Jeremy R. Azrael (eds), *US and Russian Policymaking with Respect to the Use of Force* (Rand Corporation, 1995). Payin and Popov were members of the President's analytical centre, and so have a certain interest in defending Russian government policy, but were also strong opponents of the decision to intervene militarily.

3. Derluguian, *Chechnya and Tataria*.

4. Interview with the author, Grozny, 18 Feb. 1992.

5. At the end of 1996, the Chechen government officially renamed Grozny after Dudayev; but since throughout its history, and the latest war, it was known as Grozny, I have used the old name in this book.

6. For this perception of Maskhadov's staff, I am indebted to Colonel Charles Blandy, of the Royal Military Academy, Sandhurst, who visited Maskhadov during 1995.

7. For a report on the delegation's visit, see *Izvestia*, 7 Oct. 1991, and for Rutskoy's lack of diplomacy, see an interview with him, Itar Tass, 10 Oct. 1996, in which he described the Chechen national guards as 'bandits'.

8. See Broxup, *The North Caucasus Barrier*, p. 229.

9. Another politician (a democratic statist) who took an early hard line over Chechnya was the now forgotten Nikolai Travkin, who warned that by

not shedding a small amount of blood immediately, Russia would have to shed a great deal more later.

10. Interview with Dmitry Balburov in *Moscow News*, 12–18 Dec. 1994. For a later revolt of prisoners, Itar Tass, 13 Oct. 1994.

11. See 'Yeltsin Presents Chechen Leaders with Ultimatum, Itar Tass, 19 Oct. 1991.

12. Quoted in Tishkov and Orlov (eds.), pp. 29–30.

13. See *Washington Post*, 13 Nov. 1991.

14. Quoted in Splidsboel-Hansen, 'The 1991 Chechen Revolution'. See also *Izvestia*, 13 Nov. 1991.

15. Extracts from the Govorukhin report appeared in *Pravda*, 27 and 28 Feb. 1996.

16. Tishkov and Orlov (eds.), p. 19.

17. One should therefore perhaps not be too hard on Dudayev; quite apart from the threat from Russia – which was after all very real – a system without formal institutions of leadership, and in the midst of revolutionary change, is likely to impose the most intense personal strain on a leader, who has to compensate with personal charisma, displayed in continual public appearances, for the lack of any more solid bases for his rule. In the end, he was at least a convinced and dedicated Chechen nationalist. The strain of such leadership on the leader is movingly evoked by Tolstoy in his otherwise not very sympathetic portrait of Dudayev's predecessor Shamil in *Haji Murat*, where it is contrasted both with the 'natural', family-centred, spontaneous spirit of Haji Murat himself and with the supportive network of sycophancy, bureaucracy, hypocrisy and automatic obedience which surrounds Nicholas I.

18. Alla Dudayeva's life following her husband's death has been a murky one. She was 'arrested' by the Russian authorities on her way to Finland, and it seemed for a time as if she had made her peace with them. She also issued wild statements

about her husband's death having been the work of an American missile. At the time of writing, she is resident in Turkey. Caught hopelessly between conflicting loyalties, she is not the least pitiable victim of the Chechen War. See her interview with Anatoly Anisimov, 'Widow Sure US Missile Killed Dudayev', *Komsomolskaya Pravda*, 9 Jan. 1997, and with Thomas Goltz, 31 Oct. 1996. Reproduced in Johnson's Russia List.

19. Tishkov and Orlov (eds.), p. 8.

20. Cf. his press conference on 1 Dec. 1994, at which he said that the prisoners would be tried by Islamic courts.

21. See for example the television address in the collection of Dudayev's speeches, statements and interviews, *Ternisty Put' k Svobode* (Vilnius, 1994), p. 45.

22. See John Thornhill, 'Chechen in Russia Threat', *Financial Times*, 30 Jan. 1997. Thus Raduyev told Reuters in January 1997 that the guerrilla war against Russia should continue, and that 'at least three Russian cities must be burned to cinders. We are working on a major operation codenamed Ash.'

23. For an example of Chechen arrogance and a patronising attitude towards the other Muslim Caucasians – although he is careful to quote an Abkhaz – see Zelimkhan Yandarbiyev in his book, *V Preddvery Nezavisimosti*, pp. 31–2, in which he implies not just that the Chechens are the best Muslims of the region, but also that they led all the major revolts against Russia and suffered the worst casualties.

24. This is also pre-eminently true of the region often considered the next possible flashpoint in the North Caucasus, Karachai-Cherkessia, which is divided between the Turkic Karachai (31 per cent of the population), the Circassian Cherkess (10 per cent) and Russians of largely Cossack origin (42 per cent), in a way that makes it extremely difficult for either of the

indigenous nationalities to demand greater independence without sparking immediate reactions from the other two.

25. For the difficulties involved, see an interview with Leonid Smirnyagin, 'Russian Can't Blockade Chechnya in Case of Conflict', Itar Tass, 12 Aug. 1994.

26. See Emil Payin and Arkady Popov, *Chechenskaya Politika Rossii: 1991–1994 gg.* (The Chechen Policy of Russia, 1991–1994), p. 13.

27. Tishkov and Orlov (eds.), p. 34.

28. See *Nezavisimaya Gazeta*, 11 Feb. 1994.

29. The Govorukhin report of the Duma alleges that:
'In 1993, 559 trains were attacked and 4,000 cars and containers worth a total of 11.5 billion roubles were completely or partially plundered. During the first eight months of 1994, 120 armed attacks were committed, resulting in the plundering of 1,156 cars and 527 containers. Losses came to more than 11 billion roubles. In 1992–4, 26 railroad workers died during robberies of railroad rolling stock.'
This is almost certainly a gross exaggeration; as usual, Govorukhin does not give any specific incidents, and I myself never heard of any railway workers being killed by the Chechens. Incidents of armed robbery were, however, indeed numerous. Even Dudayev, when I asked him about this in an interview, did not deny the robberies – he simply blamed them on the Russian 'special forces', who, as usual, were 'carrying out provocations to discredit Chechnya and my government'.

30. See Sharip Asuyev, 'Chechen–Russian Negotiations: Details', Itar Tass, 22 Sept. 1992.

31. For the Tatar government's very real ability to make its own economic policy (for good and evil) and with withold taxes due to the centre, see Michael Gerschaft, 'Tatarstan's Soft Entry into the Market', *Jamestown*

Foundation Prism, 18 Aug. 1996, part 3.

32. For Shaimiyev's tactics up to the coup of 1991, see *Nezavismaya Gazeta*, 13 Aug. 1981.

33. See *Russia Briefing* 2:5 (May 1994).

34. That is not to say that, as the Russians allege, Turkish agents and Islamic sympathisers may not have played a part in supplying the Chechens through Georgia, Azerbaijan and Daghestan; but if so, their role was limited to supply. They did not do the actual fighting.

35. Full text on Itar Tass, 28 Dec. 1994.

36. See for example the statement of Vyacheslav Mikhailov, Deputy Minister for Nationalities, reported by Itar Tass on 4 Dec. 1994.

37. For a Russian analysis of the reasons for intervention, see Stepan Kiselyov and Azer Mursaliyev, 'Who Stands to Gain from the Invasion?', *Moscow News*, 23–29 Dec. 1994.

38. For a general survey of the Caspian energy region and the pipeline issue, and of the state of play as of 1996, see Rosemarie Forsythe, *The Politics of Oil in the Caucasus and Central Asia* (Adelphi Papers, Oxford University Press, 1996). It is however advisable to remember that the author is a US diplomat, and her portrait tends to emphasise the benign nature of US policy while playing down the US commercial interests involved. On the role of Lukoil and the shift in Russian policy in the second half of 1996, see Carol J. Williams, 'Caspian Sea Change', *Los Angeles Times*, 8 Dec. 1996.

39. For a very well-informed and insightful Russian account of Yeltsin administration politics in the months before the war, which oddly omits altogether to mention the hijackings, see Maria Eismont (a correspondent for *Segodnya*), 'The Chechen War: How It All Began', *Jamestown Foundation Prism*, 11 Mar. 1996, part 4.

40. For the different theories concerning the hijackings, see Alexander Yevtushenko, 'Tragic Thursdays', *Kom-*

somolskaya Pravda, 12 Aug. 1994.

41. Quoted in Tishkov, 'Chechen War', p. 2.

42. See 'Chechen Conflict Must Be Settled by Peaceful Means', Itar Tass, 2 Dec. 1994.

43. See Tishkov, op. cit., Shaimiyev told Tishkov this himself, and said that he had been told it by Yeltsin personally when the Russian President visited Kazan in March.

44. Quoted in M. A. Smith, *A Chronology of the Chechen Conflict*, Vol I (Conflict Studies Research Centre, Sandhurst, 1996).

45. In *Segodnya*, 18 Aug. 1994, Stepashin explicitly ruled out military intervention.

46. For the Provisional Council's hostility to Khasbulatov, see the interview with Avturkhanov on Itar Tass, 16 Aug. 1994. For the bitterly hostile response of the Dudayev regime to Khasbulatov's return, see Lyudmilla Perkina, 'Chechen Congress Condemns Avturkhanov and Khasbulatov', Itar Tass, 10 Aug. 1994.

47. Payin and Popov, 'Chechnya'.

48. For Avturkhanov's exaggerated sense of his own potential at this time, see *Izvestia*, 15 Oct. 1994.

49. See *Obshchaya Gazeta*, 12–18 Aug. 1994.

50. Eismont, 'The Chechen War'.

51. Itar Tass, 29 Nov. 1994.

52. See Lawrence Sheets, 'Grozny Defiant after Nine Killed in Air Raids', Reuters, 2 Dec. 1994.

53. Smith, *Chronology*, p. 13

54. See Lawrence Sheets, 'Khasbulatov Quits Chechnya', Reuters, 4 Dec. 1994.

55. Payin and Popov, 'Chechnya'.

56. See Jonathan Steele, *Eternal Russia: Gorbachev, Yeltsin and the Mirage of Democracy* (London, 1994), and Bruce Clark, *An Empire's New Clothes: the End of Russia's Liberal Dream* (Vintage, London, 1995).

57. Charles Fairbanks, 'The Legacy of Soviet Policymaking in Creating a New Russia', in Leon Aron and Kenneth M. Jensen (eds), *The Emergence*

of Russian Foreign Policy (US Institute of Peace, Washington DC, 1994), p. 57.

58. I am indebted for this insight to Dr Shermann Garnett.

59. See for example Vladimir Yemelyanenko, 'Chechen War Threatens to Blow Up Russia', *Moscow News*, 9–15 Dec. 1994, in which the author suggested that numerous volunteers from elsewhere in the Caucasus were gathering to defend Chechnya. For earlier Chechen attempts to win support from the other peoples of the region, see Sharip Asuyev, 'Chechens Trying to Rally Caucasian Nations', Itar Tass, 9 Sept. 1992. For a remarkably frank exposition of Russian goals and fears in the Caucasus, see Pavel Baev, 'Russia's Policy in the North Caucasus'.

60. The most famous such raid into Georgia – even at the time it was world famous – was that of Shamil's forces on the Alazan valley in July 1854, which captured the ladies of the distinguished Chavchavadze family and their French governess. They were later exchanged against Shamil's son, Djemal al-Din, who had been a Russian hostage since 1839. For a romantic account of this episode, see Lesley Blanch, *The Sabres of Paradise* (Quartet, London, 1978), vol. 2, pp. 302–36. For a brief account by a contemporary historian, see Moshe Gammer, *Muslim Resistance to the Tsar: Shamil and the Conquest of Chechnya and Daghestan* (Frank Cass, London, 1994), pp. 270–2.

61. For a good general survey of the North Caucasus region up to 1994, see Helen Krag and Lars Funch, *The North Caucasus: Minorities at a Crossroads* (Minority Rights Group, Copenhagen, 1994). The Tass survey of that year, 'Northern Caucasus: a Key Point in World Politics', contains some useful basic information. See also 'The Caucasus Powder Keg', *Eastern Europe Newsletter* 6:20 (Oct. 1992).

62. See Valery Shanayev, Itar Tass, 18 Aug. 1994.
63. See *OMRI Daily Digest* 3 Apr. 1996.
64. On the especially strong links of the North Caucasus Communist leadership of the Brezhnev period with the mafia, see Arkady Vaksberg, *The Soviet Mafia* (Weidenfeld and Nicholson, London, 1991).
65. For the early history of Kabardin–Muscovite relations, see Chantal Lemercier-Quelquejay, 'Cooptation of the Elites of Kabarda and Daghestan in the Sixteenth Century', in Broxup, *The North Caucasus Barrier*, op. cit.
66. For a wonderful picture of traditional Abkhaz society and the effects of Soviet rule, see Fazil Iskander's novel, *Sandro of Chegem*, translated by Susan Brownsberger, King Penguin, London, 1983, and 'The Goatibex Constellation'. Iskander himself is the grandson of a Muslim cleric, but Islam plays very little part in his portrait.
67. For demographic statistics, see Muzayev and Todua, *Novaya Checheno-Ingushetia*.
68. In a television address, 13 Dec. 1994.

3 The Course of the Chechen War

Epigraph from Harry Holbert Turney-High, *Primitive War: Its Practice and Concepts* (University of South Carolina Press, 1949), p. 12. Perhaps the words 'mathematical' or 'electronic' might today be substituted for 'athletic' in his description of the nature of 'fire fights for their own sake'.

1. Cf. Pascal, 'Had Cleopatra's nose been shorter, it would have changed the whole face of the world.'
2. See Pavel Baev, *The Russian Army in a Time of Troubles* (Sage, London, 1996), p. 143.
3. Pavel Felgenhauer, 'A War Russia Cannot Afford to Lose', *Transition*, 31 May 1996.
4. Quoted in M. A. Smith, *A Chronology of the Chechen Conflict* (Conflict Studies Research Centre, Sandhurst, 1996), vol. 2, p. 15.
5. See the statements of Grachev and Kvashnin on the Grosny battle reprinted in *Krasnaya Zvezda*, 2 Mar. 1995.
6. See Yuri Golotyuk, 'Russia on the Brink of Catastrophe', *Segodnya*, 5 Jan. 1995.
7. Interview with the author, Stary Atagy, 11 Jan. 1995. This picture was confirmed by other Russian prisoners I interviewed, both those taken during the assault in early January, and the smaller numbers captured in the clandestine operation to support the Chechen opposition attack on Grozny on 26 November – for example, Private Andrei Chasov of the Kantemir Guards Motorised Infantry Division (supposedly a 'crack' unit), who also said that his group were given no maps and no instructions. 'They didn't tell us anything. We had no idea where we were. We got into town, and then the Chechens who were supposed to be leading us ran away.'
8. For an overview of the Russian press approach at this time, see Timothy Heritage, 'Russian Newspapers Scorn Official Chechnya Story', Reuters, 5 Jan. 1995; for an example of misinformation, Interfax, 5 Jan. 1995, in which a Russian government statement has 'enemy groups retreating from the Chechen capital deep into Chechnya'; for lies about the Russian army not bombarding civilians, see Ron Popeski, 'Yeltsin Orders Halt to Chechnya Bombing', Reuters, 5 Jan. 1995.
9. A crazily brave British photographer, Nigel Chandler, remained in the headquarters to within three days of the end.
10. Interview with the author, Stary Atagy Hospital, 11 Jan. 1995.
11. This reality may be contrasted with the absurd hyperbole of Russian military statements like the following, addressed to the civilian population,

who soon came to mock them: 'The modern technical capabilities of the army are such that we can suppress the fire of a single AK-47, not to speak of whole groups of fighters... We can easily determine where fighters and their headquarters are located. We track them night and day, and even when there is cloud cover.'

12. Dmitry Kamyshev, 'Forty-Eight Hours without War', *Kommersant Daily*, 22 Aug. 1996.

13. For the ebb and flow of popular (i.e. cheap) and aristocratic or imperial (i.e. expensive) military technologies in history and their impact on states and societies, see Michael Mann, *The Sources of Social Power* (Cambridge University Press, 1986), and William H. McNeil, *The Pursuit of Power: the Technology and Organisation of Armed Force* (University of Chicago Press, 1982).

14. Sebastian Smith of AFP made repeated visits to Bamut on the Chechen side during the war, at great personal risk, and I am indebted to him for his remarks on the defence.

15. See for example Frederick S. Voss, *Reporting the War: the Journalistic Coverage of World War II* (Smithsonian Institution Press, Washington (1995), p. 166.

16. See *Izvestia*, 2 Mar. 1995.

17. Smith, *Chronology*, vol. 1, p. 31.

18. For the Russian Foreign Ministry response to the initial proposal for the mission, see Andrei Kozyrev's remarks reported by Interfax, 26 Jan. 1995.

19. I was exposed to these arguments personally when I testified on Chechnya to the OSCE Committee of the US Congress in March 1996. The two others giving evidence were Sergei Kovalev, the most noted Russian critic of the Russian army in Chechnya, and Ambassador Jack Matlock, perhaps the most noted American defender of the Russian record in Chechnya – which made me very much the pig in the middle.

20. See *Izvestia*, 17 June 1995 and *Segodnya*, 17 June 1995 (for casualties). For Basayev's own justification of his action, see Colin Peck's interview with him, 'Unrepentant Basayev Blames Russia', *Moscow Times*, 4 Aug. 1995.

21. See the account of Basayev's press conference in *Nezavisimaya Gazeta*, 12 Mar. 1996.

22. Lee Hockstader, 'Latest Chechen Guerrilla Attack Presents Yeltsin With a No-Win Situation', *Washington Post*, 11 Jan. 1996.

23. Alexander Goltz, 'When Will We Finally Wake Up?', *Krasnaya Zvezda*, 17 June 1995.

24. Otto Lacis, 'Cruelty Breeds Only Cruelty', *Izvestia*, 20 June 1995.

25. Carl von Clausewitz, *On War*, ed. and trans. by Michael Howard and Peter Paset (Princeton University Press, 1976). See for example Col. John A. Warden III, USAAF, 'Employing Air Power in the Twenty-First Century', in Richard H. Shultz Jr and Robert I. Pfaltzgraff Jr, *The Future of Airpower in the Aftermath of the Gulf War* (Air University Press, Maxwell, Ala, 1996), p. 62.

26. John Keegan, *A History of Warfare* (Pimlico, London, 1993), pp. 3–24, 385–92 and *passim*.

27. Interview with the author, 25 May 1996. For the Russian fear of entering supposedly 'liberated' Shali, see also Thomas Goltz, who went up to the edge of the town with a Russian military police unit four months later. They would not go into the town even in their armour. Thomas Goltz, 'Diesels, Drunks and Devastation', *Soldier of Fortune Magazine*, May 1996.

28. See 'The Military Balance, 1994–1995', and the one for 1995–96, published by Brasseys for the International Institute for Strategic Studies, London.

29. To this end, the Russians frequently employed demands and appeals actually or ostensibly written by their

Chechen allies. Thus in February 1995 Russian aeroplanes dropped the following typical 'appeal' from the 'Provisional Council of the Chechen Republic' on to the town of Shali (hundreds of such appeals were dropped in the course of the war): 'Residents of Shali!

All of Chechnya is watching you! How could it happen that in your proud settlement, without your permission, bandit formations appeared that prepare only for your annihilation? One shot from Shali and fire will be opened upon the whole village. Remember how much unhappiness one single anti-aircraft gun parked in the hospital courtyard brought? Tens of innocent people died, and the bandits that fired at the plane escaped … You must immediately kick the bandits out of Shali. Hurry and make your choice.'

(Quoted in 'Russia: Three Months of War in Chechnya', *Human Rights Watch Bulletin* 7:6 (Feb. 1995) (Helsinki))

30. For an accurate (though very overoptimistic) analysis of the Russian strategy following the storming of Grozny in February 1995, by a journalist considered very close to the Russian General Staff, see Pavel Felgenhauer, 'Russia's War of Deception', *Segodnya*, 16 Feb. 1996. See also Ken Fireman, 'A Two-Track Approach to Peace', *Moscow Times*, 1 Mar. 1996, and Thomas de Waal, 'New Chechnya Envoy Looks to Peace', *Moscow Times*, 31 Jan. 1996.

31. For the French strategy of *regroupement* in Algeria, see Alastair Horne, *A Savage War of Peace: Algeria 1954–1962*, rev. edn (Penguin, London, 1987, pp. 220–1, 338–9 and *passim*.

32. See the report of the medical coordinator of Médecins sans Frontières in Samashki on 1 Apr. 1996; and of US diplomats with the OSCE mission to Chechnya, dated 18 Mar. 1996 and subsequently unclassified (US State Department).

33. OSCE/US State Department report, ibid.

34. Report by Hussein Hamidov, Chairman of the Chechen Casualties of War, movement', on 'Respect for Human Rights in the Chechen Republic' and 'The Fate of Persons Who Have Disappeared or Are Forcibly Detained'. This report was given to me by the OSCE mission in Grozny in December 1995, in their translation, quoted here. The report says that with the assistance of Hussein Hamidov's group, by December 1995 360 people had been freed from Russian 'filtration points' (interrogation centres), and 350 bodies had been found and given to relatives, out of 780 corpses altogether found in mass graves. It does not say, however, how many of these were victims of the bombardment of Grozny, and how many were or appeared to be the result of extrajudicial executions. For abuses in the first months of the war, see 'Russia: Three Months of War in Chechnya'.

35. 'Civilians Targeted: a Doctors without Borders/Médecins sans Frontières Report on Violations of Humanitarian Law in Chechnya', 18 Apr. 1996.

36. See Carlotta Gall, 'Chechnya Observes "Independence" in Peace', 7 Sept. 1995, and 'Premier Named, Grozny Rallies', 25 Oct. 1995, *Moscow Times*.

37. See Michael Specter, 'Russians and Chechens Sign a Partial Peace Agreement', *New York Times*, 31 July 1995.

38. See Mathias Brueggman: 'War in Chechnya Enriches Muscovites – Billions are Flowing into Strangers' Pockets', *Die Welt*, 15 Aug. 1996; Yulia Starostina, 'Paying General Antonov's Bill's, *Moskovskiye Novosti*, 29 Oct.–5 Nov. 1995.

39. See Michael Specter, 'Russians Assert Radioactive Box Found in Park Posed No Danger', *New York Times*, 25 Nov. 1995.

40. See *Nezavisimaya Gazeta*, 9 Dec. 1995, and Elizabeth Fuller in *Transi-*

tion, 31 May 1996.

41. See Richard Boudreaux, 'Bitterness Fills Chechnya as "2nd War" Replaces Peace Pact', *Los Angeles Times*, 3 Jan. 1996.

42. See David Hoffman, 'Separatists Free 2,000 Hostages', *Washington Post*, 10 Jan. 1996, and 'Chechen Guerrillas Harden Demands in Russian Hostage Crisis', *Washington Post*, 11 Jan. 1996.

43. See *OMRI Daily Digest*, 31 July 1996.

44. Pavel Felgenhauer, 'Russia's War of Deception', *Segodnya*, 16 Feb. 1996.

45. For my information about this period, I am indebted to Andrew Harding of the BBC, who was in Chechnya at the time and witnessed these events personally.

46. *Obshchaya Gazeta*, 14–20 Mar. 1996.

47. For this and previous peace attempts, see Elizabeth Fuller, 'The Desperate Search for a Compromise in Chechnya', *Transition*, 31 May 1996.

48. Smith, *Chronology*, vol. 3, p. 25.

49. For accounts of Dudayev's death and the immediate Chechen reaction, see David Hoffman, 'Chechen Separatists Vow to Fight On Despite Leader's Death', *Washington Post*, 25 Apr. 1996; Susan Caskie in *Transition*, 17 Apr. 1996; and Charles Blandy, 'Cutting the Chechen Knot', *The World Today*, June 1996.

50. See Maria Eismont, 'The Peace Process in Chechnya: Nobody Has Any Illusions', *Jamestown Foundation Prism* (2 Aug. 1996), part 2.

51. For the Security Council report, see *Moskovsky Komsomolets*, 4 Dec. 1996.

52. See Lee Hockstader, 'Beyond Swagger, Chechen Guerrillas Are among the World's Most Deadly', *Washington Post*, 18 Aug. 1996.

53. See John Thornhill, 'Yeltsin Returns with Harsh Words for Lebed: President is Trying to Distance Himself from the Chechen Debacle', *Financial Times*, 23 Aug. 1996.

54. See for example *Komsomolskaya Pravda*, 12 Oct. 1996. The paper carried out a poll of 1,000 Muscovites on 7–9 Oct. 1996, asking them what they thought of the Lebed–Maskhadov agreement. Sixty-five per cent approved and only 7 per cent denounced the agreement, though another 17 per cent said that they approved some aspects and opposed others.

55. John Thornhill, 'Yeltsin Faces Flak over Troop Pullout', *Financial Times*, 25 Nov. 1996.

56. Sergei Shargorodsky, 'Yeltsin OKs Chechnya Pullout', Associated Press, 23 Nov. 1996.

57. See Richard Beeston, 'Pullout Sets Seal on Chechen Debacle', *The Times*, 3 Jan. 1997, and Lee Hockstader, 'Moscow Weighs Costs of War in Chechnya, *Washington Post*, 3 Jan. 1997.

58. See Richard Dion, 'The Chechens Lack Friends', *Moscow Times*, 13 Feb. 1997.

59. See Dmitry Zaks, 'Russia, Chechnya Sign Historic Accord', *Moscow Times*, 13 May 1997.

60. See Interfax, 11 July 1997. The full text is in the BBC's *Monitoring Summary of World Broadcasts*, SUW/0495, 18 July 1997

61. See Chrystia Freeland, 'Yeltsin Staves off Chechnya Crisis', *Financial Times*, 19 Aug. 1997.

Part II: The Russian Defeat

Epigraph from *The Heritage of Russian Verse*, ed. and trans. Dmitri Obolensky (Indiana University Press, Bloomington, 1976), pp. 172–5.

4 The Masque of Democracy

1. 'Liberal capitalist' as a description is much to be preferred to 'bourgeois', a word so chewed over as to have lost all flavour and meaning. As Alfred Cobban and others have convincingly argued, even when applied to the

classic (in Marx's own analysis) 'bourgeois revolution', that of France, the term is highly questionable. Rather than arguing about sterile definitions of class, it makes more sense to look at ideology, tactics and results. Certainly in Russia today, it is impossible to talk of a real bourgeoisie with a defined interest – and as for the idea that a Soviet bourgeoisie overthrew Communism, that would be self-evident nonsense. It is, however, already possible to speak not just of economic 'clans' in the administration and political elite, but also of economic group interests which motivate in the same general direction political figures who appear on the surface to be opposed to each other.

2. Vladimir Shlapentokh: 'Russia as a Medieval State', *Washington Quarterly* 19:1, 1996. For another view of the new Russian oligarchy, see the June 1997 report on Russia by the prestigious Stockholm International Peace Research Institute (SIPRI), which states that Russia is turning into a corrupt and criminalised oligarchy with a monopolied private sector dependent on extracting state favours.

3. Gerald Brenan, *The Spanish Labyrinth* (1943; reprinted Cambridge University Press, 1982), p. 11.

4. I hasten to add that these are not intended as exact analogies or parallels – Yeltsin is not Porfirio Diaz or Camillo Cavour; Lebed is not Pancho Villa or Mussolini – but only as useful and interesting ones, from which tools of analysis may be drawn for the interpretation of Russia today.

5. Molly Moore, 'Three Years after Mexico Embraced Free Trade, Rural Poor Still Flock to Capital', *Washington Post*, 31 Dec. 1996. A later article in the same series, 'As China's Economy Booms, Inequality Divides its People', 1 Jan. 1997, quoted statistics saying that the real income of 41 per cent of families in Shenyang, Nanning and Chonqing dropped in 1995.

6. See Alexei Bayer, 'A New Capital for a Capitalist Russia', *Wall Street Journal*, 17 July 1997.

7. Charles C. Cumberland, *Mexico: the Struggle for Modernity* (Oxford University Press, New York, 1968), pp. 165, 199.

8. Ibid., pp. 204–10; Alan Knight, *The Mexican Revolution*, vol. I, pp. 94–7.

9. Mark Whitehouse, 'Eurobond Sparks Blue-Chip Rally', *Moscow Times*, 30 June 1997.

10. See John A. Davis, 'The South, the Risorgimento and the Origins of the Southern Problem', and Adrian Lyttelton, 'Landlords, Peasants and the Limits of Liberalism', both in John A. Davis (ed.), *Gramsci and Italy's Passive Revolution* (Croom Helm, London, 1979).

11. See Jonas Bernstein in *Moscow Times*, 4 July 1997.

12. The fictional hero of Ilya Ilf and Yevgeny Petrov's *The Twelve Chairs*.

13. See '"Mafiosi" Spread Capitalist Message in Siberia', Reuters, 27 Dec. 1996.

14. David Remnick, 'Can Russia Change?', *Foreign Affairs*, Jan.–Feb. 1997.

15. David Satter, 'The Lawlessness of Russian Reform', *Jamestown Foundation Prism* 2:11 (May 1996). For a masterly description of the feelings of ordinary Russians concerning privatisation, and the justification for them, see also his 'The Lawlessness of Russian Reform', *Wall Street Journal*, 4 June 1996.

16. All the different motivations came together in a passionate desire for freedom to travel abroad. Nothing was so bitterly resented by the younger Soviet elites as the restrictions on travel to the West – especially because under Brezhnev, more and more children of the very top officials did in fact get state jobs which gave them such opportunities, whetting the appetites of the remainder to fever pitch.

17. See Charles H. Fairbanks, *Clientelism and the Roots of Post-Soviet Dis-*

order (1993).

18. See Arkady Vaksberg, *The Soviet Mafia*, trans. John Roberts and Elizabeth Roberts (Weidenfeld and Nicolson, London, 1991). For changing attitudes to private property and commercial activity in the Soviet intelligentsia in the 1970s and 1980s, see James Millar, 'History, Method, and the Problem of Bias', in Frederic J. Fleron and Erik P. Hoffman (eds), *Post-Communist Studies and Political Science: Methodology and Empirical Theory in Sovietology* (Westview Press, Boulder, 1993); and David S. Mason, 'Attitudes Toward the Market and Political Participation in the Postcommunist States', *Slavic Review* 54: 2 (summer 1995).

19. See for example Claire Sterling, *Thieves' World* (Simon and Schuster, New York, 1994).

20. The most balanced brief introduction to the post-Soviet organised criminal world is probably Phil Williams, 'How Serious a Threat Is Russian Organised Crime', in Phil Williams (ed.), *Russian Organised Crime: the New Threat?* (Frank Cass, London, 1997). The standard longer account in English of the origins of Russian organised crime and its activities in the years of the Soviet collapse is Stephen Handelman, *Comrade Criminal: the Theft of the Second Russian Revolution* (Michael Joseph, London, 1994).

21. For his view, see Jim Leitzel, *Russian Economic Reform* (Routledge, London, 1995). For the workings of the Sicilian Mafia as commercial judge and enforcer, see Diego Gambetta, *The Sicilian Mafia: the Business of Private Protection* (Harvard University Press, Cambridge, 1993); and Federico Varese, 'Is Sicily the Future of Russia? Private Protection and the Rise of the Russian Mafia', *European Journal of Sociology* 23:2 (1994). Phil Williams quotes Andrei Nechayev, president of the Russian Finance Corporation:

'Law-abiding businessmen would much rather take their grievances to the courts (as they do in the rest of the world) than to gangsters. Regrettably, in our present situation a person can either petition a court, wait months for a decision, pay bribes … and still have no guarantee that his wishes will be fulfilled, or he can go to the gangsters, pay them a certain fee, and have the highest expectation that his wishes will be fulfilled. This however gives rise to the colossal danger. As soon as you appeal to the world of crime for help, you automatically become its hostage.'
See *Literaturnaya Gazeta*, 29 Nov. 1996.

22. Louise Shelley, 'Post-Soviet Organised Crime: a New Form of Authoritarianism', in Williams, *Russian Organised Crime*.

23. Douglas Farah, 'For International Criminal Links, Russian Crime Finds Haven in Caribbean', *Washington Post*, 7 Oct. 1996. For a fraud in the USA by officials of another major Russian bank, Inkombank (but in this case, probably without the knowledge of its leadership), see Olga Kedrina, 'In Bed with the Banker', *Moskovsky Komsomolets*, 25 Sept. 1996.

24. See Oleg Yuryev, 'The Business Cocktail: a Mixture of Petrol, Engine Oil and Crime', *Moskovsky Komsomolets*, 31 Aug. 1996; and Pavel Voshchanov in *Komsomolskaya Pravda*, 5 Nov. 1996.

25. For 1996 figures, see Valentin Kunin, 'Doing Business in Russia is an Increasingly Hazardous Enterprise', *Ria Novosti*, 3 Dec. 1996, and Zakhar Vinogradov in *Nezavisimaya Gazeta*, 5 Dec. 1996.

26. See Richard Lapper in the *Financial Times*, 18 Oct. 1996.

27. See Louise Shelley, 'Privatisation and Organised Crime in Russia', *Kennan Institute Report* 14:6 (1997).

28. See Joseph Blasi, Maya Kroumova and Douglas Kruse, *Kremlin Capitalism: Privatising the Russian Economy* (Cornell University Press, Ithaca,

1997), pp. 33ff.

29. Quoted in ibid.

30. A fascinating insight into this possible alternative path for Russia, and into the psychological roots of the cruelty and ruthlessness of the urban Communists during collectivisation, is to be found in an essay of Maxim Gorky of 1922, 'On the Russian Peasantry'. On the one hand, he assumes the peasantry's future dominance. On the other hand, he hates them for their cruelty, 'dreadful darkness' of superstition, anti-intellectualism and indifference to the starvation in the cities during the Civil War: 'I am reluctant to speak of the crude taunting, the vengeful mockery with which the village greeted the hungry people of the town.' He concludes that Russia's future rulers 'will not be a very "nice and likable Russian people", but this will be finally a businesslike people, distrustful and indifferent to everything which is not directly related to its needs.' Maxim Gorky, 'On the Russian Peasantry' (1922), in R. E. F. Smith (ed.), *The Russian Peasant, 1920 and 1984* (Frank Cass, London, 1977). The other essays, articles and short stories in this collection also deal, either in an optimistic or pessimistic spirit, with the future of an essentially peasant Russia.

31. Even to a considerable extent, as Stephen Kotkin has noted with reference to Magnitogorsk, from kulak or rich peasant families – precisely because these tended to be more dynamic and better educated than the rest of the peasantry. See Stephen Kotkin, *Magnetic Mountain: Stalinism as a Civilisation* (University of California Press, Berkeley, 1995).

32. For a depressing picture of apathy and acceptance of social and political evils among ordinary Russians, see Vladimir Shlapentokh, 'Bonjour Stagnation', *Washington Quarterly* (winter 1996–7).

33. For Gramsci's discussion of the meaning of 'passive revolution', see *Selections from the Prison Notebooks*, ed. Quintin Hoare and Geoffrey Nowell Smith (Lawrence and Wishart, London, 1971), pp. 106–14.

34. Davis, *Gramsci and Italy's Passive Revolution*, p. 23.

35. *Selections from the Prison Notebooks*, p. 90.

36. His classic view, which has critically shaped the whole modern analysis of totalitarian systems, is in C. J. Friedrich and Z. Brzezinski, *Totalitarian Dictatorship and Autocracy* (Praeger, 1966).

37. Petro G. Grigorenko, *Memoirs*, trans. Thomas P. Whitney (W. W. Norton, New York, 1982); Irina Ratushinskaya, *In the Beginning* (Sceptre, 1990).

38. See George Schopflin, 'The End of Communism in Eastern Europe', *International Affairs* 66:1 (1990).

39. For Yeltsin's loss of interest in appealing to the people, and reversion to 'managerial' (or autocratic) type after the defeat of Gorbachev, see Timothy Colton, 'Boris Yeltsin, Russia's All-Thumbs Democrat', in Timothy J. Colton and Robert C. Tucker.

40. For an insightful and very informative survey of Russian privatisation (which suffers however from a soft spot for Chubais and his cronies), see Blasi et al., *Kremlin Capitalism*.

41. This is the assessment of Professor Olga Kryshtanovskaya of the Institute of Sociology in the Russian Academy of Sciences; see *Kennan Institute Report* 13:15 (1996). See also Martin Malia, 'The Nomenclatura Capitalists', *The New Republic*, 22 May 1995.

42. Quoted in Layard and Parker, *The Coming Russian Boom*, p. 165.

43. Blasi et al., *Kremlin Capitalism*, p. 83.

44. See David Lane, *The Rise and Fall of State Socialism* (Polity Press, 1996), p. 161.

45. For portraits of Vladimir Potanin and his career, see John Thornhill, 'Unbuttoned Capitalist: Vladimir Potanin', *Financial Times*, 17 Aug.

1996; 'O Lucky Man: Mr Potanin Goes to Moscow', *The Economist*, 31 Aug. 1996; and 'Russia's Takeover Kings', *Forbes*, 7 Oct. 1996.

46. See John Thornhill, 'Russia's Jewish Emigrés Seek to Invest in Their Homeland', *Financial Times*, 1 Feb. 1997.

47. For Berezovsky's early and extremely dubious business career, see Oleg Yuryev, 'The Business Cocktail: a Mixture of Petroleum, Engine Oil, and Crime', *Moskovsky Komsomolets*, 31 Oct. 1996. See also *Forbes*, Nov. 1996.

48. See 'Moscow's Group of Seven', *Financial Times*, 1 Nov. 1996.

49. For evasion of taxes by the oil companies, see Mikhail Berger, 'Tax Collection Can Be a Very Risky Business', *St Petersburg Times*, 11 Nov. 1996.

50. See Robert C. Tucker, 'Post-Soviet Leadership and Change', in Colton and Tucker.

51. George F. Kennan (under name 'X'), 'The Sources of Soviet Conduct', *Foreign Affairs* (July 1947).

52. Gramsci, op. cit., *Selections from the Prison Notebooks*, p. 138.

53. For the Yeltsin administration's adoption of the threat of bankruptcy against companies to force them to pay their taxes – and the great difficulty of actually implementing this threat, given both official corruption and the extraordinary nature of Russian accounting systems – see Vanora Bennet, 'The Tax Man Cometh for Russian Companies', *Los Angeles Times*, 28 Dec. 1996.

54. See also David Filipov, 'Evasion Schemes Tax Russia's Economy', *Boston Globe*, 28 Oct. 1996, and 'Carving up Russia', *Financial Times*, 29 Nov. 1996.

55. See Stephanie Baker-Said, 'State Set to Submit Tax Code', *Moscow Times*, 26 Apr. 1997.

56. See Carol Matlack, 'Where the Taxman Cometh – Very Carefully', *Business Week*, 16 June 1997.

57. For further passages from my interview with him, see chapter 10.

58. See Gary Peach, editor of *Capital Markets Russia*, in *Moscow Times*, 24 June 1997.

59. See Larisa Beloivan, Vladivostok, *RIA Novosti*, 13 Jan. 1997.

60. On the raw materials trap, see the work of Jeffrey Sachs and Andrew Warner, quoted in Fred Hiatt, 'Is Russia Too Rich for its Own Good?', *Russia Review*, 10 Mar. 1997. In Hiatt's words, 'The kind of transparency in government and faithfulness to the rule of law with which Estonia and Singapore attract foreign investment are death to such diamond-guzzling elites.' For the raw materials trap in Latin America, see Thomas Skidmore and Peter E. Smith, *Modern Latin America* (Oxford University Press, 1997).

61. For a political portrait of the region to 1994, and especially of the ascendancy of Governor Yevgeny Nazdratenko, see Peter Kirkow, 'Regional Warlordism in Russia: the Case of Primorsky Krai', *Europe–Asia Studies* 47:6 (Sept. 1995). It includes a picture of the way in which the local regime distributed licences for the lucrative fishing trade in such a way as to reward themselves and their friends and consolidate support.

62. For example, in the sale of a large stake in Sibneft in May 1997, from which foreign bidders were excluded. See *Moscow Times*, 15 May 1997 and 3 June 1997.

63. See Matthew Kaminski, 'Barriers to a Cash Flood', *Financial Times Russia Survey*, 9 Apr. 1997. For the reasons for this shortfall, see also the surprisingly frank criticisms by Deputy US Treasury Secretary Lawrence Summers in his speech to the Kennedy School of Government, Harvard, 9 Jan. 1997, recorded by the US Information Agency. See also Sergei Kashlev, 'Foreign Capital Plays it Careful', *Nezavisimaya Gazeta*, 29 Oct. 1996.

64. See *Novaya Gazeta*, 31 Jan. 1997; the paper declared that the government

should be ashamed 'before the people, before God and their own consciences'. See also Sophia Coudenhove, 'Hunter Chernomyrdin Blasted for Cub Shoot', *Moscow Times*, 1 Feb. 1997; and 'Premier Defends Bear Hunt', *Moscow Times*, 4 Feb. 1997. Journalists on the magazine *Ogonyok* claim that after they joined in the criticism, an attempt was made from within the government to stop their pay, though this was later abandoned due to adverse publicity.

65. Blasi et al., *Kremlin Capitalism*, p. 171.

66. Figures in the Economist Intelligence Unit profile of Russia, 1995–6. See also Vladimir Mikhalev, 'Social Security in Russia under Economic Transition', *Europe–Asia Studies*, 48:1 (Jan. 1996).

67. For example, the Economist Intelligence Unit Profile of Russia, 1995–6, which describes Russian privatisation as 'undoubtedly one of the success stories of post-Communist reform in the former Eastern bloc' – despite the fact that as of 1996, it had neither stopped steep economic decline nor led to higher investment either by the new Russian owners or from abroad, nor increased the productivity of Russian industry, nor improved the living standards of the population. So the success was simply, it would appear, that it had happened – in other words, privatisation is praised as a good in itself, irrespective of its results.

68. Figures quotes in Blasi et al. *Kremlin Capitalism*, p. 77.

69. Albert Speransky, 'Master and Man in Today's Russia', *Jamestown Foundation Prism* 2 (Nov. 1996), part 4.

70. Andrei Piontkovsky, 'Reformer or Oligarch?', *Moscow Times*, 11 Mar. 1997. For the arguments of Berezovsky and Malashenko that the 'robber barons' are converting themselves into productive and legal figures and 'reducing poverty and creating a middle class', see 'Difficult

Days for Overnight Billionaire', *Financial Times Survey of Russia*, 9 Apr. 1997. For the repetition of this by Western sympathisers, see Layard and Parker, *The Coming Russian Boom*, pp. 171–2.

71. The remarks by Kovalyev and Gaidar appear in Chrystia Freeland, John Thornhill and Andrew Gowers, 'Moscow's Group of Seven', *Financial Times*, 1 Nov. 1996.

72. See Reuters, Moscow, 25 Nov. 1995 for Oneximbank's acquisition of Norilsk Nickel; 24 Nov. 1995 for the Duma's appeal to Yeltsin to stop the loans for shares auctions; and 12 Jan. 1996 for the cash raised by the government. See also 'Russian Privatisation Officials Accused of Abuse', Reuters, 22 Mar. 1996, for the accusations by the State Audit Chamber (the parliamentary financial watchdog) against two of Chubais's deputies. For an overview of 'loans for shares' and the role of this deal in the 1996 election, see Peter Reddaway, 'Beware the Russian Reformer', *Washington Post*, 24 Aug. 1997.

73. For the difference between the privatisation of Gazprom and the oil companies, see John Thornhill, 'Two Routes to a Common Objective', *Financial Times Survey of Russia*, 9 Apr. 1997. For a general portrait of Gazprom as of 1996, see MC Securities Ltd, 'Gazprom: a Strategic Assessment', 7 Oct. 1996.

74. For a searing personal portrait of Igor Malashenko, president of the 'independent' television channel NTV (controlled by Vladimir Gusinsky's Most Bank) turned Yeltsin PR chief, see Chrystia Freeland, 'Mover, Shaker, President Maker', *Financial Times*, 28 June 1997.

75. See 'All The News that Fits: Russia's Media Moguls', *The Economist*, 15 Feb. 1997; and Grigory Simanovich, 'Dependent Television Endangers Democracy', *St Petersburg Times*, 18 Nov. 1996.

76. Patricia Kranz, 'The Making of a Russian Political Machine', *Business*

Week, 4 Nov. 1996.

77. Quoted by Jonas Bernstein in the *Moscow Times*, 23 May 1997.

78. A rare piece of hypocrisy this. For if anything might cause a wave of anti-semitism in Russia, it would of course be precisely the perception that a group of Jewish bankers had got control of the government and were using it to enrich themselves. In fact, no such backlash has occurred, beyond some statements by politicians concerning Berezovsky himself.

79. For Berezovsky on his Israeli citizenship and other matters, see his interview with Yevgeny Kiselev on the *Itogi* programme of NTV, 17 Nov. 1996 (reprinted in *Johnson's Russia List*). See also Pavel Voshchanov, 'Are Those Who Are Not with Berezovsky Anti-Semitic?', *Komsomolskaya Pravda*, 5 Nov. 1996. For the original news of Berezovsky's Israeli citizenship, see *Izvestia*, 1 Nov. 1996.

80. Chrystia Freeland, John Thornhill and Andrew Gowers, 'Wealthy Clique Emerges from Kremlin Gloom', *Financial Times*, 31 Oct. 1997, and 'Moscow's Group of Seven', *Financial Times*, 1 Nov. 1997. See also Vladimir Alexandrov, 'The Magic Seven. Who Are They, These Saviours of Russia?', *Interfax-Argumenty I Fakty*, nos 1–2 (Dec. 1996); 'The Election Stakes Were High for Russia's New Industrial Plutocracy', *International Herald Tribune*, 5 July 1996; and Timothy Heritage, 'Russian Tycoon's Rise Shows Business Circle Power', Reuters, 1 Nov. 1996.

81. See Jonas Bernstein, 'The Ties That Bind', *Moscow Times*, 23 May 1997, and Jeremy Weinberg, 'Chubais' Career Marked by Relentless Efficiency', *Moscow Times*, 11 Mar. 1997. For Dyachenko's appointment and the allegations of a romantic involvement with Chubais, see Dmitry Zaks, 'Yeltsin Gives Daughter Post as Image Manager', *Moscow Times*, 1 July 1997.

82. For an accurate portrayal of this process by one of Russia's leading business newspapers, see Yelena Babak, 'Capitalist Bridge', *Dyelovoi Mir*, 10–14 Nov. 1996.

83. See 'Russian Bank MFK Says No Plan to Sell Steel Stake', Reuters, Moscow, 13 June 1997.

84. See 'Russia's Oneximbank to Take Part in Norilsk Tender', Reuters, Moscow, 7 July 1997, and Poul Funder Larsen, 'Miner's Threats Loom over Norilsk Reform', *Moscow Times*, 8 Feb. 1997.

85. See John Thornhill and Chrystia Freeland, 'Setback for Russia's Banking Barons', *Financial Times*, 19 Mar. 1997.

86. See Peter Henderson, 'Fight Seen Brewing over Prize Russian Oil Firm', Reuters, 8 May 1997.

87. *Moscow Times* (leader), 15 May 1997.

88. See 'Analysts Say "Rigged" Bid Gives Menatap Control of Vukos', Dow Jones, Moscow, 23 Dec. 1996.

89. MC–BBL Monthly Valuation Analysis, 3 June 1997.

90. See Nigel Stephenson, 'Russia Moves to End Row over Surgut Share Issue', Reuters, Moscow, 10 Dec. 1996.

91. Figures in the Economist Intelligence Unit country report on Russia, 4th quarter 1996.

92. See Lynnley Browning, 'Russian Oil Exports Seen Stable', Reuters, Moscow, 11 Oct. 1996.

93. At least one great international fortune has also been built as a result. David and Simon Reuben of London-based Transworld Metals were able to use their links with a pair of Russian businessmen with close links to part of the Yeltsin administration to corner 5 per cent of world aluminium production. See Julia Flynn and Patricia Kranz, 'Grabbing a Corner in Russian Aluminium: Transworld Has Snapped Up Half of Russia's Production', *Business Week*, 16 Sept. 1996; Ian King, 'Aluminium Tsar Accused', *Guardian*, 12 Mar. 1997; and Rufus Olin: 'Revealed: Britain's Metal Tsar', *Sunday Times*, 4 Aug. 1996.

94. See the World Bank's *Statistical Handbook 1996: States of the Former USSR*, in the series Studies of Economics in Transition, pp. 379–407.

95. See Skidmore and Smith, *Modern Latin America*, esp. pp. 42–52.

96. See the *London Property News*, Feb. 1997.

97. Of course, a key role in procuring the June 1996 was played by Moscow Mayor Yuri Lushkov; and it is probable that in future he will be a rival of other members of the Yeltsin administration for the presidency. The point however is that all these figures will aim at redistributing the personalities in both government and government-linked business, but certainly not at changing the whole system.

98. For relations between Moscow and the richest of all the autonomous republics, Sakha-Yakutia, see Marjorie Mandelstam Balzer, 'Nationalism, Interethnic Relations and Federalism: the Case of the Sakha Republic (Yakutia)', *Europe-Asia Studies* 48:1 (Jan. 1996). In 1992, the centre and the republic agreed to split the proceeds of the republic's diamond wealth 32 per cent each, with employees (i.e. largely the management) getting 23 per cent. But as Daniel R. Kempton points out, in the years that followed, the weakness of the centre (and especially the 1993 crisis with the parliament) allowed Yakutia considerably to improve its position in a variety of ways. See Daniel R. Kempton, 'The Republic of Sakha (Yakutia): the Evolution of Centre–Periphery Relations in the Russian Federation', *Europe–Asia Studies* 48:4 (June 1996).

99. On the extraction of loans by the republics and regions, and the way the centre has tried to use this as a lever, see Daniel Treisman, 'The Politics of Soft Credit in Post-Soviet Russia', *Europe–Asia Studies* 47:6 (1995).

5 'Who Would Be a Soldier If You Could Work in a Bank?'

Epigraphs from Carl Maria von Clausewitz, *On War* (Penguin, Harmondsworth, 1974), p. 185); Kostomarov quoted in Maxim Gorky, 'On the Russian Peasantry', in R. E. F. Smith (ed.), *The Russian Peasant, 1920 and 1984* (Frank Cass, London, 1977), p. 12.

1. All figures from the *Statistical Abstract of the United States, 1996* (US Department of Commerce, Washington DC).

2. Projection by the Russian demographic expert Anatoly Antonov, *Washington Times*, 22 Sept. 1996.

3. Richard Pipes, *Russia Under the Old Regime* (Collier, New York, 1974), pp. 15–16.

4. Figures from the State Statistics Commission of the Russian Federation, *Dyelovoi Mir*, 3 Dec. 1996.

5. For a portrait of hunger and misery in one medium-sized provincial industrial town (Zavolzskie, in Ivanovo Oblast), see Alexander Kalinin, 'The Art of Living without Paycheques', *Izvestia*, 26 Apr. 1996. For the desperate conditions in the countryside, especially the increasing proportion of elderly, the best source is the newspaper *Selskaya Zhizn*. I am indebted to Frank Durgin for bringing these sources to my attention, through *Johnson's Russia List* on the Internet.

6. On the growth of the Muslim population throughout the Soviet Union in its last decades, see for example Sergei Panarin: 'Muslims of the Soviet Union: Dynamics of Survival', *Central Asia Survey* 12:2 (1993). On the general change in fertility patterns, see A. J. Coale, B. A. Anderson and E. Harm, *Human Fertility in Russia since the Nineteenth Century* (Princeton, 1979).

7. See Mark Tolts, 'The Modernisation of Demographic Behaviour in the Muslim Republics of the Former

402 Notes to pages 189–203

USSR', in Yaacov Ro'i (ed.), *Muslim Eurasia: Conflicting Legacies* (Cass, London, 1995).

8. Figures from the Soviet censuses, quoted in Valery Tishkov, 'The Russians in Central Asia and Kazakhstan', in Ro'i, *Muslim Eurasia*. For an early Western perception of these growing tensions and fears, based on the accounts of Soviet emigrés, see Rasma Karklins, 'Ethnic Relations in the USSR: The Perspective from Below' (Allen and Unwin, Boston, 1986).

9. See Martha Brill Olcott, 'Demographic Upheavals in Central Asia', *Orbis* (Fall 1996).

10. Figures from the Soviet censuses.

11. Hélène Carrère d'Encausse, *L'Empire éclate* (Flammarion, Paris, 1978).

12. For a survey of the various traditions of 'Eurasian' thinking, and their reappearance under Mikhail Gorbachev, see Milan Hauner, *What Is Asia to Us: Russia's Asian Heartland Yesterday and Today* (Routledge, London, 1992).

13. For Trubetskoy's views, see ibid. pp. 60, 65.

14. Fifteen years earlier, my uncle had been an officer with the Gurkhas, but he did at least speak Gurkhali, thanks to the strict policy of the British Indian army in this regard.

15. Interview with the author, Afghan frontier, Pyanj District, Tajikistan, 27 Apr. 1995. For the extreme unwillingness of the wives of border guards officers to accept their husbands serving anywhere in Central Asia, see Deborah Adelman, *The Children of Perestroika Come of Age: Young People of Moscow Talk about Life in the New Russia* (M. E. Sharpe, London, 1994), pp. 29–31.

16. See *Itogi*, 17 Dec. 1996: 'SSSR – Eto Kitezhgrad'. Kitezh is the miraculous city of Russian myth, which was taken into the sky to save it from the Tatars. See also the poll results published in *Nezavisimaya Gazeta*, 10 Dec. 1996.

17. See Matthew Wyman et al., 'Public Opinion, Parties and Voters in the December 1993 Russian Election', *Europe–Asia Studies* 47:4 (June 1995).

18. Excerpts from Vladimir Zhirinovsky's book, *Posledniy Brosok Na Yug*, quoted here are from the partial translation by Mark Greaves in *Index on Censorship*, 1 Feb. 1994, pp. 61–71.

19. All the figures in this section are from polls conducted by the independent All Russian Centre for Research on Public Opinion, directed by Yuri Levada.

20. Post-election speeches by Zyuganov showed that he now recognised that the language of revolution held little appeal for the Russian electorate. See Marina Shakina, 'Communists without Socialism?', *RIA Novosti*, 7 Aug. 1996.

21. Taken from personal observations in Russia during the election campaign.

22. For attitudes to military service, and youth culture in general, see Hilary Pilkington, *Russia's Youth and its Culture: a Nation's Constructors and Constructed* (Routledge, 1994), p. 191 and *passim*; and for youth culture (official and counter-) in the later Soviet period, Jim Riordan (ed.), *Soviet Youth Culture* (Indiana University Press, 1989).

23. See the interviews in Deborah Adelman's extremely evocative collections, *The Children of Perestroika: Moscow Teenagers Talk about Their Lives and the Future* (M. E. Sharpe, New York, 1991) and *The Children of Perestroika Come of Age*.

24. Taylor E. Dark, 'No Illusions: Russia's Student Generation', *National Interest* (spring 1996).

25. Cf. Igor Kon, 'Moral Culture', in Dmitri Shalin (ed.), *Russian Culture at the Crossroads: Paradoxes of Post-Communist Consciousness* (Westview Press, Boulder, 1996), p. 203.

26. Tatyana Kutkovets and Igor Klyamkin (Institute of Sociological Analysis), '"Special Path" of Russia:

Myths and Paradoxes', *Moskovskiye Novosti*, 25 Aug. 1996.

27. For a short but brilliantly perceptive account of the extent to which Soviet mass culture shaped itself from below (at least after Stalin's death), see Richard Stites, *Russian Popular Culture: Entertainment and Society since 1900* (Cambridge University Press, 1992). For the diminishing effects of Soviet state propaganda about the 'Great Patriotic War' on Russian youth, see Nina Tumarkin, 'The War of Remembrance', in Richard Stites (ed.), *Culture and Entertainment in Wartime Russia* (Indiana University Press, 1995).

28. For Soviet films from the perestroika era set in the war, see Anna Lawton, *Kinoglasnost: Soviet Cinema in Our Time* (Cambridge University Press, 1992), pp. 29–32, 167–8, 225–6. Since the end of the Soviet Union, the genre seems to have disappeared completely, through lack of funds as well as lack of interest among the younger audience.

29. Interview with the author, 14th Army HQ, Tiraspol, 24 Feb. 1994.

30. See Christopher Duffy, *Russia's Military Way to the West: Origins and Nature of Russian Military Power, 1700–1800* (Routledge, London, 1981).

31. The classic study of this factor remains John Howes Gleason, *The Genesis of Russophobia in Great Britain: A Study of the Interaction of Policy and Opinion* (Harvard University Press, 1950). See also David Gillard, *The Struggle for Asia, 1828–1914* (Methuen, London, 1977), esp. pp. 18–43.

32. See Leo Tolstoy, *War and Peace*.

33. Roger R. Reese, *Stalin's Reluctant Soldiers: A Social History of the Red Army, 1925–1941* (University Press of Kansas, 1996). See also Carl van Dyke, 'The Soviet–Finnish War of 1939–40', Ph.D dissertation, Emmanuel College, Cambridge, 1994, p. 284. This thesis however focuses mainly on the tactical ill-preparedness and inflexibility of the Soviet army, and its tendency to launch bludgeoning frontal attacks and suffer correspondingly high casualties – a tendency which stems in part from a lack of interest on the part of the High Command in the lives of the ordinary soldiers, and which continued through the Second World War. I am grateful to Dr van Dyke for sending me a copy of his thesis.

34. Leo Tolstoy, *Anna Karenina* (Penguin, 1977), esp. pp. 839–43.

35. Vsevolod Garshin, *From the Reminiscences of Private Ivanov, and Other Stories* (Angel Classics, London, 1988), p. 176. For a recent Western military history of the Russian army's performance in the wars of 1877–8 and 1904–5, see Bruce W. Memming: *Bayonets before Bullets: the Russian Imperial Army, 1861–1914* (Indiana University Press, 1992).

36. A partial exception is Malaya, but there the war was not against the Malays but the mainly Chinese-backed Communists, which put the British troops in a much better position – and the British forces in Malaya were largely in fact Gurkha. Casualties were also very slight compared to the other wars under consideration. By comparison, this was not really a very serious war.

37. Hans Binnendijk and Jeffrey Simon, 'Baltic Security and NATO Enlargement', study no. 57, Institute for National Strategic Studies, National Defence University, Dec. 1995.

38. Kon, 'Moral Culture', p. 204.

39. Quoted in Jo Durden-Smith, 'Russia Struggles in Its Chains', *St Petersburg Times*, 28 Oct. 1996.

40. Milovan Djilas, *Wartime*, trans. Michael B. Petrovich (Harcourt Brace Jovanovich, New York, 1997).

41. Primo Levi, *The Truce*, trans. Stuart Woolf (Penguin, London, 1979), pp. 231–2.

42. Figures presented by Professor Yuri Levada to the conference of the American Association for the

Advancement of Slavic Studies (AAASS), Boston, Nov. 1996.

43. Harry Holbert Turney-High, *Primitive War: Its Practice and Concepts* (University of South Carolina Press, 1949), p. 52.

44. See Thomas E. Ricks, 'The Widening Gap between the Military and Society', *Atlantic Monthly* 280:1 (July 1997). In an earlier article, 'The Military: the Great Society in Camouflage', *Atlantic Monthly* 278:6 (Dec. 1996), he says, 'Accountability, diversity, sobriety, hierarchy – all this and a sturdy safety net too, have put the US Army on a different road from the rest of America.' He also points out that the army is the only section of American society to have established something like genuine racial equality and career opportunities for blacks. However, he also warns of the dangers of a gap between the military and society. Ricks makes the point that for all these reasons, there is a growing risk of the army coming to see itself as superior to a corrupt and decadent society, and even developing a belief that it has the right of political intervention 'to save the nation'.

45. For a moving account of his first encounter with the British regimental spirit, see John Keegan, *A History of Warfare* (Pimlico, 1994), pp. xv–xvi.

46. Words used to me by several officers and soldiers in Chechnya. They were not as yet saying that the army itself should take over – indeed, that would be a ridiculous position to take, given the glaring evidence of the army's own weakness and corruption. But in their eyes the new political order, let alone the Yeltsin administration, had no legitimacy whatsoever. They just could not work out what to put in its place.

47. Deborah Yarsike Ball and Theodore P. Gerber, 'The Political Views of Russian Field Grade Officers', *Post-Soviet Affairs* 12:2 (1996).

48. In a talk at the Woodrow Wilson Centre, Washington DC, May 1996.

6 Failure of the Serbian Option, 1

Translated by Judith Deutsch Kornblatt, in *The Cossack Hero in Russian Literature: a Study in Cultural Mythology* (University of Wisconsin Press, 1993).

1. Georgy Derluguian, 'Parade, Prayer, Patrol: Sources and Constraints of the Reinvented Kuban Cossacks', paper presented to the United States Institute of Peace, Washington DC, 1997.

2. Declaration of the *Soviet Atamanov Soyuza Kazakov*, Apr. 1992, quoted in Barbara Skinner, 'Identity Formation in the Russian Cossack Revival', *Europe-Asia Studies* 46:6 (1994).

3. See for example Bruce Clark, *An Empire's New Clothes: the End of Russia's Liberal Dream* (Vintage, London, 1995). For an optimistic overview of the position of the Cossacks in 1993, see Alexander Kaltakhchan, 'Russian Cossacks: Between Past and Future', *Novoye Vremya*, no. 19 (1993). For a much more sceptical look four years later, see Carlotta Gall in the *Moscow Times*, 12 May 1997.

4. For a look at the commercial background to this 'treaty', see Vadim Dubnov, 'Tales from the Cossack Lands', *Novoye Vremya*, Nov. 1994.

5. Interview with the author, 24 June 1996.

6. For an Interior Ministry view of the Cossacks, see the interview with General Yuri Kosolapov, then Commander of the Internal forces in the North Caucasus: 'Russia's South', *Rossiiskiye Vyesti*, 21 July 1993.

7. See Dmitry Zaks, 'Cossack Representative Asserts Will to Defend Chechen Land', *Moscow Times*, 18 Jan. 1997. See also the piece by Yury Budya of *Novoye Vremya*, 'Cossacks: No Protectors', *Moscow Times*, 20 Jan. 1997.

8. For a Cossack view of the Ossete–Ingush conflict, see the Tass

interview with Alexander Starodubtsev, 10 Aug. 1993.

9. Patrick Kamenka, 'Cossacks Volunteer by Thousands for Chechen
War', Agence France Presse, 4 Mar.
1995.

10. Igor Rotar, 'Dudayev Threatens to
Fight in Stavropol Region', *Nezavisimaya Gazeta*, 25 Mar. 1995. For similar threats, see 'Chechen Crisis. On
the Verge of War?', *Izvestia*, 3 Dec.
1994. It is perhaps hardly surprising
that Russian as well as Western journalists have taken Cossack claims
more seriously than they deserve,
given the importance of the Cossack
myth in Russian culture and especially literature.

11. For even more grotesque Cossack
claims, see Vladimir Mezentsev, 'A
Third Force to Stop Bloodshed in
Chechnya', *Rossiyskaya Gazeta*, 31
Oct. 1995, which has the chief Don
Cossack Ataman, Nikolai Kozitsyn,
claiming that he could muster
15,000 armed men within twenty-
four hours, and 150,000 in three
days. Doubtless not by coincidence,
this was about the number of Cossacks mobilised by the Russian imperial army in August 1914.

12. Maria Korolova, 'Cossacks Accuse
Chechens of Terror Tactics', Reuters,
27 Mar. 1994.

13. Interview with the author, Grozny, 4
Dec. 1995.

14. Interview with the author, Krasnodar,
2 Oct. 1994. *Kunachestvo* means a
formalised friendship in the Caucasian languages. This was true in the
past of the Cossacks and the Ossetes,
and to some extent the Kabardins.
For the rest, this is a considerably ide-
alised picture, albeit an amiable one.

15. Interview with the author,
Naurskaya, 5 Dec. 1995.

16. For a portrait of the Cossack behaviour in Budennovsk, see the
despatches of Elaine Monaghan to
Reuters, 16–20 June 1995. For Cossack threats to Chechens living
around Budennovsk, see Nikolai
Grichin in *Izvestia*, 16 June 1996. For

the reaction among the Kuban Cossacks, and threats not just to
Chechens but to 'Caucasians' in that
region, see Viktor Zhilyakov, 'Kuban
Cossacks Demand that Caucasians
Leave Krasnodar Region', Tass, 23
June 1995. By widening their attack
to include all Caucasians, the Cossacks involved displayed their own
blind chauvinism, their lack of real
concern for the Chechen War, and
indeed their real priority, which was
not so much to expel the Caucasians
as to extort protection money from
them.

17. See 'Cossacks Present Ultimatum to
Terrorists in Budennovsk', Interfax,
17 June 1995.

18. See Sebastian Smith, 'Yeltsin Brings
Back Cossack units', AFP, 18 Apr.
1996. See also Interfax, Budennovsk, 17 Apr. 1996.

19. Anatol Lieven, 'Cossacks Sign Up as
Mercenaries in New Wars of Conquest', *The Times*, 28 Mar. 1992. For
a report on this meeting, see also
Eastern Europe Newsletter (back-
grounder on the North Caucasus, 11
May 1992).

20. For a portrait of the Terek Cossacks
and their internal splits as of mid-
1995, see *Russia Briefing* 3:5 (May
1995).

21. For a split between descendants of
Reds and Whites on the Don in the
years of the Soviet collapse, see *Russia Briefing* 2:12 (Dec. 1993).

22. The first 'Russian' (i.e. 'Rusian', as
from Kievan Rus) penetration into
the region was a Varangian expedi-
tion to the Caspian in AD 914, and
there were also intermittent contacts
and trade between the Caucasian
people and Muscovy. A sixteenth-
century Cossack song runs:
'No grey geese cackling there, in the
field;
No eagles that scream in the under-
sky;
But Greben Cossacks before the Tsar;
The Tsar Ivan Vassilievich.
"Little Father of us all, Orthodox Tsar,
What will you give and grant unto us?"

"I will give and grant, little Cossacks mine,
The Terek River that runs so free,
From the ridge itself to the wide blue sea,
To the wide blue sea, to the Caspian.'"

23. Interview with the author, 21 Dec. 1995. See also Sergei Panarin, 'Muslims of the Soviet Union: Dynamics of Survival', *Central Asia Survey* 12:2 (1993). Chechen and Ingush demonstrations took place in 1973, and followed ones by the Armenians in 1963, calling for the transfer of Karabakh to Armenia from Azerbaijan. This shows the level of nationalist discontent during the later Soviet decades, and also the extent to which this was being expressed – something of which the West knew nothing – or possibly in some cases chose to know nothing.

24. A directive signed by Yakov Sverdlov on 24 Jan. 1919 ordered the Communist Party and the Red Army 'to conduct ruthless mass terror against all Cossacks who have directly or indirectly participated in the fight against Soviet power'.

25. See Svetlana Alieva (ed.), *Tak Eto Bylo: Natsionalnye Repressii v SSSR, 1919–52 Gody* (Moscow, 1993) and Albert Seaton, *The Horsemen of the Steppes* (London, 1985), pp. 229–37.

26. Milovan Djilas, *Land without Justice* (Harcourt, Brace, New York, 1958) and *Wartime* (Harcourt Brace Jovanovich, New York, 1977).

27. For a completely serious warning of the power and menace of the Cossacks – written *after* they had proved their complete inefficacy in Chechnya – see 'Cossacks Ride Again along the Don', *New York Times*, 4 Apr. 1996.

28. Eric Hobsbawm and Terence Ranger (eds), *The Invention of Tradition* (Cambridge University Press, 1983), the seminal work on this theme – now followed by numerous others.

29. A classic account of the importance of pre-existing traditions in the for-

mation of modern national identities is to be found in Anthony D. Smith, *The Ethnic Origins of Nations* (Blackwell, Oxford, 1986), esp. ch. 8, 'Legends and Landscapes', pp. 174–207. For the tremendous importance of already existing religious identifications in the formation of what may well be totally new national identifications, see Linda Colley's *Britons: Forging the Nation, 1701–1837* (Yale University Press, 1992). For a recent collection of essays on historiography and nation-building in Britain, see Alexander Grant and Keith Stringer (eds), *Uniting the Kingdom: the Making of British History* (Routledge, London, 1995).

30. For a longer discussion of this debate against the background of my experiences in the former Soviet Union, see my essay in the *National Interest*, winter 1997.

31. Benedict Anderson, *Imagined Communities* (Verso, London 1983).

32. Ernest Gellner, *Thought and Change* (London, Weidenfeld and Nicholson, 1964), p. 169.

33. Anderson, *Imagined Communities*, p. 6.

34. Tim Ingold (ed.), *Key Debates in Anthropology* (Routledge, London, 1996), pp. 115–16.

35. See Anatol Lieven, 'Gruff General Reveals Scars that Made Him', *The Times*, 23 June 1996.

36. Interview with the author, 24 June 1996.

37. By 1989, Krasnodar had 700,000 inhabitants, Novocherkassk 145,000 – both clearly totally different cities from the Cossack provincial capitals they once had been.

38. See Vladimir Seleznev, 'Mafia Seeks to Control Cossack Movement', *Rossiiskie Vyesti*, 24 Aug. 1994; and Sander Thoenes, 'Proud Cossacks Seek New Role in Market Economy', *Moscow Times*, 9 Sept. 1994.

39. See A. Andrusenko, 'Cossacks of Southern Russia: Legends and Facts', *Kultura*, 13 Feb. 1993.

40. David Ljunggren, 'In Southern Rus-

sia, Cossacks Becoming Impatient', Reuters, 20 Apr. 1996.

41. For the way in which political 'outsiders' in Krasnodar used the Cossack movement in an effort to get into power, see Derluguian, 'Parade, Prayer, Patrol'.

42. The Ataman's deputy, 'security chief' and general factotum (and brother-in-law, via one of the Ataman's previous wives) described to me his own transition from a retired Soviet police colonel in Volgograd to a businessman's sidekick in words that can stand for a whole generation of the more honest and honourable Soviet people, caught in social and economic changes which they had never asked for and could not control:

'In 1991, I took early retirement, and by early 1992, my pension hadn't been paid for three months. One day I went walking with my small son. He wanted to buy an ice cream, and I couldn't afford it. Two years before, on a salary of 500 roubles a month, I could afford most things in the Soviet Union of those days. And now I couldn't even buy an ice cream, and my son was crying. You can't imagine what that does to a man, an officer after all ... You hate society, the government, yourself, the whole world. You have no self-respect. You feel capable of anything. So I bought him a tin whistle, and when we got home, I sat down and drank a whole bottle of Armenian brandy that my mother had given me for my birthday, and thought what to do. The next day, I used my contacts from my police days in Volgograd to borrow money and buy some petrol, which I sold in Ukraine where it was in short supply, and made a small profit. It didn't come easily to me. Speculation was still an ugly word for me, as you can imagine; but I built up a small trade, including with the Ataman here, whom I'd known one way and another for a long time. When the Ukrainians introduced their customs and the petrol trade became diffi-

cult, I came here and joined him, and now I am his chief of staff, deputy Ataman and deputy director of the business, and of course I am also working for Lebed's re-election.

But still, I understand the Communist voters. Pensioners here have not been paid for three months, teachers for two, and now they are being sent on two months unpaid summer holidays. I know how they will vote, and I don't blame them.'

43. Interview with the author, 24 June 1996.

44. See the interview with Ataman Vladimir Naumov in *Nezavisimaya Gazeta*, 18 Feb. 1994.

45. See Elaine Monaghan, 'Yeltsin Gives the Cossacks a Pre-Election Spur', Reuters, 23 Jan. 1996, and 'Over Twenty Cossack Units to be Formed within Russian Army', Interfax, 16 Aug. 1996. For a general list of government decrees, and statistics concerning the Cossacks, see the Itar Tass special report, 'Kazachestvo v Sovremennoi Rossii', 1995.

46. For the regularisation of the Cossack hosts in the last decades of Tsarist rule, see Robert McNeal, *Tsar and Cossack, 1855–1914* (St Martin's Press, New York, 1987).

47. See John Keegan, *A History of Warfare* (Pimlico, 1994), pp. 7–24, 221–5. For Clausewitz's description of the Cossack's behaviour in 1812, and his contempt for them, see Roger Parkinson, *Clausewitz* (Wayland, London, 1970), pp. 175–6.

7   Failure of the Serbian Option, 2

Epigraph from George F. Kennan (under name 'X'), 'The Sources of Soviet Conduct', *Foreign Affairs* (July 1947).

1. I must say, as someone who was in Moscow as a Western correspondent at that time and shared in the bias, that although understandable, and on balance correct in view of the real issues involved, our reporting of

those events did not do much honour to our objectivity, and we may well have missed the extent to which the fighting which ended the fortnight-long stand-off was deliberately set up by the Yeltsin side. See Bruce Clark, *An Empire's New Clothes: the End of Russia's Liberal Dream* (Vintage, London, 1995) and Jonathan Steele, *Eternal Russia: Gorbachev, Yeltsin and the Mirage of Democracy* (London, 1994).

2. For the Cossacks in Abkhazia, see Michael Hetzer, 'Cossacks for Hire', *Moscow Times*, 16 July 1993.

3. See Vladimir Socor, 'Dniester Involvement in the Moscow Rebellion', *RFE/RL Research Report* 2:46 (Nov. 1993). The Transdniestrian security and deputy interior ministers 'Vadim Shevtsov' and 'Nikolai Matveyev' had been OMON officers in Riga under their real names, Vladimir Antyufeyev and Oleg Goncharenko. They were implicated in the OMON seizure of the Latvian Interior Ministry in January 1991, in which five people died, and were suspected of planning the murder of seven Lithuanian border guards in August of that year. I should like to say, on a personal note, that whatever the evils of the present order in Russia, if such men had triumphed in October 1993 the result would have been a good deal worse.

4. See Reuters, 13 Oct. 1993.

5. As a 14th Army lieutenant, born in Transdniestria, told me in September 1994:
'We can't withdraw from here. Whatever order Moscow gives, we will have to stay, because this is our home. But whether we'd stay as Transdniestrian soldiers, or become civilians, I don't know. It would depend on the situation. Certainly we would never agree to be citizens of Romania, though that looks likely now ... If they try to pull the army out quickly, it will disintegrate, criminals and extremists will seize the arms, and then we will have a Karabakh here, or

worse. But Lebed is determined to stop that happening, and we will all obey him. He is a fine commander, and what he says, he does.'

6. Interview with the author, 19 Sept. 1994.

7. See Jeff Chinn and Steven D. Roper, 'Ethnic Mobilisation and Reactive Nationalism: the Case of Moldova', *Nationalities Papers* 23:2 (1995); Charles King, *Post-Soviet Moldova: a Borderland in Transition* (Royal Institute of International Affairs, London, 1994), pp. 21–7; and William Crowther, 'The Politics of Ethno-National Mobilisation: Nationalism and Reform in Soviet Moldova', *Russian Review*, no. 50 (Apr. 1991).

8. James Rupert, 'Regional Tensions Trip Up Ukraine's Quest of Stability', *Washington Post*, 27 Oct. 1996. See also Sherman W. Garnett, *Keystone in the Arch: Ukraine in the Emerging Security Environment of Central and Eastern Europe* (Carnegie Endowment, Washington DC, 1997), pp. 30–2.

9. See Vladimir Solonar and Vladimir Bruter, 'Russians in Moldova', in Vladimir Shlapentokh et al. (eds), *The New Russian Diaspora* (M. E. Sharpe, London, 1994), and Crowther, 'The Politics of Ethno-National Mobilisation'. See also the chapter on Moldova in Jeff Chinn and Robert Kaiser, *Russians as the New Minority: Ethnicity and Nationalism in the Soviet Successor States* (Westview Press, Boulder, 1996).

10. See Vladimir Socor, 'Moldovan Proclaimed Official Language in the Moldovan SSR', Radio Liberty Report on the USSR, 22 Sept. 1989.

11. For the importance of the Popular Front's commitment to union with Romania for sparking the Transdniestrian secession, see Paul Kolstoe and Andrei Edemsky with Natalya Kalashnikova, 'The Dniester Conflict: Between Irredentism and Separatism', *Europe-Asia Studies* 45:6 (1993). The programme and ideology of the Popular Front is described

and analysed by Charles King in 'Moldovan Identity and the Politics of Pan Romanianism', *Slavic Review* 53:2 (summer 1994).

12. This information appears in Kolstoe et al., 'The Dniester Conflict', p. 975. Russians of Old Believer descent beyond Russia's borders have in recent years often sided with local national movements, presumably because of their historic alienation from the Russian state, which drove them to emigrate in the first place.

13. For the Cossacks in Transdniestria, their motivation and ambitions, see *Nezavisimaya Gazeta*, 20 June 1992.

14. For a critical view of the Transdniestria Cossacks at the height of the fighting, see Robert Seeley, 'A Nasty Little War', *Spectator*, 16 May 1992.

15. See *Nezavisimaya Gazeta*, 22 Sept. 1992.

16. This action by General Lebed formed the basis for his mystique, both as a military leader and a peacemaker. In particular, it is suggested that he showed great moral courage and independence by taking the action he did without orders from Moscow. This may be so – and he is certainly an exceptionally brave and determined man – but I have also been told by informed sources that the General received a private nod from the Defence Ministry in Moscow that it was all right to go ahead.

17. For a Western view of the essentially common identity and culture of the Romanians and Moldovans – along the lines of the West and East Germans – see Jonathan Eyal, 'Moldovans', in Graham Smith (ed.), *The Nationalities Question in the Soviet Union* (Longman, London, 1990).

18. For Romanian attitudes and policies in 1992, see Dan Ionescu, 'Romanian Concern over the Conflict in Moldova', RFE/RL Research Report.

19. See Dan Ionescu, 'Media in the Dni-

ester Moldovan Republic: a Communist Memento', *Transition*, 20 Oct. 1995. In his words, which I can confirm from my own experience, 'reading the Dniester press is like taking a trip back to the Brezhnev era.'

20. Interview with the author, Tiraspol, 24 Feb. 1994. See also *Izvestia*, 3 Feb. 1994.

21. Interview with the author, Tiraspol, 24 Feb. 1994.

22. Cf. for example the articles in *Transition* 1:19 (Oct. 1995): 'Moldova: a Test Case for Russia and the Near Abroad?'

23. See Anatol Lieven, *The Baltic Revolution: Estonia, Latvia, Lithuania and the Path to Independence* (Yale University Press, 1994), pp. 191–201.

24. Paul Kubichek, 'Variations on a Corporatist Theme: Interest Associations in Post-Soviet Ukraine and Russia', *Europe-Asia Studies* 48:1 (Jan. 1996).

25. 'A Political Portrait of Ukraine', *Democratic Initiative* 4 (Feb. 1994).

26. See for example William E. Odom and Robert Dujarric, *Commonwealth or Empire* (Hudson Institute, Indianapolis, 1995). For a more recent exposition of this prejudice, see Jonathan Sunley, 'Post-Communism, an Infantile Disorder', *National Interest* (summer 1996).

27. For a fuller description of these attempts, see Lieven, *The Baltic Revolution*, op. cit.

28. For the 1994 elections, see Andrew Wilson, 'The Elections in Crimea', *RFE/RL Research Report* 3:25 (June 1994).

29. For the best and most dispassionate analysis of the Russian–Ukrainian security relationship, see Garnett, *Keystone in the Arch*.

30. Interview with the author, Simferopol, 24 May 1994.

31. For the contemporary political organisation and programme of the Tatars, see Mustafa Cemiloglu, 'A History of the Crimean Tatar National Liberation Movement: a

Sociolopolitical Perspective', in Maria Drohobycky (ed.) *Crimea: Dynamics, Challenges and Prospects* (American Association for the Advancement of Science, 1995) and David Marples and David F. Dute, 'Ukraine, Russia and the Question of Crimea', in *Nationalities Papers* 23: 2, June 1995, and Andrew Wilson, 'A Situation Report on the Crimean Tatars', *International Alert*, 1994.

32. For ethnic relations up to 1995, see Volodymyr Yevtouch, 'The Dynamics of Interethnic Relations in Crimea', in Drohobycky.

33. For a general view of the position of the 'Russians' outside Russia as of 1995, see Chinn and Kaiser, *Russians as the New Minority*; Neil Melvin, *Russians beyond Russia: the Politics of National Identity* (Royal Institute of International Affairs, London, 1995), esp. pp. 78–99 for Ukraine. See also Paul Kolstoe, *Russians in the Former Soviet Republics* (Hurst, London, 1995). See Igor Zevelev, 'Russia and the Russian Diasporas', together with the comment on it by Gail Lapidus, *Post-Soviet Affairs* 12:3 (1996).

34. See Nikita Khrushchev, *Khrushchev Remembers: the Last Testament*, ed. and trans. Strobe Talbott, introd. Jerrold L. Schecter (Little, Brown, Boston, 1974). For a critique of the language of Khruschev's memoirs and what it reveals, see Andrei Sinyavsky, *Soviet Civilisation* (Arcade, New York, 1990). He speaks of 'the language of the government elite, the muzhik seated on high. On the one hand, his head is full of the artificial language made up of abstract formulas, and on the other, of the natural, crude and semi-literate language he has known from childhood' (p. 200).

35. *OMRI Daily Digest*, no. 158, part 2, 15 Aug. 1996.

36. I visited coal mines in Donetsk in March 1994 and August 1995.

37. For a picture of the Donbas miners between the strikes of 1989 and 1993, with extensive interviews, see Lewis H. Siegelbaum and Daniel J. Walkowitz (eds), *Workers of the Donbas Speak: Survival and Identity in the New Ukraine, 1989–1992* (State University of New York Press, Albany, 1995). It includes many valuable insights into the reasons for failure of the democratic protest movement of 1989 to consolidate itself into effective long-term structures, whether political or trade unionist, and into the growing irritation of the miners with the new Ukrainian state. For a comparison with the character and behaviour of steelworkers in Magnitogorsk, a Urals industrial city, see Stephen Kotkin, *Steeltown USSR: Soviet Society in the Gorbachev Era* (University of California Press, Berkeley, 1991).

38. Andrew Wilson, *Ukrainian Nationalism in the 1990s: A Minority Faith* (Cambridge University Press, 1997), p. 195.

39. Interview with the author, 22 Aug. 1995.

40. Theodore H. Friedgut, *Iusovka and Revolution* (Princeton, 1989), vol. 1, pp. 327–8.

41. For a fascinating but deeply depressing picture of lack of basic democracy and of social demoralisation and disintegration in Russian urban post-industrial society, see Sarah Ashwin, '"There's No Joy Any More": the Experience of Reform in a Kuzbass Mining Settlement', *Europe–Asia Studies* 47:8 (Dec. 1995).

42. Of course, it has been pointed out, most notably by Mancur Olson, that even in Western societies, by no means all the groups and occupations who might have been expected to mobilise for protest in fact do so. See Mancur Olson, *The Logic of Collective Action: Public Goods and the Theory of Groups* (Harvard University Press, 1965).

43. This threat was recognised – and indeed exaggerated – by the Kuchma administration in its heavy-handed

response to the Donbas miners' strike of the summer of 1996, which government representatives warned 'threatened Ukrainian territorial integrity', though in fact demands for regional autonomy played only a small and relatively peripheral part in the protests.

44. Interview with the author, Dnipropetrovsk, 20 Aug. 1995.
45. Dominique Arel, 'Ukraine: the Temptation of the Nationalising State', in Vladimir Tismaneanu (ed.), *Political Culture and Civil Society in Russia and the New States of Eurasia* (M. E. Sharpe, New York, 1995), p. 177. See also his 'Language Politics in Independent Ukraine: Towards One or Two State Languages', *Nationalities Papers* 23:3 (1995). For the language question in 1994–5, see Yaroslav Bilinsky, 'Primary Language of Communication as a Secondary Indicator of National Identity: the Ukrainian Parliamentary and Presidential Elections of 1994 and the Manifesto of the Ukrainian Intelligentsia of 1995', *Nationalities Papers* 24:4 (1996). For the situation as of 1996, see Ustina Markus, 'The Bilingualism Question in Belarus and Ukraine', *Transition*, 29 Nov. 1996.
46. See John Armstrong, 'Ukrainian Nationalism' (University of Colorado Press, 1990), pp.111ff.

8 'A Fish Rots from the Head'

1. *Rossiiskiye Vesti*, 12 Sept. 1996.
2. Stephen J. Blank and Earl H. Tilford, 'Russia's Invasion of Chechnya: a Preliminary Assessment', US Army War College, Jan. 1995. By November 1996 Dr Blank had changed his mind and was arguing that Russia is not just a weak but a failed state, akin to those of Africa, also a gross exaggeration.
3. Richard L. Kugler: 'Enlarging NATO: the Russia Factor', National Defence Institute, June 1996, p. 127. The misrepresentation of Russian military strength in this report stems in part from a more general failing typical of much Western and especially American security analysis. This is to add up the number and quality of tanks and guns belonging to different countries, and assume that the result provides a final answer concerning their security capability. It is, as so often, an approach divorced from any attempt to understand the historical, cultural and social context. On the other hand, for a sober and accurate assessment of Russian military strength from an analyst at RAND, see Benjamin S. Lambeth, 'Russia's Wounded Military', *Foreign Affairs* (Mar.–Apr. 1995).
4. See General William Odom, 'Russia's Military – Down But Not Yet Out', *Wall Street Journal*, 27 Aug. 1996, where he writes: 'We have not seen Russia's best units in Chechnya. No airborne division is committed there. Nor are the better tank and motor-rifle units.'
5. See also a report by another Western journalist who covered the war on the ground, Michael Specter, 'Strolling at Will, Chechen Rebels Mock Russian Army', *New York Times*, 1 Feb. 1996.
6. Interview with the author, 8 Sept. 1996 (during the Russian–US joint peacekeeping exercise at Totskoye military base, Orenburg).
7. Yuri Khots and Andrei Shtorkh, 'Russia to Have Fully Professional Army from the Year 2000', Itar Tass, 17 May 1996.
8. See *Izvestia*, 10 Feb. 1997. For the identity of Baturin's and Rodionov's views on this, see Pavel Felgenhauer, 'Not the Time for Volunteers', *Moscow Times*, 6 Mar. 1997.
9. See *Trud*, 1 Aug. 1996; interview with the Director of the Institute of Religious Rights, Anatoly Pchelintsev.
10. For the state of contract service before the Chechen War, see Stephen Foye, 'Manning the Russian

Army: Is Contract Service a Success?', *RFE/RL Research Report* 3:13 (Apr. 1994). For malnutrition in the military, see a report of *Moskovsky Komsomolets*, 6 Jan. 1997, citing the military procuracy.

11. See Geoffrey Jukes, 'The Soviet Armed Forces and Afghanistan', in Amin Saikal and William Maley (eds), *The Soviet Withdrawal from Afghanistan* (Cambridge University Press, 1989). For a more admiring – but since discredited – portrayal of Soviet military adaptability and effectiveness in Afghanistan, see Stephen Blank, 'Soviet Russia and Low Intensity Conflict in Central Asia: Three Case Studies', in Lewis B. Ware (ed.), *Low Intensity Conflict in the Third World* (US Air University Press, 1988). For the impact of the Stinger anti-aircraft missiles on the Soviet decision to withdraw, see Diego Cordovez and Selig S. Harrison, *Out of Afghanistan: the Inside Story of the Soviet Withdrawal* (Oxford University Press, 1995), pp. 198–201, 257.

12. For the tasks and composition of the Defence Council, see *Krasnaya Zvezda*, 30 July 1996.

13. Quoted by *RIA Novosti*, 26 Jan. 1995.

14. See Stephen Foye, 'Confrontation in Moscow: the Army Backs Yeltsin – for Now', *RFE/RL Research Report* 2:22 (Oct. 1993); and Richard Woff, 'Options for Change – Russia's Defence Minister', *Jane's Intelligence Review* 6:8 (Aug. 1994) and 'Trial in Public is Hard for "Hero" Pavel Grachev', *Jane's Defence Weekly*, 19 Nov. 1994.

15. See Pavel K. Baev, *The Russian Army in a Time of Troubles* (Sage, London, 1996), esp. pp. 66ff. As he remarks concerning Grachev's rhetoric, 'If this campaign was a success anywhere, it was primarily among Western security experts, who had been seeking to prove that there still existed a security threat from the East' (p. 70). Dr Baev's work is the best and most comprehensive to date on the Russian armed forces in the mid-1990s.

16. See Pavel Felgenhauer, 'Military Reform after Chechnya', *Segodnya*, 25 Dec. 1996. He points out that it was poor command and training, not lack of numbers, which led to the Russian defeat: 'In early January 1995 the 131th Maikop brigade, which was part of the group under the command of General Kvashnin, was routed in Grozny. During the August battle for Grozny, incommensurate losses were sustained by the 205th SKVO brigade. Both brigades were well manned. Nevertheless they were smashed.'

17. According to Western intelligence sources, interviewed by the author.

18. See Robert F. Baumann, *Russian-Soviet Unconventional Wars in the Caucasus, Central Asia and Afghanistan*, Leavenworth Papers, no. 20 (1993), pp. 141–3, 152–63; Edward R. Girardet, *Afghanistan, the Soviet War* (St Martin's Press, New York, 1985); and General Alexander Lebed, *Za Derzhavu Obidno* (Moscow, 1995), pp. 64–128. The Mujahidin with whom I travelled in Afghanistan in 1988–9 described having been very much harassed by Soviet heliborne troops in the first years of the war, though they added that this had greatly declined after the introduction of the Stinger anti-aircraft missiles.

19. 'Russian Airforce Dwindling', Associated Press, 3 Dec. 1996.

20. See Oleg Levitsky, 'Chaos in the Army', *Moscow News*, 13–19 June 1996; Yuri Maslyukov (the last Chairman of Gosplan) in *Zavtra*, no. 31 (Aug. 1996); and the figures given in *Rossiiski Vesti*, 24 Sept. 1996.

21. See Levitsky, 'Chaos in the Army', and Lambeth, 'Russia's Wounded Military' and Alexander Nicholl, 'Russian Air Force Hit by Lack of Money', *Financial Times*, 15 Oct. 1997.

22. See Lambeth, 'Russia's Wounded

Military'. The detail about the test pilots was given to me by a NATO military attaché in Moscow, and confirmed by a Russian contact.

23. See ITN report by Lawrence McDonnell, 6 Oct. 1996.
24. See Nadezhda Anisimova, 'Chubais and Lebed Meet to Discuss Army Reform', Itar Tass, 1 Oct. 1996.
25. See Andrei Tarakanov, 'The Rise of Russia's Military Opposition', *Transition* 2:16 (Aug. 1996). For the state of the conscription system by 1996, see 'Army Drafts Half of Required Strength', *Rossiiskaya Gazeta*, 1 Oct. 1996 and Lt-Col. Vladimir Mukhin and Col. Sergei Soboyev, 'Younger Generation Dodges Conscription: Change System Now', *Nezavisimoye Voennuoye Obozreniye*, 26 Sept. 1996.
26. Quoted by Interfax, 26 Jan. 1995.
27. *Krasnaya Zvezda*, 30 Sept. 1995.
28. Report by *RIA Novosti*, Moscow, 4 Oct. 1996.
29. See Timothy Heritage, 'Yeltsin under Fire over Military Reforms', Reuters, Moscow, 18 July 1997.
30. 'The Russian Armed Forces will be Unable to Defend this Country if the Current Situation Persists', *Nezavisimaya Gazeta*, 29 Aug. 1996.
31. *Jamestown Foundation Monitor*, 30 Aug. 1996.
32. Interview with the author, 15 Feb. 1996.
33. Fyodr Dostoyevsky, *The Brothers Karamazov*, trans. David McDuff (Penguin Classics, 1993), pp. 124–31.
34. Pavel Felgenhauer, 'Foul Play with Officers' Pay', *Moscow Times*, 30 Jan. 1997.
35. Sergey Selyutin, 'Military People Attack the Government and Seem to be Losing', *Obshchaya Gazeta*, no. 1, 9–15 Jan. 1997.
36. 'Russian Defence Chief Tells Wife "No Pay Today"', Reuters, Moscow, 5 Sept. 1996. See also David Hoffman, 'Russian Forces Disintegrating: Even Officers Seek Way Out of a Military Facing Collapse', *Washing-ton Post*, 5 Oct. 1996. For military theft, see Alexander Igorev, 'Generals Steal More Often, Military Investigators Note', *Obshchaya Gazeta*, no. 37, 19–25 Sept. 1996. See also Simon Saradzhyan, 'Russia: Soviet Soldiers "Going Begging" – Not Just an Expression', *RFE/RL Report*, 27 Sept. 1996.

37. Maria Eismont, 'The Peace Process in Chechnya: Nobody has Any Illusions', *Jamestown Foundation Prism*, 2 (Aug. 1996), part 2. What she says about armoured vehicles is entirely true; the Chechen capacity to create major considerable forces simply by capturing them from the enemy is perhaps unprecedented in the history of modern war.
38. Thomas Goltz, 'Diesels, Drunks and Devastation: SOF Rides with Russian Road Warriors in Chechnya', *Soldier of Fortune*, May 1996. For accounts of this kind of behaviour at the very start of the Chechen operation, see Ilya Bulavinov in *Kommersant Daily*, 25 Jan. 1995.
39. Draft document on national security policy of the Russian Federation, 1996–2000, prepared by the office of Yuri Baturin, national security assistant to President Yeltsin; printed in *Nezavisimaya Gazeta*, 23 May 1996; points 44, 48, 49.
40. See 'The Military Balance 1994–1995', International Institute for Strategic Studies, London, Oct. 1994, pp. 107–19.
41. Colonel Valery Borisenko, 'Gendarmerie or Army', *Moscow News*, no. 6, 15–21 Feb. 1996.
42. Quoted in *Rabochaya Tribuna*, 23 Aug. 1996.
43. *Nezavisimaya Gazeta*, 24 Feb. 1996. For an appeal by another branch, see the interview with the Chief of Staff of the Strategic Missile Forces, General Viktor Yesin, 'The Strength of the Rocket Forces: the Nuclear Defence of Russia is in Good Hands', in the same paper.
44. See 'Army Must Fully Inquire into Hazing', *Moscow Times*, 15 Apr.

1997. See also Svetlana Alexievich, pp. 51, 53, 137 and *passim* for *dedovshchina* in Afghanistan. As one of her interviewees, a military doctor exclaims, 'Christ! So much blood being spilt, and they do this to a young soldier far from home!' The boy in question had been beaten and then starved for two weeks by his elders because when he brought one of them his tea, a fly was in it. See also Oleg Yermakov, *Afghan Stories* (Secker, London, 1993).

45. See Alexievich, p. 41 for fragging in Afghanistan. 'Fragging' is American slang for 'killing with a fragmentation (anti-personnel) grenade'. Tossed into sleeping quarters at night, this was the easiest and safest way of getting rid of an unpopular officer or NCO. It became shorthand for any action of this kind.

46. Interview with the author and Sebastian Smith of AFP, Shali, 25 May 1995 (I should like to express my gratitude to Sebastian for introducing me to this charming and impressive family, and to the Damayevs for their hospitality in Shali). Incidentally, it is not quite true that Chechens do not use the Russian expression, 'xxxx your mother!' when speaking to each other; but they only do so *when speaking in Russian* – in which language, among Russian men (thanks partly to generations of military service), it has become so common under Soviet rule as to lose all meaning. Spoken in Chechen, I was told, this would indeed be a killing matter.

47. See the portrait of Lebed by Benjamin Lambeth, 'The Warrior Who Would Rule Russia', RAND Corporation for Project Air Force, Santa Monica, 1996, and Lebed's own memoirs, *Za Derzhavu Obidno* (Offended for the state).

48. Interview with the author, Totskoye base, 8 Sept. 1996.

49. For Rodinov's views on reform and Yeltsin administration policy, see his essay in the supplement to *Nezavisi-*

maya Gazeta, 19 July 1997: 'The Problems of Military Reform are Being Transformed into Political Speculation.

50. 'The Military Balance, 1995–1996', International Institute for Strategic Studies, London.

51. See for example 'Russians are Engaged in a Fierce Debate over their Military's Future', *International Herald Tribune* (New York Times Service), 1 Mar. 1997, and 'The 66-year-old President Wants to Turn the Armed Forces into a Smaller and More Efficient Fighting Force', Reuters, Moscow, 21 July 1997.

52. See for example Alexander Goltz, military correspondent of *Itogi*, in *Moscow Times*, 20 Dec. 1996.

53. 'Yeltsin Must Set Course for Army', *Moscow Times*, 23 May 1997.

54. See the *Jamestown Monitor* 2:167 (Sept. 1996).

55. Interfax, 4 Oct. 1996; and 'Russians Disagree on Army Pay', *International Herald Tribune*, 5 Oct. 1996.

56. See Alexander Goltz, *Itogi*, 9 Dec. 1996.

57. Yuriy Golotyuk, 'The Paratroops' Resistance to Reform has Finally been Crushed, Although the Airborne Troops Managed to Retain a Number of Strategic Bridgeheads', *Segodnya*, 15 Dec. 1996.

58. To be fair to Russia, this pattern also affects the West – by 1994, the Royal Navy had more admirals than major warships, and in 1996, the US Marine Corps, while reducing the number of its troops, asked to be allotted a considerably increased number of generals.

59. Jeremy Weinberg, 'Top General Takes Hit in Yeltsin's Graft War', *Moscow Times*, 21 May 1997; and Dmitry Zaks, 'Paratroops Plead in Face of Cuts', *Moscow Times*, 11 July 1997. He reports amusingly that the frantic paratroopers were beginning to use the autonomy of the US Marine Corps as an argument, and were displaying a book by Tom Clancey to back this up.

60. Carlotta Gall, '"Indignant" Yeltsin Fires Defence Minister', *Moscow Times*, 23 May 1997.

61. Dmitry Zaks, 'Yeltsin Hands Military Reform to Liberals', *Moscow Times*, 11 June 1997.

62. For Chernomyrdin's views, see Gennady Yezhov, 'Army Reform Calls for Streamlining of Spending', Itar Tass, 9 July 1997.

63. I am indebted for this insight to Dr Sherman Garnett of the Carnegie Foundation, who as a former senior Pentagon official has a particular awareness of problems of civilian indifference to military concerns.

64. See Pavel Felgenhauer, 'Ruining Once-Proud Army', *Moscow Times*, 17 July 1997.

65. The full text of his appeal was published by the Duma Defence Committee.

66. Quoted by Reuters, 'Ex Defence Minister Slams Yeltsin over Reform', 18 July 1997. See also James Meek, 'Yeltsin Orders Military Cuts', the *Guardian*, 17 July 1997.

67. See Ivan Rodin, 'Pro-Government Legislator Blasts Own Party', Reuters, 3 July 1997.

68. See Timothy Heritage, 'Rokhlin's Movement Worries Kremlin', Reuters, 21 July 1997.

69. For the full text of Yeltsin's speech, see *Izvestia*, 18 July 1997.

70. See Pavel Kuznetsov, 'Russia to Up Defence Spending', Itar Tass, 19 June 1997; and 'Yeltsin Endorses Military Reform', Itar Tass, 19 June 1997.

Part III: The Chechen Victory

Epigraph from *The Koran*, trans. with notes and parallel text by N. J. Dawood (Penguin Classics, London, 1995), p. 510.

9 The Two Hundred Years' War

Epigraphs from Pavel Felgenhauer, 'A War Russia Cannot Afford to Lose', *Transition*, 31 May 1996; *Svobodny Kavkaz*, no. 4 (1952), quoted in Lowell Tillett, *The Great Friendship: Soviet Historians on the Non-Russian Nationalities* (University of North Carolina Press, Chapel Hill, 1969); p. 130.

1. See Marie Broxup (ed.), *The North Caucasus Barrier: the Russian Advance towards the Muslim World* (New York, 1992), p. 1.

2. For example, Bariatinsky's deportation of the inhabitants of Khan Qala in December 1852, see Moshe Gammer, *Muslim Resistance to the Tsar: Shamil and the Conquest of Chechnia and Daghestan* (Frank Cass, London, 1994), p. 220. For a pro-Cossack view of settlement patterns in the sixteenth to eighteenth centuries, see Valery Tishkov and A. S. Orlov (eds), *Chechensky Krisis*, (Moscow, 1995), pp. 11–14.

3. Cf. Y. Anchabadze and N. G. Volkova, *Etnicheskaya Istoria Severnogo Kavkaza* (Moscow, 1993), pp. 78–84. Interestingly, among those described as moving voluntarily to Russian-held territory near the Terek at the end of the eighteenth century are the 'Khasbulatovtsi'. Ruslan Khasbulatov's base and main area of support in his struggle against Dudayev in the autumn of 1994 was the town of Tolstoy Yurt (formerly Doeky Yurt, renamed under Soviet rule) near the south bank of the Terek, where many of his clan relatives apparently still live. The accusation that 'Khasbulatov's ancestors served the Russians' is one of the insults which has been thrown at him by the pro-Dudayev forces – though it must be said that they use this accusation against all their Chechen enemies.

4. The first cyrillic-based Chechen alphabet was developed in the late nineteenth century by a Chechen,

Kedy Dosoyev, with the help of a Russian specialist, Professor Uslar. It was however only introduced into the school system under Soviet rule in the 1920s, as part of a general process underway at that time among the numerous Soviet peoples whose languages did not possess a written form.

5. 'Chechen' is the Turkic and Russian word for these people from the name of a particular village. The Chechens call themselves Nokhchi ('The People') – a name which is mentioned by Armenian writers of the seventh century. The Chechens' origins in the Caucasus however go back even further, in fact far beyond the dawn of recorded history. Their language belongs to an East Caucasian language group called the Nakh, to which Ingush and an almost extinct language of Georgia, Tsova-Tush, belong. Nakh in turn is part of the East Caucasian-Daghestani group of languages, which are indigenous to the Caucasus and totally separate from all other known world language families. See Johanna Nichols, 'Who are the Chechen?', *Central Asian Survey* 14:4 (1995), and Tishkov and Orlov, *Chechensky Krisis*, p. 10.

6. Yermolov is not actually on record as having said this, but his own memoranda leave no doubt as to the savagery of his policy. In his words, 'I desire that the terror of my name should guard our frontiers more potently than chains of fortresses, that my word should be for the natives a law more inevitable than death. Condescension in the eyes of Asiatics is a sign of weakness, and out of pure humanity I am inexorably severe. One execution saves hundreds of Russians from destruction, and thousands of Mussulmans from treason' (quoted by General V. A. Potto in *Kavkazkaya Voina*, vol. 2, p. 15). For a present-day (very critical) Russian liberal view of Yermolov, in the light of the latest Caucasian War and the methods used by the

contemporary Russian army, see Yakov Gordin, 'The Legend of General Yermolov', *Novoye Vremya* (Mar. 1995).

7. For a contemporary fictional description of such a raid, by an officer who took part in several, see Leo Tolstoy, 'The Raid', in *How Much Land Does a Man Need, and Other Stories*, trans. Ronald Wilks, introd. A. N. Wilson (Penguin Classics, London, 1993). A much harsher, and probably more accurate description, involving not just looting but the murder of civilians, forms part of *Haji Murat*. The difference reflects Tolstoy's move from the Russian patriotism of his youth to the pacificism and anticolonialism of his old age.

8. See John F. Baddeley, *The Russian Conquest of the Caucasus* (Longman, London, 1908), p. 350, for an incident when, to compel an Ingush to hand over two Chechens he was seeking, Shamil had one of his eyes put out, and later burned his family alive; and see an early work by Tolstoy, *Prisoner of the Caucasus*, for a naive but moving fictional account of a Russian prisoner in Chechen hands, based on the testimony of former prisoners.

9. Colonel Charles E. Callwell, *Small Wars: Their Principles and Practice* (General Staff-War Office 1899; repr. EP Publishing, Wakefield, 1976), p. 148. (Today's spelling and transliteration in the quotation would give Matabele and Abd al-Qadir.)

10. Baddeley, *Russian Conquest*, p. 163.

11. The Chechens in 1991 also destroyed the monument to Lermontov, an action cited by local Russians as a sign of Chechen barbarism, but hardly unfair, given that Lermontov had been a Russian officer in the war against them, and his protagonist, Pechorin, had behaved disgracefully towards at least one 'tatar' family.

12. Quoted in Baddeley, *Russian Conquest*, pp. 319–20.

13. Gammer, *Muslim Resistance to the Tsar*, pp. 244–5.

14. For a portrait of Shamil's contemporary and fellow Muslim resister, Abd al-Qadir, as Sufi ruler around this time, see Raphael Danziger, *Abd al-Qadir: Resistance to the French and Internal Consolidation* (New York, 1977), pp. 180–211. For an extended comparison between the experience of Abd al-Qadir and Shamil, see Austin Lee Jersild, 'Who was Shamil? Russian Colonial Rule and Sufi Islam in the North Caucasus, 1859–1917', *Central Asia Survey* 14:2 (1995). For the (also rather ineffectual) state-building efforts of the leader of the anti-French tribal resistance in Morocco in the 1920s, Abd al-Krim, see D. S. Woolman, *Rebels in the Rif: Abd al-Krim and the Rif Rebellion* (Oxford University Press, 1969); and for the role of Islam in their struggles, see P. Shinar, 'Abd al-Qadir and Abd al-Krim: Religious Influences on their Thought and Action', *Asian and African Studies*, no. 1. For a general portrait and analysis of Islam among the Berbers of Morocco, there is the famous work by Ernest Gellner, *Saints of the Atlas* (Weidenfeld and Nicholson, London, 1969).

15. Baddeley, *Russian Conquest*, and Gammer, *Muslim Resistance to the Tsar*, as cited above; Lesley Blanch, *The Sabres of Paradise* (Quartet, London, 1978); Robert F. Baumann, *Russian-Soviet Unconventional Wars in the Caucasus, Central Asia and Afghanistan*, Leavenworth Papers, no. 20 (1993). For a brief general survey of the whole region in this era, see Firuz Kazemzadeh, 'Russian Penetration of the Caucasus', in Taras Hunczak (ed.), *Russian Imperialism: From Ivan The Terrible to the Revolution* (Rutgers University Press, 1974).

16. Notably the multivolume *Kavkazsky Sbornik*, a collection of contemporary Russian official documents, reports and memoirs. See also V.

Potto, *Istorichesky Ocherk Kavkazskikh Voin* (Tiflis, 1899).

17. Baddeley, *Russian Conquest*, p. xxxv. For a vivid eye-witness description of an episode of this kind, see 'The Woodfelling' by Leo Tolstoy, who served as a junior officer in several such expeditions in the early 1850s (the most recent English translation is in *How Much Land Does a Man Need?* (Penguin, London, 1993).

18. Rudyard Kipling, *Kim*, introd. Edward Said (Penguin Classics, 1987), p. 85. See also Malcolm E. Yapp, *Strategies of British India: Britain, Iran and Afghanistan, 1798–1850* (Clarendon Press, Oxford, 1980); Firuz Kazemzadeh, *Russia and Britain in Persia, 1864–1914: a Study in Imperialism* (Yale University Press, 1968); Halford L. Hoskins, *The British Routes to India* (Longman, 1928); Robert A. Huttenback, *British Relations with Sind, 1799–1843: an Anatomy of Imperialism* (Berkeley, 1962); David Gillard, *The Struggle for Asia, 1828–1914* (Methuen, London, 1977).

19. Cf. Gammer, *Muslim Resistance to the Tsar*, pp. 24, 277; Baumann, *Russian-Soviet Unconventional Wars*, p. 5.

20. Baddeley, *Russian Conquest*, p. 112.

21. Quoted in Kazemzadeh, *Russia and Britain in Persia*, pp. 8–9.

22. From an early draft of *Haji Murat*, quoted in Susan Layton, *Russian Literature and Empire: Conquest of the Caucasus from Lermontov to Tolstoy* (Cambridge University Press, 1994), p. 285.

23. The orchestrator of these efforts was one David Urquhart, briefly a British diplomat in Constantinople but essentially acting as a free agent. For the attempts of Urquhart and others to get the Circassians (including the Abkhaz) to combine against the Russians, see Edmund Spencer, *Travels in Circassia* and *Krim-Tartary*. (London, 1839); James Stanislaus Bell, *Journal of a Residence in Circassia dur-*

ing the Years 1837, 1838 and 1839 (London, 1840), pp. 135ff., 333ff.; and J. A. Longworth, *A Year among the Circassians* (London, 1840). It is interesting to note that most of the 'British' involved in these missions of Urquhart's were actually ethnic Scots – as if they had transferred to the Caucasians a variety of 'mountaineer' or 'highland' nationalist emotion to which, for equally good but more pragmatic Scottish reasons, it would have been pointless to give voice in contemporary Victorian Britain. For a general overview of their efforts by a contemporary scholar, see Paul B. Henze, 'Circassian Resistance to Russia', in Broxup, *The North Caucasus Barrier*, and also G. H. Bolsover, 'David Urquhart and the Eastern Question, 1833–37: a Study in Publicity and Diplomacy', *Journal of Modern History* 8 (Dec. 1936).

Baddeley (*Russian Conquest*, p. 348) takes a dim view of what he calls 'Urquhart's machinations', suggesting that by making promises on behalf of the British government which he had no possibility of keeping, he encouraged the Circassians to fight on and drew down on them a crueller fate in the end. On the other hand, the affection and admiration of these men for the Circassians was clearly genuine, and very understandable. It is difficult not to be moved by the farewell words of a 'Circassian dignitary' to a correspondent for *The Times* who travelled with Bell, J. A. Longworth:

'So then you are leaving us, Bey, forever. You have been so long amongst us, that we had begun to consider you as one of ourselves; but happily for you, you have a country to go to where you may live in peace and where there is yet no dread of the Muscovite. We, alas! have no other home to fly to; nor, if we had, would we leave that of our forefathers, in which we were born, which Allah has given to us, and for which it is our

duty to die.' (Longworth, *A Year among the Circassians*, p. 336, quoted in Henze, 'Circassian Resistance to Russia', p. 86)

24. For accounts of the Circassian exodus and estimates of the numbers involved, see Willis Brooks, 'Russia's Conquest and Pacification of the Caucasus: Relocation Becomes a Pogrom in the Post-Crimean War Period', *Nationalities Papers* 23:4 (1995); Justin McCarthy, *Death and Exile: the Ethnic Cleansing of Ottoman Muslims* (Darwin Press, 1996); and Henze, 'Circassian Resistance to Russia'.

25. See Brooks, 'Russia's Conquest and Pacification of the Caucasus'.

26. For the role of Soviet pressure on Turkey in the origins of the Cold War, see J. P. D. Dunbabin, *The Cold War: the Great Powers and their Allies* (Longman, London, 1994), pp. 64–5, 72, 126.

27. On the Civil War period, see Stephen Blank, 'The Formation of the Soviet North Caucasus 1918–24', *Central Asian Survey* 12:1 (1993), pp. 13–32; and Marie Broxup, 'The Last Ghazawat: the 1920–21 Uprising', in Broxup, *The North Caucasus Barrier*.

28. Alexandre Bennigsen and Enders Wimbush, *Mystics and Commissars: Sufism in the Soviet Union* (Berkeley, 1985), p. 24.

29. The first major Western account of the deportations was Robert Conquest, *The Soviet Deportation of Nationalities* (1960), which in adapted form appeared as *The Nation Killers* (Macmillan, 1970). See also Alexander Nekrich, *The Punished Peoples: the Deportation and Fate of Soviet Minorities at the End of the Second World War* (New York, 1978), and Svetlana Alieva, *Tak Eto Bylo: Natsionalnye Repressii v SSSR, 1919–52 Gody* (Moscow, 1993).

30. These documents are reproduced in the collection of President Dzhokhar Dudayev's speeches, interviews and decrees, *Ternisty Put' k Svobodu* (Vil-

nius, 1994), pp. 26–7.

31. Interview with the author, 30 Nov. 1994.
32. Interview with the author, 3 Dec. 1994.
33. See Zelimkhan Yandarbiyev, *V Preddvery Nezavisimosti* (Grozny, 1994), pp. 6ff.
34. Figures from the Soviet censuses.
35. Interview with the author, 20 Dec. 1995.

10 'We are Free and Equal like Wolves'

Epigraph from Giuseppe Tomasi di Lampedusa, *Il Gattopardo* (Feltrinelli, Milan, 1974), p. 239. (Passage translated by the author.)

1. One of the odder aspects of the Chechen War was the mixture of Chechen and Soviet/Communist symbolism in some of the Chechen rhetoric. 'No Pasaran' was of course the war-cry of Communist and other Republican troops defending Madrid against Franco in the Spanish Civil War, and reached Chechnya through the Soviet school system, films and so on.
2. In Turney-High's words, 'There are tribes with social control adequate enough for other purposes ... but which is so ineffective, so lacking in authority, team work, cohesion and co-operation that they could not indulge in a fight that could be called a battle ... The military horizon is one of social organisation and has next to nothing to do with the state of weaponry' (Harry Holbert Turney-High, *Primitive War: Its Practice and Concepts* (University of South Carolina Press, 1949), p. 23.
3. R. Brian Ferguson (ed.), *Warfare, Culture and the Environment* (Academic Press, 1984), p. 3.
4. Interview with the author, 23 Sept. 1994.
5. I was informed of this very surprising defection by Sebastian Smith of AFP, who knew Islam from an earlier visit and took me to stay with him.
6. See Georgy Derluguian, *Chechnya and Tataria* (United States Institute of Peace, Washington DC, 1997), ch. 3. Pursuing the analogy, Professor Derluguian points out that while Chechens have always practised forms of egalitarianism and tribal democracy among themselves, they have also always been slave-owning; people captured in war and raids have become the house slaves of Chechen families since time immemorial, and the Chechens also sold their slaves (especially young female ones) to the Ottoman markets of the Black Sea (personal communication, 1996).
   Slavery has to all intents and purposes revived in our own time: before the war, the Russian press carried reports of Russian drifters and homeless people being kidnapped or lured by Chechens, taken to mountain villages and effectively turned into field slaves. This was confirmed to me by a Chechen friend, though I never met any of these slaves. During the war, I did however see Russian prisoners who had effectively become house slaves of Chechen military units, doing their cooking and cleaning and pouring their tea.
7. Anthony F. C. Wallace, 'Psychological Preparations for War', in Morton Fried et al. (eds), *War: the Anthropology of Armed Conflict and Aggression* (National History Press, 1968), pp. 173ff.
8. Robert Montagne, *The Berbers: Their Social and Political Organisation*, trans. and introd. David Seddon, preface by Ernest Gellner (1931; Frank Cass, London, 1973), p. 35.
9. Sergei Arutiunov, 'Ethnicity and Conflict in the Caucasus', in Fred Wehling (ed.), *Ethnic Conflict and Russian Intervention in the Caucasus* (Institute for the Study of Global Conflict and Cooperation, University of California at San Diego, 1996), p. 17.
10. For the social background, disci-

pline, motivation and general character of the classical Greek hoplite phalanx, see Michael Mann, *The Sources of Social Power* (Cambridge University Press, 1986), vol. 1, pp. 200ff., and John Keegan, *A History of Warfare* (Vintage, 1994), pp. 244–51.

11. D. S. Woolman, *Rebels in the Rif: Abd al-Krim and the Rif Rebellion* (Oxford University Press, 1969), pp. 82ff.

12. See E. E. Evans-Pritchard, *The Nuer: a Description of the Modes of Livelihood and Political Institutions of a Nilotic People* (Oxford University Press, 1940). For a recent study of the Nuer, based on Evans-Pritchard's work while bringing out how Nuer society has been changed by firearms, modernity and the Sudanese civil wars, see Sharon E. Hutchinson, *Nuer Dilemmas: Coping with Money, War and the State* (University of California Press, London, 1996), esp. chs 3 and 6.

13. See Montagne, *The Berbers*, pp. 56ff. Of great interest for a comparison with Chechnya are also the various works of Ernest Gellner on Muslim frontier societies. See for example the essays in Ernest Gellner and Charles Michaud (eds), *Arabs and Berbers: From Tribe to Nation in North Africa* (Lexington, 1972). It is interesting that while at first sight, the Berbers seem much more rigidly structured along clan lines than the Chechens – and among the latter there is nothing as strictly defined as the Berber moieties – a closer examination of the Berbers also reveals a much looser society than the model put forward by the Berbers themselves would suggest.

14. Ibn Khaldun of Tunis, *The Muqaddimah: an Introduction to History*, ed. N. J. Dawood, trans. Franz Rosenthal (Routledge, London, 1987), esp. chs 2 and 3, pp. 91–155. In Ibn Khaldun's words, which are very relevant to the Chechen victory over the Russians:

'Thus greater fortitude is found among the savage Bedouin than among people who are subject to laws ... Those who have no one of their own lineage [to care for] rarely feel affection for their fellows. If danger is in the air, such a man slinks away and seeks to save himself, because he is afraid of being left without support ... Such people, therefore, cannot live in the desert. [But] such a nation [as the Bedouin] is better able to achieve superiority and full control, and to subdue other nations. The members of such a nation have the strength to fight other nations, and are among human beings what beasts of prey are among dumb animals ... Their sustenance lies wherever the shadow of their lances falls.' Ibn Khaldun of Tunis, *The Muqaddimah*.

15. The Pashtun are commonly regarded as a free, 'anarchic' and ungovernable people; but historically they had far more contact with various Muslim imperial states than the Chechens ever did. There is no Chechen equivalent for the ancient Pashtun saying that 'feuding eats up the mountains, and taxes eat up the plains,' for the simple reason that until the Russians conquered them, the Chechens paid no state taxes to anyone.

16. An index of Chechen isolation – and also perhaps of their stubborn adherence to their own traditions – is the quite extraordinary length of time it took for Islam to spread (at least at a more than superficial level) to Chechnya from southern Daghestan, where it had already been strongly present in the ninth century (and where Sufism was already a major force in the thirteenth century).

17. A very intriguing example of what might be called the Iron Law of Pirdom – that is to say, the tendency in Sufi-influenced Muslim societies for socio-religious prestige, or *baraka*, to become hereditary – may be the case of General Ibragim Suleimeinov (I say 'may' because the circumstances

of Suleimeinov's rise are far from clear). Suleimeinov was one of only three Chechens to achieve the rank of general under Soviet rule. He is a direct descendant of the sister of the famous anti-Shamil Sufi leader Kunta Haji, and this is said to have influenced his adoption by the Soviet nomenulatura, who assumed that he would possess natural influence within Chechen society, which they could exploit. (It could also be that the Kunta Haji tradition influenced Suleimeinov in the direction of compromise with the regime.) To a limited extent this may also have been true, though his prestige and influence as a general were doubtless greater. In any case, Dudayev was certainly scared of him, had him arrested, and may have ordered the murder of his brother.

18. See John Armstrong, *Nations before Nationalism* (University of North Carolina Press, 1982). The literature on the origins and nature of nations and nationalism is so huge as to be hardly listable. It should be clear from the discussion that I reject – at least with reference to relatively small, compact and homogeneous ethnoses like the Chechens – the more simplistic ideas associated with the name of Elie Kedourie, which would connect the growth of nationalism worldwide above all with the spread of a particular set of European ideas; as also those of neo-Marxists who would root it in a mixture of ideas and specific class formations. In general, I have been most influenced by the approach of Anthony Smith and his school, while trying to take due account of the cogent criticisms of this approach made by Ernest Gellner and others.

19. Anthony D. Smith, *The Ethnic Origins of Nations* (Blackwell, Oxford, 1987), p. 15 and *passim*.

20. For a study of the comparable effects of the genocide of 1915 on the Armenian psyche, see Ronald Grigor Suny, *Looking toward Ararat: Arme-*

nia in Modern History (Indiana University Press, 1993), pp. 94–115, 213–30.

21. Benedict Anderson, *Imagined Communities: Reflections on the Origin and Spread of Nationalism* (Verso, London, 1993). I am not for a moment challenging the validity of Professor Anderson's thesis when it comes to Indonesians and Filipinos, and it is also extremely helpful when it comes to the origins of modern nationalism in India and other large and heterogeneous imperial territories.

22. The degree of antiquity of some Chechen rules of behaviour, for example hospitality and blood brotherhood, is a matter of dispute among anthropologists. Jan Chesnov believes that they are of great antiquity; Mahomet Mamakayev and Georgy Derluguian think that they may at least have been greatly strengthened by the process whereby the Chechens moved down into the plains during the sixteenth century, supplanted the Turkic nomads and fought with the Cossacks – in other words that these too were a product of warfare and the needs of fighting solidarity. They point out that these traits are less strongly marked among the Ingush, who descended from the mountains much later.

23. Tom Nairn, *The Break-up of Britain: Crisis and Neo-Nationalism* (New Left Books, London, 1977), p. 340.

24. See Anatol Lieven, *The Baltic Revolution: Estonia, Latvia, Lithuania and the Path to Independence* (Yale University Press, 1993), pp. 175–80.

25. Jan Chesnov, 'Civilisation and the Chechen', *Anthropology and Archaeology of Eurasia* 34:3 (winter 1996).

26. For a criticism of the 'mythopoetics', as he calls them, of some aspects of Russian liberal and Western reporting of the Chechen War, see Valery Tishkov, 'Explaining, Representing and Categorising the Chechen War', paper presented to the Carnegie Endowment in Washington DC, Dec. 1996.

27. The most famous study of such colonial stereotyping is of course Edward Said's *Orientalism* (Routledge and Kegan Paul, 1978), the approach of which has been applied to the Russian literature of the Caucasus by Susan Layton, *Russian Literature and Empire: Conquest of the Caucasus from Lermontov to Tolstoy* (Cambridge University Press, 1994). For a study of French colonial stereotyping of the Berbers, see Edmund Burke III, 'The Image of the Moroccan State in French Ethnological Literature: A New Look at Lyautey's Berber Policy' (in Gellner and Michaud, op cit) – with the difference that because they hoped to split them from the Arabs (and in some cases, because the officers concerned were personally attracted to the feudal, or archaic, or pre-modern – but in any case romantic world of the Berber tradition) the French stereotyping of the Berbers was largely a positive one.

28. Alexander Lebed, 'The Chechen War is Over for Russia', *Washington Post*, 9 Oct. 1996.

29. See for example the account by Yusup Soslambekov, *Chechnya (Nokhchichob) – Vzglyad Iznutri* (Moscow, 1996), esp. pp. 39ff.

30. For a Chechen nationalist portrayal of the present lack of significance of teips, in the context of the 'electrification of the whole people' by the national struggle, see Zelinkhan Yandarbiyev, *V Preddvery Nezavisimosti* (Grozny, 1994), pp. 97–8. However, Yandarbiyev also says that in contemporary Chechnya, one reason for the decline of the teips is the rise of modern political parties, which is certainly not the case.

31. See Olivier Roy, *The Civil War in Tajikistan: Causes and Implications* (United States Institute of Peace, Washington DC, 1993). Professor Roy is probably the greatest Western expert on the Afghan and Soviet Tajiks, and the OSCE representative in Dushanbe in 1994–5.

32. For a comparison with the on the whole more stratified and government-influenced mountain peoples of Daghestan, see M. A. Aglarov, *Selskaya Obshchina v Nagornom Daghestanye, v XVII–Nachalye XIX Vyeka* (Academy of Sciences, Moscow, 1988). On the other hand, some of the most remote of these, like the Ingush, were so isolated that they remained in effect pagans until the early twentieth century.

33. Mahomet Mamakayev, *Chechensky Taip v Period Ego Razlozhenia* (The Chechen teip in the period of its decomposition), (State Publishing House, Grozny, 1973), p. 33.

34. According to Jan Chesnov, the traditional ordering of Chechen society is as follows:
'What is a teip from the point of view of a Chechen? First of all, a teip is a group which characterises his or her personality. A Chechen uses as a surname the name of one of his or her immediate ancestors. [Author's note: surnames as such were however only introduced under Russian and especially Soviet rule.] A surname might go back to a 'fourth father' (great-great-grandfather), or even beyond. A group of such relatives bearing the same surname is called *neck'ii*. The immediate family is known as the *doizal*. A wider group of relatives forms a *gar*. This could be called a lineage. A teip unites several gars...

It is difficult to determine the exact number of Chechen teips. Some gars, which grew in size, now pretend to the name of teip. Today, there are more than 150 teips. In the middle of the last century, there were more than 100, and at the beginning of that century, according to legend, there were only 59...

The Tukum is a group immediately below the Chechen ethnos as a whole, which historically lived in a particular territorial area. Such regional grouping emerged from alliances between various teips in one region – for example the Shatou Tukum, based in the mountain region of Shatou. The total number of Tukums differs from seven to thirteen according to different legends …' (Jan Chesnov, 'It is Difficult to Be a Chechen: Teips, their Past and Role in the Present', *Nezavisimaya Gazeta*, 22 Sept. 1994).

This picture corresponds to that given earlier by Mahomet Mamakayev. He, however, puts the number of nineteenth-century teips at 35, and the number of tukums at nine, which shows that you never can tell with these teips…

Chesnov himself quotes an amusing Chechen legend showing that the Chechens themselves have never been able to determine authoritatively how many 'genuine' teips there were even in the past. The story goes that when the original teips descended from the mountains to the plains, they carried with them a huge copper cauldron (a symbol of ethnic-kin unity in many cultures, recalling the old Russian phrase describing the extended family, 'those who eat from the same pot'). Unfortunately, the new or 'unrecognised' clans stole the pot and melted it, and since then no one has been able to say which is a truly genuine or original teip.

35. Soslambekov, *Chechnya*, p. 41.
36. Or as Professor Valery Tishkov, Director of the Ethnographical Institute of the Russian Academy of Sciences, told me, 'When I was a minister in '91, a delegation of Ingush came, and the younger ones pointed to the old people and said, "These are our elders; their word is law for us" – but in fact they just parroted what the activists told them to say. It is no different in Chechnya.' Professor Tishkov also played down the role of teips today: 'Once upon a time, a strict teip system did exist, but even in the nineteenth century other forces were more important – Islam, warrior democracy. Today, it is

family links and family coalitions which are most important.'
37. Interview with the author.
38. Now given back its old name of Deukr Aul – it was renamed under Soviet rule because Tolstoy had been stationed there while a Russian officer, and several of his early works are based on his experiences there.
39. I am indebted for this information to Professor Aslan Dukayev.
40. Originally, these cemeteries seem to have been founded by and reserved for a particular teip, but they have gradually become 'ancestral' in a looser sense.
41. Alexander Solzhenitsyn, *The Gulag Archipelago*, trans. Harry Willetts (Harper Collins, New York, 1992), vol. 3, pp. 401–5.
42. For a brilliant monograph on one institution of 'ordered anarchy' in pre-revolutionary Afghanistan, see G. Whitney Azoy, *Buzkashi: Game and Power in Afghanistan* (University of Pennsylvania Press, Philadelphia, 1982).
43. In what appears to be a veiled apology for some of the failings of the Chechen state in this period, the then Vice-President, Zelimkhan Yandarbiyev, quoted the Russian philosopher Lev Shestov, who asked, 'Why should a prisoner need virtues? He has only one goal, one desire – to be free. With this in mind, he values only those qualities which will help him to fulfil his dream' (Yandarbiyev, *V Preddvery Nezavisimosti*, p. 77).
44. Montagne, *The Berbers*, pp. xiii, xxxi, 28–44.
45. Quoted in Tishkov, *Chechensky Krisis*, pp. 11–12. After intense criticism both from Russians and from pro-Russian Chechens, Barsukov was forced publicly to repudiate this remark. An opinion poll published in *Nezavisimaya Gazeta*, 21 Nov. 1992, had 40 per cent of Muscovites polled describing Chechens as a 'criminal nationality'.
46. John F. Baddeley, *The Russian Conquest of the Caucasus* (Longman,

London, 1908), p. xxxvii.

47. Private communication, March 1997. See also Robert Chencinier, *Daghestan: Tradition and Survival* (Curzon, London, 1997), pp. 69–70.

48. Oleg Kutasov and Stanislav Romanov, in *Nezavisimaya Gazeta*, 16 Feb. 1996.

49. Nikolai Modestov in *Segodnya*, 3 Aug. 1996 (excerpt from his forthcoming book, *Moskva Banditskaya*), quoted in Phil Williams (ed.), *Russian Organised Crime: the New Threat?* (Frank Cass, London, 1997), p. 248.

II 'The Prayers of Slaves Are Not Heard in Heaven'

Epigraph from *The Koran*, trans. with notes and parallel text by N. J. Dawood (Penguin Classics, London, 1995), p. 38.

1. The most comprehensive survey of Adat that I have read is by Mahomet Mamakayev, *Chechensky Taip v Period Ego Razlozhenia* (State Publishing House, Grozny, 1973), pp. 24–33. He views Adat as 'a juridical norm of the teip structure', and lists twenty-three main obligations and rules.

2. See Alexandre Bennigsen and Enders Wimbush, *Mystics and Commissars: Sufism in the Soviet Union* (Berkeley, 1985).

3. Psalm of Shamil, 'Composed by Him to Replace All Profane Songs', and sung in chorus by his Murids as they rode with him. Quoted in John F. Baddeley, *The Russian Conquest of the Caucasus* (London, 1908). According to Baddeley, this version (originally presumably in Arabic) is translated from the Russian version of Professor Mirza Alexander Kazem-Bek.

4. Contemporary Chechen national song, loosely translated from the Russian by the author. Why this song is in Russian – whether because this is the language of pop-music across the former Soviet Union, or because the Chechen singer who sung it

could not in fact speak Chechen, or for some other reason – I do not know. Georgy Derluguian pointed out to me that both the title and several of the verses strongly recall the Cuban revolutionary song 'Liberta or Muerte', and given that the Chechens all went through a Soviet school system at which such international Communist songs were taught, it could very well be that this was an influence – another piece of evidence that they have moved a long way from Shamil.

5. See John F. Baddeley, *The Russian Conquest of the Caucasus* (Longman, London, 1908), pp. 231–51; Moshe Gammer, *Muslim Resistance to the Tsar* (Frank Cass, London, 1994), pp. 238–40.

6. See for example Ernest Gellner, 'The Unknown Apollo of Biskra', in his *Muslim Society* (Cambridge University Press, 1981), p. 167. He quotes an official French circular of 1933 stating that 'most heads of orders and main saintly families venerated by the natives are sincerely converted to our dominion and see themselves threatened by a grouping which, by an active and skilful propaganda, recruits new adherents daily.' This would almost certainly have become the case with hereditary Sufi leaders in the Russian empire, had it continued, but the Soviet regime, both for ideological reasons and because it could not of course allow major accumulations of property through donations, could not exploit this factor.

7. Baddeley, *Rugged Flanks*, p. 209. Baddeley also reports the persistence of pagan customs in Ingushetia, Chechnya and Daghestan into his own day: for example, the ritual ending of a blood-feud by having the guilty party suck the breast of the mother or sister of the man he had killed, thereby becoming the 'brother' of those seeking vengeance. This custom, evidently of immense antiquity, appears to have

parallels to one among the ancient Etruscans, or – who can say – may even have originated in some common primeval root. For, according to Ingrid D. Rowland,
'The decorative back of a bronze [Etruscan] mirror, now in Florence, shows Hercle's [Etruscan for Hercules] final introduction into Olympus, where he is ritually suckled by the goddess who first caused him all the trouble, Uni, the Etruscan version of Hera. All is forgiven in a rite that is utterly non-Greek and strangely, affectingly primal.'
See Ingrid D. Rowland, 'Beyond Art' (a review of *Etruscan Art* by Otto J. Brendel), *New York Review of Books*, 19 Sept. 1996, p. 47.

8. Interview with *Literaturnaya Gazeta*, 12 Aug. 1993, quoted in Alexei Malashenko, 'Does Islamic Fundamentalism Exist in Russia', in Yaacov Ro'i (ed.), *Muslim Eurasia: Conflicting Legacies* (Frank Cass, London, 1995), p. 46.

9. Dzhokhar Dudayev, *Ternisty Put' k Svobode* (Vilnius, 1994), pp. 6–10.

10. Zelimkhan Yandarbiyev, *V Preddverri Nezavisimosti* (Grozny, 1994), p. 77.

11. I am indebted for my knowledge of Gantemirov's previous activities in Moscow to Dr Georgy Derluguian.

12. Interview with the author, 15 Feb. 1992.

13. See Carlotta Gall, 'Troubled Dudayev Seeks Islamic Law in Chechnya', *Moscow Times*, 22 Nov. 1994.

14. For developments in Daghestan to 1997, see Robert Chencinier, *Daghestan: op. cit.* As well as a highly evocative personal portrait of the region and its people, this book contains a great deal of anthropological information about contemporary Daghestani religion and society.

15. Baddeley, *Russian Conquest*, records a sermon of Shamil against feuds, in which he used the example of a quarrel over a hen which led to a feud which lasted three centuries and led to hundreds of deaths (p. 245).

16. Interview with the author, Grozny, 25 May 1995.

17. See for example A. Avksentyev, *Islam na Severnom Kavkaze* (Islam in the North Caucasus) (Stavropol, 1984): 'Adherents of Islam were drawn mostly from local feudal lords. The ideology of obedience which penetrated all Muslim dogma corresponded to the class interests of the feudal lords. This ideology helped them to keep the working mountaineers in obedience, and distracted them from class struggle and revolutionary actions' (p. 11). Typically for such propagandists (whether Russian, Soviet, French and even contemporary American), he rarely uses the word 'Muslim' without attaching to it the words 'fanatic' or 'fanaticism'.

Conclusion

Epigraph from C. V. Wedgwood, *The Thirty Years War* (Methuen, 1981), p. 459.

1. Francis Fukuyama, *The End of History and the Last Man* (Free Press, New York, 1992).

2. Alan Knight, *The Mexican Revolution*, pp. 21–2.

3. Quoted by Christian Lowe, 'Can't Beat em, So Zyuganov Joins Them', *Moscow Times*, 18 Dec. 1996: 'with the 149-strong Communist faction toeing the government line in the State Duma, the parliamentary opposition has to all intents and purposes ceased to exist.'

4. Oleg Schedrov, 'Russian Election Losers Got Consolation Prizes', Reuters, Moscow, 1 July 1997.

5. I first expressed the following theses in an article for the *Washington Quarterly*, autumn 1996.

6. These different but related streams in Russian thought have been most famously traced by Nikolai Berdyayev in *Russian Thought* (Macmillan, London, 1948), even though, writing in the shadow of the Bolshevik Revolution and Stalinism, he was in my view too ready to see all the streams

426 Notes to pages 375–383

of Russian idealism flowing towards one apocalyptic conclusion. For a recent study of the contemporary exhaustion of Russian idealism and messianism, see Tim McDaniel, *The Agony of the Russian Idea* (Princeton University Press, 1996).

7. Regis Debray, 'Marxism and the National Question', *New Left Review*, no. 105 (1977), quoted in Anthony Smith, *The Ethnic Origins of Nations* (Blackwell, Oxford, 1986), p. 175.

8. See the interview with presidential aide Georgy Satarov in *Rossiiskaya Gazeta*, 14 Nov. 1996.

9. Martin Malia, 'The Dead Weight of Empire', *Times Literary Supplement*, 20 June 1997.

10. By far the best study of the development of the Russian empire as a non-national, multi-ethnic state is Andreas Kappeler, *Russland als Vielvoelkerrreich* (C. H. Beck, Munich, 1992).

11. Interview with the author, Dnipropetrovsk, 20 Aug. 1995.

12. See my forthcoming book on the subject, to be published by the United States Institute of Peace, Washington DC.

13. Alexander Lebed, press conference, Moscow, 24 June 1996.

14. Roman Szporluk, 'Statehood and Nation-Building in the Post-Soviet Space', in Szporluk (ed.), *National Identity and Ethnicity in Russia and the New States of Eurasia* (M. E. Sharpe, New York, 1994), p. 10.

15. Letter to *Izvestia*, 25 Nov. 1991.

16. Lowell Tillett, *The Great Friendship: Soviet Historians on the Non-Russian Nationalities* (University of North Carolina Press, Chapel Hill, 1969), p. 422.

17. Andrei Sinyavsky, *Soviet Civilisation* (Arcade, New York, 1990), pp. 243–5.

18. Interview with the author, Kharkiv, 4 Aug. 1995.

19. G. M. Tamas, 'Ethnarchy and Ethno-Anarchism', *Social Research* 63:1 (spring 1996).

20. Interviewed in *Freedom Review* (Sept.–Oct. 1994).

21. See for example John Keegan, 'Tales of Combat to Come', in the *Washington Post*'s Book World, 1 Dec. 1996.

22. James Pettifer, *The Turkish Labyrinth: Ataturk and the New Islam* (Viking, London, 1997), p. xxxv.

Index